PSYCHIATRIC TREATMENT
CRISIS / CLINIC / CONSULTATION

PSYCHIATRIC TREATMENT
CRISIS / CLINIC / CONSULTATION

C. PETER ROSENBAUM, M.D.
Associate Professor
Department of Psychiatry
Stanford University School of Medicine

JOHN E. BEEBE III, M.D.
Department of Psychological and Social Medicine
Pacific Medical Center
University of the Pacific

McGRAW-HILL BOOK COMPANY
A BLAKISTON PUBLICATION

New York   St. Louis   San Francisco   Auckland   Düsseldorf   Johannesburg   Kuala Lumpur   London
Mexico   Montreal   New Delhi   Panama   Paris   São Paulo   Singapore   Sydney   Tokyo   Toronto

Library of Congress Cataloging in Publication Data

Rosenbaum, C   Peter, date
    Psychiatric treatment.

    Includes index.
    1. Psychotherapy. 2. Crisis intervention
(Psychiatry) I. Beebe, John E., date joint
author. II. Title. [DNLM: 1. Crisis intervention.
2. Psychotherapy. 3. Referral and consultation.
WM420 R813p]
RC480.5.R667   616.8'91   74-22026
ISBN 0-07-053710-0

PSYCHIATRIC TREATMENT: Crisis, Clinic, and Consultation

1 2 3 4 5 6 7 8 9 0   VHVH   7 9 8 7 6 5

This book was set in Press Roman by Reprographex, Inc. The editors were
J. Dereck Jeffers and Michael Weber; the designer was Rich Chafian;
the production supervisor was Judi Frey. The drawings were done by
John Foster. The cover was designed by Pencils Portfolio, Inc.
Von Hoffmann Press, Inc., was printer and binder.

NOTICE
Medicine is an ever-changing science. As new research and clinical
experience broaden our knowledge, changes in treatment and drug therapy
are required. The editors and the publisher of this work have made every
effort to ensure that the drug dosage schedules herein are accurate and
in accord with the standards accepted at the time of publication. The
reader is advised, however, to check the product information sheet
included in the package of each drug he or she plans to administer to be certain
that changes have not been made in the recommended dose or in the contraindications for administration. This recommendation is of particular
importance in regard to new or infrequently used drugs.

Contents

List of Contributors

C. Peter Rosenbaum, M.D.
Department of Psychiatry
School of Medicine
Stanford University
Stanford, California

John E. Beebe III, M.D.
Department of Psychological and Social Medicine
Pacific Medical Center
San Francisco, California

Diana Silver Arsham, Ph.D.
Department of Psychological and Social Medicine
Pacific Medical Center
San Francisco, California

John D. Asher, M.D.
Department of Psychiatry
School of Medicine
Stanford University
Stanford, California

Philip A. Berger, M.D.
Department of Psychiatry
School of Medicine
Stanford University
Stanford, California

H. Keith H. Brodie, M.D.
Department of Psychiatry
School of Medicine
Duke University
Durham, North Carolina

Varda P. Ganz, M.D.
Counseling and Psychological Services
Cowell Student Health Center
Stanford University
Stanford, California

Leo E. Hollister, M.D.
Veterans Administration Hospital
Palo Alto, California

John I. Maurer, M.D.
Emanuel Mental Health Center
Turlock, California

Frederick T. Melges, M.D.
Department of Psychiatry
School of Medicine
Stanford University
Stanford, California

Karl A. Menninger, M.D.
The Menninger Foundation
Topeka, Kansas

Warren B. Miller, M.D.
Department of Psychiatry
School of Medicine
Stanford University
Stanford, California

Mario P. Sassano, M.S.W.
Family Service Agency of Santa Clara County
San Jose, California

Cary Lee Stone, M.S.W.
Department of Psychiatry
School of Medicine
Stanford University
Stanford, California

Robert L. Taylor, M.D.
Marin County Community Mental Health Services
San Rafael, California

Jared R. Tinklenberg, M.D.
Department of Psychiatry
School of Medicine
Stanford University
Stanford, California

Robert J. Underwood, Ph.D.
Department of Psychological and Social Medicine
Pacific Medical Center
San Francisco, California

Preface

Beginning therapists know they have available to them supervisors, consultants, and seminars — that multitude of training experiences that will help them develop into the competent therapists they want to be. But at the beginning, there is still the patient and his or her predicament. The clinical situation regularly challenges therapists before their training can tell them what to do, and it does so in ways their supervisors cannot always predict. A major task of clinical teachers is to guide therapists as they enter into therapeutic work.

One way of preparing therapists has been to recommend readings on psychiatric work. As teachers we have found many books to recommend, but no one book has seemed to address the range of situations beginners will have to face. Many excellent books presuppose previous supervised clinical work and concentrate only on intensive psychotherapy. Other books can be used by beginning therapists but have a narrow focus in that they deal only with certain kinds of problems or clients and present only one kind of approach. Recommending many books may discourage beginners. In this book we have tried to present enough different theories and suggestions for treatment to permit new therapists to get started.

A second way of preparing therapists has been to expose them to clinicians well trained in the practice of different theoretical approaches. In this country there are many excellent teachers of individual and group psychotherapy, crisis intervention and brief psychotherapy, supportive psychotherapy, biological psychiatry, and hospital consultation. In seminars these teachers often work to define the relevance of their theories to actual clinical situations and to explain where the given theory does and does not apply in practice. Too few of these qualifying explanations have found their way into print, and thus beginners often use a good treatment at the wrong time, with the wrong person, or in the wrong way. Also experienced clinicians often avoid an unfamiliar approach because they have no guide to tell them how to use it. As a resident said, "We need a theory to tell us when to use which theory." This book tries to put these considerations into print and provide the needed keys.

In presenting a rationale for the work therapists do, we soon realized that relying on tradition is not enough. Nor is practice explained because it fulfills the promise of a single theory, is backed by clinical experience, or follows a set of prescriptive rules drawn up for use with certain kinds of patients. As we progressed in writing this book, it became evident that we needed to define why a given approach was appropriate in a given situation.

Repeatedly we reexamined our theories, our clinical experience, and our "rules," always asking ourselves if the traditional ways really met the test of practice and thus deserved to be passed along to a new generation of therapists and patients. We also attempted to integrate the lessons and the language of newer work that has appeared within the past fifteen years.

Thus the more experienced reader will find both familiar and unfamiliar words, behaviorist concepts along with phenomenological ones, Rogers and Jung cited with Sullivan and Freud, and theories of learning set beside theories of meaning.

We use these many different concepts as part of our basic clinical language because we have found it practical to do so. Equally we have eliminated some old words from our working vocabulary. Moving from one clinical situation to another often requires a shift in style, stance, and vocabulary, and we have tried to avoid language that makes it hard to make these shifts. Sometimes we have introduced concepts that will ease the necessary transitions from one traditional vocabulary to another.

The reader will also notice a consistent effort to introduce the situational and ecological dimensions of therapy into our formulations, along with the traditional ones of diagnosis and psychodynamics. This effort required a fuller statement of common problems and pushed us in a phenomenological direction. Thus a patient wrestling with a suicidal feeling must be helped to deal with that feeling, whether he or she be called "depressed," "obsessional," "alcoholic," or "hysterical." In turn these diagnoses say as much about the patient's relationship to others in his or her social field as about the suicidal feeling.

We hope this book will give working therapists ways to link their experience with a given patient both to the clinical tradition and to the newer formulations prevalent in the literature. This book is designed to help practitioners, whether they are just beginning their work or are reexamining the foundations of a long-standing practice. We believe we have dealt with a basic issue for therapists working within our field: the need to find concepts that accurately express the nature of treatment. Ideally such concepts define approaches that work in a language that considers the persons as well as the conditions therapists are called upon to treat.

C. Peter Rosenbaum

John E. Beebe III

Acknowledgments

We had the good fortune to be present when two major training centers in psychiatry found new inspiration and were reorganized: the Department of Psychiatry of the School of Medicine at Stanford University under David Hamburg, and the Department of Psychological and Social Medicine of the Pacific Medical Center under Allen Enelow. This book reflects not only the great interest in finding new ways to teach psychiatry that both centers have encouraged, but also the contributions of the many excellent people we met there. Members of the San Francisco Psychoanalytic Institute and the C. G. Jung Institute of San Francisco also contributed to a more informed understanding of current analytic thought.

Many colleagues reviewed one or more chapters, gave valuable advice and criticism, helped to clarify formulations, and provided case examples. We want to acknowledge especially the contributions of Charles Casella, Richard Chapman, Randolph Charlton, James Corby, Norman Dishotsky, Cleo Eulau, Loma Flowers, Hector Goa, Robert Goodwin, Nancy Hale, Sylvia Hammond, Joseph Henderson, Elizabeth Osterman, Ruth Rosenblum, Alan Rosenthal, Neil Scott, Alice Serbin, Oscar Serbin, Philip Spielman, Eva Strock, Michael Tiktinsky, Bruce Wermuth, Andrew Whyman, and Irvin Yalom.

We are especially grateful to Dr. Robert G. O'Briant, who made a detailed criticism of Chapter 6, and Cary Lee Stone, who clarified the writing of Chapter 1 at a critical stage.

Special mention must be given to the contributions of the late Alfred E. Weisz, whose lectures on emergency psychiatry were the inspiration for the crisis section of this book. Indeed the two chapters on suicide build on his original presentations given in the summer of 1968 and utilize notes he made available shortly before his death.

Several persons were responsible for preparation of the manuscript, the typing and checking of references, and the keeping of order when chaos threatened over a four-year period. Eileen Rogers did most of the preparatory work; Nancy Phillips worked with her. Joan Wolfe helped from start to finish. Beatrice Belmont did several middle-draft chapters, and Sarah Collins, Maxine Harris, Valarie Munden, and Jan Olszewski prepared final versions.

Jeanne Kennedy was our thorough indexer.

The editors learned from each other during this collaboration. Indeed we talked together so often and reviewed each other's chapters so many times that frequently it is difficult to know where the ideas of one leave off and the ideas of the other begin, even in the chapters which bear our separate names.

Both friends and family helped in the work and tolerated the demands we placed on them. David Mackey reviewed many of the chapters to ensure that the sense, feeling, tone, and intention preserved human values, and he was an indispensable consultant to the editors in making their collaboration more effective. Eva Rosenbaum helped the idea for the book to take shape; she assisted in formulating concepts for several of the chapters as well as in the typing of them and she provided support and encouragement throughout.

We must also acknowledge our debt to our patients. In presenting their material, we often had to disguise and substitute to protect their privacy.

We tried to preserve the feeling-values of our original contacts and to retain the clinical truths we learned from them. We believe our patients will understand the many compromises we had to make.

Finally we thank the therapists in training at Stanford and the Pacific Medical Center who patiently heard us out while we presented the ideas that were to become this book. Their vigorous response to our preliminary efforts was like good therapy, enabling us in the end to speak for what was most ourselves. We hope they will be pleased with the result.

C. Peter Rosenbaum

John E. Beebe III

PSYCHIATRIC TREATMENT
CRISIS / CLINIC / CONSULTATION

Principles of
Crisis Intervention

The following example has been adapted from a first-year psychiatric resident's case description written her first day on the emergency service. The example will be cited repeatedly throughout this chapter because it is typical of the kinds of situations with which the emergency therapist is faced.*

> *Example 1–1, Anna.* Anna, a 24-year-old single, black mother of two, was brought to the emergency room by her cousin, Betty, with whom she had been living since she lost custody of her children to her mother-in-law six weeks before. Betty demanded "total psychiatric" care for Anna: "You have got to put her in the hospital!"
>
> Until Anna moved in with Betty, she had lived in a foster home in a neighboring community. She had been there since early adolescence. Her parents were dead, and she had no family in the area. She had been in continual trouble with the law, mostly in connection with heroin addiction.
>
> Cousin Betty was 25, rigid, and a disciplinarian. She saw herself as a reformed sinner;

vis-à-vis Anna her role was that of the strict mother. She found herself rapidly running out of patience with Anna's behavior, which she viewed as irresponsible and bad. On this particular evening she had become furious at Anna for lying, and in the midst of their argument had made the threat of "total psychiatric care" and forced her to come to the emergency room.

When the emergency therapist first saw her, Anna was tearful and upset, frightened, and angry with her cousin. She was oriented and reasonably cooperative, and her feelings and behavior were within a socially acceptable range. She was able to think rationally. The therapist learned that at Betty's insistence Anna had seen another therapist, Dr. Jones, at the neighborhood health center, and that Anna had an appointment there the next day. The emergency therapist also learned that Dr. Jones was Betty's regular therapist.

This case is typical of the kinds of emergency situations the emergency therapist will be called upon to solve. The reader may wish to ask himself before proceeding how he would have approached the crisis of Betty and Anna. Later in this chapter we shall discuss how the case was actually handled by the emergency therapist.

---

*In this, as in all other case material presented in this book, data that might identify patients and their families have been changed to ensure privacy.

A CRISIS AS A PLAY IN FOUR ACTS

C.G. Jung[1] has suggested that a typical dream is like a play in four acts, an idea we shall develop in our chapter on dreams (Chapter 22). A dream is a sort of miniature, nocturnal emergency in which there is a libidinal upset and a rallying of coping mechanisms to deal with the disturbance and to provide resolution. A typical crisis also has four acts. This four-act model can be used as an aid in collecting and sorting the clinical data in crisis intervention. In the first act the setting is defined and the protagonists are shown; we observe their lifestyles. In the second act a situation develops: a new character appears, or an action or event produces change, with its attendant uncertainty and tension. In the third act the development culminates in a peak of tension. In the fourth act a solution is reached.

These same four stages are present in the evolution of an emergency. The emergency therapist should train himself to identify (1) the protagonists and their natural setting; (2) the development, or that which emerged before the emergency required professional attention; (3) the point at which the greatest stress or tension was felt; and (4) the solution that is anticipated or expected by each of the participants.

The job of the emergency therapist is to help the protagonists find the solution that has the most capacity for benefit and safety in all their lives. Until, however, he has taken all aspects of the crisis into account, including the principals' own ideas about what a good solution would be, he is in a poor position to achieve this goal. Even if he is wise enough to see what the optimal resolution should be, he still has to assess what portion of this hypothetical best solution is likely to be acceptable to the individuals involved.

The emergency therapist is advised, therefore, to proceed cautiously, gather information about the crisis methodically, and not let himself be drawn too quickly into the drama. If he follows the four-stage model, he is unlikely to lose his professional head. As he gains experience he can go faster, but at first he should take his time.

ASSUMING THE NECESSARY ROLE

To function effectively the therapist should be in a setting that is comfortable and in which he feels adequately supported by the law and by expert consultants to whom he can turn in obscure situations. Most emergency room and training situations do provide such a structure. If he has these resources at his command, the therapist should recognize the extent of his power. However insecure he feels about his abilities, the participants in the crisis see him as the person who has the authority to resolve the situation. He can ask individual family members to leave or to remain in the office while he talks with the "identified patient." He can recommend for or against hospitalization. He is the one who calls the police in if the situation requires legal restraint.

He also incarnates an ancient role, that of the village wise man who knows the way to end distress and is justified in using whatever procedures he believes will achieve his end. The patients expect to have expectations made of them, and the emergency therapist is in a position to define the situation. He should not shirk this responsibility. It is this role that gives him the edge over the participants in the emergency, many of whom may actually understand the emotions involved and the total situation far better than he.

The model described here can serve as a point of departure for each therapist to work out a system that best fits his own needs and talents. Many of the ideas presented can serve as a first approximation for therapists who are in process of letting their own styles evolve. The central task is the same however it is approached: to assess the emergency situation, analyze its components, search for possible outcomes, and assist with the resolution.

A MODEL OF CRISIS INTERVENTION

Step 1—Basic Information Gathering

Using paper and a pencil to record the answers, the therapist must ask basic questions of the people involved: the names, addresses, and phone numbers of the identified patient and of the people with whom he lives or most frequently interacts. The therapist is asking, in effect, who are the protagonists? Often at this point vital details are omitted, including mention of the existence of some of the most significant actors in the crisis. Only later do they appear, and often only after detailed questioning. Such dramatic forgetting is characteristic of emotional stress, and the therapist has a good clue to the most charged issues by the omissions made at this point that later come to light. It is helpful therefore to record what is said at first. The purpose in listening for omissions is not to trap the patient but to understand his conflicts.

The therapist can grasp the ego functioning of the participants by the manner in which they answer basic initial questions. Their ability to communicate, remember, and organize basic information about their lives reveals a good deal about their mental states.

History taking is also therapeutic. Frequently it lets people in crisis know that the particular situation which seems so hopeless or out-of-hand began at some point in time and presumably will end at some point in time, and that in spite of the current investment in the traumatic peak of stress and tension, the persons involved have more of a history and future together than they momentarily believe. Harry Stack Sullivan[2] has said:

> Severe anxiety probably contributes no information. The effect of severe anxiety reminds one in some ways of a blow on the head, in that it simply wipes out what is immediate proximal to its occurence. If you have a severe blow on the head, you are quite apt later to have an incurable, absolute amnesia covering the few moments before your head was struck. Anxiety has a similar effect . . . .

In a psychiatric emergency, the participants are often quite anxious. The therapist's job is to help uncover the events and feelings about which the participants are partially amnesic so the emergency can be placed more rationally into the context of the past that led up to the anxiety. In this manner the future can be ordered to help diminish the effect of the crisis.

At this point the therapist should also ask everything he must know to place the participants in a social context he can understand. Where do they work? What do they do? Where do they live? What religion, if any, do they practice? In general, where do they exist in society? Unless the therapist makes this conscious effort, it is easy to make projections that are unwarranted in terms of the protagonists' actual standards, attitudes, and experiences.

One trap in gathering information is that one of the principals may want to bind the therapist with *pseudoconfidentiality* by asking him to promise not to reveal some particular "family secret" to the others. Agreement to such a request is almost inevitably detrimental to successful intervention for several reasons. First, it sets up a special alliance of "we have a secret" between the therapist and informant that estranges the therapist from the others. Second, it ties the therapist's hands because he cannot utilize information valuable in seeking a resolution. Third, a family secret is almost always a pseudosecret; everyone has known it all along and has pretended ignorance. In fact, everyone else may breathe sighs of relief when a member's drinking, incestuous advances to a child, bizarre thinking, murderous or suicidal impulses, and so on are brought into the open and discussed as a problem that needs to be dealt with instead of buried.

When a participant in a crisis situation approaches the therapist with "Promise you won't tell the others, but . . . ," it is best for the therapist to take the position that although he is interested in hearing what everyone has to say, he needs to be free to use that information in as helpful a way as he can. He *can* promise that he will make every effort not to use the information in an embarrassing or hurtful manner. He explains that to intervene effectively he needs to know what the informant can offer, even though he cannot promise confidentiality. Usually this explanation convinces the informant to give the necessary information. If not, the therapist may inquire about what the informant fears will happen if he divulges the information. If it becomes apparent that his fears are illusory, such as divulging a family secret that is already known or suspected by the others, the informant will usually provide the information. Often anxiety about keeping a secret betrays a real desire to be unburdened of it.

Step 2–Understanding the Development of the Crisis

There are three main considerations in step 2: (1) finding the sequence of events; (2) structuring the interview; and (3) avoiding the dangers of premature catharsis.

The emergency therapist must determine the *sequence of events* preceding the crisis. Patients usually are eager to focus on the peak of stress, but the therapist is interested in firmly understanding how the situation developed.

Thus the emergency therapist wanted to know how Anna lost custody of her children and came to live with her cousin. She wanted to hear how the two women had been getting along during the six weeks they had been living together. At first Betty maintained that the situation had been terrible the whole time. Nevertheless, they had been under the same roof for six weeks, and the therapist reasoned that they must have faced difficulties in living together before and had found ways of resolving them.

Learning about their first weeks together was part of learning about the development of the situation that brought them to the emergency room. By being forced to accept this focus, Betty and Anna obtained some perspective on the crisis they were facing. In turn, they gave the emergency therapist valuable information concerning the coping options they were likely to exercise in dealing with the present crisis.

Usually a therapist is more successful in having patients accept a solution already in their repertoire than he is in having them try a new solution. Many patients have a solid repertoire of healthy coping strategies, but in the development of the crisis events occur that cause the actors to disqualify or discard them. In learning about the development of the crisis, the therapist can frequently identify a strategy that had been effective previously. The discarding of it can be identified and called into question. "Why did you give that up since it was working for you?" the therapist may ask.

Orderly history taking is itself a treatment modality. The patient benefits by watching the emergency therapist bring logical order to what seemed a chaotic situation. The therapist's ability to cope comes through too; there is a great deal of modeling or *ego borrowing* at this phase of the interview.

It is obvious that the emergency therapist will have to be firm in *structuring the interview* if he is to succeed in having patients explain the development of the crisis. The patient may want to jump ahead or avoid elements of clarification because of an overinvestment in the dramatic, insoluble tension. It seems to be human nature to perseverate on traumatic points of anxiety or anger. This tendency of the patient's must be firmly countered or the crisis intervention will become crisis amplification, with the therapist becoming a passionate advocate for the patient's sense of injury.

Premature catharsis can be dangerous. A common error made by beginning therapists is to identify with the patient and to precipitate injudicious catharsis. With homicidal patients, as we shall see in Chapter 4, this can be a dangerous procedure. Freud's[3] famous dictum, "Where id was, there shall ego be," is especially pertinent in emergency work. The emergency therapist strives to give the patient two ways of protecting himself from his overwhelming emotion: structure and distance. This is not to say that the therapist is uninterested in letting the patient express emotion, but that he must strive to create a situation which can contain the emotion expressed. Indeed, the creation of an ego structure large and solid enough to hold the emotion of the patient is a task of the therapist at all times during all forms of therapy.

If he has been successful in creating structure, the therapist can proceed safely to the next stage of understanding the crisis: reliving with the patient the experience of peak stress or tension.

Step 3—Re-experiencing the Peak of Tension in the Crisis

In this step the emergency therapist has four tasks to attend to, namely, (1) approaching the emotion, (2) using special interview techniques, (3) hearing each person out, and (4) mediating catharsis.

When the emergency therapist has been able to slow down the participants enough to find out who they are and how the present turmoil developed, he is ready to *approach the underlying emotion* by asking them to recount the issue that brought them before him, and relive the peak of stress or tension. It is surprising how many patients do not know what it is that set them off, what the last straw was, what hurt most. Here the therapist uses all the skills of the empathetic, open-ended, emotion-releasing questioning and commenting that he has been taught.

Certain *special interviewing techniques* may be helpful. Carl Rogers[4] described the reflection of feeling as a therapeutic method. To release emotion the therapist reflects back to the patient the affective quality of what he has just said, restating the feeling and emotional meaning rather than details of content.

Attention to content can also work. For instance, note taking can be a powerful stimulus for the patient to open up more. It is all right for the therapist to continue to satisfy his own desire for accurate information by note taking, provided he communicates that his main interest is in grasping the feelings of the patient.

Other therapists will prefer to put their pencils down at this point and to emphasize by direct, wordless eye contact that a critical point in the interview has been reached and feelings are now more necessary than facts.

Whatever technique the therapist uses, it is important that *each person has his say*, that each is heard. Again, the therapist offers treatment by listening. To paraphrase John Perry:[5] There is no anger quite like the anger of the person who is not being heard. One reduces anger by listening fully. Relatives must not be allowed to interrupt each other, and each participant may have to be interviewed separately if each is to have his say. It is important that each person feel the therapist has understood his particular stress and has taken in the news of his suffering.

The therapist must *mediate catharsis* for some patients. Certain patients in crisis offer, instead of anger, a blank, dazed, depressed, or retarded affect. The therapist may have to mediate catharsis by making statements such as, "I can imagine with the amount of confusion you have described to me that you must have felt terribly upset just then," or, "I'm positive that being alone for so many weeks after the loss of your wife made you feel tremendously lonely and grieved." With schizophrenic and very depressed patients, the therapist's putting into words what the normal human feeling would be can have a profoundly releasing effect. The schizophrenic patient may suddenly talk sense; the silent, depressed patient may burst into tears.

Anna (cont'd.). When the emergency therapist tried to learn from Anna what she had been lying about, cousin Betty interrupted persistently. It took considerable persuasion to establish Anna's right to speak for herself, but the therapist elected to let Betty remain in the room. It turned out that Anna had lied to her cousin about the time of her appointment with Dr. Jones and that Betty knew she was lying because she had called Dr. Jones earlier in the day to ascertain the exact time.

As soon as this fact emerged, Betty began to

weep. Sensing that an important feeling of a private nature was emerging, the therapist asked Anna to wait outside. Alone with the therapist, Betty said, "I guess you realize I don't like sharing Dr. Jones with Anna." She then related how much it meant that Dr. Jones held her in high regard and how much she feared Anna's telling him things that might make him think less of her. Betty's father, like Anna's, had run off with a woman when she was a little girl, and this point of empathic identification had suddenly become a source of competition.

The emergency therapist asked to see Anna alone while Betty waited outside. From Anna the therapist learned that she had known all along it "wouldn't work" if she saw Dr. Jones, but that Betty kept insisting she go. Anna had even suggested seeing a Dr. Gregg, who had more experience with heroin users, at the same clinic, but Betty had not allowed her to make the arrangements. Finally, sure that Betty was going to be jealous, Anna lied about the appointment time. She planned to miss the appointment and pretend she had the time wrong.

Anna's main emotion centered around the impossibility of doing anything to please Betty.

With knowledge of the background, the therapist found it much easier to understand the impasse that had developed between Betty and Anna and was ready to make plans for them. Betty and Anna were united in trusting the therapist, who had heard both their points of view, and they were noticeably less antagonistic toward each other as the therapist proceeded to help them find a practical solution to the problem of Anna's therapy.

In this third stage the therapist must use all his skill to elicit the peak of stress or tension from the patients, either by hearing it from them or saying it to them. If he has done this job well, he will have the patient's confidence and will be in a

strong position to search for the solution to the crisis.

Step 4—Finding the Solution

The solution lies within the system, not within the therapist. Implicit in all that has been said so far is that the emergency therapist has been working toward a solution to the crisis. If he has conducted the interview properly up to this point, he will already have done much about resolving the problem. There needs to be, however, a specific resolution by the participants, who will now be called upon to do a major share of the work. The therapist should remember he is a consultant to a system, not its savior. Even when he hospitalizes, refers, or prescribes, he should be carrying out solutions that have emerged logically from his consultation with all the participants and for which they are willing to take their share of the responsibility.

The following five tasks are to be accomplished in step 4: (1) bringing the participants together to redefine the situation; (2) gathering from all participants their expectations about the outcome; (3) enhancing the emergence of previously omitted information; (4) suggesting possible solutions to the principals to solicit their reactions; and (5) carrying through with the resolution that seems most likely to work.

Each member of the system in crisis must fully understand the crisis intervention. After the therapist has learned about the development and peak of tension, it often helps to *bring the participants together* and *redescribe the situation* in understandable human terms.

One of his responsibilities is to make explicit certain issues that had been treated as unknowns or secrets. For instance, an alcoholic patient, trying to bind the therapist with pseudo-confidentiality, may say, "I've been drinking heavily, but don't tell anyone." As with other pseudosecrets, the problem is closed communication: everyone knows the patient has been drinking, but he has been unable to say so directly to the people around him. When the group is gathered together the therapist can open the communication channels by saying, "Mr. Williams has been drinking quite heavily in the past week and has been making a number of problems for himself and for all of you, and he is well aware of this." A statement like this can relieve a bind of several days' duration, in which Mr. Williams has steadfastly refused to acknowledge verbally to his concerned relatives the obvious fact that he has been drinking. The emergency therapist frequently has to mediate important self-disclosures in this way.

When gathering *expectations about outcome,* the participants (and outside therapists) should be asked what they think the outcome should be. Preadolescent children may see with clearer vision than older people. Outside therapists, as the case of Anna will show, may possess information unavailable to the emergency therapist that will drastically change his view of the situation.

The participants may have withheld information for fear it would result in moral or legal problems, and the emergency therapist should seek to *enhance disclosure.* He can do so by saying, "I think I have a fair understanding of the situation which brought you here, but it may be that there are some important things I don't yet know. Is there anything that's been left out or anything you think I should know about before we try to make a decision?" If Anna's emergency therapist had been successful in such an attempt, she might have saved herself some embarrassment.

The emergency therapist should *suggest possible solutions* to the patient and the others to see what their reactions will be. Sometimes a shake of the head or a reavealing look will show that one of the participants has qualms about an apparently reasonable solution. These qualms should be aired. The therapist may say, for instance, "I get the feeling, Mrs. Green, that there is something about that idea which doesn't sit well with you." The therapist should seek a solution that is reasonable and that the patient and his social system can

make work. The solution need not meet with the approval of all concerned; it should have a good chance of working and of not being undermined. This principle is especially helpful when *involuntary hospitalization* is indicated. Then everyone has to hear the reason for internment but need not necessarily agree with it. There will usually be no lasting grudge against the decision, despite temporary anger, if the therapist has proceeded responsibly and explained the reasons for his actions.

Finally, the emergency therapist, after having assessed the situation as completely as possible, should *carry through with the solution* that seems best. He should do so simply and unambivalently. This clarity of intent is especially important if the solution involves doing something the patient or others oppose or are highly ambivalent about, e.g., injecting a tranquilizing medication or forcing an involuntary hospitalization. If others are ambivalent, the therapist must not be; he should carry through expeditiously with what needs to be done. An insecure family will often voice doubt over a wise decision mainly to *test* the therapist.

Anna (cont'd.). At this point the emergency therapist called the outside therapist, Dr. Jones, and told him about the cousin's pressure, what its possible origins were, and what the effects had been on Anna. Being new to emergency consultation, she even suggested a referral to Dr. Gregg.

Dr. Jones surprised her by saying, "Aren't you going to hospitalize her there?" When the therapist started to explain that Anna seemed quite rational, Dr. Jones said angrily, "I think you had better evaluate her more carefully," and abruptly ended the call by saying he was in the middle of an appointment and could not talk more for another hour.

The emergency therapist was angry but realized she must not have all the facts. After all, both Betty and Dr. Jones had said that Anna belonged in the hospital, even though the therapist assumed Anna felt coerced by this possible solution.

The therapist asked Betty what her idea of a solution was. Betty said, "I still think Anna needs to go into the hospital."

She asked Anna what she thought, and to her surprise Anna said, "I know I should be there." Anna then revealed that one of her children was with her and that she had come at the little girl with a knife earlier that day. Because she had thought she was going to be admitted, she had not told the therapist about this part of her dilemma; she had assumed controls would be instituted and had talked only about the part of the trouble with Betty that was making her so angry.

It turned out that Betty had withheld all information about the presence of the little girl in their home and about the assault because she feared getting Anna into further trouble with the law and that Dr. Jones (who was black) had gone along because he thought that the emergency therapist's agency could not understand the problems of minority group patients. Betty had told Dr. Jones all the facts, and it was he who had suggested she bring Anna to the emergency room for admission.

If she had gathered expectations about hospitalization from all the participants before she jumped to a solution (referral to Dr. Gregg) based on her preliminary formulation of the case, the therapist could have spared herself embarrassment and avoided the danger of an inadequate crisis resolution. However, her ultimate willingness to listen to the participants saved the day.

Anna was hospitalized, and the emergency therapist called Dr. Jones to inform him. Dr. Jones said that he would have Dr. Gregg visit Anna in the hospital and take over the case when she was ready for discharge. He had not appreciated the depth of Betty's jealousy over him. He even thanked the emergency therapist for calling this fact to his attention. It helped him to understand some angry silences in his recent hours with Betty.

SEVERAL ASPECTS OF CRISIS INTERVENTION

Theories of the Nature of Crisis

A full replaying of the literature on crisis and crisis intervention will not be attempted here. Excellent reviews and reformulations of the current views are provided by Rapoport,[6] Darbonne,[7] Bartolucci and Drayer,[8] and Hirschowitz.[9] Crisis has been seen and studied as the change in an *individual undergoing transition,* as the cumulative toll of major *life-change events,* and as the signal of *strain in a social system.* Strategies of intervention follow naturally from the aspect of crisis that is emphasized, but a complete approach must deal with the individual, the event, and the social system. Some theoretical comments about each of these aspects will be offered as a guide to the overlapping viewpoints in this expanding field.

In the *individual undergoing transition,* crisis is often viewed as disequilibrium, an "upset in a steady state"[10] of the reacting individual who finds himself in a hazardous situation. Lydia Rapoport[6] has written that there are three sets of interrelated factors which can produce a state of crisis: (1) a hazardous event that poses some threat; (2) a threat (to an instinctual need) which is symbolically linked to earlier threats that have resulted in vulnerability to conflict; and (3) an inability to respond with adequate coping mechanisms. Generally the term *crisis* is preferred to the older term *stress* because it offers the idea of a positive turning point rather than the image of a burden or load under which a person either survives or breaks.

The *crisis state* has been carefully studied in light of Erich Lindemann's classic observations of the *acute grief reaction* following the 1943 Coconut Grove nightclub fire, which left many Boston families suddenly and unexpectedly bereaved.

Lindemann[11] identified five points which establish the diagnosis of grief:

1. Somatic distress, including sighing respiration, lack of strength and exhaustion, and loss of appetite and digestive function

2. A sense of unreality about everyday surroundings coupled with a preoccupation with the image of the deceased, which may lead to copying the appearance or behavior of the deceased

3. Guilt

4. Hostile reactions

5. Loss of patterns of conduct

He went on to discuss the *grief work,* which he defined as "emancipation from the bondage to the deceased, readjustment to the environment in which the deceased is missing, and the formation of new relationships." He showed how the therapist could play a constructive role in helping the patient overcome the major resistance to this grief work, the tendency "to avoid both the intense distress connected with the grief experience and the necessary expression of emotion."

If grief work were not accomplished, the following manifestations of an *inadequate grief* were noted:

1. Overactivity without a sense of purpose or loss

2. The acquisition of symptoms belonging to the last illness of the deceased

3. A recognized medical disease such as ulcerative colitis, rheumatoid arthritis, or asthma

4. Alteration of relationships with friends and relatives

5. Furious hostility against specific persons

6. Absence of emotional display, to a schizoid level

7. Lasting loss of patterns of social interaction

8. Unwise social, business, and professional decisions

9. Agitated depression

Lindemann's conclusion was that "sharing the patient's grief work" at the time of normal bereavement could completely prevent the appearance of such late, highly damaging "distorted reactions."

This classic study became the paradigm of much later work in crisis intervention; even the time period for working through normal grief (four to six weeks) became the standard for brief, crisis-oriented psychotherapy. Much literature on the crisis state betrays the origins in the grief state. For example, Caplan[12] defines crisis as

> ... a state provoked when a person faces an obstacle to important life goals that is, for a time, insurmountable through the utilization of customary methods of problem-solving. A period of disorganization ensues, a period of upset, during which many abortive attempts at solution are made. Eventually some kind of adaptation is achieved which may or may not be in the best interest of that person and his fellows.

Others have tried to define the *phases* of the period of upset that constitutes the state of crisis. Tyhurst[13] identified the period of impact, period of recoil, and the posttraumatic period. Bowlby[14] noted three distinct phases of the separation trauma of a young child entering the hospital: protest, despair, and denial. Kubler-Ross[15] notes that the usual response to news of a fatal illness is a sequence of personality states: shock, denial, anger, bargaining, depression, and acceptance.

Based on these and other important studies, Hirschowitz[16] has provided a useful "crisis sequence." He sees the crisis as proceeding through the phases of impact (lasting hours), recoil-turmoil (lasting days), adjustment (lasting weeks), and reconstruction (lasting months). Each phase is characterized by its own time perspective, emotions, thoughts, goal orientation, and behavior.

Thus far the crisis states we have described have been precipitated by life "hazards," which Caplan[17] points out involve a sudden *loss*, a *threat* of loss, or a *challenge* to new adaptation. Erikson[18] calls these crises "accidental crises," and he distinguishes them from his well-known "developmental crises," which are periods of disorganization marking the transition from one developmental phase in the life cycle to another.

Crisis as an opportunity has been stressed by Tyhurst[19] and Rapoport,[20] and Dabrowski[21] has postulated a developmental instinct that operates by means of a "positive disintegration" of existing personality structures. Crisis thus becomes a normal and to-be-expected transition state at nodal points in development.

Certainly crisis can serve as a catalyst to growth by disturbing old habits and evoking new responses.[22] But against the idea of crisis as a "call to new action,"[6] we have to recall that it can also be a major chance for failure, a "mess," or just another turn of a "maladaptive cycle." Part of the confusion lies in the use of the word "crisis."

Bartolucci and Drayer[23] have observed:

> The use of the term "crisis" to mean periods of acute emotional distress is now well established in the literature. "Crisis" is defined in the Oxford English Dictionary, however, as a "vitally important or decisive stage in the progress of anything, a turning point." Erikson's[24] use of the word in his discussion of developmental phases is therefore correct. On the other hand, the word "predicament" is defined as "a state of being, condition, situation, position, especially an unpleasant, trying, or dangerous situation." It may be presumed that a person going through the stresses of a developmental crisis may be more predicament-prone than at other times. However, initial intervention, as in an emergency room, is obviously aimed more at the presenting predicament than at the possible developmental crisis in the background.

The idea of predicament helps to avoid some of the overtones of an intense, cataclysmic disaster, which seems to be the connotation of the term crisis. The emergency therapist may be called upon to offer *routine service* and to spot *pseudocrises* as part of his emergency duty. He should recognize these predicaments as a valid part of his emergency room caseload.

Routine service for all medical complaints is now sought at all emergency rooms by patients who cannot leave their work or children to come at routine hours. Their predicament is the problem of entry into the health care system. They know they must be seen if they come to the emergency room and choose this way of calling attention to their needs. Persons ambivalent about applying for psychiatric help are notorious in adopting this method of seeking help, and the emergency therapist's primary responsibility is to help the patient clarify his own need and to accept referral to the regular clinic. The emergency therapist should not demand that his patient be "in crisis" before he offers this simple and helpful service.

Alternatively, some people can ask for help only by manufacturing a crisis. Often the style of an entire family may be histrionic; they will appear together in a pseudocrisis that is easily resolved. One of the tasks of crisis intervention is to help such individuals develop a repertoire of less dramatic, more effective ways of communicating their distress.

The life events that lead to crisis have been studied by Holmes and Rahe,[25] who have adopted the interesting approach of establishing a mean value for the stress potential of each of these events. As the score of mean values mounts, the likelihood of crisis increases. When the score is higher than 300,[26] a major depression or physical illness is likely within a year. An adaptation of their scale is presented in Table 1-1.

Crisis as a response to life events leads naturally to the idea that crisis strikes not just a single individual, but a unit of interacting individuals. The unit most studied, of course, is the family, and Parad and Caplan[27] have offered the concept of "family lifestyle" to describe the repertoire of solutions that are available to a family unit in crisis. The crisis intervention must work within the family style if it is to succeed.

Table 1 - 1   Social Readjustment Rating Scale

Rank	Life Event	Mean Value
1	Death of spouse	100
2	Divorce	73
3	Marital separation	65
4	Jail term	63
5	Death of close family member	63
6	Personal injury or illness	53
7	Marriage	50
8	Fired at work	47
9	Marital reconciliation	45
10	Retirement	45
11	Change in health of family member	44
12	Pregnancy	40
13	Sex difficulties	39
14	Gain of new family member	39
15	Business readjustment	39
16	Change in financial state	38
17	Death of close friend	37
18	Change to different line of work	36
19	Change in number of arguments with spouse	35
20	Mortgage over $10,000	31
21	Foreclosure of mortgage or loan	30
22	Change in responsibilities at work	29
23	Son or daughter leaving home	29
24	Trouble with in-laws	29
25	Outstanding personal achievement	28
26	Wife begins or stops work	26
27	Begin or end school	26
28	Change in living conditions	25
29	Revision of personal habits	24
30	Trouble with boss	23
31	Change in work hours or conditions	20
32	Change in residence	20
33	Change in schools	20
34	Change in recreation	19
35	Change in church activities	19
36	Change in social activities	18
37	Mortgage or loan less than $10,000	17
38	Change in sleeping habits	16
39	Change in number of family get-togethers	15
40	Change in eating habits	15
41	Vacation	13
42	Christmas	12
43	Minor violations of the law	11

Recently, Gregory Bateson[28] has argued that all mental life is really an ecological event, the individual's way of experiencing the circuit of interdependence he shares with his environment and other individuals in it. The experience in the mind of the single individual is always, he argues, "news of a difference" traveling through an entire ecological circuit, and the difference is in the circuit, not the individual. Seen this way, the individual in crisis is carrying news of a difference in an ecological system, and logically we should look for signs of strain not only in the single individual who comes in upset, but also throughout his social system. Bateson's ecological view helps to explain some otherwise puzzling crisis phenomena, such as related crises occurring at nearly the same time in the lives of persons who live or work within the same social system.

An elegant study by Yoshiko Ikeda[29] describes a wave of emotional disturbance in a leprosarium in Japan during the spring of 1960, when eleven nurses required psychiatric hospitalization and many other staff members and patients were upset. Much of the turmoil seemed to be a reaction to a new general head nurse who was insensitive in her attempts to bring more modern nursing values to a traditional setting, but the tensions between the old and new ways within the leprosarium also reflected tensions in the larger Japanese culture of that time. Indeed, the staff situation became for a time a national political scandal.

In the smaller unit of the family, a single member's heart attack may coincide with developments in the lives of other members, for instance, elopement, unwanted pregnancy, unemployment, and so on. Most families can recall "one hard year" in which everything seemed to go wrong. Occasionally an emotionally sensitive family member may *anticipate* a period of family crisis with a personal crisis of his own. Acute schizophrenia may appear in a sensitive adolescent who senses the incipient fragmentation of his parents' marriage even before they have faced their incompatibility.

Warren Miller[30] has advanced a theoretical bridge useful to the understanding of such data:

> It is important to consider the patient and the social environment playing a role together in making a psychiatric emergency. In order to facilitate this point of view, I have introduced a concept called the *ecological group,* which refers to the patient and those people in the social environment with whom he has major dynamic relationships. It may include people in the family environment, the work environment, or the medical environment. In short, it cuts across various social systems to include all those people who currently provide sources of gratification and control for the patient and for whom he does the same.

We can now take Bateson's philosophic view and Miller's clinical concept to advance a final statement on the nature of crisis. *Crisis is news of a difference affecting the pattern of relationships within an ecological group.* Thus a single individual's anxiety will be mirrored in physical distress, marital discord, vocational disruption, or social dislocation in the lives of other individuals in the ecological group. The wise therapist will look for signs of strain in other members of the group, as did Anna's when she found strain in Betty, Betty's therapist, and herself before the crisis resolution was completed.

Crisis Intervention as Consultation

In essence, the emergency therapist serves as a consultant to a system in crisis; he must therefore be familiar with the theory of psychiatric consultation, as described in Chapter 31 ("Psychiatric Consultation in the General Hospital"). In practice, certain role obligations fall upon the psychiatric consultant, whether he functions in the emergency room, on the medical ward, or in a community mental health agency.

The Consultant Defines His Role. It is incumbent upon the emergency therapist to identify himself. He must know in his own mind and make clear to the persons he treats whose agent he is. If he is working in a county emergency room, he is the agent of that county, and his primary duty is to promote the mental health and safety of the citizens of that particular county. If he is working in a private capacity, he defines himself as a consultant to the *situation* rather than as the personal advocate of any of the *participants.*

As a consultant, the emergency therapist listens for a *theme* in the information during his work-up of a crisis situation. The feelings of other professionals—police officers, hospital staffs, and secretaries—bear the imprint of the emotion generated by the crisis itself. If he takes these feelings into account, he will gain valuable insight into the specific character of the crisis. A crisis often has a kind of theme that can be recognized only if each new piece of information is viewed as an emotional communication.

In Anna's and Betty's crisis, the theme was competition. Only when the therapist could resist the temptation to compete with Dr. Jones for control of the case could she break through the competitive atmosphere that had grown up between Betty and Anna. This change from competition to cooperation allowed new information about Anna's competition with her mother-in-law over control of the children to emerge, permitting a real resolution to the crisis.

If the beginner can learn to adopt a *consultative set,* he will be able to deal effectively with many of the contingencies that arise. In the example, the emergency therapist decided, as part of the solution, to phone the regular therapist. This is a recommended procedure when a patient is already in therapy. Such a call is more than a courtesy or means to a quick "disposition"; it is part of the intervention.

In this call the outside therapist must be listened to consultatively. It is easy to make one of two false assumptions: that the outside therapist is more competent, or that because he works for a different agency he is suspect. It is better to regard the outside professional as a participant who is intimately involved in the crisis. His identity and role in the development of the crisis and his own experience of the tension must be listened to and evaluated just as the other participants are. He has a unique contribution to make and is a potential strength in resolving the crisis. And he is a member of the ecological group, not a consultant to it.

If the outside therapist sounds angry or rejecting, it is better to listen consultatively than moralistically, to keep from competing with him. The competitive consultant wins a Pyrrhic victory in which he establishes the other professional's lesser competence only to find that that person is now unwilling to cooperate in any plan to help the patient.

Knowing Disposition Resources

The emergency therapist should know what options are available *before* he discusses them with the patient. It is fruitless to discuss brief hospitalization with a patient when the nearest psychiatric facility is a distant state hospital with a reputation for stays of three to six months. Therefore the therapist will have to give himself time away from the patient to think and to check. For the therapist who is unfamiliar with community resources, telephone consultation with a knowledgeable mental health professional can prove invaluable. (A psychiatric social worker is often helpful.) Indeed, it is wise for someone starting a tour of emergency room duty to review and have with him a list of the local resources before he sees his first patient. When the list proves inadequate to handle a given situation, a phone call will often

reveal additional resources. Such calls or consultations should be made with the patient *out* of the room, leaving the therapist free to discuss various options. (Once the referral *decision* is made, the therapist may wish to contact the referral sources with the patient *in* the room so the patient can hear how and why he is being referred and have a sense of what the next person to treat him expects.)

The emergency therapist should be able to effect recommendations to patients *immediately*. For instance, if Anna needs hospitalization, the therapist should already have ascertained that a bed is available and that Anna or a social agency can pay for it. He should not suggest the improbable or impossible, only to then have to betray the patient's expectations. A suicide attempt may occur when a therapist suggests hospitalization and then cannot arrange a bed, vacillates and reverses himself, schedules an outpatient appointment, and sends the patient home more frightened than before.

A good principle for the disposition phase is *never leave the patient in midair.* When you refer him, make sure he knows where he is going, when, and why. Be sure he knows how to contact you if the initial plan proves unworkable.

The use of the telephone has become such an important part of contemporary psychiatry that we have devoted a separate chapter to it (Chapter 24). It is good to become as flexible as possible in using the telephone so that absent members of an interacting social system can talk with each other. Frequently the therapist finds himself handing the phone to the patient so he can talk with another therapist or with a family member who is not present but who has potential to resolve the situation.

Phoning can be a helpful way to make referrals, particularly with patients who are marginally motivated or fearful of rejection. When treating an alcoholic patient, some therapists make it a rule to call the referral resource in his presence, describe his problem to the resource person, and hand the phone to the patient for him to make the rest of the arrangements. With considerate referral, the percentage of alcoholic patients following through will be extremely high, as Chafetz, Blane, and Hill[31] have shown.

Strategies of Crisis Intervention

In crisis intervention, as in many other areas of psychiatry, process is as important as content in conveying implicit messages to the participants. The act of bringing the participants in a crisis together in the same room (or by phone) implies that they can interact to create a successful solution. In his official role as a representative of psychiatry, the emergency therapist refuses to condemn people for having created a system that failed but instead gives them permission to try again to find a common, acceptable solution.

In each case the consulting therapist should do everything possible to help the system find its own solution. It is all right to use therapy or hospitalization to aid the system in finding its own solution, but it is unfortunate when members of the system come to believe that the initiative is no longer theirs and that only their passive compliance with medical orders can make the difference. Medical paternalism quickly extinguishes many of the healthy coping strategies that even marginal patients and families can bring into operation.

The *extended emergency contact*[32] allows the system to find a solution over a period of several days or weeks if one cannot be formulated the first evening. Knowing that there is an interested person who, by acting as a consultant to the ecological group, is assisting it in finding its own solution can be the necessary catalyst. If the system is unable to find a solution, the emergency therapist can offer the alternative of hospitalization at any time.

In general it is more effective to appeal to the strengths of people rather than to underscore their weaknesses. Even when hospitalization is used, the interacting members of the ecological group should be encouraged to stay involved; the ulti-

mate burden of finding a solution remains with them. If the hospitalization is effected in the proper manner (see Chapter 10, "Acute Inpatient Intervention"), *discharge planning* begins the minute the patient enters the hospital.

The emergency therapist has several *important prerogatives* in dramatic situations and can exploit the element of drama in a therapeutic way. Because he is working in an emergency context, he has a right to call anyone, however far away, and make unusual demands, such as that the person participate in family interviews or communicate with others in the ecological group. No one is going to blame the emergency therapist for doing everything he can do to respond to the emergency.

Exploiting the drama that has been used by patients to make the situation seem more drastic than it is is an effective means of encouraging the members of the ecological group to interact in a healthier manner. At a time of crisis, long-standing defenses can be dropped because the situation is exceptional. At such a time individuals can communicate openly, cry in each other's presence, make admissions of a personal nature that in another context would be too damaging, and not suffer unduly.

The reason for these changes is that everything occurs under the aegis of "the emergency"; to some extent the emergency therapist can bear the onus for what is revealed. Such revelations, he implies, are part of resolving this particular crisis; they do not mean that from now on life will be a series of endless confessions. Nevertheless, steps taken now by the therapist and by the system that he is influencing may have a long-lasting effect.

Often intervention is best done *near the original setting* of the crisis by a team of mental health professionals who can share the tasks of working with the participants. Often the team is based in a regional mental health center.[33] The "social network intervention" of Speck and Attneave[34] extends further into the community to visit the homes of families in crisis and is capable of assembling as many as forty friends and neighbors for a *network meeting* to help in the emergency. (Some other ways of organizing emergency work are discussed in Chapter 11.)

Patients often remember emergencies with respect. If it is properly handled, the emergency can provide a new model to an ecological group, one in which problem solving becomes more important than winning or losing hateful confrontations.

REFERENCES

1. Jung, C. G.: "On The Nature of Dreams," in *The Structure and Dynamics of the Psyche, Collected Works,* Pantheon, New York, 1960, vol. 8, pp. 294–295.

2. Sullivan, Harry Stack: *The Interpersonal Theory of Psychiatry,* Norton, New York, 1953, pp. 151–152.

3. Freud, Sigmund: *New Introductory Lectures in Psychoanalysis,* Norton, New York, 1933, p. 112.

4. Rogers, Carl: *Client-Centered Therapy,* Houghton Mifflin, Boston, 1951.

5. Perry, John W.: Personal communication, 1970.

6. Rapoport, Lydia: "The State of Crisis: Some Theoretical Considerations," in Howard J. Parad (ed.), *Crisis Intervention,* Family Service Association, New York, 1965, chap. 2.

7. Darbonne, Allen R.: "Crisis: A Review of Theory, Practice and Research," *Psychotherapy: Theory, Research and Practice,* **4**(2): 49–56 (1967).

8. Bartolucci, Giampiero, and Calvin S. Drayer: "An Overview of Crisis Intervention in the Emergency Rooms of General Hospitals," *Am. J. Psychiat.,* **130**(9):953–959, September 1973. Copyright 1973, The American Psychiatric Association.

9. Hirschowitz, Ralph G.: "Crisis Theory: A Formulation," *Psychiat. Ann.,* **3**(12):33–47, 1973.

10. Lindemann, Erich, and Gerald Caplan: "A Conceptual Framework for Preventive Psychiatry," unpublished paper cited in Rapoport, loc. cit.

11. Lindemann, Erich: "Symptomatology and Management of Acute Grief," *Am. J. Psychiat.,* **101**:141–148, September 1944.

12. Caplan, Gerald: *An Approach To Community Mental Health,* Grune & Stratton, New York, 1961, p. 18. By permission.

13. Tyhurst, James C.: "The Role of Transition States—Including Disasters—in Mental Illness," *Symposium on Preventive and Social Psychiatry,* Walter Reed Army Institute of Research, Washington, D.C., 1970, p. 150.

14. Bowlby, John: "Separation Anxiety," *Internat. J. Psychoanal.,* **41**:89–113, 1960.

15. Kubler-Ross, Ellsbeth: *On Death and Dying,* Macmillan, New York, 1969.

16. Hirschowitz: op. cit., p. 38.

17. Caplan, Gerald: *Principles of Preventive Psychiatry,* Basic Books, New York, 1964, p. 35.

18. Erikson, Erik H. *Childhood and Society,* Norton, New York, 1963.

19. Tyhurst: loc cit.

20. Rapoport: loc. cit.

21. Dabrowski, Kazimierz: *Positive Disintegration,* Little, Brown, Boston, 1964.

22. Thomas, W. I.: *Social Behavior and Personality Contributions of W. I. Thomas to Theory and Social Research,* E. Volk (ed.), Social Science Research Council, New York, 1951, pp. 12–14, cited in Rapoport, loc. cit.

23. Bartolucci and Drayer: op. cit., p. 954.

24. Erikson, Erik H.: "Growth and Crises of the Healthy Personality," *Psychol. Issues,* **1**:1–171, 1959.

25. Holmes, Thomas H., and Richard H. Rahe: "The Social Readjustment Rating Scale," *J. Psychosom. Res.,* **11**:213–218, 1967.

26. Holmes, Thomas H., and Minoru Masuda: "Life Change and Illness Susceptibility," in John P. Scott and Edward C. Senay (eds.), *Separation and Depression,* American Asso-

ciation for the Advancement of Science, Washington, D.C., 1973, pp. 161–186.

27. Parad, Howard J., and Gerald Caplan: "A Framework for Studying Families in Crisis," in Howard J. Parad (ed.), *Crisis Intervention,* Family Service Association, New York, 1965, chap. 4, pp. 53–74.

28. Bateson, Gregory: *Steps to an Ecology of Mind,* Ballantine Books, Inc., New York, 1973, p. 454.

29. Ikeda, Yoshiko: "An Epidemic of Emotional Disturbance among Leprosarium Nurses in a Setting of Low Morale and Social Change," *Psychiatry,* **29**:152–164, May 1966.

30. Miller, Warren: "A Psychiatric Emergency Service and Some Treatment Concepts," *Am. J. Psychiat.,* **124**:924–933, 1968. Copyright 1968, the American Psychiatric Association.

31. Chafetz, Morris, Howard T. Blane, and Marjorie J. Hill: "Engaging the Alcoholic to Enter into Treatment," *Frontiers of Alcoholism,* Science House, New York, 1970, chap. 2.

32. Miller: op. cit., p. 931.

33. Lieb, Julian, Ian Lipsitch, and Andrew Slaby: *The Crisis Team: A Handbook for the Mental Health Professional,* Harper & Row, New York, 1973.

34. Speck, Ross V., and Carolyn L. Attneave: "Social Network Intervention," in Clifford L. Sager and Helen S. Kaplan (eds.), *Progress in Group and Family Therapy,* Brunner/Mazel, New York, 1973, pp. 312–332.

Evaluation of the Suicidal Patient

> . . . The sociologists and clinical psychiatrists, in particular, have been peculiarly unstoppable. Yet it is possible—in fact, easy—to plow through any of their innumerable books and articles without once realizing that they deal with that shabby, confused, agonized crisis which is the common reality of suicide.
>
> A. Alvarez, THE SAVAGE GOD[1]

EVALUATION

Evaluation is emphasized because it is critical to all psychiatric work. Evaluation implies judgment, and judgment implies *feeling,* a function of consciousness,[2] without which the gathering and logical ordering of factual data remain as preliminary as catgut knots tied in orange skins by surgeons studying to do a procedure. Psychotherapists must be in touch with their own and their patients' feelings if they are to make reasoned judgments. And they *do* make judgments (feeling-decisions) constantly, despite stereotypes to the contrary; what they strive to avoid making are stupid, impulsive, or moralistic judgments.

Evaluation is especially important in working with suicidal patients because the wish to kill one's self is almost always the end state of feeling-confusion, of being in the *closed world*[1] of ambivalence about whether to live one's own feelings or the internalized feelings of others. Suicide may not represent a clear-cut decision to die, but rather the end of a tortured inability to find one's own life to live. If he is to be helped at all, the suicidal person must find someone who can guide him in the process of evaluating his own life.

The current literature on "suicidology" (as this mechanical name implies) often deals in statistics and sociology. Facts and theories are important in understanding suicidal crises in general but neglect the emotional impasse of the individual patient. Exceptional books by Hillman[3] and Alvarez deal directly with suicidal emotion. This chapter too will present some statistics and sociology to be used as a background against which feeling-understanding can be brought to individual situations.

This chapter does *not* assume that under all circumstances suicide is to be prevented, although prevention is an obvious and usual medical goal. To postulate a dogma of prevention is to deny the individual nature of evaluation. We do not wish to bypass the slow, even painful, feeling-decisions. What suicide must be prevented by involuntary hospitalization? What choice rests with the patient? What suicide is justified? Resolving these questions takes time, for feeling as a process is slower than thinking; the impression develops rather like a photographic negative, by saturation.

There is no substitute. The argument against an

automatic policy of prevention belongs not so much to civil liberties as to therapy itself. Unless the emergency therapist has worked faithfully to evaluate the patient, he cannot counsel survival convincingly. He will be just another stranger telling the patient how to feel. If he has come honestly by a feeling-judgment that alternatives to suicide exist, his patient will surely hear him. If he knows no more than he wants to work with the patient and share the pain of the ongoing feeling-struggle, the care exercised in evaluation will rarely have been in vain. Usually the patient's closed world will have opened.

THE SCIENTIFIC STUDY OF SUICIDE

Introduction

Suicidal behavior has received enormous scrutiny during this century. A unique summary of the literature available in English up to 1970 is provided by Lester.[4] This is a definitive presentation of research findings and major theoretical perspectives, and it is well worth the careful study of workers in the field. Available books on suicide that introduce the emergency therapist to current suicidology are Farberow and Shneidman's[5] *The Cry for Help* and Stengel's[6] *Suicide and Attempted Suicide.* The following section provides a summary of this broad field.

Theories of Suicide

Many theories have been advanced to explain suicide, but four major types of theory are noteworthy[4]: (1) suicide seen as a disturbance in the individual's relation to society (Durkheim)[7]; (2) suicide seen as an expression of the individual's struggle with aggressive impulses (Freud)[8]; (3) suicide seen as the attempt to manipulate others in the environment (Adler)[9]; and (4) suicide seen as concretizing the symbolic process of death and rebirth (Hillman).[10]

Suicide as a Sociological Disruption. Durkheim postulated two characteristics of the societal group, each of which has a role in determining the suicidal behavior of its members. These were the degree of *integration* of the societal group, and the degree of *social regulation* it imposed upon its members.

Integration of the society means that its members possess shared beliefs and sentiments, interest in one another, and a sense of devotion to common goals. If integration is high, *altruistic suicide* is common, as for example by kamikaze pilots loyal to the Japanese Emperor in World War II. If integration is low, *egoistic suicide* is common, as for example in modern Hungary, where a Durkheimian explains the high rate by the lack of political ties that allows excessive individualism to develop.

Social regulation is the control exercised over members. Where social regulation is high, *fatalistic suicide* is common, as was the case on many slave ships. Where social regulation is low, *anomic suicide* is common, as President Eisenhower mistakenly assumed was the case in Sweden, where he felt social welfare made life too easy for its inhabitants.

Suicide as a Struggle with Aggression.[4] Litman[11] in reviewing Freud's writing on suicide, has shown that by 1910:

> Freud had recognized many clinical features of suicidal behavior: guilt over death wishes toward others, identification with a suicidal parent, refusal to accept loss of libidinal gratification, suicide as an act of revenge, escape from humiliation, or as a communication, and the connection between death and sexuality.

In *Mourning and Melancholia*, Freud[8] cited his first theory of suicide. He argued that suicide was the outcome of the ego's struggle to deal with loss. When an ambivalently loved object is lost, the energy that has been bound up in the loved one is relocated in the ego; the *identification* with the lost loved one is equally ambivalently perceived, and mourning takes a pathological turn and becomes melancholia because the hostile feelings once directed toward the loved one are now being turned against a part of the self. Ambivalence is particularly likely to occur after a death because a primitive anger at being abandoned collides with guilt that attends the expression of negative feelings toward the loved one. This guilt is sustained by tradition: "Speak no ill of the dead." Litman notes that *ego splitting* is an inevitable consequence of loss, even if there is no ambivalence, because room must be made in the ego to restore the lost object. Thus a complexity of emotion comes to be directed toward a part of the ego, and an intense inner dialogue may be set in motion by loss: now love, now hate, now *ambivalence,* the conscious pain of feeling-confusion. Such dialogue contributes to the pathological introspectiveness, the exhaustion, and the paralysis of melancholic individuals who often cannot stop it. Sylvia Plath's[12] poem "Daddy" is a vivid example of this internal dialogue that splits and exhausts the ego. Plath's father died when she was 9, and she spent years preoccupied with him and his fate. Her poem, addressed to him, shows her intense desire to be "finally through" with him and his introject, "the vampire who said he was you."

Suicidal people often struggle with an intense preoccupation with dead parents. Presumably this is based on inadequate grief, following the Lindemann observations in Chapter 1. If grief work is not accomplished, as in a dazed, denying family, *perseveration* of aspects of grief goes on. One of these aspects of normal grief is desire for reunion with a lost loved one, and it feels to the patient whose grief was blocked as if the loved one is somehow forever pulling him into death, where they can be together. This obsessive idea feels morbid and annoying to the suicidal person, who is kept back from progress in his own life, but until he has accomplished the grief work, death

absolutely will not go away, and the patient is locked in ambivalent combat with the emotional claims the dead person has on him.

In *Beyond the Pleasure Principle*, Freud[13] explored his later idea of a primary drive toward death. This theme was too metaphysical for most of Freud's followers, but it was adopted by Melanie Klein and Karl Menninger, who view it as a primary aggressive drive, the source of aggressive energy. Their observations relate suicide to *ambivalence* and *variations* in the directing of this aggressive energy, the death-dealing part of the personality.

Melanie Klein relates the development of ambivalence to the internalization of the death instinct, or aggressive drive. Klein[14] feels this instinct is originally identified in projection onto the mother whose "bad breast" is felt to be the cause of the child's hunger and pain. The baby feels at one with the "good breast," which is responsible for his feelings of satisfaction and relief. The bad breast is outside him, split off and dreaded: this is the paranoid-schizoid position of earliest infancy, with its intense *persecutory anxiety*. Only at a later stage does the infant learn that "when he loves and hates his mother, it is one and the same person whom he desires and attacks."[15] Then he has to weigh his pain when hungry against her pain when attacked, and the conflict of ambivalence starts. Ambivalence is the core of the infantile depressive position. Furthermore, the infant's belief in the power of his destructive impulses is greater than his belief in the power of his loving impulses, and he suffers intense fear that his negative feelings will destroy his mother or her love for him. This is *depressive anxiety*. Only gradually is it outgrown, and only if the mother establishes that the infant's negative feelings do not in reality destroy her.

Hendin[16] has applied psychoanalytic findings in his study of the effects of different national styles of child-rearing on the way adult suicidal patterns appear in three Scandinavian countries. In Denmark, a long period of dependency is encouraged, and aggression against the parents is severely checked to ensure "proper" dependency gratification. The child is disciplined by arousing his guilt. Suicide rates are high. In men, suicide follows the loss of a mother or wife; in women it follows the birth of the children, thus reflecting the frustration of their own dependency needs. The depressive pattern is a classic retarded involutional depression with ambivalence and guilt over repressed hostility.

In Sweden, separation from the mother comes early. Direct expression of both anger and dependency is discouraged, and the major anxiety is intense self-blame over performance failure. The resultant depression is anxious and agitated, connected with shame and a striving to improve a failing performance. The suicide rate is high. Men kill themselves in the grip of self-hatred over job failures, women from a sense of failure in their heterosexual relationships.

In Norway, both aggression and dependency are encouraged by a mother who centers her emotional life on her child. Neither guilt nor shame are invoked in child-rearing. Rather, the culture instills fear of envy rather than fear of failure, and a national style of injustice collecting and nursing grudges develops because blame for failure is projected onto others. The suicide rate is low.

It would seem that depression and suicide are least likely to occur if the mother is able to *accept* the projection onto her of the withholding bad breast and most likely if the mother has to present herself as *only giving,* thus forcing her child to experience his aggression as a threat to his dependent needs. The implications are obvious for a country like the United States, where the "positive mother" is glorified in holidays such as Mother's Day, and the "negative mother" is not admitted to exist.

The death instinct has been most specifically explored by Karl Menninger[17] in *Man against Himself.* In all suicidal motivation, Menninger discovers three strands: a wish to kill, a wish to be killed, and a wish to die. Each relates to the use of the aggressive drive.

A practical application of these dynamics is made in referral decisions. Successful psychotherapy of suicidal patients usually involves a strong recapitulation of attitudes toward the original mothering figure and of the wish to kill, the wish to be killed, and the wish to die. It is a good idea to establish early in evaluation the nature and strength of these attitudes and drives to determine whether treatment is best conducted in a private practice setting, where dependency, anger, and guilt are likely to be more focused and intense (because there is only one mothering figure), or in a clinic setting, where the institution shares some of the mothering function and receives some of the anger and blame. Often the "Swedes" (patients with anxiety about performance failure) do better in private settings, and the "Danes" (patients with guilt over hostile dependency) do better in clinic settings. Very hostile patients do best in clinic settings.

Suicide as the Attempt to Manipulate Others. One motive of many suicidal fantasies and acts is the suicidal individual's knowledge that he can attain from or do to others in suicide what he cannot easily attain or do in life. The suicidal patient may assume that his death attempts will attract the desired attention and devotion; provide a real or symbolic reunion with loved ones; cause anguish, grief, and guilt in those who have "let him down," overburdened him, or treated him unjustly.[18] Or as Adler[9] argued, death may be perceived as finally establishing a validation of his worthlessness and proof that he is not worth caring about. (For patients with long-standing inferiority feelings, with rage and envy at "healthy" others, suicide is the ultimate vengeful victory of the *inferiority complex.*)

These complex and often contradictory emotions may result in a paradox: although the suicide attempter may wish to establish that he cannot be loved, the successful suicide often acts as if he will be around to receive the love and attention which will come to him posthumously.[19] The paradox obtrudes into both evaluation and treatment.

When the manipulative intent is transparently obvious to the harrassed therapist or internist (although it may not be obvious to the patient), there is a strong temptation to speak disparagingly of a "suicide gesture" and dismiss the patient as a "hysteric" who should, in effect, go home, grow up, and learn how to express conflict in a more mature manner. What may not be obvious in such an incident is the intensity of feeling which precipitated the "gesture" and the realization that at least in this stage of the patient's life a gesture may be the closest he can come to expressing how he feels.

Indeed, the patient may present his "childish" behavior in such a way (or at such a time, 4 A.M. being one of the favorites) that he elicits punishment for it. If the therapist is led into becoming an angry parent figure, the patient has succeeded in bringing a child he cannot control to a father who will give him a scolding. Occasionally such scoldings help. More often they succeed only in further alienating the patient from his own infantile parts that, like a real infant's, find it necessary to act up still more to regain attention. When the therapist takes the infantile signal for attention seriously, he interrupts this vicious cycle and allows the "infant" in the patient to enter treatment along with the bewildered adult.

This split between more and less mature portions of the personality is found frequently in suicidal people, who are notorious for neglecting their dependent needs because they are ashamed of them. When they begin to overcome their antipathy to the less mature parts of themselves, they can be taught to take care of their own dependent needs, and the need to manipulate others into doing so lessens. This is sometimes spoken as *learning to take care of the child within* and is a critical step in the psychotherapy of hysterical patients.

Suicide in the Evolution of Identity. There are certain life crises of identification in which people find themselves hopelessly locked into a lifestyle which is no longer successful; yet they do not know how to aid themselves in their evolution to the next phase of life. It is as if both personal and cultural rites of passage or initiation were not available to them. The person perceives suicide as the only means of shedding an outworn identity state, as a snake must shed its skin, for the new self to emerge magically after death.[20]

One common complex of this sort found in gifted young adults is called by Jungians the *puer aeternus,* a particularly "inflated" offshoot of the familiar Wunderkind.[21] *Puer aeternus* means eternal boy and is exemplified by the myth of Icarus, who flew too close to the sun on wax wings built by his father, and plunged to his death in the sea. Many young people who show promise are extravagantly praised for being gifted. Influenced by an older generation's aspirations for them, they are reluctant to become adults by confronting the issue of how to develop their gifts and idealism into realistic productivity.[22] Some resolve the dilemma by becoming dilettanti, others by becoming perpetual graduate students who style themselves Renaissance men. A few refuse any compromise (as did Zelda Fitzgerald) and find that their inability to relinquish the godlike prerogatives of eternal youth leads to a psychiatric crisis of catastrophic proportions.[23]

A more common resolution of "puer inflation" is a suicidal crisis. Alvarez[24] describes his own unsuccessful suicide attempt at age 31, in the midst of great precocious success as a critic, in terms which suggest it was a death-of-the-puer experience.

Active suicidal fantasies develop in this extreme form, often without relation to major setbacks in the outer world; it feels to the patient like an attack from within. If this *death experience*[25] is allowed to occur symbolically, a giving up of the puer adaptation and a maturing of the personality often ensues. If the death experience is blocked by well-meaning friends and therapists who attempt to help the young person retain his airy imperviousness to life, it may assert itself in a suicide attempt. Alvarez describes his own experience as follows:[24]

The truth is, in some way I *had* died. The overintensity, the tiresome excess of sensitivity and self-consciousness, of arrogance and idealism, which came in adolescence and stayed on and on beyond their due time, like some visiting bore, had not survived the coma. It was as though I had finally, and sadly late in the day, lost my innocence.

... Certainly, nothing has been quite the same since I discovered for myself, in my own body and on my own nerves, that death is simply an end, a dead end, no more, no less.

... Before the pills was another life, another person altogether, whom I scarcely recognize and don't much like—although I suspect that he was, in his priggish way, far more likeable than I could ever be. Meanwhile, his fury and despair seem improbable now, sad and oddly diminished.

Thus suicidal phenomenology becomes an unconscious way out of the ego impasse. The therapist tries to make the process at least somewhat more conscious, to locate which part of the patient needs to be sacrificed to make way for new growth. His goal is to lead the patient to a voluntary sacrifice of old, no longer viable attitudes so that life itself may be preserved.*

Classification of Suicide

Classifications of suicide are more helpful to sociologists than to therapists in evaluating patients.[27] Furthermore, each classification introduces its own bias as to what will and will not be considered suicidal behavior. Nevertheless, each system helps identify individuals who seem consciously or unconsciously headed toward self-

destruction. The English coroner system distinguishes these four classes of death: natural, accidental, suicidal, and homicidal (giving rise to the acronym NASH). It is an imperfect system: the chronic drinker, frequently warned by doctors, dies a "natural" death of cirrhosis; the soldier, no longer wishing to live, volunteers for and is killed on a dangerous mission, dying an "accidental" death, which makes him a posthumous hero; the actress unwittingly takes a lethal overdose, thinking it sublethal, and dies a "suicide," even though her death was unintentional.

Shneidman[28] introduces the concept of intentionality into the classification of deaths and distinguishes between *unintentioned, subintentioned, intentioned,* and *contraintentioned.* The drinker's death was subintentioned; the soldier's, intentioned; the actress', contraintentioned. It is the therapist's job to see if individuals whose words and acts suggest subintentioned and intentioned self-destruction can be swayed from their lethal paths and if those flirting with death can find safer ways to express themselves. At times fate itself appears to deny the intention to die.

Example 2-1. A 29-year-old man crashed two small planes without injury and was captured by a policeman who shot to kill and missed. The policeman reported, "He begged me to go ahead and kill him. He said he wished my aim had been a little better." The man's wife had announced her intention to leave him. He went for a flying lesson and forced his pilot-instructor to crash the airplane nose first onto the ground. The policeman's first shot, aimed at his head, missed, and the second shot succeeded only in knocking the rifle out of this hijacker's hand. Despite the two crashes and two shots, he remained unharmed.[29]

Lester[30] has argued that it makes sense to recognize that all acts of suicide fall on a continuum of lethality from thoughts through threats, attempts, and completed deaths. A particularly difficult problem for the emergency therapist is evaluating the lethal intent of a suicide threat,

---

*Nevertheless, patients are encountered for whom the solution of total physical death subbornly insists upon itself. It is the only solution the patient finds satisfactory, no matter how many alternatives are explored. Hillman[26] has argued that we must respect the choice of suicide when it is made responsibly. Jung emphasizes that death is part of nature: it has a place in the ecology of a healthy personality and on occasion is the only way an unhealthy personality can bring its sickness to an end.

whether it is made verbally or through "gesture." He must first dismiss the popular idea that those who threaten suicide rarely attempt it. In fact, most patients who make serious or successful attempts at suicide have threatened to do so in the preceding days and weeks. Likewise, many persons whose blatantly nonlethal attempts have been dismissed as "hysterical gestures" may later make lethal ones. For every seven attempts at suicide, one succeeds.[31–33]

Some [34–39] have attempted to discriminate between suicidal acts that are lethal and nonlethal in intent. This work is preliminary, and we prefer this principle: *anyone who threatens suicide or makes a suicidal gesture needs to be taken seriously and evaluated carefully.*

Suicide Statistics

Official statistics underreport suicides.[38] In recent years in the United States, approximately 22,000 persons will have been adjudged suicides each year; another 5,000 to 8,000 are assumed to have killed themselves but have not been adjudged suicides by a coroner's jury. Officially, more than 11 of each 100,000 people in this country take their own lives each year. Compared to other countries studied by the World Health Organization, the United States is about midway in incidence. Greece, Northern Ireland, and Italy have official rates below 6.0 per 100,000; West Germany, Austria, and Hungary above 20.0 per 100,000; and West Berlin 41.3 per 100,000.

Data from attempted suicides allow sociologists to define characteristics of groups that have the highest and the lowest risks for suicide. From these data, suicide danger-rating scales have been constructed. From knowledge of these risks, predictions can be made about suicidal behavior for a class of people, but it is always the individual and members of his immediate group with whom the emergency therapist is concerned. To date, no danger-rating scale discriminates absolutely between the person who will probably not make a suicide attempt and the one who probably will.

The data in Table 2-1 demonstrate sociological factors in the United States correlated with low and high risk for suicidal behavior. Whenever a patient falls in several of the high-risk categories, the emergency therapist's index of suspicion about suicide potential should be high and his evaluation more careful.[40–43]

Even though a patient may fall primarily in the lower-risk categories of Table 2-1, he is not immune from suicidal risk.

> *Example 2-2.* A young black engineer with a devoted fiancée, a good work record, and no problem with alcohol had little known present stress, no known physical problems, and excellent interpersonal resources. On most suicide-rating scales he would seem to be a low risk. However, he had a past history of an LSD trip on which he "learned" the insignificance of life, and he had made several serious attempts at suicide. Moreover, this time he had a plan of action for completing suicide. His doctor wisely hospitalized him.

It would have been easy for this man to disguise his distress in an interview conducted to screen him and to agree to psychotherapy on an outpatient basis. His deep preoccupation with death would have been missed.

The studies from which Table 2-1 was derived suggest that emotion isolation is an important factor. Sociology confirms common sense: lack of participation in the human group drives people to suicide. Also, recent studies point to anger, energy depletion, and difficulties in adaptation to rapid changes as contributors. In some cases the collection of better suicide data from a population follows new understanding of its problems[44]: witness studies of black suicide undertaken only at the end of the decade of James Baldwin, Eldridge Cleaver, and the Watts riot.[41]

A few aspects of Table 2-1 deserve amplification. Suicide increases with age, showing, as Alvarez[45] notes, the fallacy of the serenity of old age. The steady rise is shown in Figure 2-1, based on the work of Choron.[46] The low suicide rates for

Table 2-1   Sociological Factors and Suicide Risk in the United States

Factor	Lower Risk	Higher Risk
Age	Childhood, adolescence (see Figure 2–1)	Middle, older age (see Figure 2–1)
Sex	Women (30%)	Men (70%)
Family status	Over 24 years old, married with children Over 35 years old and never married	Separated, divorced, widowed
Race	Black*, Oriental	White, American Indian
Religion	Jewish, Catholic	Protestant
Profession	Noncompetitive and/or low demand for interpersonal giving, e.g., white-collar workers, craftsmen, taxi drivers, machine assemblers	Competitive and/or demanding of interpersonal giving, e.g., doctors, lawyers, policemen, housekeepers, nurses
Employment status	Employed at job or at home	Unemployed
Geographic		
1. Local	Stable areas and neighborhoods; suburbs; homeowners	Transitional and slum urban areas; renters
2. National	East coast, midwest	West coast (especially San Francisco)
Health	Good; no history of chronic depression or alcohol abuse	Poor, and/or chronic depression or alcohol abuse
Political	Wartime; political or religious persecution	Peacetime; little persecution

*However, see Hendin[41] for possible change in this trend.

married people may reflect not only the companionship of marriage but also its outlet for aggression; one wonders what would have happened to George and Martha in Albee's *Who's Afraid of Virginia Woolf?* had they not had each other to fight. Rates are lower during times of war and religious persecution, when an external enemy increases group solidarity and provides a focus for aggression.

Personal Factors

We move from the anonymity of statistics to the feeling-uncertainty of the individual patient; the case of Alice will be cited often as an example. This chapter focuses on understanding why Alice behaved suicidally; the next chapter describes the treatment of Alice and other suicidal patients.

Example 2-3, Alice. Alice, a 45-year-old divorced woman, was brought into the emergency room by the police, whom she had called earlier that evening to report that her husband was threatening to kill her. In response to the call, the police met Bradley, a 50-year-old man who had been living with Alice and with whom she had just taken a year-long business tour of the United States.

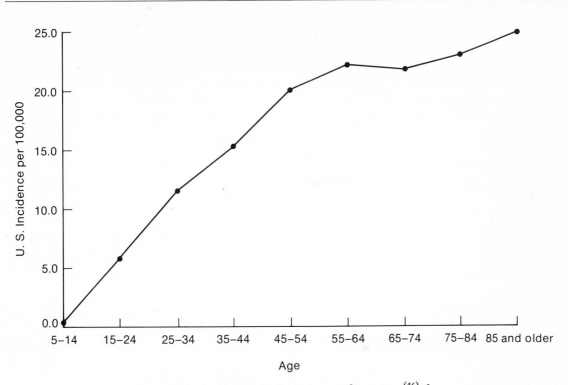

Figure 2–1   Incidence of suicide by age. [Based on [46] .]

This tour had included a visit to her son in jail. Bradley and Alice had been drinking and quarreling, but Bradley agreed to the policeman's suggestion that he leave for the night. After he left, Alice called a taxi to take her to "some motel, it doesn't matter where," spent her last $10 on a room, swallowed a bottle of Sominex, called the police, and said, "You'd better come and get me, I just took something."

In the emergency room she was given ipecac. Later, when the first-year psychiatric resident saw her, she insisted tiredly she could take care of herself. The record showed similar attempts three and four years before; both times she had been released from the emergency room without follow-up plans.

This time the psychiatrist, noting she had no resources and would not return to Bradley, recommended hospitalization and threatened to sign a seventy-two-hour hold until the situation was clarified. Alice finally agreed to enter voluntarily at county expense. The admitting diagnosis was "depressive reaction in a passive-aggressive personality, possible alcoholism." She insisted on returning to the hotel to get her things, so the resident drove her there in his car. When she was admitted to the psychiatric unit she said, "I didn't know anything this nice was here," and prepared to go to bed.

The resident felt that Alice might attempt suicide again in spite of the impulsiveness of her previous gesture and her request for help. He was willing to impose the seventy-two-hour involuntary hospitalization to obtain time for further evaluation and because he knew that the risk of a repeat attempt is highest in the three days after a suicide attempt.

From a sociological point of view, this patient was high risk. She was outside society, in transit, divorced, jobless, restless, and she drank. But her first suicide attempts belonged to the period before her present rootlessness began. Old records revealed that her husband had held a managerial position in a munitions firm. What lay behind her immediate problems?

Chronic Predisposing Factors. Usually even a sudden, impulsive suicidal act has an extensive background. Often there is evidence of a *death trend,* in which deaths of family members, deaths of aborted or live-born children, and so on are prominent in the patient's history. Such losses, often under dramatic and tragic circumstances, were found in nearly all fifty suicidal patients in one study,[47] and three-quarters of the losses had occurred by the patient's adolescence. Again we recall Sylvia Plath's adult preoccupation with her father, who died when she was 9.

The link between past loss and present depression may be the *anniversary reaction* described by Hilgard and Newman.[48] This reaction surfaces at a time that evokes the memory of the loss—on the anniversary of suffering. Obvious reminders are the actual dates of loss, such as the yearly anniversary of a spouse's death.[49] Less obvious reminders come when a patient reaches the same age as a parent who died or when the patient's child becomes as old as the patient when a parent was killed. Seasons can bring on reactions: one woman became depressed every March, when the first warm days reminded her of her contact with an abortionist. Frequently women who lose babies, whether by therapeutic, illegal, or spontaneous abortion, find themselves unaccountably depressed and even suicidal on the day the baby would have been born.

Alice (cont'd.). The day after admission, Alice willingly told the resident about her life. Her father had left home when she was 14; her mother raised her and her brother, who had become a policeman. Alice was unable to give up her father, however, and when she was 17 followed him after work and discovered that he lived with another woman. Shortly after

this incident her father was killed in a fire. Talking about this event, the patient suddenly burst into tears and was surprised at the intensity of her feelings.

Shortly after her father's death, Alice met Fred. He was a handsome, charming man, and they quickly married. She became pregnant with Don, and while she was carrying him she learned that Fred had escaped from prison in Missouri. Fred became brutal and began to drink heavily and was physically cruel and frequently unfaithful to her. She left Fred soon after their second child was born. The day before she attempted suicide Alice had visited her son Don in prison. Until the age of 17 he had been an outstanding student. On his seventeenth birthday he was in a car accident in which three people were killed; he was sentenced by an outraged court to five years in prison, in spite of the fact that Alice tried vainly to have the sentence commuted. Two years after Don went to prison, Alice made her first suicide attempt.

Don was 17 when he was sentenced; Alice was 17 when she learned of her father's infidelity. Alice was 19 when her father died in the fire; when Don reached 19, Alice made her first suicide attempt. Delinquency and death have their eerie anniversaries. Alice appeared to be reacting to Don's imprisonment as she had to her father's disappearance and death: by following him into exile and punishing herself for his loss.

Although distant or recent loss is not prominent, most suicidal patients, even if their attempts appear impulsive, have been thinking about death for some time. Alvarez, while intoxicated on Christmas Eve, took an overdose of sleeping pills after a marital squabble. He too had "been incubating this death for longer than I recognized." When things went badly for him as a youth, he recited a litany to himself, "IwishIweredead . . . IwishIweredead." One day, he writes, ". . . suddenly I heard the phrase as though for the first time. . . . I repeated the words slowly, listening. And realized that I meant it. It seemed so obvious, an answer I had known for years and never allowed myself to acknowledge."[50]

In addition to hearing about the current distress, the emergency therapist must learn about old losses, anniversary reactions, previous suicide attempts, and other long-term incubations of the wish to die. Often the lethal risk is clarified only after the chronic background is revealed.

Personality Styles. *Predisposing personality styles* for suicide are the (1) impulsive, (2) compulsive, and (3) risk-taking. Some patients cannot control *impulses,* such as reactions to minor stress, and become suicidal. A San Francisco man became frustrated in the midst of a traffic jam, left his car, and jumped off the Golden Gate Bridge; a housewife stabbed herself with an ice pick when her children refused to do the dishes. Such people are usually more prone to attempt than to complete suicide.

The impulsivity of persons who make dramatic life decisions to communicate feelings they cannot put into words is more lethal. Alice's dramatic search for her father and her impulsive marriage show the beginnings of a stubborn, impulsive streak that surfaced in her conflicts with men. Such impulsivity combines willfulness with an inability to put the same feelings into words.

Alice (cont'd.). The day after Alice was admitted, Bradley called her therapist to confide that she was "kind of peculiar." Alice habitually called the police when she was angry with Bradley and had had him locked up twice. This made Bradley "sore," even though he "liked her spunk." He compared her to Don, who a few hours after her visit had made an impulsive attempt to escape from prison. He had been caught immediately and sentenced to solitary confinement with a loss of parole, all of which Alice had read about in the newspaper. That night she had started the quarrel with Bradley which ended with two calls to the police and a suicide attempt.

Alice admitted to feeling anger toward the policemen who responded to her first call,

because they did not do more to protect her. She said she called the police right after taking the pills because she was still angry with them. The fact that calling them led to her life being saved seemed less important to her than that she had taught them a lesson about how to treat people in trouble.

Compulsive personalities are high-achieving and perfectionistic. They have difficulty adjusting their needs and goals to changing circumstances and are inflexible in their habits. In middle and later life they are predisposed to involutional depression. They may for a short time become acutely and dangerously suicidal. When this personality pattern is recognized in a depressed person past the middle of life, the clinician must be alert to the high lethal risk. To some extent compulsive defenses appear with age, and the ability to adjust to minor stress lessens. And *anyone* can fall apart with too drastic a change in life pattern.

Whether a person is compulsive or not, an *erosion of life style* deprives him of many personal and social gratifications and defenses against loneliness, anxiety, and depression. Previously bound or sublimated impulses push for expression with greater urgency, and suicide as an egoistic or anomic event becomes progressively more thinkable. As one suicide note put it, "Why suicide? Why not?"[51] In Alice's life a definite erosion of stability rendered her more vulnerable to suicide.

Alice (cont'd.). When Don was 6 and his brother Joe was 4, Alice entered into a second marriage with Rolfe, an engineer who was very strict with her boys ("to keep them from turning out like their father"), but who babied the son born a year after their marriage. Their social life was stable; for many years Alice made friends and participated in the PTA, country club, and other social activities.

After Don's car accident, Alice silently blamed Rolfe's heavy-handed discipline for Don's behavior, became increasingly dissatisfied with the marriage, and listened to her friends' suggestions that she leave Rolfe. At the same time that Joe was being dishonorably discharged from the Army, Alice filed separation papers. She anticipated going into business with Joe and Don, who was within two months of discharge on parole. Shortly thereafter Don and Joe pulled an armed robbery together; both received five-year sentences.

This did it. Alice withdrew from her friends, started drinking, and met Bradley, who quickly left his wife and moved in with her. They drank and went through Alice's money, and she completely fell away from her old friends and activities. She and Bradley started traveling across the country. Bradley promised to set up a business and divorce his wife, but he succeeded only in passing a few bad checks and skipping from one town to the next.

For some, *risk-taking* is a way of life. One woman, in a showdown with her boyfriend and the other woman, took an overdose of sleeping pills. Later she said, "All my life I've been a gambler; I wanted to show them I was willing to gamble my own life." For a long time this woman had played the stock market and enjoyed the risk-taking involved. She transferred this psychology to the resolution of her romantic dilemma.

For many, risk-taking is part of the "good life." Perhaps the Kennedy family is the most noteworthy public example of the risk-taking style of high-achieving, flexible people. In examining the role of the victim in assassination attempts, Weisz and Taylor[52] suggest that the propensity of the victim to take risks increases his likelihood of being murdered.

Obviously, *chronic predisposing psychiatric conditions* play an enormous role in the choice of suicide. Among the more important are

1. *Drug or alcohol problems.* Fifty percent of the male suicides have measurable blood alcohol levels. Ruth Fox[53] says the suicide rate is fifty-five times higher for alcoholics. It is estimated that about 10 percent of addicts, alcoholics, and drug abusers will die by suicide, not counting their many accidental deaths.

2. *Manic-depressive disease.* The depressed phase is a highly dangerous time, and the patient should almost always be hospitalized.

3. *Depression.* People tend to commit suicide more often when depression is improving or after a period in which they have begun to feel better. Two reasons have been advanced to explain this pattern. First, patients who have been slowed by the intense psychomotor retardation of an exhausting psychotic depression do not have the energy to kill themselves or to formulate a plan. When they begin to improve, their energy returns, and suicidal behavior again becomes a possibility. Second, these patients dread a return to their formerly depressed states. A minor setback after a period of improvement may threaten the patient with another long bout of emotional paralysis. Recognizing that chronic depression is just around the corner, a patient may choose a time when he is feeling relatively well to kill himself. Experienced clinicians are very cautious during the improvement of severe depression and often resist pressure from the patient and family for premature discharge into an environment where suicide can be accomplished.

4. *Schizophrenia.* The schizophrenic patient most often commits suicide during the early phase of his illness, in contrast to the depressive patient, who commits suicide during the convalescent phase. Schizophrenic patients also commit suicide during times of change. Times such as when they enter the hospital, go into or come out of the psychotic phase, or when they are discharged are especially high risk.

5. *Personality disorder.* Most clinicians would describe Alice as having a personality disorder. Her distress became part of her character and led her to seek out partners who would hurt her. Menninger[54] uses the term *chronic suicide* to describe this process. From the time she made her first choice, choosing a husband, Alice seems to have been acting unconsciously

against herself. Suicide attempts were just one aspect of an overall pattern of self-destruction. Much of this pattern appeared as an adverse fate over which she had no control. But had she nothing to do with the choice of four alcoholic men and with two sons being sent to jail? When she did consider this, the insight seemed malignant and only made her hate herself more.

6. *Past suicidal history.* The *history of a previous suicide attempt* is the single most important prognosticator of suicidal potential. Alice had made two such attempts. In a man over the age of 50, a serious attempt within the past ninety days would almost certainly demonstrate a period of high risk.

Other forms of self-destructive activity should be regarded as part of the suicidal history. It is customary for therapists to regard these as *suicidal equivalents.* Alice, for instance, chose brutal, alcoholic men and a lifestyle (presumably motivated by shame and guilt) that amounted to social suicide in the group to which she had belonged. Other patients give even clearer histories of actions that although not directly suicidal are self-destructive. A formerly suicidal woman may turn to prostitution or heroin addiction. A suicidal air force officer may volunteer for an unnecessary mission. A young psychiatrist may begin treating his own anxiety with barbiturates. An adolescent girl may have many therapeutic abortions. At any point in his history the patient may exchange one of these suicidal equivalents for suicidal behavior. (An overzealous therapist may precipitate a suicidal crisis by forcing a patient to give up some "masochistic" behavior whose real motivations neither he nor the patient understand).

7. *Negative therapeutic history.* It is common to find in the histories of those who kill themselves a dismal story of *past failures in psychotherapy and unsuccessful medical treatment.*

Alice (cont'd.). After Don's first imprisonment, Alice saw a psychotherapist three times, did not find therapy helpful, and did not return. The therapist remembered her as "very skittish; underneath I had the feeling she was very confused, maybe crazy." For two years preceding her most recent suicide attempt she had been having heavy menstrual bleeding. Gynecologists had recommended a dilatation and curettage, but in her travels with Bradley she had never found the money for this minor surgery.

Recent Precipitating Factors

The chronic background of most suicidal crises can be summarized as the combination of negative life expectation with a character style which does not leave the environment much room to counter that expectation. The immediate background is a major current frustration. Suicidal patients act when the going gets tough. Certain acute life situations are especially apt to precipitate the suicidal act in susceptible individuals. These include loss, health problems, social disgrace, loss of the reason to live, and plastic surgery.

Loss. Loss stands out in almost every suicidal history. In an otherwise normal person the loss of a loved one can precipitate suicidal thinking. In the person with a chronic expectation of loss, starting with the loss of a parent in childhood, further loss can be catastrophic. Thus the emergency therapist finds himself taking an inventory of loss as he talks to his potentially suicidal patients. What may be difficult to remember is that the *threat of loss* can be as upsetting as actual loss. It may be likelier to precipitate suicide and is far more difficult to identify.

Alice (cont'd.). Alice's therapist was puzzled about why Alice attempted suicide at that particular time. Don's escape attempt had probably contributed, but some pieces of the puzzle were still missing. Alice insisted she was through with Bradley and seemed to believe that leaving him would be a gain, not a loss. The resident and ward staff supported her decision.

Therefore the resident was surprised to learn a day later that Bradley was visiting Alice and holding hands with her. In a joint interview he learned that Bradley was threatening to leave Alice and return to his wife, and that Alice's threats to leave Bradley were mostly a strategy to convince him to obtain his divorce and marry her. Since her sons' imprisonment, Bradley was the only person that mattered to her. Whatever society thought, she loved him, and she held the secret belief she could change him enough so that they could be happy together. She had been deeply threatened by his new talk of going back to his wife at a time when she wanted to make final arrangements for a permanent move across the country. At this point the resident perceived that he was dealing with a couple problem.

As Freud pointed out, loss hits harder when the thing lost is regarded ambivalently. But any loss is hard: death, divorce, military duty, urban renewal. Almost always the individual regrets not having done the best with what he had, and self-recrimination is usual.

A common issue in the lives of suicidal patients is the loss or threat of loss of a supportive professional. Frequently a therapist's vacation precipitates a suicidal crisis, a syndrome called the *caretaker crisis*. Often only the caretaker can resolve it by returning or promising to return. Although the issue is dependency, the caretaker crisis does not occur only in passive-dependent individuals. High-achieving, compulsive personalities, who usually have strong guilt feelings over dependency and stoically deny their needs feel the absence of nurturant others most. And they are the ones who find it most difficult to ask for substitute help. Quite frequently they signal their needs by serious suicide attempts. For this reason, discharge planning for patients with involutional depressions is extremely difficult. Patients may move compliantly through the planning stage of discharge and make serious attempts soon after they return home. In some cases they are not able to *say* that they still felt the need for support. As a matter of routine, many therapists tell their patients: "You probably won't agree, but in the first days at home you are going to miss this place a great deal, whatever you think now, and you should expect a return of the suicidal feelings. I expect you to call me when this happens, even though you may think it is unimportant."

Health Problems. Loss of another sort comes when a healthy person, proud of his body and used to activity, is forced into invalidism, and the patient may doubt that life is worth continuing. Two-thirds of the old people who commit suicide have painful or disabling diseases.

In checking up on the patient's health, *medications that have a depressing effect* should be identified. Rauwolfia alkaloids, prescribed for hypertension, have precipitated severe depressions that look primary. Diazepam (Valium®) and chlorpromazine have also been reported to have this effect. Surgical residents in particular are prone to overprescribe diazepam, which causes later appearance of depressive symptomatology in hospitalized patients.

Social Disgrace. Here too a kind of loss is involved—the loss of face. Suicide may follow sudden arrest or bankruptcy, disclosure of child molesting, and so on.

Some suicidal crises occurring after encounter groups are of this type, seemingly caused by too rapid a dissolution of the ego defenses that acted as supports.[55] Loss of face can occur in a group as small as two, and traditional one-to-one psychotherapy can also be a place where social disgrace occurs. Some patients seen in emergency rooms are in flight from therapeutic situations that have brought about confrontations with extremely unacceptable parts of themselves. *Homosexual panic* can also lead to suicide.

Loss of Reason to Live. To understand suicidal metapsychology, Freud started with the question, "Why should the normal instinct for self-preservation fail?" In evaluating suicidal patients, the emergency therapist must learn to reverse the question: "Why does this person live?" In searching for the factors that affect an individual's potential for suicide, it is easy to forget to ask this question. Yet when a suicide is actually completed, it is often because the one reason for staying alive no longer exists. The late actor George Sanders perhaps epitomized the *existential suicide* when he wrote, "I am committing suicide because I am bored."

Others stay alive because they harbor hopes of future interests. If a symbolic purpose keeps them alive, its disappearance may be unknown to anyone else. And they themselves may not always know what it was. Alice apparently found her reason to live in her dream of establishing a new life with Bradley. When this hope became threatened, the suicidal impulse, strengthened by her tragic background, broke through.

A paradigm for this type of suicide is the *vacation suicide.* For many, a vacation is anticipated as the solution to long-standing problems. When at last the vacation comes, but not the expected relief, a suicidal crisis may appear "out of the blue."

Plastic surgery too may precipitate a suicidal crisis. The issue again involves false hope. The surgery was expected to work magic by restoring long-absent self-esteem.

SPECIFICS OF INTERVIEW EVALUATION

Focus on Recent Changes

Despite its chronic background, the decision to commit suicide is always an acute event. In the emergency room the key question is "Is the patient moving in a suicidal direction now?" In the short range the prognosis is *worse* when the onset of self-destructive behavior is recent. (Of course,

the long-term prognosis is better for those whose pattern is not chronic.) Recent loss, recent appearance of depressive signs, and recent concern on the part of friends and relatives are all important signs. If suicide is an issue, evaluation should be prompt and follow-up frequent. The patient should not have to wait several days before the therapist can see him. Here, as with the evaluation of possible homicide, information about the development of the immediate crisis is essential. The resident decided to hospitalize Alice almost entirely on his evaluation of her present circumstances. Here, he reasoned, is a divorced, middle-aged woman in the acute period of a romantic breakup, with no job, no place to live, and a suicidal gesture, who says, "Next time I'll do it right." Whatever the long-range prognosis for her ending her life, another rejection now (in the form of accepting her denial and letting her go) could tip the balance in favor of suicide. Only later did the resident learn about the long lead-up to her attempt.

Inquire about Suicide Planning

Beginning therapists often find it difficult to ask detailed questions about the patient's fantasies of killing himself and about the steps he has taken to do so. Usually there are two reasons for this reluctance. One is the fear that detailed questioning will suggest suicide to a patient who has not thought of it. Actually, there is *no* evidence that it is detrimental to ask these questions. The therapist should be reassured that no suicide has been recorded in which the patient got the idea from a therapist.[56] There is probably more danger of intensifying suicidal intent if the patient feels he *cannot* talk about his ideas with anyone; the suicidal motivation thrives when it is closed off from communication.

The second reason the inexperienced emergency therapist is reluctant to delve into suicidal planning is a feeling of awkwardness. This is a specialized interviewing skill, but the principles are the same as for any other awkward interview topic. The therapist tries to lead into the subject naturally by following a stepwise line of questioning. A typical sequence of questions might be: "I gather things have been falling apart for you lately?" (Pause) "And that you're getting pretty depressed?" (A pause for the patient to reply, cry, or ventilate.) "Has it reached the point that you've thought of taking your life?" (The therapist deliberately implies that this is a normal part of the depressive process and that he recognizes the extremity of suffering necessary before such usually unacceptable thinking starts. This should enable the patient to answer honestly.) "Have you actually found yourself thinking of a way you might kill yourself?" Often the patient resists at this point with a vague answer such as, "All kinds of ways." But the therapist can insist, "I mean, have you thought of a specific way of ending your life?" *The answer to this question is the central one in any suicide evaluation.*

> *Alice (cont'd.).* The resident did not ask Alice what ways she had thought of for ending her life. After all, she had made a suicide attempt with pills. Moreover, her two previous attempts had been with pills. As we shall see, he should have asked what other ways she had thought of and what she meant by her ominous statement, "Next time I'll do it right."

Facts about the Suicide Plan. *Suicidal thoughts* must be distinguished from actual planning, and in evaluating the degree of intent the *lethal potential* of the plan, the *availability of means,* and the *sophistication of the patient* must be taken into account.

Probably more than half the population has had suicidal thoughts. The ratio of people who think about it to those who act on it is very large. Thus the fact that someone has thought about suicide is not sufficiently important to consider him a serious risk.

The plan provides the bridge between a passing thought and a definite action, and here the *lethal potential of the plan* is the most important issue. When the patient mentions shooting himself,

jumping off a bridge, or taking poison, his determination to die is obvious.

However, the interviewer should discover if the intended means are available. In New York, where jumping from high buildings is the method in 15 percent of all suicides,[57] a threat of suicide by this method is realistic. In a rural community, a plan to use this method would probably be a dramatic statement. The common threat, "I think I'll jump off the bridge," is more than a figure of speech in San Francisco, where 20 percent of the suicides occur when people jump off the Golden Gate Bridge. Guns and pills are available everywhere, and specific inquiry into whether the patient keeps a gun at home or has sleeping pills is a necessary part of evaluation. Alvarez, for instance, reports that he had been stockpiling barbiturates for months before his "impulsive" suicide attempt.

In deciding the degree of suicidal risk from the plan, *the degree of sophistication of the patient* must be taken into account. The university professor who thinks of shooting himself but who has no gun can use the same skills that earned him tenure to acquire one. The adolescent girl who swallows a bottle of aspirin in a slum may really think it will work. Lack of sophistication should be regarded as a high-, not a low-risk, factor because the chances for accidental death are greater. In their study of equivocal deaths Litman et al.[58] reported the following case:

> *Example 2-4.* When her husband threatened to divorce her, a woman ingested poison in front of him. He immediately took her to a hospital. After emergency treatment for arsenic poisoning she felt better and told the doctors she did not really want to die. However, she developed severe kidney damage and died after two weeks of uremia and cerebral hemorrhage. After some consideration, the recommendation was suicide.

The resident who treated Alice acted wisely by assuming she meant to kill herself, even though she used an over-the-counter medication. She had said, "I thought on top of the alcohol it would work."

Learn about Past Suicide Attempts. Incredibly, it is easy to forget to inquire if the patient has tried suicide in the past. The patient is often glad to leave an old attempt buried.

The full history has an important bearing on the prognosis. It should be taken carefully, with attention given to the method, timing, circumstances of the attempt, feelings about death, and the reasons why death was successfully prevented.

Notice How the Patient Communicates in the Interview

Eli Robins' group's[59] classic study on the communication of suicidal intent revealed that more than two-thirds of those who committed suicide had communicated suicidal ideas and 41 percent had specifically stated their intent. In the majority of instances the suicidal communications had been recently and repeatedly espressed in words, and to many persons. A neglected conclusion is that 31 percent of suicides do *not* communicate their intent clearly. Another 28 percent do not state directly that they plan to kill themselves. And some of the direct communications are made in such a joking or offhand way that they are not recognized as statements of intent. Thus *indirect* communication, as well as direct threats, must be picked up and heeded by the emergency therapist.

Affective Clues to Suicide. In the interview situation, three kinds of moods suggest the possibility of suicide: *hopeless resignation, euphoria,* and *psychomotor retardation.*

Resignation, a calm communication of hopelessness, is an extremely serious clinical finding. Rare but lethal, extreme calm is the mark of a paranoid person who may be planning homicide and suicide in a logical, methodical way. In the interview situation, the paranoid person with a well-organized delusional system may show studied calm. If paranoia is a defense against depression, the paranoid system may include a nonemotional plan for suicide as the last step in a well-worked-out strategy for revenge that also includes murder.

Depression followed by euphoria of recent onset is also a serious finding. Here the dynamic reason for improvement in mood may be that a decision has been reached. Suicidal people are notoriously ambivalent. Not knowing whether to live or die exhausts them, and there is great relief in finally knowing that they have decided to die. In Robins'[59] study, the husband of a 42-year-old woman said, "On the morning of the day of her suicide she was sweeter and more attentive than ever before, she kissed me better than she ever had before."

Psychomotor retardation, i.e., long reaction times to questions and a generally slowed, immobile appearance, is the hallmark of severe depression. At this stage many patients do not have the energy to commit suicide, but some might. This condition, possibly the end stage of long-standing ambivalence and confusion about living, is extremely painful for the patient. Suicides *do* occur in the retarded phase of this malignant process often enough.

Fantasy Clues to Suicide. There are several common fantasies, one or more of which may accompany the suicidal affect. The emergency therapist should ask the patient to imagine out loud his own death, its effect on others, and its long-range outcome. Often one of the fantasies will become apparent, and the therapist can use it in treatment. The most common fantasies are revenge against the hated self (as in the puer aeternus or incomplete Renaissance man), revenge against others, death as reversible sleep, and death as a reunion with loved ones.

As revenge against others, patients may express a version of "You'll all be sorry (and guilty) when I'm dead and gone." The others usually are members of the patient's immediate ecological group (lovers, spouses, parents, therapists). The patient's fantasy may be that after the suicide they will all feel intense guilt for the rest of their lives for their sins of omission and commission. After hearing out this fantasy, the therapist can point out two contradictory elements of reality. One is that although everyone would probably feel some grief and sadness if the patient died, each would, after a suitable period of mourning, return to the business of living, and the patient's death would recede to the background of his consciousness. The second is that however much anguish the patient's death causes others, the patient will not be around to see and enjoy it. For these two reasons the therapist can argue that although the patient's vengeful feelings toward others are understandable, there are more effective ways of expressing them than through suicide.

The concept of death as irreversible (except perhaps in religious persons with a strong belief in the afterlife) does not become fixed in the ego until the age of 5 or 6. Before that time children believe death is a variant of sleep from which they will always awaken. They play "Bang, bang; you're dead": the victim falls limp on the floor for a moment, and then comes back to life. Certain patients with primitive ego functioning have never fully assimilated the irreversibility of death, and this may come out in fantasy. When it does, the therapist can point out to the patient that dead is dead, that there will not be any physical reawakening to see the effect of the death on others. Surprisingly, the therapist's challenge to this fantasy may be sufficient to cause the patient to relinquish a fixed idea that suicide can be used in a temporary way.

Lonely patients may view death as a reunion with already departed loved ones; they will find the company and comfort in heaven that they cannot find on earth. To the extent that this fantasy is a remnant of magical childhood fantasies about afterlife (rather than a carefully developed adult philosophical view), the therapist can challenge the unrealistic hopes for reunion and at the same time offer a real relationship on earth.

Indirect Suicidal Communications. Many suicidal people communicate their despair indirectly, even seek to deny it, only to turn with vengeful anger on the therapist who has failed to appreciate the depth of their distress. Above all, suicidal people have difficulty locating their own feelings, and often they cannot communicate them clearly. The

wise therapist will not restrict himself to what the patient knows or admits about his feeling-life; he will look at other material.

Dreams provide valuable clues. Typical suicidal dreams involve the opening of a door onto a black, forbidding territory, escaping into a peaceful unknown territory, or jumping through a window. Dreams of enclosed spaces and of falling also may hold a suicidal meaning.

Self-deprecating remarks should not be taken lightly. In involutional depressions, statements such as, "I'm no good, you don't need me around, I'll only depress you," are extremely common. Frankly psychotic statements arguing, "I have sinned, I deserve to die," are often expressed by patients in severely depressed states. Cynicism in describing himself may identify the potential suicide to a sensitive listener who should be cued to inquire more deeply about those depressive ideas.

Behavioral clues are abundant. In Robins'[59] study, a patient phoned his ex-wife's mother and asked her to burn a candle for him. Another repeated a pantomime of shooting himself without a gun in his hand. A would-be suicide may begin to plan for his death by showing increased concern for others, visiting his friends for a series of intense chats, and giving away prized possessions. He may buy a gun, increase his life insurance, or change his will. Often the entire sequence can be reconstructed only when several people in the patient's social surroundings have been interviewed. Each will have seen only part, yet the patient may feel that everyone should have understood his intention clearly.

Direct Suicidal Communications. Robins' study positively contradicts the idea that those who threaten suicide never commit it. Among the direct statements his team collected were "I won't be here tomorrow," "Don't be surprised if you find I walked into the water," "You won't see me again except in a hearse," and, when a physician suggested an appointment with a psychiatrist, "By that time it will be too late." Such comments can be made so casually that others may not believe they are sincere. Suicidal patients are past masters at self-disqualification, and it is easy to be misled into believing they do not mean what they say. Also, the statements may be made in an altered ego state, in the heat of a quarrel or when drunk, for instance. When he returns to his "normal" state, it is easy for the patient to say that he did not mean it. If he has a drinking problem or is a frequent quarreler, he is likely to enter that "abnormal" state again and kill himself. It is good practice to *note down the patient's statements of intent* as made in the interview and as quoted by others. Often the meaning of these statements will become apparent later, although in the confusion of the initial interview they may seem trivial.

Alice (cont'd.). The initial notes of the resident who saw Alice read, "She took 'everything I had on hand'—seven Darvon, Sominex (some)—thinking, 'On top of the alcohol I'd had, it would work.' Then she called the police to 'Come get me, take me to jail. . .' She was brought to the emergency room and stated she would 'do it right' next time. She saw the situation as a 'mess' and refused to go into a mental hospital for fear 'of what it would do' to her youngest son."

Reading these notes much later, the resident was impressed by the amount of meaning lost in his later, inexact translations. He remembered her as saying to the police, "You'd better come and get me, I just took something." The distorted wording was deliberately left in the initial description to show how progressive clarification is part of the evaluation process. There is a definite threat and the hint of an "I have sinned" motif in the patient's curt "Come get me, take me to jail." Suicidal patients often show *discrepancies between words and deeds.* Despite her overt rejection of help, Alice's actions were an invitation to someone to intervene. The resident was correct in insisting that her veiled communication suggested suicide if help were not offered. His insistence on

hospitalization was his way of communicating to a denying patient that he would not participate in her denial, that he had heard her. If he had let her go, Alice might easily have made a suicide attempt to revenge herself against his heedlessness, just as she had in part acted against the police and Bradley earlier in the evening. The treating person is often sorely tested by the patient's verbal denials.

Example 2-5. A 30-year-old nurse came to the emergency room from her doctor's office. She was staggering. Tests showed some barbiturate in her blood. "It's just a bad habit," she insisted. When she was offered hospitalization, she said she could not afford time off from her job; she'd been out sick too often already and her invalid mother was dependent on her for support. She insisted she had no suicidal intent. The emergency therapist instituted involuntary hospitalization for seventy-two hours until her situation could be clarified. He said that her unexplained actions spoke louder to him than her vociferous denials.

At the beginning it is extremely difficult to learn the art of listening to the patient's behavior rather than to what he says. Patients, however, are grateful when their behavioral cues are taken seriously. They often feel rejected when their words are accepted at face value.

Alice (cont'd.). Alice and Bradley formed a strong, positive attachment to the resident who had hospitalized Alice. Alice told him he was the best doctor she had ever met. When her situation remained uncertain, she asked if she could stay on the ward longer than seventy-two hours. She was surprised to learn she had been on voluntary status all along and was glad to continue on that basis.

Response of the Ecological Group

The context of suicide may involve a large and surprisingly varied network of people. Because people related by blood or law may not be the only important participants, this system is not best described in terms of the family. Indeed, the idea that only family members can be contacted may be restricting, as seen in the example of the young resident who felt he did not have a right to contact Bradley because he and Alice were not legally married.

Warren Miller[60] uses the term *ecological group* for the social network. He argues that suicide, like other crises, may be seen as an event registering strain in the entire system, *ecostrain*. Thus a suicide may appear in an ecological group that has recently suffered a move, cancer, a heart attack, or a graduation in one of its members. The suicidal crisis may be a ripple effect in a long wave of strain that has been triggered by a major shift in the structure of the group, as, for instance, from some important member's marriage, death, or divorce. (This view of crisis as "news of a difference" is developed in Chapter 1.)

Thus data from other members of the ecological group are important in understanding the dynamics of the crisis. They also contribute corroborative data that can give factual backup to an intuitive sense of high suicidal risk. Important data on suicidal potential can come from interviewing significant members of the ecological group. Finally, and very importantly, *interpersonal resources open to the patient* can be evaluated by interviewing the significant others in his life.

The Immobilization Response. The question of interpersonal resources is raised when the reaction of family members faced with a suicide warning is examined. Robins' series of cases points up a curious nonreaction in the face of clear suicidal messages. This nonreaction seems to occur when relationships regress to almost nonverbal, symbiotic states. Litman[61] has coined the term *immobilization response* to describe this nonreaction. Generally the immobilization comes from a stronger member who fails to react to a weaker member's plea for support in an interpersonal situation.

Alice (cont'd.). Bradley sounded angry when he called the resident who had hospitalized Alice. And he did not appear on the psychiatric ward until well into her second day. The nurses did not like him, and they felt his handholding with Alice was a kind of grandstanding. Moreover, he confided to the resident that he was "getting kind of tired" of her complaining. He wanted to know how sick she was. "Could she be depressing me is what I want to know? I don't want to be dragged down, if you understand what I mean."

Often the nonreaction comes from the therapist who himself is suffering a loss and does not hear his patient's complaint of neglect.

Alice (cont'd.). The emergency resident had not originally planned to take Alice as a patient. The ward was not his primary assignment, and his own caseload was already full. But both full-time residents were having marital problems, and they were tired and irritable. Neither wanted Alice in his caseload. Each was sure she would be too great a drain.

The Lifeline. An understanding of isolation and immobilization has led to the concept of *lifeline*. The single most important question for a therapist to ask himself when evaluating a patient is, "Is there a lifeline open to this person?" A lifeline is one or more interested persons who want the patient to stay alive. An immobilized other, no matter how significant, is not a lifeline. In fact, if he is immobilized enough, he may unconsciously drive the patient to suicide.

When a suicidal patient is referred, the experienced therapist takes a consultative set as he listens to the referring therapist. If the therapist on the other end of the phone is rejecting, moralistic, and stereotypes the patient in a pessimistic manner ("This is a masochistic gal. . . ."), the emergency therapist can assume that an immobilization response is present. If, on the other hand, the referral is made in a sympathetic and encouraging manner, he can assume that the patient has a lifeline. (The presence of a lifeline becomes especially important if the patient is ready for discharge.)

In all fairness, it must be recognized that the closed world of suicide can produce contagious exhaustion. Endless ambivalence, vengeful dependency, repetitive pressure for reassurance, and frustrating denial wear out those who want to help. Passive negativism is so exasperating that it regularly elicits lecturing and rejection.

> *Alice (cont'd.).* Whenever the nurses talked to Alice about Bradley's limitations they met with denial. She insisted her love would change him, despite the fact that he divided his time between her and his wife and blatantly teased her about her jealousy. Gradually the nurses began to tease the resident, saying, "You sure know how to pick patients." The effect of this was to make him insist that Alice could be treated. Secretly he wondered *how.* Bradley used their joint sessions not to assist in planning for Alice, but to parade his own symptomatology before the resident in a scene-stealing fashion while he dropped hints about his ambivalence about Alice. Because Alice could not conceive of life without Bradley, the resident continued the couple's sessions on an outpatient basis. If their relationship could stabilize, possibly a way out of the impasse would emerge. In this way the resident quietly became the lifeline for Alice, and the couple's therapy her main avenue of hope.

In the next chapter we shall examine the treatment of suicidal patients in both the crisis intervention and the longer-term phases. The case of Alice will again be used to illustrate problems that occur frequently. The reader now may wish to ask himself: How would he proceed, confronted with the same patient? How would he formulate the situation, and what would his treatment plan be? He can check his approach with the suggestions offered in the next chapter.

REFERENCES

1. Alvarez, A.: *The Savage God,* Random House, New York, 1972, p. xiii. Copyright 1972, Random House.

2. Jung, C. G.: "Psychological Types," *Collected Works,* Princeton, Princeton, N.J., 1971, vol. 6, p. 433.

3. Hillman, James: *Suicide and the Soul,* Hodder, London, 1964.

4. Lester, David: *Why People Kill Themselves,* Charles C Thomas, Springfield, Ill., 1972. (Originally published as "Suicidal Behavior: A Summary of Research Findings," supplement to *Crisis Intervention,* vol. 2, no. 3, Suicide Preventation and Crisis Service, Buffalo, N.Y., 1970.)

5. Farberow, Normal L., and Edwin S. Shneidman (eds.): *The Cry for Help,* McGraw-Hill, New York, 1965.

6. Stengel, Erwin: *Suicide and Attempted Suicide,* Penguin, Baltimore, 1969.

7. Durkheim, Émile: *Suicide,* Free Press, Glencoe, Ill., 1951.

8. Freud, Sigmund: "Mourning and Melancholia," in *The Complete Psychological Works of Sigmund Freud,* Hogarth, London, 1957, vol. 14, pp. 243–258.

9. Adler, Alfred: "Suicide," *J. Individ. Psychol.,* **14**:57–61, 1958.

10. Hillman: loc. cit.

11. Litman, Robert E.: "Sigmund Freud on Suicide," in Edwin S. Shneidman (ed.), *Essays in Self-Destruction,* Science House, New York, 1967, pp. 324–344.

12. Plath, Sylvia: "Daddy," in *Ariel,* Harper & Row, New York, 1966, p. 51.

13. Freud, Sigmund: *Beyond the Pleasure Principle,* J. Strachey (trans.), Liveright, New York, 1950.

14. Klein, Melanie, Paula Heimann, and R. E. Money-Kyrle: *New Directions in Psychoanalysis: The Significance of Infant Conflict in the Pattern of Adult Behavior,* Basic Books, New York, 1955.

15. Heimann, Paula: "A Contribution to the Re-Evaluation of the Oedipus Complex—The Early Stages," in ibid., p. 25.

16. Hendin, Herbert: *Suicide in Scandinavia,* Grune & Stratton, New York, 1964.

17. Menninger, Karl A.: *Man Against Himself,* Harcourt, Brace & World, New York, 1938.

18. Lester: op. cit., p. 132 (orig. pub.).

19. Ibid., p. 146 (orig. pub.).

20. Hillman: op. cit., p. 67.

21. Von Franz, Marie-Louise: *The Problem of the Puer Aeternus,* Spring Publications, The Analytical Psychology Club of New York, Inc., 1970.

22. Henderson, Joseph: *Thresholds of Initiation,* Wesleyan, Middletown, Conn., 1967, pp. 22–29.

23. Milford, Nancy: *Zelda,* Harper & Row, New York, 1970.

24. Alvarez: op. cit., pp. 279–283.

25. Hillman: op. cit., pp. 56–76.

26. Ibid., pp. 92–94.

27. Neuringer, C.: "Methodological Problems in Suicide Research," *J. Consult. Psychol.,* **26**:273–278, 1962.

28. Shneidman, Edwin S.: "Sleep and Self-Destruction," in Shneidman (ed.), *Essays in Self-Destruction,* Science House, New York, 1967, pp. 510–539.

29. *Palo Alto Times,* Palo Alto, Calif., Feb. 23, 1972, p. 30.

30. Lester: op. cit., p. 5 (orig. pub.).

31. Farberow and Shneidman: op. cit., pp. 19–74.

32. Parkin, D., and Erwin Stengel: "Incidence of Suicidal Attempts in an Urban Community," *Brit. Med. J.,* **2**:133, 1965.

33. Stengel: loc. cit.

34. Schmidt, E. H., Patricia O'Neil, and Eli Robins: "Evaluation of Suicide Attempts as a Guide to Therapy," *J. Am. Med. Ass.,* **155**: 549–557, 1954.

35. Weisz, Alfred E., Donald C. Staight, Peter Houts, and Michael Volen: "Suicide Threats, Suicide Attempts, and the Emergency Psychiatrist," *Proceedings of 4th International Conference for Suicide Prevention,* Norman L. Farberow (ed.), Delmar Publishing Co., Los Angeles, 1968.

36. Beall, Lynette: "The Dynamics of Suicide: A Review of the Literature, 1897–1965," *Reflections,* **5**(5):12–38, 1970.

37. Delong, W. B., and Eli Robins: "The Communication of Suicidal Intent Prior to Psychiatric Hospitalization," *Am. J. Psychiat.,* **117**:695–705, 1961.

38. Dublin, Louis, in Erwin Stengel, op. cit., p. 33.

39. Robins, Eli, Seymour Gassner, Jack Kayes, Robert Wilkinson, Jr., and George Murphy: "The Communication of Suicidal Intent: A Study of 134 Consecutive Cases of Successful (Completed) Suicide," *Am. J. Psychiat.,* **115**:724–733, 1959.

40. Dorpat, T. L., and H. S. Ripley: "The Relationship between Attempted Suicide and Completed Suicide," *Compr. Psychiat.,* **8**:74–89, 1967.

41. Hendin, Herbert: *Black Suicide,* Basic Books, New York, 1969.

42. Retterstol, Nils: *Long-Term Prognosis After Attempted Suicide,* Charles C Thomas, Springfield, Ill., 1970.

43. Lester: op. cit., p. 194 (orig. pub.).

44. Douglas, Jack: *The Social Meanings of Suicide,* Princeton, Princeton, N.J., 1967.

45. Alvarez: op. cit., p. 81.

46. Choron, Jacques: *Suicide,* Scribner, New York, 1972.

47. Moss, Leonard M., and Donald Hamilton: "Psychotherapy of the Suicidal Patient," in Edwin S. Shneidman and Norman L. Farberow (eds.), *Clues to Suicide,* McGraw-Hill, New York, 1957, pp. 99–110.

48. Hilgard, Josephine, and Martha F. Newman: "Anniversaries in Mental Illness," *Psychiatry,* vol. 22, May 1959.

49. Weiss, E.: "The Clinical Significance of the Anniversary Reaction," *Gen. Pract.,* **17**:117–119, 1958.

50. Alvarez: op. cit., pp. 268–269.

51. Ibid.: p. 128.

52. Weisz, Alfred E., and Robert Taylor: "The Assassination Matrix," *Stanford Today,* pp. 11–17, Winter 1969.

53. Fox, Ruth: *Alcoholism,* Charles C Thomas, Springfield, Ill., 1967, p. 245.

54. Menninger: loc. cit.

55. Yalom, Irvin D., and M. A. Lieberman: "A Study of Encounter Group Casualties," *Arch. Gen. Psychiat.,* **24:**16–30, 1971.

56. Litman, Robert: "Management of Acutely Suicidal Patients in Medical Practice," *Calif. Med.,* **104:**168–174, 1966.

57. Massey, J. T.: *Suicide in the United States,* PHS Publication 1000, ser. 20, no. 5, U.S. Department of Health, Education, and Welfare, 1967.

58. Litman, Robert, T. Murphey, Edwin S. Shneidman, Norman L. Farberow, and N. Tabachnick: "The Psychological Autopsy of Equivocal Deaths," in Edwin S. Shneidman, Norman L. Farberow, and Robert E. Litman (eds.), *The Psychology of Suicide,* Science House, New York, 1970, chap. 30.

59. Robins, et al: loc. cit.

60. Miller, Warren: "The Ecological Group," this book, chap. 32.

61. Litman: loc. cit.

Treatment of the Suicidal Patient

Some people turn to suicide to resolve interpersonal struggles; others want only to be done with struggle. For the first kind of patient, the seemingly introverted act of suicide has the extraverted meaning of influencing another person. The second type has given up on the extraverted world, and an introverted plunge into self-destruction seems the only way out of despair.[1] If the patient uses suicide to influence others, the therapist should aid at helping him find another way of getting himself heard. If suicide expresses loss of connection, the therapist must try to reconnect the individual with life. Both themes may be present in a given patient whose ambivalence reflects a tension between his extraverted and introverted feelings.[2,3] At different stages of treatment, one or the other theme may be dominant, and the therapist must be guided accordingly. Throughout the treatment the therapist must expect to be *active* and vitally involved with the patient in seeking alternatives to suicide as the solution to external and internal problems.

THE ACTION RESPONSE

The therapist counters the immobilization response (Chapter 2) of the patient's ecological group by a strong *action response*. By word and deed he indicates that he is vitally interested in keeping his patient alive and that if need be he is willing to be the lifeline. He counters the patient's ambivalence with firmness. For instance, the therapist may sit through a meal hour with an elderly patient who will not talk and insist that he eat all the food on his hospital tray.

The therapist must also open the patient's closed world to the feeling-responses of others and mobilize those in the ecological group who have been immobilized so they can share the extremity of the patient's predicament and stay involved with the treatment.

Finally, the action response dictates that the therapist be available to the patient in both the physical sense of being readily accessible by phone and willing to set up extra appointments as they are needed and in the emotional sense of being able to put his own feelings into clear, unambiguous verbal statements. In addition to talking, considerable caring behavior is required.

Example 3-1, Alice (cont'd). The resident working with Alice soon found that if he were slightly late for his appointment she would be sullen and uncommunicative. He made a point of being on the ward when he said he would, and the sessions became more productive. Throughout, Alice maintained that she could not understand why he should bother about her and said she did not need therapy:

The therapist soon will be tested to show that he has mastered nonverbal language, that he understands behavior signaling distress, and that he is able to convey concern by his own behavior. To pass the test, the therapist must express verbally what the patient's behavior leads him to feel and conjecture and must show by his own behavior what he wants the patient to understand.

> *Alice (cont'd).* The night Alice was admitted the resident told her, "The fact that you want to leave this emergency room without any more plans than you had when you took the pills makes me think you still feel like killing yourself. Therefore I have to keep you in the hospital until I'm convinced you aren't going to take your life."
>
> Alice immediately said, "If I tell you I won't take my life, will you let me go?"
>
> The resident replied, "No, because your situation hasn't changed."
>
> Alice then said, "I can get a lawyer to make you let me go."
>
> The resident replied, "If I put a hold on you, you're entitled to a lawyer. But I'll say in court what I've said to you: your situation makes me think there's a great risk of suicide." He maintained his position through several minutes of cross-examination by Alice, who was keeping her eyes averted.

The resident used the style of communication he had learned to use with suicidal patients: (1) he told Alice in words what her behavior said to him, and (2) he backed up his verbal expression of concern with caring behavior, in this case a willingness to place a seventy-two-hour police hold on her if she did not accept voluntary hospitalization. This action response was in marked contrast to those made on her two previous discharges from emergency rooms after ingestions, when she was let go without recommendations for further treatment. A verbal statement of concern along with an offer of outpatient therapy would have seemed perfunctory to this hardened veteran of rejection.

THE ECOLOGICAL GROUP APPROACH

Rationale of the Approach

The members of the patient's ecological group should be included in the treatment process from the beginning. Too often, however, the therapist feels he has adequate information for treatment decisions from interviews with the patient alone. Failure to include others often results from binds the patient tries to place on communication.

> *Alice (cont'd).* Although the resident did rather well in standing up to Alice's denials of the precariousness of her situation, he was considerably less effective in establishing his right to talk to several others who might have been included in her treatment planning. Because of Alice's assertions that she was "through with Bradley," the resident felt inhibited about including him in what seemed to be a confidential relationship. Her ex-husband Rolfe was now ill with cancer of the liver, and their 14-year-old son Billy lived with Rolfe and his new wife. Don and Joe were in jail. Alice's brother, a stable, married policeman, lived across the country, as did her mother, who had a heart condition.
>
> Alice and Rolfe's new wife were concerned about Rolfe's terminal illness and the planning that should be done for Billy. Alice wanted to take Billy to live with her and Bradley after Rolfe's death, but the resident did not feel he had the right to contact Rolfe and his wife and make them participants in Alice's current treatment. Alice had said she did not want Billy, a shy, wilting adolescent, involved. She said, "That kid's been through enough already." Neither did she want her brother involved in her current difficulties with Bradley, even though he had offered Billy a home. The jailed sons seemed inaccessible. Alice did not want to worry her mother and possibly aggravate her heart condition.
>
> The resident and the ward staff were trapped by Alice's denial and her insistent focus on her

romantic vicissitudes with Bradley. They failed to deal with other areas of significance to Alice, especially with Billy's future. This major error in focus was reinforced by the patient's and staff's almost total avoidance of Rolfe's terminal illness. It was as if not talking about it would make it go away.

Unconcious collusion of the therapist and ward staff with a patient's denial is not uncommon. Careful supervision by someone outside the treatment process can be of great help in avoiding such collusion. The decision to exclude members of Alice's ecological group drastically limited the scope of the crisis intervention. Although the immediate threat of suicide was reduced by the strategy adopted (couple therapy), Alice's entire course of psychotherapy was affected by the failure to start with the widest possible evaluation.

When information is not obtained from members of the ecological group, the immediate results may be tragic.

Example 3-2. A previously active 45-year-old divorced mother of one married daughter and two teenagers had been paraplegic for two years following an auto accident. The week after losing a $150,000 lawsuit she visited her urologist, who noted a serious exacerbation of her chronic depression. Although she was adamant in refusing to see a psychiatrist, the urologist sought psychiatric consultation anyway. The emergency therapist called the patient at home.

Over the telephone she described her recent suffering, and when asked if she were unhappy enough to kill herself, she replied that she had often thought of it but did not plan to commit suicide for at least two or three years because she still had two teenagers to take care of.

The reassured resident discussed outpatient psychiatric treatment with her, but she continued to resist the idea. He left his name in case she decided to seek help.

Three weeks later the patient killed herself by hooking a newly purchased garden hose to the exhaust of her car and starting the motor.

The resident interviewed the patient's three daughters. The eldest, 22, told him, "Mother threatened every day to everyone that she was going to commit suicide. Sometimes she was sarcastic, sometimes she was bitter, and sometimes she was humorous about it." She said that all her mother's hopes had depended on the court case, and she had noticed the depression following its loss. She felt this was "only normal." This daughter had discovered the newly purchased garden hose sitting in the front seat of the car. She had asked her mother about it and was told in a characteristically dry way that this hose would be more effective than the old one.

The 18-year-old daughter had also noted the recent purchase of the hose. She lived in the house but took no action because "She was always threatening, I couldn't watch her day and night." She added that during the past week the mother had visited several wheelchair clubs and had commented with surprise on the happiness of the members.

The youngest daughter, 14, said that her mother had frequently confided her despair to her. She said she had repeatedly said to all of them, "If I try to kill myself, I don't want to fail."

This case illustrates the danger of an individual approach to the resistant suicidal patient. The emergency therapist blundered in relying on the patient's statement that she would stay alive to take care of her children. If he had insisted on interviewing them, he would have recognized their immobilization. The children could have been advised that the depression they accepted as usual in their mother was a treatable illness, and hospitalization could have been pursued. In later treatment their anger and immobilization would be important targets for intervention if the mother's hopeless feeling about herself were to be countered.

Crisis Resolution by Means of the Ecological Approach

After a suicide threat or attempt, the therapist gathers together the patient and key members of the group and states openly that the patient has been having suicidal feelings and is a definite risk. He tells them that the danger poses a problem for all of them and that he wants to help them as a group to find a solution to the crisis and any issues which have led to it.

In the drama that ensues, and with the supportive presence of the therapist, members of the ecological group are often able to resolve long-standing difficulties (see Chapter 1, "Principles of Crisis Intervention"). This way of working with the suicidal patient has particular advantages. First, it reinforces the effectiveness of verbal communication because the therapist's authority lends credence to the patient's stated threat to die. His own words translate the patient's ambiguous or nonverbal communication into intelligible statements. Second, sufficient drama and attention are given to meet whatever threatrical need-signaling is present in the patient. The drama of a group confrontation in the therapist's office accomplishes much that an actual attempt might. It gives others the message that the patient is suffering and allows them to present evidence of their concern.

Finally, the ecological approach enables the therapist to discover to what extent the group is providing a lethal context for the patient. Key members may wish the patient gone or dead. (Studies of voodoo deaths show dramatically that group wishes can be fulfilled.) When the group is bent on extruding the patient, the therapist may have to help the patient realize that membership in *this* group is no longer a viable option.

Example 3-3. A 25-year-old man was brought into the emergency room by his parents-in-law. Their daughter had left him, and he had recently taken to hanging despondently around their kitchen. At first he insisted his wife would return and refused to accept their assertions to the contrary. Their patience and sympathy for the son-in-law began to wear thin. When he began talking openly about suicide, they were relieved to have a legitimate reason to get him out of their house and into the hands of "someone who could talk some sense into him." They made it clear to the emergency therapist that their involvement with the patient was now at an end. They felt that they had discharged their responsibility by bringing him to treatment.

Thus the ecological approach can help to mobilize resources or identify the permanent extinction of old resources. Often this approach has two outcomes: (1) the patient is helped to achieve some long-desired interpersonal goal (e.g., a mother-in-law agrees to baby-sit or a husband to quit his second job) or (2) the group is helped to dispose of the patient. In either case the ecological group approach attempts to do in a life-preserving way what a suicide attempt might try to accomplish self-destructively.

This neat formulation of suicidal crisis resolution somewhat obscures the *ambivalence* that pervades the suicidal process in the ecological group as well as in the patient. Although group members often make superficial changes to please the patient and the therapist, it is usually more difficult to find out from them whether, at bottom, they really want relationships with the patient.

Alice (cont'd.). In couple therapy and on the ward, Bradley acted eager to help and to make a new attempt at a relationship with Alice. But when the resident was leaving the ward, Bradley would often follow him, saying, "Do you think she's really schiz? I mean I don't want to get stuck with a psycho on my hands, if you know what I mean."

The resident was troubled by Bradley's ambivalence, but he didn't know what to do about it. Following advice he had been given, he tried not to see Bradley or Alice individually once the couple sessions had begun. He did see Alice alone during the time she was on the ward, but her suspiciousness made him wary of seeing Bradley without her.

Uncertainty in the ecological group about the patient's belonging is a major factor in the patient's ambivalence about living or dying. This uncertainty cannot be well resolved without a frank discussion of the possibility of separation. The significant others cannot work through their negative feelings about the patient in a setting where they are not able to air their views. The presence of a recently suicidal person is distinctly inhibiting to direct expressions of disaffection. The therapist, therefore, should also hold separate individual sessions with group members. He should not allow himself to be bound by pseudoconfidentiality; he must be judicious about sharing what he hears. He should make it possible for the various group members to state their feelings honestly, fully, privately, and without the fear that in doing so they will provoke the patient to suicide.

Example 3-4. A 28-year-old woman brought her 25-year-old husband to the emergency room. She tearfully admitted that he was suicidal because of her; she could not make up her mind whether or not to leave him. Couple therapy started, but no progress was made. The wife continued to vacillate, and the husband remained suicidal. The therapist decided to see them separately.

The wife revealed in her individual session that she was in love with another man and the only reason she stayed with her husband was her fear he would kill himself so that she could be free. This thought made her feel extremely guilty.

The therapist asked the husband what he would do if his wife actually left. (In the couple sessions the answer to this question had always been unequivocal: "I'd kill myself for sure.") The husband said, "I'll tell you *this*. If my wife really left for good, I don't think I'd kill myself. I'd ask you to put me in some quiet place, and I'd cry on somebody's

shoulder until I was ready to get out and find somebody else."

Before the next joint interview, the therapist encouraged the wife to tell her husband the truth, and he prepared to support the husband. The husband first broke down, then accepted hospitalization. After a week of hospitalization and a week of day care he was able to enter productive outpatient psychotherapy without a return of serious suicidal feelings.

His wife did not continue in therapy. During her husband's hospitalization she filed for divorce. Eventually she married the other man.

When Not to Use the Ecological Approach

Obviously not every suicidal patient should be approached through his ecological group. Experienced therapists may well be dismayed by the recommendation for *routine* use of extensive contacts with significant others. They know of well-motivated patients who have sought individual therapy at a time of active suicidal thinking and have done well in it, without any outside contacts. Such patients are capable of recognizing when a formerly sustaining social ecology has dried up, and they are capable of initiating contact with new people to put their lives in order. For them therapist-initiated contacts with others might well be infantilizing or restricting and might possibly inhibit movement *out* of an undesirable life situation. Also, the therapeutic relationship is often more effective when it is kept entirely between two people.

Example 3-5. A 40-year-old single, professional woman contemplated suicide when a five-year homosexual relationship ended. She sought therapy a week after a mild overdose of pills. At the initial interview she seemed ready to begin depth therapy with an experienced, analytically oriented therapist. She soon formed a close bond with him.

During the first months of therapy the patient was able to enter into a sexual relationship with a man. A year and a half after treatment began the patient married. She continued therapy through the first year of her marriage and terminated when the marriage seemed assured of going well. Throughout the course of treatment, the analyst's only contact was with the patient.

Experiences similar to this one are common in private practice, where the fee and the referral process tend to select patients who are highly motivated to change and able to use an intense transference relationship positively. When the patient is met in the midst of crisis in an emergency room setting, his degree of motivation for change is still unknown, and the ecological group approach offers the best chance for adequate crisis intervention. The occasional disadvantages of overinvolving others in a patient's treatment are far outweighed by the advantages this approach holds for opening up a potential suicide's closed world.

THE INITIAL INTERVIEW

The initial interview is particularly critical for the suicidal patient: if it goes badly, it may be the *only* interview. Mintz[4] suggests a checklist of tasks the therapist ought to accomplish during the initial interview. The checklist, with slight modifications, is

1. Obtain the necessary personal data immediately. These include the patient's name, age, telephone number, place of occupation, residence, and the names of his closest friends and family members.

2. Bring the subject of suicide into the open. Also obtain information about suicidal thoughts, plans, preparations, and attempts.

3. Insist on the removal of all firearms and potentially lethal medications from the patient's home.

4. Notify and arrange to meet with one or more significant responsible others in the patient's life.

5. Discuss the natural history of depressive illnesses and their favorable responses to treatment.

6. Formulate and communicate a specific initial treatment plan.

7. Specifically schedule a next appointment for patients who are not hospitalized.

8. Be sure the patient is able to contact you.

There are a number of other points to be considered in utilizing Mintz's suggestions and conducting the first interview. First, even though the interview may be conducted by a nonmedical mental health worker, it should take place in a hospital, clinic, or other place where medical tradition and authority are in evidence. An atmosphere of medical authority can help to influence the ambivalent patient and ecological group to take seriously the life-protective measures that are recommended.

The therapist must consider how he presents psychiatric intervention to the patient. His primary concern is to preserve the patient's life, but if he tries to accomplish this in an overzealous, authoritarian manner he may drive the suicidal impulse underground, and it will surface again in a lethal form when he is unavailable. This is as true for involuntary as for voluntary patients. Consistently the therapist must regard the patient as someone who is, or soon can be, responsible enough to choose treatment when its goals are made clear to him. It follows that the patient is, or soon will be, free to withdraw from any treatment he finds unreasonable. For this reason a special challenge is to demonstrate sufficient courtesy, compassion, and tact to induce the involuntary patient to continue treatment.

Finding out the patient's name, address, and phone number *immediately* can be crucial because many suicidal people isolate themselves by using unlisted phone numbers, post office box addresses, and changed names. The anonymous patient is difficult or impossible to trace if he hurriedly leaves his office or becomes disconnected on the phone. Some patients even call the emergency room, give only meager identifying data, and announce they are going to kill themselves. The emergency therapist must make it clear from the beginning that he wants to establish and maintain contact. He should keep phone numbers and other information with him for later use in case of an emergency.

Example 3-6. A 30-year-old alcoholic man called his former therapist several months after he had broken off treatment. He asked the therapist to forgive him for what he was about to do and hung up. When the therapist called the telephone number the patient had given his answering service, he found the line busy. A check with the telephone company revealed that the phone was unlisted, and no address could be found. Fortunately the therapist still had the address and phone number the patient had given him at the time of their first contact. The phone number was the same, and the therapist called the police to investigate at that address. They found the patient nearly comatose from barbiturate ingestion. His life was saved in a nearby emergency room, and a crisis team took over his care. Two days later the patient called the therapist, thanked him, and announced his intention to enter an alcohol treatment program administered by the local hospital.

To bring suicidal thinking into the open, the therapist should permit the patient to talk about his thoughts, plans, preparations, and attempts. Suicidal emotion thrives if it is not disclosed. To share his frightening, "selfish," or "immoral" suicidal thinking with someone else is almost always a great relief to the patient, and his gratitude is the beginning of a firm bond with the therapist. The few patients who become angry at this questioning usually become less depressed and are determined to prove the therapist wrong.

Example 3-7. A gruff teamster in his mid-50s, widowed and alcoholic, became increasingly depressed following prostate surgery for a benign enlargement. When he refused food, the nurses became alarmed and notified the surgeon, who in turn called in a psychiatric resident consultant. The young man inquired gently about the teamster's state of mind and met with stiff, resistant denial that anything was wrong. Finally the resident asked if the teamster had ever thought of suicide. The older man became furious, delivered a dressing down to the resident, and loudly threatened to sue the hospital for "vile insinuations." It turned out that he was a good Catholic and suicide was against his religion. The nurses asked a priest to see him, and the priest arranged a reunion with a widowed sister who was glad to arrange care for him during his convalescence. Although he never ceased to berate the "headshrinker" who visited him, everyone noticed that from the morning of the psychiatrist's visit the patient began to eat heartily and show signs of his former vigor.

If weapons, poison, or pills are in the home, every attempt should be made to have them surrendered. It is wise to involve other members of the family in this effort. In some cases they are the suppliers of the weapons, and in others they have knowledge of the stockpiled drugs or weapons. Often it is easier at a first interview to insist upon "total disarmament" than it is later in treatment, when transference resistance may push the patient into an "arms race" of escalating suicidal riskiness with his therapist.

Example 3-8. A middle-aged man came to the Veterans Administration (VA) Hospital one afternoon. He was well-dressed and appeared healthy. He admitted to the resident that since the breakup of his marriage several weeks before, he had grown despondent. The resident asked if he felt the need to enter the hospital. The patient broke down in admitting that he did and confessed he had thought of killing his former wife and himself. The resident asked if he had a means to do it, and the patient revealed that he kept a loaded pistol in the glove compartment of his car. The resident arranged admission at once and walked with the patient to his car, where the gun was surrendered. The patient said, "I was going to use it on myself if I didn't get admitted today."

It is important to secure the permission of the patient before contacting others in his life. When the patient is present, the therapist can phone the other person and explain that there is a serious risk of suicide. This procedure provides an initial model for talking openly and directly about the situation. The therapist also establishes his right to communicate with others and to act as the patient's advocate in discussing a painful subject. With extremely rigid, compulsive personalities who feel guilty about burdening others, a stern insistence that frank communication is necessary usually works to secure the needed permission.

Depressive illnesses remit and respond to treatment. Without treatment, a depressive illness may last a few weeks or months. With treatment, improvement begins in days or weeks. The depressed patient and his ecological group should be told that his present suffering will not last indefinitely because depressive illnesses tend to remit with a full return of usual function.[5,6] Therefore, the emergency psychiatrist can counter stereotyped notions about the irreversibility of "mental illness" as far as depression is concerned. Firmness is necessary to deal with the pessimism characteristic of depression.

The therapist should formulate a specific initial treatment plan. The suicidal person lives in a vague, indecisive state, and the decision to die usually comes when there is nothing definite in his life. The therapist must give direct, unambiguous statements that leave no doubt about what he means. His initial plan should be simple, clear, and definite, and he should take pains to be sure that the patient understands exactly what is expected of him.

If the plan involves a trial period of outpatient treatment, the therapist may say to the patient,

I would like you to start treatment immediately. I want us to meet twice a week for the next three weeks. Our sessions will be fifty minutes long, and we will try to understand together what is causing this depression and what can be done to help you find relief. Between sessions you may feel panicky or upset, and I expect you to call me. If I am going to be away, I will let you know, and someone who knows that you may be calling will be available.

Under no circumstances are you to hesitate to call if you feel upset. If you feel pressed to act on your suicidal feelings, I expect you to call me before you act. During the next three weeks I will be in touch with people who are close to you, and we will schedule joint sessions when necessary. I will expect them to call me if they have any concerns. At the end of the three-week period we will all evaluate the situation again and make a decision on where to go from there.

If the therapist is not this definite, the patient may conclude that he does not care or appreciate the depth of his confusion. The patient may then signal his dilemma by a nonverbal "appeal" such as a suicide attempt.

It is important that the other members of the ecological group also understand the plan. Occasionally the treatment plan that seems reasonable to the patient and therapist will not meet with favor from important others. Their feelings are significant and should be taken into account. For example, an anxious wife may want to be present during her husband's interview or may not want to assume the burden of having him remain an outpatient. The wise therapist will not regard her as a nuisance, even if her presence complicates the therapy. He will recognize that he needs her active cooperation if treatment is to succeed, and he may have to make concessions to secure that cooperation. A good plan must be acceptable to the entire ecological group and must give all the members a sense that they are in competent hands and have a good chance of resolving their difficulties. Unspoken disapproval of the treatment plan may result in immobilization toward the patient and thus increase the risk of suicide.

The therapist should not end the first session until a next definite appointment has been made, even if the patient has not yet agreed to enter psychiatric treatment. For example, when the paraplegic woman in Example 3-2 declined treatment on the first contact, the psychiatrist left her his phone number in case she changed her mind. Instead, he could have said, "I want you to take a whole day to think about your decision to decline treatment, and I want to hear from you between four and five tomorrow. I will be in my office waiting for your call. This is my telephone number." If he had heard from her at that time, the resident could have continued negotiating about treatment and might possibly have secured an agreement to talk by telephone at regularly scheduled intervals during the period of acute crisis. If he had not heard from her, the resident could have telephoned her to express his continued concern. He could probably also have expressed his concern about her to her urologist, who might have helped him to persuade family members to attend an emergency strategy meeting.

In short, the definite appointment becomes a focus around which the degree of suicidal intent can be gauged and can also be used to demonstrate concern to an ambivalent patient. A patient's failure to keep the appointment can be interpreted as a presuicidal communication and should be responded to immediately. A failure on the therapist's part will be interpreted by the patient as a lack of concern. The therapist must take care in noting down and arranging to keep the appointment he makes. This is true whether the appointment is set up over the telephone or in the office.

The patient must be able to reach the therapist. Confused patients easily forget names, and they tire of fighting busy switchboards and indifferent answering services. Before the first interview ends, the therapist should write down his name, professional address, and phone number, preferably on an appointment card or prescription blank, and give it to the patient. The patient should be able to say the therapist's name, know his exact title, and know how to reach him in case this written information is mislaid. The first interview can be brought to an end with the lines of communication clearly established and with the explicit understanding that the patient and therapist expect to use the channels discussed.

It is the therapist's responsibility to make sure emergency room staff, clinic secretaries, hospital or answering service operators, and members of his own ecological group know how to reach him at all times. It is his responsibility to ascertain that the intermediaries between him and the patient have sufficient information to communicate for him during his temporary absences. It helps for the therapist to explain to the others that the patient is a suicide risk and that if he cannot be reached in a reasonable time, he wants a backup professional to be notified.

Sometimes an emergency therapist will conclude the first interview by referring the patient to another professional. As a consultant, he should ensure that the patient will be able to reach the professional and that a definite appointment has been made. Almost always he will need to speak personally to the other professional. He must also serve as a backup until the patient is solidly established in treatment with the other person. Thus the referring emergency therapist could say to the patient, "I expect you to call me back if any difficulties arise with this referral. I will be checking with your therapist to see that you have started." And he must do so. Again, if the therapist is not meticulous in following up on his referral, the patient may feel rejected and act out his ambivalence about treatment by attempting suicide. Even after he has referred a patient, the emergency therapist must assume that he is the lifeline until the patient is connected to another source of support.

THE DECISION TO HOSPITALIZE

The resident handled many of the tasks of the first interview by hospitalizing Alice. Although this decision relieved him of immediate anxiety concerning Alice's committing suicide, it also created problems in treatment. In this section we shall examine the criteria for hospitalization and the problems that occur after the decision to hospitalize has been made.

Initial Aspects of Hospitalization

The criterion for hospitalization is simple. If the therapist does not trust the patient to call him before making an attempt on his life, he should recommend hospitalization. This criterion does *not* mean that hospitalization, any more than outpatient treatment, guarantees the patient will not kill himself or that the therapist can assume final responsibility for the patient's decision about death. What it does mean is that the therapist stands against the *impulsive* decision to die. The strategy is similar to the use of Antabuse® with alcoholic patients. The drug cannot assume the responsibility for the patient's decision about abstaining from alcohol, but it does give him three days, the time it takes the medicine to leave his system, to think about returning to alcohol. Seventy-two-hour involuntary hospitalization is permissible in the state of California when a patient is unable to care for himself or is a danger to himself or to others.

The therapist can say, "I would like you to come into the hospital for at least three days. During that time we will all be able to take a closer look at this situation and come to a decision about how to proceed with treatment. It may be that a longer period of hospitalization will be necessary, or it may be that we can continue on an outpatient basis after that. I do think we need to make this decision inside, not outside, the hospital." The therapist neither presents hospitalization as a "cure for suicide" nor as a judgment of the patient's and the group's ultimate ability to resolve the crisis. He presents the hospital as an environment more conducive to the therapeutic process that hopefully will reconnect the patient with his normal desire to live. The same need for his cooperation, the same need for outside support, and the same ultimate risk follow the patient into the hospital. After all, he is the same patient.

Certainly the therapist should not be afraid to use the hospital. Keeping the patient *out* of the hospital becomes an end in itself for some therapists, almost a proof of therapeutic macho. Others fear the anger patients sometimes show when hospitalization is suggested. Such considerations obscure the initial purpose of therapeutic work with suicidal people—the clear, unambivalent expression of concern. Neither the therapist's vanity nor the patient's anger is important when hospitalization becomes the appropriate expression of that concern.

Once the decision to hospitalize has been made, a new crisis occurs. Having just been told that a professional does not think he can control himself, the patient should not be sent home unguarded to pick up a toothbrush, razor, or any other personal belongings. Also, the therapist should recognize that the anxiety which attends entry into a new environment can lead to a suicide attempt the first night on the ward.

Ideally the therapist should take the patient to the ward himself, introduce him to the head nurse, explain in his presence that the patient has had impulsive thoughts of suicide, and request the ward staff's or family's help in bringing personal necessities from the patient's home to the ward. Such arrangements are usually easy to make. Occasionally the therapist may have to accompany the patient home to pick up the items.

Alice (cont'd.). After he had made it clear to Alice that he was determined to put her in the hospital, the resident met with stiff resistance over the issue of getting her belongings. She raised a number of objections to being accompanied by Bradley or by her son but finally acceded to the resident's suggestion that he go with her. Her small, ugly hotel room with clothing strewn around was a reminder to the resident of the squalor of her life. She gave the pills in the room to the resident and collected her possessions. They returned to the psychiatric ward.

The resident introduced Alice to the night nurse and explained that she had made a suicide attempt earlier in the evening, that they had gone together to get her belongings, and that she would have to remain on the ward until he could see her the following day. He told Alice that he would see her at 2 o'clock the following afternoon and left her in the care of the night nurse. He wrote a brief admission note, admitting orders (including ward restrictions and suicidal precautions), and his home phone number in the chart.

Medical Hospitalization

Patients who have attempted suicide with pills (especially aspirin, barbiturates, and tranquilizers), poisons (especially arsenic and carbon monoxide), or violence (knives or guns) *must* be medically treated and cleared before they are admitted to a psychiatric ward. Contrary to occasional belief, psychiatric wards usually are *not* equipped to evaluate either the acute symptoms or delayed complications of physical trauma. Patients whose medical status is in doubt should be treated on a medical or surgical ward by internists, neurologists, and surgeons, and they should stay on the medical ward until they are given medical clearance.

The psychiatrist should make himself available to the medical staff as a consultant and should use the principles described in Chapter 31. Internists may want to make a premature transfer of patients to the psychiatric ward because they are afraid that the patient will make another suicide attempt while he is under their care. Psychiatric consultation can help to assure and support the medical staff in their treatment of the patient as well as assist with proper referral for further psychiatric treatment on either an in- or an outpatient basis.

Psychiatric Hospitalization

The advantages and disadvantages of psychiatric hospitalization for suicidal patients are many and varied. Some of the themes to be discussed are developed further in Chapter 10 ("Acute Inpatient Intervention"), which treats hospitalization as a separate topic.

Psychiatric hospitalization per se performs no miracles. The patient may use the period of hospitalization to plan for death while he makes a token "recovery" to convince his therapist that he has "gotten over being silly." The ecological approach to establishing a lifeline can be used with a maximum degree of safety in the hospital.

The therapist should present a detailed history to the ward staff, and together they should work out a careful treatment plan with explicit goals. The patient should be told about these considerations so he can allow the staff to help him open up his closed world. As time goes on, the staff can offer the often lonely and discouraged therapist consultation and companionship through personal contact and nursing notes. He in turn can serve as a model to the staff by telling them what he is trying to accomplish. The staff that is listened to by the therapist is more likely to listen to the patient, and, as we have already seen, suicidal people require much support in making their feelings heard.

Alice (cont'd.). One positive feature of Alice's hospitalization was the degree of give-and-take between the resident and the ward staff. The resident made a point of talking with the nurses each time he visited Alice on the ward. The nurses in turn gave him a great deal of information about their contact with Alice, and they paid a good deal of attention to her. Alice's mood improved markedly as the hospital stay continued. From her initially guarded, suspicious style of communication, she moved toward an increasingly friendly openness and began to reach out to other patients. The ward staff regarded this change as progress, and they began to like her.

Structure and Expectations. The patient should be expected to participate in a structured program, i.e., attend group meetings, eat meals, observe ward rules, and so on. Patients often test the concern of others by failing to participate in any or all of these activities, disappearing without notice, and so forth. The therapist must carefully observe the patient and consult with the nursing staff during his daily visits so he will be able to detect such testing and bring it to the patient's notice. This is further proof to the patient of the therapist's unambivalent wish for him to live.

The therapist does not have to be a "nice guy" to set limits. Rather, his should be a clear and unemotional stance that insists on participation, that will believe the patient's stated interest in treatment when it is demonstrated by his behavior. The therapist may have to stand over an ambivalent, psychotically depressed patient and insist that he eat his food. He may say, "No, you have to stay here, you have to finish your plate; no, I expect you to eat," and so on.

If the patient makes a suicidal gesture in the ward (usually minor wrist cutting with a stray razor), the therapist should make it clear that he will not tolerate this behavior and should immediately offer an acceptable way for the patient to signal his distress to the ward staff in the event a similar situation arises. If a more serious attempt on life is made, the therapist should arrange a special conference between himself, the ward staff, and the patient. In addition to hearing the patient out, the therapist should make it clear that he expects the patient to communicate verbally to someone when he feels driven to hurt himself. A patient will almost always hear this message when it is given in the atmosphere of crisis following a serious attempt in the ward. The experience may be the turning point for a depressed patient in taking the ward and his treatment seriously.

Potential Dangers. Before a patient is hospitalized, it is important to be aware of the potential negative effects of the inpatient experience. Among these are the opportunities the hospital affords the chronically suicidal patient to establish *hostile dependency* on the unit, to *split the staff*, and to form *"sick" friendships*. These themes are illustrated by some of the events that took place during Alice's stay in the hospital.

Alice (cont'd.). Alice accepted hospitalization only grudgingly in the first place. After all, it had been the psychiatric resident's idea, not hers. Technically, however, hers was a voluntary admission. She lived in a state that offered medical insurance to indigent patients, and to avoid a large bill she had to establish her inability to pay.

Alice simultaneously passively thwarted efforts by the hospital business office to establish her eligibility for assistance and complained to the resident that she didn't see how she could pay her bill. He didn't want to be bothered with what seemed to him trivial paperwork and mistakenly assumed it would automatically be taken care of at some point. The matter came to haunt the later course of Alice's treatment.

While the resident was taking a short vacation, Alice made an issue with the ward chief about the impossibility of paying her bill, refused to accept his reassurance, and angrily signed out against medical advice. This action defined her as a financial delinquent on the hospital records and precluded readmission until she paid her bill.

Alice expressed her anger at being taken care of through passive-aggressive tactics. She would not clarify her financial position, complained that it prevented her from being helped, and thus turned a resource into a liability. Hostile response to dependency is typical of the suicidal person's ambivalence.

Frequently the patient's ambivalence can be discerned by the way a staff splits in its response to him. Part of the staff believes one treatment should be used, and the rest believes another.

Alice (cont'd.). Alice's insistence on returning

to Bradley infuriated the nurses, who had spent many hours trying to talk her out of it. The resident found the idea at least plausible if not ideal, and in heated staff discussions he pointed out that if Alice and Bradley did separate, they would only seek out similar new partners. The staff told the resident he was a hero for wanting to try with Alice and that if she improved he would have performed a therapeutic miracle. The first-year resident was still naïve and susceptible to seeing himself in a heroic role. After Alice left the hospital he started outpatient treatment without first seeking consultation. If he had, he could have taken the middle course of neither encouraging nor discouraging the relationship with Bradley.

Sometimes it seems that an inpatient staff is furnishing adequate consultation when it is not. The resident and the inpatient staff, including the ward chief, thought that a reasoned decision had been made. No one recognized how much Alice's ambivalent psychology influenced everyone to accept both the hopelessness of her relationship with Bradley and the impossibility of her survival without it.

Another potential hazard of hospitalization is the opportunity it furnishes patients to find other people with whom they can interact in a mutually self-defeating manner.

> *Alice (cont'd.).* After Alice left the hospital she moved in with Frank, a depressed patient on day care. She took care of him and in return he gave her money and a place to stay. Bradley moved in almost immediately. He and Alice reported this arrangement to the resident at the first couple therapy session after his vacation. To Alice's mind, this arrangement met the therapist's demand that she have a place to live and a means of support.
>
> For several weeks Alice and Bradley systematically took advantage of Frank, who even signed over his car to Bradley. Finally Frank's exasperated therapist called the resident during a session with Alice and Bradley and handed

the phone to Frank. Frank told the startled resident, "Tell Bradley to stop using me."

Long-Range Aspects of Hospitalization. Patients recovering from a severe depression may become more suicidal as they recover from emotional paralysis and regain energy and initiative. *They must be carefully observed during this period.* Proposed shifts from total hospitalization to day care or discharge may seem desirable to the therapist but may feel like imminent abandonment to the patient. He must be allowed to express this feeling. The therapist may even take the initiative in exploring such feelings by saying:

> I know it feels fine now, and that's progress, but you are just past a period when you were at the brink of despair. Conflicts have a way of coming back, and I think you should expect some bad days in the near future. You should expect more depression, especially when you think there's no one around to contact, and you should be willing to try doubly hard to ask for help when that happens. If it occurs on a day when I'm away, I expect you to contact my partner, Dr. Smith.

The rationale of such a *negative prediction* is both to inform the patient with a program of action for further relapses and to employ the healing properties of a paradox. The prediction protects the patient in that, like the watched pot which never boils, the unconscious finds it hard to move in where consciousness is awaiting it. If depression does reappear, the patient will have the therapist's words in mind and will know this is expected behavior for him, not a sign that his treatment is a failure. His attitude can then be like the driver's who steers in the direction of the skid.

SPECIFIC THERAPEUTIC STRATEGIES

Drug Therapy

Therapists are concerned with two kinds of drugs: those the patient has been taking (frequently alcohol, barbiturates, narcotics, or stimulants) and those he is thinking of prescribing (usually antidepressants). He should take a careful history of self-medication and employ generally accepted principles in effecting withdrawal. Often depression, anxiety, and insomnia are caused by these drugs and diminish markedly or disappear when their use is discontinued. If the use of drugs has been heavy, or the patient's ability to withdraw is doubtful, he should be hospitalized for supervised withdrawal.

The therapist should evaluate the patient in the drug-free state so he has a base line against which to measure change. Some patients are drug-free on first contact or on admission; others need to be withdrawn. Many hospitalized patients will improve significantly within the first week of admission and will show considerable diminution of the target symptoms of depression, guilt, anxiety, insomnia, psychomotor retardation, agitation, and loss of appetite.

Patients undergoing a severe unipolar or involutional depression are often in such piteous condition that they should be hospitalized and placed immediately on antidepressant medications. Similarly, patients with documented manic-depressive illness in the depressed phase may benefit from lithium carbonate treatment.

Depressed, suicidal patients in milder or reactive depressions who do not respond to an initial drug-free period of treatment, whether or not in the hospital, should be started on tricyclic antidepressants (Chapter 28, "Treatment of Mania and Depression"). These drugs can be used in suicide attempts, and so long as suicide remains a substantial risk they should be prescribed in sublethal doses of at most a week's supply at a time. The "bother" of a patient's having to see a therapist frequently to refill a prescription is an advantage because it enforces regular contact and is a nonverbal statement of the doctor's concern.

Drugs, like hospitalization and legal restraint, should be employed unambivalently in both dosage and timing. Published dosage schedules for the tricyclic antidepressants often border on the homeopathic; consult the schedules in Chapter 28. The dose should be brought into the therapeutic range in three to five days.

Insomnia is a private hell for otherwise only mildly depressed patients and can be peculiarly intractable to psychotherapeutic intervention. (If the patient is severely depressed, the insomnia usually responds to antidepressant medication along with the other symptoms.) Currently two agents surpass all others in safety for treatment of insomnia: flurazepam and chloral hydrate. Neither should be given in large quantities. Other available agents cannot be recommended for use with suicidal people; their "track record" for completed suicides is frightening. Barbiturate sleeping medications particularly have *no* place in the treatment of suicidal people; they are often stockpiled by patients who dissimulate en route to a serious, and often lethal, attempt (vide Alvarez).

It is also important to establish good consultative relationships with other professionals in the patient's life because they may become additional sources of drugs. These include internists, surgeons, dentists, and pharmacists. They need to know that the patient is suicidal and in psychiatric treatment. Their own use of psychotropic drugs in treatment of the patient should be curtailed as much as possible and coordinated with the psychiatrist's. Usually they will be glad to defer to his instructions. Courtesy and tact are essential in consultation, and communication between members of the treatment ecological group is more important than complete agreement.

Alice (cont'd.). From the beginning, drugs were a problem in the treatment of Alice and Bradley. Both were chronic drinkers (Alice's two husbands had been, too). Bradley had signs of cirrhosis; Alice did not. Both agreed to take disulfiram (Antabuse®). The resident prescribed it, hoping that if they could not drink to excess, they could not recreate the circumstances of her suicide attempt.

Alice still complained of insomnia. The resident, unaware of its potential depressant qualities, prescribed limited doses of chlor-promazine at bedtime (remembering her old therapist's conjecture, "Underneath . . . she is very confused, maybe crazy"). Initially she responded well to 100 mg at bedtime.

As Alice became quieter, Bradley grew more restive. He complained she was "like a zom-bie" on chlorpromazine; her immobile sleep on the drug upset him. He disliked disulfiram because it made him feel tired. Alice came to one session alone while Bradley was out on the road trying unsuccessfully once more to reacti-vate his promotional advertising business. She said, "I don't mind telling you this, Brad is a happy drunk. He hasn't used that pill you gave him since the first week, and I don't mind. I take mine, though. And the other one. I couldn't sleep without that one."

Psychotherapeutic drugs can quickly become a part of the patient's world, to be used in ways not originally intended by the therapist. Therefore any prescription of drugs must be clearly thought out in advance.

Electroconvulsive Therapy

Electroconvulsive therapy (ECT) is of proven worth in treating severe recurrent and involu-tional depressions. It should be considered seri-ously if psychotherapy and medication fail. Suicidal ideation per se is *not* an indication for the use of ECT, nor is the frustration of a therapist who has difficulty tolerating a patient's ambiva-lence and seeks a quick solution to long-standing conflict. Two possible risks of ECT are the social consequences of receiving a treatment linked to "the snake pit" in the public's mind (for instance, the response to the revelation of Democratic vice-presidential candidate Thomas Eagleton's ECT history during the summer of 1972), and the still-debated possibility of irreversible memory changes. ECT is sometimes withheld when its use would be life-saving.

Example 3-9. A 55-year-old lumberjack was brought by his wife to a minimally staffed hospital. She complained that she was tired of watching him, that he had been threatening suicide, and that he was "all slowed down." He was treated on a medical ward that had locked rooms for severely ill psychiatric patients and seen daily by a psychiatrically oriented general practitioner who was supervised by an over-worked psychiatrist. He recommended joint sessions for the husband and wife and a trial period of amitryptyline. The joint sessions were used by the wife to complain of her husband's irritability and by the husband to deny the accusations. Outside the sessions the patient looked bleak and showed signs of psychomotor retardation.

After spending several days in the locked room, the patient thought he could manage on the ward. Although he still looked depressed, the physician let him out on the advice of the psychiatrist, who said, "You can't keep him locked up forever." On the next morning the patient became irritated at a nurse who was calling him to breakfast and jumped out of an upper story window. He was killed instantly.

In retrospect it is clear that he should be been referred for ECT after the failure of the antidepressants and psychotherapy.

Psychotherapeutic Strategies

Intensive psychotherapy with suicidal patients is a specialist's art, and there are certain techniques the therapist must master if he is to be effective. These include mediating catharsis, interpreting anger and hostility, separating the thought from the act, having the patient imagine his own death, encouraging activity, using the telephone, and involving the law.

Ambivalent suicidal patients often find it diffi-cult to express negative feelings in words. When this impasse occurs, the therapist can *mediate catharsis* by expressing negative feelings for the patient.

For instance, after hearing a circumstantial account of a difficult marriage, the therapist may say, "Under the circumstances a person would be forced to feel quite angry at his wife." Or in family sessions the therapist might express what he thinks are the patient's feelings directly to the wife. This provides a model for the patient that tells him it is permissible to express such feelings.

Initially the therapist does not insist that the patient take responsibility for these feelings because he realizes they pose too much of a burden. Instead he acts as a kind of midwife to the process of catharsis and performs a certain amount of therapeutic work until the patient gains sufficient courage to acknowledge the feelings on his own.

But it can be brutal to both the patient and his family to focus on hate and ignore love. It is better, in fact, to have the patient acknowledge his love for the members of his family first; it is easier for them to accept criticism from someone they know loves them. Indeed, the suicidal patient is usually acutely aware of his own potential for destructiveness and feels a great need to protect his loved ones from it. (Suicide notes that say, "My darling wife, I don't want to hurt you anymore, I love you," express this poignantly.) Almost every depression causes grief and exasperation in others, and the suicidal person knows only too well that he can be a burden to his loved ones. Encouraging the patient to put his negative feelings into words directed to his loved ones may seem to him to be adding insult to injury.

Interpretations therefore must voice *both* halves of the patient's ambivalence, not just the aggressive component. Thus the therapist will say to a man in a bind of hostile dependency with a controlling wife, "It must be very hard, when your wife has been so good to you, to admit that there are times when, good as she is, you find yourself angry with her." This careful, even protective, wording gives the patient a chance to express the complexity of his feelings without guilt.

Without such respect for the patient's ambivalence, the therapist may lead him into expressing extreme anger and bring on another bout of depression when the patient guiltily reflects on what he has said. Worse yet, the patient may grow uncontrollably angry in a process of injudicious catharsis. Then the therapist has replaced a suicidal crisis with a homicidal one.

The therapist can encourage the open expression of feelings, but he should nevertheless refrain from joining in any attack on significant others. He can do this by making statements such as, "It is terribly important that you know you are angry and that you let the feeling live. We can't condemn her of course, since she does what she does out of her own character and for her own reasons." Indeed, the therapist may have to take a stiff line against absolute judgments so the patient will not feel he has succeeded in making the therapist an accomplice in his homicidal feelings or his therapy a place where the reputation of others is damaged. If the patient regards his therapy as a place where a symbolic murder is taking place, he will feel intensely guilty. Over and over the therapist will have to protect his patient from the backlash of guilt by making it clear that he is not judging the loved one and by pointing out the loved one's position: "She has to be angry at you sometimes; you aren't always right." As this process advances, the patient will feel increasingly safe about saying what he feels because he knows the therapist will not let it lead to actual or symbolic harm to others.

Part of the dilemma of suicide is the blurred distinction between fantasy and action—inner feelings must be acted upon to be acknowledged. Thus suicidal action is often the only way a patient can find of expressing himself. One of the most valuable acts a therapist can perform is to teach the patient that there is an *inner* world of fantasy and emotion with its own laws, and this world is not the same as the outer world of action.

The therapist must recognize that the suicidal patient is often quite concrete, i.e., has only a weak ability to distinguish fantasy from action, and may take the therapeutic dialogue literally after the session. The therapist must explain repeatedly that emotion is not to be naïvely acted upon. He should explain at the outset that he is going to encourage the patient to express his feelings, but if the patient feels compelled to act on them outside the therapeutic situation, he must call the therapist.

Example 3-10. An intelligent divorced woman in her middle 50s entered psychotherapy after a suicide attempt brought on by her rage at an indecisive boyfriend. She called her therapist after a session in which she had begun to ventilate her long-suppressed anger at the man, whom she had previously mothered and forgiven. She said that she felt like killing him. The therapist said those feelings were important but that they belonged to the psychotherapy, and if she felt like acting on them, she should come in immediately. At the next psychotherapy session the therapist inquired about her homicidal concern, and she said "I've got it under control now." She reported a dream she had the night after she spoke to the therapist. In it she was holding a knife. In front of her was a wall on which the word KILL was written. Gripping the knife tighter, she moved to the right and saw the word MURDER. She was so frightened she dropped the knife, and from this point impulsivity was not a problem.

Imagining the Effect of One's Death. It is instructive and often therapeutic to ask the suicidal person to imagine out loud how he thinks he will die. Such exploration may lead to a confrontation with the fact that the effect of death is often different from what the patient imagines. Some patients need to pursue suicidal fantasy to overcome it. As mentioned in Chapter 2, the fantasy may be one of killing a hated part of the self, of inducing enduring guilt and grief in others, of coming back to life and watching them suffer, or of being reunited with loved ones in heaven.

Example 3-11. A 35-year-old divorced mother of one had since childhood been entwined in a frustrating, symbiotic relationship with her clergyman father. She pathetically sought but rarely received his approval unless it was accompanied by extensive moral admonitions. During therapy she struggled, with occasional success, to free herself from this tyranny. Her therapist was struck by how primitive (although not psychotic) her defenses were and had thought of her as "a flamboyant, childlike, hysterical character."

Usually he presented her bill at the end of each month, and she paid it promptly. During a midmonth session she uncharacteristically asked him, "How much do I owe you for this month?" and took her checkbook from her purse. The therapist asked her why she wanted to pay her bill then. Was it because she was thinking of suicide and wanted to leave no hard feelings? She was indeed. She had received a depressing letter from her father and felt pessimistic. She believed that *nothing* would ever please him, was tired of trying, and wanted to take her son with her to heaven.

With the therapist's encouragement, she described how wretched her death would make her father feel and how he would finally come to see how he had failed to appreciate her. She looked forward almost gleefully to the retribution. The therapist asked the patient to estimate how long the father's grief would continue, given his long record of imperviousness to her feelings and tendency to moralize away the meaning of her existence. She soberly estimated that he would probably "get over it" in several weeks at most. The therapist asked her how she would be able to perceive and enjoy even those several weeks. She had never thought of this before. The patient realized that if she were dead, she would not be able to see her father suffer, and her effort would have been in vain. She put her checkbook back into her purse, and the two began to talk of more effective ways by which she could register her disappointment.

Other patients need to be confronted with the

uncertainty of death and the brutal reality of suicide. In a letter to an anonymous correspondent, Jung[7] said:

Anon.   *19. Novb. 1955*
I am glad that you do understand the difficulty of your request. How can anybody be expected to be competent enough to give such advice? I feel utterly incompetent—yet I cannot deny the justification of your wish and I have no heart to refuse it. If your case were my own, I don't know what could happen to me, but I am rather certain that I would not plan a suicide ahead. I should rather hang on until I can stand my fate or until sheer despair forces my hand. The reason for such an "unreasonable" attitude with me is that I am not at all sure what will happen to me after death. I have good reasons to assume that things are not finished with death. Life seems to be an interlude in a long story. It has been long before I was, and it will most probably continue after the conscious interval in a three-dimensional existence. I shall therefore hang on as long as it is humanly possible and I try to avoid all the foregone conclusions, considering seriously the hints I got as to the *post mortem* events.

Therefore I cannot advise you to commit suicide for so-called reasonable considerations. It is murder and a corpse is left behind, no matter who has killed whom. Rightly the English Common Law punishes the perpetrator of the deed. Be sure first, whether it is really the will of God to kill yourself or merely your reason. The latter is positively not good enough. If it should be the act of sheer despair, it will not count against you, but a willfully planned act might weigh heavily against you.

This is my incompetent opinion. I have learned caution with the "perverse." I do not underestimate your truly terrible ordeal.

In deepest sympathy,
yours cordially,
C. G. Jung

"Stick to your last" is wise advice for anyone who is depressed. *Self-assertion* in relatively conflict-free areas provides one channel for the problematic aggressive drives. The patient should be encouraged to go to his job or, if he is on a ward, to structure his day. Activity outside therapy builds self-esteem and lessens the risk of severe conflicts over dependency.

The *telephone* is a nuclear element in suicide prevention. The patient should be encouraged to use it whenever he feels the need. This channel may be used in the early phase of therapy—as it was by the intelligent but overcontrolled woman in Example 3-10—to mention particularly unacceptable thoughts and feelings for the first time. Always its use extends and dramatizes the emotional lifeline with which the therapist is trying to provide the patient. It is particularly helpful in dealing with a suicidal crisis over a weekend or holiday because the therapist can schedule specific telephone appointments and force the patient to stay in touch. If the telephone appointment is not kept, the therapist is probably being tested for concern and should telephone the patient himself. If the patient does not answer, the therapist may take this as a presuicidal signal and call other members of the ecological group or the police.

The therapist should be willing to take *legal steps* to prevent suicide when the patient impulsively breaks contact or makes specific suicidal threats. Police officers are usually helpful to suicidal people, and their presence expresses concern. The best way to use the law is as a means of bringing the patient into custody long enough for an evaluation to be made. When the therapist does use the law (see Example 3-6), he is making an unambivalent statement that he wants the patient to live. Sometimes in the later stages of treatment the therapist may say to a patient who habitually threatens to kill himself, "When you tell me you plan to kill yourself, I will take you seriously, and I will have to inform everyone concerned, including the police, that this is what you plan to do." Alternatively, the therapist may state, "If you are absolutely set on killing yourself, I can't stop you, and I'm not going to chase you. I will make sure that everyone around you knows the risk."

COUNTERTRANSFERENCE PROBLEMS

Countertransference means reactions in the therapist, unwittingly called forth by the patient, that stand in the way of the therapist's attention to and understanding of the patient's dynamics. Suicidal patients can be draining in their demands and negativism. The therapist should recognize his limitations. Probably he should serve as a lifeline to no more than one actively suicidal person at a given time.

He also must come to terms with his own negative feelings. Sooner or later every therapist realizes that there is a patient in his caseload whose death would unburden him. The therapist must be on guard against his own tendency to immobilize. Probably his best protection is to share his burden with a colleague and to communicate fully and often his difficulties in working with the patient. When the colleague starts to immobilize, perhaps it is time to change colleagues or patients.

Usually it is bad to refer a patient in crisis. It is, however, acceptable when a therapist is unable to summon the energy to continue supporting a patient to be honest about his own limitations. Without impugning the patient, the therapist can explain that he feels as a professional he cannot offer the best treatment. The reason lies in the therapist's own limitations at this time, and he would like the patient to accept referral to another professional who can help him. This message is usually accepted by patients because it is an expression of continued concern and not a repudiation.

Many countertransference problems can be resolved successfully when the therapist perceives that he has become an agency through which the patient's ambivalence is being expressed. The therapist who wonders if the patient would not be better off dead should realize that he is taking over the patient's fantasy. Although the exact process may be obscure, therapists who work with suicidal people should recognize that it is possible to feel the patient's emotions. In fact, the patient may be working unconsciously to make the therapist give up hope and behave rejectingly so that the suicide will become justifiable.

When the bind is intense, skillful consultation may be required to free the therapist to recognize that his hostile feelings are being elicited by the patient. Then the therapist can confront the patient with what he is doing, often to good effect. Some therapists say, "Stop putting your anger into me." Others may say, "I find that you are communicating with me in a way that makes me feel hopeless too. You shouldn't try to bully me into agreeing with your depression. When you do, I will confront you with what you are doing. Because you feel hopeless now doesn't mean I have to agree with you that it will always be this way."

Finally, every therapist who works with suicidal people has to accept the possibility of failure. His own skills may not be equal to the demands of a particular suicidal process. The failure to help may be a force in furthering professional growth if the therapist accepts that his own process is one of continuous development in the face of difficult challenges.

Alice (cont'd.). Alice killed herself. She had left the hospital against medical advice, with an unpaid bill that prevented her readmission. The resident had started outpatient couple therapy with Alice and Bradley and hoped, if not to restore the relationship, at least to let it dissolve amicably. They enjoyed the sessions, but Bradley used them to talk about himself, and Alice used them to watch Bradley and obtain refills of her chlorpromazine prescription. She said virtually nothing about her emotional life.

After several months Alice and Bradley left again for the East Coast. While they were on the trip, both Alice's mother and ex-husband died, and she and Bradley had to take care of

Billy. They returned to the resident. Alice was much more depressed, but could not talk about it. She and Billy moved away from Bradley. She took a job selling dresses, became more depressed, and made another suicide attempt with alcohol and drugstore medications. She was sent to a state hospital for three days, then returned to the resident and was morose and taciturn. When Billy reported finding her in the kitchen one day with the gas turned on, the resident again sought to help. He found another therapist who agreed to treat her at another hospital with county financing. The resident and the other therapist discussed the possible use of ECT.

The resident's consultant heard the case and recommended that when Alice was released he wait for her to ask for help before trying to rescue her. Among other things, the consultant said, "This is a dead woman."

Alice stayed in the other hospital a week, felt better, and called the resident to make an appointment. On the day of this appointment she called to say she had car trouble but that she would be there the following week. Following his consultant's advice, the resident waited.

Three days before the appointment Alice drove to the railroad station, parked her car, and lay down across the tracks. She was cut in half by the morning express. When he was interviewed later with Alice's brother, who had come to get him, Billy expressed great relief that his mother was dead. "She was always threatening, and I was tired of coming home from school wondering if I was going to find her dead. Do you know what happened that day her car broke down? She was driving to the railroad station then, and her car broke down on the way. You did everything you could."

Privately the resident wondered. Had he immobilized at the end, or was his consultant right to make him wait until Alice asked for treatment? He wondered if he knew all along that she would kill herself if he stopped reaching out actively. Turning to the record he kept of his dreams for his own analysis, he discovered the following one. It had been written down on the morning of Alice's suicide a few minutes before her death:

"Am in some kind of subway or train station. I have with me the briefcase in which I keep my patient's records, only instead of tan it is unaccountably black. There is a woman who is living in one state and tells me she wants to go to another. She has had troubles with her husband. We are talking on the lower platform, and I know I have plenty of time to catch the train. Suddenly I realize I've left my briefcase on the upper platform. I rush up to get it, and I pick it up just as the train is pulling in, just in time."

The resident's dream reflects the paradox of his experience with Alice. On the one hand, he did not succeed in rescuing her, and this failure blackened his feeling about himself as a clinical worker. On the other, he came to accept this disappointment as a corrective to his overconfidence and was able to function at a higher level of clinical understanding.

REFERENCES

1. Stengel, Erwin: *Suicide and Attempted Suicide,* Penguin, Baltimore, 1969.

2. Jung, C. G.: "Psychological Types," in *Collected Works,* Princeton, Princeton, N.J., 1971, vol. 6, pp. 354–356, 387–388.

3. Hillman, James: "The Feeling Function," *Lectures on Jung's Typology,* Spring Publications, New York, 1971, pp. 101–102.

4. Mintz, Ronald S.: "Basic Considerations in the Psychotherapy of the Depressed Suicidal Patient," *Am. J. Psychotherapy.,* vol. 35, January 1971.

5. Lesse, S. (ed.): *An Evaluation of the Results of the Psychotherapies,* Charles C Thomas, Springfield, Ill., 1968.

6. Kalinowski, Lothar M.: "Convulsive Shock Treatment", in S. Arieti (ed.), *American Handbook of Psychiatry*, Basic Books, New York, 1959, vol. 2, pp. 1510–1511.

7. Adler, Gerhard (ed.): *Selected Letters of C. G. Jung*, Princeton, Princeton, N.J., 1975. Reprinted by permission of Princeton University Press.

JOHN E. BEEBE III, M.D. CHAPTER **4**

Evaluation and Treatment of the Homicidal Patient

We have presented suicide as a personal decision to end life, as an ego decision. Treatment is also largely directed to the patient's ego, his awareness and ability to take responsibility for his often overwhelming feelings and thoughts.

To understand homicide, we must go deeper. The motivation for most homicide does not lie within the ego, in its internal self-divisions or its external failures of integration into society. Rather, homicide arises in the more impersonal and instinctive area that Freud called the "id" and Jung called the "collective unconscious." Homicidal motivation belongs usually to the purposes of the id, not to the decisions of the ego; to collective prejudices, not personal values. The suicidal patient may tell the emergency therapist, "I wanted to die"; the potential homicide is likely to report, "Something in me wanted to kill."

Thus homicide, for the therapist, is a greater challenge than suicide. In addition to rational clinical skills, he needs to develop a feeling for the irrational, an intuitive sensitivity to the logic of emotion. Effective intervention in homicidal crises requires the ability to appraise areas of functioning of which the patient himself may be totally unconscious. Effective intervention also requires

the ability to recognize the patient who is not equipped to exert his own controls so that appropriate external restraint can be provided. Finally, effective intervention requires the ability to face human destructiveness as a reality and see it without the sentimental or wishful thinking that avoids the human, and frequent, desire to harm others.

PEOPLE WHO KILL

With the important exceptions of those who kill on military assignment or for monetary gain, people who kill are enacting a primitive response to an impasse for which they perceive another person as being responsible. The choice of the primitive killing response seems to be conditioned by a long, maladaptive background that is present in nearly all homicide offenders. The actual killing is usually triggered by an immediate frustration. Anger[1] often appears when

... the development of the situation is such that the possibility of any resolution to the situation, any reasonable prompt satisfaction of need or elevation of self is contradicted by elements of the situation.[2]

Anger, of course, relocates the blame for the impasse outside the suffering individual, avoiding the continued experience of pain, uncertainty, and anxiety. By engaging in violent, homicidal behavior, the aggressive person punishes someone in the outer world and completes the process of putting all his distress outside himself.

In actual practice, people who kill show *varying* degrees of being out of touch with their own pain and of relocating it in the outer world. Thus pain, denial of pain, anger, denial of anger, homicidal fantasy, denial of homicidal fantasy, homicidal action, and denial of having acted homicidally may all occur at different times in the life of a potentially violent individual. An important part of the treatment of a homicidal individual occurs through his learning to experience pain, anger, and hostile fantasy without turning to action.

Homicidal individuals differ in their relationship to fantasy. Of course many people experience homicidal fantasy as an accompaniment to anger. Some persons, frightened by this fantasy, repress it, and the hostile content appears only in dreams or other symbolic substitutes such as hostile jokes and teasing. Other people retain the fantasy but repress the anger that goes with it. They entertain extremely violent thoughts in a "split-off," unemotional way. When a mild-mannered person of this type kills, everyone is usually surprised because he has not shown even anger, let alone a potential for violence. Megargee[3] calls such people "chronically overcontrolled types." Indeed, the majority of those who kill never commit another violent act,[4] and the only clue to homicide is the pre-existence of homicidal fantasies.[5]

Other violent persons seem to have much anger but little fantasy. Habitually aggressive patients show an impoverished fantasy life and little recognition of internal states. Pain is repressed in favor of the direct expression of rage.[6] Often a depression exists, unrecognized because it is masked by the angry behavior.[7] For persons in this group—whom Megargee calls the "undercontrolled agressive types"—homicide seems but a side effect of a habitual pattern of rage response to frustration.[8]

The Homicide Offender

Most of what is known about homicidal behavior comes from studies of arrested persons. "Criminal" homicide includes murder and manslaughter (both voluntary and involuntary); it excludes killing in self-defense, excusable and "justifiable" homicide, and homicide performed "as a legal duty" by a peace officer or executioner. Generally speaking, the therapist will find himself taxed by the need to prevent the loss of control that leads to criminal homicide. Psychotic homicide is much less frequently a problem for him, as the indications for intervention are so clear-cut. (The treatment of psychotic states is discussed in Chapter 5.) Rational, premeditated homicide is rarely discussed with a therapist, nor is "justifiable" homicide. Therefore much of the data relevant to everyday preventive work are drawn from the records of those who have lost control and have been held legally culpable, from studies of prison populations of convicted slayers, and from records of persons arrested for murder.

Marvin Wolfgang[9] has summarized much of what is known sociologically about criminal homicide:

> The typical criminal slayer is a young man in his twenties who kills another man only slightly older. Both are of the same race; if Negro, the slaying is commonly with a knife; if white, it is a beating with fists and feet on a public street. Men kill and are killed between four and five times more frequently than women, but when a woman kills she most likely has a man as her victim and does it with a butcher knife in the kitchen. A woman killing a woman is extremely rare, for she is most commonly slain by her husband or other close friend by a beating in the bedroom.

A recent report[10] on the epidemiology of murder gives the following facts and statistics:

Of the urban murders in this country, 66% are between blacks; 24% between whites, and 4% whites killing blacks. The black murder rate is 16 to 17 times that of the white rate; black females murder three times as frequently as white males.

In 62% of all murders, men kill men; in 18% females kill males; in 16%, males kill females; and in 4% females kill females . . . .

According to the Federal Bureau of Investigation's statistics, the circumstances of U.S. murders break down this way: spouses killing spouses, 12.5%; parents killing children, 2.9%; other family killings, 8.9%; "romantic triangles and lovers' quarrels," 7.1%; other extramarital arguments, 41.2%; murders committed during lesser felonies, 22.1%; and murders committed during possible felonies, 5.3% . . . .

Firearms are the preferred weapons of murderers, who use them 66.2% of the time. Handguns account for 54% of the killings, followed by knives or other sharp instruments in 19% of cases, and bodily force in 8.2% . . . . Among murdering spouses, wives tend to use knives twice as often as husbands. Murdering husbands outnumber murdering wives, 52% to 48%.

. . . Of all crimes of violence, murder is the likeliest one to result in arrest. In fully 86% of homicides, the perpetrator is taken into custody.[11]

From these and other statistics, generalizations can be made about homicide. People tend to kill people who resemble them in age, sex, and race; they know each other and act under circumstances in which it might be difficult to predict who would be the killer and who the victim.[12-15] When the killer and victim are of different sexes, the killer is more often a male who kills his wife or girlfriend. Even though only one-half as many women as men are killed in the United States each year, women living with potentially homicidal men are at a considerably greater risk.[16-19]

Persons in the 20- to 24-year age group are most

likely to kill; the median age of killers in one study was 31.9 years, of the victims 35.1 years.[19] In 1960 nonwhites comprised about 11 percent of the total population but suffered 53 percent of the homicides.[20] Mortality rates for homicides per 100,000 population by race for 1959 to 1961 were Japanese, 1.5; Chinese, 3.0; white males, 3.6; American Indians, 12.9; blacks, 22.6.[21, 22] Of the 18,000 homicides in 1972, 70 percent of the victims were black; "the typical murderer in the U.S. is a young urban black; a male who is either out of work, a student, or a laborer."[10]

Backgrounds of People Who Kill. In contrast to suicide, homicide is primarily a problem of the lowest socioeconomic classes. Detroit has the highest homicide rate of any city in the United States, but the highest rate in the country for nonurban areas is found in the rural South, twice as high as the rest of the United States. (This increased rate still holds when only Southern whites are compared to Northern whites. The simplest explanation is that Southern whites are more likely to carry handguns.)[10]

Areas with the highest homicide rates also have the largest proportion of persons who did not reach high school. Convicted murderers have lower IQ and school achievement scores than other inmates of prisons. The educational level of convicted murderers is lower than the average for males committed for all crimes. There is a high positive correlation between homicide and social maladjustment, as indicated by juvenile delinquency, child neglect and dependency, private agency child placing, and illegitimate birth rate. Gillin's[23] study found that, during the boyhoods of murderers, the subjects' mothers were almost twice as likely to work outside the home as the average American mother.

The subject had often had to assume early economic responsibility for family support; in seven out of ten cases he was 14 years of age when he began, and in over nine out of ten cases he contributed to family earnings before he was 21. Furthermore, there was one chance in three that his family had had a history of intemperance and at least one chance in five of insanity, epilepsy, or mental defect in his family.

    ... the murderers left school earlier, had full-time jobs before the age of 14 in significantly greater numbers, married women with more education than they themselves had had in significantly greater numbers, lived less harmoniously with their wives, and remained on their jobs for shorter periods of time than their brothers.[24]

Wolfgang and Ferracuti[25] have postulated that these sociological conditions have brought into existence a "subculture of violence" that puts a high premium on physical rather than verbal forms of mastery:

    A male is usually expected to defend the name and honor of his mother, the virtue of womanhood ... and to accept no derogation about his race (even from a member of his own race), his age, or his masculinity. Quick resort to physical combat as a measure of daring, courage, or defense of status appears to be a cultural expression, especially for lower socio-economic class males of both races. When such a culture norm response is elicited from an individual engaged in social interplay with others who harbor the same response mechanism, physical assaults, altercations, and violent domestic quarrels that result in homicide are likely to be common.

Early History. In addition to the predisposing subcultural background, the personal background of the eventual murderer suggests considerable disequilibration within the family and within himself. Menninger and Modlin[26] list five factors commonly present in the personal childhood histories of those who later commit murder:

1. *Severe emotional deprivation or overt rejection in childhood:* prolonged absence of one or both parents, a chaotic family life, or actual removal of the child from his family to live with friends or relatives.

2. *Parental seduction:* ranging from subtle forms such as offsprings' sharing their parents' bedroom through adolescence; through overt actions such as a mother's bathing the early adolescent boy, or parading nude before him, or a father's forbidding his four adolescent daughters ever to close the bathroom door under any circumstances, or inflicting painful corporal punishment; to frank incest.

3. *Exposure to brutality and extreme violence:* witnessing violent episodes involving parents, neighbors, or others in the community, and/or being subjected to violent attacks and punishments by parents or parent-surrogates. This witnessed and/or experienced violence is often associated with sexual behavior . . . .

4. *Childhood fire-setting:* "accidental" arson, building bonfires, homemade fire bombs, etc.

5. *Cruelty to animals or other children:* as evidenced by intentional destruction or injury of a sadistic sort; setting fire to animals, torturing them, etc.

Hellman and Blackman[27] discovered that a triad of bed-wetting, fire setting, and cruelty to animals in childhood could be demonstrated three times as often in the early history of those who had committed violent, antisocial crimes as in the histories of those whose crimes were not violent. They consider this triad highly predictive of a potential for violence. John M. Macdonald[28] studied convicted offenders and control groups and found that the homicide-threat group and the homicide-offender group both had a higher incidence of four factors (when considered together): parental brutality, parental seduction, childhood fire setting, and cruelty to animals. The homicide-threat group had the highest incidence of attempted suicide; the homicide-offender group had the lowest incidence of attempted suicide. If the homicide offenders had taken more than one life, been more sadistic, or killed strangers, one factor—cruelty to animals—was significantly higher in the childhood background. Other factors such as alcoholism, a police arrest record, and arrest for assault were distributed evenly among the three groups. He was unable to verify an initial impression that fire setting was a predictive factor taken by itself.

The literature gives an overwhelming impression that the childhood of the person who kills is one in which the child's feelings are not heard and his privacy not respected, in which he is used by adults as an outlet for their aggressive and sexual needs, and in which he turns increasingly to highly antisocial, nonverbal ways of expressing his resentment: soiling, burning, and torturing objects in his environment. Within the subculture of the deprived, those who later commit homicide are the particularly deprived; those most mistreated in youth become the most violent later.

Character Traits of Undercontrolled Patients.
Menninger and Modlin[29] have noted the following characteristics of habitually violent patients:

1. A marginal tolerance for anxiety and tension
2. A proneness to act rather than use thought, words, and symbols
3. Limited, superficial, or highly ambivalent relations with others
4. Intense self-centeredness, with a tendency to see others as very powerful and themselves as weak, inferior, and inadequate
5. A tendency to make suspicious assumptions about the hostile intent of the actions of others

The effect of these traits is to make a relatively minor stress a major crisis, for the sensitivity of these patients is great, and their repertoire of response explicitly physical.

Kinzel[30] has researched this hypersensitivity in an ingenious manner: by measuring the closest distances tolerated on approach from an experimenter by violent and nonviolent prisoners. This distance is called the "body buffer zone"[31] and is defined as the "area around a person within which anxiety is produced, if another enters." This distance is known to ethologists as "reaction distance," and violation of it produces sham or actual violence in an animal.[32] Anthropologists have shown that different cultures define different comfortable limits for intimate, personal, social, and public distances.[33]

Kinzel discovered that assaultive prisoners were hypersensitive to physical closeness to others: their body-buffer zones were almost four times larger than those measured for nonviolent prisoners. Furthermore, the violent prisoners had larger rear zones than front zones, whereas the nonviolent prisoners had larger front than rear zones. After twelve weekly determinations, the zones of both groups decreased to one-half their original size. This decrease indicated that some desensitization could occur as the experiment grew familiar, but the difference between groups remained significant. Kinzel concluded that the large zones for the violent group reflected what he called "a pathological body image state," which was supported by misperceptions of the experimenter as "looming" or "rushing" at the subjects: "Violent individuals tended to perceive nonthreatening intrusion as attack." Many also experienced tingling or goose pimples across their shoulders and backs when approached from the rear. The same subjects tended to be highly defensive about homosexuality, denying it despite histories of homosexual contact (standard for prison populations) and stating strong aversion to taking the "feminine" homosexual role. One subject appeared to experience homosexual panic during the experiment.

These data demonstrate what the personal consequences of a history of parental brutality and seduction may be. Outside prison, violence-threatening patients often complain of too-close approach by heterosexual partners. Paradoxically, the background of parental neglect may cause the same people to make great demands on partners for a maternal sort of support. The combination of an unusual need for mothering and an unusual need for physical distance creates tension in a partner who is trying to meet these contradictory expectations. The patient too is tense, for usually he cannot meet one of his emotional needs without sacrificing the other. Thus the partnership is likely to produce anxiety, resentment, and the potential for violence, each partner misreading the nonverbal cues as the other approaches or draws away physically. Because neither partner may be skilled in the use of words, the process is likely to proceed without either being able to define what is occurring. Instead, each is likely to behave with hostility to the other's presumed affronts, and an escalating pattern of violence is set in motion.

Megargee[34] has called the sort of person showing these habitually aggressive responses to minor stress "the undercontrolled aggressive type":

> The Undercontrolled Aggressive person corresponds to the typical conception of an aggressive personality found in the literature. He is a person whose inhibitions against aggressive behavior are quite low. Consequently, he usually responds with aggression whenever he is frustrated or provoked. Since inhibitions are specific to the situation, he will, occasionally, be inhibited from expressing his aggression. For instance, he might not attack his mother or a judge even though they frustrate him. In such cases, however, the Undercontrolled Aggressive person will readily use the mechanism of displacement and find a substitute target for his aggression, or he may resort to the mechanism of response generalization and make a less drastic response to the original frustrating agent. .

Character Traits of Overcontrolled Homicide Offenders. Megargee[35] spells out the differences this group has from habitually aggressive persons:

> The Chronically Overcontrolled type behaves quite differently, however. His inhibitions against the expression of aggression are ex-

tremely rigid so he rarely, if ever, responds with aggression no matter how great the provocation. These inhibitions are not focused on a few specific targets, as was the case with the Undercontrolled Aggressive type, but instead are quite general. He is, therefore, unable to make use of the mechanisms of displacement or response generalization. The result is that . . . his instigation to aggression builds up over time. In some cases, the instigation to aggression summates to the point where it exceeds even his excessive defenses. If this occurs where there are sufficient cues to aggression in the environment, an aggressive act should result.

Megargee[36] describes some examples:

> In case after case the extremely assaultive offender proves to be a rather passive person with no previous history of aggression. In Phoenix an 11-year-old boy who stabbed his brother 34 times with a steak knife was described by all who knew him as being extremely polite and soft spoken with no history of assaultive behavior. In New York an 18-year-old youth who confessed he had assaulted and strangled a 7-year-old girl in a Queens church and later tried to burn her body in the furnace was described in the press as an unemotional person who planned to be a minister. A 21-year-old man from Colorado who was accused of the rape and murder of two little girls had never been a discipline problem and, in fact, his stepfather reported: "When he was in school the other kids would run all over him and he'd never fight back. There is just no violence in him."

After the aggressive act, the overcontrolled person reverts to his usual rigid (though brittle) controls. In a study of fifty-three Michigan murderers, Tanay[37] found that 68 percent had overly strong superegos and "a self-image of benevolence, cooperativeness, and self-sacrificing love," a view that was shared by most of their associates.[38] Such persons experienced anger "primarily in the form of sudden explosions" and had noted an altered state of consciousness prior to the murder.

This is the type of murderer who may carry a schizoid or schizophrenic diagnosis. Indeed, mass murderers such as Winnie Ruth Judd and Emil Kemper are extremely complicated problems for psychiatric management because they may appear well integrated both before and after a bizarre crime is committed.

Some persons of this type experience loss of control because they have been under the influence of alcohol or amphetamines. Others are experiencing psychotic episodes at the time of the murders. Indeed, Tanay found that 14 percent of his subjects were psychotic. In dealing with people with rigid, brittle defenses, it is well to imagine what might happen if the defenses were to be undermined by some means, not what the *usual* level of control is. When an altered ego state appears in this kind of person, and he presents himself for psychiatric help, he should be evaluated carefully.

THE PREASSAULTIVE CRISIS

In Chapter 1 we defined crisis as "news of a difference affecting the pattern of relationships found within an ecological group." For homicidal people, the pattern of relationships is already unstable, tending toward rupture, and the difference that precipitates violent action is one that a member of another ecological group might easily take in stride. The first sign of crisis is often an *affective state.*

Rarely does a patient in the preassaultive state present himself to an emergency room therapist saying, "I'm afraid I'm going to kill someone." Rather, the patient's complaint is likely to be a nonspecific tension state. He will be manifesting affective cues such as tremulousness, breathlessness, and rapid pulse and be experiencing a vague uneasiness. He may be alarmed by the tension

building within and say, "I'm afraid I'm going to blow." The patient makes a paranoid projection of his distress onto the other person who then "becomes" the anxiety, as in Kinzel's experiments in which the disequilibration was pictured as the looming or rushing in of the experimenter, not as an internal process of the subject. How all this looks in an actual patient can be illustrated by the following case:

Example 4-1, Ronald and June. Ronald was a 35-year-old white man who had spent half his years in jails and prisons for car thefts, assaults, and forgery. He had met his wife, June, two years younger than he, when he was on parole at age 28. He liked her because she was "game for thieving"; after living together for several months they married.

For four months preceding their first psychiatric visit their marriage had become increasingly strained, and they had quarreled constantly. During an argument a week before their first visit, Ronald choked June until she lost consciousness. As she fell to the floor Ronald "felt all the feelings for her I had never let myself feel," meaning love, concern for her safety, and remorse for what he had done. He ran out of the house; when he returned she had recovered and was gone. He was terrified that she had left for good. He drove around looking for her and nearly gave in to the temptation to drive into a brick wall at ninety miles an hour. When he returned the next morning, she was back, after having spent the night at a male neighbor's. They agreed to try to talk things out; Ronald hinted at a definite suicide attempt if she left him.

They came to the clinic. After the initial interview, first together and then individually, Ronald's care was taken over by a male psychiatric resident and June's by a female social worker. It seemed at the time that each would be more comfortable with a therapist of the same sex.

Ronald's past was amply documented with instances of brutality, neglect, exploitation, delinquency, shallow interpersonal relationships, and academic failure. His father drank and had often beat him. One of Ronald's elder brothers constantly bullied him, and many years later Ronald still felt he would like to "pound my brother into the ground." He recalled his mother as a "beautiful person" who understood him but would not intervene in his or anyone else's problems and who was subjugated by her brutal husband. Curiously, Ronald told his therapist that he still liked his father and wished he could be closer to him.

Ronald did poorly in school, rejecting teachers' efforts to reach out to him. He was first arrested at age 11 for stealing $20 from his school. Later he was arrested on several charges of car theft (he claimed he did it only for joy riding) and spent considerable time in reform schools during his adolescence. Later he was sent to a state prison for similar offenses. He had always been fascinated by cars and had become an expert mechanic.

Ronald was on parole when he met and married June. She became pregnant, but before the birth he was returned to jail for a parole violation. June and the baby visited faithfully every weekend. A prison psychiatrist asked Ronald if he had ever thought of having sex with his mother, and Ronald knocked him out with one punch.

The baby died after a few months of what was diagnosed as crib death. Ronald was released five months later, and June quickly became pregnant again. The second baby's delivery was normal, but when it was nine weeks old, it too died suddenly. Ronald rushed the lifeless infant to the hospital where an autopsy was performed; the diagnosis again was crib death. Ronald worried that these deaths were the result of either "something bad in my blood" or of negligence on June's part.

Four years elapsed between the death of the second child and their first psychiatric visit. During those years Ronald had become increasingly dependent upon June. They had spent only three days apart during that time, and he insisted that she always be near him, an intense demand she found difficult to tolerate. Although she remained present physically, both sensed that she was becoming psychologically distant. Privately, she was thinking of leaving him. It was this impasse between Ronald's intense need for June and her growing restiveness that produced the brutal quarrel that brought them into treatment.

Ronald had been helpless in dealing with his father, his brother, his wife, his teachers, and his schoolmates. Repeatedly he had resorted to action: robbing the school, stealing cars, punching the prison psychiatrist, rushing his dead baby to an autopsy, choking his wife. Sadly, these actions had served only to complicate his life. For Ronald the problem always had been "out there" somewhere, and it is easy to imagine him thinking that the right course of impulsive action would finally resolve it. For Ronald, life had been chronically insecure; he needed to rely more and more on his wife to stabilize him. This chronic disequilibration gradually became a haunting fear that she would leave and it could at any time flame into an acute crisis were she to indicate that she actually planned to do so.

During the crisis with June, Ronald had been flooded with a violent impulse. Presumably choking her promised to relieve the immediate situation, however unfortunate the long-term consequences for him. In the language of dynamic formulation, an unconscious, archaic solution had appeared in response to an impasse Ronald did not know how to resolve at the ego level. It is important to look more closely at this solution, at its meaning for Ronald in terms of unconscious problem solving. We turn now to the common meanings of the homicidal solution.

Meanings of the Homicidal Solution

Homicide As Freedom. Studies on the body-buffer zone measure the degree of physical proximity people can tolerate before they lash out to free themselves from intrusion. The therapist measures the degree of psychological, emotional, or subjective proximity his patients can tolerate and the subtlety of means at their disposal to free themselves from a sense of crowding or oppression from another's closeness. Often the therapist finds that a partner triggers an unconscious introject of the devouring mother who cripples the infant's initiative while perpetuating his dependent ties upon her.[39] Murderous rage toward a wife may be a continuation of anger toward a mother, as would appear to be the case with Ronald. If suicide is frequently an attempt to achieve an extraverted end that wears an introverted mask, homicide is often the reverse: an attempt to achieve introverted freedom by acting upon an external situation which threatens to engulf the homicidal person.

Homicide As Power. There is an archaic belief that if a man kills another man or an animal, the life force (or mana) of the other creature belongs to him.[40] This primitive idea seems still to operate in many homicidal people and is well supported by their surrounding cultures. In our own country, Mafia dons have a charismatic appeal, as exemplified by the success of *The Godfather*. This same psychology may operate for some persons who find the homicidal solution appealing. In their daily lives they are weak and ineffective; through murder they at last demonstrate power.

Homicide As Mastery. In analytic treatment, there is a class of "killing dreams" in which the patient stabs or shoots a threatening figure or is witness to a killing. (Some examples are given in Chapter 22.) The dreamer often feels profound satisfaction (an emotion that may alarm him when he wakes). After such a dream the patient often takes active steps toward mastery of a long-standing intrapsychic conflict. A phrase such as "getting to the heart of the matter" suggests the positive meaning of the homicidal idea.

There are some persons who turn to homicide to experience mastery of long-term interpersonal conflicts. Indeed, some murderers have reported that immediately following the killing they felt profound emotional relief, often for the first time in a long time.[41]

Homicide As Connection. Often homicide is a way of establishing a connection with a person who is felt to be so powerful or remote that no other form of communication suffices: physical force becomes the only way of being heard.

An example of this theme can be found in Shakespeare's *Julius Caesar*, in the scene in which the conspirators are pressing their arguments to Caesar, who imperiously brushes them away. Casca, the least articulate of the group, finally shouts, "Speak, hands for me!" and plunges the first dagger into Caesar's breast. The rest of the conspirators join him in stabbing the Emperor. Clearly Caesar was a man who could be reached only by attack.

Similar dynamics operate in everyday life. Every therapist knows some patients who dislike words, fear the verbal prowess of the therapist, and must be approached in nonverbal ways such as through painting or gestalt techniques. Outside therapy, less inarticulate patients frequently resort to physical means to settle disputes or to relate to others.

> *Example 4-2.* A 24-year-old woman who had excelled in sports was experiencing great distress in her relationship with her husband, a highly articulate and argumentative young professor of English. She subtly provoked him to assault until he pushed her down to the floor and began to choke her. She said later that she felt considerable satisfaction because she thought that it was a fairer fight than their usual verbal battles.

Her husband, it developed, had harbored conscious homicidal feelings toward his mother for some years, and she was taking a great risk by provoking him in the area of this strong residual hatred. Confronted by her therapist with the potential danger, she could for a long time reply only, "I know that, but I can't fight back when he uses words, and I can fight back when he attacks me physically."

Homicide may also represent a sexual connection, as shown in the frequent association of stabbing with sexual molestation. Homicidal fantasy directed toward wives often erupts in men who have become impotent. Presumably the aggressive impulse compensates for the fear that emotional connection has become impossible. Severely depressed men, humiliated by associated impotence, may resort to homicide to establish the desired connection with the powerful wife.

THE DECISION TO ACT

Many overcontrolled people enjoy Walter Mittylike fantasies of homicide; many undercontrolled people engage in at least verbal altercations. Few of either group actually commit homicide. Four factors illuminate the conditions under which the danger of turning fantasy or quarrels into violent acts becomes great: a history of past violent behavior, sanction of the ecological group, sanction of the victim, and impairment of individual ego functioning.

Patients who have a history of *past violent behavior* used as a mode of conflict resolution are more likely to employ it in the future than those who do not. Wherever the violence has been "successful," i.e., winning fights or receiving plaudits rather than punishment, the tendency will have been reinforced, as Berkowitz[42] has shown in a study of nursery school children.

It is true that the way people responded to stress and conflict in the past is the best single predictor of how they will respond in the future. In evaluating potential for violence, the emergency therapist should learn about a patient's history of fights, arrests and convictions for violent crimes, reputation for toughness among his peers, and having caused previous deaths in civilian or military life. He should gauge the patient's general regard for the value of the lives of others: are people subjectively real, or objects to be disposed of if they get in the way?

Homicide occurs more frequently when it has the *sanction of the ecological group,* as in the subculture of violence Wolfgang has described. Macdonald[43] describes the following case:

> *Example 4-3.* A wife who had been threatened sent for her father-in-law, who told her in her husband's presence, "If my son had killed you tonight, I wouldn't have blamed him."

Macdonald shows that often the family will provide the murderer with the weapons he uses to kill.

Murder often takes place with the *sanction of the victim*. In many cases, the victim was the first to show and use a deadly weapon, to strike a blow, or to start the interplay involving physical violence. In some cases the victim (usually a wife) virtually challenged the partner to kill her.

> *Example 4-4.* One case involved a wife who suffered repeated beatings and homicidal threats. In her living room she displayed a gift from a neighbor man with whom she had lived during a period of separation from her husband. Macdonald insisted that she get rid of this gift, and she did so, but only as far as her mother's mantelpiece, where her husband discovered it on the couple's next visit. Following a threat with a loaded shotgun, the wife said, "Go ahead, you might just as well kill me." Whenever the husband announced his intention of selling the shotgun, the wife would insist he keep it.[44]

Whenever homicide is threatened, the emergency therapist must ascertain whether the victim is actively provoking the homicidal attacks. Often considerable therapeutic pressure must be applied to counter ecological group pressure to a homicidal solution.

Homicidal behavior is id behavior. A healthy ego usually inhibits criminal homicide for the obvious reason that criminal homicide is not in the ego's best interests. Under circumstances of *impaired individual ego function,* homicidal impulses can break through more easily to concrete expression. These circumstances include the influence of drugs and alcohol, organic brain disease, psychotic conditions, and unusually strong emotion.

Saturday night is the time of the highest incidence of homicide,[45] and usually both the victims and offenders have been drinking. [45, 46] Homicide rates, like suicide rates, are highest where alcoholism rates (as measured from deaths from cirrhosis of the liver) are highest.

Drugs that may reduce ego control include LSD, cocaine, and barbiturates, but the most dangerous are amphetamines, which produce in the withdrawal phase symptoms nearly identical with paranoid schizophrenia. In a recent study of homicide offenders,[47] amphetamines were the most commonly used drug at the time violent crimes were committed (16 percent) by both habitual and nonhabitual violent offenders. Cocaine, incidentally, works like a very short-acting amphetamine and may lead to outbursts of suppressed rage in susceptible individuals.

Organic brain disease is a potential cause of violence.[48] Menninger's[49] concept of *dyscontrol* is important. He describes it as "varying degrees of disturbance in organization, failure in coping, escape of disruptive impulses, disruption of orderly thought processes, and confusion." If organic brain disease is present, dyscontrol occurs with minimal stimulation and greatly increases the potential for violence. Organic conditions associated with dyscontrol include psychomotor-variant dysrhythmia, temporal lobe dysrhythmia, occipital dysrhythmia, and brainstem glioma. Alcohol may unmask temporal lobe epileptoid states and associated violence in susceptible individuals. The possible relation of the chromosomal XYY karyotype to violence is still under investigation. [50, 51]

Any patient who complains of sudden outbursts of unexplained rage or struggles with uncontrollable homicidal thoughts should see a neurologist for a full evaluation, including a sleeping electroencephalogram (EEG). In many instances, an abnormal EEG will be the only finding. The therapist will be charged with helping the patient to cope with occasional outbursts of disruptive affect under minimal stimulation, just as he must help the patient deal with affects produced by emotional interaction.

Certain *psychotic conditions* predispose individuals to homicide, especially involutional paranoid psychosis and paranoid schizophrenia. The risk is much greater for schizophrenic patients who drink than for those who do not. The male involutional psychotic murderer often kills himself after killing his spouse, whom he unconsciously sees as possessing the soul he must regain. This kind of murder is illustrated in the film *The Blue Angel*, in which a rigid, 50-ish professor falls under the power of a young woman cabaret singer (Marlene Dietrich) and is progressively degraded by her. Eventually he is driven to make an attempt on her life, trying to regain himself, even at the cost of ruin. In evaluating depressed patients in middle life, it is important to explore ideation concerning the spouse; this may be the area where paranoid ideation lies hidden.

THE EVALUATION OF HOMICIDE RISK

Dealing with Homicidal Threats

The emergency therapist will see patients who impress him as high-risk for homicide as well as those who seek him out because of their own fears about violence. Macdonald[52] studied 100 patients who threatened to kill; at five-year follow-up 3 had killed, and 4 had committed suicide. His study suggests that when someone threatens to kill, it is impossible to predict what the outcome will be, except that the probability of a lethal outcome is very low. Nevertheless, the threat to kill indicates a troubled emotional state and must be taken seriously.

Often young mothers present fantasies of killing their new babies. Such fantasies are common and rarely acted upon. The mother should be evaluated for the ideational, affective, and behavioral strength of these fantasies. Although she is plagued by the idea, has she felt herself giving in to strong emotion to strangle, strike, or drown the baby? Has she felt herself to be on the verge of acting on any such urges? Has she struck the child or left it in a potentially dangerous situation and walked off? How much does she fear loss of control over her fantasies?

If the fantasies are almost entirely ideational, i.e., if she has not felt surges of anger and if she has not impulsively struck the child, then she can be reassured that such fantasies are common, and outpatient psychotherapy should be arranged. The goal of therapy is to allow her to understand better the disequilibrium in her life brought about by the birth. If others can help take care of the baby for a few hours a day, she may appreciate both the relief from being a full-time mother and the implied approval that it is natural to want to do something else.

If the fantasy has strong affective and behavioral components, or if the patient seems to be on the verge of a postpartum psychosis, the baby is at risk. The husband, family, friends, and social agencies must be prevailed upon to protect the child until the mother is once again able to care for it.

Many patients who think about killing are not made anxious by the presence of homicidal fantasy. Other patients are made so anxious that they deny the presence of the fantasy and experience only a nonspecific tension. Neither position is realistic. The therapist should explore any homicidal ideation patiently and in detail to enable both the content and the anxiety about the consequences of action to emerge. This is one situation in psychiatric work in which it is helpful to stimulate anxiety. Once the patient is made anxious by his own potential for violence, he is likely to be more careful. If the therapist believes a significant danger is present, it is mandatory that he communicate the risk to the patient and to significant others.

Essentials of Interview Evaluation

Few patients say outright, "I think I'm going to kill someone." Instead, they will expect the emergency therapist to recognize that people come because they fear they may be losing control. Indeed, the question, "Why did you come here?" may be met with a quiet, evasive answer, slow to come and blunted in effect.

The therapist will need to encourage his patient to talk about this area. He should indicate by his questions that he is interested in and capable of receiving information about the patient's capacity for violence. He does not from the outset lovingly assume good faith or virtue in the patient by a show of "unconditional positive regard" which is in fact deeply conditional and indicates to the patient that he would be disappointed to hear selfish, angry, or negative data. In short, the psychiatrist's stance should indicate that he is accustomed to the bad as well as the good in people, and that he wants to get down to specifics for the practical purpose of assisting the patient. As in other aspects of crisis intervention, the therapist seeks to understand the origins of the crisis, its current status, and its possible future outcome.

Past behavior is the single best predictor of how the patient is likely to behave in the future. Psychiatric history repeats itself. Has there been an association with anyone's violent death, accidental or otherwise? Has the patient been the cause of anyone's death, for whatever reason? Has the patient ever tied anyone up with a rope? Has he used knives or guns? Was he ever arrested or jailed? Has he been known to engage in fights? What has his behavior been like when he drinks? Have there been homicidal thoughts, plans, preparations, or attempts in the past? What was his childhood like?

Did he experience parental brutality or seduction, wet his bed, set fires, or torture animals? What is the current status of his homicidal thoughts, plans, preparations, and attempts? Does the patient have a weapon at hand? Does he have ready access to a weapon? What is his current drinking pattern? Has he been anxious or depressed without apparent cause? Is he actively quarreling with anyone, or jealous of someone? Has anyone provoked him to attack? In many cases the therapist must obtain permission to talk to the family or friends to hear the full story of the patient's recent destructiveness. Quite often they have brought the patient in and are sitting in the waiting room assuming naïvely that he will tell the therapist everything that has concerned them. They should be interviewed privately and assured that the information they give will not be used in an impulsive way which could harm them. They should be encouraged to air *fully* any uneasiness they have about the patient. They should also be evaluated as potential accomplices and as willing victims: do they add to the homicidal risk?

Are there any future conditions under which the patient would resort to a homicidal solution? (A mild-mannered man may answer, "If my wife ever left me for someone else, I'd get the gun out of my top drawer and shoot them both.") What are the patient's attitudes toward punishment? (Some patients welcome punishment as a final, suicidal curtain to a homicidal drama.) Has the patient considered killing himself?

In the evaluation interview, it is helpful to consider those psychiatric patients who are especially likely to commit homicide:

1. Anyone who has made homicidal preparations
2. Involutional paranoid psychotic patients
3. Paranoid schizophrenic patients who drink
4. Antisocial personalities who are starting to settle down (Ronald falls into this category)
5. Either member of a sadomasochistic marital couple
6. Schizophrenic mothers

ESSENTIALS OF PREVENTION

The Psychological Approach

The key to controlling homicide is control of impulsivity. The psychiatrist should take the necessary steps to help the patient separate the thought of homicide from the act. The therapist "lends" his own ego to the patient's weakened ego-control by standing squarely against impulsive emotional discharge. The therapist should proceed slowly and systematically with such patients and avoid excessive emotionality of his own. He stands for thinking things out, coming to decisions only after time, and for order. Therefore, from the outset he should make it clear that he will not be rushed into impulsive decisions, especially these which involve therapy. For instance, if the patient suddenly decides he wants to switch from individual to couple therapy, the therapist should find out why before he hurries to the waiting room to invite the wife in. Abrupt cancellations of appointments should be questioned, and the patient should be confronted with his impulsivity if it manifests itself in treatment.

The therapist must explore all homicidal thinking thoroughly, but he should not side with these ideas. He guards particularly against a therapeutic process of injudicious catharsis in which the patient is allowed to rant at a family member without contradiction from the therapist. If the therapist does not actively point out the "other side" and the dangers of premature action, often such sessions are perceived as license to act on the feeling that has been expressed. A basic condition of psychiatric treatment is that the patient is free to feel, but not necessarily to act, and it is especially important that the therapist stress this distinction when homicidal emotion is discussed.

Another basic principle is that the ultimate responsibility for homicidal behavior rests with the patient. The therapist should make it clear that therapy is no guarantee that a murder will not be committed and cannot be used as a justification for committing this crime. He reminds the patient that if he is firmly launched in the direction of committing murder, there is no way a therapist can stop him or protect him from the consequences of his act. In the emergency setting, he makes it clear he will communicate with peace officers and those in danger to avert loss of life but that in the end the patient must learn to control himself.

Environmental Manipulation. In the early phase of intervention, the therapist is often called upon to *separate the warring parties*. He may have to advise a wife or husband to move out of a house or even a city to avoid harm. He may effect hospitalization to separate people who are likely to kill each other.

The therapist also needs to *undercut potential accomplices*. He does this by exposing them in the act of condoning homicidal behavior and by making them anxious about their responsibility for a possible lethal outcome.

He must also *identify the willing victim* and encourage that person to enter treatment. She is often the wife of a man with a drinking problem or severe personality disorder who feels responsible for his failings. She may want to leave him, but she may be so filled with guilt (partly as a result of his guilt-provoking tactics) that as soon as she expresses her desire she wants to be punished for it. Clearly this situation can provoke homicide because the man is not only aroused to anger but also encouraged to attack, and decisive therapeutic intervention is required for the woman to understand her role. Often a basically healthy woman gets caught up in this bind. Once she learns to stand up to the man she is leaving without provoking him, her later therapeutic progress can be highly gratifying. Early treatment, however, is a relentless pointing out to the potential victim what she is doing to invite attack.

Generally, it is effective to make the patient, his "accomplices," and his "victim" conscious of every prehomicidal communication. As with other impulsive behavior, homicide appears when it is

not expected. Therefore, in dangerous situations it seems wise to teach everyone to expect trouble. (The watched pot is less likely to boil.)

Appealing to Narcissism. Homicidal people often have severe personality disorders, including major deficits in conscience. Because ethical imperatives or moral considerations are not generally inhibiting to antisocial people, therapeutic pessimism about their treatability has prevailed. A current useful tactic that makes use of one of their characteristics is a direct appeal to their narcissism. Antisocial people are often good-looking, enjoy life, and pride themselves on getting what they need without being "hung up" by the needs of others. These defenses against feeling can be mobilized against aggression.

> *Example 4-5*. A Mexican-American man in his late 20s was referred for treatment by a facial surgeon who was concerned about the patient's violent anger at his ex-wife, an Anglo. She had stood by and laughed while her current boyfriend broke the patient's nose when he had dropped by, drunk, to harrass her. Now he was in the hospital to have the nose reset and could think of nothing but revenge against the wife. Even his dreams were full of it.
>
> His therapist suggested that the wife was trying to degrade him further by stimulating him to revenge. "She just wants to see you in jail. Why should you let her drag you down to that level and wind up serving time yourself just to satisfy her?" Gradually the patient began to take pride in not letting his ex-wife "drag him down." He was able to find another woman who respected him, and he congratulated himself no end for being "too smart" to let his ex-wife "fix him for good."

Avoiding Complacency. No matter how stable a patient looks in the office, the therapist who treats homicidal patients must always fear the worst. At the beginning, a firm stand on alcohol and illicit drugs should be taken, and the therapist should insist that all weapons be removed from the home. As treatment proceeds, the therapist must listen carefully for communications that tell him the destructive situation is still raging outside the office—information about drinking bouts, quarrels, gun collections. He should continue to reflect the lethal possibilities to the patient whenever he hears such information.

Particularly, the therapist should recognize and not be fooled by the "mask of adequacy" in improving borderline people. At the first blush of improvement, they will try to leave treatment: it is almost as if they are testing to see if the therapist perceives their continuing potential for violence. If he has honest doubts about their ability to sustain a nonviolent adaptation, the therapist is thoroughly justified in being quite firm with them about their need for continued treatment.

Ronald and June (cont'd.). Ronald and June saw their therapist almost every day during the acute crisis. Ronald quickly formed an attachment to his therapist and thought of him as a benign older brother who was sympathetic to his concerns, who could offer sensible reflection and advice, and who could help him find more successful ways to deal with June. The therapist worked consistently with Ronald to help him convert his feelings into words instead of inarticulate rages and to help him anticipate situations instead of responding with impulsive violence.

At the beginning of his therapy, Ronald described episodes of "blindness" while driving. These episodes occurred only when someone was with him and forced the other person to tell him how to manipulate the car to the side of the road. Fifteen minutes later Ronald's sight would come back. A neurological examination was negative, and Ronald agreed with the therapist that these episodes were an expression of some unknown and overwhelming feelings and that he should let others do the driving for the time being.

June discussed with her therapist her ambivalence about living with Ronald and also mentioned it to Ronald. During the third week of treatment, Ronald toyed with a large hunting knife while he talked with June at home. The next morning it appeared at her bedside. She was terrified and called her therapist. They discussed the options of June's leaving the house and calling the police. Her therapist did not minimize the danger, and informed Ronald's therapist of the incident. June decided to stay with Ronald for the time being. Ronald's therapist discussed the knife with him and pointed out how terrified June had been. Ronald denied any sinister motive and elected to lock up the knife in a trunk for June's peace of mind.

Following this step, June decided to stay with Ronald permanently. Both gained considerably in their ability to talk about difficulties, first with their therapists and then with each other, and the risk of a violent confrontation diminished steadily. Ronald's trust of his therapist grew, and he was able to reveal things that he had never been able to tell anyone. In fact, Ronald had never even articulated many of these matters in his own mind. His therapist could, from his position of trust, transmit some of his own social and personal wisdom, lending Ronald some of his ego. Together they came to see how damaging and self-defeating Ronald's unthinking, impulsive actions could be.

The frequency of the visits diminished. For six months Ronald and June had been living together in greater harmony and were able to talk about and resolve their differences. The homicidal crisis had long since passed, and therapy ended by mutual agreement.

The turning point of the case was the handling of the hunting knife. Its appearance symbolized the dramatic potential for violence. June's prompt reporting of the knife to her therapist testified to her reluctance (not previously so clearly established) to play the role of a victim. The therapists' emphatic demand that the issue of the knife be dealt with and Ronald's decision to lock it up marked the moment when the violence model was abandoned, the verbal model was accepted, and the preassaultive crisis was resolved.

Learning to Relate to the Inner World. John R. Lion[53] has said of the explosive and antisocial personalities he treats at the outpatient violence clinic of the University of Maryland School of Medicine:

> . . . It is common to hear this type of patient tell what he would *do* about an unpleasant situation, but not how he would *feel*.
>
> Therapeutically, therefore, I have regarded one of the main tasks of therapy as promoting in these violent patients an ability to feel and appreciate the depression that accompanies any kind of frustration. It is my experience that if the patient can merely recognize some of his feelings and briefly reflect on them, less impulsive, aggressive action is apt to occur. . . .
>
> Second, it is extremely useful to deal with the fantasies and imaginations of this group of patients. Many patients with impulsive personality disorders seem to have an impoverished ability to fantasize, to think about the possible consequences of behavior, or even to indulge in any kind of daydreams connected with their feelings. To counter this, I spend time with the patient in getting him to elaborate upon the possible consequences of actions he plans, in talking about the possible solutions to his problems, and generally in getting him to talk about his feelings and fantasies concerning a particular act. This is a vital step for a violence-prone patient.
>
> The patient who tells me he wants to kill his wife, for example, must be made to dwell upon the fantasies surrounding the actual murder and the end result of his homicide— incarceration. Likewise, the patient who drives recklessly under the influence of alcohol must

be made to fantasize about the possible occurrence of an accident, revocation of his license, and jail, down to the last detail, for with the detail comes the affect. The fantasies surrounding incarceration are particularly important to elaborate on so as to bring home fully to the patient the consequences of his actions. These usually stir up many depressing feelings and make the patient squarely face his own vulnerabilities and limitations. These are what the violent patient must come to grips with. A violent patient is violent only insofar as he is unable to come to grips with his own weakness and helplessness and to tolerate the depression associated with realizing these feelings.

This excellent description of a difficult task in the treatment of homicidal people—opening up the inner world without eroding controls—shows how fantasy and affect can be used to strengthen the ego. Dream material, too, can be used in this way, especially when the dream content shows the undesired outcome of some particularly charged aggressive release.

> *Example 4-5 (cont'd)*. The Mexican-American man who wanted to kill his wife had a dream in which he kept shooting at her until she was filled with holes. Still she continued to stand in front of him with a mocking expression on her face. Filled with rage, he walked around her only to find he had been shooting at a cardboard image. It was easy for his therapist to point out that the flesh-and-blood woman had been gone for a long time and that he was locked into a fruitless, exhausting struggle with a memory. This dream and its interpretation were the point at which he was able to grieve for the loss of his wife and to engage seriously with another woman.

Lion's way of working with fantasy is to *relate* it to real-life issues. This method has much to offer the overcontrolled person, too. Potentially homicidal people who are overcontrolled need to discover their hurt and anger, not hide it behind rigid defenses. Their capacity for *unrelated* fantasy must be counted as one of the rigid defenses. Although violent fantasy may be present, even pleasurable, it is not integrated. The overcontrolled person does not relate it to his feelings or to the possibility that this fantasy is one he could enact. He needs to be taught to relate his violent fantasy to his life, not to discount it, and to assume that his usual controls will continue to serve him. He should accept the possibility that he may be rehearsing[54] for a big, one-time violent action, and he should be taught to look for the feelings which lie hidden behind the violent images. As these emerge, the patient will become more anxious, less in control, and more in need of therapeutic support. For the first time, he may need limit setting and reminding of the real-life consequences of violent behavior.

Pharmacologic and Physical Approaches

Psychological means alone are often not sufficient to bring homicidal patients under control. Sometimes drugs are helpful in reducing powerful affective states. A discussion of the use of drugs in combination with psychotherapy is found in later chapters.

Diazepam (Valium®) has rapidly become a popular psychotropic drug because it provides quick relief in a way most patients find pleasant. However, dissociative reactions, including rage reactions, have been reported with its use. The combination of diazepam and alcohol may lead to a classic "blackout" in which the patient behaves aggressively and later cannot remember doing so. Clearly diazepam is an inappropriate drug for control of homicidal behavior.

Phenothiazines and related compounds are preferable. Both trifluoperazine (2 to 5 mg one to three times a day) and haloperidol seem useful in controlling chronic anger and haloperidol seems especially useful in treating psychotic patients with a hypomanic component. Both drugs often cause Parkinsonian side effects.

All these drugs have atypical reactions. In general, close contact with the doctor is required if these agents are used. They should also be regarded as adjuncts to therapy, not as substitutes for psychotherapeutic intervention with the patient and his ecological group.

Some violent patients must be restrained. Many emergency rooms provide locked rooms for obstreperous patients who are dangerous or "high" on drugs or alcohol. Judicious restraints should be used with such patients. It is wise not to underestimate an acutely intoxicated or psychotic patient's potential for violence.

Most schizophrenic patients need not be restrained, and schizophrenia alone is not a indication of potential violence. Schizophrenic patients who are violent may require the same restraints as intoxicated patients. There is no contraindication to the use of physical restraint when a significant doubt exists concerning the patient's immediate potential for violence. The therapist should, however, have some positive sign or recent history of destructiveness before he applies restraints.

The most agitated patients require, in addition to restraints or a locked room, an injection of 75 mg of chlorpromazine followed four hours later by another injection or oral administration. Dosages depend on the size of the patient, the degree of agitation, and the degree of intoxication. Phenothiazines react synergistically with alcohol, barbiturates, and sedatives; lesser doses should be administered to patients already intoxicated on these drugs. The immediate goal, in any case, is to quiet or "snow" the patient safely when he cannot be controlled in any other way.

Assuming physical control of a situation is an art in itself. When he takes control, the therapist must accept that he has assumed total responsibility for the patient's behavior. It is up to him to see that the controls are instituted firmly, unambivalently, and smoothly.

It is best to make a concrete display of power that gives the patient no opportunity (in even his foggiest, most concrete state) to misperceive the situation. This is effectively accomplished if four or five men enter a room together. If restraint is to be applied, it should be administered without hurting the patient or allowing him to hurt himself. If an injection is to be administered, the nurse may give it as the male staff members hold the patient. Whenever possible the patient should be given a choice of drinking his medication or receiving it by injection. The male staff should stand by to ensure that no one gets hurt.

External controls administered this way offer security to the patient who is unable to control his violent impulses. When inadequate staff is used, chase sequences upsetting to both the patient and the staff are likely to ensue. There is every chance that someone will get hurt.

The treatment of homicidal patients involves a special sensitivity to their emotional needs, a willingness to be active, direct, and decisive in intervention, and the ability to avoid one's own impulsivity in dealing with them. A common and gratifying result of therapy is the patient's discovery of the use, rather than the misuse, of aggressive energy.

REFERENCES

1. Stearns, Frederic R.: *Anger: Psychology, Physiology, Pathology*, Charles C Thomas, Springfield, Ill., 1972.

2. Sullivan, Harry Stack: in Stearns, ibid., p. 3.

3. Megargee, Edwin I.: "Undercontrolled and Overcontrolled Personality Types in Extreme Antisocial Aggression," *The Dynamics of Aggression*, Harper & Row, New York, 1972, pp. 108–120.

4. *Medical World News*: "The Mind of a Murderer," **14** (43):40, Nov. 23, 1973.

5. Menninger, Roy W., and Herbert C. Modlin: "Individual Violence: Prevention in the Violence-Threatening Patient," in Jan Fawcett (ed.), *Dynamics of Violence*, American Medical Association, Chicago, 1971, pp. 71–73.

6. Gallup, Palmer: "Pain and Rage in Personality Disorders," unpublished paper.

7. Spiegel, Rose: "Anger and Acting Out: Masks of Depression," *Am. J. Psychotherapy* **21**: 597–606, 1967.

8. Tupin, Joe P., Dennis Mahar, and David Smith: "Two Types of Violent Offenders with Psychosocial Descriptors," *Diseases of the Nervous System*, **34**:356–363, October/November 1973.

9. Wolfgang, Marvin E.: "A Sociological Analysis of Criminal Homicide," in Marvin E. Wolfgang (ed.), *Studies in Homicide*, Harper & Row, New York, 1967, p. 15.

10. *Medical World News*: op. cit., pp. 42–43.

11. Ibid.

12. Menninger and Modlin: op. cit., pp. 71–78.

13. Garfinkel, Harold: "Inter- and Intra-racial Homicides," in Marvin E. Wolfgang (ed.), *Studies in Homicide*, Harper & Row, New York, 1967, pp. 45–65.

14. Iskrant, Albert P., and Paul V. Joliet: *Accidents and Homicide*, Harvard, Cambridge, Mass., 1968.

15. Federal Bureau of Investigation: *Crime in the United States: Uniform Crime Reports*, U.S. Government Printing Office, Washington, 1963.

16. Macdonald, John M.: *The Murderer and His Victim*, Charles C Thomas, Springfield, Ill., 1963.

17. Cole, K. E., Gary Fisher, and Shirley S. Cole: "Women Who Kill: a Socio-psychological Study," *Arch. Gen. Psychiat.*, **19**:1–8, 1968.

18. Langberg, Robert: *Homicide in the United States, 1950–1964*, National Center for Health Statistics, ser. 20, no. 6, U.S. Government Printing Office, Washington, D.C., 1967.

19. Wolfgang: loc. cit.

20. Langberg: loc. cit.

21. Macdonald: loc. cit.

22. Wolfgang: loc. cit.

23. Gillin, John: "Murder as a Sociological Phenomenon," *Ann. Am. Acad. Polit. Soc. Sci.* **284**:20–25, 1952.

24. Iskrant and Joliet: op. cit., pp. 119–120.

25. Wolfgang, Marvin E., and Franco Ferracuti: "Subculture of Violence—a Socio-psychological Theory," in Marvin E. Wolfgang (ed.), *Studies in Homicide,* Harper & Row, New York, 1967, p. 275.

26. Menninger and Modlin: op. cit., pp. 74–75.

27. Hellman, Daniel S., and Nathan Blackman: "Enuresis, Firesetting, and Cruelty to Animals: A Triad Predictive of Adult Crime," *Am. J. Psychiat.,* **122**:1431–1435, 1966.

28. Macdonald, John M.: "Homicidal Threats," *Am. J. Psychiat.,* **124**:475–482, 1967. Copyright 1967, the American Psychiatric Association.

29. Menninger and Modlin: op. cit., pp. 76–77.

30. Kinzel, Augustus F.: "Body Buffer Zone in Violent Prisoners," *Am. J. Psychiat.,* **127**:99–104, 1970.

31. Horowitz, Mardi J., Donald F. Duff, and Lois O. Stratton: "The Body Buffer Zone: An Exploration of Personal Space," *Arch. Gen. Psychiat.,* **11**:651–656, 1964.

32. Hediger, Heini: *Studies of Psychology and Behavior of Captive Animals in Zoos and Circuses,* Geoffrey Sircom (trans.), Criterion Books, New York, 1955.

33. Hall, Edward T.: *The Hidden Dimension,* Doubleday, Garden City, N.Y., 1966.

34. Megargee: op. cit., p. 111.

35. Ibid.

36. Ibid., p. 110.

37. Tanay, Emanuel: "Psychiatric Study of Homicides," *Am. J. Psychiat.,* **125**:1252–1258, March 1969.

38. Tanay, Emanuel: *Medical World News,* op. cit., p. 41.

39. Hillman, James: "C. G. Jung's Contributions to 'Feelings and Emotions': Synopsis and Implications," in Magda B. Arnold (ed.), *Loyola Symposium on Feelings and Emotions, 1968,* Academic, New York, 1970, pp. 125–134.

40. Jung, C. G.: "The Mana Personality," *Two Essays on Analytical Psychology,* Meridian Books, The World Publishing Company, Cleveland, 1956, p. 240.

41. Wertham, Frederick: *The Show of Violence,* Doubleday, Garden City, N.Y., 1949.

42. Berkowitz, Leonard: "Experimental Investigation of Hostility Catharsis," in Jan Fawcett (ed.), *Dynamics of Violence,* American Medical Association, Chicago, 1971, pp. 139–144.

43. Macdonald: "Homicidal Threats," op. cit., p. 480.

44. Ibid., p. 481.

45. Wolfgang, op. cit., p. 22.

46. Ibid., p. 83.

47. Tupin, et al.: op. cit., p. 360.

48. Gross, Mortimer: "Violence Associated with Organic Brain Disease," in Jan Fawcett, (ed.), *Dynamics of Violence,* American Medical Association, Chicago, 1971, pp. 85–91.

49. Menninger, Karl A.: *The Vital Balance,* Viking, New York, 1963.

50. Jacobs, Patricia A., Muriel Brunton, and Marie M. Melville: "Aggressive Behaviour, Mental-Subnormality and the XYY Male," *Nature,* **208**:1351–1352, 1965.

51. Kessler, Seymour, and Rudolph Moos: letter to *Science,* vol. 165, Aug. 1, 1969.

52. Macdonald: "Homicidal Threats," loc. cit.

53. Lion, John R.: "The Role of Depression in the Treatment of Aggressive Personality Disorders," *Am. J. Psychiat.,* **129**:347–349, 1972. Copyright 1972, the American Psychiatric Association.

54. Bandura, Albert: *Aggression: A Social Learning Analysis,* Prentice-Hall, Englewood Cliffs, N.J., 1973.

Evaluation and Treatment of the Psychotic Patient

WHAT IS PSYCHOSIS?

The initial contact with a psychotic patient can be a confusing, upsetting experience. One does not want to relate to the patient in this state; one wants to bring him or her out of it so a normal interaction can occur. The first suggestion of the diagnosis of psychosis, then, often comes with the interviewer's discomfort with a patient's way of being-in-the-world, a sense that the patient is somehow too extreme or dreadfully lacking. Thus the patient's behavior is too bizarre, too happy, too sad, too confused, too confusing, too aggressive, or too withdrawn; or it is not usual enough, not well-enough modulated, not clear enough, not logical enough, not "under control," not "in contact." In short, the patient's failure to meet others as they expect to be met is *drastic*. The professional judgment that someone is psychotic simply registers the fact of his drastic departure from the basic expectations of others.

> *Example 5-1.* Late at night, the police brought a woman in her 20s to the emergency room. She had been trying to hitch a ride on a dangerous stretch of freeway when they picked her up.
>
> She wore a torn, faded granny dress, was barefoot, and her curly mop of blonde hair was flung out in all directions. Unlike many similarly dressed young adults, she had a look of pitiful terror on her face.
>
> When the therapist asked her what was wrong, her eyes widened in terror, her whole body shook, and her head moved back and forth furiously. She could have been saying, "I'm not allowed to talk." To any question she repeated this violent gesture of refusal. Otherwise she would stare, peacefully enough, straight ahead, with a half-smile on her face, and seemed not to care about the impression she made.
>
> She had said nothing to the police and had not resisted arrest. On her the police had found an envelope with the name of a mental hospital in a distant state, with the name Bob and a telephone number written on it.
>
> The therapist asked her if he could call this number. She did not respond. He dialed the number, received a recorded message that the number was not in service, and let the patient hear the recording. She started to weep. Almost immediately the tears stopped, and she again stared ahead with the half-smile on her face.

"Do you miss Bob?" the therapist asked. She responded with a burst of high-pitched laughter. After this, no question brought any response other than a shrug, a shudder, or a half-smile. After half an hour, the therapist had not even learned his patient's first name.

A formal definition of psychosis is given in Freedman, Kaplan, and Sadock[1]:

> *Psychosis.* Mental disorder in which a person's mental capacity, affective response, and capacity to recognize reality, communicate, and relate to others are impaired enough to interfere with his capacity to deal with the ordinary demands of life. The psychoses are subdivided into two major classifications according to their origin: psychoses associated with organic brain syndromes and functional psychoses.

The traditional dichotomy between organic brain syndromes and functional psychosis is oversimplified and can be misleading. What appears to be typical paranoid schizophrenia (functional) can arise as the result of impaired cerebral circulation in an austere hospital setting or as a result of amphetamine use. The patient in Example 5-1 may have been schizophrenic, but she may also have had a brain tumor or have been reacting to drugs.

Thus two uncertainties must be taken into account in working with psychotic patients: the patient's uncertainty about reality (or in the case of some paranoid schizophrenic patients, an overcertainty about a reality others cannot perceive) and the therapist's uncertainty about the nature and causes of the psychotic phenomena in the patient he is trying to evaluate and treat. Throughout this chapter we shall give guidelines on (1) how the therapist can refine his abilities to make an accurate diagnosis without prematurely stereotyping the patient with an incorrect label, and (2) how best to initiate treatment.

Example 5-1 (cont'd). When the patient remained mute, the therapist handed her a pencil and pad and asked her to write her name. She took the pencil and drew four interlocking ellipses that looked like a highway cloverleaf. With a look of great urgency she handed the paper to him.

The therapist accepted the drawing but he could not understand it. He then ordered 200 mg clorpromazine for her. She sniffed it, then swallowed it all. He told her he was arranging for her admission to a hospital. She did not respond. He placed her on a seventy-two-hour hold and arranged for transportation to the nearby state hospital, the only facility that would take her and had a bed open.

The transfer diagnosis was "acute schizophrenia, suspected," and the admitting physician at the state hospital promised follow-up information that never came. The therapist heard no more about the patient.

Such episodes are common. Contact with the psychotic patient is limited and confusing. A tentative diagnosis is made on the basis of limited information, and drug and hospital treatment is offered (often with only implied consent, sometimes with no consent) based on the tentative diagnosis. It is not suprising that strong criticisms have been leveled at the current practice of psychiatry with psychotic patients.[2,3] On the other hand, studies indicate that these same practices lead to a later, voluntary entry into treatment by two-thirds of the patients who are so treated.[4] Indeed, it is probable that this woman would start to talk within a day or two and that a more precise understanding of the nature and origin of her peculiar communicative state would become possible.

Nevertheless, several chances for error in the brief interventions that make up most first contacts with psychotic patients exist. Foremost is the chance for *diagnostic error.* The therapist decided to give the young woman chlorpromazine because he suspected "acute schizophrenia." Such a precise diagnosis was impossible to make from the data at hand. In addition to chlorpromazine, he gave his patient a label that will now accompany her as others treat her. Such labels are like old bandages clinging to an inadequately cleaned wound, infecting it further; often they must be removed and changed before adequate healing can occur.

On the other hand, not making a diagnosis is a dangerous practice. Without diagnosis the patient cannot be given the best care. The proper use of ECT (shock therapy), lithium, antipsychotics, and psychotherapy proceed from diagnosis. It is especially important to know if the psychosis is of organic origin, for unrecognized it often means irreversible brain damage or death. Changes in the central nervous system, first detectable by psychological interview, are the earliest signs of many serious somatic illnesses.

Organizing the Interview Data into Syndromes

Making an exact diagnosis of a psychotic patient is seldom easy. The diagnostic interview may reveal many symptoms that could belong to several diagnoses. Lorr, Klett, and McNair[5,6] have sought to arrange such data with the methods of factor analysis. They have shown that psychotic symptoms detectable through interviewing techniques fall into ten basic psychotic syndromes. These syndromes,

which may be present in varying combinations in different psychotic illnesses, and the patient symptom variables that make up each of them, are shown in Table 5-1. Lorr has shown that eight of these syndromes can be organized around a circle (Fig. 5-1) showing their frequency of association. The distance of the syndromes from each other in the circle represents the likelihood of their appearing together in a given psychotic state. Adjacent syndromes appear together frequently, opposite syndromes infrequently.

A patient showing motor disturbance is likely to show conceptual disorganization or disorientation but less likely to exhibit paranoid projection. A patient showing paranoid projection is as likely to show grandiose expansiveness as anxious intropunitiveness. Such associations become important when, as often happens, a patient shows one syndrome prominently. Then the circle guides the interviewer in what to look for next.

Organizing the Syndromes into Diagnoses

In the case of the psychotic hitchhiker in Example 5-1, the syndromes of motor disturbances and retardation and apathy were present.

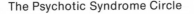

The Psychotic Syndrome Circle

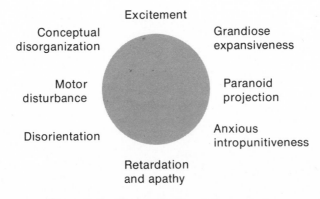

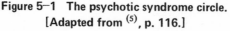

Figure 5-1   The psychotic syndrome circle.
[Adapted from [5], p. 116.]

Table 5-1   Psychotic Syndromes and Patient Variables Associated with Them*

Psychotic Syndrome Name	Patient Variables Included
Excitement	Expresses feelings without restraint Manifests speech that is hurried Exhibits an elevation in mood Exhibits an attitude of superiority Dramatizes self or symptoms Manifests loud and boisterous speech Exhibits overactivity, restlessness Exhibits an excess of speech Tries to dominate the interview
Paranoid projection	Preoccupied with delusional beliefs Believes people talk about him Believes he is being persecuted Believes people conspire against him Believes people control his actions Believes external forces influence him
Hostile belligerence	Verbally expresses feelings of hostility Expresses an attitude of disdain Manifests a hostile, sullen attitude Manifests irritability and grouchiness Tends to blame others for problems Expresses feelings of resentment Complains and finds fault Expresses suspicion of people
Perceptual distortion	Distressed by hallucinatory voices Hears voices that accuse or blame Hears voices that threaten punishment Hears hortatory voices Sees visions Reports tactual, gustatory, or olfactory hallucinations Familiar things and people seem changed
Anxious intropunitiveness	Tends to blame or condemn self Anxious about specific matters Apprehension re vague future events Exhibits an attitude of self-depreciation Manifests a depressed mood Expresses feelings of guilt and remorse Does not show a lack of insight Preoccupied by suicidal thoughts Preoccupied by unwanted ideas Preoccupied by specific fears Believes he is unworthy, sinful

Retardation and apathy	Manifests slowed speech
	Indifferent to own future
	Exhibits a fixed facial expression
	Manifests slowed movements
	Deficient in recent memory
	Manifests blocking in speech
	Apathetic to self or problems
	Exhibits a slovenly appearance
	Manifests low or whispered speech
	Fails to answer questions
Motor disturbances	Exhibits peculiar, rigid postures
	Manifests overt signs of tension
	Grins or giggles inappropriately
	Exhibits peculiar grimaces
	Exhibits peculiar repetitive gestures
	Talks, mutters, or mumbles to self
	Glances around as if hearing voices
Conceptual disorganization	Gives answers that are irrelevant
	Gives incoherent answers
	Tends to drift off the subject
	Uses neologisms
	Repeats certain words or phrases
Disorientation	Does not know he is in a hospital
	Does not know where hospital is located
	Does not know name of one other person
	Does not know season of year
	Does not know calendar year
	Does not know own age
Grandiose expansiveness	Exhibits an attitude of superiority
	Hears voices that praise and extol
	Believes he has unusual powers
	Believes he is a well-known personality
	Believes he has a divine mission

*Drawn from material found in Lorr et al.[5], pp. 35–38, based on a factor analysis of ratings using the Inpatient Multidimensional Psychiatric Scale (IMPS).

The interviewer should have checked more carefully for signs of disorientation. It was not clear from the information whether the young woman's tears and laughter had any relation to the name Bob, or whether she intended the cloverleaf diagram to be an answer to the command to write her name. If the disorientation syndrome were present, it is likely that this young woman had an organic brain syndrome manifested by motor disturbances, disorientation, retardation, and apathy.

On the other hand, if the police description had stressed symptoms resembling those of an excitement syndrome on the freeway, the apathy she exhibited in the office could have been discounted and signs of conceptual disorganization should have been sought. If the cloverleaf diagram were an answer to the command to write her name, this impression would be confirmed. Acute catatonic schizophrenia manifested by motor disturbances, conceptual disorganization, and a history of recent excitement would be likely.

Treatment in the first instance would be an intensive search for the organic cause of the underlying disturbance; in the second, it might be a referral to a setting specializing in the treatment of acutely psychotic young adults. [7,8]

Three Approaches to Taxonomy

The American Psychiatric Association. In 1952 The American Psychiatric Association published its first *Diagnostic and Statistical Manual of Mental Disorders (DSM-I).* [9] The current edition, *DSM-II* [10] was published in 1968 and contains the preferred nomenclature. By and large, *DSM-II* preserves the traditional dichtomy between organic and functional psychoses and presents concise and useful descriptions of the various diagnostic entities, e.g., that *schizophrenia* can be broken down into subtypes of *simple type, hebephrenic type, catatonic type,* and so forth. The entities described in *DSM-II* are amplified upon by Freedman, Kaplan, and Sadock. [11]

Menninger. Karl Menninger and colleagues [12] took a different approach. They organized their basic patterns of psychosis around five major configurations of emotional, perceptual, and cognitive dysfunction: (1) pervasive sadness and guilt; (2) erratic disorganized excitement; (3) autistic regression; (4) delusional preoccupation; and (5) confused delirium. Any of these patterns encompasses a variety of the more traditional states. Menninger thinks that all of them represent a similar level of "dyscontrol" or ego failure.

A useful aspect of the Menninger approach is that it is phenomenological; i.e., it describes phenomena that the interviewer sees in his work with patients. Thus, if the interviewer notes pervasive sadness and guilt, or erratic disorganized excitement, he can then see what other symptoms

and signs described in those configurations are present. This approach may guide him to a more accurate diagnosis (which may be a traditional one) to aid him in treatment planning.

The five basic patterns of psychosis described by Menninger et al. [13] are

1. Pervasive feelings of sadness, guilt, despondency, and hopelessness, with convictions of inadequacy, incompetence, unworthiness, or wickedness—or several of these. Psychomotor retardation is usually present, sometimes stupor or restless activity, even agitation. Delusions or delusional trends appropriate to feelings of guilt, defection, unworthiness, and self-disparagement are common—such as fantasied offenses or fantasied punishment to come. (This picture has been called *melancholia, depression, thymergasia, affective disorder,* and other names.)

2. More or less continuous erratic, disorganized excitement, accompanied by a corresponding excess of verbal and motor production and emotional heightening, elation, excitement, irascibility, and so on. In this syndrome overactivity, volubility, and impulsivity may be at times self-injuring, at times bizarre, meddlesome, exhibitionistic, and socially annoying. The characteristic feature is the great and continuing overflow of poorly controlled energy. (This picture may be found in conditions variously called *mania, hypomania, delirium, furor, frenzy, recurrent mania, hyperthymergasia, moria, dysergasia, catatonic schizophrenia (excited stage), status epilepticus,* and many others.)

3. Autistic regression and self-absorption, silliness, mannerisms of speech and behavior, bizarre delusional ideation, irrelevancy and incoherence of speech, posturing and gross (apparent) indifference to social expectations. Inertness or automatonlike behav-

ior, often mutism or hallucinations, apparent indifference to the external world, but occasional sudden "impulsive" outbursts of speech or action are also typical. (This picture may be found in such conditions as *hebephrenia, parergasia, amentia, autism, chronic delirium, dementia simplex, catatonic schizophrenia (stuporous stage), chronic deterioration, regressed states, nuclear schizophrenia,* and many others.)

4. Delusional preoccupation with one or several themes, usually persecutory in trend, and usually accompanied by defensiveness, resentment, suspiciousness, grandiosity, condescension, irascibility, and so forth. A facade of dignity and sensibleness may partially or occasionally obscure the underlying picture. (This picture has classically gone under many compound names containing the noun *paranoia* or the adjective *paranoid*.)

5. Confused, delirious states with disorientation, bewilderment, amnesia, confabulation, and sometimes hallucinations and hyperactivity. These are commonly seen with severe injury, intoxication, or inflammation of the brain, hence with encephalitis, arteriosclerosis, alcoholic and other poisonings, Huntington's disease, Alzheimer's disease, and so forth. (These pictures have also been called *dementia* and *delirium.*)

Lorr, Klett, and McNair. Lorr et al.[14] used an empirical approach to taxonomy based on their earlier, phenomenologically defined psychotic syndromes. They tested several populations of acutely and chronically psychotic patients to see which syndromes were present or absent and how those syndromes that were present clustered together. They were able to establish nine regular types of psychosis for men and nine for women, representing different combinations of the basic syndromes.

All these psychotic types fell under four major categories: (1) paranoid, (2) disorganized, (3) excited, and (4) intropunitive. We shall use these four categories in the section on differential diagnosis.

From the work of Lorr et al. it is apparent that "disorientation," long considered the hallmark of organic psychosis, is in fact but one aspect of *psychotic disorganization,* which manifests itself along several dimensions: conceptual, affective, and orientative. In actual clinical situations, the sharp textbook distinctions between "functional" and "organic" illness do not hold up well: catatonia and hebephrenia are not always easy to distinguish from dementia and delirium.

THE DIFFERENTIAL DIAGNOSIS OF PSYCHOTIC STATES

The emergency therapist should accept the uncertainty of the initial contact with psychotic patients and explore the range of diagnostic possibilities. This chapter will attempt to help the therapist think intelligently about the range of diagnostic possibilities for any clinical situation. The material is organized under the four basic categories stemming from the work of Lorr et al.

Differential Diagnosis of Paranoid Conditions

Paranoid thinking may appear by itself (classical paranoia, rare) as a reaction to stress (common), or as part of another psychosis. It always involves a delusional interpretation of the motives, behavior, or intentions of others. The basic forms of paranoid thinking are *paranoid jealousy* (a profound, relentless suspicion that a partner is unfaithful, based on scant evidence and excessively argued), *paranoid eroticism* (the assumption that someone else, often a famous person, is infatuated with the patient and that even his avoidant actions are motivated by love), *paranoid grandiosity* (the patient's grossly inflated estimate of his own power), and the *persecutory paranoid state* (which may be the patient's nonspecific fear of retaliation for some hostile act or an active program of self-defense against a delusional "pseudocommunity"). The pseudocommunity, a typical part of the chronically paranoid patient's delusions, is "a group of real and imagined persons" assumed by him to be "bent on destroying his reputation or his life."[15]

The most common conditions under which paranoid thinking occurs are the paranoid stress reaction, the involutional paranoid state, schizophrenia, psychoses associated with drug use, organic brain syndromes associated with physical illnesses, and the manic phase of manic-depressive psychosis.

Paranoid Stress Reaction. This state is, as its name implies, an acute response to a crisis. Bellak says that the acute paranoid condition

> . . . consists of an episode of delusions brought on by exhaustion or by a psychologically determined precipitating cause and is characterized by illusions which gradually develop into hallucinations and delusions. After the episode is over the personality is well-preserved and integrated.[16]

In *DSM-II,* this condition is classified under "other paranoid state." It is seen frequently in military settings and is part of the identity turmoil of young men. It can, however, occur at any age.

Involutional Paranoid State. This is a paranoid psychosis characterized by delusion formation that begins in the involutional period. Many feel that this condition is an alternate form of involutional depression. Divorced or separated women are at especially high risk. Twice as many women as men are hospitalized for involutional paranoid states. [17,18] Often, the wish fulfilling component of the dynamics is transparent, as in the following case:

> *Example 5-2.* A 47-year-old woman was admitted to the hospital from the emergency room, where she had been brought by her daughter. The woman had been living alone for the past ten years since her divorce. She had become extremely agitated that day after listening to the radio. During the interview, she said she believed herself to be engaged to a famous entertainer and had expected him to sing "their song" that day. When the song was not included in the broadcast, she became distraught and called her daughter.

Paranoid Schizophrenia. A question that should be asked early in the evaluation of anyone showing evidence of paranoid thinking is, "Is this schizophrenia?" Usually thought is more disorganized and delusional notions are more bizarre when schizophrenia is present than when paranoia occurs by itself. Kurt Schneider [19,20] has listed symptoms of first-rank importance for the diagnosis of schizophrenia:

1. Audible thoughts
2. Voices heard arguing
3. Voices heard commenting on one's actions
4. The experience of influences playing on the body (somatic passivity)
5. Thought withdrawal—the experience of having one's thoughts taken from one's mind
6. Thought insertion—the experience of having someone else's thoughts put into one's mind
7. Thought diffusion (thought broadcasting)—the experience of having other people directly privy to one's inner thoughts
8. Delusional perception—the crystallization of a set of delusional inferences on the basis of an everyday perception
9. "Made" feelings—the experience of having feelings which are felt to be the work of others

10. "Made" impulses—the experience of impulses to act which are felt to be implanted from outside

11. "Made" motor acts—the experience of being completely under the control of an external influence as one acts

This list of symptoms can be used to distinguish between paranoia and schizophrenia. Both paranoid and schizophrenic people are disturbed in relationship to an ecological group. The paranoid person has a suspicious, isolated relationship to his ecological group, fears its actions, mistrusts its motives, and misperceives its intentions. His ecological group is, in addition, a pseudocommunity: some of its members do not exist, although he behaves as if they do.

By contrast, the schizophrenic individual has an overly concrete relationship to his ecological group. Emotional participation, usually unconscious, with other persons is experienced by the schizophrenic person as a direct involvement in his conscious thinking. Moreover, the ecological group to which he relates is largely anonymous, such as arguing *voices* or *influences* playing on his body.

Finally, both paranoid and schizophrenic individuals are overly concerned with ordinary events and public experiences, for instance, with events they read about in newspapers or see on television, or with experiences with strangers on public transportation. The paranoid person personalizes public contacts; the schizophrenic person concretizes them. A paranoid schizophrenic patient may do both.

Some authors[21] doubt the existence of "pure paranoia," a state in which a single, fixed, false assumption underlies an intricate and internally consistent logical system, and mental functioning is normal in all other areas. These authors feel that schizophrenic thought disorder is always present in such cases, although it may be difficult to detect. In any event, some people who organize experience in a highly paranoid fashion exhibit few of the symptoms of the schizophrenias described by Schneider,[22] Bleuler,[23] and others.

Paranoid Psychoses Associated with Drug Use. Both schizophrenic and nonschizophrenic paranoid states may be associated with many organic conditions. Withdrawal syndromes from alcohol, amphetamines, bromides, barbiturates, and appetite-supressing drugs such as phenmetrazine may closely resemble paranoid schizophrenia. Amphetamine, LSD, marihuana, and cocaine may produce frightened or hostile paranoid thinking in the "high" state, with associated destructive or self-destructive behaviors (see Chapters 6, 8, and 9). Obtaining a single urine sample during an emergency can lead to identification of many of these substances if the patient is unable or unwilling to admit their use. In paranoid states of unknown etiology, it is always wise to suspect drug use and to be on the lookout for other signs of withdrawal or intoxication.

Paranoid Psychoses Associated with Other Organic Conditions. Sometimes a seemingly isolated paranoia in a clear sensorium is the first sign that a major organic illness is present. Patients over 45 who develop paranoid schizophrenic symptoms should receive careful neurological examinations for brain tumors. Cancers in other organs may also occasion paranoia; it is as if the patient senses a threat and projects it outside his body. When the patient confronts the reality of his physical illness, he can share the stress of preparing for an operation or for death with a physician, and the paranoia often disappears. As usual in psychosis, uncertainty appears to do more emotional harm than painful reality.

Paranoid reactions are common in physically ill patients who are confined to hospitals under conditions resembling sensory-deprivation experiments. In addition to environmental isolation, many chronically ill patients have organic brain syndromes that subtly or grossly impair their abilities to process information. Often these patients make paranoid explanations to themselves for poorly understood hospital procedures, personnel changes, or illness. In the treatment of such states, simple explanations, a lighted room at night, and frequent human contact often work wonders. These easily reversed paranoid reactions suggest that paranoia is a response to physical and emotional isolation and that it tends to disappear when the isolation can be interrupted through authentic contact with reality.

Manic-depressive Psychosis. An acute manic episode involves psychotic symptoms that progress through a sequence of stages. After the illness reaches its height, it remits by retracing the stages.[24] In the initial stage, the patient is *euphoric*; he talks too fast and demands too much. Kraepelin[25] called this picture "acute mania." In the intermediate stage, *anger and irritability* prevail, and the patient becomes angry and explosive. It is in this stage that paranoid delusions, both persecutory and grandiose, may appear, along with the classical flight of ideas. Kraepelin called this picture "delusional mania." In a final stage, the patient is *panicked*. He looks helpless. His thought processes, which are incoherent, are marred by loose associations, by bizarre and idiosyncratic paranoid delusions, and by ideas of reference. His movements are frenzied and pathetic. He may be disoriented or hallucinating. The picture is similar to that of a disorganized paranoid schizophrenia or to a delirium. Kraepelin called it "delirious mania."

The way to distinguish the intermediate delusional state of a manic episode from other paranoid states is to note the associated affective tone. The manic patient is irritable, and paranoid thinking emerges naturally from his anger. He can be talked out of it, distracted, mollified. As one therapist expressed it, "The way I could tell he was manic was that I still liked him when I was talking back to him." By contrast, the patient in a paranoid state is likely to present his delusions with reserved, controlled hostility and to remain unlikeably cool as he insists on preserving them.

One way to distinguish the final delirious stage of mania from deteriorated paranoid schizophrenia is to use Schneider's first-rank symptoms of schizophrenia. These first-rank symptoms were devised to distinguish schizophrenia from affective psychotic illness. None of these first-rank symptoms appeared in twenty manic patients studied by Carlson and Goodwin,[26] who established the three-stage sequence of mood changes in the manic episode. Another way to distinguish is to focus on the evidence for affective illness.[27] It should be noted that the progression from one mood stage to another can occur in a few hours or might take several days, but the sequence of stages seems to occur uniformly. Therefore, rapid progression of a seemingly paranoid psychosis through a series of moods in the stages described indicates a manic-depressive illness, and the therapist needs to consider lithium treatment (see Chapter 28).

Differential Diagnosis of Disorganized Psychotic States

Under these conditions, the ego fails to operate as a consistent center of consciousness and control. This failure may be represented in frank conceptual disorganization, disorientation, or the fragmentation of emotional responses so that thinking, sensory input from the outer world, and affective reactions are not properly integrated. When integration fails, the patient is in a vulnerable condition, at the mercy of his own uncontrollable reactions and of stronger people's wills.

When evaluating psychotically disorganized patients, the therapist must remember this *impressionability* and guard against premature feeling-reactions, diagnostic "labels," and treatment plans that encourage the patient to assume a *facade of pseudoorganization*. This facade conforms to the therapist's ideas, but the patient has not actually integrated his own experience. Indeed, many psychotic diagnoses are not made because the patient perceives that the therapist cannot tolerate "craziness," or the therapist structures the interview so that "crazy" material does not emerge.

In the differential diagnosis of disorganization, the most important distinction is between the *schizophrenias* (defined as "functional" psychoses having no clear basis in brain pathology) and the many *organic brain syndromes* (a change in the tissue structure or metabolism of the brain is the cause of the psychosis). A less frequent cause of the disorganized psychotic picture is the *third-stage mania* that has already been described.

The Schizophrenias. These disorders are a group of different behavioral responses to a similar kind of psychological deficit, involving the patient's inability to organize and maintain a consistent attitude toward his experience. There are many ways to understand this deficit,[28, 29] but Kurt Goldstein[30] offered a particularly clear formulation:

> ... an impairment of attitudes toward the abstract in the schizophrenic resulting therefore in concrete behavior similar to that in patients with brain disease. The abstract attitude of which Goldstein writes consists of: abilities to assume a mental set voluntarily, to shift voluntarily from one aspect of the situation to another, to keep in mind several aspects, to grasp the essentials of a whole, to break these up into parts and isolate them, to abstract common properties, to plan ahead, to assume an attitude of the possible, to think and act symbolically, to detach the ego from the outer world.[31]

The fact that often he does not utilize symbols in an abstract way does not mean the schizophrenic patient is impoverished in their use. Unlike the brain-injured patient whose language is frequently banal, the schizophrenic patient may show an arresting talent for metaphor. And although schizophrenic language is often difficult to comprehend, it is frequently interesting and intriguing. The major drawback is that the patient does not label the fact that he is using metaphors.[32] The effect is a little like a poet starting to speak modern poetry in the midst of an ordinary transaction.

Example 5-3. The senior editor of this book was doing therapy with a young schizophrenic woman. One day she greeted him with, "Hello, Mr. Rosenbaum, do you have any roses in your garden?" He responded that he didn't have a garden. Later he thought this answer missed the point. Translated (and taken in context), the question was: "Leaving your medical credentials aside, can you tell me if you are my therapist in name only, or do you really know how to make me bloom?"

A *symbolic mode* has come to replace the *cognitive mode* of ordinary communication. Moreover, the shift to the symbolic mode is not a conscious choice. Instead, the symbolic mode is substituted in situations that call for the cognitive mode. The patient may make these inappropriate substitutions most of the time or only some of the time. Almost all schizophrenic patients retain some healthy ego and can use the cognitive mode in well-structured situations. It is in ambiguous or unstructured situations that they turn most often to the symbolic mode.

Use of the symbolic mode is not in itself abnormal, of course; as Deikman[33] has recently pointed out, we all shift from the cognitive mode to a much more loosely structured mode of consciousness when we meditate or make love. The ability to daydream is part of mental health. What is abnormal is the *interference* with usual thinking by symbolic mode activity, the *archaic nature* of the symbolic intrusions, and the very substantial *loss of the normal ability to coordinate* cognitive mode with symbolic mode activity. As both Jung and Sullivan have noted, schizophrenia is like being unable to awake from dreaming as one tries to pursue everyday activities. The result is a disastrous fragmentation of personality. As Buss and Lang[34] note:

> ... when a schizophrenic is faced with a task, he cannot attend properly or in a sustained fashion, maintain a set, or change the set quickly when necessary. His ongoing response tendencies suffer interference from irrelevant, external cues and from "internal" stimuli which consist of deviant thoughts and associations. These irrelevant, distracting, mediating stimuli prevent him from maintaining a clear

focus on the task at hand, and the result is psychological deficit.[35]

Enoch Callaway[36] has compared schizophrenic thought processes to programs run in a computer constructed with unreliable components: the ability to make some reliable operations remains, but the risk of interference and interruption in the running of normal programs is ever-present.

The archaic nature of the symbolic mode in schizophrenia has been stressed by Freud and Jung, who saw striking comparisons to the preconceptual thinking of infants and to prescientific myths. Often the most archaic symbolic communications conceal the strongest affects. If this affect is discovered and released, the need to use symbolic communication is markedly reduced, as will be shown in Example 5-10.

Appropriate affective response is needed for the normal mediation between the symbolic and cognitive modes. When affect is lost, either mode can extinguish the other, with resultant disastrous restriction of personality. In the florid schizophrenic states, the symbolic mode tends to overrun the cognitive mode. In latent and residual schizophrenia, the cognitive mode gains a brittle, uneasy ascendancy, creating personality imbalance. Many observers have noted that such "borderline" patients are overly logical, poor in fantasy, and unable to relax. Instead of having a comfortable ability to loosen up, they use rigid defenses to wall off the symbolic mode, which is portrayed in dreams as a tidal wave threatening to break through. If affective response returns, some of the normal ability to shift into the symbolic mode may return, and the tidal wave subsides in the unconscious. If affective response does not return, the risk of a psychotic break is ever-present.

Bowers[37] has described the pathogenesis of an acute schizophrenic episode. First there is the *impasse*. The prepsychotic individual may be in considerable panic, unable to decide how to act or to communicate with others at a crucial point in his development. He may feel betrayed or rejected by a loved one, and he may be harboring intense hatred and destructive fantasies toward the loved person. He cannot or dare not express these fantasies. This inability to communicate may stem in part from the patient's negative self-image. As Arieti[38] points out, recent failures in living may have confirmed a negative self-concept acquired much earlier in life. The patient really is a "bad me"; the world (like some earlier Terrible Parent), a "Malevolent Thou." Then, writes Arieti,

> In the totality of his human existence, and through the depth of all his feelings, the individual feels himself as totally defeated, without any worth or possibility of redemption.
>
> In most cases, only one solution, one defense, is still available to the psyche: to dissolve or alter his cognitive functions, the thought processes that have brought about conceptual disaster and that have acquired an ominous resonance with the original and preconceptual understanding of the self.[39]

At this point there is *destructuring of perception and affect*. The prepsychotic panic gives over to frank psychosis as the symbolic mode is allowed to overrun the cognitive mode. For many patients the experience is at first beatific, transcendent, and mystical. The patient may be elated by what he perceives as a "peak experience" of heightened awareness, and he will often want to share this "high" with others. The symbolic mode brings with it *symbolic perception*:[40] ordinary things take on a special meaning. Magical coincidences occur and are hailed. (Such perception is not quite delusional, but more like that of the Tarot reader who makes some accurate inferences by occult symbolic means but also may allow untoward associations to creep in.) *Projective identification* also occurs more easily in the symbolic mode: unacceptable parts of the self are rediscovered as a lurking presence of evil in the outer world, and "ideas of reference and influence" begin. (At this point the therapist may be viewed suspiciously or with scorn, even if he makes an effort to understand the patient's vision of the world. Any mention of the patient's former negative feelings is especially unwelcome, a sign of the therapist's "bad faith.")

Next, a *destructuring of the sense of self* occurs. The cognitive mode now gives way altogether to the symbolic mode. Identity dissolution begins and may be characterized by changes in the patient's mental image of himself, including major and bizarre changes in his body image. (For example, his left side may no longer seem to belong to him or his face may look unreal.)

Finally, *delusions are formed* as the symbolic mode supplies explanations for these changes to the shattered cognitive processes. The pressure to make sense of the experience aids in overcoming the realistic uncertainty that the delusional ideas are true, and crude delusional explanations may be welcomed with relief by ordinarily sophisticated patients. (A doctor with much experience in electronic technology may be satisfied that his room is bugged.[41]) Often the newly psychotic person naïvely shares his delusional explanations in an elated way.

A particularly common delusion is for the patient to believe that he is a messianic hero,[42] often Christ. In this case, the symbolic mode appears to be exerting its *reparative function*. Correcting the patient's helpless, evil, bad me, this delusional self-image not only improves the patient's self-esteem but gives him the energy to rechannel his life energies, especially his aggressive drives.[43] In this state the patient is often able to enter treatment, as Example 5-11 will show.

The *time course* of these stages is highly variable. The cognitive mode can disappear suddenly in response to overwhelming stress (such as the exhaustion of combat). The patient is likely to react to this sudden loss of ego with panic, excitement, and confusion (often expressed as the fear of being dead or of dying). These responses characterize "reactive schizophrenia," for which the prognosis is good.

Or the cognitive mode may be eroded insidiously (as in a family that subtly prevents vulnerable members from attaining a consistent point of view). The patient is able to make compensations for chronic interference with ego function, and panic does not appear. Instead, we see a major inability to think or to form coherent feeling-responses behind a facade that may be sad, silly, quizzical, apathetic, or paranoid—in any case, *resigned* to the presence of a deficit. This facade tends to put others off and to hide the schizophrenic person from himself[44]; it helps him do what his ego can not do, but at the cost of a permanent acceptance of dysfunction. This is the picture of "process schizophrenia," which has a poor prognosis. Prognostic features in schizophrenia are shown in Table 5-2.

Table 5-2 Prognostic Features in Schizophrenia [Herjanic [45]]

Associated with a Poor Prognosis
Insidious onset (more than six months)
Hebephrenic clinical picture
"Massive" delusions of persecution
Clear sensorium
Schizoid personality
Family history of schizophrenia
Striking emotional blunting

Associated with a Good Prognosis
Prominent depressive symptoms
Family history of affective disorders
No family history of schizophrenia
Good premorbid adjustment
Confusion
Acute onset (less than six months)
Precipitating factors
Concern with dying and guilt

The diagnosis of schizophrenia often implies a treatment fate. Certain typical courses for reactive and process schizophrenia have been described, each with a characteristic treatment. Involvement in aftercare becomes a major part of many schizophrenic patients' lives and strongly affects their ecological groups. According to Herjanic[46] and Rosenbaum,[47] typical courses are:

1. Acute onset with complete recovery. A later stress may precipitate another psychotic episode, which also responds to treatment. Response to psychotherapy is gratifying. A short hospitalization with or without antipsychotic medication may suffice; when high-dose phenothiazine treatment is used, the patient may be able to return to his usual activities in one or several weeks.[48]

2. Acute onset followed by recurrent episodes, with increasing residual impairment between episodes. Here antipsychotic drugs are needed intermittently, and long-term psychotherapy is indicated.

3. Insidious onset and chronic course broken by acute exacerbations and slight improvements. Both long-term phenothiazine treatment and long-term supportive psychotherapy are commonly used.

4. Insidious onset and slow progressive deterioration without acute exacerbation. Here long-term phenothiazine treatment and long-term social supervision are needed. Often such patients live in halfway houses, boarding homes, or state hospitals.

Despite many advances in society's understanding, tolerance, and treatments for the schizophrenias, they are not benign conditions. According to Herjanic, long-term follow-ups reveal that about one-sixth of untreated patients are eventually considered "cured with mild defect" (meaning a somewhat eccentric lifestyle and a blunted emotional life), another one-sixth show a moderate defect, and the remaining two-thirds become severely disabled. (Such statistics exclude the schizophrenias with the best prognosis as variants of affective illness.) A key point is that the patient be encouraged to seek treatment when schizophrenia is suspected.

In the emergency room, the therapist will see many forms of schizophrenia and many kinds of crisis situations. The patient may appear because he is distressed by the changes in his personality, or some peculiar feature of his behavior may distress a significant other. If his ecological group is in crisis, the schizophrenic person is more likely to appear in the emergency room. Affects belonging to the group in crisis are often perceived symbolically as direct interference with the patient's own thoughts. Yet if he communicates this distress, it may be the last straw for an already strained ecological group. His presenting picture will often be only part of a larger crisis situation. (This includes times of national crisis, which can be extremely trying for schizophrenic individuals.)

The schizophrenic patient's need for specific intervention and the ecological group's need for crisis intervention must be kept separate. It is true that the patient will settle down when the emotion in his group becomes less intense, but failure of the cognitive mode requires special individual support that an ecological group approach alone cannot provide. The balancing of these two needs is described in Chapter 10, which presents the treatment of an acutely schizophrenic young man and his ecological group.

The diagnosis of schizophrenia is not easy because of the wide variability in presenting pictures. In many instances acute schizophrenia is difficult to distinguish from delirium. If confusion and disorientation predominate, organic causes, including intoxication, must be ruled out before the diagnosis of schizophrenia is made. Chronic schizophrenia may resemble organic dementia or mental retardation.[49]

In describing the signs and symptoms of the schizophrenias, and from these a typology of schizophrenia, Bleuler[50] drew heavily from the work of Kraepelin. A primary symptom is *autism,* which reflects the shift from the cognitive to the symbolic mode. Some cognitive mode function always remains to the ego, but it is often grossly impaired by the continual intrusions of the symbolic mode. As a consequence, *attention* is no longer focused for tasks but scans the perceptual field; it ignores usual boundaries and becomes overinclusive. We have already stressed the loss of appropriate *affective response,* which may trigger the turn to the symbolic mode. *Ambivalence* characterizes emotions that are communicated by the symbolic mode; entire response tendencies organize into pairs of opposites and paralyze decision making. Finally, will, behavior, and activity undergo changes. A concise review of Bleuler's original descriptions may be found in Rosenbaum.[51]

Recently, Schneider's first-rank symptoms of schizophrenia (already described) have gained considerable importance in diagnosis. Some therapists insist on their presence before the diagnosis can be made; others remain faithful to Bleuler. A useful table of the symptoms that have been related to schizophrenia has been prepared by Herjanic (Table 5-3).

The last step in diagnosis is the classification of the kind of schizophrenia. Usually it is not difficult to distinguish acute from chronic schizophrenia, paranoid from hebephrenic (silly) or catatonic (excited or stuporous) schizophrenia. Subtleties emerge when the schizophrenic picture grades into one resembling affective disorder (schizoaffective schizophrenia, excited or depressed), neurosis (pseudoneurotic schizophrenia), or sociopathy (pseudosociopathic schizophrenia). In *DSM-II,* the latter two schizophrenias are called "latent schizophrenia." Additional labels include simple, residual, childhood, and chronic undifferentiated schizophrenia. Since Bleuler and Kraepelin there have been few changes in this unsatisfactory classification. Further discussion of the differential diagnosis of the schizophrenias is beyond the scope of this book, but the reader is referred to others [52, 53] who also provide a key to the current taxonomy.

Organic Brain Syndromes. Frequently disorganization is found in organic brain syndromes.[54] Because they may occur in an entirely clear sensorium, organic brain syndromes are difficult to distinguish from schizophrenia. Usually there is a reduction in the *level* of awareness and a reduction in the *efficiency* of cognitive functions that suggests organic difficulty. Spheres of mental

Table 5-3   Symptoms Related to Schizophrenia [Herjanic [45], p.76]

A.   Almost Pathognomonic Symptoms
Audible thoughts
Voices conversing with one another
Voices commenting on one's own actions
Somatic passivity experiences
Thought withdrawal
Diffusion of thought
Delusional perception
Feelings of being controlled by others
Flat affect
B.   Highly Suggestive Symptoms
Neologisms
Tangential speech
Blocking
Catatonic symptoms
rigidity
waxy flexibility
posturing
Autism
C.   Symptoms Commonly Seen
Incongruous affect
Delusions
persecution
reference
body change
Hallucinations
auditory
somatic
Apathy
Inappropriate or bizarre behavior
Social isolation
Poor occupational or academic performance
Poverty of thought

functioning in which impairments are most likely to appear can be remembered from the acronym EMOJIAC;

Emotion
Memory
Orientation
Judgment
Intellect
Attention
Concentration

Emotion becomes labile and shallow; recent memory is more impaired than past; orientation to time and place is more impaired than to persons; judgment of social realities may be poor; intellectual functioning (such as the ability to compute) is compromised; attention to environmental events is reduced; concentration on work and the general level of mental functioning is reduced.[55] All these issues are treated more fully in Chapters 14 and 30 and the appendixes.

Delirium derives from a Latin word meaning "derailed." It implies a sudden insult to consciousness that is based on a failure of brain metabolism or depression by toxins. The effects of this sudden "cerebral insufficiency"[56] are a reduction in the level of consciousness, a lessening of the ability to attend, and a marked disturbance in cognitive function. Diffuse slowing in the EEG "is a regular finding in delirium regardless of the cause" and provides "an accurate reflection of the metabolic adequacy of cortical neurons."[57] The EEG is slowest when the level of awareness is lowest; it tends to recover as treatment produces a return of a clear sensorium and is the most reliable indicator of the continued presence of the delirium. These EEG findings are not present in schizophrenia.[58]

The delirious patient may not look ill to cursory examination, or he may be obviously "out of his head." Profiles of patients include the (1) quiet and torpid, (2) blandly confused, (3) anxious and panicky, (4) hallucinating, and (5) muttering and incoherent patients. Types 1 to 3 are easily confused with depressed, habitually stupid, or neurotic patients; only a careful mental status examination can reveal the underlying cognitive defect.[59]

Dementia, which denotes a permanent loss of function in higher cortical neurons, produces an irreversible intellectual deficit. The deficit is stable, marked by a *loss* of function rather than by a distortion of function, as is delirium. Disturbances in memory stand out, and the personality deteriorates as the patient becomes progressively more unkempt, lacking in initiative, and emotionally unstable. In addition to diffuse loss of higher intellectual functioning, *judgment* fails in the demented patient. Occasionally a patient will be admitted to a psychiatric unit with the diagnosis of acute schizophrenia or affective psychosis, and only later will the diagnosis of dementia of recent onset become apparent. Among the causes of dementia (which will not be considered further in this book) are (1) senility; (2) degenerative brain diseases (such as Alzheimer's and Pick's diseases, and Huntington's chorea); (3) arteriosclerosis; (4) syphilis; (5) encephalitis of other cause; (6) brain injuries; (7) brain tumors; and (8) end-stage alcoholism.[60]

Psychoses Associated with Drug Use.* The most common drugs are amphetamines, alcohol, LSD, marihuana, and cocaine. *Amphetamine withdrawal psychosis* may closely resemble acute paranoid schizophrenia. In the early withdrawal phase there may be frightening visual and auditory hallucinations, disorientation and confusion, irritability, muscle cramps, headaches, sensations of heat and cold, sweating, and alternations of weakness with aggressive and sometimes violent behavior. Amphetamine and its metabolites, which can be demonstrated in the urine, lead to the diagnosis. Both during intoxication and after withdrawal, other symptoms may be very similar to those of chronic paranoid schizophrenia. [61]

Alcoholic psychosis include acute and pathological intoxication, delirium tremens, alcoholic auditory hallucinosis, and the Wernicke-Korsakoff syndrome. All these conditions are described in detail in Chapter 6.

LSD psychosis is discussed in Chapter 8. In contrast to schizophrenia, a "bad trip" on LSD is characterized by predominantly visual hallucinations and a heavy dose of what Sullivan called the "uncanny" emotions: awe, dread, horror, and

---

*Psychoses associated with drug use, toxic conditions, and diseases of the body and the brain are other kinds of organic brain syndromes. Because it is important to consider their individual characteristics, we shall consider them separately from the organic brain syndromes just described.

loathing. The average LSD trip lasts eight hours and can be managed successfully by "talking the patient down" with occasional support from diazepam (see Chapter 8). However, LSD use has precipitated a full-blown paranoid psychosis in susceptible individuals, so the emergency therapist should not be complacent when someone comes in on a bad trip. Unknown agents mixed in street drugs—the most common being strychnine and arsenic—also produce organic psychoses if they are taken in quantity.

Marihuana psychosis[62] has been reported in patients who required admission to a hospital after they smoked marihuana. Initially they exhibit aggressive behavior, gross motor disturbances, bizarre grandiose delusions, passivity, and amnesia. Later there may be an indefinite period of amnesia, flattening of affect, and mild-to-moderate thought fragmentation. When cannabis and alcohol are combined, visual hallucinations can also occur.

The effects of *cocaine* are similar to those of a short-acting amphetamine. When the user is high, or during the early withdrawal phase, he may become belligerent and grandiose. In four to six hours the trip ends. Damage to the mucous membranes of the nose (nosebleeds) are a sign this drug has been used.

Carbon Monoxide Psychosis. Cases of carbon monoxide poisoning are becoming more frequent. The clinical picture combines confusion with the expression of anger that would ordinarily be suppressed. Headaches and a characteristic cherry-red color to the skin suggest this diagnosis. Although leaking home refrigerators are the commonest cause, this syndrome has been reported after freeway driving. It also may result from a suicide attempt.

Metabolic and Endogenous Psychoses. Tumors of the brain and endocrine system can produce schizophrenic pictures. Other endocrine abnormalities can also produce significant behavioral alterations.

Brain tumors are the bane of the emergency therapist's existence because he usually forgets to consider them as a possible cause of psychological illness. Patients who develop paranoid schizophrenia after the age of 40 should always be evaluated for brain tumors. A good neurologic evaluation is part of the routine treatment for the first appearance of any psychotic state in a person of any age. Psychosis and confusion may be a compensation for compromise or loss of brain tissue.

Hypoglycemia may produce a range of symptoms from passive-aggressive behavior to psychosis. Many prediabetics show hypoglycemic symptoms, although the most florid symptoms are found in diabetics who use too much insulin and in patients with insulin-secreting tumors of the pancreas. The symptoms usually include a sense of "jitteriness inside," hunger pangs, sweating, muscle weakness, apprehension, disorientation, and delusions. Hyperactivity of reflexes and seizures have been reported.

The patient may be brought raving into the emergency room. If hypoglycemia is suspected, a blood glucose determination should clarify the diagnosis, and, if confirmed, an intravenous injection of 50 cc of 5% glucose should produce a dramatic clearing of the symptoms. Such glucose infusions should be made only after it has been ascertained that the patient has not been drinking heavily. A comatose alcoholic patient may be unable to metabolize glucose because of an excess of pyruvic acid secondary to thiamine deficiency. Unless thiamine is administered first and given time (usually thirty minutes) to take effect, a serious or fatal reaction to glucose may ensue.

Other endocrine conditions that may produce behavioral alterations are hyperthyroidism, pheochromocytomas, and high doses of steroids. Often the organic nature of these conditions is betrayed by the *lability* of the patient's affect. In the most severe forms the symptoms mimic delirious and manic states.

Infections and Inflammations of the Brain. Psychosis characterized mainly by confusion and a clouding of consciousness is one of the first signs of *meningitis* and *encephalitis.* Additionally, *temporal arteritis* may manifest itself in this way. Often the patient is well until a few hours before the appearance of the symptoms; the family is anxious but otherwise normal, and there is no history of stress. Often the psychosis is present before other signs of organic disease such as fever or underlying pneumonia can be demonstrated. There will be pressure from a medical service to accept this patient as a "schizophrenic." Generally, nonspecific psychosis characterized mainly by confusion without other signs indicating schizophrenia should be evaluated medically for several days before the patient is transferred to a psychiatric unit.

Epilepsy.[63] It is well known that the "psychic seizures" of *temporal lobe epilepsy* can produce a schizophrenialike picture. These episodes may last for days or weeks and may not be accompanied by EEG changes that clearly diagnose epilepsy. On the other hand, temporal lobe EEG changes are present in many patients diagnosed as schizophrenic. All of Schneider's first-rank symptoms of schizophrenia may be present. Other psychotic reactions belong to the "twilight state" following a *grand mal seizure.* Periods of excitement may occur and in rare instances last several days. These periods are characterized by extreme agitation, paranoid ideation, hallucinations, and delusions that cause aggressive outbursts.

Differential Diagnosis of Excited Psychotic Conditions

Alcoholic psychoses, hypoglycemia, epilepsy, and LSD are common organic causes of psychotic excitement. Among the functional psychoses, the *manic phase of manic-depressive psychosis, acute catatonic schizophrenia, acute homosexual panic,* and the *sociopathic personality in a state of rage* are the most frequent excited conditions. And certain *side effects of phenothiazine drugs* and *chronic schizophrenia in exacerbation* can lead to excitement.

The Manic Phase of Manic-depressive Psychosis. This phase was partially described before to distinguish it from paranoid schizophrenia. To make the diagnosis of primary affective disorder, manic type, Feighner and his associates[64] seek

   A. Euphoria or irritability

   B. At least two of the following:
     1. Hyperactivity
     2. Push of speech
     3. Flight of ideas
     4. Grandiosity
     5. Decreased sleep
     6. Distractibility

   C. At least a two-week course before reaching the hospital

It must be emphasized, however, that in a single, brief contact the patient may look quite good—quiet, reasonable, and charming—not at all as described by his ecological group. The therapist may emerge from the initial interview feeling that he alone understands the patient and that those who insisted he come to the emergency room are scapegoating him. Splitting the therapist and the ecological group is characteristic of the acutely manic patient: he has an unparalleled ability to manipulate.

Indeed, on initial contact the therapist's only clue to the presence of mania may be the "interpersonal havoc"[65] that the acutely manic patient can create. Janowsky et al. observed in a recent article, "Playing the Manic Game":

> Possibly, no other psychiatric syndrome is characterized by as many disquieting and irritating qualities as that of the manic phase of manic-depressive psychosis. These characteristics seem specific to the acute attack. . . .
>
> The acutely manic patient is often able to alienate himself from family, friends, and therapist alike. This knack is based on the facile use of maneuvers which place individuals relating to the manic in positions of embarrassment, decreased self-esteem, and anxious self-doubt.[66]

These authors found that the manic patient uses five types of activity to induce discomfort in those around him:

1. Manipulation of the self-esteem of others: praising or deflating others as a way of exerting interpersonal leverage
2. Perceptive exploitation of areas of vulnerability and conflict
3. Projection of responsibility
4. Progressive limit testing
5. Alienating family members

Thus, one way to recognize the manic patient is from the size and exasperation of his ecological group. Many people will call the emergency room, angry with the patient and with each other, each with a different idea of what must be done. The appearance of a *manipulated ecological group* at war with the patient and with each other is strong evidence of mania.

Acute Catatonic Schizophrenia (Excited Phase). This syndrome differs from mania in the *fragmentation* of the patient's personality. The patient is wildly excited by vivid hallucinations and delusions that he may or may not offer freely to the therapist. This form of schizophrenia often has a good prognosis. The patient often shows considerable insight into psychotic material and is intensely interested in sharing it with a therapist; thus he is a good candidate for psychotherapy.

The patient's willingness to share his psychotic attempts at regaining his sanity poses problems for the emergency therapist. A real liability of many paranoid and manipulative psychotic patients is their need to impose their idiosyncratic solutions upon others. The therapist can help such patients only if he stands up to this psychotic attempt at problem solving and insists that the patient come to terms with his deficit in realistic thinking.

On the other hand, many schizophrenic patients are seriously engaged in rebuilding their own egos, and they use their fantasies to help them, not to exert power over others. They behave as if the

symbolic mode is helping them. The therapist who cannot accept the archaic solutions presented by the symbolic mode may pressure his patients to substitute cognitive mode thinking. He will get it, but only by forcing his patients to assume a facade. The symbolic thinking will continue beneath this facade but will not develop into cognitive thinking because the patient has been taught to distrust it.

The acutely catatonic patient may be either wildly excited or stuporous and may require several days of tranquilizing medication before he is able to open up.

Acute Homosexual Panic. The picture of this syndrome is described by

. . . intense agitation and panic, confusion, delusions and hallucinations of persecution, occasional assaultiveness, and considerable preoccupations with homosexuality and fears of homosexual attack per anum. [67]

There is often a precipitating event, such as

. . . seductive closeness or actual attempt at seduction by a member of the same sex, loss of a close friend of the same sex, failure in heterosexual performance, separation from home and friends, etc. [68]

Recently Ovesey[69] has demonstrated that apparently homosexual concerns are often really *pseudohomosexual* in many men, who symbolize their conflicts over power and dependency in terms of sexual submission to a feared or envied rival. Whenever their power is threatened, such pseudohomosexual men often turn to violence, as in the following case reported by Woods:[70]

Example 5-4. A businessman entered treatment because of severe depression precipitated by competitive defeat at the hands of an old business rival. The patient's fantasy of wealth and status was shattered by his rival's completely legal but unethical manipulations which won a coveted contract. In treatment the patient alternated between fits of depression and fits of rage with plots of vengeance and violent destruction. He finally hired someone with instructions to beat and cripple the offender on the anniversary of the incident. The patient clung to his plan until one day he appeared panic-stricken following a dream. In the dream he encountered a cripple on the street whose attempts to walk appeared ludicrous and caused the patient to laugh loudly. However, he jumped into the cripple's immensely powerful arms and was promptly stipped naked and impaled upon a huge erection. A crowd gathered and hooted at his humiliation.

Clearly, such men live close to panic, and psychotherapy may precipitate a frank psychosis. As Woods points out:

> Patients may experience psychotherapy as having their nose rubbed in their passivity and dependency, and the therapist's interventions as the equivalent of rape. They view the unfolding of their inner life as a submissive humiliating surrender of masculinity. Such patients often have strong paranoid dynamics, and when there is significant or psychotic ego disorganization the therapist may indeed be in danger.[71]

It is important to remember that the patient in a homosexual or pseudohomosexual panic is likely to turn to violence. Often the treatment resembles the treatment of the homicidal patient described in Chapter 4, but with the frequent additional need for brief hospitalization.

The Sociopathic Personality in a State of Rage. This kind of patient is excited, hostile, and manipulative. The usual explanation is that he has begun to fail in his attempts to manipulate others or in his attempts to control himself. Usually his psychosis reflects the ambivalence between his need for help and his desire to dominate. The following case is adapted from Lorr's illustration of his excited-hostile type:

Example 5-5. A 38-year-old white male, unemployed, married, and the father of two children, was admitted to the hospital when he complained of feeling as if he were "losing his mind." His long drinking history had begun in the military service.

Six weeks before his admission to the hospital he had come to the city to look for work. He started drinking before he was on the bus, played card games, and passed checks on a closed account. He thought of jumping out of his hotel room window, but the idea struck him as so ridiculous he became hysterical. One day he awoke in "somebody's boathouse." He felt ill, vomited frequently, and was so frightened by the ideas flying through his head that he came to the hospital for help.

After his admission, the patient acted anxious to please and promised never to get into trouble again. He worked well at hospital jobs and had a good memory and good orientation. He was continuously boisterous and jocular on the ward and in groups because, he said, he would rather be that way than cry. In spite of his promises to do better and his anxiousness to please, he refused group and individual therapies because he felt he had only two problems: financial difficulties and the fear of his wife's leaving him. A week before he was to be discharged he became upset when he received legal papers for his wife's divorce. He became destructive and disturbing to other patients on his ward and was discharged. He was diagnosed as a sociopathic personality with alcoholism.[72]

Often in retrospect such admissions appear to be the sociopathic patient's attempts to obtain sympathy, an excuse for misbehavior, and an appeal for a second chance. He may try to fulfill these needs by simulating any of the psychotic syndromes just described, especially mania and panic.

Often the manipulative patient is alienated and needs a treatment setting to satisfy his wish to complain with the theater's aging salesman, Willy Loman, that "Attention must be paid!" Like Willy, the manipulative patient may need to hide his dependent need behind a belligerent, help-rejecting facade. It may be adequate therapy to pay attention briefly, even if the hospitalization ends when the patient, no longer feeling the need for help, angrily departs against medical advice.

Side Effects of Phenothiazine Medications. Certain side effects of phenothiazine medications resemble excited psychotic conditions. The most important are *akathisia* and *tardive dyskinesia*.

Akathisia appears *early* in treatment with phenothiazines. Akathisia

> . . . is the inability to sit still. The patient experiences symptoms of restlessness and tends to move about. Inactivity produces a feeling of extreme discomfort, resulting in shifts of the legs, tapping of the feet, or rocking the body. The patient who is unable to remain seated and must get up and walk about is said to have tasikinesia.[73]

A clue to this untoward reaction to phenothiazines (usually trifluoperazine and fluphenazine) is the patient's complaint that he finds the medication unpleasant. However, he may complain of being unable to sleep and to lie down, and the emergency therapist, noting his restlessness, pacing, and anxiety, may assume that the patient's hyperactivity represents an exacerbation of his psychosis. Tardive dyskinesia occurs *late* in treatment with phenothiazines (see Chapter 26).

Of course, excitement is often the reason for long-term phenothiazine treatment, not the result of it. Recently Kline[74] reported the case of a schizophrenic woman whose tendency to hostile, belligerent excitement has required high-dose treatment with phenothiazines for eighteen years. She has shown no physical ill effects from these drugs and has maintained an adequate social recovery.

Chronic Schizophrenia in Exacerbation. This pro-duces dramatic, excited picture, often when the patient stops his medication in defiance of someone who has displeased or expected too much of him. Such patients are often dragged by police into emergency rooms in astonishing states of excited disorganization that require several men to contain. Occasionally a patient will come himself for a "booster dose" of a phenothiazine drug that helped him in the past.

> *Example 5-6.* The wife of a middle-aged man called to say that her husband was coming into the emergency room. His previous therapist also called and said that this man would probably come in as he had seven years before, screaming loudly that he was going to lose control. After a single dose of chlorpromazine, his former therapist predicted, "He will most likely calm down and be able to go home." The therapist offered to see him in his office the following day.
>
> The patient came in screaming, "I'm going to blow, I'm going to blow!" and had a pale, "possessed" look that was distinctly frightening. The emergency therapist immediately gave him 200 mg of liquid chlorpromazine to drink; the patient quieted down almost immediately, and his wife said there would be no problem at all taking care of him until he could see his therapist.
>
> The entire transaction took less than an hour and was an exact repeat of the patient's behavior seven years before.

Differential Diagnosis of Intropunitive Conditions

Intropunitive means the continuous self-torture of the psychotically depressed individual. The neurotically depressed patient's jury is still out, but the psychotically depressed patient has already been found guilty and has begun to serve his sentence. When he accepts this internal judgment, the patient may become anxious or resigned, and his preoccupations leave no doubt that he feels he has sinned and must pay through incessant self-questioning, a period of inactive silence, or death. Thus agitation, psychomotor retardation, or dread may be the predominant affective symptoms, and the depressive thought content may involve obsessive concerns with bodily decay, the conviction that life is over, or accusation by voices that insist on self-mutilation or execution. Where neurotic ambivalence centers on the degree of guilt, psychotic ambivalence concentrates on how the sentence may be carried out: suicide (a risk in all depressions) is most likely here.

The important diagnostic considerations for intropunitive psychotic states are *psychotic depressive reactions, primary affective disorders, schizoaffective schizophrenia, depressions related to drug use,* and *depressions caused by organic illness*. Many examples of patients with psychotic depressions are found in Chapters 2 and 3, together with material concerning the dynamics of depression. Here we shall concentrate upon the diagnosing of such states. Depressions belong to the class of psychiatric illnesses that have been called "the affective or mood disorders." The current classification of these disorders by George Winokur[75] is depicted in Figure 5-2.

Psychotic Depressive Reactions. Most people react to loss or precipitating stress with a certain degree of depression. Some, especially so-called depressive characters, may react with a depression so severe and incapacitating that it assumes psychotic proportions. The depression may occur in response to a loss or threatened loss, such as the death of a loved one, the onset of old age, a major life-threatening illness, or major surgery. Or depression may occur with pre-existing psychiatric illness, such as hysterical personality, anxiety neurosis, antisocial personality, alcoholism, or drug addiction.[77] Winokur[78] found such depressions frequently among patients admitted to a psychiatric hospital for a variety of primary diagnoses, such as neuroses, acute and chronic brain syndromes, schizophrenia, and alcoholism. He suggests we call such depressions "secondary depression," noting that it is entirely possible they are reactive "to a chronic life of psychiatric disabilities" caused by the primary disorder. Our chapters on suicide and alcoholism (Chapters 2, 3, and 6) give much information concerning the lives of persons chronically susceptible to such "secondary depression," which can in fact be more

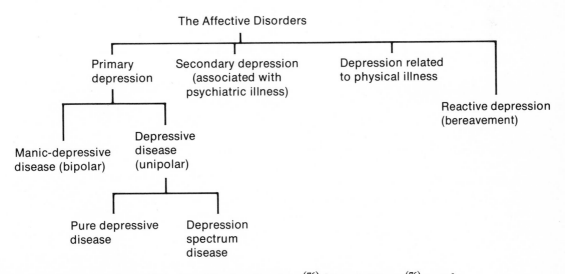

Figure 5-2 The affective disorders. [76] [Adapted from [76], p. 2.]

incapacitating than the primary disorder, requiring intensive acute intervention without prejudice based on the prognosis for the underlying chronic condition.

Primary Affective Disorders. In the primary affective disorders the symptoms are thought to arise primarily from biological and physiological causes and only secondarily as a response to life stress. Often there is a family pattern of mood disturbance, indicating a hereditary aspect.

Some psychotic depressions are part of a manic-depressive cycle. The patient has had clearly documented episodes of mania and depression,

usually with a normal period separating them, although sometimes one phase proceeds directly from the other. This is called *bipolar* affective disorder, and it seems to run in families.

Patients who become psychotically depressed one or more times and who have never had a manic period are said to have a *unipolar* affective disorder.[79] Usually their families are also free of a history of mania. A special kind of unipolar disorder is involutional melancholia, which is profound depression arising in the middle age of persons who had been previously extraordinarily conscientious, virtuous, and responsible.

Some patients with *unipolar* depressions are the

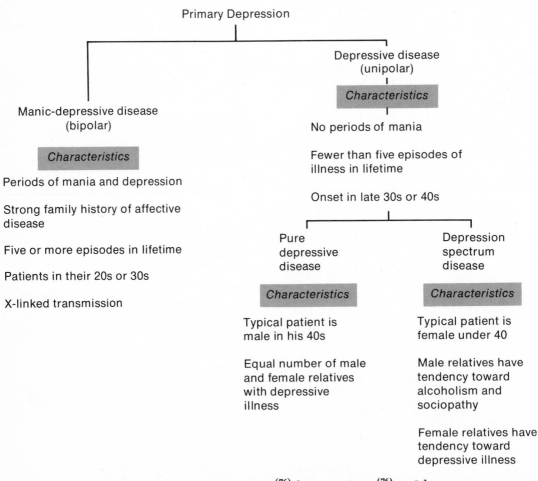

Figure 5–3 Primary depression. [76] **[Adapted from** [76]**, p. 3.]**

only members of their families to become depressed. Others have relatives who show depressive equivalents such as drinking and sociopathy. On this basis Winokur[80] distinguishes pure depressive disease from "depression spectrum disease." His summary of the kinds of primary depression is given in Figure 5-3.

Even though all these kinds of psychotic depressions may seem quite similar clinically, making such distinctions is important for treatment: lithium carbonate seems to offer prophylaxis against the depressive as well as the manic phase of bipolar illness; ECT may work wonders in unipolar depression; and tricyclic antidepressants should not be used in bipolar depressions. (Drug treatment of depressions is discussed in detail in Chapter 28.)

Three stages in the development of a psychotic depression have been described, akin to the three stages of a manic attack. The *first stage* of a depressive attack is marked by fatigue, inertia, and dissatisfaction. The patient may cease to take care of himself, report bodily discomfort with bizarre tinges ("his chest is heavy as a stone . . . he feels no sensations but his weight"[81]), start to berate himself, or make suicide attempts. Typically, the patient will have difficulty falling asleep, wake early in the morning, feel worst just after getting up, and feel most like himself in late afternoon.

The *second stage* is sometimes called the acute stage. It brings major focus on the body and its sensations, but the explanations for the physical distress are weird. We hear from the patient that "his brain is melting, his bowels are stopped up, his heart fails to beat, his stomach is rotting away."[82] One patient said, "I had a bowel movement several months ago that took the life out of me." In addition to such *somatic delusions*, the fixed belief that a major illness is present may appear. Furthermore, a kind of negative grandiosity appears: the patient has become the worst person in the world, the source of its evils and problems; he thinks he has engendered wars and catastrophes. He feels unreal, and hallucinations and paranoid ideas appear. Although he expects death, he fears poisoning and stops eating. (At this

point food has lost its flavor and looks peculiar.)

The *third stage* is stupor. The patient refuses to get up, talk, or respond visually to stimulation. He will not eat, go to the bathroom, or control his urination or defecation. Such patients often develop major fecal impactions or bladder infections. He is preoccupied with fantasies of sin and death, delusions, and hallucinations.

Anxiety comes early in the depressive process; weight loss is late. Early in depression the patient may try suicide; later he may starve to death.

Abstracting from these and other descriptions of psychotic depression, Feighner and colleagues[83] propose these criteria to make the diagnosis:

A. Dysphoric mood (depressed, sad, blue, and so on.)
B. At least four of the following:
  1. Anorexia or weight loss
  2. Sleep difficulty
  3. Loss of energy
  4. Agitation or retardation
  5. Loss of interest in usual activities (includes decreased libido)
  6. Self-reproach or guilt
  7. Diminished ability to think or concentrate
  8. Recurrent thoughts of death or suicide
C. At least a one-month course prior to admission to the hospital

Schizoaffective schizophrenia is distinguished by the evidence of conceptual disorganization favoring the symbolic mode, which is characteristic of schizophrenia. Many clinicians feel that this disorder is a variant of primary affective illness, from which it is sometimes indistinguishable.

Depressions Related to Drug Use and Organic Illness. Serious depressions are seen after alcohol and amphetamine withdrawal, during active marihuana and barbiturate use, and as a side effect of reserpine and diazepam (Valium®) medication. The psychotic manifestations tend to clear when the patient has been free of all drugs for several weeks, although the amphetamine and alcohol user may show sleep disturbances for months after withdrawal. These issues are discussed in greater detail in Chapters 6 to 9.

Organic illnesses, such as anemia, cancer, and heart disease, may show the dispiritedness, anxiety, retardation, sleep disturbances, and weight loss of a primary depression yet be entirely secondary to the hidden physical condition. They are a reminder to the therapist to wonder always if a true organic condition lies behind the psychotic somatic delusion. Endocrine abnormalities—such as hypothyroidism, diabetes mellitus, and estrogen insufficiency—provide a realistic basis for weird-sounding complaints of bodily decay and depletion of vital force.

One of the aftereffects of an attack of viral influenza may be serious depression in depression-prone individuals. Suicides have been known to occur two to four weeks after apparent recovery from such an infection.

INITIAL TREATMENT OF PSYCHOTIC PATIENTS

The therapist's job is to protect a personality that is disintegrating. He must be conservative (to avoid further disintegration) and constructive (to set the stage for reintegration). It is helpful to think of the therapist's responsibilities in the initial contact in terms of *mistakes to be avoided* and *steps to be taken*. We start with a discussion of mistakes because the management of psychotic patients is one area of psychiatry in which the therapist can do harm if he does not act with restraint. Then we shall look at initial intervention in various psychotic conditions.

Mistakes to be Avoided

Basically the therapist must avoid making the same kinds of mistakes with the psychotic patient that the patient has made with himself. Just as the psychotic patient may resort to paranoid, disorganized, excited, and intropunitive methods of coping with uncertainty, the emergency therapist may find himself tempted toward the comple-

mentary responses of (1) false structuring of the situation (paranoia), (2) inappropriate refusal to put a basic treatment plan together (disorganization), (3) maneuvers that exceed his own executive limits (excitement), and (4) unnecessary guilt over his own inadequacies in the treatment situation (being intropunitive).

False Structuring of the Situation. In spite of the complexity involved in reaching a diagnosis, many therapists, out of anxiety, turn to labels and drugs before they have clarified what is wrong with the patient. In Example 5-1, such a false structuring occurred when the therapist gave the patient chlorpromazine to drink and wrote "acute schizophrenia, suspected" on his admission note. Such rote behaviors tend to reinforce each other in a sort of delusional logic: "I gave her chlorpromazine, so she must be schizophrenic; I've called her schizophrenic, so I must give her chlorpromazine." Then "evidence" for the diagnosis may take on the quality of a delusional perception: "I saw her sniff the chlorpromazine and not mind the smell; in fact she drank it—only schizophrenics do that—she *must* be schizophrenic!"

In this particular case the emergency therapist should have written, "acute psychosis, characterized by mutism, withdrawal, disorganization, and possible disorientation." These are not indications for immediate drug treatment but for further evaluation, and he should have withheld drugs. If the patient appeared to be grossly agitated, the best drug would be injectable diazepam, which acts for a short duration, does not block autonomic responses, and does not confuse the diagnostic picture. Thus the patient's treatment would have been appropriate for the many kinds of psychosis she might in fact have had.

Refusal To Make a Treatment Plan. This is the opposite of false structuring. The therapist in Example 5-1 did not fail his patient in this area. Even though the therapist could not have known from the evidence at hand the exact type of psychosis the patient demonstrated, there was considerable evidence of poor judgment and inability to fend for herself: mutism; a shallow, labile affect; and above all, being picked up at night while attempting to hitch a ride along a dangerous stretch of road. Thus, putting this patient on a seventy-two-hour hold until she could demonstrate her ability to take care of herself was a reasonable, caring action.

Therefore some treatment can begin before the diagnosis is clear. Provision always should be made for the acutely psychotic patient's safety. Like the suicidal patient, the psychotic patient need not be hospitalized if others, through crisis support, can arrange for his care. Members of the ecological group can avoid his hospitalization by providing limit setting, administering drugs, and supporting reality with the help of occasional visits by a crisis intervention team. But when no ecological support system exists, the therapist cannot allow a grossly disorganized patient to refuse treatment and walk out of the emergency room unless it is evident that he retains enough ego strength to avoid major mishaps. Involuntary detention is the next logical move.[85] If the therapist decides not to use involuntary detention, he must find a safe alternative: he cannot just let his patient go.

Often a good middle way to work with patients who are not so disorganized that they should be detained automatically but who seem on the verge of losing control is to share concern with the ecological group. It is entirely appropriate to say to a disorganized patient, "I'm concerned for you; I think you need help, and I'm going to tell the others that I want you to come into the hospital." To the others, the therapist can say, "I'm not sure what is wrong, but I'm afraid this situation will get out of control if he continues on the outside." Usually this honesty will bring the therapist, the patient, and the ecological group together in the attempt to find out what is wrong. Even if the patient does not enter treatment immediately, he usually returns to the setting and the therapist who has offered to help him find his way.

Exceeding One's Executive Limits. It has been said that one way to become psychotic is to try to control a situation one cannot in fact control. The same therapists who are able to assert themselves in the face of psychotic disorganization may fail to recognize that borderline patient whose ambivalence prevents any immediate resolution.

Example 5-7. A woman in her early 30s who had been in analytically oriented treatment for years came to the emergency room and announced that she had terminated with her therapist and was about to walk out of her marriage. Almost immediately she said that this wasn't what she wanted to do, she wanted to try couple therapy. She agreed to be seen with her husband. He was called and said he would be right over. Immediately after the therapist had placed this call, the patient said she didn't really want to face her husband, she was going to go off alone.

She started to walk out of the emergency room, then came back and said, "I'd better tell you that I made a suicide attempt when I left my first husband eight years ago."

The therapist asked her about suicide and obtained a strong suicidal history. She had talked frequently with her former therapist, who was now on vacation, about killing herself.

The husband arrived, and the patient's ambivalence mounted. He turned out to be a patient, boyish young man who tried to reason with her to no avail. She could not decide whether to come home or go off and kill herself.

Finally the therapist decided to place the patient on a hold. He learned that there were no involuntary holds at his facility and he would have to arrange transportation to the nearby county hospital if he wanted to detain her. Arranging transportation was a nightmare: the ambulance would have to cross a county line, which it could not do with an involuntary patient. It was a Saturday night, and the police and sheriff's office were tied up with criminal work. The therapist was afraid to send her alone with her husband.

Assuming his presence would be authoritative enough, the therapist agreed to go with the patient and her husband in their car. She jumped out of the car into the traffic on a main highway and screamed for help. Her husband honked his horn, to signal a police car to stop. Because the couple's car was over the county line, the police were able to flag down a county ambulance, which took her to the facility.

A more experienced clinician at the county hospital diagnosed pseudoneurotic schizophrenia and sent her home to a friend with a return outpatient appointment to him. (She kept the appointment.) In retrospect, the first emergency therapist should have accepted his inability to reach quick closure.

Often the inexperienced therapist overreacts to the borderline patient. Careful history taking of such patients usually reveals latent psychosis and often suicidal or homicidal potential. The conscientious therapist may overstep his bounds in trying to deal with the potential for crisis, forgetting that it is a *chronic* potential in such patients.

If the patient's first responses to offers to help seem ambivalent or help-rejecting, it is often better for the therapist to listen to the patient, and to avoid the temptation to engage him in treatment. Frequently the pattern of a paranoid personality or a hysterical character appears in what the patient tells about his life, and the personality diagnosis will be more appropriate than the soft signs of psychosis, such as ambivalence, restlessness, and poorly controlled rage. It is essential not to try to do more for the patient than can be done and to let the movement for treatment come from the patient. An appeal to listen to ambivalence is not a request for intensive treatment, but a need for attention. It is emphatically not a signal for active, self-defeating crisis intervention.

In many more serious crisis situations, especially those involving manic patients who have not yet started to "crash," the therapist must also wait for the right moment to intervene actively.

Unnecessary Guilt. Psychotic patients are particularly skilled in making therapists feel inadequate. They do this by taking advantage of the fact that there is no good way for the therapist to establish contact with a patient whose ego is not in control.

Example 5-8. A young therapist was asked by a patient to see a friend who was becoming disturbed. The friend turned out to be a large, bearded, sensitive young man who was disturbed by the emergence of paranoid feelings. After he had begun to tell these to the therapist, he stopped. The therapist asked, "How long have you been feeling this way?"

The patient said, "You can't help me," and walked out of the office.

The therapist wondered what he had done wrong. Had his stiff, clinical questions driven the sensitive patient away? He worried about what the patient who had referred the young man would think.

A month later the young man called the therapist, apologized for "putting you up tight," and explained that he hadn't had the courage to ask for a letter recommending exemption from the military draft because he feared he would be turned down.

No therapist, no matter how experienced, is able to understand the meaning of everything a patient says. Rather than assuming he is defective in his powers of comprehension, the therapist is better off to say, "I'm afraid I don't follow you. Can you try explaining that to me again?"

Provoking guilt can be a way for the patient to rid himself of it by passing along a "bum rap." The schizophrenic person often has been made to carry the guilt for an entire family.[86] The therapist sets an example for his overburdened patient by showing that it is possible to refuse such undeserved guilt.

Steps to be Taken: Initial Intervention in Various Psychotic Conditions

This section illustrates various interviewing techniques and procedures that may be used to approach paranoid, disorganized, excited, and intropunitive patients. The problems posed by working with a psychotic patient's ecological group are described in detail in Chapter 10. If psychosis is a response to crisis within the group, the process of crisis intervention is as described in Chapter 1. Detailed specific treatment of the separate syndromes is beyond the scope of this book.

Initial Intervention with Paranoid Patients. The therapist must be firm and emphatic in standing up with common sense and realistic medical authority to his patient's psychotic attempts to maintain control. The following case of Enelow's[87] illustrates this stance:

Example 5-9. Mr. B.G. was a 25-year-old old engineer who was first seen in the emergency room at the community hospital. The patient had attempted to purchase a Cadillac in the middle of the night. On finding the automobile agency locked up, he attempted to force an entry. The police overpowered him and they took him to the emergency room for treatment of his wounds. Here the intern found him to be suspicious, sullen, and delusional. He spoke of having been hypnotized by someone he was unable to identify. He felt that he was being secretly groomed for the presidency of the engineering firm at which he worked. He was offered hospitalization on the psychiatric ward and refused. A psychiatrist was called; he made a rapid examination and then in a friendly but firm way, said: "I want you to come into the hospital and to take some medication." "On what basis?" Mr. G. inquired suspiciously. "On the basis that I am a doctor and know you need it," the psychiatrist replied. "Oh!" said

Mr. G. and quietly signed the admission sheet. Phenothiazines were begun at once. One week later, Mr. G. was discharged, free of psychotic symptoms, to outpatient care.

Initial Intervention with Disorganized Patients. Often the most helpful approach is to *talk to the patient's affect.* For acutely disorganized patients, a suppressed affective issue is often behind the shift from the cognitive to the symbolic mode.

Example 5-10. Perry[88] has described a woman in her early 30s, a nurse who was admitted to the hospital with a diagnosis of acute catatonic schizophrenia. She was often wildly excited and would draw furiously during her therapy sessions. One drawing revealed an "archetypal" symbol, a serpent hung upon a cross. For several days Perry sought to find what connection this archaic symbol might have to her present life. During this time his patient was especially turbulent.

Finally, realizing that the serpent resembled a caduceus, Perry asked his patient if the drawing had anything to do with her feelings about her profession. "I hate it!", she exclaimed, and explained that her widowed mother, who depended on her for support, ironed her uniforms as if she were her husband. The patient had begun to feel she had no life of her own. Expressing this, she cleared.

To help a disorganized and confused patient make sense out of what is happening, the therapist often has to do much of the talking.[89, 90] The therapist should tell the patient why he makes his statements so he does not reinforce the fear that he or others can read the patient's mind ("thought broadcasting"). The therapist may say, "From the way your hands are trembling and the scared look on your face, I would guess you're feeling pretty frightened" (rather than "You're feeling pretty frightened"). The therapist can state facts he *does* know, e.g., "It looks as if you've been having a pretty rocky time recently," or "Your husband says you haven't been getting much sleep," or "From the way you're looking all around the room, it must be difficult to concentrate on what I'm saying."

Often such reflections provide the bridge the patient has been looking for to enable him to engage with the therapist. If the patient makes symbolic references or uses unlabeled metaphors, the interviewer should listen most attentively. This does not mean that he shakes his head in understanding if he does not or that he agrees with delusions that he does not agree with, but rather that he tries to enter into the patient's experiential world, that he is willing for the time being to hear "crazy talk," and that he wants to hear about feelings which, however symbolized, are real and important to the patient. By doing so, the therapist can begin to establish rapport and start treatment.

Example 5-11. A 32-year-old chemist was picked up by the police on a freeway where he had been carrying a placard with a political slogan. He was unkempt, wore a long beard, had a messianic gleam in his eye, and told the emergency therapist that he had been instructed "by the forces of God" to campaign for this candidate. He also said he had been instructed by such forces in the past, that he had been locked up in a mental hospital with a diagnosis of schizophrenia, and that he wasn't going to talk with this therapist further if he were going to do the same.

The therapist said he'd have to know the patient better before he'd say or do anything and asked him to describe what had been going on in his life recently. The patient described an increasing preoccupation with political and religious matters, racing thoughts, inability to concentrate on his work, and loss of sleep and weight (all brought about by his efforts to get his candidate elected).

The therapist told the patient that he didn't think his political tactics were as effective as

those a candidate of this stature deserved. Because his thoughts were racing and his concentration poor, the patient couldn't give good, coherent speeches. Because of his unkempt appearance, he would put off those who might be favorably disposed to the candidate, and so on.

This criticism made sense to the patient. The therapist asked him if he would take some medication to slow his thoughts and improve his concentration. The patient asked if this meant the therapist thought he was schizophrenic. The therapist said he hadn't reached any diagnostic conclusion (he hadn't, although he was thinking of paranoid schizophrenia, schizoaffective disorder, and manic-depressive illness, manic phase, as possibilities), but that he thought the medication would help, whatever the diagnosis might be. The patient accepted the medication and returned for regular visits. Hospitalization was avoided as his psychosis was treated and cleared.

Not every success in connecting the patient's affective response to a dynamic issue in himself or the ecological group means that a psychosis is resolved.

Example 5-12. A 52-year-old woman was brought into the emergency room by her husband and two teenage daughters. She had had radical breast surgery for carcinoma and was receiving large doses of steroids as part of her treatment for metastasis. She had not seen her doctor for two months; her next appointment was a month away. Her husband reported numerous wild behaviors, including failure to take her steroid medications.

The therapist learned that her surgeon and her husband had agreed not to tell her of the recurrence of the cancer. Feeling that this was a pseudosecret, the therapist obtained their permissions to tell the patient the truth. She seemed almost relieved to hear the painful news, and her mood improved and her erratic behavior diminished.

Nevertheless, she continued to ramble, and her husband found it exhausting to care for her. On a return trip to the emergency room, a consultant examined her with the therapist. Noting her lability, the consultant said he strongly suspected organic factors were involved and recommended that she be admitted. The final diagnosis turned out to be steroid psychosis, secondary to her antitumor medications. Only when these medications were changed did she improve for good.

Initial Intervention with Excited Patients. Medications and restraints must often be used with this group of patients. Often the patient will be brought in by the police, who should be asked to escort him to a locked room. Before they leave they should give full documentation of what he has done, how he was picked up, any threats, concealed drugs or weapons, and the names of significant others. Often the interview with the police (who may be in a hurry to leave) is the best information that will be available for days or hours and provides the basis for a working diagnosis.

A significant portion of these patients will have been drinking, but this does not exclude manic-depressive disease, acute catatonic schizophrenia, or chronic schizophrenia in exacerbation, all of which may lead to heavy drinking. Barbiturate intoxication may also unleash psychotic excitement. (The treatment of drinking and addicted patients is discussed in Chapters 6 and 9.)

Having obtained all available history and determined (if possible) the presence or absence or intoxication (not discounting the mimic, hypoglycemia), the therapist must proceed to calm the patient. Often this means the involuntary administration of tranquilizing drugs.

The *way* these drugs are offered to excited patients is important. The nurse or doctor emphatically should *not* go to the patient's room alone with a loaded syringe or medication cup. This practice is a form of "exceeding executive limits." The sudden relaxation of controls by recent captors in favor of a benevolent expectation of cooperation invites the patient to overstep his limits and may cause him to panic.

Instead, it seems wisest to demonstrate control by entering the room with five strong men who are prepared to hold down the patient. This procedure is called "show of force" and is meant to be appreciated by the concrete patient. A choice is offered to the patient's remaining healthy ego: he can take the medication voluntarily or be held down and injected. (These issues are discussed further in Chapters 10 and 25 to 28.)

Initial Treatment of Intropunitive Patients. We discussed in Chapter 3 the unambivalent, firm style of caring behavior that is most effective in dealing with intropunitive patients. Evaluation of the suicidal risk and protection of the patient from himself are the overriding concerns in initial management. Antidepressant medications (or, in manic-depressive illness, lithium) should be started as soon as possible.

ECT should be available wherever the psychotically depressed individual is hospitalized. Patients with recurrent depressions may show benefits only from this method of treatment, and hospitalization should be arranged with ECT in mind.

Not all intropunitive patients need to be hospitalized. Much depends on the quality of interpersonal resources in the ecological group. Many patients will be hospitalized on a milieu ward (see Chapter 10). A locked ward may be safer for very suicidal (often bipolar) depressive patients. The patient and his family should be given realistic hope: most depressions respond to treatment.

SUMMARY

Psychotic problems, which are met with in every aspect of psychiatric work, require difficult treatment decisions and a specialized vocabulary. Treatment is most effective when the therapist does not flinch from sharing the psychotic patient's uncertainty and when he defines the reasons for the steps he takes. To accomplish these goals, the therapist must be able to define for himself what he means by psychotic difficulties. When the therapist has a working understanding of psychosis, he will not mystify himself or his patient.

REFERENCES

1. Freedman, Alfred M., Harold I. Kaplan, and Benjamin J. Sadock: *Modern Synopsis of Comprehensive Textbook of Psychiatry,* Williams & Wilkins, Baltimore, 1972, p. 788.

2. Szasz, Thomas: *Law, Liberty, and Psychiatry,* Macmillan, New York, 1963.

3. Cooper, David: *Psychiatry and Anti-Psychiatry,* Ballantine Books, New York, 1971.

4. Spensley, James, James T. Barter, Paul H. Werme, and Donald G. Langsley: "Involuntary Hospitalization: What For and How Long," *Am. J. Psychiat.,* **131**:219–222, 1974.

5. Lorr, Maurice, C. James Klett, and Douglas M. McNair: *Syndromes of Psychosis,* Pergamon, New York, 1963.

6. Lorr, Maurice (ed.): *Explorations in Typing Psychotics,* Pergamon, New York, 1966.

7. Perry, John W.: *The Far Side of Madness,* Prentice-Hall, Englewood Cliffs, N.J., 1974.

8. Grinker, Roy R.: "Changing Styles in Psychoses and Borderline States," *Am. J. Psychiat.,* **130**:151–152, 1973.

9. American Psychiatric Association: *Diagnostic and Statistical Manual of Mental Disorders,* 1st ed., Washington, D.C., 1952.

10. American Psychiatric Association: *Diagnostic and Statistical Manual of Mental Disorders,* 2d ed., Washington, D.C., 1968.

11. Freedman et al.: op. cit., pp. 202–215.

12. Menninger, Karl A., Martin Mayman, and Paul Pruyser: *The Vital Balance,* Viking, New York, 1963, pp. 260–261.

13. Ibid.

14. Lorr et al.: Acute Psychotic Types," chap. 4, in op. cit., pp. 33–75.

15. Freedman et al.: op. cit., pp. 250–251.

16. Bellak, Leopold (ed.): *Schizophrenia: a Review of the Syndrome,* Logos Press, London, 1958, p. 157.

17. Freedman et al.: op. cit., p. 249.

18. Tyhurst, James C.: "Paranoid Patterns," in A. H. Leighton, J. A. Clausen, and R. N. Wilson (eds.): *Explorations in Social Psychiatry,* Basic Books, New York, 1957, p. 31.

19. Schneider, Kurt: *Clinical Psychopathology,* M. W. Hamilton (trans.), Grune & Stratton, New York, 1959, p. 133.

20. Mellor, C. S.: "First Rank Symptoms of Schizophrenia," *Brit. J. Psychiatry,* **117**:15–23, 1970.

21. Rosenbaum, C. Peter: *The Meaning of Madness: Symptomatology, Sociology, Biology and Therapy of the Schizophrenias,* Science House, New York, 1970, p. 37.

22. Schneider: loc. cit.

23. Bleuler, Eugen: *Dementia Praecox, or the Group of Schizophrenias,* J. Zinkin (trans.), International Universitites Press, Inc., New York, 1950, p. 213.

24. Carlson, Gabrielle A., and Frederick K. Goodwin: "The Stages of Mania: a Longitudinal Analysis of the Manic Episode," *Arch. Gen. Psychiat.,* **28**:221–228, 1973.

25. Kraepelin, Emil: *Manic-Depressive Insanity and Paraphrenia,* R. Mary Barclay (trans., ed.), E. S. Livingston, Edinburgh, 1919.

26. Carlson and Goodwin: op. cit., p. 224.

27. Taylor, Michael Alan, and Richard Abrams: "The Phenomenology of Mania," *Arch. Gen. Psychiat.,* **29**:520–522, 1974.

28. Rosenbaum: loc. cit.

29. Grinker, Roy R.: "An Essay on Schizophrenia and Science," *Arch. Gen. Psychiat.,* **20**:1–24, 1969.

30. M. L. Simmel (ed.), *From the Reach of the Mind: Essays in Memory of Kurt Goldstein,* Copyright 1968 by Springer Publishing Co., Inc., 400 Park Ave. S., New York. By permission of the publisher.

31. Grinker: "An Essay on Schizophrenia and Science," op. cit., p. 14.

32. Bateson, Gregory, Don D. Jackson, Jay Haley, and John Weakland: "Toward a Theory of Schizophrenia," *Behav. Sci.,* vol. 1, 1956.

33. Deikman, Arthur: "Bimodal Consciousness," *Arch. Gen. Psychiat.,* **25**:481–489, 1971.

34. Buss, Arnold H., and Peter J. Lang: "Psychological Deficit in Schizophrenia: I. Affect, Reinforcement, and Concept Attainment," *J. Abnorm. Psychol.* **70**:20, 1965.

35. Ibid.

36. Callaway, Enoch: "Schizophrenia and Interference: An Analogy With a Malfunctioning Computer," *Arch. Gen. Psychiat.,* **22**:193–208, 1970.

37. Bowers, Malcolm G.: "Pathogenesis of Acute Schizophrenic Psychoses," *Arch. Gen. Psychiat.,* **19**:348–355, 1968.

38. Arieti, Silvano: "An Overview of Schizophrenia from a Predominantly Psychological Approach," *Am. J. Psychiat.,* **131**:241–249, 1974. Copyright 1974, the American Psychiatric Association.

39. Ibid., p. 245.

40. Whitmont, Edward: "Prefatory Remarks to Jung's 'Reply to Buber,'" *Spring,* 188–195, 1973.

41. Hoch, Paul: "Differential Diagnosis in Clinical Psychiatry," in Margaret O. Strahl and Nolan D. C. Lewis (eds.), *The Lectures of Paul H. Hoch,* Science House, New York, 1972.

42. Perry, John W.: "The Messianic Hero," *J. Anal. Psychol.,* **17**:184–198, 1972.

43. Levinson, Fritz: "Religious Delusions in Counter-Culture Patients," *Am. J. Psychiat.,* **130**:1265–1269, 1973.

44. Laing, Ronald: *The Divided Self,* Tavistock Publications, London, 1960.

45. Herjanic, Marijan: "Schizophrenia: Pieces of the Puzzle," *Medical World News, Psychiatry* 1972, Eli Robins (ed.), pp. 75–77.

46. Ibid.

47. Rosenbaum: loc. cit.

48. Donlon, Patrick T., and Joe T. Tupin: "Rapid 'Digitalization' of Decompensated Schizophrenic Patients with Antipsychotic Agents," *Am. J. Psychiat.,* **131**:310–312, 1974.

49. Bleuler: loc. cit.

50. Ibid.

51. Rosenbaum: op. cit., p. 10.

52. Rosenbaum: ibid.

53. Perry: "The Messianic Hero," loc. cit.

54. Freedman et al.: op. cit., pp. 268–311.

55. Ibid., pp. 268–269.

56. Engel, George L., and John Romano: "Delirium, a Syndrome of Cerebral Insufficiency," *J. Chron. Dis.,* **9**:260, 1959.

57. Freedman et al.: op. cit., p. 270.

58. Ibid., p. 271.

59. Ibid., p. 272.

60. Ibid., pp. 272–273.

61. Grinspoon, Lester, and Peter Hedblom: "Amphetamine Abuse," *Drug Therapy,* **2**:83–89, 1972.

62. Spencer, D. J.: "Cannabis Induced Psychosis," *Brit. J. Addiction,* **65**:369–372, 1970.

63. Slater, E., A. W. Beard, and E. Glithero: "The Schizophrenia-like Psychoses of Epilepsy," *Brit. J. Psychiat.,* **109**:95–150, 1963.

64. Feighner, J. P., Eli Robins, S. B. Guze et al.: "Diagnostic Criteria for Use in Psychiatric Research," *Arch. Gen. Psychiat.,* **26**:57–63, 1972.

65. Janowsky, David S., Melitta Leff, and Richard S. Epstein: "Playing the Manic Game: Interpersonal Maneuvers of the Acutely Manic Patient," *Arch. Gen. Psychiat.,* **22**:252–261, 1970. Copyright 1970, American Medical Association.

66. Ibid., p. 253.

67. Rosenbaum: op. cit., pp. 30–31.

68. Ibid., p. 31.

69. Ovesey, Lionel: *Homosexuality and Pseudohomosexuality,* Science House, New York, 1969.

70. Woods, Sherwyn M.: "Violence, Psychotherapy of Pseudohomosexual Panic," *Arch.*

Gen. Psychiat., **27**:255–258, 1972; quote is on p. 257. Copyright 1972, American Medical Association.

71. Ibid., p. 257.

72. Lorr, Klett and McNair: op. cit., pp. 254–255.

73. Raskin, David E.: Akathisia: A Side Effect to Be Remembered," *Am. J. Psychiat.,* **129**: 345–347, 1972; quote is from p. 345. Copyright 1972, the American Psychiatric Association.

74. Kline, Nathan S.: "18 Years on Chlorpromazine," letter to the *Am. J. Psychiat.,* **113**: 228, 1974.

75. Winokur, George: "Diagnostic and Genetic Aspects of Affective Illness," *Psychiat. Ann.,* 3:6–15, 1973.

76. Winokur, George: "Depression: The Clinical Perspective," *Pract. Psychiat.,* 2:2, 1974.

77. Guze, S. B., R. A. Woodruff, and P. J. Clayton: "Secondary Affective Disorders: A Study of 95 Cases," *Psychol. Med.,* 1:426–428, 1971.

78. Winokur: "Diagnostic and Genetic Aspects of Affective Illness," loc. cit.

79. Ibid.

80. Ibid.

81. Kaplan, Harold I., and Benhamin J. Sadock: "An Overview of the Major Affective Disorders," *Psychiat. Ann.,* **4**:31, 1974.

82. Ibid.

83. Feighner et al.: loc. cit.

84. Kessler, David: "Preventing Psychiatric Hospitalization: A Crisis Intervention Approach," talk given at Pacific Medical Center, San Francisco, Calif., Mar. 8, 1973.

85. Spensley et al.: loc. cit.

86. Stabenau, James R.: "Schizophrenia: A Family's Projective Identification," *Am. J. Psychiat.,* **130**:19–23, 1973.

87. Enelow, Allen J., and Murray Wexler: *Psychiatry in the Practice of Medicine,* Oxford University Press, New York, 1966, p. 263.

88. Perry: *The Far Side of Madness,* op. cit., chap. 12.

89. Gendlin, Eugene T.: "Research in Psychotherapy with Schizophrenic Patients and the Nature of That Illness," *Am. J. Psychotherap.,* **20**:4–16, 1966.

90. Rosenbaum: op. cit., chap. 14.

JOHN E. BEEBE III, M.D.

CHAPTER 6

Evaluation and Treatment of the Drinking Patient

THE DIFFICULTIES

Drinking patients appear frequently in emergency rooms. They are dealt with in a variety of ways, depending on how their physicians view drinking and alcoholism, but the pattern reflects a major prejudice. Studies conducted by a group led by Morris Chafetz[1] show that patients with jobs, family, and insurance are likely to be admitted to a medical service with a medical diagnosis, and even though the drinking problem is recognized, no psychiatric referral is given.[2] The diagnosis of alcoholism and referral to an alcohol treatment program is reserved for "skid row" persons without signs of social competence who are the poorest treatment risks. The referral is made in a cold, disinterested manner, with little attempt to instill motivation.[3] The poor follow-through of patients who are referred in this manner is used to justify the idea that drinking problems and alcoholism cannot be treated. Thus the best candidates for treatment of such problems are protected from treatment, and the patients who are hardest to treat are pushed toward alcohol treatment programs in a way that greatly reduces their chances of successful entry into therapy.

Thus the emergency therapist who receives a drinking patient on referral must fight hard against a medical stereotype: the alcoholic patient is a childish pest who has brought all his problems on himself and little can be done for him. The psychiatric version of this stereotype is that drinking patients do very poorly in psychiatric treatment too, and therefore any extensive contact with them is wasted professional time. This moralistic approach begs the real question, which is to find the *right* treatment for a drinking patient and to offer it to him in the right way.

Indeed, patients who drink do tax the emergency therapist to develop skills in many areas of competence. Drinking presents a continual challenge to many levels of the patient's existence—biological, spiritual, marital, vocational—all demanding expert attention, some later, some at the moment. Particularly demanding is the acute problem of a drug-induced syndrome that involves a change in state, shifting rapidly over a short period of time, with quick variations in the kind of distress felt and the kind of intervention required. The beginning therapist needs to develop a feeling for the ways patients change in response to chemical stress. This is not an easy skill to master. Almost as difficult is to "open" treatment, not only to members of the patient's ecological group, but also to other health professionals—the internist, the vocational counselor, the social worker at the family service agency, and the visiting public health nurse—whose skills may be required to master particular problems. The therapist almost always has to share the drinking patient with other professionals. It becomes obvious why problem drinkers have been rejected so often: they need (as well as demand) more than average therapeutic skills.

This chapter, which presents basic information, attempts to bridge the distance between the general therapist's skill and the problem drinker's need. First, it will survey the vexing problem of the classification of emotional problems that involve alcohol use and will examine kinds of problem drinkers and criteria for the diagnosis of alcoholism. Next, it looks in detail at the biological effects of alcohol use, examines the organic response to alcoholic intoxication and withdrawal, and suggests methods of treatment for this pharmacologic crisis and its complications. Finally, it presents major psychological considerations in the therapeutic management of patients with drinking problems.

Throughout, two emphases will be apparent. One will be upon the appraisal of the patient's acute state, whether biological or psychological. The second will be upon using a multidisciplinary approach to the resolution of chronic problems. Once the therapist has mastered these difficulties and the different time frames to which they apply, he can offer considerable help, even to those who appear to be the most unpromising candidates.

CLASSIFYING ALCOHOL PROBLEMS

A Matter of Definitions

Not everyone whose psychological difficulties are associated with alcohol should be classed as an alcoholic. In 1967 the Cooperative Commission on the Study of Alcoholism[4] specifically rejected the use of alcoholism as a "collective term for a family of problems correlated with alcohol," or to describe "any use of alcoholic beverages that causes any damage to the individual or society or both."[5] Instead, the Commission's report suggested that the term *alcoholism* be reserved for "a condition in which an individual has lost control over his alcohol intake in the sense that he is consistently unable to refrain from drinking or to stop drinking before getting intoxicated."[6]

Additionally, the Commission's report noted that the term "loss of control" usually includes two phenomena. The first is the inability to do without alcohol or to manage personal tensions without drinking, often called the "inability to abstain." The second is the inability of the individual to stop drinking after he has started. These phenomena are consistent with the conception of alcoholism as a disease characterized by a "pathological dependency on ethanol," which is how alcoholism is classified by the American Psychiatric Association.[7] This latter definition set the stage for the first presentation of uniform criteria for the diagnosis of alcoholism by the National Council on Alcoholism in 1972.

Problem drinking is now the term preferred to refer to "a repetitive use of beverage alcohol causing physical, psychological, or social harm to the drinker or to others."[8] This term makes it possible to discuss persons with alcohol problems without classifying them as suffering from the disease alcoholism, an approach that can all too easily lead to a stereotyped, inflexible approach to evaluation and treatment. At the same time, some problem drinkers are indeed alcoholics.

Kinds of Problem Drinkers

Kissin[9] says that the population of problem drinkers is "completely heterogeneous," ranging from the skid row type (less than 5 percent) through the inner-city dweller (20 percent), the blue-collar worker (40 percent), the middle-class citizen (30 percent), to the upper-class executive (more than 5 percent). In the United States there are thought to be 9 million alcoholics and problem drinkers, as opposed to only 250,000 "hard drug" addicts.

This section offers some impressionistic profiles of the different kinds of problem drinkers who may seek help and gives some preliminary guidelines for intervention. Each one presents a different psychodynamic picture and requires a different kind of psychiatric help. Any given patient, however, may have the characteristics of several profiles. Nevertheless, experience has shown that definite types do exist; the following text introduces some of the common ones. The section ends with current information about the drinking problems of women and the young, both of whom are still poorly defined groups.

The Reactive Drinker. Some people, when faced with emotional stress, turn reactively to alcohol for relief of emerging anxiety and depression. When the stress is resolved, the excessive drinking ends.

> *Example 6-1, Andy.* Friends bring a drunken Andy to the emergency room. He is a good-looking man in his 30s. The friends report that his drinking has increased noticeably in recent months and that tonight he tried to set fire to a wedding picture on the mantel. Andy spills out the story of having been separated from his wife and children for six months, of the sexual difficulties he and his wife had while they were together, and of the loneliness of his recent life. The scene borders on bathos, but the pain is real. The emergency therapist sets an appointment for two days later, asks the friends to take Andy home, put him to bed, and remind him about the appointment when he is sober.
>
> Andy shows up, sober and well-groomed, for the appointment, and remembers only vaguely what he said in the emergency room. The therapist tells Andy what he remembers from the session, and Andy quickly enters into brief psychotherapy to grieve the loss of his wife and to start building a new life for himself.

> After six sessions these goals have been accomplished; he has a new girlfriend and his drinking is no longer excessive.
>
> Six months later he requests a single therapy session to discuss a possible new marriage and some potential in-law problems. The session helps him to obtain a better perspective on these problems; his drinking has remained under control. The therapist last hears from him a year later, when Andy happily reports the birth of his first child in the new marriage.

Reactive drinking frequently appears when a love problem or a crisis at work cannot be resolved. Not all reactive drinkers are as easily or successfully treated as Andy, but most experience a similar process. Once psychotherapy uncovers the underlying life issue, the patient usually decides on his own that excessive use of alcohol affords poor relief and is in fact adding to his problems. (This is in marked contrast to the course of psychotherapy with patients who habitually manipulate their lives into crisis, to have an excuse to drink.)

Reactive drinking sometimes is an attempt to reduce the tensions felt in developmental crises (adolescence, the end of early youth in the late 20s, the onset of mature middle age in the early 40s). Patients who turn to alcohol at these times may be using it (wrongly) as an antidepressant. Indeed, successful psychotherapy for them may require the adjunctive use of an antidepressant drug as they approach the deep problematic issue. It is as if the patient needed to switch from alcohol to a more effective medication while he works out the problems of his life.

The Schizophrenic Drinker. Some schizophrenic patients use alcohol as a tranquilizer to mask the disquieting symptoms of chronic anxiety, sense of unreality, threatening hallucinations and delusions, and so forth. In other instances, marginal or poorly compensated borderline characters drink, and the ensuing loss of psychological and physical defenses allows the emergence of frankly psychotic ideation and behavior. Some nonschizo-phrenic persons suffer from an aftereffect of chronic drinking called alcoholic hallucinosis, which may be difficult to differentiate from paranoid schizophrenia. Finally, many schizo-phrenic patients stop taking phenothiazines when they start drinking.

Example 6-2, Bill. Police have picked up Bill, a 35-year-old veteran, for assaulting union pickets outside a movie theatre. There was no discernible motive.

The emergency therapist learns that Bill lives alone on a VA pension of 100 percent psychi-atric disability and that he has been in and out of VA psychiatric hospitals since his separation from the service for psychiatric disabilities. His last outpatient visit was three months ago. He evades the interviewer's glance, grimaces when asked a question, and gives largely evasive answers until, in a single rush of breath he says, "Yeah, the voices told me to do it—why don't you get it done?" At this point he is willing to be hospitalized. He later reveals that he had started to drink heavily a week before, when the voices had first started to get louder, and that he had tried to keep them under control by drinking a quart of gin a day. At that time he had discontinued the chlorpro-mazine which had been prescribed for him. On the day he had been picked up, the main voice had gotten particularly loud, insisting he "Go beat up that picket!"

The diagnoses of schizophrenia and alcoholism are often used by federal and local health facilities as much for administrative purposes as for medical ones. Public funds may be available for the treatment and support of patients with one diag-nosis but not the other. The emergency therapist should make his own, independent judgment rather than rely too heavily on records from VA, state, and local hospitals. Some schizophrenic patients are also alcoholic, but most alcoholic patients are not schizophrenic. In either event, withdrawal from alcohol (often in a hospital) is the first order of business. After that, schizo-phrenic patients can be returned to a safer and more effective tranquilizer. Alcohol interferes with the judgment of a schizophrenic patient as much as it does with anyone else's, and the rate of violence and crime for schizophrenic patients is much higher when they have been drinking than when they have not been.

The Cyclothymic Drinker. There is a small but highly memorable group of people who seem extraordinarily dependent on the praise and es-teem of others to feel good about themselves. The external reassurances must be many and constant; these people are exquisitely vulnerable to narcis-sistic injury and often expend prodigious energies in manipulating others to meet their needs. Their moods go up and down; their lives seem to be muted forms of a manic-depressive cycle, hence the term "cyclothymic." Sober, they often appear to be charming extraverts; when they are drinking, their charm may become pathetic and irritating.

Example 6-3, Cal. Cal has just awakened from a night during which he had slept off a drunk in a holding bed in the emergency room. He is past 40, but he pushes his weather-beaten face into the puckish grin of a 9-year-old child. He asks you your whole name and proceeds to call you by your first name from the first minutes of the interview. He inquires where you went to medical school (especially if you are not a physician) and proceeds to name various doc-tors in the city where you say you studied. Anything you reveal about yourself may be-come the focus of Cal's next sentence.

During the interview, Cal has more history than you can possibly assimilate: he seems to have done everything, lived everywhere, met everyone. The names of people, places, and jobs pour out of him.

Finally exasperated, you ask Cal what is troubling him now, and he starts to cry. His pain is genuine: he has no resources, his friends have deserted him. Only you can help him.

You ask him what you can do. "I'm not sure," Cal says, "I have no place to stay." He implies he will talk more about treatment plans *after* he has been admitted; it is beneath his dignity to discuss plans when he has no roof over his head. He tightens the yellow scarf around his neck and winks at you, behind his tears. "You doctors have a tough time," he says, and smiles kindly. Treatment? It's your move.

In such patients alcohol is part of the up-and-down cycle of ego inflation and deflation. The vicissitudes of the drug effect, its joys and miseries, its anxious highs and depressed lows, have become integrated into the lifestyle of the patient. Would he be less cyclothymic if he abstained from alcohol? Probably, but one of the functions of his drinking is to keep him on the exciting roller coaster of mood swings that follow the rhythm of alcohol intoxication and withdrawal. Indeed, other drugs such as LSD, marihuana, cocaine, amphetamines, and barbiturates are used along with alcohol to exaggerate the ever-shifting pattern of highs and lows such patients seem to require. The increased use of alcohol by frankly manic-depressive patients during the manic phase has recently been reported. [10]

In treatment, the underlying mood disturbance, the problem of self-esteem, and the need for a cycle of success and defeat must be recognized. Alcoholics Anonymous (AA) may provide such patients a model program. Bateson [11] notes that for the grandiose, power-loving person who insists on his ability to master every situation, AA tends to do what alcohol does: it reduces his inflation. The "first step" for the individual in AA is to admit that he is powerless with regard to alchohol. When he takes this step and admits weakness, he is given much attention, praise, and peer support; indeed, he will be criticized for proclaiming any strength in being able to hold his liquor. This paradox undercuts the power motivation and places the individual in a more realistic position vis-à-vis others and his own instincts.

The Heavy Drinker under Pressure. Some persons start drinking heavily and steadily during high school, college, or military service. They are able to handle their drinking relatively well for many years; perhaps they even take perverse pride in never missing a day's work. Although they are not terribly happy at how inefficient their hangovers make them, they pride themselves on being able to hold their liquor and dismiss the protestations of their wives and the curious glances of their supervisors. The years catch up with them. The iron constitution starts to rust, and the ravages of chronic alcoholism, even while the drinker tries to deny them, become increasingly apparent to families and employers.

Example 6-4, Don. Don is 38, married and has children of ages 8 and 4. He has worked as an airline mechanic for fifteen years. His wife Diane leads him firmly to the psychiatrist's office in the emergency room. He is tremulous and red-eyed. Her upper lip quivers, but she has a determined look. She announces that Don wants to enter the hospital for treatment of alcoholism.

The psychiatrist asks Don what he feels, and Don says, "If you think that's what I should do, Doc." The psychiatrist asks Don what *he* wants to do, and Don says, "You're the doctor."

Diane says pleadingly to the psychiatrist, "We hoped you'd admit him. It's taken a lot to get him here." She mentioned that she has told Don that if he doesn't get treatment for his alcoholism, she is going to leave him. Additionally, he is under the threat of suspension from work unless he participates in an alcohol treatment program. Don hands the psychiatrist the name of the airline doctor who wants to be called after a decision has been made.

The patient who likes to drink appears for treatment only when the drinking problem poses a threat to another vital need. When this crisis is the threat of the loss of a job, a marriage, or a lover, an involved person may bring the patient in. The therapist may well be tempted to try to stand between the patient and this outside pressure, noting that when the others "lay off" the patient becomes less anxious because his is not the motive force for change. The therapist should consider the positive value of the pressure and the anxiety it engenders. Without it, would the patient realize anything was wrong? Thus the wise therapist often *supports* the ecological group when it applies pressure to the patient. He reminds the significant others that the patient's tentative entry into therapy is not a signal for them to reduce this pressure: the ambivalent patient will continue to need outside insistence on change if his own motivation to abstain from drinking is to persist.

On the other hand, scapegoating the drinking person for all work and family problems should not be supported. As part of the pressure toward health, the others should be encouraged to enter treatment along with the patient and avail themselves of consultation or therapy to work toward an understanding of roles they have played in producing the alcoholic solution to conflict. When the patient is well into mastering his drinking problem, members of the ecological group may try to maneuver him into "being to blame" because of his past behavior. These attempts usually reflect difficulties on the part of the others in looking at their own contributions to family conflicts. A patient's alcoholic "slip" after a long period of remission is a particularly good time to observe and identify such scapegoating behavior. Often it will develop that the family has literally pushed the patient into drinking again. Family members can be helped to see their destructive influence when the effects of it on the patient's drinking are immediate rather than long-range.

Generally, when a drinking person is brought in for help by someone else, it is a good idea to evaluate whether the other person desires to motivate or to scapegoat the patient. Usually, provoking anxiety is motivating and provoking guilt is scapegoating. Much progress in treatment depends upon the therapist's ability to recognize

when to side with, and when to question, outside pressure. For patients who have been drinking heavily for a long time, outside pressure to stop, however brusquely presented, is almost always caring behavior and a motivation for change. Such pressure should be supported.

The Heavy Drinker without Funds. Some heavy drinkers run out of money and need food and shelter. County jails have served as semisatisfactory halfway houses for such patients; hospital emergency rooms are another portal of entry to institutional care. Hospitals are not hostels, and inhospitable doctors are often hostile to patients who do not present an interesting set of medical or psychiatric symptoms. Some alcoholic patients have become expert at playing the roles of "interesting patients."

> *Example 6-5, Earl.* Earl is a man in his early 50s. His hair is still blonde, and he dresses eccentrically in toga and sandals. He wears a look of benign philosophical understanding. There is alcohol on his breath. When asked what is wrong, Earl gazes through an open window and says, "Young man, my spirits have sunk down." Asked to explain, he responds condescendingly, "Young man, have you ever heard of the planet Venus?" He explains that he is in daily contact with higher intelligences from the cloudy planet, and that he has single-handedly saved the Earth from invasion. Now he feels too weak to continue without rest. It is the twenty-second of the month, and he must be strong when the first comes.
>
> Earl is admitted with a diagnosis of chronic paranoid schizophrenia in acute exacerbation. His airy imperviousness resists therapeutic efforts for eight days. On the first of the month, Earl's pension check arrives, and he asks for discharge. When asked what he has got from being hospitalized, he finally confides, "A place to crash, you fool."

Many alcoholic patients have learned how to con

a hospital into a free ride while they wait for their disability checks. It is wise to confront their lack of financial resources directly. Helping the alcoholic patient without funds to find temporarily safe shelter is a wholly appropriate task for the emergency therapist. The hospital is an inappropriate "hotel."

A penniless patient may still want treatment. Often a good test of motivation is to ask the patient if he is willing to take disulfiram (Antabuse®) after detoxification is effected. If he is, the patient is probably motivated to participate in an alcohol treatment program. Another approach is to refer the patient to a public hostel but to invite him to return for inpatient treatment after the first of the month, when definite detoxification can be undertaken. In either case, the therapist reserves the hospital setting for those who seriously desire treatment.

The Middle-aged Alcoholic in Crisis. Many middle-aged drinkers manage to keep functioning over the years until, because of an accident, malign fate, or physical deterioration, they cannot cope any longer. They turn to alcohol even more until a single event or a succession of events makes life a burden, and a self-destructive or suicidal crisis builds.

Example 6-6, Fritz. Fritz is 57 years old. He comes to the emergency room with a stricken look; his chart contains many previous diagnoses of problem drinking and alcoholism. Earlier in the evening he developed chest pains and came to the hospital to be checked. His EKG shows no change; indeed, the surgical intern suggests he may have a hyperventilation syndrome. He refuses to leave the hospital; psychiatric consultation is requested.

He says, "Doc, I think I may be killing myself." He tells you that lately, since the death of his wife from cirrhosis ("We both drank a lot, Doctor"), he has been drinking even more. Two days ago he accidentally set a fire in his apartment. Tonight, he had chest pain that lasted an hour. He admits to being depressed, and when asked about suicide, he starts crying and says, "I bought a gun today. I figured if I got drunk enough, I'd have guts enough to pull the trigger." He had tried to fire the gun at himself, but missed. He hoped that his heart reading would be "just off enough" to ensure his admission to the hospital for a few days. "But I know, Doctor," he concludes to the therapist, "that it's your department I need."

The diagnosis of alcoholism does not preclude other diagnoses. The therapist should probe especially deeply for suicidal and homicidal concerns because this is the population in which both suicide and homicide occur most frequently. A visit to the hospital is often a "cry for help," as is the case with Fritz. His need for shelter and emotional support should be respected: he is asking for a lifeline. It is sometimes difficult to distinguish Fritz from Earl. Despite Fritz's alcoholism, his appeal for help is typical of the proud, compulsive, widowed older man who is high-risk for suicide. The crisis of his depression may be the springboard for treatment that was impossible before. Often, older patients will be willing to give up alcohol for health reasons when in younger, healthier years they could not be persuaded to do so. As one man in his 50s put it, "It finally caught up with me."

The Woman Problem Drinker. In this country women who drink have been far less numerous than men. According to Verdery,[12] the ratio of women to men who drink excessively is 1:5; in England, 1:2; and in Norway, 1:23. Many observers feel the United States ratio is increasing because women are growing less inhibited about drinking in public.

The woman problem drinker is frequently divorced, in the crisis of middle life, has grown children, and no future career to inspire her. She may be very hard to engage in treatment, harder than a man, possibly because most treatment programs are predominantly oriented to male needs. Frequently another sympathetic woman can be the bridge to treatment. The visiting public health nurse can perform this service.

> *Example 6-7.* In one such case it took seven years of a growing and deepening relationship, punctuated by help given in a variety of critical family events, for a mother of many children, a capable and very worthwhile person with a long alcoholic history, to ask the nurse to go with her to a treatment clinic. Up until then she had refused any such suggestions and had reacted to a meeting of Alcoholics Anonymous with scorn and revulsion. She stuck with the treatment, which was reasonably successful, though it involved quite a few backsliding incidents. [13]

The case of Alice (Chapters 2 and 3) is a sustained description of a woman with a drinking problem who faces the crisis of middle life. She is in a state of almost total psychosocial disruption yet is attempting to achieve the dignified married role traditionally required of noncareer women. Her story also points up the high suicide risk present in all problem drinkers.

The Young Drinker. A burgeoning alcohol problem is appearing among the young. A recent review article [14] notes that

> The National Parent-Teacher Association estimates that of the 75% high school students who drink, more than one-half have a serious alcohol problem. Alcoholics Anonymous (A.A.) reports that 10% of its membership of 400,000 is currently under 21 years old, and one 10-year-old member recently marked his first anniversary with Alcoholics Anonymous, capping a drink-free year.

No one personality profile typifies these young problem drinkers, although sexual identity conflicts and parental alcoholism seem to play important roles.

The Diagnosis of Alcoholism

Which of these problem drinkers are alcoholic? In the past there has been a tendency to overdiagnose alcoholism once the problem of alcohol use has been uncovered. To qualify as a *disease,* alcohol use must have been sufficient to lead to transient or permanent deterioration of psychosocial and/or physiological function. (These changes may occur within two years after the individual has started to drink, and in early adolescence.) Isolated episodes of inebriation, however unfortunate their consequences, cannot be considered as evidence of the disease of alcoholism.

A major contribution in the definition of the physiological and behavioral criteria of alcoholism came in 1972 with the simultaneous publication of a system developed by the National Council on Alcoholism in the *American Journal of Psychiatry* [15] and the *Annals of Internal Medicine.* [16] Some of the tabular data of that system has been adapted in Table 6-1. We strongly encourage those who are going to work with alcoholic patients to read the original article.*

In the Council's system, signs and symptoms of possible alcoholism are grouped into two tracks: Track I is a list of physiological and clinical indicators, and Track II consists of behavioral, psychological, and attitudinal indicators. Each track is subdivided into major and minor criteria, and each of these is assigned a diagnostic level. A criterion with a diagnostic level of 1 is clearly associated with alcoholism; a level of 2 is highly suggestive of alcoholism, and a level of 3 indicates possible alcoholism or an incidental finding.

For example, see Track I, Major Criteria, Item A1, physiological dependency: physiological dependence as manifested by evidence of a *withdrawal syndrome* when the intake of alcohol is interrupted or decreased without substitution of other sedation: (*a*) gross tremor; (*b*) hallucinosis; (*c*) withdrawal seizures; (*d*) delirium tremens. Each

---

*Reprints are easily obtainable from any local office of the National Council on Alcoholism.

**Table 6-1: Major and Minor Criteria for the Diagnosis of Alcoholism
[National Council on Alcoholism]** [15]

MAJOR CRITERIA

Criterion	Diagnostic Level	Criterion	Diagnostic Level

TRACK I. PHYSIOLOGICAL AND CLINICAL

A. Physiological Dependency

1. Physiological dependence as manifested by evidence of a withdrawal syndrome when the intake of alcohol is interrupted or decreased without substitution of other sedation.

    (a) Gross tremor   1
    (b) Hallucinosis   1
    (c) Withdrawal seizures   1
    (d) Delirium tremens   1

2. Evidence of tolerance to the effects of alcohol. (There may be a decrease in previously high levels of tolerance late in the course.)

    (a) A blood alcohol level of more than 150 mg. without gross evidence of intoxication.   1
    (b) The consumption of one-fifth of a gallon of whiskey or equivalent daily for more than one day, by a 180 lb. individual.   1

3. Alcoholic "blackout" periods   2

B. Clinical: Major-Alcohol-Associated Illnesses, in a person who drinks regularly. In such individuals, evidence of physiological and psychological dependence should be searched for.

Fatty degeneration in absence of other known cause   2
Alcoholic hepatitis   1
Laennec's cirrhosis   2

Pancreatitis in the absence of cholelithiasis   2
Chronic gastritis   3
Hematological disorders:
Anemia: hypochromic, normocytic, macrocytic, hemolytic with stomatocytosis, low folic acid.   3
Clotting disorders: prothrombin elevation, thrombocytopenia   3
Wernicke-Korsakoff syndrome   2
Alcoholic cerebellar degeneration   1
Cerebral degeneration in absence of Alzheimer's disease or arteriosclerosis   2
Peripheral neuropathy (see also beriberi)   2
Toxic amblyopia   3
Alcohol myopathy   2
Alcoholic cardiomyopathy   2
Beriberi   3
Pellagra   3

TRACK II. BEHAVIORAL, PSYCHOLOGICAL AND ATTITUDINAL

All chronic conditions of psychological dependence occur in dynamic equilibrium with intrapsychic and interpersonal consequences. In alcoholism, similarly, there are varied effects on character and family.

1. Drinking despite strong medical contraindication known to patient.   1
2. Drinking despite strong, identified, social contraindication (job loss for intoxication, marriage disruption because of drinking, arrest for intoxication, driving while intoxicated).   1
3. Patient's subjective complaint of loss of control of alcohol consumption.   2

Table 6-1 (cont'd):   Major and Minor Criteria for the Diagnosis of Alcoholism

	MINOR CRITERIA			
Criterion	Diagnostic Level		Criterion	Diagnostic Level

TRACK I. PHYSIOLOGICAL AND CLINICAL

A. Direct Effects (ascertained by examination)

  1. Early: Odor of alcohol on breath at time of medical appointment   **2**

  2. Middle:

    Alcohol facies   **2**

    Vascular engorgement of face   **2**

    Toxic amblyopia   **3**

    Increased incidence of infections   **3**

    Cardiac arrhythmias   **3**

    Peripheral neuropathy   **2**

  3. Late (see Major Criteria, Track 1, B)

B. Indirect Effects

  1. Early:

    Tachycardia   **3**

    Flushed face   **3**

    Nocturnal diaphoresis   **3**

  2. Middle:

    Ecchymoses on lower extremities, arms or chest   **3**

    Cigarette or other burns on hands or chest   **3**

    Hyperreflexia, or if drinking heavily hyporeflexia (permanent hyporeflexia may be a residuum of alcoholic polyneuritis)   **3**

  3. Late: Decreased tolerance   **3**

C. Laboratory Tests

  1. *Major — Direct*

    Blood alcohol level at any time of more than 300 mg/100 ml   **1**

  2. *Major — Indirect*

    Serum osmolality (reflects blood alcohol levels): every 22.4 increase over 200 mOsm/liter reflects 50 mg/100 ml alcohol   **2**

  3. *Minor* — Indirect

    Results of alcohol ingestion:

      Hypoglycemia, hypochloremic alkalosis   **3**

      Low magnesium level   **2**

      Lactic acid elevation, transient uric acid elevation, potassium depletion   **3**

    Indications of liver abnormality:

      SGOT elevation   **3**

      SGPT elevation; BSP elevation; Bilirubin elevation; Urinary uroblinogen elevation; Serum A/G ratio reversal   **2**

    Blood and blood clotting:

      Anemia: hypochromic, normocytic, macrocytic, hemolytic with stomatocytosis, low folic acid   **3**

      Clotting disorders: prothrombin elevation, thrombocytopenia   **3**

    ECG abnormalities:

      Cardiac arrhythmias, tachycardia: T waves dimpled, cloven, or spinous; atrial fibrillation; ventricular premature contractions; abnormal P waves   **2**

    EEG abnormalities:

      Decreased or increased REM sleep, depending on phase   **3**

      Loss of delta sleep   **3**

      Other reported findings   **3**

      Decreased immune response; Decreased response to Synacthen test; Chromosomal damage from alcoholism   **3**

Table 6-1 (cont'd):   Major and Minor Criteria for the Diagnosis of Alcoholism

MINOR CRITERIA (cont'd.)

Criterion	Diagnostic Level	Criterion	Diagnostic Level

TRACK II.   BEHAVIORAL, PSYCHOLOGICAL AND ATTITUDINAL

Criterion	Diagnostic Level	Criterion	Diagnostic Level
A. Behavioral		**B. Psychological and Attitudinal**	
1. Direct effects		1. Direct effects	
Early: gulping drinks	3	Early: When talking freely, makes frequent reference to drinking alcohol, people being "bombed," "stoned," etc., or admits drinking more than peer group	2
Surreptitious drinking; morning drinking	2		
Middle: Repeated conscious attempts at abstinence	2	Middle: Drinking to relieve anger, insomnia, fatigue, depression, social discomfort	2
Late: Blatant indiscriminate use of alcohol	1	Late: Psychological symptoms consistent with permanent organic brain syndrome (see also Major Criteria, Track I, B)	2
Skid Row or equivalent social level	2		
2. Indirect effects		2. Indirect effects	
Early: Medical excuses from work for variety of reasons; Shifting from one alcoholic beverage to another; Preference for drinking companions, bars, and taverns; Loss of interest in activities not directly associated with drinking	2	Early: Unexplained changes in family, social, and business relationships: complaints about wife, job, and friends	3
Late: Chooses employment that facilitates drinking; Frequent automobile accidents; History of family members undergoing psychiatric treatment; School and behavioral problems in children; Frequent change of residence for poorly defined reasons	3	Spouse makes complaints about drinking behavior, reported by patient or spouse	2
		Major family disruptions: separation, divorce, threats of divorce	3
		Job loss (due to increasing interpersonal difficulties), frequent job changes, financial difficulties	3
Anxiety-relieving mechanisms, such as telephone calls inappropriate in time, distance, person, or motive (telephonitis)	2	Late: Overt expression of more regressive defense mechanisms: denial, projection, etc.; Resentment, jealousy, paranoid attitudes; Symptoms of depression: isolation, crying, suicidal preoccupation	3
Outbursts of rage and suicidal gestures while drinking	2		
		Feelings that he is "losing his mind"	2

of those four manifestations of withdrawal carries a diagnostic level of 1; a patient showing one or more of them should be considered alcoholic.

By similar logic, patients satisfying other clinical or behavioral *major criteria* are at a diagnostic level of 1 alcoholic. Patients satisfying several *minor criteria* are most probably alcoholic, especially if those criteria are drawn from one track. Note that a blood alcohol level of greater than 300 mg/100 ml is a major criterion, even though it may be associated with several minor criteria of a clinical nature. In many cases the minor criteria categories also help differentiate between early, middle, and late stages of alcoholism. The presence of only minor criteria indicators at a diagnostic level of 3 is probably *not* diagnostic of alcoholism.

In short, these criteria (described in greater detail in the original publication) afford the therapist a set of relatively easily determined physiological and psychosocial standards by which he can assess a patient's degree of alcoholism at the initial evaluation. The therapist can reassess the patient's condition as treatment progresses to document improvement, stability, or deterioration. Proper use of these criteria can protect the overzealous therapist from the pitfall of diagnosing alcoholism when only a few level 3 criteria are satisfied. They can aid him in properly making the diagnosis when one or more level 1 features are present.

In estimating daily consumption, the whiskey equivalent chart (Table 6-2) is useful. Alcoholic patients are notorious for underestimating their consumption with statements such as, "Oh, I only drink a couple of beers or so." The interviewer should ask specific questions; for instance, ask the patient to examine a typical day's drinking. Does he drink in the morning; at lunch; before, during, or after dinner? What does he drink at each of those times (whiskey, gin, wine, beer)? How much at each juncture? How many shots go into each hard drink? How big are the shots (one ounce, doubles?) And so on. When totaled, even the patient may be surprised at the quantity of ethyl alcohol he consumes in its various guises during a twenty-four-hour period. Often, however, it is quite difficult to obtain an accurate drinking history from the actively drinking patient, and he must be questioned about other criteria.

Table 6-2: Whiskey Equivalents of Consumption of Wine and Beer

Equivalents are based on:
  0.8 quart = one-fifth gallon
  32 ounces = 1 quart
  Whiskey contains 43 percent ethyl alcohol
  Fortified wine contains 20 percent ethyl alcohol
  Table wine contains 12 percent ethyl alcohol
  Beer contains 4 percent ethyl alcohol

Person's Weight (pounds)	Whiskey (quarts)	Fortified Wine (quarts)	Table Wine (quarts)	Beer (quarts)	Beer (12-oz. bottles)
220	1.0	2.0	3.6	11.0	29
200	0.9	1.9	3.2	9.7	26
180	0.8	1.7	2.9	8.6	23
160	0.7	1.5	2.5	7.5	20
140	0.6	1.3	2.2	6.5	17
120	0.5	1.0	1.8	5.4	14

THE PHARMACOLOGY OF ALCOHOL

We turn from the identification of alcoholism in the problem drinker to the specific effects of the drug alcohol on the central nervous system. Both its enormous appeal and the great capacity of this drug to do harm can be traced to its specific pharmacology. Additionally, patients appear at various stages of intoxication or withdrawal, and it is necessary to develop skill in recognizing the various states that are produced during these pharmacological stages.

Acute Alcohol Intoxication

It is easy to believe that the experience of being drunk is so universal that no description is necessary. In fact, drunkenness is a great mimic of other psychiatric syndromes, and a great deal of time is wasted by the beginning emergency therapist in gathering "psychiatric" data from patients in the drunken state. The intoxicated person, for his part, is all too eager to bend the listener's ear and can be quite skillful at impersonating hysteria, schizophrenia, depression, or whatever seems to be required to hold his psychiatric audience.

A survey of the stages of intoxication is in order. These resemble the stages of anesthesia, from excitation to depression. The best description of them is an old one: verbose, jocose, lachrymose, bellicose, and comatose. A classic description of alcohol intoxication shows how these stages progress:

In a mild state of intoxication there are unnecessary vocal efforts, pathos which is incongruent in view of the unessential content of conversation, exaggerated expressions of affect, laughter, and exaggerated motorics. With this comes an increase in the subjective feeling of well-being. After larger alcohol intake there is impairment of sensory function, the thought processes become superficial, and conversation becomes flatter. There is a tendency towards flight of ideas. Judgment is clouded and self-criticism, especially [recognition of the] disproportion between the increased ego feeling and the objective ability to produce. This contrast is sometimes vaguely felt by the intoxicated person and results in a feeling of insecurity. On the basis of this mood tone then develop symptoms of irritability and readiness to paranoid reactions. In a severe state of intoxication there is ataxia, staggering gait, slurred speech and finally, severe impairment of perception. The intoxicated person becomes apathetic and falls into a deep sleep. Although some personality characteristics break through into the picture of intoxication it is not possible to construct a law of relation between type of alcohol reaction in personality, especially if the picture may change on different occasions in the same person. The degree of drunkenness is related to the alcohol concentration in the blood only in a very broad way. [17]

Others have pointed out the disruption of perception, as did the philosopher Kant, who wrote that "Drunkenness is the unnatural state of inability to organize sense impressions according to the laws of experience." Psychiatrists are fond of noting that "Conscience is that portion of the personality which is soluble in alcohol."

All these observations make it clear that a person who is acutely intoxicated may show disorders of thought, affect, perception, or judgment and that an observer may be led into thinking the drunken patient is schizophrenic, manic-depressive, organic, or antisocial, depending on his state at the initial evaluation. The important clue to intoxication, when breath odor or history are not diagnostic, is the extreme lability: no other condition involves such dramatic changes of state over so short a period of time.

Pathological Intoxication

In some individuals, dissociative, rage, or psychotic reactions appear after only minimal amounts of alcohol have been consumed. Following a period of grossly disruptive behavior, the patient may fall into a profound sleep. This untoward response to alcohol should not be confused with similar reactions appearing after large quantities of alcohol have been consumed. Sufferers from this condition often have explosive (or "epileptoid") personalities. They need to abstain from alcohol altogether.

Limitations of Interviewing the Drunken Patient

The therapist should guard against making any psychiatric diagnosis while the patient is still in the drunken state; base-line ego functioning can be appraised only when the patient is sober. Similarly, the therapist must be cautious about the significance he attaches to alcoholic monologues. Although these can be extremely meaningful, even beautiful, to the listener who has not heard them before, the patient may not derive much benefit from what he reveals when drunk. The deep material is analogous to the material obtained through amytal interviewing. Many of the ordinarily repressed emotional conflicts rise to the surface with refreshing immediacy, but the same material sinks down again without a trace when the patient is fully conscious. The meaning, as well as the content, is again repressed; along with it goes the feeling of rapport with the listener. All that is left for the patient may be a vague sense of uneasiness at having somehow exposed himself against his will.

However, what is observed about the patient's personality and behavior during the drunken state is valid for predicting how the patient is likely to behave the next time he is drunk. Therefore, the therapist should take careful note of the kind of pathology that belongs to the patient's drunken state, not as a psychiatric diagnosis in itself, but as a means of determining how alcohol influences his potential for suicide, homicide, psychosis, and antisocial behavior.

Acute Alcohol Withdrawal

The emergence of disturbing symptoms upon withdrawal is the proof of dependency on any drug. In alcohol-dependent patients, withdrawal symptoms appear forty-eight to seventy-two hours after the intake of alcohol is abruptly stopped or sharply reduced. The main symptoms are (1) tremor, (2) convulsions, (3) hallucinosis, and (4) clouding of the sensorium. (When the fourth is of sufficient degree, it is called delirium tremens, which is the most serious stage of alcohol withdrawal. In the past it has had a 15 percent mortality.) It must be pointed out that these symptoms may appear even though the patient continues to drink: withdrawal symptoms may appear when the rate of intake is *reduced* (with a consequent dip in the blood level of alcohol); absolute cessation of intake is not required.

Some withdrawal symptoms are direct effects of

depriving a dependent nervous system of alcohol, others indirect effects of the nutritional disturbances that also affect the brain. Therefore it is important to realize that symptoms of *acute intoxication*, symptoms of *withdrawal*, and symptoms of *nutritional deficiency* may all be present at the same time, contributing to impairment of brain function and to the "alcohol withdrawal syndrome."

By the time a drinking patient comes to the emergency room his brain function may be seriously compromised. Most of the early indications that this crisis is developing are subjective: he feels awful and cannot organize his thinking properly. It is imperative that the significance of his subjective discomfort be grasped so appropriate treatment can be instituted before the crisis results in death or permanent brain injury.

Milton Gross[18] has defined the withdrawal syndrome as advancing through a series of stages: early, prodromal, and advanced. This outline will be followed to present basic information about the course of alcohol withdrawal.

Early Phase. Not every alcoholic bout ends in withdrawal symptoms. Usually there is a severe depressive reaction involving a loss of appetite and sleep disturbance, which leads to a great intensification of the desire to drink. Alcohol intake becomes extremely heavy, but the patient may not feel his drinks as much as usual. They only seem to cancel the major depressive symptoms. This is the point at which the person finds himself drinking around the clock yet feels sober much of the time. Alvarez[19] describes such depressive drinking:

Mostly, I'm a social drinker. Like everyone else, I've been drunk in my time but it's not really my style; I value my control too highly. This time, however, I went at the bottle with a pure need, as though parched. I drank before I got out of bed, almost before my eyes were open. I continued steadily throughout the morning until, by lunchtime, I had half a bottle of whiskey inside me and was beginning to feel human. Not drunk: that first half-bottle simply brought me to the point of calm where I usually began. Which is not particularly calm. Around lunchtime a friend—also depressed, also drinking—joined me at the pub and we boozed until closing time. Back home, with our wives, we kept at it steadily through the afternoon and evening, late into the night. The important thing was not to stop. In this way, I got through a bottle of whiskey a day, and a good deal of wine and beer. Yet it had little effect.

The culmination of Alvarez' drinking was a suicide attempt on Christmas Day. The holiday drinking obscured his own marked increase in intake. Although treatment of withdrawal is not indicated at this stage of drinking, recognition of the pattern of depressive drinking and evaluation of the suicide risk is imperative. (Alvarez called his old therapist on Christmas Eve and was given an appointment for the day *after* Christmas, on the face of Alvarez' statement that it could wait.) This is the phase of withdrawal in which the prompt cessation of alcohol intake and transfer to an antidepressant drug can avoid major physical and psychiatric complications. Without prompt intervention, progression to a stage in which withdrawal symptoms will appear is almost certain—unless, as in Alvarez' case, another self-destructive act supervenes.

Prodromal Phase. The patient begins to experience (in addition to intoxication) the toxic organ effects of prolonged excessive drinking, disturbances secondary to nutritional deficiencies, and the early effects of alcohol withdrawal called "impending DTs." This phase involves gastrointestinal, perceptual, motor, vegetative, and sleep disturbances. It need not lead to frank delirium tremens.

The gastrointestinal symptoms include nausea and vomiting. "Dry heaves" appear when the patient awakes, presumably because of relative alcohol withdrawal during sleep. There may also be gastritis and an increased loss of appetite, leading to still further dependence on alcohol for caloric needs.

Perceptual disturbances are found in auditory, visual, and somesthetic disturbances. The most common auditory symptom, according to Gross, is *tinnitus*, a ringing, blowing, or whistling sound in the ears. Some patients experience clicking, popping, or shotlike sounds. (These have been related to spasms of the tensor stapedius muscle in the middle ear and are considered by some to be the basis for the later appearance of frank auditory hallucinosis, as the organism attempts to integrate the unfamiliar input.) Visual symptoms are spots, flashes of light resembling falling rain, and blurring of vision. Bodily sensations include paresthesias and numbness. Motor disturbances include marked tremulousness, weakness or severe cramps in the extremities, and impairment of gait.

Massive autonomic (vegetative) nervous system discharge is marked by a rapid pulse, fever, hypertension, and profuse night sweats accompanied by itching and increased tremulousness. Sleep disturbance is great, starting with insomnia (which eventually cannot be relieved by alcohol) and leading to brief periods of restless sleep punctuated by nightmares.

At this stage, intellectual functions start to become impaired, and the first signs of confusion appear. This is the stage at which many authorities recommend hospitalization and at which many alcoholic patients seeking help experience professional rejection.

Advanced Symptoms. The next stage is the appearance of frank psychotic symptoms and autonomic reactions that can lead to death in as many as 15 percent of those treated.

Gross[20] calls this stage the *Walpurgisnacht* of the actual acute withdrawal. Serious failure of mental functions and hallucinatory manifestations occur. Delusions may be present. Recent memory, concentration, integrative and synthetic functions, and orientation to time and place are all impaired. As stable internal points of reference for contact with reality disappear, patients are driven to seek cues from external sources. When these are absent (as at night when the patient lies alone in the dark, afraid or unable to sleep), psychotic manifestations emerge.

Because a certain percentage of the alcoholic population is schizophrenic, it becomes important to distinguish organic psychosis in the phase of alcohol withdrawal from paranoid schizophrenia. Both conditions involve delusions and auditory hallucinations. In schizophrenia, however, the voices appear before other signs of toxicity (such as disorientation) and persist after the toxic effects of withdrawal are gone. Moreover, the voices are more plausible in cases of withdrawal psychosis, and their statements are exclusively in the third person. ("He did that; look at him," and so on.) Finally, suspiciousness and hostility are usually present in withdrawal psychoses only when the physician is not identified as a professional, whereas in paranoid schizophrenia the physician may be seen as an enemy even when his medical role is fully grasped.

Convulsions are another advanced symptom, occurring in as many as 60 percent of patients treated at this stage. Electroencephalographic evidence shows multiple disturbances in sleep. In addition to rebound of fast-wave rapid-eye-movement (REM) sleep, there seems to be an interruption of deep, dreamless delta-wave sleep. Recovery from the withdrawal accompanies the reestablishment of delta-wave sleep, experienced subjectively by the patient as "the first good night of sleep." Anxiety and confusion may also play a role in lowering the seizure threshold, pointing to the need for good environmental support.

The autonomic discharge of the prodromal period is intensified, with a pronounced rise in fever over 100°F in dangerously ill patients. Usually the term delirium tremens is reserved for cases that show *both* marked clouding of sensorium *and* this massive, life-threatening autonomic discharge. Lesser degrees of withdrawal psychosis, characterized primarily by tremulousness and auditory or visual hallucinations, are not as serious and

are usually spoken of as "acute alcoholic hallucinosis."

TREATMENT IN THE PHASE OF ALCOHOL WITHDRAWAL

Management of Uncomplicated Alcohol Withdrawal

Properly treated, alcohol withdrawal usually runs its course within five days. Convulsions may appear forty-eight to seventy-two hours after treatment has begun and yet be directly related to the withdrawal. Fevers and hallucinations appearing twenty-four to thirty-six hours after treatment has begun often point to a complicating medical or psychiatric condition. We shall discuss complications later in this chapter.

It is helpful to learn a standard method for handling withdrawal. The following list of procedures was adapted from Gross,[21] then modified by suggestions taken from O'Briant:[22]

1. *Vitamins.* On first contact, the patient is given an injection of 100 mg of thiamine. Thereafter he is given 50 mg of thiamine three times a day orally, and vitamin-B complex three times a day.

2. *Aluminum hydroxide gel and a bland diet.* It is wise not to feed the patient until half an hour after the thiamine is administered: severe thiamine deficiency blocks the body's ability to metabolize foodstuffs, and deaths from pyruvic acid poisoning after patients have eaten have been reported.

3. *Fluids.* Until recently it was thought that the therapist should "force fluids" with alcoholic patients on the premise that alcohol (a diuretic) causes dehydration. Recent research[23] has shown that overall a relative retention of fluid occurs after heavy drinking, so fluids should be administered moderately during the first twenty-four hours. In well-nourished patients, the total body water level should decrease to

normal in about four days, with no specific fluid or electrolyte therapy. [23]

4. *Environmental support.* The setting may be an alcoholic rehabilitation center, a recovery home, or a general hospital ward. The purpose is to help the patient maintain contact with reality by keeping the light on at night, talking with him, reminding him where he is, to whom he is talking, and why he is there.

Often it is best not to accomplish this work in a medical setting but in a social treatment setting where the caretakers are committed to the long-term rehabilitation of the alcoholic person. The detoxification ward should be reserved for severely ill patients with frank DTs. A rehabilitation unit with medical back-up support is ideal, but the earliest contacts should be with alcohol treatment workers, not with nurses and doctors who are committed only to easing immediate bodily pain. [26]

In any setting *talking down alcoholic hallucinations* can be accomplished easily. The patient may be asked, "Do you see something?" ("Yes.") "Where?" (The patient indicates that the vision, often an animal, is by his bed or chair.) "Close your eyes." (The patient does.) "Do you still see it?" (The patient indicates that he does.) "Then you know it isn't there!" [22]

Contact with people experienced in alcohol rehabilitation at this time of greatest fear and need may well facilitate a *religious conversion* to the ideal of abstinence, one of great benefit to the marginally motivated, despairing patient.

5. *Psychopharmacological treatment to end and reverse the acute withdrawal state.* In a sense, this is replacement therapy, and in some specific situations the most practical solution will be to have the patient return to alcohol. Or, the therapist may use a sedative-hypnotic drug that can be interchanged with alcohol (such as a barbiturate). However, the clinical challenge has been to find a drug that will

"cover" for alcohol without posing the same toxic and addictive risks.

Currently, three agents are preferred: chlordiazepoxide (Librium®), paraldehyde, and hydroxyzine (Vistaril®). Chlordiazepoxide has the advantages of being nonodorous, easily palatable, and pleasantly sedative. It has the disadvantages of having no effect in restoring terminal delta sleep, or not reaching sufficient terminal delta sleep, of not reaching sufficient stration) to cover the severest forms of withdrawal, and of becoming part of an addictive cycle. Chlordiazepoxide by injection is a rapid and effective means of bringing patients in the prodromal stage of alcohol withdrawal under control.

The following regimen has been found to be effective. At first contact with a tremulous, nonpsychotic patient, administer 100 mg of thiamine and 100 mg of chlordiazepoxide intramuscularly in the same syringe. If the patient is hungry, give him something to eat after half an hour. After giving the drugs an hour to take effect, continue the evaluation. During the first twenty-four hours of treatment, repeat oral, 100-mg doses of chlordiazepoxide every six hours if the patient is not vomiting, or give it by injection if he is. On the second day, continue 25 mg of chlordiazepoxide every six hours; on the third day continue it at the 10-mg level. If more sedation is needed, 1 gram of chloral hydrate can be given and the dose repeated once or twice an hour as necessary. Such a program is effective and does not produce undesirable oversedation.

Paraldehyde is often touted as the drug of choice for patients in advanced alcohol withdrawal. Although it is addictive, it is decidedly effective. Experienced alcoholic patients and ward nurses prefer it: it produces good, delta-wave sleep, which mimics natural, terminal sleep. It is therefore a rational treatment for withdrawal. Unfortunately, its chemical structure resembles that of ethyl alcohol, and its degradation uses the same enzyme system in the body. Accordingly, it may cause stress to the diseased liver and add a new risk of toxic injury. Its use is being increasingly questioned. [22]

When paraldehyde is used, it should be given on a regular schedule. It is malodorous and produces vomiting in sensitive patients. Previous administration of aluminum hydroxide greatly increases its chance of being held down. Injections of paraldehyde sting, and they may cause sterile abscesses. It is hard to find a rationale for their use. A standard schedule is 10 cc orally every four hours (every six hours in patients past 45 to avoid cardiac arrythmias) during the first twenty-four hours; 10 cc orally every six hours during the next twenty-four hours; and 10 cc only at bedtime on the third and fourth days. If there is an acute infectious or inflammatory process, the dosage schedule of the first twenty-four hours is maintained until the complicating condition is brought under control. If there is hypersomnolence in response to paraldehyde, the dose should be reduced and the possibility of Wernicke's encephalopathy (which responds to thiamine) or other brain syndromes (including trauma) should be explored.

Currently, hydroxyzine (Vistaril®) is coming into favor with clinicians such as Dr. Robert G. O'Briant. [22] He reports success with the following schedule: 100 mg of hydroxyzine is given intramuscularly (IM) initially, together with 100 mg of thiamine. The 100-mg hydroxyzine IM is repeated as needed every two to three hours for two doses. Then 75 mg is given as needed every four to six hours. Chloral hydrate, 1 gram, is used for sleep. This regimen is effective for about 95 percent of withdrawing alcoholic patients and is conducted with their immediate participation while they are still in the withdrawal phase and under a program of social treatment aimed at alcoholic rehabilitation. Only the most severe cases require admission to an intensive care detoxication unit. For them, injectable diazepam can be used, 10 mg IM as needed every three to four hours until the most severe stage of withdrawal is under control.

This hydroxyzine regimen avoids the potential dangers of both paraldehyde (possible stress to diseased livers) and chlordiazepoxide (a new habit-forming drug). Moreover, it is not oversedating. (Patients do not becomed "spaced" on hydroxyzine, and later they do not seek to obtain mellow "highs" by combining it with alcohol. Patients who have experienced a pleasant withdrawal on chlordiazepoxide sometimes do try to achieve later highs from that particular combination.) Hydroxyzine also controls vomiting.

Only after the patient has gone for twenty-four hours without psychotic manifestations or medication is he ready for release from all medical management of the alcoholic withdrawal.

Common Complications and Their Management

We shall discuss the most commonly found complications of excessive drinking; descriptions of others can be found in standard medical texts. The syndromes to be presented are the Wernicke-Korsakoff, infections, and gastrointestinal and psychiatric complications.

The Wernicke-Korsakoff Syndrome. The various manifestations of this syndrome have been called Wernicke's encephalopathy, alcoholic cerebellar degeration, Korsakoff's psychosis, and "the alcoholic psychoses." It is the result of prolonged B-vitamin (especially thiamine) deficiency often found in patients who drink but do not eat.

Victor, Adams, and Collins [24] have traced the progression of symptoms. Initially the sensorium is mildly clouded, followed by global confusion, dullness, and apathy. When the confusion clears, there is a severe memory deficit marked by (1) loss of past memories, invariably coupled with an inability to form new memories or to learn; (2) relatively minor but definite impairment of perceptual and conceptual functions; and (3) diminution in spontaneity and initiative. Often the patient will *confabulate,* that is, make up a past he cannot remember, and in the past this colorful symptom was taken as a hallmark of Korsakoff's psychosis, even though it is not always present. If the condition is severe or treatment has been withheld, a permanent deficit, without confabulation, may remain; this deficit is called "alcoholic dementia."

The first indications of the disease are eye signs and incoordination of gait, ataxia. The eye signs include paralysis of ocular muscles (reported as double vision) and nystagmus on fixed lateral gaze. Ataxia suggests cerebellar dysfunction. If thiamine is administered to patients who manifest only ocular and cerebellar symptoms, improvement occurs in hours or days, and Korsakoff's psychosis is prevented. The amnesic psychosis responds to thiamine in 80 percent of the cases; its continued administration for days and weeks will cause marked improvement in many of the others.

> *Example 6-8.* A 50-year-old man brought himself for his first emergency room visit. He seemed tired, listless, superficially in contact with his surroundings, and only marginally attentive. A careful mental status examination revealed the degree of his memory deficit. Of the last six presidents, he could name only Kennedy, Truman, and Roosevelt. His eyes showed paralysis of conjugate gaze and nystagmus. He spontaneously reported seeing double images. He was given a shot of 100 mg of thiamine. An hour later the patient reported that his vision was clearing and that he was feeling much better. Asked again to name the last six presidents, he said, "Nixon, Johnson, Kennedy, Eisenhower, Truman, Roosevelt" without hesitation.

Infections. Alcoholic patients in withdrawal often have fevers. In the absence of other signs of autonomic hyperactivity (such as sweating, tachycardia, and dilated pupils), fever must be regarded as the result of infection. Pneumonia is the most common; often tuberculosis must be ruled out. Consultation by an internist is virtually mandatory when fever, gastrointestinal complaints, or other medical complications are present.

Gastrointestinal Complications. During alcohol withdrawal, bleeding episodes from severe gastritis, a duodenal ulcer, or esophageal varices are not uncommon and require immediate medical consultation. Additionally, pain and risk to life from acute pancreatitis may be present. Finally, severe acute alcoholic hepatitis, which is the probable precursor to cirrhosis of the liver, may cause nausea and jaundice. It is a reason for prolonged hospitalization, as continued drinking in the presence of this condition will surely produce cirrhosis. All alcoholic patients should have complete liver profiles on the third or fourth hospital day to check for hepatitis. If it is present, strenuous measures should be taken to see that the patients do not have opportunities to drink again soon.

Psychiatric Complications. According to Gross,[25] 14 percent of the alcoholic population are also schizophrenic. Chronic schizophrenic patients may also discontinue phenothiazines when they start drinking. Alcohol withdrawal may trigger a full-blown psychotic break in a usually borderline individual, who must then be treated as for a functional psychosis. (See Chapter 5, "Evaluation and Treatment of the Psychotic Patient.") Phenothiazines can be given after the second hospital day if the patient's liver function permits, but they will lower the seizure threshold. Because the high-vulnerability period for seizures is forty-eight to seventy-two hours after withdrawal begins,[26] an antiseizure medication such as diphenylhydantoin (Dilantin®), 100 mg, three times a day, should be administered to withdrawing patients who are receiving phenothiazines. An additional problem is posed by the potentiating effects of phenothiazines on other medications with sedating effects; care should be taken not to obtund the patient. Some patients become agitated and depressed after alcohol withdrawal, especially if they regret their behavior when they were drunk. After the patient has been withdrawn from alcohol, the risk of suicide may require his transfer to a psychiatric ward.

MEDICAL PROBLEMS OF ADVANCED ALCOHOLISM

The Therapist's Responsibility

In addition to the problems posed by withdrawal, the drinking person is generally liable to many accidents and infections, as well as to a host of diseases caused either by the direct toxic effects of alcohol on organs or by the nutritional consequences of alcoholic debilitation. These conditions may result in the crisis that caused him to seek psychiatric help: the threat to health. Although not all alcohol-related illnesses can be examined here in detail, it is the therapist's job to take his patient's suffering seriously and to be willing to refer him for careful evaluation. The patient may respond to the health crisis with a sense of narcissistic injury, which is why it comes first to psychiatric attention. The therapist may be the only one who can obtain an adequate history; he must serve as the patient's advocate in bringing key symptoms to the attention of an internist. The therapist's interest is one way of guaranteeing that the patient will receive thorough, thoughtful medical care.

The therapist who is not familiar with the signs and symptoms of the following conditions should become sufficiently knowledgeable about them so he can suspect them when symptoms develop and make the appropriate referral to an internist.

The Medical Problems

Cirrhosis. The most dreaded consequence of alcoholism is cirrhosis of the liver, a variably progressive disease in which fibrous scar tissue gradually replaces vital liver cells and interferes with the vast array of life-promoting functions of the liver. The precursor of this disease is acute alcoholic hepatitis, not fatty liver. During heavy drinking, fatty cells often occupy liver tissue, but this condition is temporary and reversible; the patient can resume drinking without inevitable progression to cirrhosis. By contrast, acute alcoholic hepatitis often leads to dangerous, permanent liver damage and requires hospitalization for about six weeks until the condition is stabilized.

Once cirrhosis is established, the alcoholic patient lives under threat. He will need to stop drinking and be supervised by an internist. From this point on, nutrition will be a paramount problem because he will absorb less fat, calcium, magnesium, and fewer selective vitamins, and he is likely to develop considerable protein deficiency. With this malnutrition, symptoms of depression grow worse, and the energy for life tasks becomes less. Equally, the patient's ability to metabolize alcohol decreases, and his tolerance for alcohol is lowered considerably.

Nutritional Disorders. Besides brain thiamine deficiency, beriberi, pellagra, and scurvy are found in alcoholic patients. Anemias resulting from iron, folic acid, and pyridoxine deficiencies are common. Finally, mineral deficiencies—including potassium, magnesium, and zinc—may appear in the course of advanced alcoholism. Any of these may materially affect the patient's well-being and have major adverse effects upon his heart, muscle, and nerve functions.

Alcoholic Heart Disease. Toxic alcohol effects weaken the muscles of the heart, causing heart failure in relatively young men. Recognition of cardiac failure may produce the anxiety that causes an otherwise well-functioning heavy drinker to seek psychiatric treatment. Reports of physical fatigue should be taken seriously, and a basic examination for heart disease should be arranged.

Accidents. Drinking patients are prone to falls, auto accidents, and fires. Although trauma victims include a large proportion of true alcoholic patients, surgeons often miss this diagnosis. Whenever the psychiatrist is given the opportunity, he should help the surgeon to share the drinking patient. Too often a patient with severe emotional problems is subject to the long confinement of a hospitalization for a fracture without any opportunity to discuss the emotional events that led to the accident. Furthermore, many "accidents" are suicide attempts that have gone unrecognized. A long hospitalization without contact with significant others becomes a semipunitive rest cure, effective for some depressions, wholly detrimental to others. The same hospitalization could be the beginning of a meaningful participation in psychotherapy or an alcohol treatment program.

Summary. Therapists must take the alcoholic patient's medical needs seriously, work with him in his struggle to recover health, help him to realize how alcohol impedes that struggle, and set the stage for discussions of psychological suffering. As one patient put it, "I'm sick and tired of feeling sick and tired." If the psychiatrist neglects these areas, sees them as "the patient's problem" or as "what he gets for drinking," he indicates that he cannot really receive the patient's own experience and discourages him from taking his treatment seriously. For the nonmedical therapist, mastering these areas is similar to entering a foreign country of vaguely hostile intent. He will be repaid for his labors by the knowledge that he is coming much closer to understanding the world in which his patient is forced to live.

LONG-RANGE TREATMENT OF THE DRINKING PATIENT

A description of all aspects of the treatment of the advanced alcoholic patient is beyond the scope of this book. What should be mastered initially, however, is a certain skill at setting the stage for definitive treatment and an understanding of the basic principles of that treatment. For a thorough description of the modern social approach, O'Briant and Lennard's[26] brief, definitive text, *Recovery from Alcoholism*, should be consulted. Hoff[27] has presented a concise statement of some initial principles of alcoholic rehabilitation, and many of his points will be summarized here.

Setting the Stage in the Initial Evaluation

The major task in the initial interviewing of the drinking patient is to keep the patient open to the idea of therapeutic intervention. This task becomes easier if certain ground rules are kept in mind.

Establish That Drinking Can Be Discussed. At first, most drinking patients are chary of revealing too much about their drinking behavior because they anticipate censure. The emergency therapist's first task is to establish that he can stand to hear about drinking. A good way is to inquire about the patient's bodily sensations in relation to drinking: does it make his head ache, his stomach get upset, his vision blur? Almost any drinking person will welcome this opportunity to talk about his body (which is probably suffering), and the therapist has established that he wants to hear about the patient's experience with alcohol.

Mediate Catharsis. Getting drunk is a way of becoming unconscious, which perforce interferes with putting feelings into words. The therapist must expect to do a good deal of the talking at first, helping the patient to articulate his feelings by verbalizing them for him. To the patient who mentions a divorce five years ago, the therapist may say, "And of course you felt extremely low when that came through." A great deal of patience is required to help the patient recapture his lost affect; the therapist should expect repression. Alcoholic patients often forget whole chapters of their lives, and considerable therapeutic patience is needed to obtain this material.

Establish Early the Right to Communicate with Others. Problem drinking is a chronic psycho-social disease; the drinker is rarely the only person involved. Despite the fact that the family knows he has a drinking problem, the alcoholic patient will often try to bind the therapist with pseudo-confidentiality. In such a role the therapist is as therapeutically confined as a bartender. Yet the patient insists on keeping their relationship confidential, claiming it would destroy the family to know that he drinks.

Usually the family knows but has developed a conspiracy of silence. The patient's insistence on confidentiality mirrors a family style of keeping feelings under wraps, as if there were a tacit rule: important emotional facts may not be discussed. The alcoholic family, like many others, adopts a strategy of denial to deal with problems for which no easy solution is at hand. This policy of denial is continued even when it has grown grotesquely ineffective. One of the therapist's first tasks is to counter this policy of denial with his own commitment to talking things out. He starts by making it clear to his patient that effective service means talking with other members of the ecological group. Indeed, it is often effective to work with a spouse *first:* the alcoholic partner will come in later.

Expect Lability. Neither the acutely intoxicated nor the acutely withdrawing patient is in a normal emotional state. He may be alternately excited or depressed. It is often helpful to indicate to the patient, tactfully, that the problem of emotional dyscontrol is recognized and that full control is not expected. Initial interviews should be short; they may often be conducted after an injection of chlordiazepoxide and between interviews with other emergency patients. The full-scale interview can be conducted after he has begun to quiet down.

Watch for Overattachment to the Interviewer. It is an oversimplification to say that all persons with drinking problems are passive-dependent or "oral"

characters. Nevertheless, chronic excessive drinking does occasion regression to more dependent stages of development, not without considerable resentment on the part of the regressing patient. At the same time, the self-isolating (and society-alienating) existence of the confirmed alcoholic patient intensifies his needs for human contact, warmth, and support. A vicious circle is set in motion whereby the patient has intensified dependency needs just when he is most ashamed of himself for being so dependent.

The therapist can unwittingly participate in this vicious circle if he gives the patient too much support, leading to the familiar situation in which the patient is telling him, by a drunken telephone call at 2 A.M., that he is the only person who ever really helped. The patient's alcoholism worsens as it becomes his only way of expressing autonomy (and anger) toward the person on whom he has become so dependent.

In some cases erotic feelings color the picture, particularly if the patient is ashamed of erotic feelings, as is often true of homosexual, hysterical, and "masochistic" patients. Then the patient must punish himself for spoiling the therapeutic relationship with sexual fantasies.

Finally, hostile feelings may reach the level of active homicidal fantasy toward the therapist, especially when the patient is drinking. Threats to the therapist's life are not uncommon from drinking borderline patients who perceive the therapist as embodying all they can never control or attain.

A classical dyadic transference neurosis, for both patient and therapist, becomes intolerable when alcohol enters the picture. The therapist becomes (and feels like) a problem drinker's spouse caught in the bind of protecting a sadomasochistic partner, feeling like a sadomasochist himself. All this undercuts the patient's learning that he can share his problem with a wider group, not focusing all his libidinal energy on one person who seems to promise acceptance.

From the beginning, the therapist should eschew manipulating the patient into accepting individual or other long-term treatment by showing excessive personal interest in him. The interview should be straightforward and matter of fact, directed toward the unexciting but realistic prospect of a conventional alcoholic treatment program involving group and family approaches. If the patient seems uninterested, the therapist should be willing to let him go. He should not appear to promise unlimited dependency gratification. Equally, any attempt by the patient to restrict therapy to a one-to-one, long-term relationship with the initial therapist should be viewed as a resistance to treatment. Beginning therapists (especially those just beginning to prize their own work) must watch for that seduction: "You're the only person I really feel can reach me." The motive, too often, is a desire for access to drugs and hospitals as a means of bolstering, not changing, the addictive process. Yet every inpatient ward has a subpopulation of patients who "cycle" through under the protective custody of doctors who cannot insist that the patient make an effort to change as part of the therapeutic contract.

Determine Where the Patient Hurts and What He Wants. Not all drinking patients can be sold on treatment. Some want only to weather the physiologic crisis of alcohol withdrawal. Others want food and shelter. Others simply want a current physical evaluation. And a few want to be sure they are not losing their minds.

Helping the patient to define his need is therapeutic. It is important that the patient have a major say in the kind of treatment he is offered. The patient should not be "trapped" in a treatment program for which he is not ready. Until the patient has reached a sober and physiologically stable condition, the therapist cannot assess his motivation for further treatment. Often, as Hoff points out, all the therapist can do is admit the patient to the hospital and accomplish a safe detoxification there. This much is surely the patient's right if he is medically ill, and it is most certainly *not* a "misuse of the hospital."

Discuss Matters with Significant Others. When treatment is started, wide communication is extremely important. Often, members of the ecological group are caught up in the conspiracy of silence, afraid to share what they know of the patient's drinking with the patient or with each other. The wife feels bound not to tell the boss; the boss is afraid to tell the wife. Yet both know, and both are concerned.

The therapist can act as a model for the group by sharing freely what he understands of the patient's dilemma. Some therapists make it a rule to interview the patient alone. They secure his permission to bring in a family member to "share with him what they have been discussing." Often the therapist asks permission to call the boss, especially if hospitalization is going to cause the patient to miss work. He may telephone other members of the ecological group who are not present and pass the telephone back and forth to let them talk to those in the office. The therapist shows by his behavior that the problem can be openly and rationally discussed, and that he thinks alcoholic treatment is dignified and effective.

Example 6-9. A man in his early 60s had been admitted to the hospital for detoxification. His wife was also a heavy drinker, and they both believed that they had kept their drinking a secret from the other members of the family.

A conference was scheduled that was to include some close cousins who had consistently expressed concern. Just before the conference was to take place, the patient told the therapist that his cousins had been good to him since childhood and that he couldn't bear for them to find out he was an alcoholic. The therapist replied that it was better if the family knew, and finally the patient said, "You tell them."

In the presence of the wife and the cousins, the therapist told about the patient's serious drinking problem, explaining that it had caused the current admission. Immediately they revealed that they had known about it for several years but had never felt free to bring it up. In a very moving way, they expressed their willingness to help.

The patient seemed relieved. He said he hadn't realized that they had known. His wife then revealed she hadn't known what to tell the patient's employer and that she had finally reported that her husband had suffered a heart attack. The patient described great affection for his boss of twenty years, and great fear of losing his job.

The therapist asked permission to talk to the boss by telephone. Perhaps because the interview with the cousins had gone so well, the patient gave his consent.

The boss was greatly relieved to learn that his employee had not had a heart attack. This "saving" lie had, in fact, been the cause of considerable pressure from others at work to terminate the patient's employment, which involved heavy lifting.

When he learned that the patient had a drinking problem, the boss expressed interest in participating in the patient's treatment. The therapist asked if he would be willing to have his secretary administer a daily tablet of disulfiram (Antabuse®) so the patient would not have to depend on his wife or himself to remember. The boss was delighted to help in this way.

Upon hearing that his boss was willing to help him, the patient readily agreed to start disulfiram. Two weeks later he was back at work, and at the end of three months was still abstinent, for the first time in twenty years. He and his wife had begun attending AA meetings.

Make Referrals Personally. Morris Chafetz'[28] research has shown a marked increase in follow-through on referral suggestions by drinking patients when the referral is made in a personal way. His method is to set up the initial appointment in a concerned manner and then send the patient a follow-up letter reminding him of the appointment.

When the telephone is used, it is good to make the referral in the patient's presence so he can hear what is said about him. (This will also make it easier for him to open up to the next therapist; it is a way of "passing the mantle.") It helps if the therapist knows the person he is calling; he can introduce the patient to the new therapist over the phone and let the patient set up his own appointment. But even if he must look up the phone number of a local alcohol treatment program in the telephone book, he can do that in the patient's presence and share the problem of "breaking the ice" with him. Again, after the therapist makes contact he hands the telephone to the patient to set up an appointment.

With experience, therapists become familiar with people who work with alcoholic patients. The referral to the internist, the AA group, or the halfway house can be made with greater confidence and more genuine personal feeling, and the patients tend to follow through.

Principles of Treatment[27]

If the emergency therapist belongs to the team that offers long-range treatment, he will want to come to an agreement with the patient. This agreement is often described in therapeutic circles as a "contract," or "covenant of treatment."[27] In it the goals of treatment, and the therapist's expectations and limitations, should be spelled out clearly. This agreement is negotiated, like a labor contract, and the bargaining that takes place between the patient and therapist is an essential part of the treatment process. As the initial stages of bargaining take place in the emergency room around the issue of hospitalization, the therapist will want to keep certain principles in mind.

What Therapy Can Offer. The patient should be given a realistic picture of what therapy can give him. For instance, every patient can be given medical attention, even if he elects to refuse psychiatric help. The patient whose drinking is symptomatic can be offered conventional psychotherapy and the reasonable hope that his depression can be treated. The confirmed alcoholic patient should be given a description of the multidisciplinary approach, with stress on the necessity for open communication. It is proper to offer the opinion that modern treatment can help.

Privilege of Abstaining from Drinking and Therapy. The therapist should make it clear that only the patient can exercise the choice of changing his drinking habits. Although the therapist has the right and responsbility to limit the patient's freedom to hurt himself or others, the ultimate decision to abstain rests with the patient. The patient should be told he must come to terms with making this choice.

The patient may balk at further therapy. The therapist must make it clear what the alcoholic prognosis is. All drinking holds a potential for addiction and organ damage. Even reactive drinking may acquire a life of its own, apart from the original conflict alcohol had been selected to treat. The patient's rationalizations should be met with a statement of what he may expect if he continues to drink excessively, whether or not he enters treatment.

What Will Be Asked of the Patient. Many psychiatric units have prerequisites to admission. Some insist on a trial of disulfiram after detoxification. Others make a rule of strict abstinence during the ward stay, and the patient who fails to comply is subject to dismissal. Still others insist upon intensive family interviewing. It is not fair to spring these demands on the patient *after* detoxification has begun. He needs to know before, when he has some choice about whether or not to surrender to treatment.

Meeting the demands of a treating institution before treatment begins can be a kind of initiation for the recalcitrant alcoholic patient. As AA has stressed repeatedly, it is not beneficial to offer too much help to drinkers who are not "ripe." It is better to give them essential medical treatment when withdrawal symptoms appear and to hold

firm on the ground conditions to be met before the doors to a long-term supportive program are opened.

Informing Significant Others. From the beginning, the family should hear that its involvement will be an essential part of the patient's treatment. Family members should be told to expect the first months of abstinence to be rocky. The patient will miss alcohol, will be in a depressed, irritable, and joyless state, and will be even more difficult to live with than when he was drinking. They should expect to find themselves wishing him back on the bottle, even subtly encouraging that solution.

They should recognize that such reactions are normal but that they will be expected to talk about their feelings with a professional. It should be made clear that therapy for them means working on their own emotional problems, not just supplying moral support to the patient in his struggle to remain abstinent. The step of defining the family members as being in need of therapeutic help in their own rights is best taken before extended treatment is planned. The family can be refused as a unit until everyone is ready to participate.

Involving the employer from the beginning, as in Example 6-9, is often strikingly effective. The timing of this intervention is a difficult matter and requires individual judgment. Often the therapist must set as a goal of treatment the patient's ability to share his difficulty with those in positions of authority. He should be told that those who get better make a strict policy of frankness: it makes it harder for them to deceive themselves, as when they call in sick for alcohol-related illnesses.

Resources for Drinking Patients

The overlapping network of treatment resources for drinking people can seem like a morass to the beginning therapist. The manipulative patient will make the most of the therapist's confusion, so it is helpful to keep in mind a structured overview of the resources available in this area. As in all psychiatric referrals, the therapist should try to avoid culture shock by matching up the patient and the program. For a merchant seaman, a recovery home run by other merchant seamen who hold AA meetings on the premises may be the ideal resource. For a lower middle-class industrial worker, the alcohol treatment program run by his own company may be ideal. An upper middle-class person may insist upon a private psychiatrist, and one skilled in the treatment of alcoholic patients is mandatory. Detailed descriptions of specific resources are found in Fox.[29]

Organizations. *The National Council on Alcoholism* offers pretreatment evaluations as a public service at most of its 125 affiliate offices in major and smaller cities throughout the fifty states. The patient may be seen on his own direct request or on referral from a professional. The National Council on Alcoholism is listed in the regular listings of the telephone directory, not as a governmental agency. No files with patient names are kept, and efforts are made to keep the consultation strictly confidential. The patient is not treated but is evaluated for treatment, and the evaluators are skilled in making the best possible referral for the patient at his stage of drinking. The therapist who is uncertain about how to proceed in making recommendations to a given patient should not hesistate to use this resource.

Alcoholics Anonymous has developed and grown during the past ten years. No longer is it a monolithic, quasi-religious organization committed to reciting the twelve steps and indulging in long monologues at its meetings. Nor is it beneficial only to lonely extraverts and cyclothymic individuals and not to other kinds of problem drinkers. It is a many-faceted, flexible organization, with as many kinds of meetings as there are subcultures of alcoholic people. In the San Francisco area there are 130 AA groups, including young people's, black, Chicano, and gay groups. A suburban AA meeting may resemble a PTA meeting. In short, it is a good place for persons like those who used to drink together to meet together without drinking.

Also, AA members often devote a certain amount of time to providing information, transportation, and moral support to persons who are becoming serious about alcohol treatment. They visit hospitalized patients on medical and psychiatric wards.

One good way to become knowledgeable about alcoholic treatment programs in individual communities is to develop a rapport with AA members who are, by and large, quite gregarious, eager to help interested persons. When he suggests the patient avail himself of AA, the therapist can call an AA member known personally to him. Simply saying to a patient, "Go to AA" is so rejecting that the therapist should hardly expect a follow-through. (A special use of AA is made by the schizophrenic alcoholic person, ambivalent about intimacy, who finds through his alcoholism a reason to socialize with others in a way both close and impersonal enough to meet his conflicting needs.) Sometimes hospitalization can be avoided during the stage of alcohol withdrawal by referral to an AA-connected recovery home. The experience of being cared for by AA members at the time of greatest need may facilitate "conversion" to an AA-based, abstinent lifestyle.

Example 6-10. A man in his 50s had been drinking for twenty-five years. He was a merchant seaman with a boisterous, extraverted personality. He came to the hospital because he was frightened by visual hallucinosis during the withdrawal phase of his most recent heavy drinking spree. He had experienced mild alcohol withdrawal symptoms many times previously without psychotic manifestations; the psychosis scared him. He seemed to be in generally good health, and his vital signs and physical examination were essentially normal.

He was given chlordiazepoxide and thiamine as an outpatient and referred to a halfway house for alcoholics run by merchant seamen belonging to AA. The empathy he found with the others in that environment permitted a dramatic conversion to abstinence. He later attributed his change to the anxiety caused by the visual hallucinosis and the support of the AA members. A year later he had continued to remain abstinent and was very active in AA. Admission to the psychiatric unit would probably have interfered with the experience of salvation that this man found in the supportive AA environment, for which he was obviously ripe.

AA is not for every problem drinker. Those persons particularly who are reactive drinkers or deeply depressed should not be encouraged to see all their problems as resulting from alcohol use and requiring only conversion to an abstinent style and membership in AA to effect a complete cure. Overemphasis on symptomatic alcohol use with such an individual may lead him to select (often masochistically) the mask of chronic alcoholism to hide from confronting an acute life situation that could be resolved. For him psychiatric treatment aimed at the specific life conflict is indicated.

Alcohol treatment programs vary in quality from city to city, county to county, and state to state. Patients who have actively concerned family members do very well in programs that have a team of psychiatrists, social workers, psychologists, and vocational and rehabilitation workers. Such programs are offered primarily by large hospitals and community mental health centers. Special mention should be made, however, of industrial programs open to those who work for specific companies. Usually treatment is combined with a period of job probation. Participation in such a program by individuals whose frequent absences from work are alcohol-related is often made a condition for continuing employment.

Residental Settings. The patient without funds who is withdrawing from alcohol needs food, shelter, and environmental support. The *recovery home* is often found in cities and is a good setting for the socially damaged alcoholic person to become motivated toward a less self-destructive life style. Such settings are no longer skid row flop houses. (In fact, there is evidence that skid row is disappearing in many cities.) AA meetings are often held on the premises. Treatment is encouraged by the banning of alcohol from the premises and the insistence on abstinence in return for admission to a program of longer-term stay and vocational rehabilitation. Personnel are not highly trained, and conditions vary.

The *alcoholic rehabilitation center,* similar to the recovery home, usually has provisions for sleeping, eating, and group meetings, as well as for intensive care detoxification. Usually a doctor will be on the premises and will provide a certain security during the withdrawal phase. Personnel are usually highly skilled in alcoholic rehabilitation. However, the medical focus can place too much responsibility on the caretakers instead of on the patients. Insistence on a social treatment model is the hallmark of the advanced rehabilitation center. It can be a center for referral to other resources. The stay at the Garden Hospital Jerd Sullivan Rehabilitation Center in San Francisco lasts three weeks, during which the patient is helped to establish a "social support system" aimed at overcoming his urge to drink. Group therapy and one-to-one counseling are offered. Members of the ecological group are involved.[26]

The *halfway house* is for alcoholic patients who require extensive residental support, often six months or longer. It provides an alcohol-free environment to come home to after work or, for some persons who work on the premises, a frank shelter from the world at large. Often there are separate halfway houses for men and for women. The directors of such houses are frequently persons with great sensitivity and skill at managing the crucial long-term problems of alcoholic people. This resource should not be the *first* step in recovery, but a choice made by the patient after he has gone through withdrawal and a period of preliminary rehabilitation. The criteria for admission to such houses usually is an authentic commitment to the goal of abstinence. As the housing cost is low, some of the patients will agitate to obtain entry to such houses without being authentically committed to change. They bring their addictive patterns with them, only to cause havoc in the house and guilt in themselves. Occasionally the therapist will find himself pressured by a patient of this type into helping him gain admission to a halfway house before he is ready for it. In this case, a pretreatment evaluation by a National Council on Alcoholism affiliate may give an official recommendation for the kind of treatment that is appropriate for the patient at his particular stage.

Outpatient Clinics. General hospitals and family service agencies offer individual, group, and family therapy to the public at large, often without specific provision for the needs of alcoholic patients. Patients whose drinking is not their primary problem may benefit from conventional evaluation and treatment. Prominently alcoholic people should not be steered toward resources that cannot provide for them simply because these resources are available.

Individual Resources. These include clergymen, internists, therapists who specialize in the treatment of alcoholism, and visiting public health nurses.

The *clergyman* is an underutilized resource. Catholic families still rely on the priest, and often he has a fund of information about the family. Usually clergymen are extremely willing to discuss their parishoners' drinking problems with interested doctors.

The *general practitioner* or *internist* is an essential resource for the patient with a drinking problem. Nowadays there is a return to the practice of home visiting and an increasing sophistication about psychological problems. Many internists in private practice have a large group of alcoholic patients whose problems they manage quite well. Often internists like to work with therapists; they turn to the therapist for help at crisis points and handle the major part of the support by themselves.

Not all internists are effective with alcoholic patients, and indeed, some perpetuate an unhealthy dependency, contributing to the addictive pattern. Nevertheless, increasing numbers of the medical profession have become interested in the treatment of alcoholism. With consultative help from the therapist, this resource can be very useful.

An *individual therapist* is in general *not* a good referral source for drinking patients unless he specializes in alcohol problems or unless the drinking is clearly of a reactive character. Reactive drinkers generally do well in individual or group therapy with a conventional focus on interpersonal conflicts and their resolution. A few therapists specialize in the treatment of drinking people and seem to know how to proceed. Individual therapy with a skilled specialist is often the referral of choice for problematic patients who do not fit the usual referral options. A word must be said against the assumption that individual therapy for the alcoholic patient can be done only by psychiatrists because they alone can admit patients to hospitals. Frequently it is better to have this medical power *out* of the therapeutic contract so that the patient can concentrate on which he can do for himself. He has the option of referral to a supportive environment if he cannot manage with outpatient therapy.

The *visiting public health nurse* can be crucial in the treatment of the woman problem drinker. Public health nurses can be contacted to provide regular home follow-up for patients who are not ready to come in regularly to an alcohol treatment program. For older, house-bound, and marginally motivated patients, this supportive resource can be of inestimable value. It is all too infrequently called upon by therapists, usually because they do not know the service exists.

Other Issues of Treatment

Quite often a drinking patient has legal problems. He may resist voluntary treatment even though he endangers himself and others. The role of disulfiram (Antabuse®) in his treatment is controversial. He often uses other drugs concomitantly. These matters will be considered in this section.

The Law. If a drinking patient is facing legal charges, the best procedure is to take care of his immediate medical needs for physical evaluation and detoxification and to insist that he settle his problem with the law before he starts lengthy rehabilitation. Otherwise, the rehabilitation program becomes part of his defense and prolongs his uncertainty about the future.

The patient should know that he can participate in the treatment program both during the legal process and after his release but that he must deal with his legal problems. Occasionally a patient will misrepresent himself as being too mentally ill to stand trial. The patient past the stage of detoxification should not be allowed to use the psychiatric treatment setting in this fraudulent way.

Involuntary Treatment. Drinking patients need involuntary restraint when they pose too great a threat to themselves or others. In acute cases, the treatment is the same as for any homicidal or suicidal patient. (See Chapters 2 to 4.) Some professionals argue that the confirmed alcoholic patient should be kept from destroying himself by drinking. In the case of very debilitated, ill, alcoholic people, involuntary treatment may precede a trial for mental incompetency. Generally, clinical experience confirms the wisdom of Hoff's[27] position that the patient retain the privilege of abstaining. Unnecessary involuntary treatment may simply intensify resistance. The therapist has to be able to let the patient go if he is not ready to accept treatment.

Disulfiram (Antabuse®). The clinical use of the drug disulfiram (Antabuse®) has staged a return in recent years. Originally it was used to produce a most incapacitating sickness in response to the use of alcohol as part of aversive conditioning. Several deaths were reported, and use of the drug declined. However, in low dosages it produces a distinctly unpleasant but not fatal response to alcohol and discourages the intake of intoxicating quantities. This property has led to its return to favor as a deterrent.

Willingness to take disulfiram can be a test of a patient's motivation to stop drinking. It gives him three days in which to decide to take the next drink. The decision to remain abstinent lies with the patient, not the pill; the patient decides when (and if) to take it. Disulfiram reactions consist of nausea, vomiting, low blood pressure, and rarely, convulsions. At doses of 0.25 to 0.5 mg/day, fatal reactions are virtually nonexistent. Every patient on disulfiram should be cautioned about the nature and duration of its effects on alcohol consumption and told to wait three days after the last dose if he intends to start drinking again. Complete instructions and an identification card prepared by the manufacturer are available and should be given to the patient when he starts to use the drug.

Other Drug Problems. Alcoholic persons often take other addictive drugs, such as marihuana, barbiturates, and amphetamines. Mixed alcohol and heroin addiction is not uncommon in the black community. The great jazz singer Billie Holiday died of complications of alcoholism, although she was famous for her heroin addiction. Alcohol use has cropped up persistently among addicts maintained on methadone: it is one drug not measured by the required urine test. The multiple drug abuser often does well in an environment such as Synanon, where active confrontation techniques are employed to break down rationalizing defenses.

SUMMARY

As Ruth Fox[30] has said, successful treatment of alcoholism is almost always multidisciplinary. Drinking problems involve such a variety of levels of functioning, from the biological to the social, that it is only reasonable to assume their cure will involve a variety of supportive professionals. Helping the problem drinker to enter treatment requires specialized knowledge, tact, and perseverance from the emergency therapist. From the beginning the therapist has to recognize that he is dealing with an acute manifestation of a chronic process and that the care and foresight with which he intervenes will have long-range consequences for the physical health, personal motivation, and social integration of his patient.

REFERENCES

1. Chafetz, Morris E., Howard T. Blane, and Marjorie Hill: *Frontiers of Alcoholism,* Science House, New York, 1970.

2. Ibid., pp. 105–155.

3. Ibid., pp. 33–73.

4. Plaut, Thomas F. A.: *Alcohol Problems: A Report to the Nation,* Cooperative Commission on the Study of Alcoholism, Oxford University Press, New York, 1967.

5. Jellinek, E. M.: *The Disease Concept of Alcoholism,* Yale, New Haven, Conn., 1960, p. 35.

6. Plaut: op. cit., p. 39.

7. American Psychiatric Association: *Diagnostic and Statistical Manual,* 2d ed., Washington, D.C., 1968.

8. Plaut: op. cit., pp. 37–38.

9. Kissin, Benjamin K.: "Alcoholism: Is It a Treatable Disease?", *Mod. Med.,* 14(20):33, Oct. 1, 1973.

10. Reich, Louis H., Robert K. Davies, and Jonathan M. Himmelhock: "Excessive Alcohol Use in Manic-Depressive Illness," *Am. J. Psychiat.,* 131(1):83–86, 1974.

11. Bateson, Gregory: "The Cybernetics of 'Self': A Theory of Alcoholism," *Psychiatry,* 34(1):1–18, 1971.

12. Verdery, Eugene A.: "The Clergy and Alcoholism" in Ruth Fox (ed.), *Alcoholism – Behavioral Research, Therapeutic Approaches,* Springer, New York, 1967, p. 273.

13. Wolff, Ilse: "The Role of the Public Health Nurse in the Treatment of the Alcoholic," in ibid., pp. 296–297.

14. Kissin: loc. cit.

15. The Criteria Committee, National Council on Alcoholism (Frank A. Seixas, M.D., Medical Director): "Criteria for the Diagnosis of Alcoholism," *Am. J. Psychiat.,* 129(2):127–135, 1972. Copyright 1972, The American Psychiatric Association.

16. Ibid., *Ann. Intern. Med.,* 77:249–258, 1972.

17. From Bowman, K. M. and Jellinek, E. M.: "Alcoholic Mental Disorders," p. 89, in E. M. Jellinek (ed.), "Effects of Alcohol on the Individual," vol. 1, *Alcohol Addiction and Chronic Alcoholism,* Yale, New Haven, Conn., 1942. Copyright by Journal of Studies on Alcohol, Inc., New Brunswick, N.J.

18. Gross, Milton: "Management of Acute Alcohol Withdrawal States," *Quar. J. Stud. Alc.,* 28:655–666, 1967.

19. Alvarez, A.: *The Savage God,* Random House, New York, 1972, p. 271. Copyright 1972, Random House.

20. Gross: loc. cit.

21. Ibid.

22. O'Briant, Robert G.: Director, Alcoholic Rehabilitation Program, Garden Hospital–Jerd Sullivan Rehabilitation Center, San Francisco, personal communication, 1973.

23. Beard, James D., and David H. Knott: "Fluid and Electrolyte Balance During Acute Withdrawal in Chronic Alcoholic Patients," *J. Am. Med. Ass.,* 204:135–139, 1968.

24. Victor, Maurice, Raymond Adams, and George Collins: *The Wernicke-Korsakoff Syndrome,* Davis, Philadelphia, 1971.

25. Gross: loc. cit.

26. O'Briant, Robert G. and Henry Lennard: *Recovery from Alcoholism: A Social Treatment Model,* Charles C Thomas, Springfield, Ill., 1973.

27. Hoff, Ebbe Curtis: "The Psychological and Pharmacological Basis for the Treatment of Alcohol Dependence," in Yedy Israel and Jorge Mardones (eds.) *Biological Basis of Alcoholism,* Wiley-Interscience, New York, 1971, chap. 14.

28. Chafetz, Blaine, and Hill: loc. cit.

29. Fox: op. cit. (Ref. 12.)

30. Fox, Ruth: "A Multidisciplinary Approach to the Treatment of Alcoholism," *Am. J. Psychiat.* 123:7, January 1967.

Overdoses of Psychotherapeutic Drugs*

The widespread use of the newer psychotherapeutic drugs has resulted in many instances of overdose, either accidentally by children or deliberately by adults. Although the general principles of the treatment of poisoning with these drugs are similar to those that apply to older sedatives and stimulants, some drugs pose specific problems.

EPIDEMIOLOGICAL CONSIDERATIONS

Despite their wide use and ready availability, psychotherapeutic drugs are involved in only a small percentage of poisonings and an even smaller percentage of fatalities. Barbiturates are far more important than these drugs as a vehicle for chemical suicide. At least 1,500 successful suicides occur in the United States each year with barbiturates. Similar figures on a proportionate basis apply to other parts of the world. But poisonings from psychotherapeutic drugs occur relatively infrequently despite their continuing popularity. The major new problem resulting from the use of psychotherapeutic drugs in recent years has been

the increasing number of instances of accidental ingestion of tricyclic antidepressants by children.[1] Because these are the most toxic of all the new psychotherapeutic drugs, and children are the most vulnerable to any kind of drug overdose, this matter is of considerable concern.

PREVENTION AND DIAGNOSIS

Limiting the amounts of drugs prescribed to a total amount that if taken all at once would be sublethal is an excellent way to prevent fatal overdoses. Such procedure is inconvenient, both to prescribing physicians and to their patients, and is still no absolute guarantee of safety. Nonetheless, it is a reasonable precautionary measure and is the responsibility of the physician. In Australia, because of increased concern about fatal ingestions of tricyclic antidepressants, fifty tablets are the maximum number permitted in any single package. By limiting packages to fifty tablets, the total dose is only 1.25 grams, generally a sublethal quantity. The Australian government has subsidized the difference to defray the extra cost to the consumer of the smaller packages. In the subsequent discussion, lethal doses of drugs will be translated into the numbers of commonly pre-

---

*Adapted with permission of the author and publisher from Leo E. Hollister, "Toxicology of Psychotherapeutic Drugs," *Principles of Psychopharmacology,* Clark and del Giudice (eds.), Academic Press, New York, 1970, chap. 43.

scribed units of each drug to provide a guide for estimating sublethal quantities.

Although the general principles of treating overdoses of psychotherapeutic drugs apply to all varieties, treatment of drug intoxication may be expedited considerably if the identity of the drug is known. Prescriptions should be labeled clearly with the generic or trade name of the drug and the unit size of the dose issued. Nothing is more frustrating than to try to identify the contents of an unlabeled bottle from a closed or out-of-state pharmacy. Clinical signs of central nervous system (CNS) involvement are not entirely reliable clues concerning the nature of the drug because many drugs ordinarily not considered to be CNS depressants or stimulants may produce prominent signs when they are taken in overdose. Aspirin, methylsalicylate, petroleum products, and organic phosphorus insecticides are examples of drugs or poisons that in toxic doses may evoke CNS symptoms and signs. Usually other distinguishing aspects of the intoxication point to the identity of the drug.

GENERAL PRINCIPLES OF TREATMENT

For the past decade the trend has been toward an increasingly conservative management of overdoses of drugs. The principles of management tend to be rather simple and are generally applicable.[2-5]

1. Rid the Patient of the Drug

The stomach may be emptied either by induced vomiting with mechanical or chemical means or by gastric lavage. The availability of syrup of ipecac as a chemical emetic is especially useful for treating overdoses of drugs in children before they arrive at the hospital. Emptying of the stomach by one means or another should probably be attempted in all cases of overdoses of psychotherapeutic drugs, even if several hours have elapsed since ingestion. The possible gains outweigh the risks because many of these drugs are absorbed slowly or tend to decrease gastrointestinal motility by their pharmacological effects. Thus, many psychotherapeutic drugs taken in overdose may persist in the gastrointestinal tract unabsorbed much longer than would be the case with therapeutic doses. Aspiration is the greatest risk in comatose patients, and after patients have been admitted to the hospital, lavage is generally preferable to induced emesis. If possible, intubation with a cuffed endotracheal tube should precede lavage to provide protection against tracheal aspiration. The return from the stomach should be saved to confirm the identification of the drug. Charcoal adsorbs many of these drugs quite well and should be administered in a dose of 30 grams/250 ml of water as soon as the stomach has been completely emptied.

If the return from gastric lavage is poor, it might be well to employ catharsis. Sodium sulfate, in doses of 30 grams, has been used to increase the passage of the retained drug through the bowel. The cathartic could be administered some time after the charcoal has been given to allow the adsorptive action to occur. On occasion large boluses of the unadsorbed drug, having passed through the stomach, may be present in the proximal intestine.

Forced diuresis may be used to hasten excretion of those drugs that may be excreted unchanged by the kidney. This is usually accomplished by the rapid intravenous injection of several liters of 5 or 10% dextrose in a water solution. The addition of two or three 0.5-gram doses of theophylline ethylenediamine to the fluid at four-hour intervals may hasten diuresis as well as stimulate depressed respiration. Urea and mannitol have been used as osmotic diuretics, and furosemide, ethacrynic acid, or hydrochlorothiazide as naturetic diuretics. Simple fluid loading alone may be satisfactory.

2. Observe the Patient Frequently

Vital signs, the state of consciousness, pupillary size and reactivity, and deep tendon reflexes should be recorded at the first examination and frequently throughout the course of treatment.

Such observations may provide the earliest indication of a worsening of the clinical state. An attempt to define a prognostic index for patients intoxicated with barbiturates, glutethimide, or meprobamate used twenty-five variables measured at different time intervals. Of all these variables, the systolic blood pressure was the best single indicator. Other indicators of value are the mean central venous pressure, the arterial pH and oxygen saturation, and arterial blood lactate.[6]

During forced diuresis, the patient's intake and output of fluid should be recorded carefully. A urine flow of 350 to 500 ml/hr or more is the goal of such treatment, but a brisk urine flow may be slow to appear until an initial state of dehydration has been rectified. Measuring central venous pressure may be mandatory to avoid fluid overload and pulmonary edema if intravenous fluids are vigorously pushed.

Serum electrolytes should be closely monitored, as should blood gases and pH. Plasma concentrations of the ingested drug may be helpful for diagnosis, but in at least one extensive study of serious overdoses with glutethimide, neither the blood nor the cerebral spinal fluid levels of glutethimide were of prognostic value.[7] Consequently, too much faith must not be placed upon the measurement of plasma concentrations of the drug.

3. Support Respiration and Blood Pressure

A clear airway is essential. If the airway is not clear, suction and placement of an oral airway are imperative. Should these not suffice, intubation with a cuffed endotracheal tube should be carried out. Central respiratory depression may be combated by artificial respiration, preferably using the mouth-to-mouth or mouth-to-tube methods until mechanical ventilators are available. Assisted respiration should be continued as long as is required to maintain optimal blood gas and pH concentrations. Tracheostomy may be required if the course of the coma is long, but the decision to perform one may be deferred twenty-four to forty-eight hours while other problems are being taken care of. Then it may be scheduled as an elective procedure with much less risk. The use of respiratory stimulant drugs is no longer regarded as proper, for at best the gains are temporary and they may decrease assiduous measures to support respiration of the type mentioned above.

Shock is managed in part by supporting respiration as well as by the same procedures used for forced diuresis. Large volumes of fluid alone often suffice to alleviate shock, although in refractory cases plasma expanders or plasma may be used beneficially. At least 1 liter of intravenous fluid should be administered when the patient is admitted, but as many as 8 or 10 liters in twenty-four hours may be required. Pressor agents are seldom needed in drug-induced shock and, in the opinion of some, are contraindicated.

SPECIAL PROBLEMS WITH SPECIFIC CLASSES OF DRUG

Antipsychotic Drugs

These drugs are represented by several different chemical classes, including the phenothiazine derivatives, thioxanthene derivatives, and butyrophenones, and poisonings with them are rather similar despite the difference in the chemical class. This is probably because the various drugs are similar pharmacologically. Poisonings with phenothiazine derivatives are probably fairly common, yet reports of them in the literature are scarce. Perhaps this rarity of case reports is a result of the almost uniformly favorable outcome. The few fatal cases from ingestion of chlorpromazine have all been in children. The minimum lethal dose for a 4-year-old child is 350 mg (14 25-mg tablets). However, adults have survived doses of 9.75 grams (195 50-mg tablets). Documented cases of overdoses with thioxanthene derivatives, such as chlorprothixene, again indicate no lethal outcome. The largest dose of chlorprothixene taken in which the patient survived was 1.075 grams (43 25-mg tablets) in a 1-year-old child, and 8 grams (80 100-mg tablets) in an adult. It would appear reasonable to expect that equivalent doses of thiothixene would be equally safe. Haloperidol has not been associated with any deaths following overdoses, and that may well prove to be the case with other butyrophenones.

After an overdose of phenothiazines, drowsiness rapidly proceeds to coma. Initially patients may become agitated or delirious, with signs of confusion and disorientation. Twitching, dystonic movements, and convulsions are other prominent neurological signs. Convulsions may be tonic, clonic or startle seizures. The pupils are miotic, and deep tendon reflexes are decreased. An electroencephalogram (EEG) shows diffuse slowing and low voltage. Tachycardia and marked hypotension are the principal cardiovascular manifestations, although an occasional patient may have a cardiac arrhythmia. The strong alpha-adrenergic receptor blocking the action of the phenothiazines may make alleviation of hypotension difficult. Hypothermia is the rule initially because of the disturbance of temperature regulation. Later, with increased activity, fever may appear, although true hyperpyrexia rarely does. The usual ranges of temperature are between 31 and 40°C. Late respiratory failure, often sudden, has been a distinguishing feature in fatal cases. A careful and prolonged vigilance is necessary so long as severe CNS depression persists. Prolonged shock and cardiac arrest have also been the causes of deaths.

Most phenothiazines are readily water soluble, so removal by gastric lavage is feasible. As mentioned, these drugs, among others, may delay gastric motility so that lavage may be successful in removing considerable amounts of drugs hours after their ingestion. Phenothiazines are tightly bound to protein, and once absorbed they become rapidly fixed in the tissues. Experimental attempts to hemodialyze 35S-labeled Chlorpromazine indicated little transfer across the cellophane membrane. Thus it is unlikely that any dialysis procedure will be useful in ridding the body of the absorbed drug. This is also very likely to be the case with exchange transfusions.

The general principles of the management of overdoses mentioned previously apply to phenothiazines, but some special problems must be met as they arise. Convulsions are best treated by intravenous injections of diazepam or sodium diphenylhydantoin. The possibility of increasing central respiratory depression with further doses of a central depressant drug should be balanced against the anticonvulsant effect and only minimally effective doses should be used. Acute hypotension not responsive to forced fluids may require the use of a pressor agent. Being primarily an alpha-adrenergic receptor stimulant, norepinephrine is the logical drug to be used in treatment. Warm blankets and heat cradles may reverse the trend toward hypothermia, but if the mark is overshot, fever will ensue. Fever should not be immediately ascribed to some infectious complication in the absence of other evidence.

Curiously enough, contrary to what might be expected with therapeutic overdoses, overdoses of phenothiazine derivatives have not been marked by the excessive development of extrapyramidal signs. Recently it has been found that very large therapeutic doses of phenothiazines produce few extrapyramidal motor reactions, quite possibly because of the stronger anticholinergic effects resulting from the larger doses of the drug.[8] Thus, it is not necessary to be overly concerned about extrapyramidal motor reactions in dealing with acute intoxications. As the patient improves and the level of drug decreases, such reactions may appear as late complications.

Antidepressants

These drugs consist of two separate pharmacological classes. One, the tricyclic antidepressants, consists of imipramine and amitriptyline and their active metabolites, desipramine and nortriptyline, as well as a somewhat different drug, protriptyline. The other class, the monoamine oxidase (MAO) inhibitors, is exemplified by tranylcypromine, a drug that chemically resembles dextroamphetamine. It would be quite fitting if drugs used for treating depressed patients, with whom suicide is an ever-present danger, were as safe as the antipsychotics. Unfortunately this is not the case. The problems from overdoses of the two separate classes of antidepressants are different.

Tricyclic Antidepressants. Amitriptyline or imipramine in doses of 1.2 grams or more is seriously toxic, and fatalities in adults are a great risk after ingestion of 2.5 grams (100 25-mg tablets). The time of death following ingestion of such large doses varies between three and seventy-two hours. As many as 5.375 grams have been taken by an adult who has survived. A 2½-year old child who ingested 2.5 grams of imipramine died within ninety minutes, but another child survived a dose of 75 mg/kg. Amitriptyline may be a bit more potent than imipramine in regard to toxicity. A dose of 1 gram (40 25-mg tablets) was fatal in a 15-month-old child, but as small a dose as 950 mg was fatal in a 70-year-old woman. However, desipramine may be less potent. A 58-year-old woman who ingested 1.15 grams became semi-comatose and hypotensive within thirty minutes, but she responded quickly to infusion of norepinephrine and was conscious three hours later. The clinical course might have been expected to be longer and more complicated with a similar dose of imipramine. Reports of overdoses of tricyclic antidepressants in children are becoming increasingly common and emphasize the great need for physicians prescribing this drug to warn patients of its toxicity. Nothing could aggravate a patient's depression more than to have a child or grandchild die of an overdose of his antidepressant drug. The specification of childproof containers when these drugs are prescribed should become a practice before it becomes a law.

Tricyclic antidepressants resemble phenothiazines chemically and, to some extent, pharmacologically. Consequently, they share many of the same clinical effects when they are given in toxic doses. A decreasing level of consciousness leading to coma is observed regularly. From the beginning, the patient may become temporarily agitated or delirious. Cardiorespiratory depression is frequent, although hypotension is less predictable than it is with the phenothiazines.

The pupils are dilated and sluggish, a reflection of the potent anticholinergic actions of the tricyclic drugs. The same problems in maintaining body temperature arise with tricyclic as with phenothiazine drug overdoses, although hyperthermia is likely to be a greater problem than hypothermia. Myoclonic seizures, twitches, increased deep tendon reflexes, and even plantar extensor reponses are frequent concomitants of toxic doses. The major distinguishing feature of intoxication with tricyclic drugs is the number of disturbances in cardiac rhythm and conduction. Usually the first disturbance to appear is a prolonged intraventricular conduction, followed by atrioventricular conduction disorders, and finally by virtually all types of arrhythmia. These include both atrial and ventricular tachycardia, and flutter or fibrillation usually with varying degrees of atrioventricular or intraventricular block. These arrhythmias may result from combined vagal block and a negative chronotropic effect of the drug.

The cardiac problems are especially difficult to manage. It is necessary to control arrhythmias in the face of impaired cardiac conduction. Thus in treating cardiac arrhythmias induced by tricyclic antidepressants, antiarrhythmic drugs that have the least possible effect on decreasing atrioventricular or intraventricular conduction should be used. Lidocaine has been used with some success in treating these overdoses. One might expect that diphenylhydantoin would also be appropriate for this particular situation. (It has the additional advantage of also controlling seizures.) The anticholinesterases, especially physostigmine, have been effective in diminishing toxicity in animals treated with amitriptyline. Physostigmine is generally preferred as an antidote rather than pyridostigmine or prostigmine because it also reverses some of the CNS toxicity induced by the anticholinergic action of the drug. Electric cardioversion is a technique to be considered in the face of persistent arrhythmias. Because of the possibility of rapid changes in cardiac rhythm or cardiac arrest, continual EKG monitoring is desirable. Provisions should be at hand for defibrillation and resuscitation.

Treatment in most other respects is similar to that outlined for phenothiazines.[9,10] The procedure used to enable the most severely intoxicated patient to recover was mannitol, used as an osmotic diuretic to hasten excretion of the drug, and dialysis used to manage hyperpyrexia. Even more than the phenothiazines, the tricyclic antidepressants tend to induce bladder and bowel paralysis because of their strong anticholinergic effects. Seizures are managed in the same way they are when resulting from overdoses of phenothiazines. It should be remembered that one of the pharmacological tests for compounds of this type is potentiation of pressor responses to tyramine mediated through norepinephrine. Pressor amines should be considered only if plasma expanders and fluid replacement fail to alleviate shock. Some patients develop profound metabolic acidosis and hypokalemia, which probably predisposes them to the persistence of cardiac arrhythmias. Sodium bicarbonate and intravenous potassium chloride may be required to restore acid-base and electrolyte balance. Frequent electrolyte and blood gas analyses are therefore highly desirable in the management of such patients.

Just as with the phenothiazines, removal of tricyclic drugs prior to absorption is easy but extremely difficult after they have been bound to protein. There is little evidence that tricyclic drugs are dialyzable, so the excretory route of choice is by forced diuresis.

MAO Inhibitors. The lowest recorded fatal dose of tranylcypromine was 500 mg (50 10-mg tablets), which was fatal for a 17-year-old girl who exhibited agitation, delirium, tremors, sweating, coma, shock, heart block, and profound hyperthermia (43.4°C) for eight hours before she died. Barbiturates were used but were ineffective. A slight fall in body temperature was achieved by tubbing. A 15-year-old girl who ingested 350 mg of tranylcypromine was subjected to hemodialysis and made a rapid recovery. Presumably the drug can be dialyzed readily. Ingestion of a dose of 750 mg (50 15-mg tablets) of phenelzine was not fatal in a patient weighing 54 kg, but ataxia, weakness, drowsiness, delirium, seizures, muscle fasciculations, and hyperthermia were encountered. Administration of chlorpromazine appeared to be an effective antagonist. That chlorpromazine was effective seemed reasonable, for most of the toxic effects of the MAO inhibitors are attributable to excessive adrenergic stimulation. In this regard, the toxicity of these drugs resembles that of amphetamines. With the declining use of MAO inhibitors for treating depression, and then only under strict observation, reports of overdoses of these drugs are declining.

Antianxiety Drugs

The benzodiazepines, diazepam and chlordiazepoxide, are the most widely used drugs. The enormous popularity of these drugs as compared with the others may result in no small part from their extraordinary safety when they are taken in overdose.

It is probably impossible to commit suicide with any benzodiazepine. No deaths were encountered in twenty-two instances of overdosage of chlordiazepoxide, even with doses as high as 2.25 grams (90 25-mg capsules). After observing 121 cases of poisoning with chlordiazepoxide in patients from 15 months to 63 years of age, the conclusion was that when used alone its symptoms were quite mild, consisting only of drowsiness and stupor. When the drug was used in combination with others, the effects of the second drug always predominated. Two instances of diazepam overdosage in children were relatively mild. The toxic effects of overdose are deep stupor and coma, marked muscle relaxation, but only a slight fall in blood pressure or respiratory depression. Supportive treatment is usually adequate. Newer benzodiazepines, such as oxazepam, have the same reputation for safety as the older ones. Oxazepam produced an unusual situation during overdose in which the blood glucose was measured at 1,680 mg/100 ml in the absence of urine glucose or acetone. Further investigation revealed that oxazepam produces a glucose reaction in vitro. One 10-mg tablet was dissolved in 2 ml of water, and the supernatant fluid was tested for glucose. It yielded values of 590 mg/100 ml by the Somogyi method and 750 mg/ml by the glucose-oxidase method. It is important to avoid the erroneous administration of insulin in an individual suffering from oxazepam overdose under the mistaken apprehension that one is dealing with nonketoacidotic diabetic coma. Such administration might lead to a hypoglycemic coma in addition to the drug-induced coma.[11] Because anxious patients are often issued large supplies of drugs between their visits to the physician, it is easy to order an amount of barbiturate that could be lethal. The availability of such safe, effective sedatives as benzodiazepines is a distinct advantage.

Meprobamate has been fatal when taken in doses as small as 20 grams (50 400-mg tablets), although recoveries have occurred after doses of 40 grams. Because sedatives are often taken in combination with other drugs or with alcohol, it is difficult to be certain about what factors contribute to death from overdose. The clinical picture of this intoxication resembles that of barbiturates, and its management is the same. The relatively small amount of meprobamate excreted by the kidney as compared to the hepatic metabolism suggests that forced diuresis may be of limited value. It should still be part of a generally supportive treatment program. Despite the ready availability and popularity of this drug, it is still a relatively infrequent cause of suicide as compared with barbiturates. A chemical congener, tybamate, has a very short biological half-life and should be free of suicide potential.

Glutethimide is perhaps the most dangerous antianxiety drug insofar as toxicity from overdose is concerned. Virtually none of the drug is excreted unchanged, metabolism being extensive. As most excretion of the drug is in bile, even comparatively small doses produce profound and lasting effects, with coma and respiratory depression predominating. Patients have taken doses as high as 35 grams (75 500-mg tablets) and recovered, which reemphasizes that the amount of the drug taken is less important to the outcome than the way the poisoning is managed. Besides the slow metabolic disposition of glutethimide, its high lipid solubility allows it to be stored in fat depots. Both factors make for a very long clinical course of intoxication, and some last as long as five days. The drug is not easily soluble, and instances have been reported in which unabsorbed drug has been found as a bolus in the intestine. Thus, almost every case of glutethimide intoxication should be treated by catharsis as well as by gastric lavage. Hemodialysis has been reported to be an effective treatment, although the drug is not easily dialyzable. Conservative treatment is probably the best procedure to take in glutethimide poisoning; in a prospective series of seventy patients treated conservatively, only one death was encountered, despite the fact that thirty-one patients were in coma when they entered and had complicated courses.[7] Thus it appears that most patients can be managed without dialysis. Hypoxia has always seemed to be greater than can be accounted for by a respiratory depression. The occurrence of methemoglobinemia in conjunction with these intoxications has been reported. Because this drug has no advantage over barbiturates or benzodiazepines, either as a hypnotic or sedative, the particular dangers associated with its overdose should militate against its clinical use in any situation.

Methaqualone, a new sedative on the American market, has already been the subject of much abuse in this country, as it was previously in Europe and Asia. Most of the reported instances of intoxication with this drug have been in the form of a combination of methaqualone and diphenhydramine, which is sold extensively in the United Kingdom under the name Mandrax.® These poisonings usually have been characterized by marked hypertonia, tonic convulsions, and relatively little respiratory depression. Other features — pulmonary edema and abnormal bleeding, spontaneous vomiting, marked tracheobronchial secretions, hypotension, and hypothermia — have also been noted. Pneumonia is a frequent complication. Plasma levels in excess of 3 mg/100 ml are considered to represent a dangerous poisoning. Despite the reputation of the drug for causing little respiratory depression, at least in one instance an overdose resembled that of usual sedatives, with thirty-six hours of apnea before spontaneous respirations reappeared. In this particular case, hemodialysis was thought to be somewhat effective because the drug is more dialyzable than most.[12]

Lithium Carbonate

Lithium carbonate is now recognized as the preferred treatment for manic-depressive disorders, both for acute episodes and for maintenance treatment. Because these patients are risks for suicide, it would be ideal if the preferred drug for treatment were nontoxic. Such is not the case, but fortunately overdoses of lithium have not been as toxic or as difficult to manage as might be expected.

Prompt treatment will minimize problems, for the exchange between lithium in plasma and cells is relatively slow. Thus there may be little relationship between the severity of the overdose and the plasma concentrations of lithium. In the beginning these may be quite high, with mild or moderate symptoms of intoxication, or lower later on, with severe symptoms of intoxication. When patients have developed coma or subcoma before treatment, the mortality may be 50 percent. Death is often caused by pulmonary complications, the result of the exceedingly viscous secretions from the respiratory tract that are difficult to remove.

Supportive measures as outlined previously and attempts to remove lithium are the mainstays of treatment. Saline infusion with or without forced diuresis and alkalinization of urine are usually sufficient. Hemodialysis has been followed by a late rebound resulting from the mobilization of sequestered lithium in tissues with a high affinity for the ion, such as bone and muscle. Peritoneal dialysis on a sustained basis has been very satisfactory. In one case, an initial plasma concentration of 4.6 Meq/liter was reduced to therapeutic levels by the fourth day of treatment, concomitant with clinical improvement.[13] No rebound was observed. The prominent symptoms and signs of lithium intoxication are exaggerations of those encountered with therapeutic overdose: retching, tremor, cog-wheel rigidity, myoclonic contractions, and coma.

Combinations of Drugs

Frequently drugs are sold in fixed combinations for ease of administration. The interactions between toxic doses of two or more drugs may create special problems. The combination of tranylcypromine and trifluoperazine, marketed in Canada and Europe but not in the United States, proved fatal in a 27-year-old man who took tablets containing either 10 or 1 mg of the drug. During a twenty-four-hour period he became restless, sweated profusely, showed signs of anxiety, and then became drowsy. Thirty hours after ingestion he suddenly developed coma, hypotension, and intense muscle rigidity. The latter was severe enough to impair respiration; death occurred thirty-six hours after ingestion. The slow onset of the marked muscle rigidity was an unusual feature in this case. It was suggested that future cases exhibiting such symptoms be treated by muscle relaxants to the point of paralysis and maintained on positive pressure respiration. This procedure was followed in a subsequent intoxication in a 42-year-old man who took sixty tablets. His respiration was impaired by a severe muscle spasm, and he developed pulmonary edema. Muscle relaxants, initially 20 mg of methohexitone and 75 mg of suxamethonium given by orotracheal tube, were followed by 4 mg of pancuronium and 10 mg of diazepam every four hours, with assisted ventilation continued for a period of thirty hours.[14] The fact that this patient responded so well to muscle relaxants and intermittent positive pressure ventilation suggests they are valuable procedures for treating this particular kind of intoxication.

A dose of 900 mg of phenelzine and 1 gram of phenobarbital was fatal in a 30-year-old man who had been taking phenelzine for two years. He developed a coma and severe hyperpyrexia, and death occurred forty-five hours after ingestion. The clinical signs were mainly those of the phenelzine overdose. A similar dose of 180 mg of phenelzine combined with 800 mg of amitriptyline led to somnolence, disorientation, labile blood pressure, and plantar extensor responses in a 38-year-old woman. Later in her course she developed bladder paralysis, presumably resulting from the anticholinergic action of the amitriptyline. Her recovery was uneventful. The patient had been on chronic therapeutic doses of amitriptyline before she took the combination. The clinical symptoms in this instance were quite different from those of intense central sympathetic stimulation (coma, seizures, and hyperpyrexia), which have occurred in patients who have taken therapeutic or toxic doses of tricyclic antidepressants following prolonged treatment with MAO inhibitors.

Sublethal individual doses of three drugs, 600 mg of imipramine, 130 mg of tranylcypromine, and 13 mg of trifluoperazine, were lethal for a 26-year-old man who took them in combination. Initial symptoms were tremors, nystagmus, and carpopedal spasms. Later he became semicomatose, developed a fever, and died.

It is always worth emphasizing the potential lethality of combining drugs and alcohol. Many unwitting suicides by patients and homicides by physicians have followed the injudicious use of barbiturates in treating acute alcoholic states—the two drugs have additive respiratory depressant effects. Sudden and unexpected deaths have followed paraldehyde therapy with alcoholism. Such deaths occurred from one-half to four hours following doses of 30 to 60 ml of paraldehyde given to nine patients in acute alcoholic withdrawal.[3,8] The autopsies revealed no morphologic cause of death. Chlordiazepoxide, diazepam, and phenothiazines are widely used for treating alcohol intoxication, and thus far no deaths have been reported from these combinations with alcohol. Hydroxyzine has also been used; in high doses it may augment the tendency to seizures. Because definite knowledge of the possible interactions between many sedatives and alcohol is lacking, their employment in patients with high levels of blood alcohol should be most cautious.

SUMMARY

The management of overdoses of the newer psychotherapeutic drugs still rests on the basic general principles applied for other sedatives and stimulants, although some special problems are associated with specific drugs. It is comforting that at least some of the newer agents are remarkably safe and that the possibility of lethal outcome is quite rare. All the drugs have a very large margin between therapeutic doses and severely toxic doses. Still, it is well to remember that patients can use these drugs for suicidal purposes or that they may inadvertently fall into innocent hands with tragic results. Ordering only small quantities in single prescriptions, identifying the prescribed drug, and treating the patient in the most expeditious and specific fashion are ways to reduce mortality.

REFERENCES

1. Brown, T. C. K., M. E. Dwyer, and J. G. Stocks: "Antidepressant Overdosage in Children, A New Menace," *Med. J. Australia,* 2:848–851, 1971.

2. Davis, J. M., E. Bartlett, and B. A. Termini: "Overdosage of Psychotherapeutic Drugs. A Review," *Dis. Nerv. Syst.,* **29**:157–164, 1968.

3. Teitelbaum, D. T.: "Poisonings With Psychoactive Drugs," *Pediat. Clin. N. Am.,* **17**:557–567, 1970.

4. Morelli, H. F.: "Rational Therapy of Drug Overdosage," in K. L. Melmon and H. F. Morelli (eds.), *Clinical Pharmacology: Basic Principles in Therapeutics,* Macmillan, New York, 1972, pp. 605–623.

5. Hollister, Leo E.: "Toxicology of Psychotherapeutic Drugs," in W. G. Clark and J. del Giudice (eds.), *Principles of Psychopharmacology,* Academic, New York, 1970, pp. 537–546.

6. Afifi, A. A., S. T. Sacks, V. Y. Liu, M. H. Weil, and H. Shubin: "Accumulative Prognostic Index for Patients with Barbiturate, Glutethimide and Meprobamate Intoxication," *New Eng. J. Med.,* **285**:1497–1502, 1971.

7. Chazan, J. A., and S. Garella: "Glutethimide Intoxication: A Prospective Study of 70 Patients Treated Conservatively without Hemodialysis," *Arch. Intern. Med.,* **128**:215–219, 1971.

8. Rifkin, A., R. Quitkin, C. Carillo, and D. F. Klein: "Very High Dosage Fluphenazine for Nonchronic Treatment-refractory Patients," *Arch. Gen. Psychiat.,* **25**:398–403, 1971.

9. Young, J. A., and W. H. Galloway: "Treatment of Severe Imipramine Poisoning," *Arch. Dis. Children,* **46**:353–355, 1971.

10. Treitman, P.: "Desipramine Poisoning," *J. Am. Med. Ass.,* **220**:861–862, 1972.

11. Zileli, M. S., F. Teletar, S. Denix, E. Ilter, and N. Adalar: "Oxazepam Intoxication Simulating Non-ketoacidotic Diabetic Coma," *J. Am. Med. Ass.,* **215**:1986, 1971.

12. Johnstone, R. E., G. T. Manitsas, and E. J. Smith: "Apnea Following Methaqualone Ingestion. Report of a Case," *Ohio State Med. J.,* **67**:1018–1020, 1971.

13. Wilson, J. H. P., A. J. M. Donker, G. K. Van Der Hen, and J. Wientjes: "Peritoneal Dialysis for Lithium Poisoning," *Brit. Med. J.,* **2**:749–750, 1971.

14. Coulter, C., T. Edmunds, and P. O. Pyle: "An Overdose of Parstelin," *Anesthesia,* **26**:500–501, 1971.

ROBERT L. TAYLOR, M.D.

JOHN I. MAURER, M.D.

JARED R. TINKLENBERG, M.D.

CHAPTER **8**

Management of "Bad Trips" in an Evolving Drug Scene*

Psychedelic drugs produce perceptual and cognitive distortions that individuals, in the majority of instances, experience as strange but tolerable, if not pleasant or even exhilarating. Although the exact reasons for a person's feeling threatened by the effects of psychedelic drugs are unknown, periodically the necessary mix of factors occurs, and a state of anxiety ranging from mild apprehension to panic evolves. The crisis created in an individual when he perceives himself to be in a threatening situation following the use of psychedelic drugs is commonly known as a "bad trip." Bad trips arise out of an extremely complex drug scene, and effective management of them is an increasingly difficult problem. Attempts at therapeutic intervention should take into account such complicating factors as the increase in the number of drugs available, impulsive use of unknown compounds, adulteration and contamination of drugs, and lethal potential of psychedelic agents.

COMPLICATIONS OF THE DRUG SCENE

The rising incidence of psychedelic drug usage is paralleled by the evolution of new drugs. The ever-increasing list of "mind-expansion" drugs now includes lysergic acid diethylamide (LSD) ("acid"), peyote, mescaline ("cactus"), psilocybin ("magic mushroom"), marihuana ("pot"), 2,5-dimethoxy-4-methylamphetamine (STP), dimethyltryptamine (DMT), methylenedioxyamphetamine (MDA), N,N-dimethyltryptamine (DMA), trimethoxyamphetamine (TMA), methoxymethylene + dioxyamphetamine (MMDA), thiocarbanidin (THC), the amphetamines ("speed"), phenylcyclidine (sernyl) (PCP), and various solvents.[1] Recently reports have appeared that describe the use of cough syrup, cold tablets, sleeping pills, heart stimulants, nasal inhalants, insecticide aerosols, asthma remedies, throat disks, and aerosol refrigerants to create the mind-expanding kick.* The rapid expansion of this psychedelic pharmacopeia is accounted for by several factors: (1) the ease with which derivative compounds can be synthesized; (2) the availability of numerous proprietary agents containing potential psychedelics,

*Adapted with the permission of the authors and publisher from an article of the same title, first published in *J. Am. Med.*, 213:422–425, July 20, 1970. Drs. Taylor and Maurer were then affiliated with the Stanford Department of Psychiatry; Dr. Tinklenberg continues to be.

*See *Medical World News*, 9:24–26, 1968.

such as atropine, scopolamine, and various solvents; (3) the desire of an increasing number of people for the psychedelic experience; (4) the prevalence of naturally occurring psychedelic agents, such as mescaline, belladonna, and marihauna; and (5) the large profit that can be realized through the sale of these drugs.

The growing number of psychedelic agents results in changing drug fads as the popularity of one drug gives way to more recent arrivals on the drug scene. As early as 1969, the medical director of the Haight-Ashbury Clinic had commented on this evolution in psychedelic drug usage: "For better or for worse, San Francisco was the 'acid' capital of the world for a long time and now it has become the 'speed' capital of the world." [2] Since then heroin, cocaine, and alcohol have in turn dominated what remains of the youth drug culture.

The tendency of drug users to ingest indiscriminately adds further to the complexity of an already complicated drug problem and creates a significant danger. Research surveying the hippie community in the late 1960s showed that almost one-half of the persons interviewed had taken unknown drugs. At a San Jose, California, rock festival, 4,000 unidentified pills were taken. In addition, the mixing of various drugs is common and results in combinations such as LSD and methamphetamine hydrochloride (Methedrine®) and marihuana "cut" with a variety of substances including amphetamines, mescaline, and opium. Contamination of marihuana with tincture of camphor containing 2.2 grams/oz of opium has been reported in California. [3]

The mixing of cheap psychoactive agents with more expensive psychedelic drugs can greatly increase profits and thus has become common practice. Unfortunately, such adulteration can create serious treatment problems. For example, the central anticholinergics, particularly the belladonna alkaloids, are frequently used for "spiking," thus making treatment of bad trips with phenothiazines potentially hazardous. The anticholinergic effects of these alkaloids are enhanced by the addition of a phenothiazine, and this combination

may lead to coma and cardiorespiratory failure. The undesirable consequences that result from the interaction between anticholinergic agents and phenothiazines have been adequately demonstrated in clinical studies. Patients receiving an anticholinergic agent treated with a representative phenothiazine showed marked central nervous system depression. [4]

The psychedelic drugs have established their lethal potential. Although deaths have been reported following the ingestion of STP (probably adulterated with belladonna alkaloids) [5] as a result of cardiovascular and respiratory effects, [6] death from the physiological effects of these drugs is rare. The psychological changes and their behavioral manifestations represent a greater threat to life. Feelings of omnipotence or panic, with an associated increase in irrational risk-taking, have led to deaths from leaps taken from high places with the intention of flying or from standing in front of oncoming vehicles in an attempt to push them back. Heavy usage of methamphetamine has been associated with an increase in paranoia and violent behavior. [7]

EVALUATION OF THE "BAD TRIPPER"

Protection of the individual from behavior dangerous either to himself or others should be a fundamental concern in treating the bad trip. For this reason the patient should not be left unattended while he is awaiting medical attention. An attempt should be made to provide a quiet place, away from unnecessary stimulation, because the patient is already overwhelmed by external and internal input. His main task is to reassemble and control this input overload, and extraneous data can only aggravate the situation. After initial safety is established, treatment of the bad trip should include an attempt to clarify the situation. Frequently bad trippers are brought in by friends who have already attempted unsuccessfully to alleviate the condition. Usually some information about what has happened can be elicited from them. Most importantly, the therapist should try to determine what drug was taken, the amount involved, and the approximate time the patient took the drug. Knowledge of the amount of drug and when it was taken will determine to some degree the course of the trip and may give the treating physician a rough idea of the amount of intervention that will be required, assuming he possesses a certain familiarity with the dosage, range, and duration of the common psychedelic agents. This area has been thoroughly covered in a recent review.[8] The experience of other drug-taking participants should be determined. This information may allow the examiner to determine whether he is dealing with an effect that is primarily the result of the unusual susceptibility of the patient. Any attempts to treat the patient before he was brought in for help should be explored, particularly any medication that might have been administered. Accompanying friends often cannot give reliable information, either because of the drug effects they are experiencing themselves or because they simply do not know what has happened. A clear history is the exception, not the rule. Fear concerning the possible legal implications of drug ingestion may block the giving of accurate information. Emphasizing the confidentiality of this information may be helpful. A history of the patient, obtained to facilitate medical treatment, comes under the rule of privileged communication and should not be shared with authorities.

Sometimes a bad tripper is brought in alone, without any history, by the police. In this situation a physical examination may yield some clues as to what drug was taken. Because of the ever-increasing problem of drug contamination, even a straightforward history that identifies the drugs should be substantiated, if possible, by physical findings.

The hallucinogens, such as LSD and mescaline, generally produce dilated pupils and reflex hyperactivity. Accompanying anxiety may mimic moderate sympathomimetic signs such as a mild increase in the pulse rate and blood pressure, sweaty palms, and tremor.[9] Anticholinergic

agents produce somewhat similar physical findings, which usually cannot be distinguished from those of other psychedelic agents. Excessive dryness of the mouth and an absence of sweating, however, may be useful clues in establishing that an anticholinergic drug was involved. Amphetamines such as "speed" produce marked sympathomimetic effects: rapid pulse rate, moderately elevated blood pressure, and excessive sweating, as well as increased motor activity. Miosis is a symptom of opiate usage. Marihuana causes dilatation of conjunctival blood vessels and creates a reddened appearance similar to that seen in conjunctivitis. There is no dilatation of pupils.[10]

A wide variety of mental states ranging in severity from mild apprehension to severe panic may be seen in persons undergoing bad trips. With high doses, a picture, best described as a toxic

Table 8-1. Physical Findings in Use of Common Street Drugs

Agent	Effects
Hallucinogens (LSD, mescaline)	Dilated pupils Reflex hyperactivity Anxiety symptoms
Anticholinergics	Dilated pupils (with cycloplegia) Reflex hyperactivity Anxiety symptoms Dry mouth Absence of sweating
Amphetamines	Rapid pulse Increase in blood pressure Increased sweating Increased motor activity (variable)
Opiates	Constricted pupils
Marihuana	Dilation of conjunctival blood vessels Rapid pulse No pupillary dilation

acute brain syndrome with disorientation and clouded consciousness, is present. Perceptual changes, such as illusions and hallucinations, are usually present and can be terrifying. A person may feel that he is going to "lose control" or "never come back." Severe feelings of depersonalization or even a total loss of the sense of identity may appear. Gross distortions of the body image may be present; for instance, the sensation that one's "brain is melting." Sensations that are experienced by one individual as extremely frightening and threatening may be experienced by another as mystical or beautiful.

An important indicator of the severity of psychological disruption is the amount of observing ego that is present. The degree to which an individual is able to "get outside" the experience and see it apart from himself as the result of taking a drug can be of important prognostic significance. The individual who develops the awareness that what he is experiencing is drug-induced and time-limited generally reintegrates successfully at the end of the experience. The absence of an observing ego, however, indicates severe disruption; if it fails to reappear as treatment proceeds, the possibility of functional psychosis triggered by the drug experience should be considered.

TREATMENT OF THE "BAD TRIPPER"

Establishment of verbal contact and a minimal use of tranquilizers should be a fundamental rule in the management of bad trips. In cases of apprehension, or even of panic, in which contact with reality is maintained by the observing ego, reassurance and a repetitive defining of reality often prove to be adequate treatment. In defining reality, the therapist should emphasize statements that attribute the distortions and frightening feelings of the experience to the drug. It is often useful to get the individual to put into words the experience he is having. Patients who are able to grasp and verbalize these experiences may thus be able to bring them under control rather than feel overwhelmed by them. One therapist found it

helpful to pick up a simple concrete object such as a book and say to the patient, "This is a book; feel the book." Simple repetitive concrete statements about person and place are useful. The temporary nature of what the patient is experiencing should be emphasized repeatedly. It can be very reassuring to a panicked bad tripper to repeatedly be told his name, that he is in a hospital bed, and in such and such a city. Concrete labeling helps the patient reassemble his reality and allows him to establish firmly that he is indeed a real person experiencing a drug-induced bad trip that is time-limited.

While a person "comes down," he experiences a phasic "in-and-out" alternation of mental clarity and confusion. This should be expected and predicted by the therapist. Reassurance should make this waxing and waning of awareness explicit. The therapist should be cautious in ascertaining that a patient who evidently has come down is truly "all the way down," not just in a temporary or transient clear spell.

The verbal "talkdown" (continuing reassurance and reality-defining) is usually effective when there is adequate time. The treating therapist, however, may not have sufficient time or staff. In these instances, medication should be used and will result, in the majority of cases, in a rapid dissolution of perceptual distortion and a reestablishment of premorbid ego functioning. Initially, if medication is used, it should be administered in a dose related to the size of the individual, not to the extent of the toxic effects. Subsequent doses, however, will depend to some degree on the severity of the symptoms and on the patient's response to the initial medication. We do not use phenothiazines in the initial treatment of bad trips for several reasons. Some drug users either intentionally or unknowingly consume anticholinergic agents that act synergistically with phenothiazines; the combination may result in an "anticholinergic crisis"[11] marked by cardiovascular difficulties. With phenothiazines, the margin between effective behavior sedation and depression of the cardiovascular system is small. Therefore, the use of phenothiazines for sedation is questionable for any clinical disorder in which the untreated course is usually benign. Also, phenothiazines may mask an incipient schizophrenic psychosis that otherwise could be detected and treated appropriately. Finally, the immobilizing properties of the phenothiazines are distressing for many patients and can increase agitation and anxiety.

If despite clarifying and supportive treatment, the patient remains distressed or becomes increasingly agitated, a drug of the sedative-hypnotic class should be administered, preferably orally. Our preference is diazepam (Valium®), in an initial dose of 20 to 30 mg orally (15 to 20 mg intramuscularly). However, the physician is well advised to use moderate doses of the short-acting sedative with which he is most familiar. Subsequent doses are determined by the patient's overall response, especially by his vital signs. The dosage schedule is determined by the time before the peak drug effects occur; to avoid suppression of cardiovascular function and excessive sedation, repeat doses should not be given until maximal drug effects can be ascertained.

Most patients with adverse drug reactions respond so favorably to supportive psychotherapy with or without medication that hospitalization is not needed. If the perceptual distortions have subsided and the patient feels comfortable enough to return home, this is a reasonable disposition. The patient should be with a responsible person for the next twenty-four hours. Thus, if he lives alone, he should be released only if he is able to stay with a friend or relative.

Certain exceptions to this disposition should be considered. Prolonged use of amphetamines often results in severe depression with increased suicidal risk when the person is "brought down." Hospitalization may be required. In addition, complicating medical problems such as abscesses and hepatitis are present in some patients treated for adverse drug reactions, particularly if the intravenous route has been used. Patients should be carefully screened for medical problems and hospitalized if necessary. Overnight hospitalization is advisable in those cases in which the observing ego fails to

return, or in which contact with reality is tenuous so that the individual does not appear to be in control of his thoughts or impulses. If these deficits persist beyond twenty-four hours, the diagnosis of functional psychosis is strongly suggested. It is a good practice to avoid the use of phenothiazines as a sleeping medication when the patient is hospitalized overnight. They may mask a psychosis and falsely reassure the therapist that the individual has reintegrated by the following morning.

Once the acute reaction is over, the emergency therapist may be tempted to investigate the reasons for the drug use. He should be cautious about this, however. A patient just recovering from a bad trip is unlikely to be ready for a general discussion of issues such as continued drug use or underlying emotional problems. At this time, the patient's decisions about future use of drugs are likely to be more in reaction to the recent bad trip than in consequence of objective self-examination, and therefore such decisions are easily reversible. The emergency therapist should confine his treatment to the immediate situation that prompted the request for help. He should encourage the patient to return for a follow-up, and at that time, when the patient is far more likely to be receptive and open, a discussion of drug use and possible underlying emotional problems could be started. Questions about drugs and the possible need for continued counseling can be explored. If there are no signs of continuing ego disruption, and the person feels no need for counseling, further follow-up is not indicated.

REFERENCES

1. Smith, D. E., J. Fort, and D. L. Craton: "Psychoactive Drugs," *Drug Abuse Papers, 1969,* Continuing Education in Criminology, University Extension, University of California, Berkeley, 1969, p. 10.

2. Smith, D. E.: "Changing Drug Patterns on the Haight-Ashbury," *Calif. Med.,* **110**(151):157, 1969.

3. Unwin, J. R.: "Illicit Drug Use among Canadian Youth," *Can. Med. Ass. J.,* **98**(pt. 2):449–454, 1968.

4. Gershon, S., H. Neubauer, and D. M. Sundland: "Interaction Between Some Anticholinergic Agents and Phenothiazines," *Clin. Pharmacol. Therap.,* **6**:749–756, 1965.

5. Snyder, S. H., L. Faillace, and L. Hollister: "2, 5-Dimethoxy-4-Methyl Amphetamine (STP): A New Hallucinogenic Drug," *Science,* **158**:669–670, 1967.

6. Solursh, L. P., and W. R. Clement: "Hallucinogenic Drug Abuse: Manifestations and Management," *Can. Med. Ass. J.,* **98**:407–410, 1968.

7. Unwin: op. cit. (pt. 1), pp. 402–413.

8. Smith: loc. cit.

9. Hollister, L. E.: *Chemical Psychoses,* Charles C Thomas, Springfield, Ill., 1968.

10. Weil, A. T., N. E. Zinberg, and J. M. Nelson: "Chemical and Psychological Effects of Marijuana in Man," *Science,* **162**:1234–1242, 1968.

11. Crowell, E. B., and J. S. Ketchum: "The Treatment of Scopolamine-induced Delirium with Physostigmine," *Clin. Pharmacol. Therap.,* **8**:409–414, 1967.

PHILIP A. BERGER, M.D.

CHAPTER 9

Management of the Addicted Patient

The addicted patient is an increasingly common sight in the emergency room. His drug of abuse is an opiate, a barbiturate, an amphetamine, one of the newer sedatives, or combinations of these drugs. His complaints stem from either acute drug toxicity or an abstinence syndrome. Responsibility for his care is split between medicine and psychiatry because tradition has not yet given drug addiction exclusively to either specialty. This chapter will focus on the emergency management of the addicted patient and briefly outline the common types of follow-up care. Of necessity it must ignore the broad social causes and implications of drug abuse and concentrate on the individual in crisis.

ACUTE DRUG TOXICITY

Acute Opiate Toxicity

Acute opiate toxicity usually results from an accidental overdose or an abnormal allergic or hypersensitivity reaction to opiates or adulterants. Addicted patients with a high degree of tolerance to a narcotic drug can become acutely poisoned after withdrawal if they return to their usual dose. Family members, especially children of patients on methadone, may inadvertently swallow a "weekend dose." Sixty milligrams of morphine or an equivalent dose of another narcotic analgesic is dangerous to an adult, and 240 mg or more may be fatal if the patient is not treated immediately.[1] Death has been reported following doses as small as 60 mg of morphine, but with careful treatment, recovery after 760 mg of morphine has also been reported.[2] Children and the elderly are more sensitive to morphine than young adults, and those with diminished vital capacity are more susceptible to the toxic effects of opiates. Hypothyroidism also increases sensitivity to the toxic effects of morphine.[3]

The patient with acute toxicity from opium derivatives or methadone usually appears with pinpoint pupils (unless anoxia or other drugs have caused them to dilate), areflexia, and either apnea or two to three shallow breaths per minute.[4] The coma is characteristically light in proportion to the degree of respiratory depression. Blood pressure is depressed, and tachycardia and pulmonary edema may be present. Convulsions are not common.[5]

Meperidine (Demerol®) toxicity results in a somewhat different syndrome. Respiratory depression, dilated pupils, and dry mucous membranes are present. Meperidine toxicity also seems to produce muscular tremors and convulsions.[6]

The treatment of acute opiate toxicity consists of immediate support of vital functions and the simultaneous administration of a specific narcotic antagonist. The patient may require prompt artificial support of his respiration or even full cardiopulmonary resuscitation. N-allynormorphine (Nalline®) or levallorphan (Lorfan®), both given intravenously, were the narcotic antagonists used until recently. However, both drugs can themselves act as respiratory depressants.[7] Naloxone (Narcan®), however, will not depress respirations and can therefore be given as a diagnostic test even to a patient with a coma of unknown etiology. The dose is 0.4 mg or 1 ml intravenously, or 0.01 mg/kg for children, which can be repeated in three minutes. If the patient does not improve after three doses, his condition is probably not caused by opiate toxicity. When the patient improves, he must still be watched carefully because the antagonism of naloxone lasts only three to four hours, whereas the depressive effects of other opiates can last much longer. Thus, further treatment with naloxone may be necessary, and the patient will require continuous observation.

Finally, the patient with acute opiate toxicity may present with other medical problems as a direct result of attempts made to resuscitate him "on the street." Stimulation is a common resuscitation technique and includes facial slaps, squeezing of nipples or testicles, and applying ice to sensitive areas. Another street technique is the injection of an amphetamine, which can cause convulsions in a hypoxic patient. In some areas street mythology has held that injected salt can "bind" heroin and that injected milk can "reverse" an overdose. Actually, the hypertonic saline will only complicate the electrolyte balance, and milk can probably cause lipoid pneumonia.[8]

Acute Barbiturate Toxicity

Acute barbiturate toxicity causes about 1,500 deaths in the United States each year. Most of these deaths represent successful suicide attempts, but some are accidental overdoses or the result of unusual sensitivity. Barbiturate toxicity reaches a peak between the ages of 30 and 50, is more common in women than in men, and is a particular problem to those with easy access to drugs, such as physicians, nurses, and pharmacists.[9]

Acute barbiturate intoxication produces confusion, emotional lability, garrulousness, and eventually sleep and coma. The neurological signs present include lateral nystagmus, ataxic gait, depressed tendon reflexes, and constricted pupils. In severe intoxication, respiration is shallow and infrequent, and the blood pressure is depressed.[10]

Severe barbiturate intoxication is a medical emergency. The patient should be managed in an intensive care unit in consultation with an anesthesiologist and other experienced specialists. Generally, the patient will require respiratory and circulatory support, careful management of fluid and electrolyte balance, and very attentive nursing care. Hemodialysis or peritoneal dialysis may be helpful. Following their recoveries from comas, some patients will develop toxic psychoses.[11] Finally, the patient whose barbiturate ingestion represents a suicide attempt will require psychiatric evaluation.

Acute Sedative Toxicity

Since 1952 a growing number of nonbarbiturate sedative drugs have been developed and introduced. They have different characteristics and therapeutic indications, but acute intoxication produces a syndrome remarkably similar to barbiturate intoxication.[12] Overdoses of ethchlorvynol (Placidyl®), meprobamate (Miltown®, Equanil®), glutethimide (Doriden®), methyprylon (Noludar®), and ethinamate (Valmid®) have been reported to cause both coma and death. Chlorodiazepoxide (Librium®) has been reported to cause coma, but fatal overdoses have not been reported.[13]

The treatment principles for sedative overdose are the same as those previously described for barbiturates. A severe intoxication requires hospitalization in an intensive care unit and the cooperation of several medical specialists. The patient can develop a toxic psychosis when recovering from the coma, and the sedative drug overdose often represents a suicide attempt. A more detailed discussion of severe sedative intoxication and its management can be found in Chapter 7, "Overdoses of Psychotherapeutic Drugs."

Acute Amphetamine Intoxication

Intoxication with amphetamines and amphetaminelike compounds produces central nervous system (CNS) stimulation, and in high doses has peripheral sympathomimetic effects. Peripheral symptoms include hyperactive reflexes, sweating, tachycardia, hypertension, and fever. CNS stimulation leads to anxiety, insomnia, hyperactivity, and confusion, and in more serious intoxications combativeness, hallucinations, and paranoid psychoses are reported. Severe poisoning may cause high fever, convulsions, coma, circulatory collapse, and death. The patient who has taken an overdose of amphetamines may require hospitalization and treatment in consultation with experienced specialists. A common pharmacological treatment for amphetamine poisoning with excessive CNS stimulation has been to administer short-acting barbiturates intravenously until the patient is sedated. Recent evidence, however, suggests that chlorpromazine in an initial dose of 1 mg/kg given intramuscularly is probably a more effective treatment.[14] If the patient has already taken a combination of amphetamines and barbiturates, a lower initial dose of 0.5 mg/kg of chlorpromazine should probably be used. Phenoxybenzamine has been suggested for use in conjunction with chlorpromazine for patients who manifest CNS stimulation and hypertension or other severe sympathomimetic symptoms.[15]

CHRONIC DRUG TOXICITY

Chronic Opiate Intoxication

The usual emergency room problem associated with chronic opiate intoxication is the withdrawal syndrome. Of the three major addictive drug categories (opiate, alcohol, sedative-hypnotic), opiates probably produce the abstinence syndrome that is easiest to manage medically. The *morphine withdrawal syndrome* has been studied carefully and can be described in some detail.

For the first eight to twelve hours after abstinence, the patient feels nothing unusual. This is followed by nervousness, restlessness, and sleepiness, but if the patient sleeps he will be restless and will soon awake. Yawning, tearing, nasal discharge, and perspiration soon appear, and restlessness increases. By the twenty-fourth to the thirty-sixth hour, the patient cannot sit still, complains of alternating chills and warmth, and may have dilated pupils and waves of gooseflesh. Appetite is decreased, vomiting and diarrhea appear, a slight fever may develop, and muscle and joint pains appear. The peak intensity of these symptoms is from the forty-eighth to the seventy-second hour after abstinence begins. After the third day the symptoms decline, but weakness, nervousness, and sleep disturbances may persist for weeks or even months.[16]

Other opiates produce abstinence syndromes that differ only in the times of onset and the intensity and duration of the symptoms. *Methadone* withdrawal is mild, begins about the third day of abstinence, but lasts longer than the morphine withdrawal syndrome. *Heroin* is converted into morphine in the body; the abstinence syndrome is therefore similar to morphine's. *Meperidine* withdrawal is characterized by early symptoms, less severe than morphine's, and rapid recovery. Abrupt cessation of *codeine* leads to slow-appearing but mild symptoms that last as long as those of morphine withdrawal. As a general rule, the greater the daily dose the more intense the abstinence syndrome.[17]

Treatment. Opiate addiction is probably best treated by substituting methadone for whatever drug the patient has been using and then gradually reducing the methadone dose. There are numerous techniques for this methadone withdrawal, and most work fairly well. One common technique is to give just enough methadone twice a day to prevent the onset of withdrawal symptoms, although some think a single dose every day is sufficient as well as more convenient to administer.[18,19] The dose required will vary as a function of the degree of tolerance, but 20 mg twice a day is usually enough. After a two- to three-day stabilization period, methadone can be reduced by 5 or 10 mg each day, or even more slowly if symptoms develop.

People addicted to heroin have a high incidence of hepatitis, pneumonia, tuberculosis, cardiac diseases, and severe diarrheas.[20] If the withdrawal is complicated by these or other medical problems, the reduction of methadone should be either slowed or stopped temporarily. If the patient also requires simultaneous barbiturate withdrawal, the time course should probably be determined by the degree of barbiturate dependence because barbiturate abstinence is potentially more dangerous.[21] Finally, many may undergo alcohol withdrawal, which is discussed in Chapter 6.

The psychological aspects of simple opiate withdrawal add to the difficulty of managing these patients. Anxiety reactions are common, and the lifestyle of persons addicted to heroin trains them well for malingering and persuasive complaining. It is probably best to be sympathetic but firm. The therapist should carefully evaluate each complaint, but changing the reduction plan is usually *not* indicated. Predicting symptoms in advance tends to reduce anxiety for some patients. Diazepam or other tranquilizers can be helpful in relieving anxiety. Massage and warm flow baths may help with muscle and joint pains. If insomnia becomes a serious problem, flurazepam (Dalmane®) or chloral hydrate can be given at bedtime.[22]

Chronic Barbiturate Intoxication

Tolerance to the effects of barbiturates, although only partial, does develop, and abrupt withdrawal from amobarbital, secobarbital, and pentobarbital after prolonged intoxication results in a characteristic *barbiturate withdrawal syndrome.*[23] Isbell,[24] who described barbiturate dependence in 1950, did a series of experiments that helped to define the abstinence syndrome. Subjects chronically taking 400 mg/day of pentobarbital had only minor withdrawal phases. Those taking 600 mg/day developed anxiety, tremors, and weakness. Seventy-five percent of those taking 800 mg/day developed convulsions, and 60 percent developed a picture similar to the delirium tremens of alcohol abstinence.

To describe the barbiturate withdrawal syndrome, it is helpful to divide the clinical picture into minor and major symptoms. The *minor symptoms* appear in almost all patients using over 800 mg/day of pentobarbital for six weeks or longer. The symptoms include anxiety, insomnia, sweating, anorexia and vomiting, muscular weakness, postural faintness resulting from postural hypotension, coarse tremors aggravated by voluntary movement, and spasmodic jerking of one or more of the extremities.[25] The *major symptoms* include grand mal seizures, psychosis similar to the delirium tremens of alcohol, and fever. The seizures usually begin during the second or third day of abstinence, and the psychosis may appear any time from the third to the eighth day after barbiturates are withheld. Finally, rising body temperature is an ominous sign in barbiturate withdrawal, and for this reason fever is included with the major symptoms.[26]

Treatment. Treatment of the barbiturate withdrawal syndrome begins with a determination of the patient's daily barbiturate intake. This is often difficult. Even a fully cooperative patient may not be aware of the capsule size or exact number of capsules he used each day. Drugs purchased illegally further complicate the problem.

Thus it is often helpful to use a procedure known as the *pentobarbital test dose,* a simple test of the patient's tolerance to barbiturates. After signs of intoxication have disappeared, the patient should be placed in bed and given 200 mg of pentobarbital on an empty stomach. One hour later he should be examined for the following clinical signs of intoxication to estimate his twenty-four-hour requirement for pentobarbital:[27]

1. If the patient is asleep or grossly intoxicated (drowsy, slurred speech, coarse nystagmus, positive Romberg sign), he probably has been using 600 mg/day or less of pentobarbital.

2. If the patient is comfortable, has normal speech, is not ataxic, and shows only a fine lateral nystagmus, his intake has probably been equivalent to 800 mg/day of pentobarbital.

3. If the patient shows no response to the test dose or even shows signs of the barbiturate withdrawal syndrome, he has probably been ingesting at least 1,000 mg/day or more of barbiturate.[28]

This testing procedure can be modified slightly if the patient admits to taking 1,400 mg or more. In this case a 300-mg test dose can be used. If the patient shows mild intoxication, 1,600 mg of pentobarbital every twenty-four hours or more will be required to prevent the abstinence syndrome. [29]

Once the twenty-four-hour requirement has been established, the patient should be given that total amount in twenty-four hours in four to six divided doses at four- to six-hour intervals. The pentobarbital test dose, however, gives only an approximation. During the first twenty-four hours of treatment, the patient should be examined for signs of abstinence just before each dose, and for signs of intoxication one hour after each dose. It is best to keep the patient mildly intoxicated. The next dose can be adjusted if abstinence syndromes appear or if the patient is grossly intoxicated. Often this stabilization takes more than twenty-four hours. [30]

After the patient has been stabilized for about forty-eight hours, the pentobarbital dose is reduced by about 100 mg/day. If abstinence symptoms become apparent, the reduction is halted until the symptoms decrease, and then reduction is continued at about 50 mg/day.[31] Seizures should not occur on this schedule, but if a convulsion

does occur, 100 to 200 mg of pentobarbital given intramuscularly can be used every hour until the patient is again intoxicated.[32]

Psychosis on admission is a more difficult situation. Intoxication cannot easily reverse this condition but should be achieved rapidly anyway to prevent agitation, insomnia, and fever. Pentobarbital should be given intramuscularly or intravenously until the patient is sedated and stable. Studies have shown that diphenylhydantion (Dilantin®) and chlorpromazine (Thorazine®) do not prevent the seizures from barbiturate withdrawal in dogs, so they are probably not useful. [33]

In addition to pentobarbital therapy, the patient with an abstinence syndrome has other needs. He should sleep in a low bed with padded side rails. The patient in severe withdrawal requires fluids, restoration of electrolyte balance, and vitamins. Finally, and perhaps most important, the patient will need follow-up psychiatric care to prevent the all too common rapid return to the dependent state.

Chronic Intoxication with Nonbarbiturate Sedatives and Minor Tranquilizers

Despite the label "nonbarbiturate" or "minor tranquilizer," this group of drugs can produce dependence, and upon withdrawal (usually from higher than recommended doses), syndromes remarkably like abstinence from barbiturates may appear. The drugs of this group include meprobamate, glutethimide, ethinamate, ethchlorvynol, methyprylon, chlordiazepoxide, diazepam, and methaqualone.

There have been many clinical reports of *meprobamate* (Miltown®, Equanil®) abstinence syndromes. In one representative study, forty-seven patients received 3.2 or 6.4 grams of meprobamate for forty days before its abrupt withdrawal. Thirty patients had insomnia, vomiting, tremors, muscle twitches, ataxia, anxiety, and headache. Eight patients had psychoses similar to delirium tremens, and three patients had convulsions within thirty-eight to forty-eight hours after the meprobamate was discontinued.[34] One death was reported following the discontinuation of meprobamate in a patient whose daily dose was probably 10 grams.[35]

The *glutethimide* (Doriden®) abstinence syndrome includes vomiting, agitation, tremulousness, disorientation, hallucinations, convulsions, and fever.[36] Thus it is very much like the withdrawal from barbiturates or meprobamate with one important difference: glutethimide withdrawal seizures have been observed as late as the sixth day after withdrawal. Experimental studies indicate that addiction occurs if the daily dose exceeds 2.5 grams.[37]

Withdrawal from *ethinamate* (Valmid®) is followed by agitation, syncopal episodes, tremulousness, and hyperactive reflexes. In a more severe syndrome, psychosis and major convulsions have been reported. Again, the syndrome is similar to barbiturate withdrawal and was produced by chronic use of 13 grams/day.[38]

Withdrawal from *ethchlorvynol* (Placidyl®) also produces generalized convulsions and psychosis. This syndrome has been reported in patients taking more than 2 grams for periods longer than six months.[39]

The *methyprylon* (Noludar®) abstinence syndrome includes confusion, restlessness, sweating, and convulsions in more severe syndromes. Daily doses greater than 2.4 grams seem to produce abstinence when they are discontinued, and one death during withdrawal was reported in a patient using 7.5 to 12 grams/day for eighteen months.[40]

Withdrawal from *chlordiazepoxide* (Librium®) produces insomnia, nausea, agitation, depression, sweating, and muscle twitching in patients using more than 300 mg/day for five or six months. It is important to note that seizures have been reported in the seventh and eighth days of the abstinence syndrome and as late as twelve days after abstinence in one patient who took 300 mg for three months.[41] However, in general the chlordiazepoxide abstinence syndrome is slower to develop and less acute than that of barbiturate abstinence.[42]

Doses of *diazepam* (Valium®) (120 mg/day) produced minor withdrawal symptoms in six of thirteen patients when they were discontinued and a grand mal seizure in one patient on the eighth day following abstinence.[43] Finally, *methaqualone* (Quaalude®, Sopor®, Parest®) must be mentioned because of the recent increase in its abuse in the face of a widespread belief that this medication is not addictive. Abrupt cessation of methaqualone in doses of at least 1,800 to 2,000 mg/day has been reported to cause tremulousness, weakness, nausea, vomiting, seizures, and delirium.[44,45] Thus methaqualone withdrawal also seems very much like the barbiturate abstinence syndrome.

Treatment of the syndromes produced by withdrawal from these minor tranquilizers and sedatives is similar to that already described for the barbiturate abstinence syndrome. Theoretically, a similar testing, stabilization, and gradual reduction program could employ the sedative on which the patient was dependent. However, it is also theoretically possible to substitute pentobarbital for the patient's usual drug and to proceed as if the patient had been dependent on barbiturates. This barbiturate substitution has been safely employed in withdrawals from glutethimide and alcohol.[46] Perhaps future clinical trials will show one of these methods to be superior, but current knowledge does not permit a firm recommendation of either the barbiturate substitution method or the gradual reduction of the drug of dependence. In either case, the appearance of seizures late in withdrawals from glutethimide, chlordiazepoxide, and diazepam using current regimens suggests that these syndromes may require more gradual reductions if the withdrawal is to be safe.

Chronic Amphetamine Intoxication

Chronic amphetamine abuse seems to occur in at least two distinct patterns. In one, the dose is increased gradually over a period of weeks or months as tolerance develops. In a second common pattern, intravenous methamphetamine is injected frequently in increasing doses over a sleepless four- to six-day period. This "speed run" is usually terminated when the amphetamine user passes out from exhaustion and sleeps twenty-four to forty-eight hours. When he awakes, the cycle may be started over again.[47]

When the amphetamine user finally abstains, he will be severely fatigued and psychologically depressed. The fatigue and depression may be extreme at first, but the symptoms gradually subside over a period ranging from weeks to months. This abstinence syndrome certainly requires less medical management than barbiturate or opiate withdrawal, but it may trigger a paranoid psychosis requiring treatment. However, the syndrome produced by continuing intoxication with amphetamines is more often a serious psychiatric problem.

Chronic amphetamine intoxication causes insomnia, anorexia, hypertension, tachycardia, and dilated pupils.[48] Psychological symptoms include anxiety, hyperactivity, suspiciousness, labile mood, and in some cases what is called *amphetamine psychosis*. This syndrome includes ideas of reference, delusions of persecution, visual and auditory hallucinations, hyperactivity, and excitement. Unlike a typical toxic psychosis, however, disorientation and memory clouding are not usually present. Thus, amphetamine psychosis presents a clinical picture remarkably like that of paranoid schizophrenia.[49]

The treatment of amphetamine psychosis presents some problems. The amphetamine user is often suspicious of hospitalization, and his hyperactivity, labile mood, and paranoid delusions make him prone to assaultive behavior. However, the syndrome does respond to abstinence and phenothiazine medication and has a relatively good prognosis. There are reports of chronic psychosis in some high-dose users, but most patients who present with amphetamine psychosis eventually recover. The most severe symptoms disappear within days or weeks, and in six to twelve months a virtually complete recovery is possible.[50] Finally, although the original amphetamine psychosis was described as a result of dextroamphetamine

intoxication, amphetaminelike drugs such as phenmetrazine (Preludin®) and diethylpropion (Tenuate®) have been reported to cause paranoid states.[51]

Chronic cocaine intoxication also produces a syndrome remarkably similar to that of chronic amphetamine intoxication. The cocaine intoxication syndrome includes tachycardia, hypertension, tremulousness, dilated pupils, and anxiety. Chronic cocaine intoxication can also produce a paranoid psychosis, with delusions and hallucinations, that is nearly identical to amphetamine psychosis and should be similarly managed.[52]

LONG-TERM TREATMENT AND REHABILITATION

Long-term Treatments for Opiate Addiction

There are at least four different approaches to the long-term therapy and rehabilitation of patients addicted to opiates:

1. Traditional individual or group psychotherapy based on the assumption that drug addiction is a symptom of deeper psychopathology.

2. Temporary drug-free communes that offer various kinds of psychotherapy, peer group confrontation, recreation, and vocational guidance. The ultimate aim of these shelters is to return the formerly addicted patient to a productive role in society.

3. Relatively permanent alternatives to society that emphasize a total commitment to a drug-free communal life style and make extensive use of group confrontation therapy. The Synanon community is the best example of this approach.

4. Pharmacological treatment programs, based in either outpatient or inpatient settings, that use methadone maintenance or opiate antagonists to prevent relapse to addiction.

Actually, the majority of programs combine

these basic approaches, and many new centers give the addicted patient his choice of several basic treatment techniques. In this chapter only the pharmacological treatments for opiate addiction will be described in detail.

Methadone maintenance is the most successful and thoroughly tested pharmacological therapy used in treating opiate addiction. Its introduction in the mid-60s was based on a biochemical theory of opiate addiction and relapse. The theory stated that a return to addiction after abstinence was caused by "narcotics hunger" which could be relieved only by the use of opiates. It was suggested that this narcotics hunger was caused by a metabolic or biochemical defect that resulted from the repeated use of narcotics.[53] Methadone would fill this theoretical biochemical need and prevent narcotics hunger. The success of methadone maintenance therapy, however, is probably also related to another aspect of its pharmacological activity: when given in high oral doses, methadone seems to prevent the euphoric effects of even relatively high doses of other narcotics. This has been called the "blockade effect," but the term is inaccurate. What methadone produces is a high degree of cross tolerance.[54]

The technique of methadone maintenance begins with gradual increases in the doses. Twenty milligrams twice a day is a frequent starting dose for patients who are using opiates at the time maintenance begins. However, some treatment centers begin with medication once a day to save staff time. The dose is then increased gradually over the next three to six weeks to the stabilization level, usually 80 to 120 mg/day, although doses as high as 180 mg have been used. However, a recent double-blind study suggests that there is very little difference between 50 and 100 mg, and because tolerance to some effects develops slowly or not at all, 50 mg theoretically would be better for the patient.[55]

Other reasons favor using a lower dosage. The diversion of methadone to illegal uses is becoming quite a problem in certain areas. Patients on methadone maintenance "take home" programs

are likely to discover for themselves that low doses are sufficient and that the excess can be sold. Another real advantage is the ease of withdrawal. When the patient decides to terminate methadone maintenance or is forced by circumstances to do so, he will have an easier withdrawal syndrome if he has been maintained at a lower level.

Methadone stabilization can be accomplished on an outpatient basis by trained medical personnel. Once stabilized, the patient comes once a day for methadone. Early side effects include sedation, poor appetite, and mood swings, but these tend to disappear with time. The major persisting side effects include constipation, which responds to laxatives, and excessive sweating. Current long-term prospective and retrospective studies show methadone to be medically safe and nontoxic when it is used as directed; further data are still being collected.[56]

The usual methadone maintenance program, however, is much more than a mere dispensing center for methadone. Counseling and rehabilitation services are an important part of the successful methadone program. Because methadone cannot prevent the use of heroin by anyone determined to use it, the patient who is accepted by a methadone program must also have made a decision to change his lifestyle. Individual psychotherapy, group therapy, vocational counseling, and good medical care enable the methadone program to reinforce the patient's decision and help him to achieve his own goals. Some programs do this supportive work well, but other methadone programs fail because these necessary services are not provided. Additionally, patients addicted to opiates must be seen as individuals, with different personalities and different needs. A successful treatment program must be ready to provide a variety of services to meet these individual needs, not just one standard regimen for everyone.

Maintenance with opiate antagonists, the second pharmacological treatment for heroin addiction, was originally based on a conditioning theory of opiate dependence and relapse. This theory notes that a formerly addicted patient, medically withdrawn from heroin, will on return to his old environment experience a classically conditioned withdrawal syndrome which in some ways resembles physiological withdrawal and can be relieved by heroin. It also notes that heroin is a powerful reinforcer of its own use because it produces euphoria and that there are many other aspects of drug-seeking behavior which become rewards in themselves.[57]

The conditioning theory of narcotic addiction assumes that addictive behavior can be extinguished by deconditioning. Thus, if on repeated injection opiates do not cause euphoria or the relief of conditioned abstinence, the opiate-using behavior will eventually disappear. It follows that what is needed is a means of preventing the pharmacological action of heroin, and an opiate antagonist offers one such means.

Cyclazocine was the first narcotic antagonist to be used as an experimental long-term treatment for addiction to opiates. Once stabilized on 4 to 8 mg/day of cyclazocine, the formerly addicted patient will obtain slight, if any, physiological effect from moderate doses of heroin.[58] Cyclazocine, however, has disturbing side effects in the induction period and a mild withdrawal syndrome.[59] Theoretically *naloxone* (Narcan®) is a better opiate antagonist than cyclazocine because it has fewer side effects. It has a serious drawback, however, since the duration of a usual dose is only four to six hours. If it is given in very large oral doses, however, e.g., as much as 3 grams, it is possible for naloxone to block the effects of moderate doses of heroin for twenty-four hours.[60]

Clinical trials with opiate antagonists have been promising but are still too limited to be used in predicting the future role of this technique in the overall treatment of opiate addiction. In fact, given current knowledge, it is probably best to keep an open mind to most treatment techniques until more extensive clinical trials reveal which are the most effective. Opiate addiction has many causes, and its treatment is likely to require several long-term treatment methods.

Long-term Treatment for the Patient Addicted to Barbiturates, Sedatives, or Minor Tranquilizers

There are presently no specific pharmacological therapies for barbiturate or sedative addiction. There are also few treatment centers specifically designed for this type of addicted patient. Thus each patient must be treated individually. Treatment for barbiturate or sedative addiction should probably begin right after withdrawal, when the patient is highly motivated.

Education should be an important part of postwithdrawal management. Ignorance on the part of patients, relatives, and even physicians of the dangers of barbiturate and sedative drugs often contributes to the development of physical dependence. The educational process can sometimes be the beginning of a favorable psychotherapeutic relationship.

A great deal has been written about the so-called addictive personality and it is likely that disorders of character and emotional expression play a major role in the genesis of sedative abuse. Although each person who abuses sedatives should be evaluated individually, a few generalizations can be made. In the original family, affective states were more often controlled than discussed, and the mothering figure was usually powerful but impersonal and likely to provoke guilt as a means of control. Thus, many patients addicted to barbiturates and minor tranquilizers must learn to find entirely new ways of adapting to stress, coping with guilt, and communicating affect to those important in their lives.[61] They must also learn to turn to people rather than to pills for help, comfort, and happiness.

REFERENCES

1. Isbell, Harris: "Opium Poisoning," in P. B. Beeson and W. McDermott (eds.), *Textbook of Medicine,* Saunders, Philadelphia, 1963, pp. 1744–1749.

2. Wikler, A.: "Addictions I: Opioid Addiction," in A. M. Freedman and H. I. Kaplan

(eds.), *Comprehensive Textbook of Psychiatry*, Williams & Wilkins, Baltimore, 1967, p. 996.

3. Isbell: loc. cit.
4. Gay, G. R., D. E. Smith, and E. I. Gutnick: "Treating Acute Heroin Toxicity," *Hosp. Phys.*, pp. 50–53, May 1971.
5. Isbell: loc. cit.
6. Ibid.
7. Dole, V.: "Methadone Maintenance," *Medical World News*, pp. 53–63, March 17, 1972.
8. Gay, G. R., and J. Vega: "Recognizing the Battered Flower Child," *Hosp. Phys.*, p. 43, July 1972.
9. Isbell, Harris: "Barbiturate Poisoning," in P. B. Beeson and W. McDermott (eds.), *Textbook of Medicine*, Saunders, Philadelphia, 1963, pp. 1739–1743.
10. Ibid.
11. Ibid.
12. Essig, C. F.: "Addiction to Non-Barbiturate Sedative and Tranquilizing Drugs," *Clin. Pharmacol. Therap.*, **5**(3):334–343, May–June 1964.
13. Ibid.
14. Espelin, D. E., and A. K. Done: "Amphetamine Poisoning: Effectiveness of Chlorpromazine," *New Engl. J. Med.*, **278**:1361–1365, 1968.
15. Ibid.
16. Isbell: "Opium Poisoning," loc. cit.
17. Ibid.
18. Ibid.
19. Goldstein, Avram: Personal communication.
20. Anderson, David: "Drug Dependence," in P. Solomon and V. Patch (eds.), *Handbook of Psychiatry*, Lange, Los Altos, Calif., 1969, pp. 208–222.
21. Ibid.
22. Isbell: "Opium Poisoning," loc. cit.
23. Isbell, Harris: "Manifestations and Treatment of Addiction to Narcotic Drugs and Barbiturates," *Med. Clin. N. Am.*, **34**:425–438, 1950.
24. Isbell, Harris: "Abuse of Barbiturates," *J. Am. Med. Ass.*, **162**:660–661, 1956.
25. Wikler, A.: "Diagnosis and Treatment of Drug Dependence of the Barbiturate Type," *Am. J. Psychiat.*, **125**(6):758–765, 1968.
26. Ibid.
27. Ewing, J., and W. Bakewell: "Diagnosis and Management of Depressant Drug Dependence," *Am. J. Psychiat.*, **123**(8):909–917, 1967.
28. Ibid.
29. Ibid.
30. Ibid.
31. Wikler: "Diagnosis," loc. cit.
32. Ewing and Bakewell: loc. cit.
33. Wikler: "Diagnosis," loc. cit.
34. Haizlip, T. M., and J. A. Ewing: Meprobamate Habituation: A Controlled Clinical Study," *New Engl. J. Med.*, **258**:1181–1186, April–June 1958.
35. Swanson, L. A., and T. Olcada: "Death After Withdrawal from Meprobamate," *J. Am. Med. Ass.*, **184**:780–781, 1963.
36. Essig, C. F.: "Newer Sedative Drugs That Can Cause States of Intoxication and Dependence of Barbiturate Type," *J. Am. Med. Ass.*, **196**(8):714–717, 1966.
37. Ibid.
38. Ellinwood, E. H., J. A. Ewing, and P. C. S. Oaken: "Habituation to Ethinamate," *New Engl. J. Med.*, **266**:185–186, 1962.
39. Blumenthal, M. O., and M. J. Reinhart: "Psychosis and Convulsions Following Withdrawal from Ethchlorvynol," *J. Am. Med. Ass.*, **190**:154–155, 1964.
40. Berger, H.: "Addiction to Methyprylon," *J. Am. Med. Assoc.*, **177**:63–65, 1961.
41. Hollister, L. E., F. P. Motzenbecker, and R. O. Deyan: "Withdrawal Reactions from Chlordiazepoxide," *Psychopharmacologic*, **2**:63–68, 1961.
42. Essig: "Newer Sedative Drugs," loc. cit.

43. Hollister, L. E.: "Diazepam in Newly Admitted Schizophrenics," *Dis. Nerv. Syst.,* **24**: 746–775, 1963.

44. Swardzburg, M., J. Lieb. and A. G. Schwartz: "Methaqualone Withdrawal," *Arch. Gen. Psychiat.,* **29**(1):46–47, July 1973.

45. Kato, M.: "An Epidemiological Analysis of the Fluctuation of Drug Dependence in Japan," *Int. J. Addiction,* **4**:591–621, 1969.

46. Essig: "Newer Sedative Drugs," loc. cit.

47. Ellinwood, E. H., Jr.: "Amphetamine Psychosis: Individuals, Settings, and Sequences," in E. G. Ellinwood, Jr., and S. Cohen (eds.), *Current Concepts on Amphetamine Abuse,* N.I.M.H., Maryland, 1972, p. 144.

48. Isbell, Harris: "Chronic Amphetamine Intoxication," in P. B. Beeson and W. McDermott (eds.), *Textbook of Medicine,* Saunders, Philadelphia, 1963, p. 1751.

49. Ellinwood: loc. cit.

50. Kramer, J. C.: "Introduction to Amphetamine Abuse," in E. H. Ellinwood, Jr., and S. Cohen (eds.), *Current Concepts on Amphetamine Abuse,* N.I.M.H., Maryland, 1972, p. 182.

51. Ewing, J.: "Addictions II: Non-Narcotic Addictive Agents," in A. M. Freedman and H. I. Kaplan (eds.), *Comprehensive Textbook of Psychiatry,* Williams & Wilkins, Baltimore, 1967, pp. 1003–1011.

52. Isbell, Harris: "Chronic Cocaine Intoxication," in P. B Beeson and W. McDermott (eds.), *Textbook of Medicine,* Saunders, Philadelphia, 1963, p. 1780.

53. Dole, V. P., and M. E. Nyswander: "Methadone Maintenance and Its Implication for Theories of Narcotic Addiction," *A.R.N.M.D. Proceedings,* vol. 46 *(The Addictive States),* pp. 359–367, 1968.

54. Goldstein, A.: "The Pharmacologic Basis of Methadone Treatment," *Proceedings of the Fourth National Conference on Methadone Treatment,* National Association for the Prevention of Addiction to Narcotics (NAPAN), New York, 1972, pp. 27–32.

55. Garbutt, G. W., and A. Goldstein.: "Blind Comparison of Three Methadone Maintenance Dosages in 180 Patients," *A.R.N.M.D. Proceedings,* vol. 46 *(The Addictive States),* pp. 411–441, 1968.

56. Kreek, M. D.: "Medical Safety, Side Effects and Toxicity of Methadone," *op. cit.,* pp. 171–174.

57. Wikler, A.: "Conditioning Factors in Opiate Addiction and Relapse," in D. M. Wilner and G. G. Kassebaum (eds.), *Narcotics,* McGraw-Hill, New York, 1965, pp. 85–100.

58. Freedman, A., et al.: "Clinical Studies of Cyclazocine in the Treatment of Narcotic Addiction," *Am. J. Psychiat.,* **124**:1499–1504, 1968.

59. Hammond, Allen: Editorial comment, *Science,* **173**:503–506, 1971.

60. Fink, M., et al.: "Opiate Antagonists in the Treatment of Heroin Dependence," in D. Clouet (ed.), *Narcotic Drugs: Biochemical Pharmacology,* Plenum, New York, 1971, pp. 468–476.

61. Ewing: loc. cit.

CHAPTER 10

Acute Inpatient Intervention

INTRODUCTION

The modern inpatient psychiatry ward, with its "therapeutic milieu," can be viewed in two ways: as a treatment *experience,* in which an entire community has been organized to facilitate ego-recovery in individuals whose adaptations have collapsed;[1-4] or as a treatment *context,* in which limits can be set on pathological behaviors and skills taught to improve social functioning. [5]

The *dangers* of hospitalization are a constant theme in the literature on this subject. Many authors express concern with preventing the "social breakdown syndrome" which is found in long-term hospital patients who have lost the social skills that could enable them to adapt to a real outside world. [6] Not wishing to encourage regression, many therapists strive to make the in-hospital experience as brief,[7] crisis-oriented, and hostile to the relaxation of ego-controls[8] as possible. A strong case has been made for *alternatives to hospitalization,* such as day hospitals,[9] family crisis teams,[10,11] and visits to the home.[12]

Others have challenged the *shallowness* of conventional hospital treatment. They feel that opportunities for growth are lost because insufficient attention is paid to the experiencing of the hospitalized patient.[13] They fear that the patient may learn only to make a pseudoadaptation to conform to staff expectations and that he will emerge from his brief hospitalization as basically unfit for life as he was before, still stuck in an unresolved developmental crisis which no one has bothered to examine but to which a pathological label has been affixed.[14] They argue for a relatively unhurried approach to the patient's recompensation, modeled less on the crisis resolutions of healthier persons[15] and more on respecting the personal and social nature of the ego-recovery process.[16]

Holmes has pointed out:[17]

> These are two different ways of relating to patients: one might be called the way of Eros, of unconditional (maternal) love, which cannot be earned, but is freely given, of concerns with the feeling and experience of the patient; the other might be called the way of Logos, of rational thought, cause and effect, reward and punishment, of (paternal) love which can be earned with good behavior, of concern with the control and correction of the patient's behavior.

As does ego development in the child, so too does the full return of ego function in the mentally ill adult require both its father and its mother. The ego returns to an adequate level of functioning both by being given real decisions and tasks[18] and by being heard and supported in resolving inner concerns. [19,20] When the therapist wants to make sure his patient is getting a consistent expectation of adult behavior, he will need to be like a father in defining the demands he would like the treating family to make. Learning how to make wise demands and how to secure the staff's cooperation in carrying them out is an important paternal task of the therapist in inpatient work.

When the therapist is alone with the patient, or listening to the concerns of the staff, he will need the receptive mode of the mother. The maternal task is to make sure he has heard the major concerns so that later demands are informed with an understanding of what the patient and staff are struggling with.

Coordinating these two ways of relating to the regressed patient's need is a major task of the inpatient therapist. He must learn when to use which, and he must guide the staff in finding which mode to use with the patient at any point in the treatment. Often the therapist will have to push the staff to be tougher; at other times he may have to protect the patient from the pressure of too many demands.

Aside from this coordination of his own responses, the hardest skill to master is cooperation with the staff. Even when the therapist has defined his own appropriate response to the patient, he will have to deal with the opinions of others in the milieu. The vast literature on social system aspects of treatment[21] repeatedly emphasizes one principle: treatment proceeds best when the involved individuals can agree about the methods and goals. This consensus must include the patient, his ecological group, the therapist, the ward staff, and the other patients on the ward.

Thus hospitalization itself is a crisis, deliberately superimposed upon the patient's original life predicament, so that treatment, via adequate crisis resolution, can occur. When the therapist admits the patient to the hospital, he effectively changes the patient's ecological group. Now the therapeutic deck is stacked with people who are trained to be helpful and who will do what the therapist wants. The therapist deliberately uses this enlarged ecological group to undercut the power that an isolated patient or a rigid family has used to maintain the pathology.

Thus hospitalization is used when it is the best available way to meet an impasse in treatment, when consultation to the patient and his usual ecological group cannot bring about a resolution. The impasse is then transferred to the milieu, which will be in crisis until the patient's treatment becomes unstuck. The therapist's work with the inpatient staff is similar to that with any ecological group in crisis. He functions as a consultant, helping the system to find its own solution, by using his knowledge of it and the patient.

Such impasses are regular occurrences in the treatment of very ill patients. They may reflect aspects of the patient's inner dynamics (for example, psychotic ambivalence) or of his family's pressure. Once their impact is felt in the milieu, however, treatment impasses are social events, accessible to resolution at a social level.

As Peplau has written: [22]

> This is what milieu therapy is all about: recognizing recurring problematic behavior patterns which had their beginning in the early childhood situations in which the child rearing tactics of the mother or of the other significant adults were not equal to the power maneuvers of the child; recognizing the replications of these patterns in subsequent school, peer group, community, and employment situations; and disrupting such replications within the day-to-day nurse-patient interactions in the ward setting.

Equally, milieu therapy is a *context* for other treatment that may become necessary. If ego functioning is so radically altered by mania, depression, or psychotic process that both psychotherapy and sociotherapy become impossible, drug therapy or ECT will be used.

The milieu can also be used as a setting to stage a massive challenge against entrenched character patterns. Abrams [23-25] has described the inpatient treatment of entire families and severely hysterical characters. He emphasizes hospitalization as a symbolic commitment to radical change and structures the ward experience as basic reeducation.

Sometimes referral to a more specialized residential setting is indicated. Among useful resources are *token-reinforcement wards* for chronic schizophrenic patients,[26] *intentional social systems* oriented to the reemployment of marginally adapted and alcoholic men,[27,28] and *anticriminal societies* that provide alternative lifestyles for previously delinquent or addicted persons.[29] In them, acculturation to a culture and its values becomes all-important, and individual psychotherapy may not even be offered.

This chapter will follow a patient through a standard inhospital experience, starting from the decision to hospitalize him and ending on the day of his discharge, to illustrate the tasks that the therapist meets in hospital work. No one patient is representative of all patients who are hospitalized, but the themes of inpatient work reoccur.

THE DECISION TO HOSPITALIZE

Example 10-1, Jerry. Jerry, a 19-year-old Coast Guard recruit, was taken to the emergency room of the community hospital near boot camp. At the end of the first week of his training, he had been found kneeling by his bunk, begging God to forgive him, and had not attended to a direct order to get up and answer the questions of his worried commanding officer. An accompanying note from the C.O. revealed that during his initial week of training he had shown "poor attention at drills and could not learn to pack his duffel bag. He would gaze into space for long periods and only answered questions the second or third time they were put to him." He had been found when he failed to turn up at the muster held before inspection.

In the emergency room Jerry was interviewed by the psychiatrist on call. He met the first several questions with silence. Finally Jerry said, "I'm with God, can't you let it be?"

Following an intuition, the psychiatrist asked, "Have you died?"

"I think so," Jerry replied. "Is this heaven?"

"Where do you think this is?"

"I think it's heaven," Jerry answered with conviction.

"Do you know who I am?"

"Someone who works for God — I know, an angel!"

Jerry responded carefully to the questions, like a small child.

"Do you know what day this is?"

"Tuesday," Jerry said, and laughed a little. Asked why he laughed, he said, "I didn't know you had time here." (In fact, the day was Saturday.) Jerry did not know the month or the day. His answers were, however, consistent with his belief that he had died and might be in heaven. It became clear that he was not sure where he was, except that he knew God was near him.

The psychiatrist said, "Actually, this is a hospital. You've been brought here because you became emotionally upset in boot camp."

"What's that?" Jerry asked.

"Basic training for the Coast Guard."

"Oh. I remember now."

"What do you remember?"

"I was in boot camp when I died."

"You aren't dead," the psychiatrist said, "so I'd have to say you're wrong about that. You got emotionally upset and had to be brought here to recover. I gather something pretty unusual happened inside you, if that's what you mean by dying. This is a hospital, and I'm a doctor. You'll have to stay here until you feel better."

"I feel O.K.," Jerry said.

"Are you frightened?"

"Yes."

"I think I can help you feel less frightened."

"You *can*?"

"Yes I can. Do you want me to help you?"

"Yes."

"It means doing what I say."

"Yes, tell me what I have to do to feel less frightened."

By relating to the patient's own view of what has happened to him, the therapist can often set up a simple contract with the patient that goes, "You feel upset, and I can help. If you do what I say, you will start to feel better." In Jerry's terror (usually the most upsetting part of an acute psychosis), the therapist found an area in which Jerry welcomed intervention. If something could be done to make him feel less afraid, he would cooperate.

From the very first the therapist started to challenge Jerry's psychotic definition of the situation. A cornerstone of the delusional thinking was the unlabeled metaphor, Jerry's assertion that he had died. The therapist called this assertion wrong and proceeded to label the metaphor: dying was Jerry's way of relating to an unfamiliar internal change. The therapist did not deny the reality of this change, or the drastic nature of it, and he indicated that his own attempts to name it would also be only metaphors.

The delusional elaboration — having died, Jerry must now be in heaven — was corrected by a simple comment on external realities: this was a hospital, and Jerry was seeing a doctor.

Finally, the therapist gave the societal definition of their transaction: Jerry had been brought to the hospital for treatment of an emotional breakdown suffered in boot camp. This statement of public fact countered Jerry's falsely individual, grandiose version of the humiliating events and showed that they could be stated. Finally, the current status of Jerry's power was explained to him. He would be made to stay at the hospital, but he retained the choice of agreeing or not agreeing to treatment.

Of course the therapist knew that Jerry did not yet believe or trust him. But he had set a basis for trust by clearly communicating what would follow when Jerry reached the ward. Then an entire society would insist upon this official version of reality instead of Jerry's psychotic interpretation of his experience. The therapist also had defined his own role as someone who would clarify reality.

ENTRY INTO THE WARD

The way the therapist arranges the admission, mentions the diagnosis, and transfers authority to the ward setting affects, for good or ill, the later course of treatment. After these procedures have been discussed, initial psychotherapeutic strategies and basic responsibilities of the admitting therapist will be defined.

Arranging the Admission

Having established that the patient needs inpatient care, the next step is to ensure (1) that a bed is available in the inpatient unit and (2) that the patient can afford to stay there. If responsible others accompany the patient, financial details should also be discussed with them.

> *Jerry (cont'd.).* Admitting Jerry was a simple task for the emergency therapist: it was the practice to admit Coast Guard recruits directly to the hospital at government expense. He already knew a bed was available on the inpatient ward, or he would not have been so explicit about Jerry's being hospitalized at this facility.
>
> Nevertheless, he placed a call to the inpatient unit to make sure the ward staff knew that he was planning to admit Jerry, so someone would be on hand to receive them. He placed the call in Jerry's presence, saying, "This is Dr. Michaels. I'm going to bring Jerry Butler to the ward. He is 19 and in the midst of an acute psychotic reaction. He looks tired, and I want to give him some chlorpromazine shortly after he arrives to make sure he gets to sleep."

Making the telephone call in the patient's presence is, of course, optional, and many therapists will prefer to have the patient wait outside while they make the necessary arrangements. With psychotic patients, however, it is often a good idea to do as little behind the patient's back as possible. The therapeutic task is to reinforce a socially shared perception of reality against the seductions of the primary process, and to accomplish it the therapist's behavior must be easy to read. Wherever possible, the therapist should act to minimize the formation of paranoid delusions, which can quickly consolidate to form a hardened front against any therapeutic alliance. When the patient listens to the therapist's way of describing his situation to others, a model is formed on which he can base his own later attempts to explain himself. Also, a certain sharing of the dilemma of explanation takes place when the telephone call is made in another's presence. This sharing of difficult ego tasks is important in the early psychotherapy of schizophrenia.

Mentioning the Diagnosis

The therapist mentioned the patient's diagnosis in the initial telephone call. Note that he did not say "schizophrenia," but rather "acute psychotic reaction." At this point the diagnosis of schizophrenia was far from being proved. The more neutral term has the advantages of saying no more than is already known and of being less frightening. If the patient asks, the therapist can explain that "acute" means of short, recent duration and that "psychotic" means confused thinking. Usually the patient will receive this more general diagnosis as a restatement of what the therapist has already told him. A more specific diagnosis given early in evaluation is sometimes received as a sentence of doom, threatening to extend the immediate confusion into a whole psychiatric career. The more general diagnosis also prevents the ward staff from assuming it knows more than it actually does about this new and still unevaluated person.

Not mentioning the diagnosis to the patient is a poor, and all too common, practice. When the diagnosis is not discussed, the patient quickly assumes that either his condition is too terrible to be revealed to him or that he is in fact not really ill and that his hospitalization is a fraud perpetrated by deceptive persecutors. A simple communication to the patient of the meaning of any terms that are going to be used in describing him goes a long way toward undercutting what Laing has called "the mystification of experience." (The patient begins to grasp that diagnostic statements, like his own psychotic statements, are simply metaphors.) Knowing that he will have to explain what he plans to say about the patient *to* the patient, the therapist will be much more careful to use terms which reflect what he really knows. And the vital relationship of trust will be furthered by the frank communication. (A good rule of thumb should not be made into a callous habit. The communication of diagnosis is always a sensitive matter, and at times the therapist will want to say to the patient only, "I'm not sure. You're certainly emotionally upset. I can't say much more than that right now.")

Transfer of Authority

Jerry (cont'd.). The emergency therapist's next step was to introduce Jerry personally into the social system that was to be his total environment for the next weeks — the acute inpatient unit.

The unit, which was cheerful and bright, resembled a well-designed motel. It was decorated in orange and brown hues. Its front door was left unlocked, but a patient or staff member was usually near the entrance to ensure that only patients with hospital privileges left the ward. The ward itself was an L-shaped wing of the first floor of the hospital and had a screened outdoor porch with a Ping-Pong table on it. A punching bag hung from a beam.

Along one side of the L was a line of patients' rooms. One room held four beds; the other five had two beds each.

The ward staff was visibly young, attractive, and mostly female. The nurses wore street clothes; they were not instantly distinguishable from the patients and volunteers. There was, however, an official-looking desk, with a roll-away Cardex file, and behind the desk was a locked, glassed-in area where medications were kept. A young woman stood inside this enclosure. She looked serious and important and had an unusually large bunch of keys. From these signs of authority, it was obvious she was the charge nurse for the shift.

The emergency therapist brought Jerry to the desk and waited. The nurse came out from her medication cubicle, carefully ensured that the door was locked, and looked at the two of them. Jerry stepped back toward the door. The therapist first introduced himself and then his patient: "This is Jerry Butler. He will have to stay on the ward because he has been extremely upset and his thinking has been confused. I will be talking with you and ordering some medicine for him. Right now, could you introduce yourself to Jerry, show him his room, and explain the ward rules?"

This transfer of authority from the therapist to the charge nurse is an essential step. It should be done quite clearly and concretely, as shown in the example. The therapist gives a ward staff member confronted with the uncertainty of a new psychotic patient essential information about the patient's emotional state and the amount of restriction that will be required. By doing so in front of the patient, the therapist provides a model for the nurse to use in talking to the patient. He also lets the patient see that the ward personnel will be aware, just as the doctor is, of the severity of his emotional and cognitive problems.

Initial Psychotherapeutic Strategies

Including the Patient. The transition from the dyadic communication between the therapist and the patient to the milieu process of the ward setting is a crucial one, and it easy to mishandle. It is possible to imagine the same scene played differently: the therapist leaves the patient at the desk, with a muttered "Wait here." Then he joins the charge nurse in the medication alcove. The two mental health professionals talk for several minutes. They are seen but not heard by the patient. The two emerge from the alcove, assume mannerisms that appear phony, and address the patient. "Miss Jones and I have just been conferring about you, Jerry, and we've decided to give you some medicine now." In an unctuous voice Miss Jones says, "Here you are, Jerry," and hands him a cup of suspicious-looking liquid she had kept hidden in her hands until the therapist spoke.

It is hard to blame a patient as concrete and confused as Jerry for making a paranoid interpretation of these events. He might bolt and force a power confrontation. Later he might reveal his fantasy that the hospital was a front assumed by agents of the devil who were conspiring to keep him from God. This fantasy would probably cause him to be labeled "acute paranoid schizophrenic," when in fact the paranoid fantasy would represent a stress reaction in this concrete, acutely psychotic young man who had been denied information that would support his fragile reality testing. The "paranoid" label, in turn, could cause the staff to relate to him in a more guarded fashion and thereby reinforce a common vicious cycle that tends to enforce a paranoid solution to the crisis of acute psychosis. Again, it is important to let the patient see and hear when vital decisions about his care are being made.

Defining the Role of Medication. In the example, the therapist introduced medication only after he had attempted to support Jerry's ego with a clear and direct communication aimed at improving his orientation and attention. Jerry heard two reasons given for the medication: it could reduce terror, and it could enhance sleep. It was not offered as the only, or even the major, kind of intervention. In short, Jerry's ego was asked to do all it could before drugs were used.

Many psychotic patients will require tranquilizing medication much sooner, of course, well before an attempt is made to enter them onto an open ward.

Theoretical Considerations Regarding Ego Support. The essence of milieu therapy is still contained in Pinel's dictum: "Treat the insane as if they were sane." When an acutely psychotic individual begins hospital treatment, two rules should be followed:

1. The patient must be protected from receiving the impression that his ego is too diseased to function. (Because he is highly impressionable, the acutely psychotic individual can quickly learn to play a sick role.)

2. The staff must make continuous demands on the patient to orient himself and attend to the social realities of the unit.

**Basic Responsibilities of the
Admitting Therapist**

Patient Should Be under Control When He Enters Milieu. Not every patient is as willing as Jerry to enter into a tentative working alliance. Some patients are already caught in a paranoid interpretation of events or are so hysterical or intoxicated that a calm discussion becomes impossible. *These patients should not be brought to an open inpatient ward until they have been brought under control.* Instead, they should be kept in the emergency room, given medication, and even kept in seclusion or restraints until they are calm enough to accept entry into the inpatient ward without belligerence and panic. Although most severely agitated patients respond to a single injection of 75 mg of chlorpromazine, there will be some patients who will need several doses of 200- to 400-mg liquid chlorpromazine orally every two hours before they have been sufficiently calmed to be safely treated on an open unit. It is best to treat these patients on a locked unit or in the emergency room while the medication takes effect. The reason is simple: access to help,

including the police, is greater on a locked unit or in the emergency room.

The combination of high doses of medication and a firm stance will usually bring a highly agitated patient under control within six to twelve hours; then he can be brought to the ward. If the patient remains seriously agitated, "sky-high," or assaultive, he should remain on a locked unit. Such patients are fortunately infrequent, but they are seen; and a rigidly liberal policy toward the civil rights of frenzied patients can involve taking unnecessary risks with the safety of an inpatient ward staff. Often it is fairer to the patient if the therapist recognizes the patient's inability to contain himself.

> *Example 10-2.* A therapist who had promised himself never to lock up anyone admitted a large, overweight man who called himself Senator Smith but was in fact an unemployed janitor. The therapist's ward was an open, patient-governed unit in a large VA Hospital. From the start, the patient was grandiose and belligerent, often clapping other patients on their backs while wearing a friendly grin that only half-concealed a sadistic sneer.
>
> The therapist responded to each provocation with a crisis interview that included a ward nurse. The urgent conferences and the increasing use of medication seemed only to provoke the patient more. Several staff members asked that the patient be transferred to a locked ward, but the therapist informed them that that was the old-fashioned way. Because he was obviously working hard on the case and his arguments were verbally convincing, the ward staff let him have his way.
>
> The patient began to drop lighted cigarette butts on the floor during community meetings, and finally he started a fire in his room. An emergency meeting of the ward was called.
>
> Several patients were among those who called for a vote on the question of a transfer to a locked ward. The therapist made a last, impassioned appeal for "one more chance." A

gruff, older man who had been hospitalized for depression spoke up sourly. "One more chance for what? To burn down the ward?"

Everyone laughed, and the controversial patient grinned at his therapist, who was sitting beside him. "Nice try, Charlie Brown," he whispered, "I've been trying to tell you." The vote was unanimous for his transfer to the locked ward.

A month later, Smith, who was now in control and had grounds privileges, saw his former therapist. "I'm O.K. now," he said. "You should have sent me there sooner; it's the only thing that works when I get high like that." A review of the records revealed that his five previous admissions had all involved stays on the locked unit. The patient had obviously come to expect this means of control. He would not accept any other, no matter how well intentioned or "modern."

The Review of Old Records. Example 10-2 illustrates another aspect of the admitting therapist's responsibility: reviewing the old record. Often what has worked in the past is what the patient expects now. Repetition of former treatment can be miraculously successful. Thus another course of ECT, a stay on the same locked ward, the exact dose of a previously used tranquilizer, can swiftly terminate an acute exacerbation of a chronic psychotic process. It is the therapist's duty to communicate the patient's therapeutic past to the ward staff so that it may replicate former successes.

Setting the Necessary Medical Work-up in Motion. Most hospitals require, and every patient should have, a physical examination when the patient is admitted to the ward. Unless the need for chemical restraint is absolutely pressing, no patient should receive large doses of tranquilizing medication until a physician has obtained vital signs and a brief medical history, and has recorded physical findings of cardiac, respiratory, and neu-

rologic status. The large doses of chlorpromazine used at the outset of the treatment of schizophrenia are sufficient to obtund many patients, and gross irregularities in heart action, circulation, breathing, and neurological function may appear as side effects. Major tranquilizers must be used cautiously in any patient with a history of chronic medical illness.

Additionally, many psychiatric patients have concurrent medical illnesses that need attention. Disturbances such as diabetes, heavy metal poisoning, tumors, infections, anemia, and hidden brain injuries can resemble acute schizophrenia, mania, depression, and character disorder. Thus a competent physician (an internist is ideal) should perform a complete physical examination soon after the patient arrives on the ward.

If drug abuse or poisoning is suspected, the therapist should be sure that the internist is alerted to order the blood and urine samples necessary to make this diagnosis. The therapist cannot assume the internist will find and follow through on any physical causes of impaired mental functioning with grossly disturbed individuals. Because his patient is not communicating normally, and he is a specialist in communication, the therapist will have to make sure that the vital information is delivered to the physician.

Problems in communication often arise between the nonmedical therapist and the nonpsychiatric physician. The therapist should arrange an unhurried time to meet with the doctor to learn about the findings of the examination. He should always ask, "Is there any possibility that a medical illness is affecting the patient's symptoms?" He should be sure to find out about any conditions that may limit his patient's comfort, activity, or employability.

Seriously disturbed patients give poor medical histories. The therapist may have to function as the patient's advocate and translator. Anxious patients often forget to communicate major details at the time of the examination and later tell the therapist, who will have to relay the information to the physician.

Summary

The admitting therapist should introduce the patient to the ward in such a way that the ward can take over the treatment from him. The therapist must see to it that his patient is in a state in which he can accept the ward environment and that the ward knows enough about the patient to make an informed intervention. From this point, until the patient is discharged, the therapist will function in an adjunctive way. He will act as a consultant to the ward and patient and will thereby facilitate their interaction. And indeed, his role will remain pivotal. But the actual healing, the return of adequate ego functioning, will come as the patient rediscovers reality in the context of the ward.

THE PROCESS OF TREATMENT ON AN INPATIENT UNIT

Four very different activities proceed concurrently in an inpatient unit: crisis intervention, milieu therapy, drug treatment, and hospital custody. Each requires highly specialized skills. A ward brings together many ambitious, highly trained people whose diverse efforts are in constant need of refinement and coordination by the ward chief. More than any other person he sets the style of the ward, its overall philosophy and ambience. No two ward chiefs are alike, and no two wards are alike. The tasks that must be accomplished, however, are common to all. The therapist must be familiar with the ward and the ward chief's philosophy of treatment.

The therapist will retain the responsibility for coordinating his own patient's treatment but will subordinate his own style to that of the ward. He will continue to direct the crisis intervention by setting up appointments with significant members of his patient's ecological group. If he is a physician, he will prescribe his patient's medications. He will be responsible for writing progress notes in the patient's record and for the admitting history. He will perform psychotherapy and usually will see his patient every day, if only briefly.

This special relationship to the patient places the therapist between the patient and the ward. He becomes his patient's advocate and, at times, his defense attorney. He will hear complaints about the patient, and he will often be blamed if things do not go right. Equally, often he will have to explain to the patient why ward procedures such as meetings, meals, and medications are important.

Overall, the therapist acts as a *troubleshooter to the treatment process*. He must ensure that his patient gets the most from the rest of the staff. Frequently the therapist will need to turn to the ward chief for advice, and he will also need to listen carefully to the opinions of staff. A good way to begin each visit to the ward is by reading the nursing report on the patient. In addition to giving him needed information, this practice creates the necessary receptive set in the therapist, and it is good public relations.

Crisis Intervention on the Ward

Involving the Ecological Group. We return now to the case of Jerry, which illustrates the therapist's direct work with the patient and his ecological group.

Jerry (cont'd.). The ward nurse took Jerry on a tour of the ward and brought him his chlorpromazine. The therapist stood by as he drank it. After the first swallow, Jerry spat out the drug and tried to run out of the room. The therapist said, "No, you're going to have to remain here." The nurse called two male aides, who entered the room. The therapist told the nurse to get another dose of liquid chlorpromazine and to draw up a syringe of intramuscular chlorpromazine. While she was out of the room, the therapist told Jerry firmly, "You will have to take your medication. You have a choice of drinking the liquid or having it injected. Which will it be?" Jerry remained silent while the therapist and the two male aides watched. (They were deliberately exposing him to a silent "show of force.") Jerry eyed them very carefully. When the nurse returned, Jerry drank the oral medication and also accepted a larger cup of orange juice she had brought him as a "chaser" for the chlorpromazine's bitter taste. Then he asked his therapist, "Is my mother dead or alive?"

The therapist asked the nurse and the two aides to leave the room. "I don't know, Jerry, let's find out."

"How?" Jerry asked, wide eyed.

"Call home."

"You mean call her?"

"Yes."

"Wow."

"Isn't it possible? She had a phone when you entered boot camp, didn't she?"

"Yes."

"Well, then dial it."

"I'm afraid."

"I'll stand by if you want."

"What'll I tell her if she answers?"

"Tell her you are in the hospital, and that I'm your doctor, and that she can call me if she wants."

Jerry dialed his father's, not his mother's number. "Hello, Dad, I'm in the hospital. You want the number? It's 483-1000. Yeah. Dr. Michaels." He hung up; his father called back right away, and the therapist answered.

The therapist told Jerry's father that Jerry had been hospitalized for emotional difficulties. The father, in a crisp, rapid, and demanding tone, wanted to know if this would ruin Jerry's chances in the Coast Guard. The therapist explained that it was too early to tell. When he asked to speak with Jerry's mother, the therapist found out that the parents had been divorced for eight years, and that Jerry had been living with his mother. She had been as dubious about Jerry's entering and succeeding in the Coast Guard as his father had been insistent upon it.

After the call the therapist told Jerry that his father really wanted him to be in the Coast Guard. Jerry responded to this with an unen-thusiastic "Yeah." Jerry then called his mother, told her he was in the hospital because he was having a breakdown, and handed the phone to his therapist.

In a tired, lackluster voice, his mother told the therapist that she didn't think she and her husband could leave their store and come to visit. The therapist told her that that wasn't necessary immediately. "You won't keep him in the service, will you?" she asked.

"We don't know."

With a faint trace of humor, she said, "Well, let me know what you decide. I don't think you will."

After telling her he would call the next day, he handed the phone to Jerry, who spoke with her for a minute and wound up by saying, "I'll be *okay*. I've gotta go." He hung up and with a hang-dog expression told the therapist, "She's alive. I thought I killed her."

In this sequence the therapist initiated the process of crisis intervention, which would be a major part of Jerry's therapy on the ward. Jerry was directly involved in the realistic communication that informed his parents of his condition and informed him that his mother was alive. At the outset, a major theme of the crisis became apparent in the conflicting parental views on the outcome of the enlistment: his father's strong desire that Jerry be allowed to continue, and his mother's equally strong doubts.

The therapist set this process of crisis intervention and reality testing in motion before Jerry was clear of psychosis. In fact, the intervention helped undercut the psychosis by showing Jerry that his mother was still alive, and it helped both Jerry and his therapist get the feel of the contradictory parental emotion underlying Jerry's decision to enlist.

It was essential for Jerry's treatment that this real conflict resurface early. It was not pleasant for Jerry to have to face, not God in Heaven, but a real father anxious for success; not a dead mother, but a doubting, live one. The therapist shared the pain of conflict with the patient, but he did not protect him from it. Thus the patient was given a crucial message early: the hospital will not be used as a place where reality can be evaded by psychosis. It is a setting where others help in confronting a difficult situation.

Goals Conference. A second task of crisis intervention is to have the patient and the hospital staff agree about the goals of hospitalization. This goals conference is vital for the ultimate resolution of the crisis. If this step is omitted, the hospitalization may acquire a "life of its own" apart from the needs of the patient's particular crisis, and the maladaptive solution of the "sick role" may supervene over any healthier resolution to the crisis.

The goals conference specifies staff tasks as well as patient goals. Lieb et al.[30] have provided the following tasks to be accomplished during a crisis hospitalization:

1. Completion of the evaluation
2. Clarification of the problems bringing the patient to the hospital
3. Communication of important decisions to significant people
4. Involvement in outpatient therapy
5. Resolution of incapacitating symptomatology
6. Reduction or resolution of suicidal or homicidal ideation
7. Completion of detoxification
8. Acceptance of the realities of the situation
9. Acceptance of structure and medication
10. Finding employment
11. Readjustment to the family system
12. Arranging an appropriate disposition

The goals conference also offers the patient a set of expectations for his inpatient stay: his daily "work" will be to perform the tasks the goals conference decides are expected of him.

Jerry (cont'd.). After he talked with his parents on the telephone, Jerry seemed much calmer, and he was able to sleep without difficulty (undoubtedly assisted by the heavy dose of medication he had swallowed). The following morning, before the community meeting, his goals conference was held on the ward.

The therapist, a nurse, a nursing assistant, and the ward chief were present. As was customary on this ward, Jerry was asked to introduce himself and to state his reason for being hospitalized. Jerry looked to his therapist for support and said, "My name is Jerry Butler. I had a breakdown in boot camp."

The therapist was asked to give a brief history of Jerry's illness. He did so.

At this point, the ward chief, a small quiet man with intense eyes, brought up the question of goals. "Jerry," he asked, "What do you expect to accomplish in the hospital?"

"I want to stop thinking things that aren't true," he said.

"Very good. Anything else?"

"I have to decide whether to stay in the Coast Guard."

The ward chief invited the therapist first and then the nursing staff to state their expectations. A nursing assistant took notes. The therapist wanted to better understand Jerry's and his parents' feelings about his enlistment. He wanted a complete physical examination, and he wanted Jerry to be able to think clearly again so that they could prepare a recommendation to the Coast Guard about his enlistment.

The nursing staff expected Jerry to pick up his medications at specific times, to attend group and psychodrama, to take KP, and to keep his area neat.

The ward chief asked the nursing assistant to read from his notes. The assistant read: "Jerry Butler, age 19, acute psychotic reaction, cause undetermined. Goals:

1. Straighten out errors in thinking

2. Decide whether to stay in Coast Guard
3. Evaluation of home situation"

The assistant enumerated the rest of the ten goals based on expectations that had been stated. The therapist, in answer to the ward chief's question, said he would see Jerry briefly every day and have two therapy sessions a week with him. This was added to the list. The ward chief asked Jerry if he agreed to live up to this contract. Jerry somewhat sheepishly agreed. The ward chief asked that the list be typed, with copies for Jerry and the staff, and said to Jerry, "We agree to hold you to this contract, which is your plan of treatment. If we *all* do what it says, your treatment should go very well."

Of course, not every feature of the goals conference was clear to Jerry at the time of this first meeting with the ward staff. He could hardly avoid receiving the impression, however, that his treatment would be a collective effort. Moreover, the staff began its work with a clear idea of what Jerry's treatment would be.

At such a conference it is important that the therapist be as candid as possible in specifying the problem areas. In Jerry's case, errors in thinking and an important decision were the major areas. Another patient might be struggling with suicidal feelings or with impulse control. The therapist should absolutely not protect the patient's privacy at this conference, but rather share as fully as possible the nature of the distress that the ward is being called upon to help resolve. This conference is similar to crisis intervention with an ecological group outside the hospital except that the ward staff is asked to function as the support system.

Discharge planning is part of the goals conference. Ideally, the discharge begins to be planned on the day the patient is admitted. A patient who does not anticipate completion of his hospitalization invites mental illness to become chronic and self-perpetuating. This is *not* to say that patients must be hurried out of the hospital, nor is it an uncritical endorsement of the current trend of brief hospitalization. There are cases on record of hospitalizations of six months to a year that have been extremely useful to the later adjustment of highly gifted individuals. The long hospitalization can offer a period of incubation and deliberate respite. However, successful long hospitalizations are usually conducted by therapists with an analytic orientation who know exactly what they are doing and when to reapply the pressure they deliberately remove for a time. Thus even the therapist who decides upon a long hospitalization anticipates the day when the patient once more will have to assume full responsibility for his life.

If the therapist adopts a "wait-and-see" attitude about planning, the patient's pathology will often mount to ensure that the hospitalization will continue. Therefore it is recommended that the therapist always try to project the length of an admission and to reason out its ultimate outcome.

Ecological Group Conferences.   The artificial ecology of an inpatient milieu, like an artificial heart, cannot be used indefinitely. (It may have to be used intermittently, like dialysis, for those individuals who fall recurrently into "toxic" emotional states. This, as Lieb et al.[31] point out, is a valid use of the inpatient milieu.) The therapist must continue to deal with the patient's relationship to his own ecological group, and conferences with everyone concerned should be scheduled as soon as is feasible.

Jerry (cont'd.).   After the goals conference the therapist called Jerry's family. At the father's home a woman answered. In a pleasant and energetic voice she informed the therapist that she had married Jerry's father five years before, that she thought the problem was Jerry's mother, who had never asked enough of the boy. She agreed to come to a conference in five days, and would discuss it with her husband.

The therapist called the mother. Her husband, Mr. Schiavo, a vague and mild man, answered the telephone and said he didn't know if he and his wife could close down their mail-order business for a day to come to the meeting. He agreed to discuss it with his wife.

The therapist called both families that evening. The Butlers energetically agreed to come. The Schiavos reluctantly said they would close down their business and attend.

In the five days before the meeting, the therapist thought about Jerry's future in the Coast Guard. It seemed likely that Jerry had enlisted over his mother's doubts to please his father. Jerry's initial confusion in boot camp may very well have reflected his lack of clarity about who had the right to make important decisions in his life. He told his therapist that when he was given an order in boot camp to carry out, he didn't seem to know who he was. He had started hearing a man's voice, very much like his father's, that talked so much he could not follow it. It also seemed that no matter what he did, his mother was there, until he thought he had killed her and he had been brought before God for judgment. The therapist thought that Jerry had unwittingly accepted a pathological aspect of his parents' communications: that they could control a part of his life that they actually could not, namely, his Coast Guard career; and that Jerry had transformed this assumption and his resentment about it into the voices giving him orders and the delusion that he had killed his mother.

The therapist's intuition told him that it was now time for the decision about Jerry's career to be made by those involved — Jerry and the Coast Guard — rather than by pseudo-omnipotent forces such as his parents. The therapist knew the Coast Guard was reluctant to have a man who might become psychotic under stress serve isolated duty either on land or at sea. Jerry, who had no interest in the Coast Guard, was relieved to know he could get out, although he was angry with his mother for implying that he wouldn't make it. It was easy to decide that Jerry should be separated from the service. Jerry and the therapist entered the family conference knowing that this key decision had already been made.

In inpatient psychiatry the therapist is often forced to rearrange, sometimes with a degree of manipulation, the "balance of power" in an ecological group. After all, the ecological group's workings have contributed to the psychosis of one of its members. Frequently a judicious use of authority will be necessary to rearrange a malignant network of communications during a family conference on an inpatient ward. Often, aspects of the solution will be "imposed" rather than "discovered" as in outpatient work. Just as the patient is not given the choice of whether to take medication, but only of how to take it, his ecological group is not allowed to decide whether he is ill, but rather how to manage the reality of his illness.

Jerry (cont'd.). The night before the scheduled meeting, Mr. Schiavo called the therapist to say that he doubted whether he could miss business for a day to come to the meeting, and that when he had spoken earlier with Mr. Butler, Mr. Butler had expressed similar doubts. The therapist countered with a firm injunction and pointed out that key decisions involving Jerry's future were involved. Everyone came.

The content of the meeting was not as important as the decision making that took place. Everyone was told that the Coast Guard was going to separate Jerry from the service when his hospitalization was over, that he would need continuing outpatient psychotherapy, and that the group had to consider how to pay for it. The father optimistically wondered if Jerry really would need further treatment; the therapist pointed out that Jerry's diagnosis was now "acute schizophrenia." The mother pessimistically wondered if he would ever get well; the therapist pointed out the good prognosis for this condition. The plan for continued treatment seemed to meet both the father's demand for action and the mother's need to see her son as ill.

The family did manage to disagree on one point, and this was who would pay for the therapy. Jerry's father insisted that part of the cost must come from job earnings (of a job Jerry had yet to acquire), and his mother felt the parents should pay "everything until Jerry gets well; who knows when he can work?" Hearing this dispute, Jerry got quite angry. In a key intervention, the therapist got all five of them to agree to defer this issue until the first consultation with the outside therapist, which was to occur the following week as part of a pass. Relieved, the group adjourned amicably.

In talking with a patient's family, the therapist can make use of the psychosis requiring hospitalization as a metaphor for the developmental crisis they need to help manage. The psychosis can stand for Jerry's previous struggle to enter life, and his treatment can stand for his capacity to grow. The family can support his treatment even if they are unable to support him.

Making conscious use of the "medical model" to rally family support, the therapist can (1) reduce uncertainty (by presenting a "medically indicated" decision to separate someone from the service, a troublesome job, or an impossible home); (2) undercut conflicting demands within the ecological group (by presenting common tasks, such as planning for outpatient treatment, that require cooperation if treatment is to progress); and (3) redefine the problem (in Jerry's case, forget the debate over what he can achieve and become concerned with finding a stable professional figure who can offer him guidance).

If hospitalization can be avoided, it should be. But once it has occurred, the therapist can use it as a trump card to deal with the power struggles and contradictory expectations so often found in the ecological group. He has a powerful tool at his disposal; he should not be afraid to use it wisely.

Goals of Ego Support Via Milieu Therapy

If long-term hospitalization is to be avoided, the patient and his ecological group will have to be convinced that his ego is in touch with everyday realities, at least enough to function on the outside. Most of the skill of milieu therapy involves knowing which ego functions to support and how to go about supporting them.

Improving the Testing of Reality. In reality testing, as elsewhere in psychiatry, the vexing concept of "reality" will need clarification. Patients usually come to the hospital because of major disturbances in their relation to one or more of three aspects of reality: (1) outer physical reality; (2) inner emotional reality; and (3) transactional reality.

In the first instance, the crucial ability is to perceive the physical world as most others do, including in and omitting from sense perception what most others include and omit. Accurate testing of outer physical reality means the perception of persons and places according to social norms. (Grossly delusional states, perceptual disturbances, and "overinclusive" thought disorders fall among the pathologies.)

The crucial ability in maintaining inner reality is the correct identification of the affects and images that make up the "inner world" of emotion. (Obsessive-compulsive personalities who become psychotically depressed, alienated from their own great grief, anger, and loneliness fail in internal reality testing.)

The issue in transactional reality is still perception, but in areas that affect judgment. The crucial ability is to recognize the rules, or power realities, by which interpersonal transactions are guided.

Failure of transactional reality testing leads to speech and actions that exceed the accepted limits within a social context and invite the "insane" label. It is often extremely hard to specify what these limits are until a group member tries to exceed them and finds himself isolated, extruded, or taken to the hospital. Often it is not so much a matter of the actual behavior as it is of the timing of behavior. Many of the "last straw" situations that precipitate a borderline individual's being hospitalized reflect a final erosion of the political sense that recognizes the lines within a social system which one must not cross.

Persons with sociopathic or hysterical character styles show major disturbances in testing transactional reality. They may become grossly unadapted despite an accurate perception of both outer physical reality and their own inner emotional reality. Some hysterical personalities are overcommitted to "affective truth," that is, to being true to their inner feelings, which they usually perceive quite accurately, no matter how much they alienate others or how bizarrely flawed their judgment. By contrast, many persons with major disturbances in the testing of outer physical *and* inner emotional reality avoid social difficulties altogether because they have learned to test transactional reality correctly. They do not openly violate the transactional norms of the persons they know. This usual ecological group may in turn have adapted itself to their gross errors in reality testing in the other areas because they "fit in so well" with the group's most-favored (or most comfortable) ways of social functioning.

An inpatient ward usually includes patients who are schizophrenic, psychotically depressed, and hysterical or sociopathic in character style. The ward must therefore undertake to help with the testing of outer physical, inner, and transactional reality. To understand what goes on inside the hospital it is necessary to realize that a milieu is a place where teaching is constantly occurring. To the nonattuned outsider, the constant pointing out of outer facts, the constant inquiry into emotional states, and the continual "holding responsible" of patients for the ways in which they communicate may appear to be horribly infantilizing, and the ward may seem to be a nursery school for adults. In fact, this teaching is entirely necessary and appropriate when it is directed to a patient's true area of weakness. Recognizing *where* the failure of reality testing occurs is a skill that grows with protracted contact with patients: probably no mental health professional has more expertise of this sort than the experienced psychiatric nurse. Much of the rapid readjustment of patients in modern settings occurs as a consequence of her work.

Setting Limits on Pathological Behaviors. Abroms[32] has described the process of a milieu therapy ward as one of "therapeutic limit setting," and he gives a list of the pathological behaviors that must be limited. This list, his "five D's of pathology," in decreasing order of severity, is

1. Destructiveness
2. Disorganization
3. Deviancy (or rule-breaking behavior)
4. Dysphoria (or disturbance in mood)
5. Dependency

In his view this "hierarchy of severity" is also a "hierarchy of intervention." The ward staff should first limit destructiveness in a given patient, then disorganization, and so on.

Teaching Psychosocial Skills. Abroms sees the milieu as "teaching skills" in four significant psychosocial areas:

1. Orientation
2. Assertion
3. Occupation
4. Recreation

To summarize, the goals of milieu therapy are to (1) improve reality testing, (2) set limits, and (3) teach skills. These goals are accomplished in the myriad of contexts provided by the treatment ward. In all these contexts, a process of ego support is occurring. In the next part of this chapter, we shall take a closer look at how ego support is actually carried out within the milieu.

EGO SUPPORT VIA MILIEU THERAPY

The handling of specific transactions in a therapeutic way is the essence of the milieu approach. We shall look at four ways ego support can be introduced into everyday ward transactions. These will be (1) orientation, (2) expectations, (3) limit setting, and (4) participation in the community.

Orientation

Jerry (cont'd.). Each day, one of the nurses asked Jerry if he knew the date, time, and place. At first he made small errors and acted as if they were unimportant. The nurse would persist, and by the end of the fourth day Jerry could say where he was, what day it was, and what time it was. In the late afternoon, when he tended to "fog out," Jerry would ask a ward attendant what day it was, where he was, and what time it was. He wanted to be sure he didn't forget. Gradually he reincorporated the habit of orienting himself to his temporal surroundings, and as he did so he appeared more alert and his paranoid feelings about the ward lessened.

Some therapists balk at using such a concrete, cognitive approach, preferring to relate to their patients' altered perceptions in terms of their accuracy as existential statements. This phenomenological approach to cybernetic error has a great appeal, but it neglects to notice that often improvement, not alienation, may follow when an "error" is corrected. Just as changes in emotion can affect cognition, so too can changes in cognition affect emotion, and simply telling a patient that "this isn't heaven, it's a hospital" can be as profoundly therapeutic as learning *how* the hospital is, in a metaphoric sense, heaven. Bateson et al.[33] have said that "The peculiarity of the schizophrenic is not that he uses metaphors, but that he uses *unlabeled* metaphors," an idea that was mentioned in the description of Dr. Michaels' initial handling of Jerry's psychotic thinking.

In his private contacts with a patient, a therapist can insist that the patient label his metaphors, or he can discourage their use altogether. Often therapists find that the use of metaphors is an effective way to communicate deep inner states. In the ward context, metaphors hinder the patient's solution of such factual outer problems as knowing where he is, what time it is, and what is going on. Poetic solutions to these problems should be discouraged. For orientation, banal, effort-requir-

ing secondary process thinking must be used. Expecting the patient to perform along this dimension (and testing his performance) helps him recover the secondary process, which proves to be of enormous help to him.

Expectations. If there were no chlorpromazine, it would probably be possible to maintain order on an inpatient ward by the judicious use of expectation. We have seen how at the outset of the hospitalization the patient is exposed to a number of transactions that indicate how much will be expected of him. The best approach is to treat the patient as if he is a business client, explaining in detail what will be required of him in the course of his treatment.

Jerry (cont'd.). Before Jerry's goals conference, Jerry's therapist explained, "You're going to be presented by me to the goals conference. You will be asked why you came to the hospital. I will say what I have found out about you. Then the staff will tell you what they expect you to do in order to get well. You can tell them anything you want, but you have to make an agreement with them to do the things that are decided on for you."

"What if I don't?" Jerry asked.

"Then the staff will call you back and ask why you didn't. If they aren't satisfied, they can transfer you off the ward."

"Where would I go then?"

"Maybe the county hospital."

"I better do what they say. I don't want to go there."

In making expectations of a patient, it is well to ask things of him that can be monitored. The therapist should not expect a patient to not make noise, for example, because the patient's degree of control over "noise" cannot be easily gauged. Rather, the therapist can tell a difficult patient, "If you want to speak after the lights go out, you have to come out to the nurse's desk." Thus uncontrollable noises are not mentioned even while the problem of unregulated verbal communication is being addressed. Equally, expectations that are too much for the patient should be avoided.

> *Example 10-3.* A middle-aged Southern seaman insisted he could not share a hospital room with a black patient. Several other patients offered to move. The acting ward chief, an inexperienced therapist who had had much luck with the use of expectation effects in bringing difficult situations under control, said, "You have to find a way of working this situation out." (He ignored the fact that the patient had appealed to the community and it was willing to give him his way.)
>
> Soon after the patient became enraged and had to be secluded. He became possessed by a fantasy of strangling his wife. He had been expected to master an anger for which he had some social support, and he did, indeed, find "a way of working it out" — regression to the level of the psychotic rage for which he had been hospitalized.
>
> Although this incident contributed greatly to an understanding of the patient's dynamics, the therapist had exceeded the patient's limits with his expectation and not helped him to discover a new area of ego control. In retrospect, the therapist should have asked the patient to find a way to spare his black roommate's feelings and acceded to his request for a different room.

Among the expectations that can be made of nearly all patients are attendance at all meals, attendance at ward meetings, daily showers, asking permission to leave the ward, taking all medications, and staying out of bed during specified hours. By insisting from the outset upon these simple rules, the therapist almost always brings the patient's ego into play and prevents him from being entirely "taken over" by feelings of panic, hopelessness, self-loathing, and inertia. Specific problems can be met with more specialized expectations.

> *Example 10-4.* A woman in her early 50s, hospitalized for an exacerbation of her chronic schizophrenia, began to lie in bed whenever the ward staff wasn't looking. Telling her to get out of bed seemed to have only a limited effect, and her behavior seemed to say, "All I can do is lie here by myself." Attempts to involve her with others produced a state of panic. The staff felt frustrated and defeated by her psychosis.
>
> Finally, the therapist hit upon a new strategy. He told his patient, "I expect you to take a walk twice each day, all the way to the hospital gate and one block beyond. Then you can come back and lie down for half an hour."
>
> Within a few days the patient had brightened considerably and stayed out of bed without being told. The walks that "earned" her her right to lie down also demonstrated the intactness of her ability to function.

Limit Setting. After the staff has established that it will do its part to clarify reality and that it has certain expectations of the patient, the staff has earned its right to question, criticize, and prohibit the patient's symptomatic refusal to live by the ward rules. Equally, there are certain rules that can be established only by limit setting.

> *Example 10-5.* A woman in her early 40s was admitted for treatment of an agitated depression. A veteran of a previous admission several years back, she presented herself to the staff as grateful to be receiving treatment again and eager to please. She cried a great deal, and she apologized for crying. Her entire stance seemed to say, "Excuse me for having such a tough time." Her husband, a kind man that the entire staff liked, stayed on the ward her first night, holding her hand and attempting to console her while the tears rolled down her cheeks.
>
> After he left, the patient went to bed, and early the next morning her therapist was summoned out of a ward staff meeting with

the news that she had cut her wrist. Without thinking, the therapist said, "That poor woman! I'll be in to talk with her immediately." The ward chief could not restrain himself. "You'll get further," he exploded, "if you tell her we don't allow that sort of thing here!"

Braced, the therapist went to his patient, and told her, "No, that's not appropriate. If you are distressed, you can always find the nurse. But you absolutely are not allowed to cut yourself." The patient attempted to apologize, but he held firm that her behavior was out-of-bounds.

By resisting the temptation to offer sympathy, an error the patient's well-meaning husband had made, the therapist was able to set limits on her capitulation to depression. Not surprisingly, the patient soon began to stand up on her own to her depression and to improve.

Limit setting is necessary when patients make infractions of ward rules or fail the expectations contained within their own "contracts." Specifically, failures to appear at a ward meeting, to take medication, or to eat meals require swift intervention because they signal major resistance to the therapeutic process. For a suicidal patient these behaviors may represent indirect suicidal communications. For a psychotic patient, the same behaviors may herald the beginning of a new regression, or a maladaptive paranoid restitution of ego functioning. For a patient with character disorder, a new bout of antisocial behavior may be warned by these first, seemingly trivial infractions.

The wise therapist will be firm. He will listen to excuses, but he will not accept them. "We expect you to be at your meals," he should say to the patient who has just explained why he "had" to miss one. The point is that these "minor" social norms are exactly those the patient, for idiosyncratic reasons, is failing to meet on the outside. An essential part of therapy is the ability to conform to minimal social requirements.

Participation in the Community. "People need people" is the premise of milieu therapy. The emphasis on orientation, the ward expectations, and the practice of limit setting tend to keep patients in the mainstream of the ward's small society[34] and involved with the staff and with each other. Usually there is a program that occupies the patients with common tasks. It is important to realize that special skills are needed to make the patients more than passive recipients of staff attention, and to get them to assume responsibility for keeping the therapeutic community going.[35]

Different wards have different styles of community participation, just as they have different styles in how they orient patients, what they expect of them, and how they set limits. In highly advanced wards, patients help in the orientation, participate in the goals conferences, function on "rules committees," assign extra work, restrict passes, and recommend transfers for other patients. Such wards work best if the turnover of patients is not too rapid and if the population of patients is somewhat uniform (as is the case with some VA wards that specialize in the treatment of marginally adjusted alcoholic men with stays of three to six months).

The community on the more acute ward usually comes together over business such as introductions, keeping the ward clean, supplying its members with coffee, and discussions of major unsettling events. Indeed, a most common topic of community meetings is how to assure that the coffee fund is kept up so that everyone can be sure of a fresh cup of coffee in a clean cup when he wants it. This seemingly banal topic, which could be decided by fiat if the staff intervened, provides endless fuel for the discussion of community conflicts. Dealing with a community task requires the ego functioning of many individuals, and this exercise of egos (not a prompt solution) is the reason for leaving simple issues to the community process.

When they are engaged together in common tasks, the members of the community will stumble over the major handicaps that a given patient has in living. In this way milieu therapy resembles long-term individual therapy in which chronic neurotic distortions appear during a mutual attempt at understanding. As in individual therapy, the therapeutic hope is that the reappearance of the handicap will be followed by its resolution. Here, most milieux hope for more than is possible; the patient simply does not have enough time to overcome more than his most obvious impediments to social functioning. The high hopes do, however, pressure most patients to the point that the obvious impediments *are* removed after a few days of milieu living.

Specialized Techniques

Techniques are the methods by which the goals and processes of milieu therapy are accomplished. Three kinds of techniques stand out: (1) techniques that improve communication, such as community and staff meetings; (2) techniques that encourage expression, such as psychodrama, small group, and family group; and (3) techniques that modify behavior, such as schedules, contracts, and reinforcements.

Techniques That Improve Communication. Because milieu therapy is a coordinated effort to bring about change, constant discussion of the rules of the game seems to improve both the skill and interest of the participants. An effective ward is one that is constantly examining its own behavior.

The *community meeting* is probably the sine qua non of a milieu ward. On most inpatient wards, it is held every morning for forty-five minutes, five or six days a week. It usually begins with the introduction of newly admitted patients, after which there is usually a silence. Then an issue of general relevance is approached by the group, which is aided by a leader who tries to interpret the veiled ways in which this "theme" was broached. Often the issue is the intolerable behavior of a patient which has upset other patients. Once

this common concern is brought into the open, the patient and the community can face their painful interaction together.

Jerry (cont'd.). Jerry became the topic of the community meeting after he had been on the unit more than a week. It seemed at one meeting, which his therapist attended, that everyone was angry. A young woman, charged with managing the coffee fund, insisted that everyone was forgetting to pay her; a nurse whispered angrily to an aide seated beside her; a stiff-postured new patient dropped a lighted cigarette. It was an atmosphere of diffuse tension. As Jerry sauntered in, late, an oppressive silence fell over the group. He took the only vacant seat, on the ward chief's right.

The ward chief said, "Can anybody explain why we're so tense today?"

A large woman said, "'Cause there's some as think they can fool everybody and some as think they're nobody's fool."

"Can you be more specific?" a young nurse asked.

"I'm as pacific as the ocean," the woman said, and would say no more. There was another uncomfortable silence.

Finally an older man on the ward chief's left spoke. "I'll tell you what you want to know, if it'll do you any good. It's Jerry here. He don't try to get better 'cause he knows he can get out of things if he don't."

It turned out that patients and staff thought Jerry was getting away with murder as far as living up to rules and expectations was concerned. He came late to meals, did not keep his area clean, and so on.

Jerry had even said, "You know I can't do that; I'm a goddam schizophrenic." After this statement, some patients had seen Jerry's mental illness as one big act. They thought Jerry's therapist (who met with him every day) supported this role of being irresponsible and fragile. The staff, too, was angry with the therapist because they felt thwarted by him in their desire to deal more openly with Jerry and his infractions.

When he heard this, the therapist said that although Jerry had indeed had a schizophrenic episode, his diagnosis did not absolve him from taking usual responsibility and that, in fact, he thought Jerry would recover a lot faster if he assumed responsibility like everyone else. This assurance greatly relieved the tension. Finally Jerry asked him, "You mean you can get better if you have schizophrenia?"

The therapist said, "Yes, if you try." At this point the new patient who had held himself so stiff seemed to relax, and suddenly got up and exchanged chairs with Jerry, who considerately gave his ash tray to him. The meeting ended with the new patient reaching over to pat the ward chief on the back, which met with comfortable general laughter.

It is obvious from the description of this community meeting how the specific problem of Jerry's laxity (which had indeed been his life problem before and during his brief try at a service career) had activated general concern. The anxiety seemed to be that the staff would label the patients and excuse them from life, and that despite the official ward ideology, mental illness could not be treated: the mentally ill would stay that way. When such a basic fear infects a ward, a general discussion is necessary to dispel it. In this meeting not only did a specific issue in Jerry's treatment unfold, but the ward itself experienced a renewal of its will to strive for health. This became graphically clear when the sickest patient took that chair to which the leader could extend his right arm in support, and Jerry, who was illegitimately clinging to that protection, gave it up.

In *Social Psychiatry in Action*,[36] Harry Wilmer describes the significance of where patients sit in community meetings. The right-hand chair to the leader's is "the sickest patient's," the left-hand, "the leader's helper's," the chair opposite the leader's, "the challenger's," and so on. Seating

diagrams and Wilmer's intuitive concepts are extremely useful ways to come to terms with the group dynamics that obtain within any ward setting. A community meeting offers a sample of the ward's group process on any particular day; its seating diagram is like a blueprint from which the process may be inferred.

The milieu therapist must always take cognizance of group processes. Otherwise he will never understand some of the puzzling emotions that are unleashed in his direction, such as the anger directed at Jerry's hard-working therapist. Once a therapist sees that a given emotional sequence can be reflective of events that are occurring on a broader social level, he can become skilled at making interventions that influence the social context positively. The community meeting is the best place for such far-reaching interventions. The right communication within this circle helps every patient's treatment. Thus, the therapist was correct in countering the ward pessimism, which seemed to say, "We can't get better and it's all *your* fault," with a firm statement that "Patients can get better," spoken to his patient in a way that everyone could comprehend. Then the ward could work on its resistances to operating therapeutically, on its overprotectiveness, and on its fear of psychotic emotion. This shift enabled the most disturbed patient to enter into treatment and freed Jerry from the pseudosick role he was so good at playing but that threatened to impede his treatment.

It is through the *staff meeting* that the emergency therapist gets to know that subculture of the ward, the treatment staff. Whenever staff members meet, their values and philosophy, their reactions to particular patients and their families, and their internal agreements and disagreements become apparent. The therapist must take the same consultative set to *this* ecological group as to the one that exists for his patient outside the hospital. He must learn to shape his interpretations, observations, and interventions in the language and grammar by which this staff operates, not in one he may have worked with previously. If he does not, he may be playing modern jazz in a Dixieland group: what's good in New York does not go in New Orleans.

The new therapist should expect a period of hostility, both toward him and his patients. Only by regular attendance of those staff meetings at which he is welcome can the therapist dispel suspicion and act effectively as an advocate for his patient's treatment.

Rehash meetings occur on many wards after community meetings, small-group meetings, and goals conferences (after any meeting, in fact, in which the patients and staff have met together). These are important meetings in which staff members discuss the nature of the processes afoot in the ward culture and critically evaluate their own responses to these processes. The staff, in effect, decides how to behave vis-à-vis the ward. It is important to attend the rehash meetings because it is at these that the therapist learns whether or not he is making interventions according to current ward policies.

The purpose of *regular* staff meetings is to generally share information and goals. They maintain the integration of the ward and usually are not for outside therapists. Some wards have regular meetings in which the staff meets with outside therapists to monitor a given patient's treatment. Here a process of mutual consultation occurs. The therapist uses his special relationship with the patient to inform the ward about the major conflict areas with which the patient needs help. The staff, in turn, helps the therapist gain objectivity by pointing out areas in which the intimate relationship has placed him in unconscious collusion with the patient's evasion of part of reality.

The "transference bond," so helpful in the treatment of neurosis, often can keep a therapist from making a necessary demand on a hospitalized patient because he seems to be "coming to grips with an internal problem." It is easy to forget that, unlike the neurotic office patient, the hospitalized patient may be using *all* his energy in trying to confront an unconscious conflict and none in

maintaining himself in the world. The staff's consultation may be invaluable in freeing the therapist from this common bind, which makes him feel that therapy is at last going well when it has only been made ridiculously easy.

Again the occasional patient for whom the pressure is deliberately removed so that he will have enough energy to confront an internal problem should be excepted. In this case, the therapist takes a calculated risk that his patient will not react to the artificial return to a supported state with a permanent commitment to infantile solutions of conflict. Nowadays, a therapist who believes in this "incubating" mode of treatment will have a fairly hard time convincing most acute hospital staffs, who have become leery of hospitalizations that last more than six weeks.

In the event of major staff disagreements about the ward ideology, the formal staff meeting, not the rehashes or the meetings over a particular patient's care, is the place to iron things out. Major philosophic disagreements should *never* be the topic of community meetings or meetings at which patients are present. Of course, this is not to say that the staff cannot openly disagree in front of the patients. Rather, patient care should not be taken over by the process of staff dispute. In meetings in which patients are present, the staff should behave professionally and confine disagreeing statements to the issues immediately at hand, not to general issues of ward philosophy, which can be intensely divisive. For the patients' sake, all members of the staff must try to play by the rules on which it has agreed, even when some would prefer to see these rules changed. A good staff will trust its own ability to make necessary changes, and the patient will not find himself in the middle of a dispute about ideology even if one exists.

Thus the techniques that improve communication are various forums in which the *rules* of the ward communication are discussed. Different kinds of discussions about rules belong to different forums. The community meeting discusses rules that govern the treatment of patients. Rehashes discuss rules by which the staff communicates its values to patients. Staff meetings discuss rules that govern the therapist's behavior and the overall rules that make up the ward ideology. Knowing these rules, and how to discuss rule changes that appear necessary, is an essential task of the therapist who is learning to function in a ward context.

Techniques That Encourage Expression. For many patients, catharsis remains a vital part of treatment. Among the techniques that encourage expression are psychodrama, small group, and family group.

Psychodrama involves role playing of a given individual's conflicts by several persons. Jerry did not engage in psychodrama, but if he had, one patient might have played his mother, another his father, and one him. Jerry could have directed them in what to do. In this way he could see his own conflict more vividly, and he could feel himself taking a direct role in its outcome. Moreover, others could criticize his way of directing. Thus various processes of catharsis, insight, and confrontation come literally into "play."

In a *small group* a few patients meet together to discuss their problems in living. Peer support in confronting problems is probably the primary effect of this time-limited group. This experience brings a sense of individual attention and intimacy to hospitalization, and it enhances the psychological set of problem solving. (Many first-time inpatients are quite unpsychologically minded and need all the help they can get in learning to view themselves psychologically, a necessary prerequisite to the effective use of psychotherapy.)

Family group enables the family to voice its concerns, and also provides an interface between the ward group and the patient's own ecological group. It can be a place where communication is improved, but more often actual change occurs in the ecological group conferences that form a vital part of the crisis intervention. Family group, usually held once a week, is an "open house" in which the family is helped to hear and see that they are not alone, that patients can be helped, and that their positive contributions are welcome. Occasionally a particular family problem will surface with glaring malignity, and the family group will resemble a difficult meeting in an ongoing therapy group. Most often it is a place where staff and family obtain information about each other.

Techniques That Modify Behavior. Increasingly, ward therapists are becoming dissatisfied with relying solely on communications and expressive techniques. Abroms'[37] work with hysterical characters points this new direction, which uses the hospital as a place where intensive reeducation can be undertaken:

> . . .We have operationally defined hysteria as the type of behaviors which emerge when the patient is required to adhere to a schedule that demands responsible self-assertion. We have thus concerned ourselves with deficits, excesses, or misdirected (indirect, displaced) forms of assertion or aggression, such as the expression of suicidal impulses, physical complaints, sarcasm, withdrawal of interest, etc. By arranging a corrective feedback system, we have assisted patients in recognizing these behaviors as unwanted — a big step in gaining control over them. Instead of the symptomatic control of others, the patient moves toward self-control, which in this context means simply the recognition and direct expression of her needs and wishes. Learning these kinds of communicative skills . . . may be approached as a current educational task.

In practice, Abroms assigns his hysterical patients to strict schedules which offer time for grooming, meetings, room cleaning, and so on. The staff then helps the patient recognize the ways in which he gets in his own way when he tries to follow a schedule. This "corrective feedback" enables the patient to eliminate his own "undesired behaviors."

Other techniques that have been used to train

patients are token reinforcements, work schedules, and ward contracts. For example, Jerry had a ward contract he had to follow; the woman who took daily walks was on a schedule. Token reinforcements have been used with severely regressed chronic schizophrenic patients, who receive tokens for socially desired behaviors such as making their own beds, eating with utensils, and so on. These tokens may be used to buy candy. In some wards they are required as payment for meals, permission to take a nap, and other basic needs. Such techniques have in common practicality, efficiency, and specificity in that they focus on definite behavioral objectives rather than on less tangible goals. Such specificity is especially good for concrete patients who cannot relate to abstract goals, and for manipulative patients who misuse abstractions for sociopathic ends.

SPECIAL PROBLEMS IN THE MILIEU

Infractions of Ward Rules

Overpermissiveness undercuts milieu therapy. When a patient acts against a ward rule, he should be told firmly that he may not do so. His first obligation is to get along in the ward society. If the infraction is severe, such as hitting another patient, a meeting of the entire ward may be called to deal with the crisis, which usually centers around whether or not the patient can remain on the ward.

After the processes of limit setting and reintegration into the ward society are complete, reasons for the infraction may be safely deferred to discussions with the therapist. In ward work the expression of hostile feelings must always take second place to limit setting because the dangers and consequences of loss of control are grave.

Minor infractions, as was stated previously, may be preludes to suicide or elopement, as well as indications of a burgeoning paranoid or antisocial attitude. They must be taken seriously.

Staff Splitting

A staff will often find itself in a bitter conflict over a patient's care: the dynamic formulation will be pitted against the organic, the phenomenological against the behavioral, the permissive against the limit setting. This widely recognized phenomenon was first described in Stanton and Schwartz' classic *The Mental Hospital.*[38] It appears that splitting more often originates in the patient's dynamics than in the staff's.[39,40]

Jerry (cont'd.). The rehash meeting that followed the community meeting at which Jerry's therapist was attacked was curious. Most members of the nursing staff stood up for the therapist's behavior, but one nurse said, "Jerry has been sicker than you let on." She felt that Jerry's treatment was going too fast and that everybody was expecting more of him than he could deliver. "I just wonder how he's ever going to put it together when he gets out of here," she finally declared. Most of the staff was incredulous that after the good, energetic resolution to the staff meeting she still voiced the pessimistic view of schizophrenia. Several staff members sought to "correct" her, but an older nurse took her side about Jerry. The therapist reiterated his statements in the community meeting and cited research data that supported his contention that Jerry's schizophrenia had a good prognosis.

Finally the ward chief noted that this conflict between the doubting nurse and the optimistic therapist sounded suspiciously like the argument between Jerry's mother and father. "And you each have your allies, as they do. Isn't it possible that you're both right? Isn't that what Jerry has to put together?"

For the first time the staff could feel what Jerry was up against. For a few minutes the group as a whole felt angry, discouraged, and very confused. Both had to be right, but what then should the staff *do*? "Now I'm confused," the older nurse said, and the tension seemed to lift.

"Well, at least we've seen how impossible it feels to be Jerry," said the therapist, who from this point on approached his patient with a certain seriousness that his work had previously lacked. He seemed less cocksure.

To the ward at large, Jerry had become a bit more real. The "doubting nurse" took pains to make a few demands on Jerry, including one speech to him that ended his failure to make his bed in the morning for once and all. "It's the least you can do," she said, penetrating his resistance as the commanding officer who tried to get him to pack his duffel bag right never could.

"Oh, *okay!*" Jerry shouted, and made the bed.

The recognition and working through of staff splits is one of the most potent aspects of milieu therapy, as the previous example shows. Their nonrecognition can lead to bitter staff battles, as a patient's ambivalent conflict, with its warring halves, is acted out by an entire ward. Such bitter disputes may require an outside consultant, who can better identify them.

Self-destructive Behavior

Minor self-destructive acts can be dealt with by limit setting, as in the case of the depressed woman who cut her wrist to relieve her inner tension in a clear-cut signal for help. Major suicide attempts on the ward constitute a crisis for the ward as well as for the patient. Often an emergency meeting of the ward will mobilize the therapeutic community to act as a lifeline for the suicidal person, who can then be kept on the ward. Repeated suicide attempts, despite mobilization of the community, will require referral to a locked facility with maximum security. Not every patient can make it on an open ward.

An actual death by suicide on the ward is a major trauma for the living who are left behind to wonder if they will be stopped from harming themselves. Often the suicide will produce a con-tagion of suicidal emotion throughout the ward, as if this solution is seen to be a possible way out of severe emotional conflict. A special community meeting that focuses on the event can serve to "bury" the suicidal solution if patients can see that staff is not going to retreat from its attempts to help patients solve problems because one made death his solution. Nevertheless, the staff can expect to have its ability to take reasonable preventive measures tested within a short time after an actual death takes place.

Example 10-6. A suicide took place on a small ward: an elderly man jumped out of a window one day after being let out of a locked room. Two other patients saw him make the jump. A community meeting was held in which everyone had his say about the event. A few hours after the meeting, one of the patients who had watched the man jump, an adolescent boy who had not previously reported suicidal feelings, informed his doctor that he felt suicidal. He was placed in a locked room at his own request. Shortly after, the other man who had watched the suicide also asked to be locked up. The two did not feel free of suicidal promptings for three days, during which time they remained in locked rooms. Later their treatment proceeded without ill effects; they expressed gratitude for being taken seriously during their time of panic and guilt.

Aggressive Behavior

It is a staff's duty to protect patients from assault. A firm rule against touching other patients is usually necessary with borderline and psychotic patients. It should be remembered that hospitalized patients are usually "mad," and that given the least opportunity their anger is apt to surface in an explosive way.

Example 10-7. An 18-year-old woman was leaving the ward after being hospitalized for a month and a half. Her recurrent problem was learning to control her anger. As she was leaving, she said to the therapist who had achieved good results by holding her responsible for her outbursts, "Gee, I'd like to give you a punch in the stomach."

Caught off guard by her good humor, the therapist said, "Go ahead." The patient proceeded to punch him as hard as she could right in the solar plexus.

This example points out that patients usually *mean* what they say to therapists. A good way to stave off trouble is to hold patients responsible for what they say, and to follow up any verbal cues that suggest an outburst of hostile behavior is being contemplated. Patients usually feel that they are being watched on an inpatient ward, and they expect this kind of careful listening from the ward staff. A ward is a good place for the therapist to learn to remember what patients say, to note down the exact words, and to allow himself to be "haunted" by seemingly trivial communications. By taking such idle remarks up in therapy sessions, the therapist can defuse many bombs.

Hostile Dependency

If a patient is hospitalized longer than he needs to be, he may become hostile and break ward rules. Some patients react negatively to hospitalization and presumably are so full of unmet dependent needs that they must constantly defend themselves with anger to hold onto their independence. If a patient becomes more and more angry the more that is done for him, the best approach is to do less. By doing more the therapist tends to "trap" the patient into the intolerable (for him) position of being indebted. By doing less, even to the point of discharging or referring him to another therapist, the therapist gives the patient the dignified "one-up" position of being able to reproach; the patient will feel less angry. This principle is often useful in the treatment of patients with character disorders.

Example 10-8. A middle-aged alcoholic woman kept pressuring a beginning therapist to admit her to the hospital. Finally he yielded to a drunken telephone call and agreed to come in at 3 A.M. to the hospital emergency room. (Previously he had told her she would have to present herself sober during regular working hours to obtain admission, and he was contradicting his own limit setting.)

The therapist immediately set up a schedule of detoxification designed to make her as comfortable as possible. He carefully explained everything that would be expected of her and thoroughly oriented her to the ward. He saw her every day and did everything to make sure she knew what was being done for her care.

At the end of the third hospital day she flew into a rage at the staff, claimed she had been hospitalized against her will, and signed out against medical advice. She called her therapist from home that evening and promised to kill him if he ever tried to control her again. Her now-frightened therapist, on the advice of a senior clinician, referred her to a long-established alcohol treatment program. After telling several professionals at the program that he had "rejected" her, the patient settled into a program that recognized her need to be in control and let the movement into therapy come from her.

Even patients who do not have severe conflicts over dependency will feel that being in a mental hospital represents a failure in their lives and will resent the "one-down" position of being cared for benevolently. Some extremely successful inpatient wards are run by ward chiefs who have harsh, abrasive styles and who do not present themselves as kind, but rather address their patients in a businesslike way. This stance allows hostile dependent patients to feel that what they do, they do for themselves and obviates their need to provoke the ward staff to find someone to resent so that they can feel better about themselves.

Example 10-9. A chronically regressed schizophrenic patient who had proved refractory to the ministrations of a series of well-meaning therapists finally perked up after a blunt, abrasive therapist took over his care. His improvement was so dramatic that after a few months he was recommended for discharge from the mental hospital where he had spent several years.

The discharge staff committee was interested in this phenomenon, and so they asked the patient, still doing well on his first review of the trial discharge, what had made the difference.

"I was sitting in my corner as usual," said the patient, "When this person suddenly was standing over me. I looked up at his mean face, and I said to myself, 'Here's a son-of-a-bitch who's going to get me well'."

Sick Friendships and Sexual Relationships

Inevitably, patients in the hospital recreate their problems in living with each other. Many therapists will not criticize their patients' relationships because they dislike commenting on the behavior of others. On a therapeutic community ward, with its seductive emphasis on patients helping each other, an uncritical acceptance of all relationships between patients can lead to trouble. Patients will sometimes "team up" to resist therapy, a phenomenon that has been described for adolescent inpatients in love when they become two against the therapeutic community. As in the case of Alice in Chapter 3, patients may live together in mutually exploitative relationships after they are discharged. The inpatient ward is not the place to make friends, but to learn to be helpful in more objective ways. When pairs do form, they should be examined.

Jerry (cont'd.). The large woman who spoke at the community meeting in such a cryptic way ("I'm as pacific as the ocean.") took a special interest in Jerry from the first day of

his hospitalization. "Come over here, honey," she bellowed into the day room a little before breakfast. "I can see you're in trouble. Sit by Ruby." Jerry obediently sat beside her.

For a few days Jerry spent much of his free time with Ruby. She claimed to be a palmist, and for long minutes would gaze at Jerry's palm. She never revealed what she saw, but the effect was devastating.

Eventually their relationship was explored in the small group to which they both belonged. It developed that Jerry's mother was active in a spiritualist church, and that she had been unable to get a favorable reading from her minister for his enlistment. Ruby had several children who had been taken away from her by court order, many years ago.

On the one hand, these two were reenacting an unhealthy mother-son relationship. On the other, this very reenactment allowed the ward staff to touch upon material that might have gone unnoticed. The depression behind Ruby's paranoia had much to do with her feelings of failure as a mother: Jerry was the first person in whom she had shown interest in many days on the ward. She had been brought in by police who found her picking trash out of garbage cans and talking incoherently to herself. Jerry, as already shown, was overimpressed by his mother's doubts. The relationship they formed on the ward brought out key issues in the illness of each.

Outside Contacts, Contraband, and Unplanned Departures

Occasionally, a patient will *misuse outside contacts* to conduct his own crisis intervention with members of his ecological group.

Example 10-10. Clare, who had been admitted following a suicide attempt after her husband had found her in bed with another man and walked out, spent much of her time on the ward telephone trying to convince him to come back. At the same time, she refused to let her therapist interview him. Eventually the problem was solved by admitting the husband to the ward. The two continued their attempts at reconciliation, but in a context where professionals could observe and help them to clarify their interaction.

This case illustrates an increasingly common clinical practice of admitting both members of a marital couple together. The therapist who uses this method saves much time in trying to convince the nonadmitted spouse that he is also "the patient," in making necessary communications a second time, and in keeping pace with the unregulated contacts between the partners.

If a member of the outside ecological group cannot or should not be included in a patient's treatment, the therapist should try to regulate their contacts. If they cannot be regulated, the therapist should reconsider whether or not this person has to be left out of the treatment. A good compromise is to have the other person be seen collaboratively by another professional: the "intruder" can be included even while the patient maintains his privacy.

> *Example 10-11.* Lois, who developed a psychotic depression her second year of junior college, could not be separated from her mother, a cheery extraverted nurse who was unconsciously crushing her daughter in her zeal to make her feel better. Mother would appear with bright bouquets of flowers which she would spend many minutes trying to arrange in a manner that would please Lois. Lois would stare quietly ahead. When they were seen together in therapy sessions, Lois would remain withdrawn and her mother would do all the talking, often acting seductively toward Lois' therapist. Following a session, Lois wandered off the ward and onto the hospital roof. She was seen there by a frightened patient on a walk.

Clearly, these joint contacts were antitherapeutic. The therapist asked that Lois' mother be seen collaboratively by the ward social worker, herself a motherly woman who was extremely responsible about not doing too much for her patients. He explained to Lois that her mother would be able to talk to the social worker every day, that she would not be attending any more of their sessions, and that her visits would be limited to fifteen minutes twice a week. Almost immediately Lois' depression began to lift, and therapy aimed at Lois' eventual emancipation got underway.

The patient must be told clearly at the beginning of his stay that he cannot keep personal stores of drugs and weapons, i.e., *contraband.* The occasional patient who uses a ward to "push" narcotics and psychedelic drugs should be discharged. The discovery of weapons and drugs threatens the security of the ward and should be made the subject of a community meeting. If a suicidal patient is found to be stockpiling potentially lethal drugs, the entire ward should be made aware of his presuicidal communication. Usually "exposing" a suicidal patient in this manner tends to undercut the feelings of isolation that lead to such behavior. The homicidal patient who harbors weapons on a ward poses a more difficult problem. The therapist should insist upon the removal and sale of all firearms as a condition of treatment. Often the ward chief will be called upon to set the limit with such patients. Sometimes the patient has to be discharged and the police notified.

Patients may arrange *unplanned departures* and leave the ward for brief periods (AWOL) or for good (elopement) without telling anyone. Or, they may leave against medical advice after having signed the necessary papers. Responsible members of the ecological group should be notified of such departures immediately. If a patient threatens to leave against medical advice, these members should be called to the ward for an emergency conference. If the patient is being held on the ward legally against his will and leaves, the police should be notified. In most other circumstances, the police should *not* be notified. A very large percentage of those who leave the ward without permission get in touch with their therapists within a few days. The ward chief will usually rule that the patient who elopes has to apply to the ward through a new goals conference before his readmission can be considered.

EFFECTING THE PLANNED DISCHARGE

Discharge planning begins when the patient first enters the milieu. If the crisis intervention and the handling of transactions within the milieu have gone well, the discharge follows naturally. Nevertheless, certain problems regularly appear when the patient reenters the world, and they are the subject of the next paragraphs.

Passes

No patient should be discharged from an inpatient unit until he has had at least one short pass to demonstrate his fitness to cope with the stresses of the outside environment. Ideally, there will be a short pass, followed by an overnight pass, and then a weekend pass, before a seriously disturbed patient is considered to be ready for discharge. After each pass the therapist should review the nurse's notes to discover the patient's emotional state upon return, whether he appeared inebriated or "high" on drugs, and the nature of his behavior on the ward on coming back. He should then discuss how the patient handled the pass. *No new pass should be written until the patient's reaction to the previous pass has been thoroughly evaluated.*

Passes should be structured around an activity. Thus a pass can allow time enough for dinner and a movie, a job interview, or a visit to a potential therapist. Long stretches of unstructured time are unwise. Patients who request such long passes without plans are usually trying to avoid the process of therapy on the ward.

Reports of behavior on passes can help the therapist spot potential sources of trouble in the patient's readaptation following his experience with hospitalization.

Jerry (cont'd.). At the end of his first week on the ward, Jerry took a four-hour pass to see a Walt Disney movie. He left and returned on time. He went to sleep immediately.

The following week, after the big conference with the members of his family, plans were made for a two-day visit home, with time also allowed for a visit to the prospective therapist's office. (Jerry's family lived several hundred miles away; the intermediate step of a one-day visit had to be omitted in his case.)

When Jerry returned he explained that he didn't have much to say to the outside therapist. "It's kind of hard to talk about yourself to a complete stranger," he said to his ward therapist, adding, "Wouldn't it be great if you could be my therapist?"

A call to Jerry's father revealed that Jerry had resisted all pressures to engage in activities by saying, "You know I'm a goddam schizophrenic."

Jerry's mother reported that her day with Jerry had gone strangely. "You should ask me to do things," Jerry had told her. She had even asked the therapist, "Do you think I don't expect enough of him?"

The pass revealed a number of problems that had grown evident on the ward: Jerry was attached to the ward therapist, and he tended to use his diagnosis as a "cop out." But it also showed that he had begun some real work in his relationship with his mother, which had been the most difficult issue in his life. The information gained from the pass helped guide the therapist in his final work with Jerry. This work involved termination and a redefinition of the meaning of his mental illness.

Options of Disposition

When a patient is discharged from the inpatient milieu, he (1) returns to his former ecological group, which stays unchanged; (2) goes to an ecological group to which new members have been added, such as a therapist or visiting nurse; or (3) enters a new ecological group (day care center, halfway house, or nursing home). The decision is reached on the basis of therapeutic contacts with members of the original ecological group, assessment of the degree of the patient's social impairment, and the resources at hand.

The general error is to be too grandiose, to try to "save" the patient from an environment that has made him ill, only to introduce him into another environment, supposedly therapeutic, in which he stays just as ill. It is often enough to make slight changes in the original ecological group, such as the addition of a good therapist. Major relocations should be reserved for those patients who are truly without social resources or who have deteriorated seriously.

Example 10-12. Annie, 76, was admitted to the hospital, failing in memory, with a history of soiling herself and setting herself afire by accidentally dropping cigarette butts in bed. After a few days of a strong vitamin regimen, enough memory returned to enable her to care for herself on the ward, although she had a clear-cut Wernicke-Korsakoff syndrome. She was visited every day by a 62-year-old gentleman who had borrowed large sums of money from her during the past year. He usually smelled of alcohol. A cousin who had emergency power of attorney revealed that Annie had confided in her that she thought he was after her money, but she loved him anyway. This man supplied her with alcohol, and it was clear that when she returned home she would quickly revert to her drinking ways.

On balance, recommendation to send her to a nursing home was made, with the cousin serving as conservator.

Discharge as a Trial of Readaptation

Transition has its difficulties for all patients. For psychotic patients, this is a time in which suicidal feelings develop. Depressive patients often experience a reactivation of suicidal intent. Patients with character disorders often become angry to the point that they leave AWOL or against medical advice a day before their planned discharge. It is well to explain to patients that they may find the discharge difficult, that it is expected that they will call the therapist if they feel unaccountably depressed, frightened, or angry, and that a number of patients find that they are not ready after all. The option of planned readmission should always be held open so that the patient does not have to stage a crisis to dramatize his need for continued support.

Jerry (cont'd.). A week after his discharge Jerry made a planned telephone call to his ward therapist at a prearranged time. He had chosen to live with his father, and he was looking for work. He had seen his outpatient therapist twice, and the therapist had seen his family twice. "He's pretty sharp," Jerry said. "He doesn't buy that schizophrenia stuff. I was pretty low for a couple of days, like you said, but everybody's trying to change for me, and I'm keeping my thoughts clear. Tell Ruby I found out I have a real long lifeline."

SUMMARY

Crisis intervention in a ward setting involves the same principles as in outpatient work, but many more people become involved, and much more of the patient's life is opened to the intervention. In using this resource, the basic skill is constant attention to the patient's transactions in the variety of situations that the process of hospitalization makes possible.

REFERENCES

1. Bettelheim, Bruno, and Emmy Sylvester: A Therapeutic Milieu," *Am. J. Orthopsychiat.,* **18**:191–206, 1948.

2. Jones, Maxwell: *The Therapeutic Community,* Basic Books, New York, 1953.

3. Wilmer, Harry A.: *Social Psychiatry in Action,* Charles C Thomas, Springfield, Ill., 1958.

4. Rapoport, Robert N.: *Community as Doctor,* Tavistock Publications, London, 1959.

5. Abroms, Gene M.: "Defining Milieu Therapy," *Arch. Gen. Psychiat.,* **21**:553–560, 1969.

6. Zusman, Jack: "Some Explanations of the Changing Appearance of Psychotic Patients: Antecedents of the Social Breakdown Concept," *Int. J. Psychiat.,* **3**:216–247, 1967.

7. Weisman, Gilbert, Alan Feirstein, and Thomas Claudewell: "Three Day Hospitalization — a Model for Intensive Intervention," *Arch. Gen. Psychiat.,* **21**:620–629, 1969.

8. Engle, Ralph P., and Elvin V. Semrad: "Brief Hospitalization, the Recompensation Process," in Gene M. Abroms and Norman S. Greenfield (eds.), *The New Hospital Psychiatry,* Academic, New York, 1971, chap. 5, pp. 67–81.

9. Herz, Marvin I., Jean Endicott, Robert L. Spitzer, and Alvin Mesnikoff: "Day Versus Inpatient Hospitalization: A Controlled Study," *Am. J. Psychiat.,* **127**:1371–1381, 1971.

10. Langsley, Donald G., David M. Kaplan, F. S. Pittman et al.: *Treatment of Families in Crisis,* Grune & Stratton, New York, 1968.

11. Langsley, Donald G., Pavel Machotka, and Kalman Flomenhaft: "Avoiding Mental Hospital Admission: A Follow-up Study," *Am. J. Psychiat.,* **127**:1391–1394, 1971.

12. Kessler, David: "Preventing Psychiatric Hospitalization: A Crisis Intervention Approach," talk given at Pacific Medical Center, San Francisco, March 8, 1973.

13. Holmes, Marguerite J.: "Influences of the New Hospital Psychiatry on Nursing," in Gene M. Abroms and Norman S. Greenfield (eds.), *The New Hospital Psychiatry,* Academic, New York, 1971, chap. 6, pp. 83–100.

14. Levene, Howard I.: "Acute Schizophrenia: Clinical Effects of the Labeling Process," *Arch. Gen. Psychiat.,* **25**:215–222, 1971.

15. Beck, James C., and Kathy Worthen: "Precipitating Stress, Crisis Theory and Hospitalization in Schizophrenia," *Arch. Gen. Psychiat.,* **26**:123–132, 1972.

16. Perry, John W.: "Reconstitutive Process in the Psychopathology of the Self," *Ann. NY Acad. Sci.,* **96**:853–876, 1962.

17. Holmes: op. cit., p. 85.

18. Cumming, John, and Elaine Cumming: *Ego and Milieu,* Atherton, New York, 1963.

19. Levene: loc. cit.

20. Perry: loc. cit.

21. Polsky, Howard W., Daniel S. Claster, and Carl Goldberg (eds.): *Social System Perspectives in Residential Institutions,* The Michigan State University Press, East Lansing, 1970.

22. Peplau, H.: "Psychotherapeutic Strategies and Its Discussion," *Perspect. Psychiat. Care,* **6**:264–286, 1968.

23. Abroms: "Group Methods in the Milieu," in Gene M. Abroms and Norman S. Greenfield (eds.), *The New Hospital Psychiatry,* Academic, New York, 1971, chap. 9, pp. 133–146.

24. Kass, David J., Frederick M. Silvers, and Gene M. Abroms: "Behavioral Group Treatment of Hysteria," *Arch. Gen. Psychiat.,* **26**:42–50, 1972.

25. Abroms, Gene M., Carl H. Fellner, and Carl A. Whitaker: "The Family Enters the Hospital," *Am. J. Psychiat.,* **127**:1363–1369, 1971.

26. Ullman, Leonard P.: "A Theoretical Overview of Behavior Modification Techniques with Schizophrenics," in Gene M. Abroms and Norman S. Greenfield (eds.), *The New Hospital Psychiatry,* Academic, New York, 1971, chap. 16.

27. Daniels, David N., and J. M. Kuldau: "Marginal Man, the Tether of Tradition, and Intentional Social System Therapy," *Community Ment. Health J.,* **3**:13–20, 1967.

28. Daniels, David N.: in C. Peter Rosenbaum: *The Meaning of Madness: Symptomatology, Sociology, Biology and Therapy of the Schizophrenias,* Science House, New York, 1970, chap. 13.

29. Yablonsky, Lewis: *Synanon, The Tunnel Back,* Macmillan, New York, 1965.

30. Lieb, Julian, Ian Lipsitch, and Andrew Slaby: *The Crisis Team: A Handbook for the Mental Health Professional,* Harper & Row, New York, 1973.

31. Ibid.

32. Abroms: "Defining Milieu Therapy," loc. cit. cit.

33. Bateson, Gregory, Don D. Jackson, Jay Haley, and John Weakland: "Toward A Theory of Schizophrenia," *Behav. Sci.,* vol. 1, no. 4, 1956.

34. Caudill, William A.: *The Psychiatric Hospital as a Small Society,* Harvard, Cambridge, Mass., 1958.

35. Ludwig, Arnold M., and Frank Farrelly: "The Code of Chronicity," *Arch. Gen. Psychiat.,* 15:562–568, 1966.

36. Wilmer: loc. cit.

37. Kass et al.: loc. cit.

38. Stanton, Alfred H., and M. S. Schwartz: *The Mental Hospital,* Basic Books, New York, 1954.

39. Burnham, D. L.: "The Special Problem Patient: Victim or Agent of Splitting?" *Psychiatry,* 29:105–122, 1966.

40. Main, T. F.: "The Ailment," *Brit. J. Med. Psychol.,* 30:129–145, 1957.

C. PETER ROSENBAUM, M.D.

JOHN E. BEEBE III, M.D.

CHAPTER 11

Organizing Emergency Work

PART 1: A FLOWCHART SYSTEM OF EVALUATION AND DISPOSITION OF PSYCHIATRIC EMERGENCIES

The preceding chapters presented ways to order, evaluate, formulate, and apply information in intervening with persons caught in crisis. Observing the patient in his particular situation, responding intuitively to the patterns inherent in the dilemma, allowing appropriate feeling to emerge from the confusion of emotion, and reasoning out possible solutions with the participants are requisites for good crisis intervention. A final skill involves the ability to take command, to orchestrate the elements of intervention into a smoothly executed plan of action. Here the emergency therapist must use his executive abilities, even if only to lend his authority to a solution he has helped the participants to find for themselves. This chapter is a kind of executive training for therapists and includes a test of mettle at its end. It is an approach to that most difficult of executive functions, *organization*.

At this stage of his work, the emergency therapist must establish relations with the patient's *ego*. He must ensure that there is enough ego functioning present to avert catastrophe. If there is not, the therapist must support the patient's ego

with his own. One aspect of ego functioning is internal and external control over the expression of sexual, aggressive, and dependent impulses. The patient must be able to avoid detrimental action as he attempts to meet his needs. One method of increasing control is through the use of environmental support; another is through the use of tranquilizing and sedative medication.

If loss of control is the major consideration, a true psychiatric "emergency" is said to exist, and Salamon[1] lists three principles of basic management: (1) deal with the healthy part of the patient's ego, (2) establish controls, and (3) use medication.

As Salamon points out, there is almost always some healthy ego to appeal to in even the most disturbed patient. The therapist must make it clear to this healthy ego that he will not tolerate uncontrolled behavior and that he will take control until the patient is able to exert his own controls again. The therapist should present medication as an aid in achieving the return of self-control.

These three principles draw heavily upon the medical model, but emergency therapists coming from a nonmedical background should avail themselves of them. (Much of the mystique attached to psychiatrists as medically trained therapists amounts merely to *comfort* in using the medical model when it is appropriate in therapy.) A psychologist or social worker should, as a mental health professional, be able to take command of a deteriorating situation with a disturbed patient, talk to the healthy ego, be able to interpose his own ego-controls, and make sure an available physician furnishes the appropriate medication. (In contemporary crisis teams, a physician need only countersign the medical prescription and the admission order; the decisions to use these modes of intervention are made by the mental health professional.)

It follows that the nonmedical therapist will have to train himself in the areas of medicine that apply to emergency psychotherapy, specifically those concerning the nature and effects of psychotropic drugs. He will also need a good working alliance with the physician who countersigns his plan of management. Indeed, unless the lines of authority and responsibility are clearly drawn, the nonmedical therapist should not accept an assignment to do emergency psychiatric work. Usually if he has demonstrated a basic ability to assume responsibility for managing the patient and seems comfortable with the medical model, he will have no trouble in his relationship with the medical man who legally supervises his emergency work.

CHOICE POINTS AND DECISION MAKING

Assuming responsibility means more than taking control; it also involves the formulation and defense of a treatment plan (in emergency work, sometimes called "the disposition"). In making decisions concerning the final plan, a series of choice points emerge, questions that must be answered before the next step in decision making can be pondered.

It helps the therapist to do his job if he asks himself a series of yes and no questions. Suppose, for example, that he is confronted with a patient who is threatening suicide, who has no interpersonal resources, and who is threatening to walk out of the emergency room. He asks himself:

1. Is the patient dangerously suicidal? Yes.
2. Is involuntary hospitalization legal in this state under these circumstances? Yes.

3. Do I have the means and facilities available to hospitalize the patient involuntarily? Yes.

The answer to each question leads to the next, and the final answer to the final question is the disposition: hospitalize the patient involuntarily.

Much psychiatric emergency work can be organized in this fashion. Each of the kinds of patients — the suicidal, homicidal, drinking, and so on — described in the preceding chapters operates under a particular set of conditions, often unique to the particular condition under consideration, which recur and which the emergency therapist must keep in mind. He must consider conditions A, B, and C for the suicidal patient; resultant choice-points may be A^1, B^1, and C^1, and so forth.

We have tried to present the most important questions that must be asked and answered by the therapist, and the logical choices that flow from their answers; these choices for several kinds of patients are presented in the flowcharts that follow. Later we shall provide an analysis in a similar form on how to organize knowledge about disposition resources.

FLOWCHART ANALYSIS FOR SPECIFIC CONDITIONS

Evaluation and Disposition of Psychiatric Emergencies: General Considerations

The most serious considerations in evaluating a psychiatric emergency center around severe incapacitation, the potential danger of the patient to himself or to others, and the degree of risk of further serious medical or psychiatric disabilities. If the death or severe disability of a patient or someone else is possible if appropriate intervention is not taken, hospitalization (involuntary if necessary) should probably be effected. Less severe probable outcomes may call for less drastic measures. The major evaluations that must be made and the decisions that result from them are shown in Figure 11-1. Table 11-1 is to be used in conjunction with this figure.

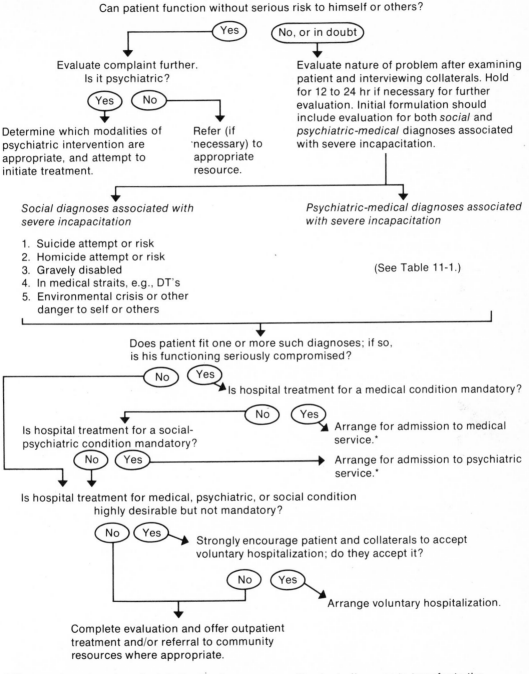

Figure 11-1 Evaluation and disposition of psychiatric emergencies. 1: general considerations.

TABLE 11-1: Psychiatric-Medical Diagnoses Associated with Severe Incapacitation

(Diagnoses often occur in combination. Once all diagnoses are made, go to the sections in this chapter that outline needed evaluation and treatment decisions in greater detail.)

Talking with collaterals can often be far more profitable than spending much time with a patient who is delirious or suffering from impaired reality testing. Always get the old chart as soon as possible; this may be a "repeat performance." Descriptions of earlier episodes may provide the guide to the treatment of this one.

I. Acute or chronic complications of medicosurgical conditions: NB: Whenever these are present to a significant degree, they must be treated adequately on a medical-surgical service *before* the patient is transferred to a psychiatric hospital where diagnostic and treatment facilities are often inadequate. Psychiatric consultation should be freely available to the attending internist or surgeon.

    A. Organic brain syndromes associated with

        1. Primary (CNS) pathology, such as

            (a) Space-occupying cranial lesions, intrinsic or the result of trauma (e.g., gunshot wounds, subdural hematoma, etc.)

            (b) Ictal and postictal confusional states

            (c) Hypertension

        2. Toxic states associated with

            (a) Alcohol

            (b) Psychotropic drugs, e.g., sedatives, especially barbiturates, glutethimide (Doriden®); methaqualone (Quaalude®); major and minor tranquilizers

            (c) "Street drugs" and "bad trips," including those from ingestion of LSD, marihauna, amphetamines, belladonna compounds, DMT, STP, cocaine, etc.

            (d) Opiate addiction

            (e) Carbon monoxide

            (f) Other poisons

        3. Metabolic and infectious diseases, especially those that may mimic functional illness

            (a) Possible mimics of anxiety and manic states: hyperthyroidism, pheochromocytoma, tertiary syphilis, hypoglycemia

            (b) Possible mimics of schizophrenia, alcoholic delirium: diabetic coma, systemic lupus erythematosis, corticosteroid reactions, Cushing's disease

            (c) Possible mimics of depression: hypothyroidism, Addison's disease

    B. Physical trauma: lacerations, stab and gunshot wounds, etc.

II. Primarily psychological states

    A. Depression and suicide (NB: Suicide risk found also in other conditions in which depression may not be significantly present)

    B. Homicide (often in conjunction with alcohol, other drug use)

C. Psychotic states
1. Schizophrenia
2. Depressive psychoses, unipolar and bipolar
3. Manic states
4. Paranoid states
D. Miscellaneous other states, including fugues, amnesias, multiple personality, and other dissociative reactions

Depression and Suicide

The major choice-points of depression and suicide center around self-destruction, by either a recent or a highly possible future overt attempt, or by "chronic suicide" (e.g., continued heavy drinking when known liver damage is present, or chronic heavy drinking in combination with barbiturate addiction), and around the recurrence of suicidal emotion after the initial intervention has taken place and treatment has been instituted (see Figure 11-2).

Homicide and Violence

The choice-points for evaluating the potentially violent patient should include his potential for violence *now,* his potential for violence *later* (especially if drinking or drug taking is not presently a problem but may be in the future), reducing the personal and social forces that may be building to a violent explosion, exerting control over the potentially violent person, and protecting the safety of potential victims (see Figure 11-3).

Psychotic States in General

Psychosis denotes only a serious impairment in the ability to perceive or respond appropriately to external and internal reality. Psychosis can result from a variety of organic states, including alcohol and other drug ingestion, brain disease, and so on, and from several kinds of so-called functional states, such as the schizophrenias, manic-depressive illness, and so on.

Once the general diagnosis of psychosis has been made, certain interventions, largely aimed at preventing the patient from doing harm to himself or others, can be made. Specific treatment (including administering drugs and ECT) depends on making specific diagnoses, and these in turn may demand that additional hours and days be spent in obtaining a history from the patient and members of his ecological group, in making observations, and in preparing a psychiatric formulation. Guidelines for pursuing both general and specific diagnostic and treatment possibilities are given in Figure 11-4.

The Schizophrenias

The basic issue in the emergency treatment of schizophrenic patients is whether the psychosis is likely to result in destructive behavior or incapacitation, not whether schizophrenia per se requires hospital treatment. There are large numbers of obviously schizophrenic people living peacefully in society, in whatever idiosyncratic ways, who constitute no threat to others and who are able to provide for their own food, shelter, and personal needs. Many such patients require help in managing their lives *outside* the hospital, which they cannot learn *inside* (see Figure 11-5).

Alcohol and its Complications

The choice-points to be considered for patients with alcohol problems almost always involve at least one other health professional in addition to the emergency therapist. (This is true whether the therapist is a psychiatrist, psychologist, or other mental health professional.) The person most frequently called upon is an internist or general physician who can help evaluate and treat the patient medically; but representatives of many social agencies (including the police) may be involved. The first major choice is that of evaluating and treating concomitant serious medical illness that may accompany the drinking. The second is the treatment of acute intoxication, and the third is treatment of the underlying psychiatric and social problems (see Figure 11-6).

Street Drugs and Bad Trips

The major question in treating a patient who has taken a street drug or is having a bad trip is, "Does the treater know what he is treating, i.e., does he have highly reliable information as to which drug(s) the patient has taken?" If he does, he can often, in addition to supportive treatment (e.g., talking the patient down), use a specific antidote. If he does not (which is usually the case), he must restrict himself to using minor tranquilizers or sedatives, such as diazepam. He must also rule out an underlying functional psychosis which may be masked by acute drug intoxication. All these possibilities are represented in Figure 11-7.

Opiate and Sedative Addictions

First the therapist needs to know whether the patient is suffering from an overdose or a withdrawal syndrome, and second whether the patient has been taking opiates, barbiturate sedatives, nonbarbiturate sedatives, or some combination of these (see Figure 11-8).

Figures 11-2 through 11-8 are located on pages 209–217. The text resumes on page 218.

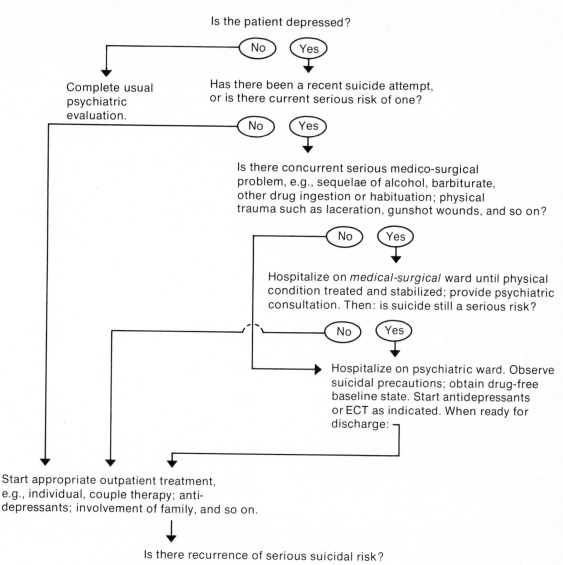

Figure 11-2 Depression and suicide.

Does patient show signs of being in a preassaultive state, e.g., one or more of the following:

1. Feeling of unbearable tension, that he might "blow".
2. Rage toward known other, often family member, with conscious thoughts of violence.
3. Recent increase of assaultive behavior, e.g., fights.
4. Toxic decrease of self-control, as with alcohol.
5. History of past violent behavior; parental brutality in past; triad of youthful bedwetting, cruelty to animals, and firesetting.
6. Arrest and prison record for violent crimes.
7. Arrest or convictions for dangerous auto crimes, e.g., speeding, hit-run driving, and so forth.
8. Well-formulated paranoid plan to "get him (them)," often in response to voices.

(No)   (Yes)

A. Further evaluation

Complete usual psychiatric evaluation.

1. Discuss with patient and collaterals the difference between thought and action; the need to exert control that psychiatrist cannot substitute for.
2. Evaluate temporary separation of warring parties, from moving in with family or friends, to motel, to psychiatric hospitalization.
3. Evaluate and discuss possible role of potential "victim" in promoting homicidal escalation.
4. Appeal to patient's narcissism, that violence on some level is "not very smart for a bright guy like you," i.e., is self-destructive, no matter how sweet the revenge. Appeal to his pride and sense of strength and control.

B. Decision making. Even with supportive psychotherapy, is the situation still high-risk for violence?

(No)   (Yes)

Continue treatment.

Advise potential victim of personal and legal rights for self-protection; use whatever professional and legal restraints (including incarceration) are necessary to control patient until acute potential for violence subsides. Patient may be more willing to accept *medical* rather than *psychiatric* hospitalization to avoid "crazy" or "psycho" label; service chief more likely to agree if psychiatrist says he will take *complete responsibility* for managing patient; can get neurological evaluation there if he suspects neurological basis for dyscontrol.

Figure 11-3 Homicide and violence.

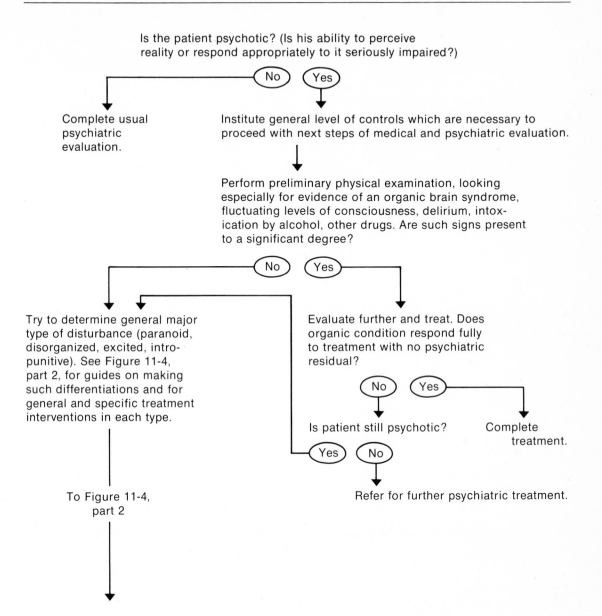

Figure 11-4 Psychotic states in general.

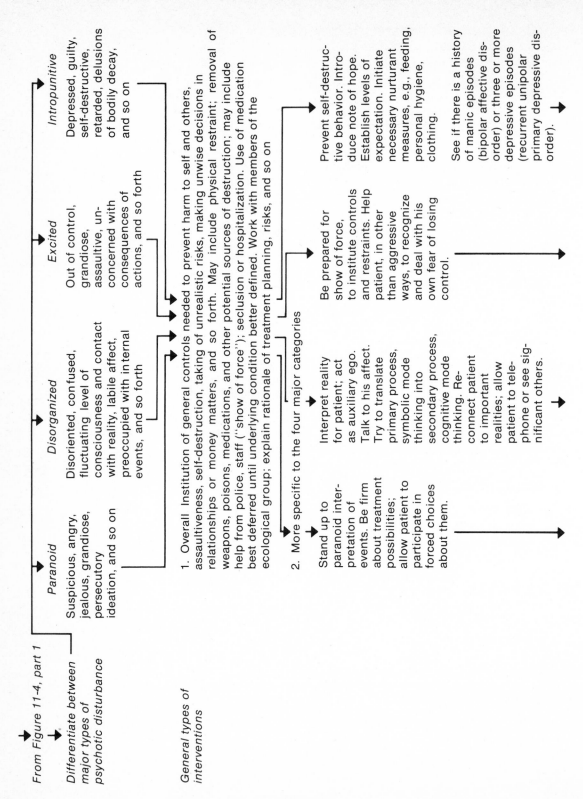

From Figure 11-4, part 1

Differentiate between major types of psychotic disturbance

Paranoid	Disorganized	Excited	Intropunitive
Suspicious, angry, jealous, grandiose, persecutory ideation, and so on	Disoriented, confused, fluctuating level of consciousness and contact with reality, labile affect, preoccupied with internal events, and so forth	Out of control, grandiose, assaultive, unconcerned with consequences of actions, and so forth	Depressed, guilty, self-destructive, retarded, delusions of bodily decay, and so on

General types of interventions

1. Overall Institution of general controls needed to prevent harm to self and others, assaultiveness, self-destruction, taking of unrealistic risks, making unwise decisions in relationships or money matters, and so forth. May include physical restraint; removal of weapons, poisons, medications, and other potential sources of destruction; may include help from police, staff ("show of force"); seclusion or hospitalization. Use of medication best deferred until underlying condition better defined. Work with members of the ecological group; explain rationale of treatment planning, risks, and so on

2. More specific to the four major categories

Stand up to paranoid interpretation of events. Be firm about treatment possibilities; allow patient to participate in forced choices about them.	Interpret reality for patient; act as auxiliary ego. Talk to his affect. Try to translate primary process, symbolic mode thinking into secondary process, cognitive mode thinking. Reconnect patient to important realities; allow patient to telephone or see significant others.	Be prepared for show of force, to institute controls and restraints. Help patient, in other than aggressive ways, to recognize and deal with his own fear of losing control.	Prevent self-destructive behavior. Introduce note of hope. Establish levels of expectation. Initiate necessary nurturant measures, e.g., feeding, personal hygiene, clothing.

See if there is a history of manic episodes (bipolar affective disorder) or three or more depressive episodes (recurrent unipolar primary depressive disorder). |

Specific interventions based on diagnosis (most commonly employed somatic treatments in parentheses)*

Paranoid	Disorganized	Excited	Intropunitive
1. Paranoid stress reaction. Removal from stress or diminution of stress (antipsychotics).	1. The schizophrenias. Reality oriented, milieu, and supportive therapy. (Antipsychotics.)	1. Manic phase of manic-depressive illness (antipsychotics, lithium carbonate; sometimes ECT).	1. Psychotic depressive reaction (antidepressants, ECT if no response).
2. Involutional paranoid state (antidepressants, antipsychotics, ECT).	2. Organic brain syndromes, delirium. Correction of organic and psychosocial factors. (Sometimes antipsychotics in low doses; vitamins.)	2. Catatonic excitement in schizophrenia (antipsychotics; sometimes ECT).	2. Primary depressive affective disorder. (a) First or second episode, unipolar type (antidepressants, ECT if no response).
3. Paranoid schizophrenia (antipsychotics).	3. Secondary to drug use. Detoxification. (Sometimes antipsychotics, sedatives.)	3. Acute panic. Milieu and supportive therapy. (Antipsychotics.)	(b) Third or more episode, unipolar type, "recurrent depression." (Lithium carbonate; ECT if no response).
4. Paranoia secondary to drug use. Detoxification. (Some times antipsychotics.)	4. Secondary to other metabolic factors, e.g., brain tumor, carbon monoxide poisoning, endocrine dysfunction. Correction of underlying metabolic disorder.	4. Sociopathic personality in state of rage. Milieu and supportive therapy. (Minor tranquilizers.)	(c) Depressive phase of bipolar, manic-depressive illness. (Lithium carbonate; ECT if no response. Avoid antidepressants.)
5. Paranoia secondary to organic brain syndromes. Correction of organic and psychosocial factors. (Sometimes antipsychotics in low doses.)		5. Side effect of antipsychotics (change or reduce offending drug).	3. Involutional melancholia (antidepressants; ECT if no response).
6. Paranoia in acute mania (antipsychotics, lithium carbonate).		6. Chronic schizophrenia in exacerbation (antipsychotics).	4. Schizoaffective disease, depressed type, first or second episode (antipsychotics, antidepressants). Third or more episode (antipsychotics, lithium carbonate; avoid antidepressants).
			5. Secondary to drug use. Detoxification. (For persistant depression, antidepressants.)
			6. Secondary to organic illness. Treatment of organic illness; milieu and supportive therapy. (For persistent depression, antidepressants.)

*"Antipsychotics" refers to medications from the classes of phenothiazines, butyrophenones, and thioxanthenes. "Antidepressants" refers to both the tricyclic group and monoamine oxidase inhibitors (MAOI).

213

Is patient in need of hospitalization? (Include following in evaluation: information from old chart, from family and friends; danger to self or others because of delusional thoughts or hallucinated commands; patient's degree of awareness or insight into psychotic process and disability; ask patient if he wants or *needs* to be hospitalized— he may know best).

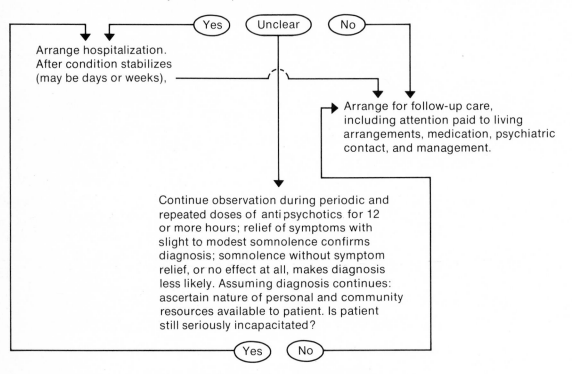

Yes   Unclear   No

Arrange hospitalization. After condition stabilizes (may be days or weeks),

Arrange for follow-up care, including attention paid to living arrangements, medication, psychiatric contact, and management.

Continue observation during periodic and repeated doses of antipsychotics for 12 or more hours; relief of symptoms with slight to modest somnolence confirms diagnosis; somnolence without symptom relief, or no effect at all, makes diagnosis less likely. Assuming diagnosis continues: ascertain nature of personal and community resources available to patient. Is patient still seriously incapacitated?

Yes   No

Figure 11-5   The schizophrenias.

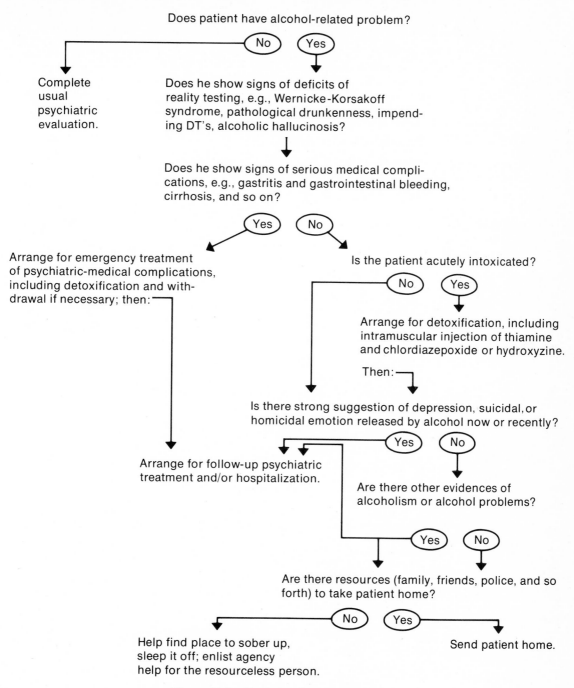

Figure 11-6   Alcohol and its complications.

Can ingredients of drugs be determined with relative certainty from patient or collaterals, including high reliability that supplier has given pure substance of named compound(s)?

No

Unclarity exists about nature, quantity, or purity of drugs taken.

Further evaluation

1. Is local toxic drug screening panel available? If so, employ to clarify or rule out substances taken.

2. Is hot line to local drug treatment center available? If so, consult with their personnel as needed.

3. Arrange constant psychiatric observation and management; help "talk patient down" from bad trip. Talking down best done in comfortable ambience, often as well or better by family or friends as by medical personnel.

4. Be *exceedingly cautious* in use of phenothiazines, whose anticholinergic effects may act synergistically with street drug to produce "anticholinergic crisis."

5. Use diazepam, paraldehyde, and related drugs for severe anxiety and agitation.

Yes

Arrange constant psychiatric observation and management; help "talk patient down" from bad trip. Talking down best done in comfortable ambience, often done as well or better by family and friends as by medical personnel. The following drugs may safely be treated with given antidote or antagonist:

Toxin	*Antidote*
1. Hallucinogen (LSD; mescaline).	1. Phenothiazines.
2. Anticholinergics, e.g., belladonna, scopolamine, related compounds. Diagnosed by "Mad as a hatter; dry as a bone; red as a lobster; blind as a stone."	2. Mild to moderate states; treat with diazepam, paraldehyde. Serious or life-threatening states: treat with physostigmine, IM, under close supervision. *Phenothiazines are contraindicated.*
3. Amphetamines; cocaine.	3. Diazepam for moderate states; phenothiazines for severe ones.
4. Opiates.	4. See Fig. 11-8 (opiates).
5. Marihuana.	5. Diazepam, paraldehyde. *Phenothiazines are contraindicated.*
6. Methaqualone (Quaalude)®; glutethimide (Doriden)®.	6. None; nondialyzable drugs. May look alert in emergency room, go into coma later. If in doubt, medical hospitalization for close observation, supportive treatment.

Has patient recovered well after 12 to 24 hours?

Yes

Evaluate need for further psychiatric treatment for underlying problems; make appropriate recommendations.

No

Consider possibility patient has taken long-acting hallucinogen, for example, DMT (dimethyltryptamine), STP and so on. Also consider possibility of underlying schizophrenia or other functional psychosis masked by drug intoxication; pursue treatment of psychosis.

Figure 11-7   Street drugs and "bad trips."

216

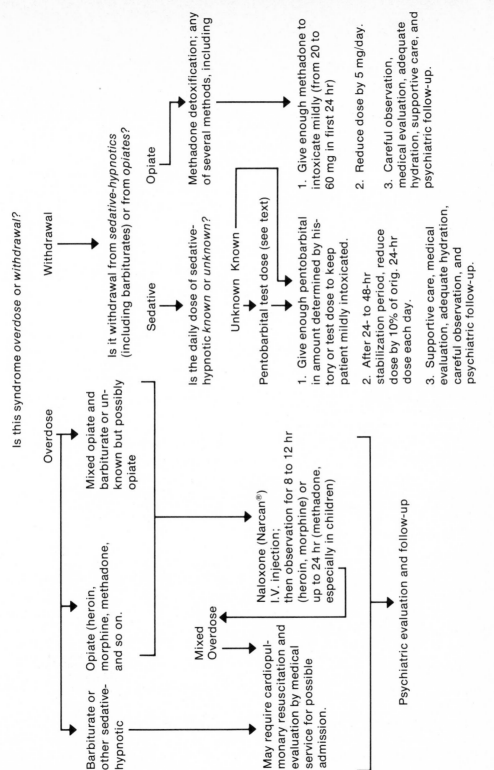

Is this syndrome *overdose* or *withdrawal*?

Overdose

- Barbiturate or other sedative-hypnotic
  - May require cardiopulmonary resuscitation and evaluation by medical service for possible admission.

- Opiate (heroin, morphine, methadone, and so on.
  - Mixed Overdose
  - Naloxone (Narcan®) I.V. injection; then observation for 8 to 12 hr (heroin, morphine) or up to 24 hr (methadone, especially in children)

- Mixed opiate and barbiturate or unknown but possibly opiate

Psychiatric evaluation and follow-up

Withdrawal

Is it withdrawal from *sedative-hypnotics* (including barbiturates) or from *opiates?*

Sedative

Is the daily dose of sedative-hypnotic *known* or *unknown?*

Unknown Known

Pentobarbital test dose (see text)

1. Give enough pentobarbital in amount determined by history or test dose to keep patient mildly intoxicated.

2. After 24- to 48-hr stabilization period, reduce dose by 10% of orig. 24-hr dose each day.

3. Supportive care, medical evaluation, adequate hydration, careful observation, and psychiatric follow-up.

Opiate

Methadone detoxification; any of several methods, including

1. Give enough methadone to intoxicate mildly (from 20 to 60 mg in first 24 hr)

2. Reduce dose by 5 mg/day.

3. Careful observation, medical evaluation, adequate hydration, supportive care, and psychiatric follow-up.

Figure 11-8 Opiate and sedative addictions.

217

DISPOSITION RESOURCES AND PRACTICES

Many communities have available a broad spectrum of disposition resources. What kinds they are, what they do and do not do, and who they do or do not accept for treatment are factors that will affect the practices of the emergency therapist. They range from facilities with locked rooms ("seclusion rooms") and high staff/patient ratios that can accept extremely disturbed, violently homicidal drunk paranoid schizophrenic patients to outpatient clinics or drop-in centers that are not equipped to deal with the out-of-control patient. In between these extremes are voluntary inpatient units, day and night care programs, emergency rooms, halfway houses, centers for the treatment of special problems such as opiate addiction, alcohol abuse, and street drugs, general outpatient clinics, and private practitioners and groups. These facilities are in marked contrast to those of two generations ago when the poor and middle-class had a choice only between a state or a county hospital in which all the wards were locked, or a public outpatient clinic with a long waiting list. The wealthy also had private sanitoriums, but with a limited range of treatments.

Not all patients are eligible for treatment at all facilities. Many county-operated facilities will not accept patients from outside the county; VA hospitals usually require that the individual have some connection with the military before they will offer treatment to him. Some insurance plans cover treatment for psychiatric problems; many do not. Some families have the money to pay for private treatment (especially short-term); many do not.

A Directory of Disposition Resources

The nature of available facilities and conditions of eligibility that must be met to enter them vary widely from one community to the next. The following directory of disposition resources is a general one that should be adaptable to the needs of a given area. The heading of Table 11-2 lists the kinds of treatment facilities that might be available in any given community; the kinds of patient eligibility that might be considered are listed along the side. (The emergency therapist can obtain some of this information from the patient or collaterals as he conducts his evaluation.) From these variables a grid is constructed and numbered; each number can be an index to a directory, available to the emergency therapist to suggest to him *all* the resources available to a given patient, not just the resources the therapist is already familiar with. Table 11-3 shows a sample excerpt from such a catalog.

Table 11-2 is reasonably comprehensive, but those who wish may refine it further. Under Partial Care Programs, one may want to insert those that deal with special populations, such as drug-using adolescents; under Special Problem Programs one may want to insert those that deal with patients from certain ethnic or socioeconomic groups, and so on. Thus, Tables 11-2 and 11-3 are to be used as models from which an emergency service can construct a catalog or directory to be used by all of its members. Such a catalog will need constant revision as new community services begin and old ones shut down.

Using a Resource Directory

Table 11-3 gives only a few of the 220 possibilities that were presented in Table 11-2. The following hypothetical situations are examples of how Tables 11-2 and 11-3 might be used. An enlisted Army man who lives in this county got drunk and belligerent and threatened to kill his wife. She called the police, who brought him into the emergency room. The emergency therapist ascertained that no medical complications were present and determined that he needed involuntary psychiatric hospitalization. Of all the categories under involuntary hospitalization in Table 11-2 (index numbers 1, 21, 41, . . ., 201), an army resource looked in principle to be the best for the patient. The therapist consulted his directory (Table 11-3), obtained the information about

TABLE 11-2: Available Facilities and Patient Eligibility

Patient Eligibility	Total Care Programs			Partial Care Programs			Special Problem Programs							Outpatient Clinics					Individual and Group Practice	
	Involuntary hospitalization	Voluntary hospitalization	Convalescent hospital and nursing home	Day treatment	Night treatment	Halfway house	Alcohol	Opiates	Other drugs	Suicide	Sexual	Geriatric	Retardation	General	Child	Crisis	Family service	Medical	Individual therapy	Couple group therapy
Federal programs																				
Military	1	2	3	4	5	6	7	8	9	10	11	12	13	14	15	16	17	18	19	20
Veterans	21	22	23	24	25	26	27	28	29	30	31	32	33	34	35	36	37	38	39	40
Public Health Service	41	42	43	44	45	46	47	48	49	50	51	52	53	54	55	56	57	58	59	60
State	61	62	63	64	65	66	67	68	69	70	71	72	73	74	75	76	77	78	79	80
This county	81	82	83	84	85	86	87	88	89	90	91	92	93	94	95	96	97	98	99	100
Neighboring county	101	102	103	104	105	106	107	108	109	110	111	112	113	114	115	116	117	118	119	120
This city	121	122	123	124	125	126	127	128	129	130	131	132	133	134	135	136	137	138	139	140
All patients above a certain income (including insurance)	141	142	143	144	145	146	147	148	149	150	151	152	153	154	155	156	157	158	159	160
All patients below a certain income	161	162	163	164	165	166	167	168	169	170	171	172	173	174	175	176	177	178	179	180
All patients without restriction	181	182	183	184	185	186	187	188	189	190	191	192	193	194	195	196	197	198	199	200
Miscellaneous other	201	202	203	204	205	206	207	208	209	210	211	212	213	214	215	216	217	218	219	220

TABLE 11-3: Some Sample Entries in a Mental Health Resources Directory

Index No.	Variable Interaction
1	*(Involuntary hospitalization)* X *(Military eligibility)* George Patton Army Hospital, 100 Main St., Greenville, 794-6000, Ext. 538, ask for medical officer of the day or report to infirmary, building 7. Limited to persons on active duty, U.S. Army, and immediate dependents.
21	*(Involuntary hospitalization)* X *(VA Hospital)* None within 50 miles
41	*(Involuntary hospitalization)* X *(U.S. Public Health Service)* None within 50 miles
61	*(Involuntary hospitalization)* X *(State Hospital)* Gardenview State Hospital, 7465 Bridge St., Gardenview, 846-8035, phasing out acute treatment facilities for mentally ill; units for the mentally retarded accepting admissions; call medical officer of the day.
81	*(Involuntary hospitalization)* X *(This county)* Morgan County General Hospital, 4739 Polk St., Hillsdale, 750-7744; 24-bed locked psychiatric unit; preference given to welfare, MediCare patients; beds often filled; admission determined at emergency room.

* * * * * * * * * * * * * * * * * * * *

86	*(Halfway house)* X *(This county)* Greenacres House, 3215 Parkview Avenue, Burlington, 893-2649, ask for supervising social worker. All residents of this county 21 years and older eligible regardless of income; fee on sliding scale; psychotic problems are their main interest. Holden Caulfield House, 5482 Oak Street, Greenville, 673-8573, ask for

youth counselor in residence. Accepts both sexes, ages 14 to 18, individual and group counseling, especially for those with drug problems and those who have left home without parental consent. No fees charged; contributions accepted.

the George Patton Army Hospital, and completed the referral.

A 17-year-old boy who lives in this county engaged in a fierce argument with his parents and went out with friends and took street drugs (a repetition of a previous pattern). He was not intoxicated when he went into the emergency room and wanted to "rap" with someone about where he might go. (He was determined not to go home.) The therapist saw that he would need a place to live away from home at least temporarily and decided on a halfway house as being the most appropriate resource. After consulting index number 86 of the directory (halfway house, this county), the therapist decided that of the two listings Holden Caulfield House seemed the better choice for this patient, who accepted the referral.

Centers with access to a computer can use it for such a directory in two ways. First, the information needed to compile the directory can be stored in the computer; for instance, the names, addresses and special features of the various treatment facilities as well as the varying kinds of patient eligibility. Second, the information can be retrieved easily from the computer. When the therapist referred the 17-year-old boy, he had only to ask the computer for the information stored in cell 86 to find out what resources were available in the community.

Actual on-call duty is the final test of an emergency therapist's executive skill. How might a therapist apply the information and the logic set forth in this and preceding chapters in a busy emergency room? The following hypothetical situation, the test of mettle we referred to previously, will give the reader a chance to apply his working knowledge of emergency psychiatry.

PART 2: EMERGENCY ROOM EXERCISE

We shall present an emergency room situation, describe the personnel and facilities available to the emergency therapist, and give a number of vignettes of the patients who are to be seen. The reader should: (1) decide in which order the patients should be seen; (2) make initial diagnostic and treatment decisions, including the use of medication and hospitalization; and (3) decide on the most efficacious use of personnel and facilities available. After noting his answers, he may then read the solutions to the problems. The reader's solutions will not be exactly like the ones given here; each person will have his own way of conceptualizing the problems. It is hoped, however, that the basic principles underlying the solutions will correspond with those in the preceding chapters.

SITUATION

It is 5 P.M. You are taking over as the on-duty (O.D.) therapist in the emergency room of a county general hospital. You can admit patients to the hospital's fifteen-bed open-ward, therapeutic community; currently it has one bed open. When its beds are full or the patient needs referral to another facility, a state psychiatric hospital (with a locked ward) is available ten miles away. You have the authority to authorize an ambulance or cab to transport patients to their residences or to other medical facilities. This emergency room has a locked room. Personnel include a surgical intern, a nurse, an orderly, and a clerk. A medical resident is on call for consultation.

The therapist who has been covering the emergency room is on the telephone with a patient who says she wants to kill herself, but who will not give her name or telephone number. He continues to listen to her and writes you a note stating that it is important that he leave soon. You signal that you will respond shortly.

You check in with the nurse. She gives you a message that the nurse on the psychiatric unit has

just called to ask you to see a 40-year-old woman who has fainted. She is being treated with chlorpromazine for schizophrenia. She was unconscious for less than thirty seconds and is now lying awake in her bed. Her pulse rate is regular at 110 per minute and her blood pressure is 90/60. There is also a patient on the unit who wants to talk to a doctor about his medication.

The nurse lists the patients waiting for you. A 22-year-old bearded man is sitting with two friends who are unsuccessfully trying to talk him down. The patient appears extremely anxious and is screaming that his mind is dissolving. Friends say that he took an unknown pink tablet that had been given to him by a stranger on the street.

An "ingestion" was brought in by ambulance five minutes ago. The patient is a 35-year-old housewife who the husband says took fifty capsules of secobarbital about one hour ago. She is presently unconscious with normal vital signs.

An adolescent girl, recently discharged from the county hospital psychiatric unit after having been treated with phenothiazines for schizophrenia, is holding her hands over her face. Her parents are with her. She is waiting to go home. She had already been seen by the previous O.D. for increasing nervousness and feeling that her "tongue was getting larger." The O.D. had examined her and found questionable swelling of the tongue, but no other signs of edema or spasm of the tissues of the neck and throat. His impression was that she was having an anxiety reaction, and he asked her to stay for further observation. The nurse points her out to you because she seems to be getting worse as she waits to go home. At that moment she shows no psychotic symptoms.

The police arrive with a violent man in handcuffs. The man's wife called the police after her husband, who had been drinking heavily, assaulted her. Three officers are required to contain him. The patient was discharged from the service with a diagnosis of mental illness and has a history of several previous hospitalizations for alcoholism.

A man and his wife are sitting with their 18-year-old son who has recently started hallucinating and has developed the idea that someone is out to get him. He has not left the house for two weeks.

You must make decisions about the following patients:

1. The anonymous, female telephone caller who is threatening suicide

2. The 40-year-old woman on the ward, diagnosed as schizophrenic, who fainted and is now conscious

3. The patient on the psychiatric unit who wants to talk to a doctor about his medication

4. The 22-year-old man who thinks his mind is dissolving

5. The 35-year-old housewife who ingested fifty secobarbital capsules an hour ago

6. The adolescent girl who is anxious and thinks her tongue is enlarging

7. The police-escorted violent man in handcuffs who had been drinking

8. The 18-year-old son who is hallucinating and thinks someone is out to get him

THE SOLUTIONS

We think the patients should be seen in the order shown for the following reasons. First, the woman who ingested secobarbital (patient 5) is an acute medical emergency. You ask the clerk to call the nurse on the psychiatric unit and tell her that an acute emergency has come in, that the woman who fainted should be kept in bed, and that you will be up as soon as you have a chance. You write a note to the O.D. going off duty to keep the suicidal patient on the telephone while you tend to an emergency. You ask the clerk to call the surgical intern to examine the comatose woman immediately, and you ask the nurse to record her vital signs and prepare for gastric lavage until the intern arrives; you call the medical resident and ask him to supervise the intern's work. You explain to the woman's husband that you are the emergency therapist, that his wife will receive emergency medical treatment first, that you would like him to wait until after you have seen some other patients so that you can speak with him about beginning psychotherapeutic treatment.

Second, you must deal with the suicidal woman on the telephone (patient 1) because her life or physical well-being is at stake. You take the phone from the O.D., talk with the patient, and ask for her name and telephone number. You explain that you cannot be of further service to her until you have this information. She continues to withhold it. You explain that you have to attend to other emergencies, and that you will refer her call back to the clerk so that the necessary registration can take place. This firm stand causes her reluctantly to give the information, including her address, and to say with some conviction that she will drive in and talk with you in person. You hang up and give the information to the clerk and ask her to inform you if the patient has not arrived in fifteen minutes so that you can call the police to investigate.

Third, you talk with the bearded man who thinks his mind is dissolving (patient 4) and to his friends because he is acutely agitated. You confirm that he has taken an unidentified street drug and explain that there is every reason to believe his current panic will pass with their support and with an injection of a medication that counteracts anxiety. You ask the nurse to prepare an intramuscular injection of 15 mg of diazepam (Valium®). As she gives it, you explain to the patient that this will reduce his terror. (You do *not* administer a phenothiazine, thereby precluding a possible autonomic crisis.) You explain to the patient and his friends that you will check back with them at intervals and that you will repeat the injection every hour as needed. When the patient is finally calm, you will arrange for follow-up care.

Fourth, you go to the police and the violent man who has been drinking (patient 7). The police have had him under control and he has not appeared to be in a medically dangerous condition. You confirm the smell of alcohol on his breath and ask the nurse to prepare an intramuscular injection of 100 mg of hydroxyzine (Vistaril®) and 100 mg of thiamine. Although the police may be impatient, you point out to them that the patient is not dangerous as long as they hold him. You ask them to take him to the locked room, have them remove his shoes, belt, valuables, and possible concealed weapons for safekeeping, make sure there is a mat in the room for the patient to sleep on, and ask the police to help hold him down for the injection. You explain to the patient why you are giving the injection and why you will be keeping him in the locked room until he regains control. The police leave. The nurse, with the orderly's help, should obtain vital signs as soon as feasible. You are prepared to check on the patient every hour and to repeat the injection in four hours if necessary.

Fifth, you turn to the adolescent girl who thinks her tongue is swelling (patient 6). She has been sitting quietly and has not appeared to be in serious distress. Her tongue *is* swelling, probably in reaction to phenothiazines. The medical resident confirms your impression and takes over her management, starting with an intramuscular injection of 50 mg of diphenhydramine (Benadryl®). He makes sure an airway is available in case there is a spasm of the tongue and muscles of the throat. She will remain for observation until the swelling has definitely subsided.

Sixth, the woman who threatened suicide on the phone (patient 1) has come in, and you interview her briefly. She has been drinking a little but she is not drunk. She tearfully describes how her boyfriend broke up with her earlier that day. After twenty minutes she seems to have somewhat recovered her composure. You explain that you want to talk with her at greater length, that there are other patients who need to be seen, and ask if she will wait until you can devote more time to her. She agrees to this, and you escort her to the waiting room. You introduce her to the clerk and ask the clerk to call you if the patient wants to leave before you have had a chance to talk with her.

Seventh, you interview the boy who has been hallucinating (patient 8) and, separately, his parents. This patient had not been in acute distress and could safely be allowed to sit with his parents while you attended to more urgent matters. You try to talk to his affect, to enter into his experiential world. You conclude he is in the midst of an acute schizophrenic episode, an impression strengthened by the parents' report of his change in behavior over the last several weeks. You explain to everyone that he is having trouble with his thinking and that he needs to enter the hospital for further evaluation and treatment. They agree, and you arrange for his admission to the psychiatric unit. Because the other patients you have to evaluate are on the ward, you accompany the patient and his parents there, introduce them to the staff, and ensure that his case will be taken over by the ward therapist in the morning. You write orders for 100 mg of chlorpromazine orally, or half of that intramuscularly, if he becomes agitated, cannot go to sleep, or seems to want to slip away. If he remains calm and can sleep, medication can be deferred.

Eighth, you see the woman on the ward who fainted (patient 2), but who now is feeling all right. You deferred her because you surmised that she probably suffered from orthostatic hypotension caused by chlorpromazine. You explain to her the necessity of shifting positions slowly, that hers is a common reaction to this kind of medication and usually goes away, and answer in simple terms any questions she has without burdening her with gratuitous technical information. If there are any suggestions of lingering aftereffects of the fall, e.g., cranial injury, you ask the medical resident to examine her. You ask the nurse to hold the next dose of chlorpromazine until the patient's standing blood pressure is up to 100/60.

Ninth, you talk to the patient on the ward about his medication (patient 3). If he wants to talk about medication change or a physical complaint unrelated to his psychiatric medications, make certain he is not asking for immediate psychological help in a veiled way. Then suggest he take the matter up with his usual doctor. If no serious immediate problem, such as a concealed suicidal or homicidal impulse, is hidden behind the seemingly trivial complaint, make sure his doctor will learn about his medical concerns by writing a note in the chart. If a problem with impulse control does emerge, help the patient deal with it.

Now you have seen all the patients. You return to the emergency room to find that the woman who ingested the secobarbital has had her stomach pumped and is under observation in the intensive care unit. The young man who thought his mind was dissolving has had his second injection and is distinctly calmer but not yet completely lucid. You will return to him later. The girl with the swollen tongue responded to medication, and the medical resident sent her home with her parents.

The alcoholic man in the locked room is both tremulous and sleepy. You order the next injection for four hours after the first one, that he be allowed to sleep there overnight, and that he be given periodic observation of his vital signs. You leave orders for the next day's O.D. to continue to observe for and treat signs of acute alcohol withdrawal, to evaluate the meaning of the drinking (whether symptomatic or addictive) and his potential for violence, and to engage the patient in follow-up treatment for his drinking (using an initial hospitalization if desirable).

You return to the woman who had broken up with her boyfriend and threatened suicide on the telephone. After a half-hour she feels better and gives you the name of some friends she might spend the night with. You call them and explain that the patient has been very upset about losing her friend and felt like hurting herself. The friends are happy to have her stay with them until she feels more in control. You put her on the telephone to work out the plans for her friends to pick her up. She is worried about sleep that night. You give her two flureazepam (Dalmane®) capsules and

arrange for a follow-up visit in the clinic the next day. She returns to the waiting room to wait for her friends.

The young man's panic has passed. He no longer fears his mind is dissolving, and he is lucid but exhausted from his ordeal. His friends are willing to have him stay with them that night. They will make sure he comes in for a follow-up visit in the clinic the next day. You give them a few diazepam tablets to give the patient in case he has difficulty falling asleep.

You interview the husband of the woman who ingested the secobarbital. You check with the intensive care unit, and they give a guardedly optimistic report on her outlook. You tell the husband, and he begins to describe a marital rift of several weeks' duration that was precipitated by his wife's learning of his involvement with another woman. Today the wife had inadvertently seen the two of them together in a shopping center, a fact she revealed in the note lying next to her in the bedroom where he had found her. Although the husband feels embarrassed and guilty about his role, he is not suicidal. He readily accepts the suggestion that he become involved in therapy as his wife recovers. He can afford private care. You give him the names of two therapists who do marital couple work and find out where you can reach him the next day around noon to find out how he is doing with the referrals. There is nothing more to be done for the time being, and he departs.

Your tour of duty is off to a busy start. You complete your paperwork and relax with a magazine until the next patient arrives.

REFERENCES

1. Salamon, I.: "Management of Psychiatric Emergencies," *N.Y. State J. Med.,* **73**: 1066–1067, 1973.

SECTION 2 The Outpatient Clinic

JOHN E. BEEBE III, M.D.
C. PETER ROSENBAUM, M.D.

CHAPTER **12**

Outpatient Therapy: An Overview

PART 1: TRANSFERENCE REVISITED

PRESENTING COMPLAINTS

As we saw in Section 1 of this book, crises often force patients to seek psychiatric help, but many enter the clinic under different circumstances. Patients come with a wide variety of presenting complaints and for many reasons. Some come because they are bothered by psychological symptoms such as anxiety and depression; they may or may not have been able to connect their symptoms with interpersonal or intrapsychic events. Some patients come, understandably anxious and depressed, because of an upheaval in their lives, e.g., the breaking up of a marriage, the end of a love affair, the loss of a job and so on. Others come because they recognize certain recurrent self-defeating or neurotic patterns in themselves that they want to change.

Certain patients may have been referred by an internist who found the patient's physical symptoms to be functional and strongly suspected an emotional cause. Some patients who have broken the law have had psychotherapy made a condition of probation (compulsive stealing and certain forms of public sexual behavior are two frequent kinds of offenses).

Section 2 deals with patients who can be treated in the clinic. This chapter describes many of the theoretical issues on which treatment decisions are based. Chapter 13 discusses the rationale for specific decisions about treatment.

PSYCHODYNAMICS

We shall begin with an overview of psychotherapy and a detailed discussion of transference, and shall then proceed to examine the kinds of approaches a modern outpatient clinic offers the patients who come to it for help. Much of this section will deal with what to the psychoanalytically educated mind has always been "psychiatry." We shall retain from the analytic tradition its belief that formulation, an understanding of the psychodynamics of the individual patient, is indispensable to any decision about treatment, but we prefer to formulate dynamics from a range of theoretical models, not just from psychoanalysis. Excellent sources of information about psychodynamics and psychopathology are White,[1] Ellenberger,[2] Hillman,[3] and Whyte.[4]

Psychodynamics broadly refers to an understanding of the interactions of conscious, unconscious, and reality; of past, present, and future.* Without clearly understanding the inner workings of the situation at hand, the therapist is really powerless to make a reasoned intervention. Still too much of psychotherapy is irrational therapy, with the disadvantage that in addition to very lucky hits there are a number of quite unlucky misses. Therapists must understand psychodynamics. Until the therapist clearly understands what the patient's behavior is accomplishing for him and what its probable antecedent causes are, he is in a very poor position to make definitive interventions.

The dynamic formulation is that part of the psychiatric examination that attempts to explain how the present situation came into being and what forces are causing it to continue to persist. It is an indispensable part of the treatment process (it is described more fully in Chapter 14).

The decision to enter therapy may be a momentous one for the patient. Very primitive emotions of hope and fear are usually operating. There is also considerable lack of clarity; patients frequently do not know, cannot say, why they seek psychiatric help. The therapist needs to develop a sensitive friendliness to the state of confusion that so frequently accompanies the entry into psychotherapy. The novelist Doris Lessing[7] describes in *The Four-Gated City* how hard it can be even for an intelligent patient if this initial feeling of confusion goes unrecognized:

> She went to her doctor, who sent her to a psychotherapist. This was a woman. The relationship lasted for a couple of confused

months. The central fact here was glaringly obvious, like the sun in the tropics: both women were stupid about people and their relationships with each other. Both were perfectionists, and managing and dogmatic by nature. Mrs. Johns . . . knew all about Phoebe from her first interview with her. Phoebe believed in self-control, doing one's duty, and behaving well even when others did not — she could not see what was wrong with this.

> The thing is, no one ever gets to that point of moral confusion where one finds oneself sitting before a human being privileged to pronounce on one's state of being without having wondered and suffered and doubted. Phoebe knew well enough that she was a sadly rigid soul. But here she was, seated opposite another! Who was Mrs. Johns to pronounce on her, Phoebe? Phoebe kept wishing that Mrs. Johns would come to the point: there must be one, surely? For it was implicit in her manner that truths were there to be seen, but every time a truth or the intimation of one emerged, Phoebe thought it was suspect.

The sort of impasse found in Lessing's example is preventable. The aim of this chapter is to give the therapist an idea about how he can get off to a different kind of start. It seems to us that good therapeutic sense begins with an understanding of transference.

TRANSFERENCE – THE KEY CONCEPT

Transference as An Intrapsychic Phenomenon

It is to Sigmund Freud, of course, that we owe the first formulation of the idea of transference. For Freud, transference referred to the *unconscious* attribution to a person or institution of qualities this "object" may or may not possess, these attributions reflecting repressed attitudes, beliefs, and feelings from childhood. As Ralph Greenson[8] says,

> Transference is the experiencing of feelings,

---

*The term *psychodynamics* seems to have originated with Jeremy Bentham,[5] who stated in 1817, "Psychological *dynamics* (by this name may be called the science, which has for its *subject* these same springs of action, considered as such) has for its basis psychological *pathology*." As Hillman[6] notes, Bentham characterized psychopathology as "the unseemly parts of the mind." Hillman points out that this nineteenth-century pathological bias is still with us when we try to formulate the "springs" of our patients' actions in the language of psychopathology.

drives, attitudes, fantasies and defenses toward a person in the present which do not befit that person but are a repetition of reactions originating in regard to significant persons of early childhood, unconsciously displaced onto figures in the present. The two outstanding characteristics of a transference reaction are: it is a repetition and it is inappropriate.

Traditional psychoanalysis directs that the therapist often make himself a blank screen so that the patient's transference projections can be seen quite clearly. This means in practice that the therapist is mostly silent and non-self-disclosing to create a situation in which the patient's perception becomes colored as much as possible by his own intrapsychic habitual modes of perceiving. What emerges is a definite neurosis in which the person of the therapist is distorted in accordance with the patient's internal dynamics. The elucidation of this "transference neurosis" is felt to be indispensable to successful treatment, for it is thought that here, in relatively pure culture, the analyst can see what typically contaminates the patient's experience.

Psychoanalysis structures the situation rather as if the patient were a slide projector, and the therapist, in addition to being a blank screen, gives the patient no slide but turns on the projector. Often an unsuspected slide stuck in the projector shows upon the screen, the very picture of an unresolved infantile conflict. The hope is that such major, distorting carryovers from the past can be worked through in psychotherapy so that the patient-projector is able to approach the world sending out a mostly clear beam, capable of projecting whatever current slide is in his projector without distortion. Psychoanalysis, then, is an attempt to modify the patient's perception of the world by freeing him from the contaminating influence of past perceptions, and the famous inactivity of the traditional analyst is felt to be essential if the contaminating past is to be identified.

The model of perception on which psychoanalysis is implicitly based has been attacked by nearly every other major school of psychology, and the inactivity of the psychoanalyst abundantly caricatured, but the *experience* of transference in the psychoanalytic situation remains one of the fundamental discoveries of our era. In a famous conversation, Freud once asked Jung what he thought about transference, and Jung replied, "It is the alpha and omega in treatment." Freud then answered, "You have understood."

Indeed, it would scarcely be possible to understand psychotherapy without appreciating the central position of transference phenomena. Furthermore, it would seem that all emotional interaction contains much of what we experience in individual psychotherapy as transference. Choices of jobs, husbands, wives, friends, penchants for behaving in certain ways, ways of experiencing others in the environment, all these involve projections based on the past, a special sort of experiential conditioning. Thus it is no accident that as a patient first enters the psychotherapist's office, he brings with him his own highly charged, individual atmosphere of feeling and perception that immediately expresses itself in the ways he reacts to the therapist and the office, and which elicit, in turn, feelings and emotions in the therapist that partly existed before the appearance of the patient.

Transference as An Interpersonal Phenomenon

When we consider that transference also involves the therapist's experience, the slide projector model is inadequate. It becomes necessary to deal with transference in its interpersonal aspects. This next step from Freud has been hard to take. Freud's original model, for all its limitations, has fascinated the modern mind, which continues to wonder at its own capacity for self-deception and projection. Therefore, attempts to expand it to include the interpersonal seem never quite satisfactory, seem always to dilute Freud. Every five or ten years another theorist still feels the need to comment on the dimension that Freud left out, only to discover that his is received as the weaker formulation.

Interpersonal theorists' formulations are considerably more complicated than Freud's in explaining countertransference, the therapist's (largely) unconscious reactions. For the interpersonalists, it is as if the patient and therapist meet together at both a conscious and a transference level — unconscious shaking hands with unconscious — so that the emotional atmosphere of one encounters the emotional atmosphere of the other, creating together a new experiential world in which both persons participate. Consciousness allows the therapist and patient to collaborate, together studying their mutual effects on each other.

Interpersonal theorists are usually less pessimistic about the unconscious than Freud; unconscious transference effects are often viewed as positive, not merely distortions, as Kaiser[9] describes so well in his *Effective Psychotherapy.* Traditional psychoanalysts have commented on the difficulties in studying the patient at all, once the therapist enters into active intervention. In interactive therapy, the therapist brings his own relationship-ego to the transference atmosphere created by the interaction of the patient's and his own dynamics, and he makes verbal use of this ability to watch from within to help the patient become more aware of the transaction in which they are both involved. Sullivan calls this method "participant-observation."

Transference as Recapitulation of Past Coping

Thus far we have discussed transference as a *process,* first as an individual phenomenon, then as an interpersonal one. Now we look at its *content.* Content is not as popular now as it once was, but content remains the ground of experiencing; content is the ultimate information about the self which can be learned in psychotherapy. Content information becomes relevant whenever psychotherapy is conceived, not merely as an unconscious transition from a less adaptive to a more adaptive state of being, but also as an educative experience

in which conscious understanding of how the individual has changed takes part. Patients want and deserve such understanding.

Transference is first of all a recapitulation of past coping strategies in the stress of a new situation. The following example is a stereotyped situation with which many therapists will be familiar.

> *Example 12-1.* A drunken, chronic alcoholic man comes into the emergency room. He is hungry, tremulous, and boisterous. He is received by the night shift receptionist who requested night duty when she became estranged from her own alcoholic husband. She calls the emergency therapist, who has a problem drinker brother-in-law and who, moreover, has been awakened at 2 A.M. four times previously this week because of drinking patients. The alcoholic patient himself despairs of receiving much good treatment for his current dilemma (and privately, in his more sober moments, he considers himself a hopeless failure, unworthy of decent care by anyone), and both the secretary and the intern find themselves quite angry at this intruder. The secretary says on the telephone to the therapist, "We have another one for you," and the therapist says back to the secretary, "Oh God! Well, I'll be down."

The interaction begins on a note that promises a highly stereotyped pattern of rejection. The patient, for his part, can be viewed as a help-rejecting complainer. The doctor is more likely than not to behave as a help-pretending rejector. And yet this is the first meeting of a new patient with a new doctor. Each brings to a situation *which is in fact new for both* old ways of operating. If both continue to behave in accordance with unconscious stereotypes, the transition will reinforce both in their belief that alcoholism is a frustrating, hopeless condition that can only be managed by grudging, temporary, ineffective support. This is, in fact, how both have coped with alcoholism in the past, and each time a new experience is forced into the old unconscious transference mold, the stereotyped solution becomes more fixed, seemingly all the more supported by evidence.

The content of both transference and countertransference starts before the patient walks in the door. The actual encounter can be said to "constellate" this content so that an unconscious decision about how treatment will proceed is reached by both participants with remarkable speed. Unless one or the other makes a conscious effort, there will be no exploration of the implicit contract, and the therapy will proceed unconsciously, and almost always in a neurotically stereotyped fashion.

The therapist has to be aware of this stereotype if he is to overcome it. Much of the early work of therapy is trying to make conscious the initial pull into an unconscious contract. Supervision often identifies a therapist's unwitting participation in the patient's pathologic approach to problem solving. Every supervisor is aware that the pretty, girlish patient who treats her therapist as if he were a father often elicits from the inexperienced therapist a certain paternal pomposity, and that the work of therapy can proceed only when one or the other takes the risk of exploding the tight bind this very common transference places on their interaction. Although it can sometimes be adaptive for a woman to behave like a pleasing little girl with men, and for a professional man to carry paternal authority, overemphasis on these styles in a recapitulation of past coping behavior precludes any new learning about the interaction of an adult man and woman.

Transference as Anticipation of Future Coping

Undue emphasis upon the regressive and maladaptive elements of transference distortions is one of the gravest drawbacks of the original psychoanalytic formulations of transference. Henri Ellenberger[10] has shown that the roots of this bias lie in the psychologies of self-deception, which were extremely popular during the late nineteenth century. Jung recognized early that transference distorts as well in a progressive direction, projecting onto the therapeutic relationship and the therapist the possibility of new development. Although at the outset of therapy the projection may be unrealistically positive, it may also contain a picture of the self the patient is able to become as a result of therapy. Similarly, the therapist can find himself responding to the patient in a new, fresh way at the outset of treatment, as if he were finding in himself a new way of relating to such persons. This anticipation of a possible new kind of coping lends hope and excitement to the process of therapy.

The beginning of therapy often is slanted toward either past experience of repetitive failure or the hope of future success in interpersonal relationships. Either transference reaction can become too extreme. Hope can be a subtle trap for both the patient and the therapist; it can substitute for the necessary acceptance of frustration which is essential to realistic functioning. Pessimism can slowly poison therapeutic life.

In general, it is wise for the therapist to pay attention to the content of initial dreams, fantasies about therapy, and comments about therapy, in himself as well as in the patient. This initial transference, often very strong, frequently tells how therapy is likely to proceed. Optimistic fantasy can give confidence; pessimistic fantasy should give pause. Is this a case in which therapy could do harm?

Particular emphasis should be given to accidents occurring outside therapy in early weeks, or to dreams portending disaster, danger, and the like. These often have predictive significance as to the impact of therapy.

The Real Relationship — A Base Line

It is necessary to have a base line upon which to gauge transference. This base line is the real relationship between the patient and therapist. The "real relationship" is perhaps a misnomer; more precisely, it is the conscious relationship between the patient and therapist. This involves events such as the therapist's behavior, his office and dress, his punctuality, all of which should be uniform enough to give the patient a certain experience of regularity and to give the therapist a certain sense of self-continuity. Most therapists will now concede it is both impossible and undesirable to maintain a totally blank screen for patients, but it is nevertheless possible to provide a certain base line against which the intrusion of emotional distortion can be measured.

The therapist's attempt to establish a base line should not be extremely rigid and punctilious. The base line should not be a straitjacket; it should be a comfortable, working rapport that enables both the therapist and patient to experience major variation as the effect of strong emotion, which can then be examined.

At a deep level, of course, even the comfortable, working relationship is a transference fiction, a still largely unconscious arrangement predicated in large part by interpersonal attraction and need. Whitehorn and Betz[11] have suggested that successful psychotherapy depends upon a kind of unconscious fit between the therapist and patient, in which the therapist's need to work with a particular kind of person may be as important as the patient's need to work with a particular kind of therapist. Although it is impossible to avoid unconscious relating, it can be examined to ensure that the fit furthers rather than hinders therapy.

In exploring transference, therapists usually do not initially interpret the base line of general mutual liking and respect. Transference interpretations are confined to intrusions of excessive positive or negative affect that interfere with the working relationship. Generally, it is not a good idea to tamper too much with the base line if meaningful work is to be done on other areas of the patient's life. There is no theoretical end to the process of making unconscious transactions conscious, but there must be a practical abstention

from too much examination of a transaction between the patient and therapist. Otherwise no other content can be discussed. Also, what is working well at an unconscious level does not *need* to be explored; we take apart the watch that *does not* tick.

Toward the end of therapy, most therapists like to get some discussion of the real relationship that has been the vehicle for therapy all along. At the beginning of therapy, such discussion merely makes the process more difficult for the patient and deprives him of the interpersonal security and unselfconsciousness that permit him to discuss openly and fully disturbances in all areas of his life.

Institutional Transference

Transference does not occur only between individuals. Important transferences are also made to institutions, including the institution of the healer's role. When patients perceive therapists as agents of societal authority more than as interested persons, therapy is comparable to going to confession and not noticing the priest. Often, the therapist is initially made to feel anonymous. Therapists who dislike this anonymity sometimes forget that their role, or the institution in which they serve, is providing an important base of their effectiveness to some patients.

Therapists and patients working in an institutional setting accord a mutual transference to that institution, and the support it gives to both should not be underestimated. Therapists who go into private practice often report what an astonishing experience it is to be without the symbolic support of an institution's walls. As one therapist reported, it was as if suddenly she were out in a boat on an open sea, alone with each patient, and her right arm grew sore from bailing out water whenever an unconscious leak occurred.

Many therapies make practical use of the institutional aspects of the transference. Chapter 18 ("Supportive Psychotherapy") illustrates this kind of treatment.

STAGES OF THE TRANSFERENCE IN ALL PSYCHOTHERAPIES

In any psychotherapeutic treatment, the transference relationship evolves with time. As therapy progresses, or if it progresses, it is possible to observe certain typical sequential stages of the transference. It is quite possible for therapy to get stuck at any of the stages. Each stage, moreover, depends upon successful evolution of the previous stage. Finally, these stages seem to be common to all psychotherapies.

In our view four distinct stages are discernible: contact, confrontation, initiation, and individuation.* Our descriptions of the stages are designed to give the therapist a sense of where he is with a given patient at a given time so he knows what he can and cannot expect of the therapy at that point. This model is intended to replace the more traditional view of psychotherapy as a three-stage process involving beginning, middle, and end of treatment.[14] These four stages are most likely to be seen in long-term, uncovering psychotherapy. In the reality-oriented therapies, perhaps only one or two of the stages will be apparent; for example, in supportive work with schizophrenic patients, the stages of contact and confrontation may predominate, and in behavior modification the stages of confrontation and initiation are the main ones.

Contact

In the first stage of therapy, the therapist and patient must make psychological contact with each other. Rogers[15] postulates psychological contact as the condition in which the client feels psychologically received by the therapist, that certain qualities in the therapist — genuineness, accurate empathic understanding, nonpossessive warmth — are requisite to successful psychother-

apy, and that the client must be able to perceive these qualities in the therapist. Much has been said in praise and criticism of Rogers' ideas of the "necessary and sufficient" ingredients of the successful therapist's personality. Less well known is his conception of neurosis as a condition in which a person becomes separated from his experiencing in infancy by the need to satisfy certain "conditions of worth" that he perceives as coming from his parents. It is Rogers' deliberate aim to remove from the therapeutic situation all such conditions of worth so that this living against (or at some remove from) felt experiencing can come to an end in an atmosphere of "unconditional positive regard."

Harry Stack Sullivan has called the ways in which neurotics avoid their natural experiencing in order to satisfy fantasied environmental demands as "security operations."[16] Franz Alexander and Thomas French[17] have talked about psychotherapy as a "corrective emotional experience," and they stress too that the therapist needs to supply an atmosphere in which constructive change is made possible.

Contact occurs between the therapist's listening or treating consciousness and the patient's preconscious experiencing. This contact is described in Freudian circles as the "working alliance." This alliance is the basis of all later therapeutic work. Unconscious factors play a part in the making of a working alliance. For example, it is often sufficient that the patient like the therapist and that the therapist like the patient for the first stage of transference to come into being and for the entire therapeutic process to be set in motion. Rogers once said in response to a beginning therapist's question that it could even be of help if the therapist felt sexually attracted to the patient. The opposite, an attraction based on power needs in the therapist, can also be effective in certain situations. Many authoritarian patients like authoritarian therapists. Some therapists intuitively relate better to men, others to women. Some therapists are able to relate well to older people but have difficulty with younger people. We are still very

*The four-stage conception is derived from the comparative study of healing systems as found in Jerome Frank's *Persuasion and Healing*[12] and C. G. Jung's *The Integration of Personality*.[13]

much in the process of learning why it is that people are able to make psychological contact with each other in some circumstances and not in others.

Often psychological contact is *implicit*. A great deal has occurred psychologically before a patient can approach a therapist and say, "I have such-and-such a symptom that I would like to overcome." To be able to make such a request, the patient must be able to accept the therapist's approach and to trust him with the responsibility of dealing with his problem. If the patient has not made psychological contact with the therapist, he simply cannot submit to treatment.

Sometimes, psychological contact is *faked*. Then we see patients who seem to be in treatment, who make verbal assurances that they are participating meaningfully in the process, but whose actual therapeutic progress is nil or marked by missed appointments, unpaid bills, dramatic evasions, and so on. The therapist needs to realize that such patients, despite their protestations to the contrary, have not made contact and thus have not really entered therapy.

Many patients find it difficult or impossible to make contact with anyone. For them, the most important part of therapy is the process of making contact. This sensitivity is particularly true of schizophrenic patients, schizoid personalities, and certain adolescents. Equally, there are some patients who can make contact *only* with their therapists and resist any movement that might lead them out of the state of symbiotic fusion with a helping person. In this group belong the "therapy addicts," including unhappy women with somatic complaints who go through long and moderately satisfying periods under the care of fatherly internists. They do not proceed beyond the stage of psychological contact in their transference relationships to their physicians, nor do they want to. They are paying for very real gratification. Erotic transferences, as Freud[18] pointed out, are a way of clinging to the therapist as a defense against further movement. In some circumstances, they must be interpreted as such.

Confrontation

For most patients, the state of being psychologically received by the therapist is not sufficient to satisfy the pressure to health. The appetite for healing asks not just a feeling of being valued or needed, but also mastery of the difficulties of living. At the stage of confrontation, patient and therapist begin to grapple with the *content* of what is wrong. The stage of confrontation has been reached when the therapist is able to make a direct comment about the patient's life without loss of rapport. At this point, the patient starts commenting on himself with an emphasis on his pathology. He begins actively to point out areas in which he feels he needs to do work.

Probably the stage of confrontation cannot proceed naturally until the stage of contact has been adequately experienced. This point is often unappreciated in the modern lust to confront. At present, confrontation is an extremely popular therapeutic technique; there are confrontation groups and confrontation wards. An almost Messianic quality is discernible in some who use confrontation; they talk as if they were rescuing psychiatry from overinvestment in gentle, passive listening. Such evangelism ignores the fact that confrontation has always been a part of psychotherapy, and although the new emphasis on confrontation is a good corrective to therapy that stresses only the contact stage of transference, meaningful confrontation grows of itself out of the condition of psychological contact in patients who are ready to go further. It is often wiser not to push. We are learning, indeed, that not everyone can handle confrontation. Harold Searles[19] pointed out that one of the several ways of driving another person crazy is to continually point to areas of himself of which he is unaware. Yalom and Lieberman's[20] report of encounter group casualties, persons who developed serious neurotic depressive or anxiety states or psychotic breaks in the course of T group or encounter group experiences, is good testimony to this.

The most common disadvantage of confronting

someone with whom the other person is not in contact is that the confrontation is not heard. Almost every experienced therapist has had his patients tell him that in therapy they learn things about themselves that friends and family members have been telling them for years. The difference is that the therapist's word is trusted and believed. If he confronts too early, it may not be.

It is common to hear experienced therapists who have worked for some time with a difficult patient say, "Well, he's finally *in treatment,*" meaning the patient is engaged and the working alliance is operating after a frustratingly slow start. This development corresponds to having arrived squarely at the stage of confrontation.

Like contact, confrontation can become an addiction. Some patients are quite willing to come to therapy for years, repeatedly telling their therapists and themselves what is wrong with them. This kind of patient frequently elicits highly critical comments from the naïve therapist, who assumes that by joining the patient's attack on his pathology he is somehow assisting him to achieve self-understanding. In fact, the therapist may only be satisfying the patient's masochistic need to recreate a childhood situation in which he was repeatedly verbally abused. Along with patients who can only be confronted, we have to mention therapists who can only confront. Sometimes therapists have to balance the urge to confront angrily with the need to confront therapeutically.

A kind of stalemate comes toward the end of the period of confrontation. It seems as if the problem, although named, can never be solved. Both the patient and therapist are likely to feel intense frustration during this period. To avoid getting stuck at the stage of confrontation, it is frequently better to admit the perplexing, defeating feel of the situation than to attempt fresh confrontation, as if to whip the unconscious into coming up with some answer. When the therapist finds himself in the bind of repeatedly confronting the same situation, it is better for him to recognize the impasse than to turn the therapy into a weekly brutal, sadomasochistic ritual. Impasse is natural,

and necessary to being convinced of the need for a new solution, which appears in the stage of initiation.

Initiation

The word initiation is used to discuss the next stage of psychotherapy because it suggests the idea of a kind of rite of passage into the stage of health. Such a rite of passage, very similar to those rites by which traditional cultures mark the move from the stage of childhood to that of adulthood, is both a natural stage in the psychology of the patient as he moves from one state of being to another, and a period of active treatment on the part of the therapist, who functions very like a shaman according to his own special skills. This is the point in psychotherapy when both the therapist and patient feel that something must be done, that something has to happen.

Here is where the schools of psychotherapy differ in all their glorious variety, just as initiation rites vary from tribe to tribe. Each school has its own idea as to the right content of the rite of passage from the "sick", undesired state to the "healthy", desired state. For psychoanalysis, initiation is "working through." For behavior therapy it is some form of new learning, conditioning, or desensitization. In Jungian therapy, it is frequently dream analysis. In client-centered therapy, it is the unfolding of the experiential process in response to accurate reflections of feeling.

At this discrete psychological stage of treatment, the patient and therapist feel that they are actively tackling the problem, that the neurotic walls are tumbling down, and that meaningful therapeutic change is occurring. This is the period during which the patient and therapist feel most intensely that therapy is working. This is also the stage during which the patient becomes most evangelical about therapy, telling family and friends how helpful it is and encouraging them to undergo the exact same initiation he is experiencing.

However, not every patient can be initiated in the same way, nor can every therapist initiate in every way. Even though it is helpful for the therapist to try to develop as large a repertoire as possible, the fact remains that each therapist becomes comfortable with some ways of guiding patients at this stage and not with others. So it is that a patient who has passed successfully through the stages of contact and confrontation and can now see what is wrong may not always be able to work on what is wrong with the same therapist. It is not inappropriate to refer a patient at the stage when he is ready for a meaningful initiation that can be conducted better by another therapist. Sometimes patients leave therapy at the point that they know what is wrong and go into a life experience that can, far more satisfactorily than therapy, provide the necessary initiation.

As with the stages of contact and confrontation, the stage of initiation also has its addicts. Among these are some therapists who become unconscionable dogmatists, expounding the joys of their own method of initiation in an inflated fashion, as if theirs were the only way to help people develop. Many initiation addicts are patients who, although they have been successfully helped by therapy through the stage of initiation, seem destined to repeat that initiation ad nauseam, bringing its once rich content into every situation, however inappropriate. Anyone finding himself in the bind of becoming too sold on the glories of what he has already experienced ought to acknowledge that he has begun to repeat himself and to wonder why this is so. For therapy can proceed beyond the stage of initiation.

Individuation

This in Jung's[21] sense is that process by which the personality becomes integrated according to its own plan, now not dependent upon models derived from the infantile, the environmental, or the therapeutic situation, but somehow differentiated into "that self which one truly is." When therapy enters this stage, the developmental process becomes conscious, and the patient actively seeks to futher his own maturation. The inappro-

priate and repetitious transference distortions from the past are no longer dominant, although some always persist: the "completely analyzed person" is a myth, but successfully treated, more independent people are many.

In the transference, this stage is heralded by a new kind of resistance, a resistance that the wise therapist will recognize as healthy. It is a resistance to the therapist's way of conceptualizing and initiating, a withdrawal from the earlier processes of contact, confrontation, and initiation that have made this stage possible, into a more actually self-defined condition. Now the Messianic inflated praise of therapy and therapist begins to fold its tent, and the patient starts taking his own life firmly in hand, withdrawing previous projections from the therapist. We believe this stage can only take place in the company of a therapist who is himself individuated enough not to need his patient to immortalize his own style. This is the stage at which the patient makes therapy his own once and for all. The therapist at this stage, according to Joseph Henderson,[22] becomes now a "symbolic friend," who helps the patient out of his general understanding of psychology wherever he can, but is in every other respect very much at the level of a peer in the patient's life. There is much less active "treating" of the patient at this stage, but the therapist stays available to further the patient's own process at any point that his information and experience might contribute.

A Jungian therapist, for instance, might be useful to a patient when a particularly puzzling dream can be elucidated by the comparative symbolism at the Jungian analyst's disposal. A behavior therapist might be able to suggest some new form of desensitizing procedure for a particular kind of maladaptive behavior that the less anxious patient might wish to work on.

As with every other stage, even individuation has its addicts: those who will not depend especially upon any particular therapeutic style or therapist but are perhaps too sold on their individual approaches to life to be comfortable in relating to others. Meaningful psychotherapy, like successful personal growth, never ends; but to the degree that therapy is successful there should be a kind of dissolving of the entire transference into some kind of living in the world so that the outlines of the now strong enough individual become less important than the experienced flexible adaptation to living. Descriptions of self-actualization are generally impossible, for the simple reason that self-actualization is a process, not a pose. Such people, innately themselves, tend to be immediate and real; and, at the risk of being flippant, it might be said that the "well-analyzed" person may in his relation to therapy be compared to the perfect haircut which conjures up no image of barber chairs either before or after.

Although formal therapy may end after a few years, informal therapy may be a lifetime process. The former patient, now accustomed to thinking about his life in psychological terms, continues to do so, especially at times of personal distress or puzzlement. He notices that he feels depressed or anxious and wonders why. Often, on introspection or thinking about his dreams, he can figure out why, and then either accept the upsetting situation more comfortably or figure out adaptive ways of dealing with it. If the distress continues, he may wish to reenter therapy to do some "postgraduate" work.

HANDLING OF THE TRANSFERENCE IN VARIOUS THERAPIES

Psychoanalysis

In this form of therapy the therapist does very little reaching out to produce contact. Rather he selects as his patient someone with a relatively strong ego who is capable of enduring a relatively low level of actual gratification in the therapeutic situation, but who accepts the basic premise that the therapist is working in his own best interest by refraining from much engagement with him. The patient's healthy ego then maintains the contact at an implicit level, while a kind of explicit frustration is undergone.

Confrontation takes place in the early weeks and months of therapy as the patient comes to see how he reacts to the therapist and to significant others in his life in neurotic and overdetermined ways that hamper his full effectiveness. As treatment proceeds, new, different, or more profound levels of conflict may be identified — the peeling of the layers of the onion — so that confrontation in one form or another extends deep into the treatment as new areas first of resistance and then of comprehension make their appearance.

As awareness of intrapsychic phenomena increases, the patient's perception of the therapy and of his interpersonal relations becomes based more on current reality and less on previous transference distortions. To the extent that insight leads to behavior change (and it often does, despite criticisms to the contrary), the patient is in the stage of initiation. Even "purely intellectual insight" (as contrasted with emotional or affective insight) can lead to behavior change. Freud[23] said, in another context, "The voice of the intellect is a soft one, but it does not rest until it has gained a hearing. Ultimately, after endlessly repeated rebuffs, it succeeds."

The combination of confrontation and initiation, the repeated assessment of neurotic perceptions and emotional responses to situations, the chipping away at the core of the neurosis, is what psychoanalysts have termed the "working through," and when it is complete the patient is into the stage of individuation.

Analytical Psychology

Jungian analysis takes a markedly different view of the transference situation. It is accepted that the therapist's own actual personality is required to "constellate" from the patient's unconscious that "archetype" that will guide him through the therapy. Thus, a patient who has suffered paternal deprivation may, in contact with a male therapist, begin to experience the father archetype that is needed to guide him in the maturation of his personality. For this reason, Jungians frequently spend much time deciding whether the patient will see a male or female, or an older or younger, therapist, and make a considerable effort to match the therapist and patient to each other according to personalities. (Often a patient will change therapists to experience another healing archetype.)

The stage of confrontation in Jungian analysis is viewed as the experience of the "shadow," or unacceptable identity, and considerable effort is made to help the patient achieve a conscious relationship to this. The stage of initiation involves the experience of positive features of the shadow which carry the seeds of new growth. These usually involve contrasexual aspects of the person's psychology, the discovery of the "anima" in a man and "animus" in a woman. A considerable amount of education is done by the therapist with the patient to help him see the value in unaccepted or unrecognized parts of himself, which formerly were encountered only in projection onto others. The stage of individuation in Jungian analysis comes when the once unowned, dissociated, and projected parts of the self are now owned as related to the conscious personality in a relationship of polar opposition. For the Jungian, finding the opposite to his own point of view and holding onto it as his necessary complement is the essence of wholeness. At this stage, few projections operate to divide the personality, and the therapist no longer carries the image of the patient's needed strength. As in Freudian analysis, the projection onto him of the guiding light of therapy is withdrawn.

Interpersonal Therapy

Sullivan conceptualizes the transference relationship as an interpersonal field in which the patient creates "parataxic distortion" of the relationship based on his early experience. The patient systematically distorts aspects of the relationship primarily by the mechanisms of selective inattention, sublimation, and obsessionalism. The therapist deals with these parataxic distortions not only by direct confrontation, but also by making use of his own experience of the interpersonal situation. The therapist becomes an expert commentator upon the interpersonal field as he knows it from "participant observation." In this interpersonal field, the therapist is well aware that he, too, makes parataxic distortions by selective inattention. By his own courageous willingness to discuss his experience of the patient in the hour, however, he renders these distortions accessible to feedback from the patient. The therapist's acceptance of correction is a model for the patient to receive feedback from the therapist in turn when he is distorting the emotional field. The therapy then becomes a kind of intense collaboration in which the major therapeutic initiation consists of working through parataxic distortions until a relatively distortion-free interpersonal atmosphere obtains.

Perhaps no one has described more fully the need for the therapist to freely offer up his own parataxic distortions to the scrutiny of the patient than Searles,[24] whose book *Collective Papers on Schizophrenia and Related Subjects* describes the handling of countertransference phenomena by means of self-analysis and self-disclosure in the service of ever-increasing clarification. It should be said that Searles' formulations are very akin to the concept of "participation mystique" in Jung's work and "projective identification" in the writings of Melanie Klein. These theorists all attempt to formulate the intense interpersonal mutuality that is integral to the phenomenon of transference. What distinguishes members of these schools is their willingness to discuss openly the ways in which the patient makes the therapist feel, in order to free the patient from an unconscious identification with him.

Adlerian Therapy

Adlerian therapy consists primarily in the rigorous examination and confrontation by the therapist of the patient's lifestyle. To Adler is owed a great deal of the understanding of the psychology of the ego and its typical adaptive and maladaptive ways of dealing with society. Once the lifestyle is grasped in the stage of contact, the relationship with the patient is used primarily to make vigorous confrontation acceptable to the patient. Advice and exhortation are common in this form of therapy.

Bierer[25] states:

> For suggestion Adler substituted persuasion, and relied upon the dialectic [which], in the case of both Adler and Socrates, starts from the assumption of ignorance on the part of both parties and endeavours a joint pursuit of truth by means of questions and answers. . . . The task of the psychologist is to prove to the patient out of his own mouth that his method of thought is a wrong one.

Typical of Adler is the view that the position of the ego is a stance, and that the neurotic syndrome is an "arrangement" by which the patient satisfies his needs for power in the world. By taking this position toward the patient's system of emotional attitudes and behaviors, the Adlerian therapist assumes from the outset that the patient has choice in his manner of presenting himself and a responsibility to find a socially satisfactory means of expressing his own individual needs for power in relationship to others. Confrontation then becomes a form of initiation. The therapist takes a strong position vis-à-vis the patient's ego, which is assumed to be basically powerful, responsible, and capable of choice, including the choice of resisting the therapist.

Client-centered Therapy

Client-centered therapy has been distinguished since its origins in Otto Rank's "will therapy"[26,27] by its emphasis upon the here-and-now experiencing of the "client." (It is consistent with Rogers' entire point of view that the medical term "patient" has been dropped.) In classical client-centered therapy the therapist does not engage in much frank self-disclosure or direct confrontation with the client, but he does vitally attach himself to the client's experiencing of the here-and-now situation during the therapeutic hour, and the therapist's every response is aimed at an accurate "reflection of feeling," emphasizing always the "affective" aspects of the client's comments in an attempt to bring to the client a profound acceptance first by the therapist and then by himself of his own experiencing. This acceptance implies confrontation with the possibility of one's own affective life as well as passive contact with the therapist. Client-centered therapists feel that it is affect which drives the process of self-actualization, and it is sufficient for healing that a client come to experience his own affective track and to follow it wherever it leads him. The therapist is thus a maximum facilitator who is using the interpersonal relationship to promote an intrapsychic process.

In this respect client-centered therapy is very similar to both Freudian and Jungian analysis in the attempt to use interpersonal dialogue as a means of promoting intrapsychic communication. The pièce de resistance of client-centered therapy is the client's discovery of his own experiential process and his moving to "greater stages of process" as he takes more seriously the affective dimension of himself.

There is remarkably little emphasis on content in client-centered therapy; thus specific dream motifs or supposedly pathogenic complexes have in themselves no interest for the traditional Rogerian. Instead, the self is considered purely as experiencing. Rogers feels that in this kind of therapy no transference neurosis develops because immediate gratification in reality is provided by the therapist's attention to the client's experiencing. The decisions about what to confront are made entirely by the client, as his own experiencing leads him into areas in which he is not happy about himself.

In a sense, individuation is assumed from the beginning of client-centered therapy, and it is indeed disarmingly individuating to the patient to have his every statement returned to him with an affective resonance by an experienced client-centered therapist. This style Rogers has always employed in responding to his critics: he simply takes the felt meaning of what they are saying to him with unconditional positive regard. More than one critic has gone away from Rogers saying, "Well he finally understood what so many others have tried unsuccessfully to tell him," without realizing that he is the beneficiary of Rogers' remarkable technique.[28]

Behavior Therapy

In this form of therapy the initiation stage of treatment is the most important. However, before a successful desensitizing or avoidance-conditioning procedure can be applied, preparations resembling the stages of contact and confrontation must be undertaken. (These preparations are described in Chapter 21.) Equally, many analysts who work with severely neurotic and borderline patients feel about behavior therapy that by the time the patients are quite clear about what is wrong with them and are willing to go to a behavior therapist, most of the work that consumes them with the patients they see has already been done. To formulate a goal clearly is not easy for many patients in therapy, and many patients who present themselves to therapy do not come to have a specific symptom removed.

Although other schools of therapy have much to offer with understanding of the stages of contact and confrontation, many of their therapists are surprisingly lacking when it comes to the specific initiatory procedures necessary to help the patient over the specific difficulties that finally emerge. It is to the credit of behavior therapists that they have brought us a whole new emphasis on specific means of helping those with specified problems.

Behavior therapy is a narrowing of the great stream of directive therapy that received so much attention before World War I, primarily as the result of Pierre Janet's major influence. Janet, as Ellenberger[29] has shown, was a master of the practical. His understanding of the destructive and constructive use of psychological energy, and his

practical suggestions for avoiding wastes of nervous force and achieving greater degrees of psychological organization (or "tension") remain a landmark of practical psychotherapeutics. The triumph of Viennese psychoanalysis over French psychological analysis led to two generations of neglect of the role of directive techniques in dynamic psychiatry. In the past decade directive psychotherapy has staged a remarkable comeback, coinciding with a general decline of faith in psychoanalysis as the sole or preeminent mode of treatment.

What is characteristic of suggestive, hypnotic, prescriptive, and behavioral techniques is that the transference relationship is assumed and manipulated rather than discussed. Nevertheless, the stages of contact and confrontation have been reached. A very specific behavioral analysis of the problem, and sometimes a dynamic formulation of it, has usually been attempted. Based on the analysis, specific procedures are recommended. So long as direction is not undertaken in a way that suggests that the therapist is able or about to take control of every part of the patient's life, the specific initiatory procedures employed by even these very directive therapists need not interfere with the patient's later individuation into someone who can learn to control his own behavior according to the techniques he has now learned from the therapist.

Comment

A final way to review the schools involves a sense of the human life cycle.[30] It has been remarked that, "If you need therapy when you are an adolescent, see an Adlerian; during young adulthood, a Freudian; and in maturity, a Jungian." Adolescents are concerned with power, autonomy, and sexuality, of establishing an arrangement with the world, and Adlerians deal with these issues. Young adults have already come to some kind of arrangement with the world, but often find the arrangement unsatisfactory and need to explore the neurotic limitations they unconsciously impose on the arrangement. Patients in their middle years have grown largely past a vital interest in struggling with their arrangement and more often seek inner ways of making their lives more rewarding and fruitful. And of course, the concerns of adolescence, young adulthood, and maturity intertwine in the emotional life of every adult, so that many therapists will find themselves working now like Adler, now Freud, now Jung, and now Sullivan, by whatever names they call themselves. And at every stage of life, the need for specific behavioral remedies for long-standing behavioral impasses will emerge. Sometimes the therapist will show the way; often, the patient will come up with a surprisingly complex behavioral program for himself, just as he had earlier surprised the therapist by his ability to befriend himself, interpret his pathology, and accept his limitations.

REFERENCES

1. White, Robert W.: *The Abnormal Personality,* 3d ed., Ronald, New York, 1963.

2. Ellenberger, Henri: *The Discovery of the Unconscious,* Basic Books, New York, 1970.

3. Hillman, James: "The Language of Psychology and the Speech of the Soul," *Eranos Jahrbuch 1968,* Rhein-Verlag, Zurich, 1970, pp. 299–356.

4. Whyte, L. L.: *The Unconscious before Freud,* Basic Books, New York, 1960.

5. Bentham, Jeremy: "A Table of the Springs of Action," in John Bulmer (ed.), *The Works of Jeremy Bentham, Vol. I,* William Keit, Edinburgh, 1843, p. 205.

6. Hillman: op. cit., p. 309.

7. Lessing, Doris: *The Four-Gated City,* Knopf, New York, 1969.

8. Greenson, Ralph R.: *The Technique and Practice of Psychoanalysis, Vol. 1,* International Universities Press, New York, 1967, pp. 154–158.

9. Kaiser, Hellmuth: in Louis B. Fierman (ed.), *Effective Psychotherapy,* Basic Books, New York, 1965.

10. Ellenberger: loc. cit.

11. Whitehorn, John C., and Barbara Betz: "A Study of Psychotherapeutic Relationships between Physicians and Schizophrenic Patients," *Am. J. Psychiat.,* 3:321–331, 1954.

12. Frank, Jerome: *Persuasion and Healing,* Schocken Books, New York, 1963.

13. Jung, C. G., *The Integration of Personality,* Stanley M. Dell (trans.), Farrar & Rinehart, New York, 1939.

14. Colby, Kenneth M.: *A Primer for Psychotherapists,* Ronald, New York, 1951.

15. Rogers, Carl R.: "A Theory of Therapy, Personality, and Interpersonal Relationships as Developed in a Client-centered Framework," in S. M. Koch (ed.), *Psychology: A Study of a Science,* McGraw-Hill, New York, 1959, vol. 3.

16. Sullivan, Harry S.: *The Psychiatric Interview,* Norton, New York, 1954.

17. Alexander, Franz, and Thomas French: *Psychoanalytic Therapy,* Ronald, New York, 1946.

18. Freud, Sigmund: "Further Recommendations on the Technique of Psychoanalysis, Observations on Transference-Love," in *Collected Papers,* Joan Riviere (trans.), Basic Books, New York, 1959, vol. 2, pp. 380–381.

19. Searles, Harold: *Collected Papers on Schizophrenia and Related Subjects,* International Universities Press, New York, 1965, pp. 254–283.

20. Yalom, I. D., and M. A. Lieberman: "A Study of Encounter Group Casualties," *Arch. Gen. Psychiat.,* 25:16–30, 1971.

21. Jung, C. G.: "Definitions," *The Collected Works of C. G. Jung,* H. G. Baynes (trans.), revised by R. F. C. Hull, Princeton, Princeton, N.J., 1971, Vol. 6, p. 448.

22. Henderson, Joseph: "Resolution of the Transference in the Light of C. G. Jung's Psychology," *Acta Psychotherap.,* 2(3):267–283, 1954.

23. Freud, Sigmund: *The Future of an Illusion,* W. D. Robson-Scott (trans.), International

Psycho-analytic Library, no. 15, Ernest Jones (ed.), Liveright, New York, 1949, p. 93.

24. Searles: op. cit., *passim.*

25. Bierer, Joshua: "Transference in the Light of Adlerian Theory and Its Developments," *Acta Psychotherap.,* **2**: 250–266, 1954.

26. Rank, Otto: *Will Therapy and Truth and Reality,* Jessie Taft (trans.), Knopf, New York, 1945.

27. Rogers, Carl R.: *On Becoming a Person,* Houghton Mifflin, Boston, 1961, chap. 1.

28. Rogers, Carl R.: "A Dialogue between Therapists," in C. R. Rogers, E. T. Gendlin, D. J. Kiesler, and C. B. Truax (eds.), *The Therapeutic Relationship and Its Impact,* University of Wisconsin Press, Madison, 1967, p. 515.

29. Ellenberger: op. cit., pp. 337–386.

30. Erikson, Erik H.: *Childhood and Society,* Norton, New York, 1950.

C. PETER ROSENBAUM, M.D.

JOHN E. BEEBE III, M.D.

CHAPTER **13**

Outpatient Therapy: An Overview

PART 2: APPROACHES TO THERAPY

Although transference phenomena in the various stages are present in all therapeutic relationships, not every school of therapy handles the transference in the same way. How, then, does the general practitioner of psychiatry begin treatment? Traditionally therapists have recognized two main approaches to therapy: the uncovering approach and the reality-oriented approach. Although the distinction reflects the era when psychoanalysis was viewed as the yardstick against which all the therapies were measured, it is still helpful for the therapist to recognize this broad division in the kinds of treatment when he is trying to decide what kind of therapy he wants to offer.

THE UNCOVERING APPROACH

This term is used whenever therapy seeks to make unconscious dynamics conscious, to uncover that which was out of awareness and bring it to awareness, and to educate the patient to his transference or "parataxic" distortions.

Nowadays it is extremely common to attack the "insight" goal, which is the main aim of the uncovering approach. Freida Fromm-Reichmann[1]

said, "Patients don't need an explanation, they need an experience." Carl Rogers[2] has questioned the value of dynamic formulations in therapy. Jay Haley[3] and Paul Watzlawick[4] feel both that (1) insight does not lead to change, and (2) insight can even be a dangerous goal, leading to that paradoxical situation in which the patient creates a hell for himself out of his pursuit of the heaven of complete self-understanding.

To answer these criticisms it is first necessary to give a careful definition of insight. We prefer the term "meaning," which implies an experiential as well as a logical and empirical approach to self-understanding.[5] The experience of meaning is very powerful indeed — leading to new experiencing. It is similar to the experience of trance or orgasm; it involves an altered state of consciousness with intense reliving and far-reaching self-consequences. Eugene Gendlin[6,7] suggests that it is upon the experience of meaning that the unfolding of experiential process depends. The purpose of an insight is not so much to change the behavior that the insight comprehends as to further the experiential process of the person who has been behaving. The worst consequence of a repetitive behavior can be its effect in trapping the patient's experiencing. The insight into the behavior may not change *that* behavior, although it often does; the insight does make it possible for the patient to experience himself in a new way and to select out of that new experiencing many new kinds of behavior.

Thus, the often quoted joke that ends with the patient saying, after several years of therapy begun when he complained of a particular symptom, "Yes, I still do that, but it doesn't bother me any more," is not so ridiculous as it seems. What is uncovered is not just the reason for that particular maladaptive or puzzling piece of behavior, but the whole experiential process which that behavior has implied. Frequently, it is the liberation of the experiential process rather than a change in behavior that satisfies the patient, providing him with the relief he was originally seeking.

> *Example 13-1.* A woman had undergone a stormy, five-year psychoanalysis during her 40s. One result was that she was able to move to the suburbs after her neurosis had kept her city-bound for many years. She took up gardening and described her situation in a letter to a relative who knew a good deal about psychotherapy, saying:
>
> "Very zany and spasmodic gardening. I find I just love ripping things out of the garden, but that does not get me the most beautiful garden in time. However, it keeps me happy. As soon as something has the temerity to push its way through the ground, I stand around palpitating until I can either cut it off or pull it out. I know what you're thinking, but I don't give a damn. Better I do it to my plants than my children. One thing analysis did for me: I got all through only to find I had the same problems I always had, but with a difference, sometimes I could do something about them, and most of the time they don't bother me very much, and that's enough for me, so I'll never find out why I enjoy ripping things out. Look at all the things I can plant for far less money. I think it's all well worth the time and money, don't you?"

Uncovering the experiential meaning of a pattern of behavior does frequently lead to change in that particular behavior. Otherwise, patients with very practical problems would be ill advised to seek help from an uncovering approach. What kinds of behaviors can be changed by an uncovering approach has yet to be completely determined. But the main advantage of uncovering therapy is its role in helping a process of maturation by freeing trapped experiencing.

THE REALITY-ORIENTED APPROACH

These approaches to therapy attempt to leave the patient's general level of experiencing pretty much alone and do not dwell too much upon the meaning of the patient's symptoms. We use the term *reality-oriented* to emphasize that the primary focus of treatment is on the two realities most easily accessible to the patient and therapist: "external, objective" reality (the patient's life situation as he perceives it and as it might be perceived by others); and "internal, subjective" reality (consciousness, awareness of how external reality impinges on the patient, how he thinks and feels about what is going on around him and inside him, including rumblings from the unconscious which may be only dimly perceived). The term *reality-oriented therapy* should not be confused with Glasser's *reality therapy*, [8] which is only one of many approaches that fall under this rubric. Crisis intervention, behavior therapy, symptom prescription and hypnosis, brief psychotherapy, supportive psychotherapy, and many other therapies have as a common and important feature the support of the patient's ego in its ability to make decisions and to modify those behaviors and their disruptive effects that interfere with harmonious living in the world. Some exponents of these approaches do not believe in the existence of a dynamic unconscious influencing consciousness and behavior. We believe that the unconscious is there in reality-oriented therapy too and that it has an important impact on treatment which must be appreciated.

In speaking of the patient's ego, both the "I," that center of consciousness the patient knows as himself, and the executive, that often unconscious part of himself that makes decisions, are meant. This definition of ego is about midway between the Freudian and the Jungian definitions, but it is empirically useful in doing reality-oriented work. This approach can be very aggressive and challenging to the patient, despite the rather nurturant connotations of the word "support," often used in this kind of therapy. Attack of a particularly self-defeating form of behavior can, paradoxically, be a form of support, if the patient receives the therapist's criticism as a concerned attempt to inject more health into his life. When this approach is used, it is frequently spoken of in therapeutic circles as "lending the patient one's ego."

In common usage, "supportive psychotherapy" is often used as a near synonym for reality-oriented therapy; by this usage, pharmacologic and behavioral approaches to symptoms are supportive techniques. (Supportive psychotherapy is described in Chapter 18.) Crisis intervention in brief psychotherapy that aims at getting the patient back to where he was, not "opening up" a new mode of adaptation to him, also is a reality-oriented approach.

COMPLEMENTARITY

In practice, the ideal therapist should be able to work in both an uncovering and a reality-oriented capacity as is needed. This ideal situation does not always obtain. Presently community mental health centers offer primarily reality-oriented therapy, and many private practitioners devote much of their professional energies to uncovering psychotherapy. Such stereotypes are not confined to professional categories. There are psychiatrists who offer primarily reality-oriented therapy and social workers who do mostly uncovering psychotherapy.

Certainly some therapists are more in touch with the needs of the ego to maintain its position and to improve its methods of coping with stress,

whereas other therapists are more comfortable with the unconscious and its need to express itself more completely and to open up new forms of experiencing. Disagreement between those who practice reality-oriented therapy and those who practice uncovering therapy has made it seem as if one or the other approach were the "real psychiatry." In fact, both approaches are needed, often with the same patient. It would be better to see them as opposite ends of a single continuum. More than one analyst has found himself giving valuable advice during a period of stress, and more than one community psychiatrist has allowed a situation to open up considerable anxiety and depression before it is able to be resolved adequately. It should be remembered that the emergency psychotherapy of grief, a cornerstone of crisis intervention theory, is essentially an uncovering approach. [9]

INDICATIONS FOR THE UNCOVERING COMPARED TO THE REALITY-ORIENTED PSYCHOTHERAPIES

Were there psychoanalysts enough and time, not every patient would benefit from uncovering psychotherapy. Many patients would not possess the strength and determination that the procedure requires, but they still could make excellent use of reality-oriented psychotherapy. Nor is attention to reality lacking in dynamic consequences. A therapist's appreciation of his patient's unconscious struggles need not be used in treatment only to uncover these conflicts; the therapist can also support reality actions that lessen or minimize these struggles.

Indications

The most common indications for uncovering and reality-oriented psychotherapies are shown in Table 13-1 and will now be expanded upon.

Motivation. The patient who is suitable for dynamic, uncovering psychotherapy is consciously

TABLE 13-1. Comparison of Indications in Uncovering
and Reality-oriented Psychotherapies

Parameter	Indication	
	Uncovering	Reality-oriented
1. Motivation	Personality change	Symptom relief; environmental change
2. Mental health	Moderate to good	Very poor to very good
3. Perception of symptoms	Ego dystonic	Ego dystonic or syntonic
4. Ego strength; capacity to endure painful affects; formal diagnosis	Strong ego; capacity to endure painful affects; symptom or character neurosis	Weaker ego; lesser capacity to endure painful affects; personality disorder, sociopathy, psychosis, organic brain syndrome
5. Quality of interpersonal relationships (including previous therapy)	Successful; useful	Unsuccessful; sparse
6. Presenting circumstances	Stable life situation	Stress, crisis
7. Age	20–40 years	Childhood to old age
8. Psychological mindedness	Considerable ("Dostoyevsky")	Moderate to negligible ("Hemingway")
9. Intelligence	Sensitive; bright	Wide range
10. Value orientation	Future: desires self-improvement and personal growth	Present or past: desires current relief or return to tradition

motivated to change his basic personality or character structure through realistic effort. (The common magical expectation that contact with a psychiatrist will ipso facto produce change cannot be counted as a sign of realistic motivation.) The usual understanding between the patient and therapist is that psychotherapy will help him to mature.

Other patients may come because they are anxious, depressed, and distraught. They may also be caught in a turbulent environmental situation. Their motivation is for relief of distress and help in controlling and improving the environmental disruption. When these objectives have been accomplished, they may very well not be interested in further exploration. Such patients are most suitable for reality-oriented therapy.

Mental Health. Some patients who are experiencing distress may strike the interviewer as basically quite healthy, with strong egos and little evidence of severe unconscous conflicts. Such patients may be caught in a life crisis for which a reality-oriented approach is indicated. Other patients have few external difficulties but are experiencing much internal conflict. Their difficulties often yield to an uncovering approach, provided their egos are strong enough. Ego strength is a concept that will be discussed later.

For the majority of patients, there is some external difficulty, some internal conflict, ego strength in some areas, and ego weakness in others. It is necessary for the therapist to understand the interactions between external reality, conscious ego, and unconscious personality structure to make the decision about how much he should use the reality-oriented approach and how much he should use the uncovering approach.

We offer the examples of Allen, Ben, Colin, and Daniel to illustrate the range of possibilities. These examples are not to be taken as rigid indications of the kinds of patients who are "suitable (or unsuitable) for uncovering (or reality-oriented) psychotherapy," but rather as kinds of presenting pictures for which different approaches to therapy are indicated. In the course of therapy, as tensions wax or wane, the same patient may come to resemble any one of the four profiles, and the approach of the therapist must change to suit the patient's needs. (Such changes may come when a seemingly healthy patient faces a major health crisis, or when a formerly psychotic patient has found the courage to separate himself from a toxic relative.) The different dynamics in each profile will be represented in the form of a diagram.

Example 13-2, Allen. Allen, a college student home for Christmas vacation, saw his father die of cancer and became engaged to a girl he had gone with for several years. On returning to school, he started having trouble concentrating, felt "sad and blue," lost his appetite, and began waking up at 5 A.M. feeling unrested. He had never experienced such feelings before, and he sought psychiatric consultation.

In consultation Allen expressed considerable concern that his symptoms might represent signs of impending insanity. The consultant reviewed his past, found that he had had many successful and gratifying social and academic achievements, and that he came from a closely knit family. He thought the student's ego was strong, that there was no evidence of significant neurotic conflict, and that, aside from the presenting symptoms, the student seemed mentally healthy.

The consultant told him he was having an acute, reactive depression, that it probably was the result of his not having been able to express all his feelings about his father's death and of being away from his fiancée, that such

depressions usually responded to psychotherapy, and that the symptoms did not portend psychosis.

Allen was greatly relieved to hear this and left the session visibly less anxious than when he had come in. He started therapy later the same week. His therapist reported that after nine sessions the patient had expressed considerable affect about the loss of his father and the separation from his girl, that there was a complete remission of symptoms, and that treatment ended by mutual consent (see Figure 13-1).

In contrast, in the case of Ben, external reality was not so stressful, but unconscious neurotic conflict was troubling him. He was motivated to change, and he seemed generally to fulfill the indications for uncovering psychotherapy described in this section.

Example 13-3, Ben. Ben, a graduate student in physics, applied for treatment of acute anxiety about a serious marital quarrel. During the course of the first few sessions, some of the marital frictions were resolved with a concomitant decrease in anxiety, but it became apparent to the therapist that the student was far from utilizing his rather considerable intellectual potential. Evidence began to emerge that conflicts about authority prevented him from working effectively with his thesis sponsor, and sibling rivalries prevented useful interchanges with his fellow students. The therapist found the patient's general level of functioning to be good, as was his ego strength.

The therapist presented these ideas and the data from which they derived in the third session, concluding, "I think you have some serious neurotic conflicts about authority, rivalry with your fellow students, and achievement, all contributing to the slowness of your progress on your thesis, and I think you need long-term psychotherapy if you are to resolve some of these problems."

Ben was taken aback by such a direct statement, but on reflection saw that there was a

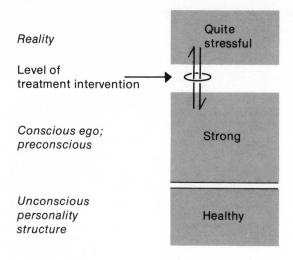

Reality

Level of treatment intervention

Conscious ego; preconscious

Unconscious personality structure

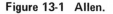

Primary conflict is between stressful reality and healthy ego temporarily unable to cope with stress. Intervention *brief*, aimed at resolution of stress and coping;   long-term treatment not called for, e.g., student with reactive depression

Figure 13-1   Allen.

good deal of merit in what the therapist had said and entered into what turned out to be a quite profitable three-year period of intensive, uncovering psychotherapy (see Figure 13-2).

Perception of Symptoms. The way the patient perceives his symptoms is closely linked to his motivation for treatment. If the patient dislikes his symptoms and what they represent, that is, if they are *ego dystonic,* he will be more motivated to give them up in intensive psychotherapy, even at the cost of experiencing anxiety and pain in the process. On the other hand, if he is relatively comfortable with them, that is, they are *ego syntonic,* he will be less motivated to change, particularly because change in intensive therapy means more work for the ego. Ben was distressed by his symptoms and was willing to suffer to give them up.

Many patients who enact their conflicts sexually

not only enjoy the actions but also dread the experience of anxiety not acting would release. Only when social disapproval of the sexual behavior, or realistic frustration of the means of gratification, is strong will the patient want therapy, and then more often to grieve the loss of a once-effective solution than to work through the original basis for taking up that solution.

Example 13-4, Colin. Colin, a 54-year-old cook who had lived homosexually his entire adult life, had recently been left by his partner of several years. In the weeks that followed he started doing two uncharacteristic things: he drank heavily, and he sought out new partners in bars and public lavatories. The police picked him up in a lavatory; he was arrested, jailed, and lectured sternly by the judge and told to seek psychiatric help as a condition of probation.

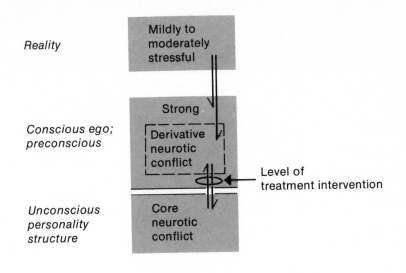

Current reality revivifies derivative conflict symptomatic
of core neurosis in patient amenable to uncovering therapy.
After initial stress resolution, *long-term* uncovering therapy
for core neurosis attempted, e.g., graduate student in physics.

Figure 13-2 Ben.

His father had brutalized Colin as a child and had favored Colin's sister. Colin's mother had ineffectually tried to protect him from his father's verbal and physical assaults. The arrest by the police and the judge's lecture stirred up Colin's fears of abuse at the hands of adult males (against which his homosexuality was presumably a reaction), and he was extremely anxious and depressed when he came for his first therapy session.

One of the first things Colin brought up was whether he was going to have to change his sexual orientation as part of therapy. After exploring the history a bit, the therapist said that it appeared to him that Colin's homosexuality had by and large worked well for him over the years, that if Colin wanted to work on it further in therapy they could, but that helping him find some relief from his current anxiety and depression seemed to be the first order of business. Colin was relieved to hear

this and did not bring up again the issue of wanting to change his sexual orientation.

Instead, therapy was aimed at finding the causes of the break with his partner, how his partner could be approached, how a new partner might be found in less self-destructive ways, and so forth. Such an approach served to make him less anxious, depressed, hopeless, and ashamed. After twelve sessions Colin felt added security about his way of life, had had some initial successes in establishing new relationships, was feeling much better, and treatment ended by mutual consent (see Figure 13-3).

The fact the symptoms are initially ego syntonic does not automatically mean a patient cannot profit from intensive psychotherapy. Sometimes one of the major tasks of the initial period of therapy is to raise anxiety in the patient's mind concerning the nature and implications of his symp-

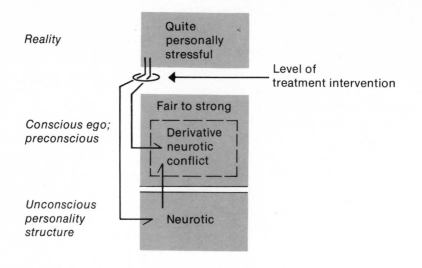

Current stress revivifies personal neurotic core conflict
in latter-day, derivative form. Patient not suitable for
uncovering therapy. Intervention *brief*, aimed at resolution
of derivative conflict; work with core neurosis not attempted,
e.g., the 54-year-old cook with conflicts over homosexuality.

Figure 13-3   Colin.

toms so that they cannot remain purely ego syntonic. In cases in which this kind of transformation seems to be a feasible goal of early intensive
therapy, the paradoxical phenomenon of trying to
make a patient feel worse about himself so that
ultimately he can feel better will occur.

Here, of course, the values of the therapist and
his judgment as to *where* to make the patient
anxious come into play. And just here, contro-
versies abound. It is well to remember that a
symptom is never an a priori item in psychiatry; it
is always a judgment involving the therapist,
the patient, and society in a complicated decision,
which is itself always open to change as part of the
therapeutic process.[10] In short, what is seen as
symptomatic at one point in therapy may not
seem so at another, depending on its meaning and
impact on the life of the individual and the
environment in which he lives.

**Ego Strength; Capacity to Endure Painful Affects;
Formal Diagnosis.** People vary in the way they
respond to anxiety and stress. Some tolerate it,
live with the anxiety, continue to function, and
seek to resolve the underlying sources of stress;
they can "muddle through," as the English did
during World War II. Such persons are said to have
a "strong ego." Others do not cope so well: they
may become paralyzed with anxiety and depression; they may discharge their feelings impulsively;
they may become psychotic. They are seen as
having a "weak ego," with the amount of weakness more or less in proportion to the amount of
incapacity or maladaptiveness of their response to
stress. Patients with compromised brain function,
such as the "syndrome of cerebral insufficiency"
(described in Chapters 30 and 31), also have a
reduced capacity to respond to stress.

Uncovering psychotherapy is itself a source of

stress because it asks that the patient be able to experience once again feelings and fantasies buried because they were painful to begin with. Therefore, uncovering psychotherapy is most appropriate for patients judged to have strong egos, those who would most likely be diagnosed as having a symptom or character neurosis. Reality-oriented therapy is most appropriate for patients whose egos are weaker, those who would most likely be diagnosed as having a personality disorder, a latent or overt psychosis, or an organic brain syndrome.[11,12]

With psychotic patients, the therapist will often have to direct his attentions to two levels of reality: he will have to help the patient with external reality and the problems of day-by-day living, and he will have to intercede against disturbing irruptions from the unconscious, as shown in the case of Daniel.

Example 13-5, Daniel. Daniel was a 22-year-old schizophrenic patient, first hospitalized when he was 18, who impulsively left his home in St. Louis, where he lived with his mother, older sister, and aunt, to fly to Los Angeles. He arrived there without warning at the home of his father, who had divorced his mother when Daniel was four. The father had remarried and started a second family. Daniel thought that if he left the women he had been living with, took up residence with his father, and also, for the first time, took his father's last name, he would somehow "become a man" (symbolically grow a penis). When Daniel's therapist in St. Louis realized he intended to complete his impulsive trip, he told him to check in at a clinic where a colleague, Dr. Hirsch, worked.

Dr. Hirsch was called to the clinic waiting room Friday afternoon and saw an obviously schizophrenic young man and an equally confused and distressed father. He saw the patient briefly, during which time the patient verified that this was the *right* Dr. Hirsch at the *right* clinic. An appointment was made for Monday.

In the weeks and months that followed, Dr. Hirsch and the patient worked to reduce the level of psychotic anxiety (using phenothiazines and interpretations based on understanding the patient's dynamics), find a suitable living situation in a halfway house (the father and his new family clearly could not take it), get the patient involved in a day care center, and, in general, stabilize his existence.

Some months later Dr. Hirsch left the clinic, and another therapist (the second of many) took over Daniel's treatment. During his first five years in Los Angeles, the patient had to have three psychiatric hospitalizations (each lasting a few weeks and often coinciding with a visit from mother), but still found a job and was largely self-supporting and self-sufficient. He required a half-hour of psychotherapy every two weeks when his life was relatively unstressful (although the time was increased at periods of stress), and he participated in community, psychiatrically based activities during much of his free time. He will probably need some psychiatric management for life (see Figure 13-4).

Quality of Interpersonal Relationships (Including Previous Therapy). Success in intensive therapy is predicated upon some degree of past success in intimate relationships with others. Not all patients can handle intimacy well: some have not developed sufficient basic trust; some cannot accept a relationship they cannot control; some must use any relationship narcissistically. Equally, some patients react to any therapist as a mother, who must be defied by means of a sequence of pranks and tricks. Others see every therapist as a father, who must be dreaded, obeyed, or defied. Whenever a patient seems to have a particularly striking pattern of creating the same relationship with every partner, the therapist should question whether intensive psychotherapy will be able to uncover the reasons for this destructive pattern or will merely be one more humiliating and costly

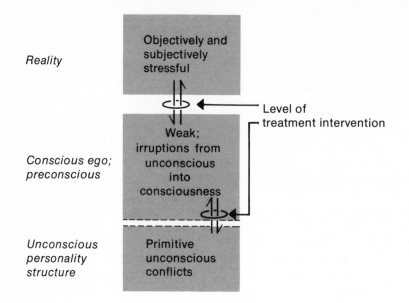

Borderline or psychotic ego defenses make patient vulnerable
to many life situations. *Brief* therapy aimed at resolution
of precipitating stress; *long-term* supportive therapy (often
with medication) needed; appreciation of unconscious dynamics
is an essential part of supplying intelligent support. Length
and frequency of sessions flexible (for instance, increased
at times of crisis), e.g., schizophrenic patient who flew
impulsively to Los Angeles.

Figure 13-4   Daniel.

repetition of the familiar sequence, "adding insight to injury."

The evidence of interpersonal success lies in the outcome of past relationships. This history is the island on which the patient must build in his relationship with the present therapist. Particularly important will be his experience with previous therapists. If the patient thinks that his other therapeutic relationships "aren't worth mentioning" or will not give the names of former therapists, then it can be assumed that things went quite badly. Often the previous therapy is frankly unfinished, and the patient would do best by going back to the former therapist at least to "close the old account." Frequently, an initial consultation for psychotherapy discovers the need to resolve an old transference, and the therapist can help the patient most by helping him end the old psychotherapy in the right way. Then the patient has a decent basis from which to start with someone else.

Of course a previous patient-therapist fit may have been wrong, and the patient may be quite a good candidate for intensive work with the present therapist. The therapist must consult his own feelings: if he feels comfortable with the patient throughout the first hour, there is a strong possibility that they can work together. If, on the other hand, he has doubts, suspicions, vague uneasiness, he should heed them: this may be a patient who cannot handle intimacy with this therapist.

Usually the patient signals early what he will be like in therapy, and the therapist should heed his message. The patient who is intensely narcissistic will ask for some tangible evidence of admiration or approval early in the session, some special favor, and the therapist should notice whether the patient can tolerate refusal. Uncovering therapy is a relatively ungratifying experience; the therapist must often withhold his opinion of what is going on, as well as expressions of admiration and support. If the patient cannot do without these, he cannot endure uncovering therapy.

Still other patients cannot stand the intimacy of fifty minutes a week with the same therapist; paranoid and schizoid patients stand out in this category. Some patients react with painful emotional storms to any suggestion from the therapist of disapproval or disinterest: here, certain hysterical characters and schizophrenic patients stand out. Patients in either of these groups may react to the end of a period of therapy or to a therapist's vacation or illness with psychotic, suicidal, or homicidal behavior. The therapist is protecting the patient and himself by not embarking on intensive psychotherapy.

If transference issues threaten to engulf, not enlighten, the patient, reality-oriented therapy may be the treatment of choice. Or, a therapist who specializes in uncovering work with patients who have certain difficult transferences may be found. (Some therapists subspecialize in work with paranoid, schizoid, hysterical, and schizophrenic patients and seem to know just what to do.)

Finally, visits of limited duration with a different therapist each time (Chapter 18) may be the right approach. This is the least transferential version of reality-oriented therapy, indicated for patients with the most difficulty accepting intimacy, frustration, and dependency.

Presenting Circumstances. The presenting circumstances of the patient who can utilize uncovering psychotherapy must include a baseline stability in his life situation.[13,14] Intensive psychotherapy is hard work, and it takes concentration and effort. If a patient is sorely beset by reality problems, e.g., job loss, eviction from home, the stress of combat, and so on, he simply does not have the psychic energy available to do the introspective work of uncovering psychotherapy.

One measure of the energy the patient has for intensive therapy is his ability to pay for it (or find a way of having it financed). Here the therapist must help him face the realities squarely. Uncovering therapy always takes months and frequently years if it is to be productive. Insurance coverage for treatment with private practitioners is limited; twice a week at $35 an hour will cost about $3,000 a year. Thus patients undertaking uncovering therapy must be able to plan on staying in the same geographical area for a year, and, if in treatment with a private practitioner, to arrange for the bills to be paid from some combination of personal resources, insurance coverage, or community support, and so on.

In contrast, most reality-oriented therapies do not take so long and do not average so many visits per week. The costs are often underwritten by community agencies, and thus the patient does not have to make so many major commitments when he starts.

Age. The age of patients suitable for uncovering psychotherapy is important in its implications about character structure and ego strength. The developmental level of adolescents can vary widely. Of two 16-year-olds, one shows a childlike, dependent orientation. He perceives himself as relatively helpless, unprepared to grow up and assume adult control over impulses and behavior, and is afraid of independence. This self-perception may reflect his family's feeling that he is ill prepared to leave the nest. He may unconsciously expect adults (including therapists) to be omnipotent and not necessarily friendly. This kind of adolescent fears entry into a therapeutic alliance whose goal is greater self-knowledge leading to a mastery of impulses and behavior, and finally to greater personal independence. Furthermore, his family senses its equilibrium would be upset if the adolescent were to make strides in a "mature" direction, and they might work unwittingly to undo whatever is accomplished in therapy. To make the work proceed at all, the therapist finds it necessary to involve the family in supportive consultations.

A second 16-year-old comes to treatment with a relatively adult ego orientation. Despite characteristic adolescent conflicts about sexuality, assertiveness and aggression, impulse control, fear of relinquishing dependent ties to the family, and so forth, somehow his storms always resolve in the direction of maturity, and his family is basically helpful. This kind of adolescent patient is psychologically much better prepared to enter into the therapeutic alliance required for uncovering psychotherapy.

At best, uncovering psychotherapy with adolescents requires an adaptation of traditional techniques to the patient's specific situation, which, because of the fluidity of character structure, defense mechanisms, coping abilities, and so on, may require session-to-session adaptations on the part of the therapist. For example, an experienced psychiatrist reported that he began to have good results with his adolescents only when he started suggesting to them that he was willing to use the therapeutic hour for a walk to the park. [15]*

At another critical period in development, by the time most people reach the age of 40 their character structures not only are consolidated but have become relatively fixed and are not easily changed. It becomes increasingly more difficult after that age to make significant changes in character structure, even when these seem called for. Nevertheless, a significant proportion of adults over the age of 40 encounter middle-life crises that

may propel them into treatment with a commitment to change only occasionally found in younger people. The dramatic changes described by Jung[18] in the individuation process are felt by him to be reserved for the second half of life; his own psychological development after age 40[19] testifies to the potential of this period.

Psychological Mindedness. This term refers to an assessment of the patient's sensitivity and perceptivity to inner, psychological events in himself and others. Some people are intuitive; others are not. Many of the characters in Dostoyevsky's novels expound at length on their own and everyone else's motivations. In Hemingway's works the characters are involved in lives of action, not contemplation. Of the brothers Karamazov, contemplative Aloysha would have been the best candidate for intensive psychotherapy; impulsive Dmitri would have been the worst. Impulsive patients can sometimes talk like psychologically minded people, but they are rarely willing to settle for the slow, hard work of uncovering; they usually argue for dramatic, new approaches if they are interested in psychology.

Intelligence. Psychoanalysis has been termed "the talking cure." In the past it has been assumed that the ability to be articulate was intimately linked with intelligence and that intelligence could be measured accurately by intelligence tests. These are dubious assumptions at best. Intelligence is not always expressed verbally; some highly gifted and creative people find it difficult to express themselves in words, although their painting, music, or mathematics are most impressive. Others may show an impressive wisdom in the business of living and coping with stress, even though they may not be able to describe how they do it.

Formal tests of intelligence are culture-bound and favor those reared in a culture similar to that of those who devised the test. Cultural differences between the therapist and patient often make it

---

*Extensive discussion of the treatment of children and adolescents is beyond the scope of this book. Readers may pursue these issues further in Weiner[16] and Caplan and Lebovici.[17]

difficult for the therapist to appreciate fully the intelligence of a patient from a markedly different background.

For all these reasons, therapists should be cautious about underrating a patient's suitability for uncovering psychotherapy on the basis of intelligence. If the interviewer has doubts, he may do well to have the patient evaluated by a colleague who can work well with inarticulate but otherwise gifted persons or who is closer in cultural background to the patient.

Value Orientation and Culture. The gratifications of uncovering psychotherapy are few at the beginning, once the novelty wears off, and the pains, both emotional and often financial, are many. The payoff is not expected to come for months or years. The goal is usually improvement of the self (rather than, say, improved loyalty to a religious faith). The means include frank self-disclosure and a willingness to be open (rather than, say, the patient's keeping shameful and guilty secrets to himself and maintaining a stiff upper lip in the face of adversity).

Spiegel[20] points out that value orientation and culture operate significantly in how both patients and therapists perceive psychotherapy. Although the predominant American culture favors a future orientation (work hard, strive, and success will come), some subcultures have a present orientation (life's gratifications are few; grab them while you can) or a past orientation (an individual's value in society is tightly connected with continuing important social and religious traditions; to change in a way that renounces those traditions is apostasy).

Traditional uncovering psychotherapy is most congruent with the values of future-oriented persons who look for individual growth through frank revelation even when it is painful, who are willing to delay gratification, and who are willing, at least to some extent, to break with tradition if it stands in the way of their own growth.

For many lower-class Americans there has been little reason to see much virtue in the delay of the few gratifications available. Therefore, if therapy promises to interfere with these gratifications, it is unlikely that the patient will engage in a therapeutic contract. The cost of therapy is one source of such interference. If it does not interfere, e.g., if insurance or the community will pay and the patient will not run up a large bill, then therapy can be considered on its other merits, and the lower-class patient often can invest himself in it.

It is sometimes argued that lower-class Americans do not have a bent for introspective thought and speech. There is much contrary evidence. Words that are quite often different from those used by middle-class therapists for feelings may not be recognized by them as introspective. Equally, therapy has not yet been available to lower-class patients until quite recently, so that its terms and formal concepts may seem unfamiliar to them. Even now therapy is frequently not explained or conducted in a culturally appropriate language, and if this failure of communication occurs, the mystified patient will wisely and understandably mistrust therapy and the intentions of the incomprehensible therapist.

Some Contrasts

The foregoing shows that most uncovering therapy takes time (months, years), that some reality-oriented therapies may be brief, and others may last a lifetime. Most uncovering therapies pay attention to unconscious phenomena, seeking to make them more explicit. Most reality-oriented therapies do not seek to make unconscious phenomena explicit or try to limit their intrusions into consciousness and day-by-day functioning; such therapies operate more at the level of the external and conscious realities of the patient. How these contrasts can be applied to the cases of Allen, Ben, Colin, and Daniel is recapitulated in Figure 13-5.

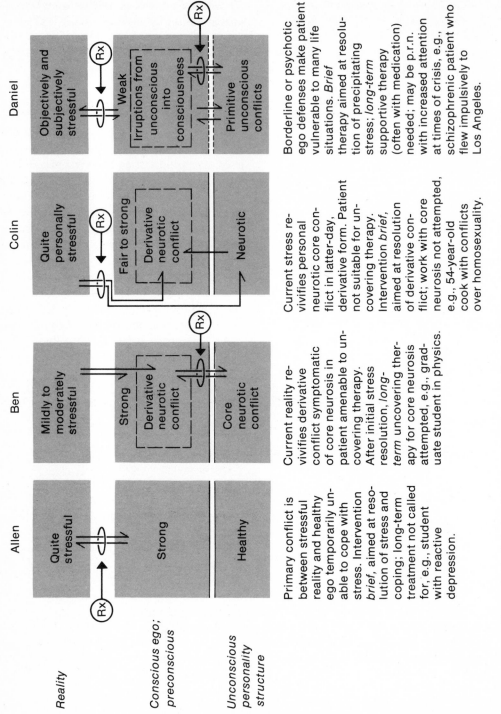

Figure 13-5 Relationship of stress and personality structure to strategy of therapeutic intervention.

BASIC PROCEDURES IN UNCOVERING AND REALITY-ORIENTED PSYCHOTHERAPIES

The basic procedures that occur most often in uncovering and reality-oriented therapies are listed in Table 13-2.

The Procedures

Advice, Exhortation, Suggestion. Into this category fall advising a patient to get a job, to assert himself more in social situations, and so forth. In insight psychotherapy, in which increased self-awareness is one goal, it may be less productive for the therapist to be drawn into the role of the helpful advice giver than to concentrate with the patient on finding out where his own decision

making tends to fail. In reality-oriented psychotherapy, on the other hand, many patients are simply not intact enough psychologically to make some of their necessary decisions, and thoughtful advice from the therapist may prove quite useful. (This is described in detail in Chapter 18.)

Praise and Criticism. Psychoanalysis has taught therapists to be stinting of praise and criticism in uncovering psychotherapy, although both are employed more frequently in the reality-oriented therapies. The rationale is (1) the therapist becomes an authority who can judge the patient, thus causing him to perform simply to please the therapist, who is now the incarnation of the patient's superego, (sometimes the therapist is referred to as "riding the patient's superego"); and (2) praise becomes a form of narcissistic gratifica-

TABLE 13-2. Basic Procedures in Uncovering and Reality-oriented Psychotherapies

Procedure	Extent of Use	
	Uncovering Therapies	*Reality-oriented Therapies*
1. Advice, exhortation, suggestion	Sparing	Frequent
2. Praise, criticism	Sparing to moderate	Frequent
3. Medication	Little	Great
4. Catharsis	Frequent	Frequent
5. Therapist initiative in establishing content areas	Little	Great
6. Relaxation of ego constraints	Considerable	Slight
7. Analysis of the transference; interpretations aimed at providing deep insights; identification of resistances	Regular	Limited
8. Discussion of dreams, childhood memories	Regular	Limited
9. Frequency of visits	1 to 5 per week*	1 per week or fewer*

*Patients in acute crises often need frequent visits, every day or even more frequently, if only for fifteen or thirty minutes. This is true for both uncovering and reality-oriented therapy.

tion for the patient; he comes mainly to be praised by a benevolent father or mother rather than to learn about himself.

Praise can have both a direct and a paradoxical effect. In its direct form, praise is encouragement. When a patient does not need encouragement, or has a neurotic need to please, praise can play into pathology. But when a patient has not had the experience of being pleasing to anybody, the therapist's praise can be as valuable as rain on a dry field; it can allow the patient to grow.

As paradox, praise can have the effect of allowing a valid feeling that is unattractively or annoyingly expressed to be more fully recognized. Often the patient has been expressing emotion in such a way as to elicit the disapproval of the therapist. The therapist's praise undercuts this self-defeating strategy. In one instance a wife continually berated her husband in an annoying, hysterical way; he shrugged off her anger because she permitted him to say to her, the therapist, and anyone else involved, in effect: "Don't pay any attention to what she says; I have a hysterical wife."

Once, as the scene was being replayed in the office, the therapist said to the wife, "You're not attacking him nearly forcefully enough." He had unexpectedly praised her emotion, even though he criticized her way of expressing it. She stopped screaming, and everyone was able for the first time to appreciate the validity of the anger she had been disqualifying with her hysterical style of expression.

Many of the same objections to praise have also been leveled against criticism: the therapist is playing the superego, is being parental. Moreover, there is a tacit assumption that therapists are supposed to be gentle, accepting people who can be too sweet from time to time without being seriously at fault, but must never err toward being too critical without immediately finding out why they are acting out a negative countertransference upon the patient.

Actually, the therapist has a powerful tool in his hands when he is able to criticize a patient who trusts him enough to hear his criticism. Construc-

tive criticism starts in the confrontation phase of psychotherapy and continues through the initiatory phase. If the therapist is going to use criticism, he does best by criticizing behavior that has really been annoying to him and owning the criticism as only his reaction to that behavior. Criticism that implies the therapist is God usually elicits a well-deserved defensive reaction.

Often an adolescent patient who has been unable to hear criticism from his parents and persists in traits that are grossly rude or maladaptive can be helped a great deal by a trusted therapist who is not afraid to tell him he is being obnoxious. Sometimes the therapist is the only person in the patient's environment who *can* criticize him and get away with it. The experience of submitting to someone else's authority can be an extremely valuable one for the patient who is used to controlling others in his environment at all times.

Medication. Patients who are severely anxious or depressed may not have the psychological energy available to them for either psychotherapy or any of life's other responsibilities, and a temporary course of the appropriate tranquilizer or antidepressant may be very useful in tiding them over a rough period. The indications and contraindications for the use of these drugs are detailed in Chapters 25 to 28.

Therapists doing uncovering psychotherapy are usually reluctant to use medication. Mild to modest amounts of anxiety in patients in uncovering psychotherapy may be an indicator that the patient is getting somewhere, that he is beginning to come to grips with unsettling but important issues which have long been buried. Such anxiety can serve both as a signal of the issue and as a spur toward its discovery. Its presence is to be welcomed rather than treated; its origins to be searched for rather than squelched.

In contrast, patients in reality-oriented and supportive psychotherapies may not be able to use anxiety profitably; its presence merely signifies that things are going wrong, not right, and medications may be called for. For chronic schizophrenic patients, long-term administration of phenothiazine drugs is often a necessary part of treatment.

Catharsis. When something has gone wrong in a person's life, it is often very helpful to him to be able to tell someone else about it. If he is in psychotherapy, whether it be uncovering or reality-oriented, the therapist, if he has proven himself an adept and compassionate listener, is a logical person to unburden himself to. Injudicious catharsis, however, is a potential hazard, particularly in patients who have trouble separating the thought from the act, as do some borderline patients with homicidal fantasies and some masochistic depressive patients who uncover feelings toward the end of a session that will be with them all week. With such patients, the therapist may model the repression of destructive affects by *suppressing* the expression of them during the hour. He will set limits, especially in the last part of an hour, on what the patient may express. Clearly, this is a technique at variance with uncovering and is a specialized skill for use only in the treatment of patients who have difficulty repressing.

Therapist Initiative in Establishing Content Areas. In uncovering psychotherapy, in which increased self-awareness is one of the main goals, therapists will often instruct patients to report all thoughts that come to mind, whether they seem important or insignificant, pleasant or anxiety provoking, proper or improper. He leaves the major burden of "producing material" to the patient. Often he lets the patient find his own way of structuring the hour. He occasionally intervenes to make a connection, direct the associations in a particular area, and so forth when a strong hunch or solid knowledge of dynamics suggests that there is some gold to be mined in a particular vein. Interactive therapists who do uncovering therapy leap in only where the patient "lives" affectively (or where he dramatically refuses to live). The cue to interest is patient emotion — strongly expressed or strongly repressed.

In reality-oriented therapies the therapist's task often is more to help the patient improve his day-by-day existence. He may much more often suggest the topics to be talked about; e.g., "How did things go when you visited your mother-in-law last weekend?" Free association can easily be irrelevant, a waste of time to both the therapist and the patient, who drifts to familiar, safe complexes, avoiding deep catharsis. Nevertheless, even in reality-oriented psychotherapy, if a given therapy hour seems to have gotten stuck, it may be useful to ask the patient to report on what is going through his mind to get things moving again.

Relaxation of Ego Constraints. When the patient in uncovering psychotherapy is asked to use free association and is assisted in this by being asked to lie down on a couch, where he cannot be distracted by the sight of the therapist and the therapist's responses to what he is saying, an opportunity for mild regression comes into being. Many of the patient's adult faculties of self-criticism, inner judgments, and so on are relaxed; a state of "willing suspension of disbelief" is called for.

Such regression allows more primitive kinds of thinking and feeling to emerge slowly. Often knowledge of these more primitive modes is crucial to understanding the development and manifestations of the neurotic behavior for which the patient originally entered treatment. As the therapist and patient learn from the patient's reports, the therapist may help the patient to make affective connections between psychological events that had not been previously perceived as related.

At the end of the therapy hour, and in the period between sessions, the patient's adult ego assimilates what has gone on; his critical abilities are implicitly called upon to reassert themselves, and the period of regression ends. Thus the regression has been in the service of the ego: it has allowed the ego access to otherwise hidden stores of information and emotion that can lead to therapeutic growth.

In uncovering therapy, such regression is sometimes painful but often profitable. In work with the marginally adapted, however, it may be a luxury the patient simply cannot afford. Borderline or overtly psychotic patients need all the reality testing they can get. The unstructured situation of being asked to free-associate to a therapist whom they cannot see may weaken already strained ego defenses and allow an eruption of disabling symptoms. In a discussion of treatment of borderline characters, Ralph Greenson[21] notes that with a neurotic patient the therapist may say, "You seem to be reacting to me as if I were your father"; with the borderline patient the therapist must say, "You seem to be reacting to me as if I were your father, but I am not your father," thus adding a needed component of reality testing to a weak ego.

Analysis of the Transference; Interpretations Aimed at Providing Deep Insights; Identification of Resistances. All these procedures are facets of a central body of technique belonging to contemporary psychoanalytic ego psychology, but they find parallels in all uncovering psychotherapies. Each is a way of trying to increase self-awareness, of making conscious the preconscious and unconscious, of bringing that which was out of awareness into awareness. The defenses (defense mechanisms), according to psychoanalysis, are those mental activities that serve to keep conflictual, anxiety-provoking thoughts, feelings, and fantasies out of consciousness. The most common defense mechanisms are repression, denial, and reaction formation. Others include isolation, undoing, intellectualization, suppression, projection, sublimation, and displacement. All are described in elegant, concise detail by Anna Freud.[22] Learning to experience defense mechanisms in action and to develop choice in their development is a major goal of psychoanalytically oriented therapy.

Discussion of Dreams, Childhood Memories. Freud called the dream "the royal road to the unconscious." Dream material can provide an astonishingly direct picture of the affective issue at hand, where free association has repeatedly led away from the central emotion. (Ways in which dream material can be utilized in both uncovering and reality-oriented therapies are presented in Chapter 22.) In general, therapists doing insight therapy will encourage patients to present dream material; in reality-oriented therapies, therapists do not usually encourage, and may even discourage, attention being paid to dreams. If dreams are used, the problem-solving aspect is more likely to be stressed in reality-oriented therapies, and the problem-revealing aspect is often emphasized in uncovering therapy. This is in line with the general principle that the patient in uncovering therapy is best confronted with a neglected problem for his strong ego to resolve, whereas the patient in supportive therapy is best left with a neglected solution for his weak ego to incorporate.

Most neuroses have their origins in childhood. Often an investigation of these origins, and of the related memories of childhood events and fantasies, can be important in uncovering psychotherapy. They are much less important in reality-oriented therapy and are less often sought after.

Frequency of Visits. In all kinds of psychotherapy, current life events and fantasies are important. Therapy occupies only one or a few of the 168 hours of each week; what goes on in the other 164 or 167 is important to know. In dynamic psychotherapy in particular, it is important to know not only what events took place, but what their private and personal meaning was to the patient. Thus the patient who reports a run-in with a boss or lover will then be asked to free-associate about that event to find out what its specific meaning was to him. The patient in uncovering psychotherapy needs time both to report life events and to search after their personal meaning. One hour a week is usually not enough to do both; it may be barely adequate for a report on the external events themselves. Thus patients in uncovering psychotherapy often need two to five sessions a week if they are to have the opportunity to do the necessary work, although instances of productive uncovering psychotherapies with only one session a week are many.

Patients in reality-oriented psychotherapy, in contrast, do not have such needs of introspection imposed upon them by the therapy; one hour a week or less may suffice. Here too exceptions certainly exist. Just as many well-motivated patients work hard on therapy between sessions and improve with an uncovering approach although they meet only once a week, many marginally adapted patients' needs for support demand that they be seen more frequently; they tend to lose their egos if the distance between sessions is too great. Generally, the frequency should enable the patient in uncovering psychotherapy to maintain contact with his unconscious and the patient in reality-oriented psychotherapy to hold onto his ego.

Being in therapy is no insurance that patients will not encounter emotional crises. Indeed, uncovering therapy may not only be an additional stress in and of itself, but it may bring to the surface upsetting and long-buried conflicts and render the patient more vulnerable to feelings of anxiety or depression about life events from which he previously was relatively well-protected by a neurotic defense structure. No matter what kind of therapy a patient is in, if he enters a period of great emotional turmoil, the therapist should see him more often than their usual contract would dictate. Sometimes these extra sessions can be less than the traditional fifty minutes; sometimes they can even be conducted on the telephone (see Chapter 24).

THE GOALS OF PSYCHOTHERAPY

At what point is psychotherapy complete? Where is the therapy going? Throughout therapy the therapist has to continually raise these questions with the patient. As to the question, "What are the symptoms?", the answers belong to the therapeutic process itself. In the first few sessions, the goals of therapy may be quite vague; it is usually impossible for a patient at the outset of therapy to state clearly everything he wants to work on. Indeed, an early goal of therapy should be to establish some idea of goals. Too conscious an emphasis on goals can lead to a kind of premature closure of psychotherapy, with the patient having mouthed a rational goal to his therapist and achieved it, but not expressed the underlying, less well-formulated concern that may have brought him to therapy. It is wise to remember the range of possible stopping points of successful therapy as a kind of guide to what may be an acceptable stopping point for the patient, even if not for the therapist. Jung[23] speaks usefully to this issue as follows:

There is in the analytical process, that is to say in the dialectical discussion between the conscious mind and the unconscious, a development or an advance towards some goal or end the perplexing nature of which had engaged my attention for many years. Psychological treatment may come to an *end* at any stage in the development without one's always or necessarily having the feeling that a *goal* has also been reached. Typical and temporary terminations may occur (1) after receiving a piece of good advice; (2) after making a more or less complete but still satisfactory confession; (3) after having recognized some hitherto unconscious but essential psychic content whose realization gives a new impetus to one's life and activity; (4) after a hard-won separation from the childhood psyche; (5) after having worked out a new and rational mode of adaptation to perhaps difficult or unusual circumstances and surroundings; (6) after the disappearance of painful neurotic symptoms; (7) after some positive turn of fortune such as an examination, engagement, marriage, divorce, change of profession, etc.; (8) after having found one's way back to the church to which one previously belonged, or after a conversion; and finally, (9) after having begun to build up a practical philosophy of life (a "philosophy" in the classical sense of the word).

The Concept of "Cure"

Many psychotherapists have posited one version or another of Bergson's "élan vital," an innate tendency toward life and development and health. It is similar to the body's response to infection or injury: physiological defenses are mobilized to deal with the insult. The physician can assist, but nature heals. Penicillin can assist the body's defenses, but when the defenses do not work, penicillin is of no avail. Psychologically, most persons seek to adjust and overcome psychological insults, and most have the defenses and strengths to make progress. The therapist's job (and the word "therapist" comes from the Greek "theraps," meaning attendant) is to assist, acting as midwife to the patient's strivings toward health. Sullivan[24] says:

> Thus we try to proceed along the general lines of getting some notion of what stands in the way of successful living for the person, quite certain that if we can clear away the obstacles, everything else will take care of itself. So true is that, that in well over twenty-five years — aside from my forgotten mistakes in the first few of them — I have never found myself called upon to "cure" anybody. The patients took care of that, once I had done the necessary brush-cleaning, and so on. It is almost uncanny how things fade out of the picture when the *raison d'être* is revealed. The brute fact is that man is so extraordinarily adaptive that, given any chance of making a reasonably adequate analysis of the situation, he is quite likely to stumble into a series of experiments which will gradually approximate more successful living.

Sullivan makes it sound easier than it is. Doing psychotherapy is hard work, and some therapists find that they cannot devote more than four or five hours a day to it before they feel spent. There are periods of discouragement, of halting progress, of slipping back into the old neurosis in virtually every course of psychotherapy, uncovering or reality-oriented.

Adding this note of caution, then, to Sullivan's statement, and combining it with Jung's, makes it apparent that the notion of ultimate "cure," a blissful renunciation of all stress and challenge and the prospect of an unruffled and tranquil future, the prospective version of an idealized, never-attained "perfect childhood" or "utopia of genitality,"[25] is neither possible nor the realistic promise of therapy. The point, again, is that therapy is a process treating a process. At its least, therapy holds out the prospect of relieving immediate discomfort and enhancing ways of coping with the factors that led up to it. At most it provides the prospect of the individual's utilizing more fully his innate strengths, intelligence, and resilience in dealing with stress, opening up opportunities to choose between self-defeating behaviors and those that can lead to self-fulfillment.

REFERENCES

1. Fromm-Reichmann, Frieda: *Principles of Intensive Psychotherapy,* University of Chicago Press, Chicago, 1950 (paperback).

2. Rogers, Carl R.: "A Theory of Therapy, Personality, and Interpersonal Relationships as Developed in a Client-Centered Framework," in S. M. Koch (ed.), *Psychology: A Study of a Science,* McGraw-Hill, New York, 1959, vol. 3.

3. Haley, Jay: *Strategies of Psychotherapy,* Grune & Stratton, New York, 1963.

4. Watzlawick, Paul: Personal communication, 1971.

5. Gendlin, Eugene T.: *Experiencing and the Creation of Meaning,* Free Press, Glencoe, 1962, p. 1.

6. Ibid.

7. Gendlin, Eugene T.: "A Theory of Personality Change," in P. Worchel and D. Byrne (eds.) *Personality Change,* Wiley, New York, 1964.

8. Glasser, William: *Reality Therapy,* Harper & Row, New York, 1965.

9. Lindemann, Erich: "Symptomatology and Management of Acute Grief," *Am. J. Psychiat.,* vol. 101, September 1944.

10. Gendlin, Eugene T.: "Values and the Process of Experiencing," in A. Mahrer (ed.), *The Goals of Psychotherapy,* Appleton-Century-Crofts, New York, 1966.

11. Fromm-Reichmann: loc. cit.

12. Rosenbaum, C. Peter: *The Meaning of Madness,* Science House, New York, 1970, chap. 14.

13. Kalis, Betty, et al.: "Precipitating Stress as a Focus in Psychotherapy," *Arch. Gen. Psychiat.,* **5**:219–226, 1961.

14. Rosenbaum, C. Peter, "Events of Early Therapy and Brief Therapy," *Arch. Gen. Psychiat.,* **10**:506–512, 1964.

15. Enelow, Allen J.: Personal communication, 1972.

16. Weiner, J. B.: *Psychological Disturbances in Adolescence,* Wiley-Interscience, New York, 1970.

17. Caplan, G., and S. Lebovici: *Adolescence,* Basic Books, New York, 1969.

18. Jung, C. G.: "A Study in the Process of Individuation," *The Archetypes and the Collective Unconscious,* R. F. C. Hull (trans.), Pantheon, New York, 1959, pp. 290–354.

19. Jung, C. G.: *Memories, Dreams, and Reflections,* Amiela Jaffe (ed.), Richard Winston and Clara Winston (trans.), Pantheon, New York, 1963.

20. Spiegel, John P.: *Transactions: The Interplay between Individual, Family and Society,* Science House, New York, 1971.

21. Greenson, Ralph: Address at American Psychiatric Association convention, San Francisco, May 1970.

22. Freud, Anna: *The Ego and the Mechanisms of Defense,* International Universities Press, New York, 1946.

23. Jung, C. G.: *Psychology and Alchemy, The Collected Works of C. G. Jung,* R. F. C. Hull (trans.), Pantheon Books, New York, 1953, vol. 12, p. 4. Copyright 1953 and © 1968 by Bollingen Foundation, reprinted by permission of Princeton University Press.

24. Sullivan, Harry S.: *The Psychiatric Interview,* Norton, New York, 1954, pp. 238–239.

25. Erikson, Erik H.: *Childhood and Society,* Norton, New York, 1950, p. 266.

Psychiatric Formulation

PURPOSE OF PSYCHIATRIC CLASSIFICATION, DIAGNOSIS, AND FORMULATION

Faced with a case in the outpatient clinic the therapist has to make some subtle judgments: what are the causes of the patient's present distress, and how are those causes related to his personality structure and his social and personal environment? What kinds of resources (including therapy) are available to him? What are reasonable therapeutic goals? What kinds of therapeutic interventions have the best chances of reaching these goals? Is the therapist equipped to help provide these interventions, or are his colleagues equipped to provide them? If the therapist is equipped, what kinds of plans for getting treatment started can he develop and share to some degree with the patient? These are questions a *psychiatric formulation* of the case attempts to answer.

Traditionally, to answer these questions therapists organize their findings and ideas around five categories, namely, the patient's *history,* the *mental status examination* (MSE), *diagnoses,* the *dynamic formulation,* and *treatment planning.* The therapist must learn about recent stress and distress, current and early life events (history); he must evaluate the level and adequacy of the patient's current emotional and intellectual functioning (MSE); he must try to see how this patient's response to stress compares with similar reactions in others, where the usual results of

treatment are known (diagnosis); he must attempt to understand why this patient is vulnerable to this stress at this time in his life (dynamic formulation); and he should use these disparate sources of information in preparing the kinds of psychotherapeutic and medical interventions he thinks can help the patient (treatment planning). These evaluations are usually made most fully and explicitly at the beginning of treatment, but they should be repeated systematically during the course of treatment if it is to progress intelligently and not founder.

And of course, there are other uses of psychiatric and psychological assessment, ones not related necessarily to treatment. Epidemiologists, sociologists, or geneticists interested in studying the incidence and prevalence of the kinds of mental disorders in given socioeconomic groups or in pedigree lines of families will use such assessments. Regrettably, sometimes diagnostic labels can be used as instruments for pseudoscientific social control over "deviant" (i.e., disfavored) behavior, as shown in the furor in the early 1970s over brain surgery on "violence-prone" prisoners and the sometimes indiscriminate use of stimulants on children alleged to have minimum brain dysfunction. Social agencies such as the U.S. Veterans Administration need to employ psychiatric diagnoses in adjudicating veterans' claims for compensation for mental difficulties presumed to be connected with military duty. Insurance carriers demand psychiatric diagnoses for settlement of claims involving psychiatric consultation and treatment. These additional, and sometimes competing, needs are not germane to the thesis presented here and will not be discussed further.

THE PSYCHIATRIC HISTORY

The patient's psychiatric history is one of several components that enter into the dynamic formulation of a case and of the treatment ideas which come from it. The techniques employed in obtaining a good history are described in detail in the chapter on Initial Interviewing (Chapter 15); the ways in which this information, which often emerges in a disorganized form, can be organized into a more coherent statement are described in the following text.

Psychiatrists have developed over the years a multitude of systems they use to record a patient's history. One of the best known and most widely used is Menninger's *A Manual for Psychiatric Case Study*.[1] (An abbreviation and modification of the Menninger system appears as The Psychiatric Interview in Appendix A.) We have selected the case of Mrs. Graves to demonstrate how the various aspects of case formulation that are the topics of this chapter can be set forth (we shall return to her case several times).

Example 14-1, Mrs. Graves. Identifying information. This is the first psychiatric contact for Mrs. Graves, a 41-year-old, white, married secretary. She has made three outpatient visits. Her third and present husband is a department store manager; her mother lives with them; there are no children by this marriage. Her only child, a daughter from her first marriage, is married and lives nearby. Mrs. Graves is a secretary in an eight-woman group working for an executive in a chemical company, and her boss asked her, more than two months ago, to consider becoming head of that office staff.

Chief complaint and present illness. Mrs. Graves has become increasingly nervous over the last three months. Particularly, she fears that she is developing arthritis in her fingers and wrists and will not be able to continue as a secretary. She finds herself short-tempered with her mother and husband, has had crying spells that are unusual for her, has noted miscellaneous aches and pains in her head, neck, and pelvis, and fears a recurrence of a cervical carcinoma which was treated successfully eight years before. Her last pelvic examination was eight months ago; no signs of infection or recurrence were found.

Two recent changes in her life are her impending promotion at work and the deteriorating relationship with her mother. The boss at work is a highly demanding man who expects work to be done promptly and efficiently and who dispenses praise and blame without restraint.

Mrs. Graves has several concerns about the job, concerns not previously discussed with anyone. The first is that when she becomes head secretary, the boss might single her out for criticism when work is not done well instead of blaming equally the eight women. She is afraid she will not be able to bear up under such criticism. A second concern is that she lacks the assertiveness to get the other women in the office to accept her direction and supervision. A third concern is that because she has been at that office only three years, a shorter time than several of the other women, she wonders if they will be resentful and spiteful because she, rather than they, was picked for promotion.

In brief, she fears the women will resent her, not accept her supervision, and do poor work, and that she will be castigated by her boss because of it. On the positive side, she feels that she is the most competent secretary in the office, she deserves to be chosen for promotion, and she probably has the ability to handle the job if her fears don't predominate.

Her marriage of six years is stable and satisfying; only after she and her husband had been married three years and felt secure about their future did they invite her mother to come and live with them. Mrs. Graves' mother, who had been taking care of her adolescent granddaughter in Ohio, was, of course, told to bring the granddaughter along. The mother has always been a difficult person, with many idiosyncracies and criticisms, but Mrs. Graves had been able to handle her until the last two or three months. Mrs. Graves has been alternately flying off the handle with her mother or dissolving into tears when criticized; either way she feels she has lost control of a situation that formerly she could handle. She thinks this loss of control may be related to her worries about the situation at work and that her mother's intrusions may be increasing.

Past personal and family history. Mrs. Graves was born and reared in Ohio. Her father, who she does not remember, deserted the family when she was three. Her mother never remarried, and there were no siblings; the mother worked as a housekeeper. Mrs. Graves has always had a dependant-ambivalent relationship with her mother, turning to her for support during times of stress.

Her childhood and adolescence were unremarkable. Mrs. Graves always did creditable school work and put herself through two years of business college. When she was 20, she married (now, she feels, partly to get away from her mother) a man with whom she had been having an affair and by whom she became pregnant. He left while their daughter was an infant. Mrs. Graves returned to her mother, who cared for the child while she worked.

At age 26 she remarried, to a man who drank more heavily than she had realized, who was verbally and physically abusive to her and her daughter, and whom she left after two years of marriage. She moved back with her mother and recalls being quite depressed for about six months. She continued to hold a job during this time.

At age 30 she moved to Chicago, and after

some temporary jobs she started working for the chemical firm where she is now employed. Two years later she met her present husband, and after three years of dating they married.

Medical history. About a year after she arrived in Chicago, a low-grade cervical carcinoma was discovered during a routine physical examination. It was treated surgically with a subtotal hysterectomy. (The ovaries were not removed.) Mrs. Graves has been faithful in going for follow-up examinations, and there has never been any hint of a recurrence. As a result of the surgery, she is unable to bear any more children, a fact that she and her fiancé accepted with equanimity. For six months to a year after the surgery she was haunted with fears that not all the cancer had been removed or that it was recurring and so visited her doctor frequently. Since then she has been unalarmed by such fears until the last three months. Other than this carcinoma, her health has generally been good. She has never been hospitalized for any other illness.

She drinks one or two glasses of wine with dinner, does not smoke, and takes no medication other than aspirin for headaches and cold tablets for colds.

Marital history. Mrs. Graves sees her current marriage as being stable and comfortable, if not exciting. Her husband had been married once before, very unhappily. Both partners, having been burned, were looking more for security and companionship than romance, and both feel things have been going well. Mrs. Graves' daughter came to Chicago and married two years later. Mrs. Graves was very tempted to "snoop" on her daughter's marriage to make sure her daughter "wasn't making the same mistakes I did," but by and large restrained herself. The two families visit approximately once a month.

Integrative functioning. In spite of the numerous emotional stresses of her life, Mrs. Graves has shown many areas of strength. She put herself through school and has an excellent work history. She has always had a number of friends and continues to be interested in church work. She enjoys an evening of bridge. She has apparently broken off the string of unhappy marriages that has run in her family. Her abilities to love, work, and play during the past several years have been good until the last few months.

The Psychobiological Timeline

Interviews are poorly organized in most instances and go from one topic and bit of information to another. Rarely does a patient present, or does an interviewer ask for, a neatly organized chief complaint, present illness, family history, personal history, and so on.

Ultimately some order must be made out of the chaos; a psychobiological timeline can help organize the data. The therapist goes over the information he has obtained from the patient and puts it into coherent and chronological order, paying special attention to life events and psychological symptoms, using a format in which the calendar year and the patient's age fall along the left margin, life events fall into the center, and psychological events fall on the right. The timeline for the patient in Example 14-1 is given in Tables 14-1 and 14-2.

Tables 14-1 and 14-2 might be constructed after the first few interviews. In subsequent interviews, the therapist might realize that the relatively blank spaces for the years 5 to 12 and 22 to 25 will suggest questions about relationships with parents, development of social and sexual relationships, hobbies and interests, and so on, that will give a more nearly complete picture.

THE MENTAL STATUS EXAMINATION

The Mental Status Examination is the psychotherapist's equivalent of the internist's physical examination. From first contact with the patient, the therapist will be curious about the quality of psychological functioning and the patient's emo-

tions, memory, orientation, judgment, intellect, attention, concentration, and so forth.

From such information, of which the MSE may be a formal or informal component, the therapist starts making his diagnosis and a dynamic formulation. Unlike internal medicine or surgery, in which the patient usually has little voice in the final diagnosis and treatment plan, the majority of psychiatric patients work collaboratively with their therapists in deciding which are the major problem areas to be worked on and how to go about it.

The formal MSE contains several parts. A form developed by Frederick T. Melges and in use at Stanford University appears in Appendix B. Tests of intellectual function usually include serial 7s (asking the patient to subtract 7 from 100, 7 from the remainder, 7 from *that* remainder, and so on), fund of general information (recent events prominent in the news), orientation to time (month, day, and year), place (where the patient is now, for what reason), and person (the patient's recognition of family, friends, and hospital staff to whom he has been introduced). Memory can also be tested by digit span (how many random digits can the patient remember in the correct order when the examiner speaks them aloud; how many can he repeat in the order opposite to the way they were given) and by naming sequences of events most people can be expected to know (for instance, the names of the last four Presidents of the United States in either chronological or reverse chronological order). Judgment and ability to abstract can be tested by asking the patient to interpret proverbs or solve a simple verbal problem (such as what he would do if he were seated in a crowded theatre and saw a fire start; or what he would do if he found a stamped, addressed letter lying on the sidewalk).

The interviewer will also note the quality and tempo of the patient's thought processes: do his thoughts seem to race; are they logically connected or do they fragment; can he stick to an essential point; does he perseverate on a single topic even when a shift to others seems to be called for; are

TABLE 14-1: Life-long Psychobiological Timeline

Year	Age	Life Event	Psychological Event
1932	0	Born in Ohio; no sibling	
33	1		
34	2		
35	3	Father deserts family; mother works as house-keeper	
36	4		
37	5		
38	6		
39	7		
1940	8		
41	9		
42	10		
43	11		
44	12		
45	13	Starts high school	
46	14		
47	15		
48	16		
49	17	Graduates from high school	
1950	18	Starts business school	
51	19		
52	20	Finishes business school; marries	Marriage in part to escape mother
53	21	Daughter born; husband deserts; patient works; mother watches child	
54	22		
55	23		
56	24		
57	25		
58	26	Marriage 2. Husband drinks, abusive	
59	27		
1960	28	Patient leaves husband; returns to mother	Depressed for six months
61	29		
62	30	Moves to Chicago; starts with present firm	
63	31	Meets fiancé	
64	32	Cervical carcinoma found; treated	Cancer phobia for 1 year
65	33		
66	34	Marriage 3. Stable to present	
67	35		
68	36		
69	37	Mother and daughter come to Chicago	
1970	38		
71	39	Daughter marries	Tempted to "snoop" on daughter
72	40		
73	41	Promotion suggested; mother more intrusive	Present symptoms begin

TABLE 14-2: Recent Psychobiological Timeline

1973, age 41

Month	Life Event	Psychological Event
January	Mother seems more intrusive	Patient becomes irritated, depressed
February	Boss first suggests promotion	Discusses with husband; initial enthusiasm
March	Is prepared to accept promotion; mother's behavior persists	Anxiety, depression; phobias start and become more severe
April	Boss asks for decision	Applies for psychiatric evaluation

his thoughts so slowed down that he pauses a long time before answering a question and then gives a minimal answer in a subdued voice?

Similarly, the interviewer notes the patient's mood and emotional state: is he happy, sad, depressed, suspicious, guilt-ridden, angry, elated, and so on? Are the contents of his thought and his mood congruent or incongruent; that is, if he is preoccupied with thoughts of death and destruction, does he laugh, weep, or merely speak in a leaden monotone? Do his thoughts and mood seem appropriate to the occasion; that is, is he cheerfully recounting major business deals after having been brought in by a family who fears bankruptcy because of his impulsive spending; do voices tell him that this is not a hospital but rather a FBI headquarters; does he believe himself to be a sinner so awful that he does not deserve anyone's concern or attention?

The interviewer also looks for signs of physical and physiological disorder: has the patient been eating and sleeping adequately, or does he look fatigued and as if he had lost weight; is there alcohol on his breath; does his state of consciousness fluctuate from attentiveness to lapses into revery or somnolence?

For patients who come into the emergency room in acute distress, often the interviewer will want to go through a formal MSE to use as an evaluation of the current situation and as a base line against which future variation can be measured. However, in the outpatient clinic, with a patient whose intelligence, thought content and tempo, judgment, memory, and mood seem to be quite intact and appropriate to the situation (which means the vast majority of patients at most outpatient clinics), going through a formal MSE is not required, even though the interviewer will be conducting an informal MSE as he talks with the patient. There is little point, for instance, in asking a moderately depressed 30-year-old patient who seems clearly to be no more than neurotic about who is President of the United States or in asking him to subtract serial 7s from 100. Such questions

serve better when the interviewer doubts the patient's capacity to respond to them. Still, there are at least two lines of inquiry, those about suicide potential and schizophrenia, that deserve special mention. Each of these can be very sensitive issues for patients, and inexperienced therapists are often reluctant to inquire about them.

As we described in the chapter on the suicidal patient (Chapter 2), such inquiries go more smoothly if a graded series of questions is used, starting with the least anxiety-provoking. By the time the interview has gotten to the crucial questions, the patient will feel more comfortable in giving an honest, if painful, answer.

Suicide Potential

We shall elaborate on material presented before. To ask the depressed patient rather abruptly in the early part of the first interview, "Are you thinking about committing suicide?" may elicit a false denial. However, if questions about depression proceed in an orderly fashion, a truthful "Yes" may emerge, and then the patient and therapist can pursue how best to manage the suicidal impulses. Following is a set of statements that can be used by the therapist; each presupposes an affirmative answer to the one preceeding it:

1. You say you sometimes feel sad and blue?

2. How do you feel when you wake up in the morning?

3. Do you often burst into tears over trifles or blow up at people when you know you should not?

4. Have you felt so blue recently that you have wondered whether it is worth it to go on living?

5. I suppose, then, that you have at least thought about harming yourself or taking your own life; most people who have felt as blue as you do have thought about it.

6. Have you made any actual plans to harm yourself — saved up pills or razor blades or something of this sort?

7. How much of a danger do you think there is that you would actually go through with it?

The answers to these questions will enable the therapist, using the guidelines described in Chapter 3, to formulate treatment plans.

Schizophrenia

If the patient starts talking about hallucinations and delusions right away, a delicate serious set of questions is not necessary to elicit other signs of schizophrenia. However, if these phenomena are *unaccompanied* by a thought disorder, the patient may well be suffering from a toxic psychosis. If the therapist suspects he is dealing with a schizophrenic patient and the patient does not show many initial overt signs, he can ask these kinds of questions:

1. Have you had any strange, unusual, or unreal-seeming experiences lately? What were they like?

2. Do your thoughts sometimes become so strong that they almost sound like voices?

3. Has your body seemed to change recently?

4. Have you had trouble with your thoughts? Do they seem disorganized, strange, or difficult to follow? Does it sometimes feel like your thoughts arē being taken away from you?

5. Have you had any thoughts or experiences which, although part of you knows they are unreal, still seem very real to another part of you, such as hearing voices?

6. Have you thought you might be having a nervous breakdown or going crazy?

With some patients the therapist is quite sure of the diagnosis of schizophrenia intuitively, even though the patient may not show any clear psychotic signs. At such times the therapist may save both himself and the patient quite a bit of time by asking, "How long have you been hearing voices?" (Not "Do you hear voices?") If the patient responds, "For a couple of years, I guess," the therapist can then ask about what the voices say, whether the patient recognizes any of the people speaking to him, and so forth.

Even though a MSE report is found in the middle of most case summaries and presentations, the therapist begins such an examination informally at first contact, whether over the phone or in person. The MSE for a seriously disturbed, e.g., psychotic, patient usually will be written up in a much more detailed fashion than that of a neurotic patient who is not in a grave crisis. (The MSE for a psychotic patient is given in Example 14-2.) The MSE for neurotic patients is usually much briefer. The one given in Example 14-1 (Mrs. Graves) is exaggeratedly long both for purposes of contrast with Example 14-2 and in anticipation of the diagnosis, dynamic formulation, and treatment plans for the same patient, which will be given later in this chapter.

> *Example 14-2.* John was a drop-in patient at the clinic. His chief complaint is that colleagues are "out to get me." He is the sole informant and his reliability is questionable, as shown by delusional thinking described below. He presents himself as a 30-year-old, white, male, graduate student of chemistry. He is neatly dressed, well groomed, fully bearded, wears eye glasses, and appears to be his stated age.
>
> *Perception.* He is attentive, alert, and cooperative. He is oriented to time, place, and person; he denies illusions, unusual perceptions, and hallucinations but reports feelings of alarming depersonalization.
>
> *Intellection.* Intelligence was not formally tested, but his appears to be in the above-average range. Past and recent memory are intact except for some mild temporal confusion concerning the few hours preceding the interview. His ability to abstract, his fund of

common knowledge, and his situational judgment are normal.

Thought processes. His speech is of generally appropriate volume and rate, except for marked pauses of several seconds at a time. He reports his thoughts to be racing at times and blocked at others. Although he is generally coherent, his thoughts are marked by considerable circumstantiality, ambivalence, tangentiality, and some perseveration.

Thought content. His thought content is marked by obsessive, fixed ideas and delusions regarding the persecutory intent of his colleagues. He reports ideas of influence, reference, and personal passivity but not thought broadcasting.

Emotions. In general, John's affect is appropriately modulated without much anxiety during the interview but is marked with occasional outbursts of inappropriate laughter with little apparent provocation and intermediate moments of apparent depression. He reports feeling relaxed but very depressed, although without suicidal feelings at present. He does report sporadic periods of severely suicidal depressive feelings in the past as recently as three months ago, marked with foiled attempts at suicide by fast driving and buying a gun. He denies angry feelings at present but reports recent anger with the intent to burn the home of a colleague.

Actions. His behavior remained placid throughout with occasional appropriate gesturing. His eye contact, however, varied from avoidance of the interviewer to brief periods of fixed staring. He demonstrated no observable tics, posturing, or mannerisms.

Impression. Although he became settled once he was established in the interview, John gives the impression of one on the brink of a more dramatic decompensation, possibly acute paranoid schizophrenia. (Voluntary admission to the inpatient service took place after the interview.)

Mrs. Graves (cont'd.). Mrs. Graves is a reliable informant who appeared moderately anxious at the beginning of the first session but has been noticeably more relaxed since then.

Perception. Normal level of alertness and accuracy.

Intellection. Appears to be of somewhat above-average intelligence, perhaps an IQ of 120 to 130, with a good fund of general knowledge.

Thought processes. Normal in tempo, rhythm, and organization.

Thought content. Normal and appropriate to matters under consideration, although some excessive preoccupation with health (fears arthritis in her fingers, which would interfere with her job as a secretary; concerned about recurrence of cervical carcinoma successfully treated eight years ago, with no evidence of recurrence).

Emotions. Anxious and a little depressed, congruent with concerns about her job and her health. No suggestion of suicidal preoccupation. Related warmly to interviewer and was pleased to accept recommendation of four to six evaluation sessions.

Actions. Somewhat stiff and closed in at the beginning of first interview; warmer and with normal facial expressions and gesticulations as the interview proceeded.

Impression. Intelligent, somewhat anxious woman with some realistic and some neurotic concerns about her job and health. She looks positively toward four to six evaluation sessions as a probable prelude for referral to a private psychiatrist for further therapy.

PSYCHIATRIC DIAGNOSIS

General Remarks

The ways in which psychiatric diagnoses have been made over the years, and the uses to which they have been put, have stirred up much controversy. Psychiatric diagnoses have been attacked on many grounds, all of which have some truth to them: they are dehumanizing; they are moralistic; they are unreliable, and psychiatrists have a hard time agreeing with each other; diagnoses can be used as instruments of social control for disapproved-of behavior; and so on.

But along with the misuses of diagnoses, the many ways they can help treatment must be considered, and it is on this constructive use of psychiatric diagnosis that this discussion will rest. We shall first explore some current issues and practices of contemporary psychiatric diagnostic formulations; then we shall apply these principles to the treatment of Mrs. Graves.

The Semantic Jungle of Psychiatric Diagnosis

The purpose of the labeling process is to imply, in an economical fashion, a large number of the attributes of the thing labeled. Thus the label "elephant" implies a huge, grey mammal with a trunk, and so on. Psychiatric diagnosis has grown into a semantic jungle in an attempt to place meaningful labels on emotional, mental, or behavioral phenomena. Szasz has pointed this out acutely in his writings.[2] But whatever semantic games psychiatry has been playing, recurrent disorders of psychological function do exist, Szasz notwithstanding, as any therapist with experience with a floridly psychotic person can testify. Such a person is crazy, whether or not the interviewer calls him, among other terms, "sick" or "schizophrenic," or thinks hospitals and medical practitioners do or do not have exclusive rights and responsibility for treatment. Likewise, someone who becomes profoundly slowed, filled with excessive guilt, and is utterly hopeless about an existence that others see as potentially rich, is depressed, whatever view is held about allowing him to take his own life, administering electroshock, and so forth.

One of the greatest areas of confusion in psychiatric diagnosis is the illogical confusion of levels of abstraction implied in the diagnosis. In common speech, if asked to pick the illogical or incongruent word from the series "chair, baseball, tomorrow, microbe, spaghetti," most people would quickly pick *tomorrow;* all but *tomorrow* are tangible things; *tomorrow* is a temporal abstraction on a different level from the others. Among psychiatric labels, if asked to pick the incongruent member of "anxiety, depression, sorrow, enuresis, elation," most would pick *enuresis;* all the others describe a relatively circumscribed mood state; enuresis implies a specific behavior. Yet, if an enuretic patient became depressed and the therapist had to make a single diagnosis, he would be hard put to describe the patient as just *depressive reaction* or just *enuresis.* Both are necessary to a reasonable description; neither is sufficient. And they are on different levels of abstraction.

To make some order of the chaos, therapists make use of a dynamic formulation in which they pay attention to the several factors of distant and recent states of the organism and for which the official diagnosis stands as a sign. To be able to do this intelligently, however, the therapist must categorize the most frequently used psychiatric labels into their levels of semantic abstraction. First we shall discuss briefly the official nomenclature of the American Psychiatric Association; then we shall examine some unofficial formulations before applying these principles to the case of Mrs. Graves.

American Psychiatric Association Formulations. The American Psychiatric Assocation issued its *Diagnostic and Statistical Manual of Mental Disorders-I (DSM-I)* in 1952; *DSM-II* appeared in 1968.[3] In *DSM-I,* many functional diagnoses ended with the word "reaction," e.g., "psychoneurotic reaction, depressive reaction." This introduced a sometimes gratuitous idea that the reaction involved was to identifiable and controllable events and therefore could be undone. For an acute depressive reaction, such is often the case; for a patient who suffered for ten years with schizophrenia, hebephrenic type, the term "schizophrenic *reaction,* hebephrenic type," hardly adds much.

DSM-II does away with calling everything a *reaction* of one sort or another, preserving the concept of reaction to identifiable external and internal stresses in the category of "transient situational disturbances," with such subcategories as "adjustment reaction to adult life." What used to be "psychoneurotic reactions" in *DSM-I* are now "neuroses" in *DSM-II*. Neurosis implies a chronic impairment of function because of unresolved intrapsychic conflicts. Where, then, is the relatively healthy person who suffers a major loss and undergoes a serious depressive reaction? In the days of *DSM-I,* "psychoneurotic reaction, depressive reaction" might have been appropriate. But in *DSM-II* the equivalent diagnosis is "depressive neurosis," with its implication of years of chronic depression before or after the loss. Yet simply to say "adjustment reaction of adult life" carries none of the flavor of depression and grief that the patient shows. No system of nomenclature is without its faults, as the contrast between *DSM-I* and *DSM-II* demonstrates. *DSM-II* is a distinct improvement over its predecessor. *DSM-II* can be used *as a beginning,* not as the end, in classification and diagnosis. The variety of colorful and descriptive words and phrases that exist must be preserved; "help-rejecting complainer" will never become part of the official nomenclature, but it tells a lot about a prevailing life style.

In the following material, some of the concepts will agree with the criteria and strategies of *DSM-II;* some will not. Tolerance for ambiguity and contradiction is a prerequisite for therapists, and this tolerance can be sorely tested when they deal with the topic of psychiatric diagnoses.

Levels of Abstraction. Part of the confusion that exists is because psychiatric diagnoses fall along different levels of abstraction, but the characteristics of the various levels are not always kept clearly in mind. Certain diagnoses, for instance, imply a long-standing set of difficulties or conflicts

that are likely to continue for months and years under natural circumstances, e.g., diagnoses of neurosis, of character or personality types and disorders, and so on.

Other diagnoses describe a symptom, e.g., "anxiety reaction," or a syndrome, e.g., a collection of symptoms and signs that naturally seems to fall together, such as a "depressive reaction," in which the emotional tenor of the conflict is demonstrated but its duration is not considered.

Still other diagnoses may tell the stage of life in which the patient is having difficulty, e.g., "adult reaction," that it is caused by situational stresses, e.g., "situational or adjustment reaction." Or there may be inferences about early life experiences that render a patient vulnerable to later stresses, e.g., "oral stage deprivation as a precursor to depression in adulthood." Some diagnostic terms reflect their psychoanalytic heritage, e.g., "anal character"; others come from the descriptive nomenclature of neuropsychiatrists and alienists who were prominent in the nineteenth century, e.g., "dementia praecox." Some diagnoses (many of which are fortunately no longer in popular use) reflect moralistic judgments, e.g., "constitutional psychopathic inferiority," although subtler forms of moralism are certainly still present.

How then to sort out matters? The diagnoses, official and informal, commonly used in several psychiatric clinics have been reviewed, and some of the common axes along which they fall extracted. What will be presented, then, is an informal review of current practices, not an ideal form of how psychiatric diagnoses should be made and used, although many in the field are trying to do just that.[4,5] Eight major sorts of diagnoses seem to be made. The reader, after reflecting on the diagnostic practices he is familiar with, may be able to identify others. The first to be described is the symptom-syndrome diagnosis.

1. Symptom-syndrome labels. Such a diagnosis is made if a specific set of psychological symptoms predominates. The symptoms are usually intrapsychic, with some conscious concern

about them. From the nature of the symptoms, the syndrome to which they belong is inferred. There may or may not be implications about the personality type, and temporality is poorly delimited. The symptoms are usually defined by a predominant emotional state or a particular psychological picture.

An example of a symptom-syndrome diagnosis based on emotional symptoms is that of "depression," in which the syndrome of depression, sadness, psychomotor retardation, difficulty in sleeping, early morning awakening, appetite disturbance, and so on occur. Sometimes a symptom-syndrome diagnosis is based more on behavior and thinking than on feelings, e.g., "obsessive-compulsive neurosis" or "conversion reaction."

2. Character and personality labels. Some psychiatrists use the terms *character* and *personality* quite differently; others use them almost interchangeably. Such confusion results in part from the intermixing of connotations applied from common speech to these terms with the somewhat more specific usages coming from psychoanalysis, anthropology, and sociology. A lucid review of these etymological issues can be found in Michaels.[6]

In general, character is seen as one component of a broader entity: personality. Psychoanalytic writers in particular have elucidated a number of character types arising from certain childhood constellations of instinct, conflict, and conflict resolution. Such conflict resolutions, appropriate and adaptive in childhood, when carried into adulthood, are often inappropriate, limiting and maladaptive. The names for such character structures may either describe the current manifestations of the character type, e.g., "compulsive character," or the stage of psychoanalytic psychosexual development in which the primary conflicts arose, e.g., "anal character."

Another common use of character diagnoses is to describe a prevailing way of meeting life, or a prevailing set of psychological defenses,

where there is no definite link with a psychosexual stage conflict, although some suggestions about earlier difficulties may be present, e.g., "schizoid character," "borderline character," and "cyclothymic character."

The term "personality," as used in psychiatric diagnosis, is more frequently connected to persons whose behavior bothers others. It is not always used in this way, but seems to be so used more frequently than the term "character." People who act impulsively and without regard for the feelings of others or the rules of society are more frequently referred to as having a "personality disorder" than as having a "character disorder," although, again, both terms are used.

Both terms connote deep and enduring patterns of behavior, thinking, feeling, and modes of dealing with others that have been present for a long time and are likely to persist. Both imply that many of the conflicts and much of the motive energy involved in character or personality development are largely unconscious, although they may be made conscious through uncovering psychotherapy.

3. Neurosis and disorder labels. Just as are character and personality, the terms "neurosis" and "disorder" are used interchangeably by some and as distinctly different concepts by others. When distinctions are made, the neurotic patient is one who seems distressed by his symptoms or his failure in adaptation; the patient with a disorder may or may not be hurting, or he may be more unhappy with society's reaction to him than with his own evaluation of himself. The neurotic patient is often seen as inhibited, overcontrolled, and unable to act because of his limitations (Hamlet); the patient with a disorder may discharge anxiety and tension too quickly and without adequate reflection into action (for example, Ronald, the violent patient in Chapter 4). It is common to see diagnoses of *personality disorder* and rare to see diagnoses of *character neurosis* applied to persons who are

impulsive, take drugs, or violate the rules of society without any apparent pangs of conscience, e.g., "impulsive personality disorder," "sociopathic personality disorder," and so on. A grouping of current, official diagnoses of neuroses and many of their related character and defense features is found in Table 14-3.

These confusing and sometimes contradictory uses of these terms lead to the following four logical possibilities:

	Neurosis	Disorder
Character	Character neurosis	Character disorder
Personality	Personality neurosis (never used)	Personality disorder

Character neurosis would most likely be applied to an inhibited, middle-class, law-abiding patient whose symptoms bother him. *Character disorder* might be applied to the same patient, or to one who is less inhibited and more prone to willful behavior or who is less upset by his emotional conflicts and incapacities. *Personality disorder* would most likely be applied to someone whose psyche might be viewed as more deeply flawed, who shows poor control over impulses, and who seems indifferent to the needs of others.

4. Organ system labels. A fourth level of abstraction is that in which a particular organ system of the body shows organic changes, and emotional factors are thought to play a part in the production of such changes. Such labels have no implications as to basic personality types, location of conflict, or temporality, although some authors have sought to make such implications. An example is that of a peptic ulcer coming on at the time of emotional stress, e.g., a "psychophysiological gastrointestinal disorder."

5. Situational labels. A fifth level of abstraction implies that whatever the symptomatology, the acute distress reflects a *current situation,* e.g., "adjustment reaction to adult life." This type of label may be used with any of the foregoing diagnoses.

6. Life-stage labels. A sixth level, closely tied in with the fifth, labels the time in the individual's life when the symptoms appear, e.g., childhood, adolescence, and adulthood.

7. Behavioral trait labels. In the seventh category, a conglomerate and miscellaneous group of labels is concerned with certain behavioral traits. Persons showing these traits are not thought necessarily to resemble others bearing the same trait in terms of underlying character structure, although such similarities probably occur more often than chance expectancy would demand. Such traits include alcohol and drug addictions, sexual deviations, and enuresis. The labels tell us no more than that the individual has had one or probably several episodes in his life during which he showed the trait or behavior pattern.

8. Etiological labels. The eighth level of abstraction is that in which etiology for the appearance of psychopathology is implied. First, genetic statements of early life experiences suggest predisposition toward the current symptomatology, e.g., early oral deprivation as a precursor for later depressions. Such statements often indicate the stage of psychosexual development affected and its subsequent inadequate resolution. The second of these levels of etiologic statement is the assessment of current threats to harmony that have caused the current eruption of symptoms, e.g., impending graduation from high school precipitates an anxiety state.

To summarize thus far, the categories or sets of levels of abstraction commonly used in psychiatric labeling are

1. Symptom-syndrome labels, e.g. "depression"*

2. Characterological and personality labels

*Beware the three uses of "depression." It can refer to a symptom, a syndrome, or a character type.

TABLE 14-3. Correlations of Levels of Abstraction Organized around Current Official Psychoneurotic Reaction Nomenclature

A	B		C	D	E	F	Characterological Labels	
DSM-II Titles and Code Numbers							G	H
Title	Code	DSM-I Titles	Former or Similar Labels	Symptoms: What the Patient Complains Of	Signs: Behavioral or Mental Traits Observed by the Examiner	Primary Defense Mechanisms	Level of Psychosexual Fixation	Miscellaneous Other Comments
1. Anxiety neurosis	300.00	1. Anxiety reaction	1. Anxiety reaction	1. Nervousness, jitteriness, feelings of impending disaster, clutched in pit of the stomach, insomnia, disturbance in eating, diarrhea, frequent urination	1. Fine tremor at rest, quavering voice, speech interrupted, jumpiness, sweating of brow and hands, hyperventilation	1. Failure of repression in face of threat to current adaptation	1. None specific	
2. Hysterical neurosis, dissociative type	300.14	2. Dissociative reaction	2. Multiple personality; fugue state	2. Inexplicable losses of consciousness; ego-alien behavior with partial or complete amnesia	2. No neurological evidence of disease; immature, primitive, magical thinking and relating	2. Massive repression and denial	2. None specific	
3. Hysterical neurosis, conversion type	300.13	3. Conversion reaction	3. Conversion hysteria	3. Inexplicable loss or alteration of function of voluntary nervous and/or musculoskeletal systems	3. No organic changes in area affected; often la belle indifference, immature, histrionic character, narcissism, opportunity for secondary gain	3. Repression, denial somatization, conversion	3. Phallic-Oedipal, with oral hidden features	3. Frequently in hysterical characters

				Symptoms	Diagnostic confirmation	Defense mechanisms	Fixation level	Notes
4. Phobic neurosis	300.20	4. Phobic reaction	4. Anxiety hysteria; psychasthenia	4. Irrational fear of specific object or situation	4. Propensity to afflict women; anxiety at prospect of phobogenic situation; recognition of irrationality of fear	4. Repression, symbolization and displacement to symbolically similar but realistically innocuous situation representing primary unconscious conflict	4. Anal, phallic	
5. Obsessive compulsive neurosis	300.30	5. Obsessive-compulsive reaction	5. Obsessive and/or compulsive; psychasthenia	5. Unending repetition of unpleasant thought or act	5. Ruminating, cautious and overqualified speech, fastidiousness, stubbornness, magic rituals	5. Displacement, symbolization, isolation, condensation, undoing, reaction formation	5. Anal a. Expulsive b. Retentive	
6. Depressive neurosis	300.40	6. Depressive reaction	6. Reactive depression (if strong fatigue component, neurasthenia)	6. Sadness, worthlessness, guilt, weariness, misc. aches, pains, gastrointestinal troubles, sleep disturbance	6. Confirmation of symptoms; psychomotor retardation, with or without agitation, suicidal thinking	6. Incorporation and introjection of ambivalently regarded object or goal: turning of hostility on self	6. Oral dependent	6. Depressive character
7. Neurasthenic neurosis	300.50	7. Psychoneurotic reaction, other	7. Neurasthenia	7. Chronic weakness, easy fatiguability, exhaustion	7. Confirmation of symptoms with *pronounced* psychomotor retardation	7. As in (6)	7. Oral dependent	7. Often is a "depressive equivalent"
8. Depersonalization neurosis	300.60	8. Psychoneurotic reaction, other	8. Depersonalization syndrome	8. Feelings of unreality, estrangement from self, body, surroundings	8. Confirmation of symptoms	8. Repression, denial, isolation	8. None specific: most frequent in "repressed" or schizoid characters	8. May be part of prodrome of schizophrenia
9. Hypochondriacal neurosis	300.70	9. Psychoneurotic reaction, other	9. Hypochondriasis	9. Preoccupation with presumed but unsubstantiated defects in bodily functioning	9. Confirmation of symptoms; suggestions of predisposition to depression as in (6), or to neurasthenia as in (7)	9. Often as in (6)	9. Often oral dependent	9. Often is a "depressive equivalent"

(a) Extended psychological symptoms, e.g., "compulsive character"
(b) Level of psychosexual fixation or immaturity, e.g., "anal retentive character"
(c) Miscellaneous other characterological labels, not implying (a) or (b), e.g., "schizoid character," "cyclothymic character"
(d) Personality labels, e.g., "impulsive personality"
3. Neurosis and disorder labels, e.g., "compulsive character neurosis," "sociopathic personality disorder"
4. Organ system labels, e.g., "psychophysiological gastrointestinal disorder"
5. Situational labels, e.g., *adjustment reaction* of adult life"
6. Life-stage labels, e.g., "adjustment reaction of *adult life*"
7. Miscellaneous behavioral trait labels, e.g., "alcohol addiction," "sexual deviation"
8. Etiological labels
(a) Genetic, e.g., "oral deprivation"
(b) Current, e.g., "recent loss"

An Attempt at Correlation of Diagnoses of Neuroses

In its category of neurosis *DSM-II* describes nine entities. Many have been known by similar names in general use for the past fifty years, or they have been known under other names. In Table 14-3, the current official names, the official names in *DSM-I*, and names in popular use are given in columns A to C.

Symptoms (what the patient complains of) are described in column D, and signs (what the examiner discerns) correlated with those symptoms are given in column E.

Psychoanalytic investigations have demonstrated that certain conflicts and constellations of impulses and defenses are commonly associated with these neuroses; the most prominent of these are given in column F (for those unfamiliar with the

psychoanalytic mechanisms of defense, a concise and elegant description of them is in Anna Freud's *The Ego and the Mechanisms of Defense*[7]).

The level of psychosexual fixation thought to be central to a given neurosis, when known, is given in column G. Miscellaneous comments about these neuroses appear in column H.

Diagnosis and Treatment Implications

How can these diagnostic considerations be used in treatment? After making as many official and unofficial diagnoses of varying levels of abstraction and inference on a given patient as seems warranted from evaluation interviews, we have a series of statements about what seems not to be working well for a patient. The diagnostic nomenclature is biased in the direction of identifying pathology, i.e., what is wrong, and it is hoped that some evaluations of strengths and what is working right will also be included. Certainly assessments of what is working right, or might work well in the future, should be part of the dynamic formulation, as shown in the next section, but they should also appear as part of the initial diagnostic statements.

Certain diagnoses have clear implications for treatment, often for milieu and somatic treatment. A diagnosis of profound depression implies to most therapists treatment with antidepressant medication or electroshock, and probably also implies hospitalization for suicidal or incapacitated patients. Schizophrenia usually implies antipsychotic medication as well as psychotherapy, manic-depressive illness, manic phase, almost always implies hospitalization, the use of phenothiazines initially, and lithium carbonate for long-term management.

Of what use are the diagnoses of less dramatic cases, of the kinds of neurotic conditions described in Table 14-3? They help therapists to decide which of the presenting symptoms (usually some combination of anxiety, fear, and depression) they can seek to relieve through psychotherapy (sometimes with the help of medication). An understanding of character structure can help the therapist to decide how to approach the patient, whether he intends to support an unconscious that, although flawed, has its strengths and is not a likely object for change, or whether he hopes to work with the patient in arriving at basic changes and growth.

Application to Mrs. Graves. The therapist is dictating an intake summary on Mrs. Graves and has come to the section on diagnoses and their implications for treatment.

1. Symptom-syndrome diagnoses. Neurotic anxiety and depression, phobic preoccupation with health and work. These are responses to situational stresses at work and home and the patient will most probably benefit from the therapist's listening to previously unexpressed concerns about these situations. The patient's ego strength and character structure are undoubtedly strong enough to handle and assimilate the emotion that would come with such expression.

2, 3. Characterological and neurosis diagnoses. Somewhat compulsive character, relatively healthy considering early life experiences, with compulsive defenses (ability to work) a definite source of strength. Ambivalent-dependent attitudes toward women (mother) and vulnerability to sadomasochistic involvement with men (father, first two husbands). These traits and attitudes are largely unconsciously being carried over into, and contaminating her ability to deal with, the current situations.

   Patient's character structure is relatively fixed and extensive change is not practical, but therapy should allow an opportunity to sort out these displacements and distortions from the past so that she can react more realistically to the current situation. Support for her characterological strengths should also prove useful.

4. Organ system diagnoses. Probably none applicable, although fears about the recurrence of carcinoma can be checked by a specialist.

5, 6. Situational and life-stage diagnoses. Adjustment reaction of adult life associated with impending promotion at work and increasing intrusiveness of mother. One of the first tasks of therapy will be to help her come to a decision about the promotion and to help her find better ways of coping with her mother.

7. Behavioral trait diagnoses. None.

8. Etiological diagnoses. Current stresses are symbolic of unresolved unconscious conflict that make Mrs. Graves more vulnerable to them. The resultant anxiety has been displaced into concerns about health. By helping Mrs. Graves see the connections between past and present, her anxiety about handling the present should be reduced. Also, her ability to accept support from benign males (husband) suggests that transference to a male therapist will be positive and will be a factor in improvement.

Thus these diagnostic labels provide a shorthand way of beginning to understand the dynamic issues of the patient's problems and some suggestions to the therapist as to where he might intervene and where he should not intervene. By weaving together recent history, past history, the MSE, and diagnostic impressions into a relatively coherent whole, the therapist constructs the dynamic formulation, the subject of the following section.

THE DYNAMIC FORMULATION AND TREATMENT PLANNING

After a therapist has had a few or several interviews with a patient, he should formulate the case. The two major purposes of the formulation are (1) to come to understand why this person is having this kind of distress at this time in his life, and (2) to see what kind of treatment should be offered.

After several interviews, the therapist draws together his disparate sets of data — observations, history, interview interactions, diagnostic impressions, hunches, and intuitions — into a dynamic formulation. A dynamic formulation is like the last movement of Franck's Symphony in D minor, in which major and minor themes from the first two movements are blended harmoniously with those of the last. For the psychiatric patient, the themes are those of the presenting picture; the development of the presenting problem; childhood and family history; the resultant character structure; assessments of strengths, interests, and resources; intrapsychic stresses and areas of vulnerability; prevailing environmental stresses; and response to current stresses (current psychological functioning). The dynamic formulation should lead logically to ideas about treatment.

The dynamic formulation and the treatment ideas that flow from it for Mrs. Graves are shown in the following example. Much of it has been anticipated and presented in the description of the patient's history and her MSE and diagnoses and should be viewed as a continuation of her case summary.

Mrs. Graves (cont'd.), Dynamic Formulation and Treatment Planning. The major external stresses for Mrs. Graves have been the impending promotion and the difficulties with her mother. The promotion has stirred up fears of her not being able to gain the respect of the women in her office, just as she had always had difficulties in gaining respect from her mother by being assertive. Rather, she had to take a passive-dependent position with her. It has also stirred up fears of another male's treating her sadistically, as she has been treated in the past.

Her first responses to these stresses were anxiety and depression. More recently these anxieties had been transformed and displaced into concerns about her body. If she has arthritis in her fingers, her boss could hardly expect her to manage a major secretarial job. Similarly, if her general health is impaired (e.g., cancer, headaches, miscellaneous aches and pains), her boss cannot expect too much of her, her mother will have to treat her as if she were an invalid, and she can withdraw to the passive-helpless position that has worked with her mother in the past. (Among her other ailments, she complained of a pain in the neck. Is this a bodily metaphor on how she is feeling about her mother now?)

There are many strengths in the situation. She is in a stable and supportive marriage. She wants to take the promotion, even though she fears it. She wants to improve the relationship with her mother. Her work history and ability to cope with stress over the years is impressive.

Treatment planning. Treatment, along with her wish to succeed, should work. She should be supported through an exploration of her underlying fears, ventilation, and clarification of the distortions and contaminations from the past, e.g., the women in her office are not her mother and are not likely to react as she fears; her boss is not a cruel man, he is, in fact, a fair, albeit critical man. Her conviction that she does have the abilities to do the job should also be supported.

Her husband sounds like a potential resource she has not enlisted. She has been reluctant to let him know how much her mother has been getting on her nerves, but he sounds as if he would give her a sympathetic hearing. This possibility should be explored further. Mrs. Graves has had previous experience with having to define limits for her mother, and ways in which these limits can be reinstituted should be explored. Probably it would be best to start setting such limits in relatively less charged areas to see if her mother gets the message early. In this way it is possible that emotional confrontations can be avoided.

Because Mrs. Graves' character structure is relatively set and she is not motivated particularly for deep personal exploration or change, use of dynamic material should be restricted to giving her a better understanding of her current stresses. Because of this, reality-oriented therapy, one session per week, for several weeks (probably eight to twelve), seems feasible. If painful anxiety, depression, or insomnia persist, medication can be prescribed. But psychotherapy itself may sufficiently relieve her distress and promote improved functioning. If this happens, it should give Mrs. Graves a stronger sense of having "done it myself," without having had to rely on pills.

The formulation and treatment plan shown here was prepared after Mrs. Graves' third evaluation session. She brought the same intelligence and determination to her psychiatric "evaluation" that she had shown in other areas of her life; evaluation rapidly became treatment. After four sessions, her symptoms had markedly diminished as she came to understand them better.

Mrs. Graves (cont'd.). In the fourth session, as Mrs. Graves was proudly telling how she had recently quietly refused her mother's suggestion of the proper perfume to wear, she had a sudden twinge of pain in her neck. Prepared for the appearance of the metaphor, her therapist suggested, "Step on a crack and break your mother's back?" Mrs. Graves nodded, saying it was hard to escape the feeling of a lifetime and describing in detail the combination of affection, irritation, dependence, and so on that she felt for her mother.

In the fifth session she said her symptoms had disappeared almost entirely. She felt confident that she would be able to handle the situation in her office. She and her mother were getting on much better, and her husband supported her when she needed it. She wondered if more treatment was necessary, as did her therapist. They agreed to stop there, with the therapist asking her to call him in a few months to let him know how things were going, or to call sooner if she felt the need.

Four months later she called to report the return of some of the symptoms. At the scheduled appointment the therapist reviewed with her some of the events since their last contact. Mrs. Graves had accepted the promotion, and the situation was generally going

well. With one exception the women in her office accepted her supervision, and she felt she could tolerate an uneasy relationship with the one woman who seemed not to like her. Her boss seemed generally pleased with the way things were going.

At home her husband had proved quite supportive in dealing with her mother. He had not appreciated the depth of Mrs. Graves' concerns, and her mother had been more responsive than anticipated.

How then to account for the return of the symptoms? Her fingers had started hurting again. Mrs. Graves said the thought had crossed her mind several times over the last few months, "What if things don't continue to work out, and my therapist isn't around to see me?" They discussed this for a while, and it became apparent to both that the pain in the fingers had been minimal, that the pain was Mrs. Graves' way of asking about the therapist's availability. The session was visible proof of it, and, as there did not seem to be much else to talk about, the session ended a little early.

Six months later, as the therapist was planning to leave the area, he called Mrs. Graves to let her know and to inquire how she was doing. She was satisfied with things, both at home and at work, and did not anticipate the need for further therapy. She was happy to take down the name of a therapist in the area, should anything come up in the future.

In this, as in most cases, the therapist alternates between activity and passivity, if actively listening to a patient can be considered passive. He must listen carefully as he hears about the distress that has brought the patient in for treatment, and he must listen carefully as he learns about those recent and remote events which make the patient's distress more understandable. He must actively seek to place this information, along with the results of his observations (the MSE, intuitions, and responses to his questions) into the coherent framework of the dynamic formulation, and if he has been diligent and thoughtful, he can offer treatment that will be both sympathetic and rational.

REFERENCES

1. Menninger, Karl A.: *A Manual for Psychiatric Case Study*, 2nd ed., Grune & Stratton, New York, 1962.

2. Szasz, Thomas: *The Myth of Mental Illness*, Harper, New York, 1961.

3. American Psychiatric Association: *Diagnostic and Statistical Manual of Mental Disorders-II*, Washington, D.C., 1968.

4. World Health Organization: *Report of the Sixth Seminar on Standardization of Psychiatric Diagnosis, Classification and Statistics*, Geneva, 1971.

5. Spitzer, Robert L., and Jean Endicott: "DIAGNO 11: Further Developments in a Computer Program for Psychiatric Diagnosis," *Am. J. Psychiat.*, **125**(suppl.):12–21, 1969.

6. Michaels, Joseph J.: "Character Structure and Character Disorders," in Silvano Arieti (ed.), *American Handbook of Psychiatry*, Basic Books, New York, 1959, vol. 1, chap. 19.

7. Freud, Anna: *The Ego and the Mechanisms of Defense*, Cecil Baines (trans.), International Universities Press, New York, 1946.

C. PETER ROSENBAUM, M.D.

CHAPTER 15

Initial Interviewing

Most patients and therapists bring hope and anxiety into the first interview. The therapist must be able to take the lead in helping both himself and his patient feel sufficiently secure so they can start working together, and he must understand the sources of the hope and anxiety if he is to initiate therapy.

The patient brings with him a hope for a cure that may lead to unconscious, or barely conscious, unrealistic expectations of quick and magical relief from an omniscient, omnipotent therapist and also a useful willingness to take therapy seriously. The patient may at the same time fear a repetition of earlier experiences of being poorly cared for, a fear supported by stories of how psychotherapy can harm. He may also bring with him a healthy skepticism. He will fear the voyage into the unknown.

The therapist may be anxious because of the pressure on him to be all the patient expects him to be, his fear that he is not expert enough to help this patient, and his own fears of the voyage into the unknown. The therapist nevertheless can, from the outset, offer the patient some things that may well be unique in the patient's experience. He offers his undivided attention in a quiet room for an hour or more. He offers the patient respect, and he takes his suffering seriously. He will attempt to be honest with the patient and collaborate with him in trying to understand better the nature of the difficulties, the feasibility of either entering into a longer-term attempt to find solutions (a psychotherapy contract), or referral to another person or form of treatment. Simply to listen attentively and empathetically for an hour may go a long way in reducing the anxieties the patient brings with him.

Some patients come in with a reasonably well-articulated problem or set of problems they want help with. Often they formulate these problems in a quite rational way, suppressing temporarily those thoughts they are afraid might seem irrational for fear that the therapist will adjudge them ridiculous or crazy. Sometimes patients have a persistent sense of uneasiness about their lives that cannot be neatly presented as "the problem," but instead bring a problem as a "ticket of admission" because they fear the therapist's contempt if they are not able to be explicit about what is troubling them. In fact, many patients are so geared to the twin patriarchal values of achievement and responsibility that they hamstring their psychotherapy by insisting too narrowly on a "goal." For them one of the first tasks is, paradoxically, to learn that relating to themselves cannot be undertaken in a goal-driven, task-oriented way; it requires a more "open," neutral attitude, like fishing or horseback riding. Or, to summarize, the patient has done a good deal of mental work before making the first contact, and the therapist must allow this work to be expressed during the course of the first few interviews.

Just as the patient enters the first interview with a set of expectations, the therapist must be prepared to meet a relative stranger in such a way that both will come to feel in the first sessions that their contact can be helpful to the patient. This is maybe not always pleasant, but it is at least helpful and not humiliating or hurtful to an already impaired sense of self-esteem. Carl Rogers[1] and his colleagues show that *unconditional positive regard, nonpossessive warmth,* and *accurate empathy* in the therapist promote therapeutic progress. These are attitudes, not postures, and they imply the therapist's acceptance of the patient and his being without moralistic judgment of what is good or bad, or right or wrong, with the patient and his problems.

FEARS AND STRENGTHS OF INEXPERIENCED THERAPISTS

Inexperienced therapists often fall prey to fears that they do not know enough to help, the patient will recognize their inexperience and challenge them on it, or psychotherapy is still an unproven quantity (even in the hands of experienced practitioners) and therefore the patient's time and money are being fraudulently spent. How, then, can the therapist thus beset by doubt bring his human qualities of warmth and empathy to bear on his work? Some do not: they retreat behind a pseudopsychoanalytic facade of sphinxlike inscrutability at first, only later allowing their human qualities to emerge as they feel more comfortable in their work. Others may be overeager to supply interpretations, reassurances, or formulations of dynamics that are premature and stifle rather than stimulate the unfolding of the therapeutic relationship.

Strengths

Inexperienced therapists often fail to give themselves sufficient recognition for what they *do* bring to therapy because of a preoccupation about what they do not. Here are some factors they should keep in mind. Most therapists begin their professional work while they are in their 20s or 30s. All have had their successes and failures in life that can allow them to empathize with their patients' concerns. Many have had a good deal of education, formal and informal, which has helped them to understand themselves and others. Most are drawn to mental health work because they want to help others. Most beginning therapists, therefore, even before the curtain goes up on their first patient contact, have been consciously or unconsciously rehearsing for this moment for a lifetime, and they bring more expertise to the situation than they often give themselves credit for. If they can grant themselves this, they can bring the wish to be helpful into the interview. They can also bring their repertoire of understanding of and sympathy with people struggling with problems and get a good start on translating these experiences into unconditional positive regard.

They can realize that however the presenting problem is formulated, the first need of the patient is to receive an attentive and understanding hearing of his concerns. The patient does not need an omniscient being who can instantly perceive all that is right and wrong with him, even though he may have had such fantasies. He *does* need someone who will attempt to understand and empathize with that which is immediately understandable but who will remain curious about matters that are obscure and perplexing, which, considering the complexity of most people, are many. It is only after a certain amount of hard work by both parties that the therapist will have a good grasp, which he has shared with the patient along the way, on the patient's primary problems in living and the beginnings of potential solutions to them.

THE THERAPIST'S JOB

Sullivan[2] defines the psychiatrist as having to be "an expert in interpersonal relationships." Unlike the expertise demanded of television quiz program contestants, whose criterion of success is coming up with the right answer before the buzzer sounds, the therapist's expertise emerges implicitly in his capacity to listen carefully, let the patient know when he is or is not following him, help the patient be able to gain a perspective on the internal and external environment from which his problems arose, and work collaboratively in exploring potential solutions. The same kind of openness to gathering information about a crisis, helping to define its antecedents, and exploring possible solutions to it that were presented in Chapter 1 are part of the initial interviewing of patients who are not in crisis when they seek help. Often these techniques can be employed in a more thoughtful and leisurely fashion in outpatient therapy because the lack of dramatic crisis gives more room for exploration and reflection.

Objectives

What should be the objectives of the initial interviews? Whether the interviewer is seeing the patient once or twice in consultation, knowing in advance he probably will be referring the patient elsewhere for continued treatment (a knowledge which should be shared with the patient from the outset so false hopes that the interviewer will be his regular therapist will not be raised), or as a prelude to possible treatment with the interviewer, the first sessions should aim at the establishment of a trusting relationship that will serve as the vehicle for a better understanding of the patient's problems and possible modes to their solution. Sullivan[3] speaks well to these issues, and all beginning therapists should be familiar with his views.

The aims of the initial interviewing are several. The first is to work with the patient to enhance a mutual understanding of the nature of the difficulties for which he is seeking treatment. Even at the end of the first session, as will be shown, the therapist can present the patient with a preliminary, working formulation. After several more interviews, the therapist will be in possession of sufficient information and intuitions to be able to

make an extensive dynamic formulation (as described in Chapter 14).

Inseparable from a formulation of problems and dynamics is the initiation of treatment. Indeed, if rapport begins to be established in the first session, the work of treatment may well have begun and will manifest itself in the first several sessions. The dynamic formulation will indicate to the therapist the levels and kinds of psychological, pharmacological, and environmental interventions that will probably be of use to the patient. The remainder of this chapter is devoted to outlining many technical features of the first interviews that can enhance the treatment process.

STARTING THE FIRST INTERVIEW

Establishing Contact

Patients may call a clinic or drop in unannounced. In either case, the therapist should talk with the patient to find out, in a general way, what problems the patient wants help with. *As important as the words, at this juncture, is the music.* The therapist should listen for the emotional tones of the patient as well as to his stated concerns. What are the initial transferences the patient brings into treatment? Does he sound seriously depressed, anxious, or angry? Is he seemingly too calm and unconcerned about matters that would trouble most people more deeply? Is he highly controlling or exceedingly impersonal? Does he give the impression of having a psychosis or a character disorder? What feelings does he arouse in the therapist: compassion, pity, attraction, irritation, anxiety, revulsion? Are the feelings he evokes in the therapist the same as those he arouses in others; i.e., is the therapist starting to participate in the same kinds of emotional interactions that the patient experiences elsewhere?

Example 15-1. A 51-year-old married businessman came to his first interview immaculately dressed, carrying his portfolio under his arm. He defined his problems as being primarily financial and was dubious about his need for psychotherapy. He described in a bland, businesslike manner, recent business losses, a brainstem stroke he had had two months before (and from which he felt he had made a full recovery), the deaths of two friends in the last six months, and a possible separation from his wife and children.

At first the interviewer and the group observing the interview (with the patient's knowledge and permission) were put off by his unemotional and uninsightful, boring, pompous manner. When the patient was asked the ages of his children, he had to consult a file he had in his portfolio; he could not remember and betrayed little concern about this lapse. The interviewer and the group then began to see that this patient had suffered a decline in intellectual functioning, that his bland and constricted interpersonal manner was part of a life-long character structure which did not allow him to see weaknesses in himself. He began to look like a pathetic, aging Willy Loman who was unwittingly alienating his clients and family when he badly needed them.

In the postinterview discussion the group speculated that he might relate well to a young man to whom he could discourse about the pressures of the business world. At the same time the therapist could, under his medical aegis, arrange for further neuropsychiatric evaluation as a prelude to helping this man "slow down a bit, as befits his age," i.e., adjust better to the social and intellectual losses that had occurred and that might be expected to occur. This approach struck a resonant note in one of the beginning therapists in the group, and he volunteered to work with the patient.

During an initial phone call or other contact, the interviewer has to assess the risk that the patient may be heading for some kind of personal disaster, that he is likely to make an attempt at suicide, flight, or assault. If this does not seem likely, if the patient sounds relatively calm and in control, an appointment can be set for the first mutually convenient time. If, however, the risks seem uncomfortably great, the caller should be seen that day; the drop-in patient should have all the time his needs of the moment demand.

Often, assessing the level of risk in cases in which the distress signals of telephone calls are ambiguous can be accomplished by saying, after hearing the initial problems, "I can understand why you want help with these problems. My first regular free time is next Tuesday at 1 P.M., but I could arrange to see you sooner if you don't think things will hold until then." Usually the patient will respond, "No, I'm sure I can manage until Tuesday," and that is that. But if the response is, "Well, I *think* I can wait until Tuesday," or, "No, I don't think I can wait until Tuesday," the patient should be seen sooner.

During the initial phone call, the therapist should get the patient's name, address, and phone number and write them down so he can reach the patient in case of a change. Because of high anxiety levels, patients often forget the name of the person they spoke to on the phone, and it is often useful to end such a preliminary conversation by saying, "Come to the psychiatry clinic a bit before 1 P.M. next Tuesday and tell the receptionist you have an appointment with Dr. Campbell; I'll tell the receptionist to be expecting you." Then tell the receptionist!

Introductions and Seating

The therapist goes to the waiting area and introduces himself to his patient: "Mrs. Mason, I am Dr. Campbell. Would you come to my office, please?" He indicates the direction to his office, and, having entered, invites the patient to be seated in a specific chair. Occasionally the patient will take the therapist's chair, even after having been shown the patient's chair. Many such patients who do this are schizophrenic, very anxious about control and being controlled, and many therapists think it best to let them sit in the therapist's chair for that first interview.

Therapists vary widely on whether to call patients by their first names, and each works out his own personal style. Generally it is wise initially to ask the patient his full name. In writing it down, ask the patient to spell it, e.g., a patient named Allen was grateful to a new therapist for asking him to spell out his name during the initial interview; a previous therapist had made his bills out to him as "Alan," and he had been unable to mention it. Similarly, ask the patient how his name is pronounced.

Adolescents and children usually feel the therapist is being unbearably stuffy if he uses anything but a given name, but he should avoid diminutive nicknames for adolescents; e.g., use "John" instead of "Johnny." Patients with sexual identity problems, especially transsexualism, may want to be regarded by their adoptive, rather than their biological, sex role and name, and the therapist should do so. In working conjointly with marital couples, using first names may be considerably less cumbersome, e.g., it is easier to say, "So, as I understand it, when you, John, come home at night, it seems to you, Martha, that John runs and hides behind his newspaper right away," than to use "You, Mr. Smith" and "You, Mrs. Smith."

Sullivan [4] recommends that the therapist's and patient's chairs be placed at 90-degree angles to each other so eye contact can be made or broken easily, as the two persons desire. Seeing a patient from behind a desk interposes one more barrier to openness and frankness and should not be done. In most instances it makes little difference to the patient whether his chair is nearer to or farther from the door, and usually both the therapist and the patient prefer the office door to be shut. Certain very anxious patients, especially those who are schizophrenic and/or paranoid, may feel trapped in the office and insist on having the seat nearer the door and the door open. Such requests should be honored initially. If a relationship of trust becomes established, the patient may later be quite willing to settle for more conventional seating arrangements.

Starting the Interview

As Sullivan [5] recommends, it is wise to start the interview by telling the patient what you know about him, either from his own self-report or from information provided by others. For example, the therapist might say, "From what you told me on the phone last week, I gather that your marriage seems to be breaking up, that you don't want it to, and that you are very anxious about what would happen to you if it does. Is that accurate?"

Outside Information. If a friend, relative, or colleague has provided information on the patient, it too should be reviewed, although items likely to damage the patient's self-esteem or cause him to distrust the therapists' interest in him should be handled tactfully. Outside information may be proffered with a certain amount of bias, e.g., "I know Joe is coming to see you today. Please don't tell him I called, but I want you to know . . . ," and therapists should be quite careful not to get trapped into a conspiracy of secrecy with outside informants. The best way to avoid this trap is to tell the caller, virtually at the outset of the call, that the therapist would like to be able to tell the prospective patient about the call and to use its content judiciously during the first interview. Most informants will agree, sometimes reluctantly. When they do not, the therapist can inquire about the informant's need for secrecy. Often the concern is that either the patient is ignorant of the information or the informant does not want the patient to know that *he knows* the information. If the informant still insists on secrecy, it is usually better for the therapist to forego the gratuitous information, telling the would-be informant that although his information might prove to be quite valuable, the therapist cannot accept it under such conditions, and he hopes it could come to him either directly through the patient or under circumstances that will allow him to let the patient know of the contact.

In situations in which the outside informant is

quite willing to have the information shared, the patient should always be acquainted with the nature of its contents. Technical psychiatric or medical terms should be translated into words the patient understands, both to avoid scaring the patient with words that may sound ominous to him (whether or not they do to the therapist) and to be sure the patient understands what is meant.

Example 15-2. A student applying to a professional school had a psychiatric interview as part of the application procedure. The psychiatrist found the student to be a social isolate, awkward, and perhaps even bizarre in his posture and mannerisms, and clearly peculiar generally. He diagnosed the student as a schizoid personality and wondered if the student might not be latently schizophrenic. He also was not sure, whatever the formal diagnosis might be, how much the student's emotional problems might hamper his effectiveness in professional training and performance. With the student's permission, he requested additional consultation and sent a copy of his own detailed psychiatric interview to the consultant.

After making the patient comfortable, the consultant started the session by saying, "Dr. Sherwood on the admissions committee asked that we talk together to see if some questions your interview raised in his mind about your readiness for professional school were warranted. Is this your understanding of the purpose of our session?" The student indicated that it was. The consultant continued, "Dr. Sherwood sent a copy of his report to me, and, in addition to some background material about your age, schooling, and so on, said his primary concerns were centered around what he saw as your feeling awkward around people, being shy and having difficulty in dealing with others, and perhaps appearing peculiar to them or to yourself. How does that square with your view of the situation?"

The student felt that this was an accurate

representation. He then went on to describe his interpersonal difficulties with considerable candor. The net result of the session was that the student happily accepted a referral for psychotherapy. The consultant felt that the student was not schizophrenic and that his awareness of his limitations and desire for help augured well for his further training. He recommended that the student be accepted for professional school.

Some special issues may come up in dealing with schizophrenic patients. Such patients understandably are afraid of or resent being labeled "crazy" or "schizophrenic." Yet they often are aware enough of their internal states so that the interviewer can establish some areas of accord without getting into an argument about ominous and odious labels. Such patients may readily agree with the interviewer that their thoughts have been racing, they have been having trouble concentrating, they have been perplexed and confused by mystifying and peculiar mental events, they are afraid their thoughts are being read or influenced by others, and so forth. If the schizophrenic patient agrees that he is troubled by one or more of these, the therapist can offer to help understand and reduce (using medication as needed) the troubling symptoms.

In any event, in the early part of the first interview, after the therapist has presented a first approximation to the patient of what he understands the major problems to be, he pauses to let the patient confirm, deny, change, or amend what the therapist has said. Once the two have more or less agreed on a problem area, the therapist then asks about other problems the patient may want help with, in addition to the presenting one. If the patient has presented a relatively innocuous problem initially as his "ticket of admission" to therapy, he may then reveal, either during the first interview or later, other problems he was too anxious, ashamed, or frightened about to mention initially. Some of these come out as "last-minute revelations," which shall be described later.

CONTINUING THE INTERVIEW

Earlier in this century, psychiatrists trained in the neuropsychiatric and medical tradition would conduct the entire interview according to the history outline they later used to note their findings, much as a very literal internist would reel off questions from the Review of Systems, without regard to how relevant they seemed to the patient's present illness or distress. Others with psychoanalytic training advised against much, if any, direction by the interviewer, and suggested instead that even initial interviews come very close to free association.

Gill, Newman, and Redlich[6] summarized some of these historical perspectives and put forth a system that considerably influenced the author's approach and that of many others. They point out the need for the interviewer to establish rapport with the patient and to attempt to keep the inquiry relevant to his conscious concerns, but still to be interested in his history and be willing to ask questions that will elicit information the interviewer needs for his formulation.

Enelow and Swisher[7] suggest, "The interviewer should move through a cycle of information-seeking behavior that begins with low use of authority and proceeds to progressively greater use of authority." By this they mean that the interviewer use general and open-ended questions early in the interview, e.g., "Can you tell me more about that?" and "How did that make you feel?" Later in the interview he may ask more specific questions, such as "Tell me more about your marriage. For instance, how did you and your husband first meet?"

Inexperienced interviewers sometimes fall into the trap of asking a series of questions that can be answered only by *yes* or *no* or by a very limited range of responses, e.g., "Has your marriage been going well recently?" or "How often do you and your wife have intercourse?" A series of such questions may "train" the patient to expect a question-and-answer format, with the questions becoming more detailed and the answers becoming shorter. Consider how much more information the interviewer might obtain if he asked, "How has your marriage been going recently?" or "What's the nature of your sexual relationship with your wife?"

This is not to say that specific and direct questions have no place in an interview. There may be times when knowing the number of acts of intercourse in a week is of importance. But such questions should be asked in the context of a more open-ended approach, with the implication that they are necessary to obtain a more rounded picture of the patient's life.

Thus, after the therapist has gained a first approximation of the patient's central concerns in the opening part of the interview, it is his task for the next thirty to sixty minutes to find out as much as he can about the context in which these concerns arose. He can save for later most of his questions that are not directly tied to his developing a broader understanding of the current stresses and confine his questions and comments to those concerns which have immediate relevancy to the patient.

Following the Affective Track

It is in this stage of the interview that the therapist's empathy should help him stay on the affective, emotional track of the patient, as client-centered therapists have emphasized. The patient's voice and manner will suggest the suppressed feelings that bother him and are striving for expression and reception. So long as the expressions of such feelings do not flood the patient's ego, do not cause extreme amounts of anxiety, shame, and so on, the therapist can reflect back the feelings as he senses them.

Example 15-3. A 21-year-old graduate student had just arrived at a university far away from home to start her first year of work. She felt alienated in the new environment. Following is a fragment from the middle of her first therapy session:

Patient. I realized the good luck charm my mother gave me was missing when I looked for it while the train was stopped in Kansas City.

Therapist. Did that seem like some kind of omen?

Patient. Yes. I was afraid to begin with, and this made it worse. I know that's silly.

Therapist. But even though it may look silly, it made you feel even less in control over the way things were going?

Patient. You don't think that was silly?

Therapist. How scared you've been feeling doesn't sound silly to me. Is there anything you've been able to do since you got here, or anything that has happened, that has made you feel less scared or more secure?

Nonverbal Cues. Patients may suggest emotions nonverbally, and therapists may help them articulate what they are feeling by commenting on what they sense.[8] If a patient's eyes begin to water and he seems to be fighting back tears, the therapist may say, "You look as if you are about to cry; you must be holding in some very strong feelings." A clenched fist with white knuckles suggests either anxious tension or anger. Depending on the context, the therapist may say, "It looks as if it makes you tense to be talking about this," or "It looks as if talking about this seems to stir up some anger."

Silences are another form of nonverbal cue. The therapist will have to use his intuition to decide what to do. If it is a reflective silence, one in which the patient is trying to gather his thoughts before proceeding, a corresponding, attentive silence by the therapist is in order. If it is an anxious and tense silence, the therapist may have to employ the abrupt transition described below. If it is a guilty and depressed silence, the therapist may have to guide the patient by making a statement along these lines: "I can see this is something which is very difficult for you to talk about, but it's important that we talk about it sometime. Should we tackle it now or come back to it later?" In any event, the therapist should not succumb to

either of the extremes of filling every suggestion of silence with an interposition simply to break the silence (as a hostess might at a social gathering), nor should he obdurately remain silent to force the patient to resume the initiative for the interview (as in a bad parody of psychoanalytic technique).

Anxiety. A certain amount of anxiety is to be expected in most initial interviews. If, however, a patient appears to become severely and uncomfortably anxious during this early part of the interview, the therapist should intervene. In addition to the usual signs of anxiety, blockage of speech in neurotic patients and increasing levels of psychotic material in schizophrenic patients are important indicators of rising anxiety. At such times it is useful to employ what Sullivan[9] refers to as an "abrupt transition," changing the topic under discussion with such startling speed that the patient does not even know what has happened.

> *Example 15-4.* A patient describing a very unsettling event got increasingly anxious and started blocking in his speech. The therapist said, "These things are important and we can come back to them later, but first I need to know a bit more about your background. You were born and reared in Ohio, is that correct?"

Widening the Circle of Inquiry

Such abrupt transitions will not be necessary with many patients. Instead, the more they talk, the more areas of their lives they allude to and thus make relevant for inquiry. In talking about a failing marriage, the patient may very well comment spontaneously, or certainly think it a relevant question on the part of the interviewer, about how he first met his wife, what they found attractive about each other, how and when they decided to get married, what each set of parents thought about the prospective spouse, and so forth. After getting a history of the marriage and its recent stresses, the therapist can return to earlier events by making maximum use of *apropos,* of connections already cited by the patient. He can say, for instance, "You said your mother never got on very well with your wife. How had she reacted to some of your previous girlfriends?" And, from the answers given, "It sounds as if your mother exerted a rather dominant influence in your life. Tell me more about your relationship with her." And here we are already talking about mother, who is always an important person to know about.

The whole point of the strategy presented so far is that the therapist has two jobs to do simultaneously: (1) he has to understand and try to help the troubled person sitting across from him, and (2) he has to gather information to help him in his, the therapist's, own private formulations as to why the patient is in the kind of trouble he is. If the therapist's interest in the second task becomes obtrusive, the patient often begins to feel that he represents little more than a repository of psychiatric and historical curiosities to the therapist. By using the system described here, the therapist can establish rapport with the patient *and* gain a great deal of useful background data in an unobtrusive manner. If rapport has been established, and the therapist still has some unanswered questions he needs to know about, he can come back to them later in subsequent interviews, saying to the patient, "As I've been reviewing our sessions, I realized that I didn't learn much about X, and it would help me if you could tell me something about it." X may be a father, early development, schooling, and so on.

Identifying Strengths and Resources

During the first interview it is exceedingly important to develop at least a preliminary idea of the patient's strengths and resources. Internists, when taking a history and doing the Review of Systems, are as interested in what is *not* wrong with the patient as in what *is*. Psychotherapists should be as interested in what the patient *can* do and *has* done that show signs of ability and

resourcefulness as in what is *not* going right presently.

Again, with the focus on the presenting situation, the therapist can say to the patient, "I think I understand your marital problems better now. But I don't yet know much about your current life situation otherwise." And then he inquires about such factors as friends, job, interests, hobbies, and use of leisure time. Many depressed patients will say that there is little in their lives, but when asked, reveal that before they became depressed they had a wide and impressive list of friends, interests, and accomplishments. One of the first major therapeutic interventions may be to push the patient to resume some of these activities, to fall back on old friends while the marriage is breaking up, and so on.

Example 15-5, Mrs. Linden. Mrs. Linden, a 45-year-old woman, sought help for unpredictable tearful outbursts and other signs of an acute depression as a chronically empty marriage was nearing its end. The children were now in high school and college, and the husband's lack of interest in the relationship was increasingly apparent. Recently he had returned from a banker's convention with a motel receipt made out to Mr. and Mrs., and his wife found it in one of his pockets as she prepared his clothing for the cleaners.

Mrs. Linden came with misgivings to her first interview with the therapist. She had been raised in a stable New England family, and some of that family's predominant values had been that an individual does not admit defeat in public, keeps a stiff upper lip, and does not give in to feelings. Thus the patient saw visiting a therapist and crying in front of him as a humiliating display of feelings and an admission of defeat in public. Likewise she had been unable to tell her close friends or family how she had been feeling and was deeply embarrassed when she suddenly burst into tears in front of friends "for no reason."

After hearing her out about the failed

marriage, the therapist asked her to tell him more about her adolescence and young adulthood, dwelling especially on those activities she had done well and that had brought her pleasure. She named several and pointed out that she had let them lapse during the years of her marriage. The therapist thought this patient might have substantial personal resources that she might develop through therapy.

At the end of the first interview he asked her to prepare a list to be gone over in the next interview of the friends, interests, and activities she might pick up on again to help give her life some new impetus. The list she brought in the next week was impressive, and she had already found some friends she could talk with frankly. She was looking at newspaper advertisements for part-time teaching jobs that might intrigue her. Her depression had started to lift.

ENDING THE INITIAL INTERVIEWS

The patient should leave the first interview with a better understanding of his situation than he came in with. First, the patient should leave with a *formulation*. He needs the anchoring security of knowing that there is a pattern and meaning to the emotional material he produces and that therapy can help him become conscious of this pattern.

Second, the patient should leave with an improved understanding of *how to use therapy*. Many of the therapist's interventions should be designed to help the patient understand his role and what is expected of him. Even at the beginning, a therapist may need to make it clear to the patient if he feels he is misusing therapy.

Example 15-6. A beginning therapist, dealing with an abundantly emotional young woman who was already adept at catharsis, found her initial response to his expressions of concern to be loud, theatrical sobbing that occupied much of the hour. Finally he said, "If you spend the whole hour crying, we just won't be

able to learn very much about you." She sat up, dried her eyes, and set about explaining her situation — to her own relief as well as the therapist's.

Third, the patient and therapist need to nail down a "contract" that will make their agreement to work together a solid, functioning pact.

Formulation and Hope

The formulation is one way of helping establish a sense of purpose. Often the information gathered in the first interview will permit a reasonable initial formulation by the therapist. Even when it does not, the therapist should make a preliminary formulation, pointing out to the patient that these are only beginning working ideas and that he would like to have one or a few more interviews to gain a better focus. Such remarks offer the patient evidence that the therapist has been doing his work during the first interview, but that he will not prematurely limit his understanding of the patient and his problems. Thus, the initial treatment contract at the end of the first interview may simply be to have the patient return. Then the therapist and patient can continue until the therapist feels he has a sufficient understanding of the patient to be able to establish an intelligent and thoughtful formulation and the treatment contract that would proceed naturally from it. The first session ends on a note of "To be continued," with both the therapist and the patient knowing why.

The emotional tone at the end of an interview may set the tone of the patient's view of himself and his life between sessions. In ending an interview with a depressed patient, it is often helpful to review with him his strengths, resources (including the possibility of further therapy visits), and what he can look forward to rather than letting the session trail off into gloom and despair.

In any event, following Sullivan's[10] lead, when the end of the first session is perhaps ten to twenty minutes away, the therapist should make some premonitory signal: "Our time is beginning to run short, and there are a few things I want to mention at this point." Then he restates what he has learned from the patient, trying to make logical connections if he can, in the form of hypotheses, that the patient is free to affirm or change. With Mrs. Linden, the depressed married woman, the therapist's formulation was of this sort:

Mrs. Linden (cont'd.). "From what you've said, then, you grew up in New England and are reasonably happy about your family, your school, and the way of life you led. In the early years of your marriage, you and your husband shared a large number of interests and activities and you found the marriage absorbing and gratifying. After the children came, you found yourself devoting a lot of time and energy to them and to assisting your husband in his career. At the same time he seemed to distance himself through his work and his traveling. Although there might have been hints then of some involvements on his part with other women, you let them pass. In the last several months these hints have become undeniable, and they have also served to highlight for you how little you were getting out of the marriage and life in general. You tried on several occasions to talk about these things with your husband, but he avoided being directly confronted with them or with discussions about separation or divorce, although you are sure these thoughts have crossed his mind just as they have yours. Yet you have also felt trapped and unable to discuss these things with your family or friends because you didn't think it right to discuss your personal troubles with others.

"Somehow his trip south a few weeks ago and finding that motel receipt when he got back was the final straw for you, and you began to notice that you burst into tears unpredictably, that your sleep and appetite were affected. You wanted to turn to your children for sympathy, but felt it wasn't fair to burden them with that. Now you are con-fronted with having to make a decision about the marriage because you no longer find the present situation endurable, and you are troubled both about the depression and crying episodes as well as about what to do with your life at this point."

The patient agreed that this was a fair recapitulation of the situation and elaborated on how difficult it was for her to make up her mind about the marriage. The therapist encouraged her to think about the advantages and disadvantages of staying together versus separating, as well as asking her to compile the list of social and personal assets previously described. She left the office with a clearer understanding of her situation and the beginnings of hope about mastering it.

Formulation and Last-minute Revelations

Sometimes patients will wait until the end of the first or second interview to make a surprising disclosure that they did not feel they could trust the therapist with initially. It may take one or more sessions for a patient to feel sufficiently comfortable with and trusting of the therapist to reveal some highly charged matter. Sometimes he may reveal definite plans he has been harboring about suicide or homicide, or a history of disturbing sexual fantasies or practices, or fears (justified or not) of becoming insane.

Example 15-7. During a first interview with a 31-year-old woman, the therapist heard about a deteriorating marital and social situation during the preceding weeks. At first the patient's presentation sounded flamboyant and dramatic. As the interview drew on, her thinking seemed more and more bizarre. After recapitulating what he had heard during the first forty-five minutes of the interview (and to which the patient agreed), the interviewer asked if there were any other concerns he should know about. She looked at him intently and said, "Yes. I think I have Lesbian tendencies. I'm worrying if I'm a homosexual."

The interviewer extended the session to hear about this concern in enough detail so that the patient knew he took it seriously but was not horrified, and the two of them could go into more detail in the session he had already set for the next day.

Thus, it is always wise at the end of a formulation to say something of this sort to the patient: "Thus far we've gotten a picture of the problems that have been bothering you. I wonder if there are any other things that are also bothering you which we haven't had a chance to talk about, or other things about yourself you think it would be helpful for me to know about?" This kind of phrasing makes it possible for the patient to bring forth more information without the implication that he has been "holding back."

Sometimes when patients do indeed come up with something "hot" at this point, beginning therapists find themselves getting irritated and wondering to themselves, "Well, damn it, that's what the *real* problem is, and here we've been fencing for a whole hour talking about trivia when we could have been talking about *that*!" And it is at just this point that the patient is most sensitive about the therapist's response. The trivia was the test, the disclosure the sign that the therapist had passed the test. Before the therapist's irritation about testing and trivia becomes too great, he should recognize how much anxiety and shame the patient must have mastered in order to make the disclosure. He should respond to the disclosure first by respecting how important and difficult it has been for the patient to make it but not (unless warranted) to be as alarmed by it as the patient is. The therapist may say, "I can see by the fact that it has taken this long for you to be able to talk about this that it is something which has been troubling you deeply. Can you tell me a bit more about it now, and then we can go into it further next time to try to get a better perspective on it." Obviously, if the disclosure indicates the patient is bent on a destructive path, the therapist should take the time necessary to deal with it in that same

hour, even at the expense of disrupting his schedule. Usually, however, full exploration of the disclosure can wait until the next session. The therapist's job is to receive the information in such a way as to show he is not frightened or horrified about what he has heard, his liking and respect for the patient have in no way been diminished, and, in fact, perhaps have been increased by the patient's willingness to mention the previously unmentionable, and he would like to work with the patient on it in the future.

Formulation and Reassurance

During the final formulation, the therapist can often *reassure* patients on several issues that may have been spoken or implied during the interview. For persons who have never experienced major emotional problems before, even a run-of-the-mill depression may portend to them a serious mental illness, and to be told that such a depression is a common reaction under the circumstances (when in fact it is), can be very reassuring. Often patients are anxious about being anxious, or anxious about being depressed, and the therapist can offer realistic and helpful reassurance at this point.

Mrs. Linden (cont'd.). When Mrs. Linden came, she was worried that she was having "a nervous breakdown." Although she knew her crying spells and loss of appetite were related to the marriage, she had never had such spells before in her life. Furthermore, she had been brought up to believe that such emotionality was akin to moral weakness. She had heard of middle-aged women having nervous breakdowns, and she was 45.

The therapist was able to tell her that what she was going through was an acute reactive depression, the symptoms were entirely understandable in view of her present circumstances, such reactive depressions usually responded well to psychotherapy, and there were effective antidepressant medications available if they were needed. He also told her he did not think her symptoms portended the serious nervous breakdown of middle-aged women that she feared. Mrs. Linden listened carefully to his statements and drew much reassurance from them.

Depressed patients often think only of their failures and weaknesses, not of their successes and strengths. In such cases, during the formulation it may be useful to add a statement such as: "Right now you are feeling very depressed, and that's understandable from what we have just been talking about. But when people are depressed, they think only about their failures and forget what they have been able to do, such as you've done here today. When your depression lifts, you will once again realize how well you have done in your job and with your family, and I think you should try to keep that in mind now, even when it is hard for you to really believe it down deep."

OFFERING THE PATIENT TREATMENT

Transference and Countertransference

A great majority of patients who see a therapist for the first time will be interested in other sessions, and usually the interviewer will agree. If the interviewer and patient feel they can work together, and time and money permit, they will continue. Sometimes one or the other does not want to continue in *this* relationship, and a referral to someone else is in order. If a therapist finds himself thinking, during a first interview, "I can't (don't want to) see this patient again," he must look into himself to seek to discover the reasons why. For therapists in training, discussions of such feelings with a trusted consultant, supervisor, or peer can be an extremely valuable learning experience.

Upon reflection and discussion, his dislike of the patient may turn out to be a manifestation of neurotic countertransference feelings. The patient may unwittingly tread on areas of the therapist's

unresolved conflicts, e.g., the homosexual patient may threaten the security of a therapist unsure about his own sexuality; the middle-aged drinking patient may upset an interviewer whose own father drank. To the extent that the therapist can fight against his inner limitations through consultation and his own therapy, work with patients who threaten him initially can lead to his growth as a therapist. He will, nevertheless, come up against patients from time to time with whom his ability to be empathic and understanding are so compromised that it would be fruitless to pretend otherwise. On such occasions he should refer the patient to someone else.

Sometimes an initial countertransference reaction, positive or negative, can be a powerful diagnostic clue, more to be listened to than acted upon. It has been said that if during a first interview the interviewer feels like kicking the patient and the patient has not been acting in a provocative manner, the patient may be more profoundly masochistic than the interviewer suspected. Likewise, if the interviewer becomes inexplicably anxious, the patient may be nearly psychotic, and the interviewer may be resonating to psychotic anxiety, which often is contagious. If the interviewer is male and the patient an attractive female, and the interviewer finds himself getting sexually aroused even though no explicitly sexual material is being discussed, the patient may be a hysteric. Or she may simply be an attractive woman.

Sometimes the patient will not want to work with the interviewer. These feelings should be carefully considered before any decision is reached. If the feelings are strong, even if they seem quite irrational, it may be better to refer the patient to someone who better fits the patient's expectations. One therapist, a relatively short man, said, "When I was a resident and patients objected to my size, I would work awfully hard to get them to analyze their neurosis about short people. Now that I'm in private practice, if my size *really* seems to make that much difference to a new patient, I refer him to one of my taller colleagues." Sometimes a patient's objections to a given therapist are fairly realistic. Again, they should be respected, as in the following example:

Example 15-8. A freshman, female college student saw a new therapist for the first time. In her shy and introverted manner, she told him about her fears of the new campus and of some of her instructors, whom she had met for the first time and who had struck her as impersonal and overbearing, and about her trying not to give in to her wish to return home and start school somewhere else.

The therapist, a first-year psychiatric resident, had worked previously on drug treatment programs, which had called for vigorous confrontation and a liberal use of expletives. He carried some of that approach into the first session with the student. He told her that her fears were neurotic (which she already knew) and that she should not give in to them (which she already did not want to do; what she wanted was help in *not* giving in to them), and so on.

At the end of the interview, she told him that she thought he understood her *problems* pretty well, but she did not think he understood *her,* and that she would like to see someone else for continuing treatment.

The resident did not commit himself to her, but instead sought out consultation after the session. He embarrassedly told his consultant he felt that he *had* jumped on this patient too hard during the interview and that she was right when she felt he had underestimated her wish not to give in to her neurotic conflicts. Both the resident and consultant were impressed with the fact that she had been able to be assertive enough to say so at the time rather than shyly keeping her misgivings to herself, as seemed to be part of her pattern. Both felt that her assertiveness should be honored rather than nullified, and a new therapist was found.

The Initial Treatment Contract and Its Components

Assuming that the therapist and the patient will continue to work together, the first session should end with a tentative initial treatment contract. Sometimes defining the contract will take two or three sessions, until the therapist has gotten to know the patient better. The components of an initial treatment contract include (1) the definition of the primary problem areas to be worked on; (2) the appropriate mode of treatment; (3) the frequency of visits; (4) fees; (5) suggestions about therapy-related projects; and (6) the use of medication when indicated.

The initial contract may often need to be renegotiated after a few sessions. The problems that brought the patient to treatment may no longer bother him, or he may see them in a new perspective. A marital partner and the therapist may come to see that couple therapy holds out the best hopes for an improved existence. A patient whose problems center around difficulties in interpersonal relationships may be best referred to group therapy. Patients who are initially upset may see a recurrent neurotic pattern in their lives for which long-term, uncovering therapy is indicated.

Thus, the initial contract may define some immediate problems that need attention, leaving the options open for further decisions to be made later. Initially the therapist and patient may contract to meet once a week for an hour, at the established fee, to help resolve the depression accompanying the disintegrating marriage, to help control the racing and confused thoughts, to find out what has been causing a previously good student to slip academically, and so on. Medication may be given. Suggestions may be given both to help illuminate some of the hidden sources of discontent and to challenge the patient into looking to himself and his social milieu as well as to therapy for possibilities for constructive resolutions of stress. The therapist and patient may conclude that the patient does not need treatment, at least at this juncture, and the contract is to discontinue.

Fees. Most psychiatric clinics operate on a sliding-scale fee basis. The therapist or the clinic financial aide suggests a fee based on the patient's ability to pay, his current financial responsibilities, and so on and arrives at a reasonable fee with the patient. Fee setting is best done just before the first or second interview so that if a patient is concerned about the fee, he can discuss it directly with his therapist.

Such matters are in the minds of virtually all patients during their first visit, and if the patient does not bring it up, the therapist should. Many middle- or low-income patients have heard that all therapists charge $35 an hour or more and are fearful that they cannot afford treatment; they may not know about the sliding scale in use in most clinics. Discussions of fees can often be a rich source of therapeutic material. For marital couples, such discussion in the first sessions may immediately bring issues of dominance and control in the marital situation into sharp focus, as in the case of a spouse who insists on doing all the bookkeeping and keeping the other in the dark on money matters.

Certain patients will offer to pay fees that they do not seem able to afford and may thus reveal a low sense of self-esteem by saying, symbolically: "No one could possibly be interested in me for myself; I'll have to buy my therapist's interest." Other patients may balk at what seems to be a realistic fee and ask to have it lowered as a special concession. These patients may be revealing such attitudes as "People have to do something special for me to show me they think I'm important," or, "There's a little larceny in everyone," or "There's nothing in the world you can't get for wholesale prices," or "I don't have much faith in psychotherapy, so why should I waste a lot of money on it?" Patients need to be helped gradually with the cynicism and despair these attitudes reveal.

Therapy-related Recommendations between Sessions

Patients frequently become patients because they have not been able to make connections between life events and the onset of their symptoms or between their symptoms and possible ways of dealing with future life situations. When some suggestions emerge during a first or second session about such connections, it is frequently useful to ask the patient to think more along these lines between sessions and see what emerges.

Mrs. Linden (cont'd.). In her second and third sessions, Mrs. Linden saw more clearly the connection between her symptoms, the pent-up frustration she had held in over the last several months, and the sense of hopelessness about her future with which she had been living.

When her husband continued to refuse to talk with her on any personal level, she came to the conclusion that the marriage was finished, even though she had not decided on the final rites, e.g., separation, divorce, who would keep the house, and so on. But she was relieved to be out of the impasse, for it gave her permission to define herself as a person seeking to construct a new kind of life, one in which greater sharing with friends, more outside activities, perhaps a job at some point, would be important. By her third session, she had noted on paper, as mentioned, an impressive list of activities she wanted to take up again or to start for the first time.

If the therapist and the patient have gone about accomplishing the tasks of the initial interviews successfully, they will share an enhanced understanding of the problems for which the patient seeks help, of some of the factors leading up to them, in an atmosphere of mutual trust and respect, and a beginning sense of how to proceed. These are all essential components in establishing the stage of *contact,* which may take some time to develop fully. Once it is established, the therapist and patient are ready to move into the stage of *confrontation*.

REFERENCES

1. Rogers, Carl R. (ed.) et al.: *The Therapeutic Relationship and Its Impact,* University of Wisconsin Press, Madison, 1967.

2. Sullivan, Harry S.: *The Psychiatric Interview,* Norton, New York, 1954.

3. Ibid., *passim.*

4. Ibid.

5. Ibid., pp. 59–62.

6. Gill, Merton, Richard Newman, and Fredrick C. Redlich: *The Initial Interview in Psychiatric Practice,* International Universities Press, New York, 1954.

7. Enelow, Allen J., and Scott N. Swisher: *Interviewing and Patient Care,* Oxford University Press, New York, 1972, p. 34 *et. seq.*

8. Ibid., pp. 44–47.

9. Sullivan: op. cit., pp. 223–224.

10. Ibid., pp. 85–93, chap. 9.

C. PETER ROSENBAUM, M.D.

CHAPTER 16

Early and Brief Psychotherapy*

EARLY THERAPY

Patients starting psychotherapy frequently feel well enough after several sessions that the goals of therapy deserve reformulation. Patient and therapist may agree that the patient has learned a lot about the circumstances which brought him into treatment, that the patient can now work competently on his own, and that this episode of therapy can end. The patient leaves, knowing he can return to his therapist should further problems arise. Sometimes the patient's relief of distress may be sufficient so that he does not see the need to continue therapy now or in the future; the present gains are enough. Such outcomes are termed "brief therapy." In contrast, even though the current distress is relieved, the patient may wish to pursue a prolonged investigation of his lifestyle in hopes of improving his future ability to handle similar circumstances more successfully.

It would be nice if every patient came away from therapy, brief or extended, with some benefit. Some do not. Some patients seem unaffected and unchanged after a period of therapy, and some are clearly worse. Sometimes impasse

comes because the therapist has gone about his work incorrectly: he may be lacking in the qualities of nonpossessive warmth and empathy that a particular patient needed, or he may have started to confront before the stage of contact had been reached. The patient's problems may not have been amenable to our current therapeutic knowledge (e.g., Alice, Chapters 2 and 3), or the patient may have been manic-depressive or schizophrenic and treated solely with psychotherapy and not with effective medications now available. We will focus in this chapter on cases where patients *did* benefit from therapy, in an attempt to elucidate the factors involved in such improvement, and will not attempt to address the issue of when psychotherapy fails and what is involved in the failure, a topic discussed more fully by others.[1-3]

Crisis Orientation

Promptness of treatment has many advantages. The natural history of an anxiety or depressive state is that it usually lasts about six to eight weeks; after that the acute symptoms tend to abate, though they may be replaced by stereotyped or limiting kinds of behavior as a defense against the unpleasant emotions. Delayed grief reactions, in which unresolved feelings about an

---

*Reprinted in part from C. P. Rosenbaum, "Events of Early Therapy and Brief Therapy," *Arch. Gen. Psychiat.,* **10**:506–512, 1964, and C. P. Rosenbaum: "Immediate Treatment and Brief Psychotherapy: Techniques and Cases," *Mental Hygiene,* **52**:284–287, 1968.

important loss inhibit spontaneity and flexibility for months or years, are common.

The patient who is hurting has maximal crisis motivation. One study[4] showed that patients experiencing the most acute distress also experienced the greatest amount of relief of distress after four weeks of psychotherapy. Though that study did not demonstrate that it was the psychotherapy per se that produced the relief, i.e., it could have been due simply to the passage of time or extra-therapy events, clinical experience suggests that the therapy was an important factor in the relief of symptoms. At times of crisis willingness to explore, think about, and experiment with changes in lifestyle and situations is great. It is a kind of motivation that can be capitalized upon in early and brief therapy.

I will describe in detail many of the factors which facilitate the early relief of symptoms and the possibility of an early satisfying end to a given episode of treatment or preparation to enter a second phase of treatment. Examples are drawn from my own experience and from cases presented in supervision. First we shall examine those therapist attitudes and techniques which affect the outcome of early therapy.

Therapist Attitudes

Therapists' widely differing attitudes about how one does psychotherapy and the ways in which these attitudes are translated into techniques, depending on their training programs, can profoundly enhance or discourage brief therapy. Some attitudes which can enhance brief psychotherapy follow.

One must assume that, whatever the patient's lifelong style of living has been, certain recent events have upset his inner and outer equilibrium sufficiently for him to seek help. Some understanding of these events and their meaning to the patient can greatly help him to restore the upset balance. Thus the first attitude of the therapist which can enhance brief therapy is an almost monotonous preoccupation with the questions:

"Why now? Why does this person come for help at this time? What recent set of stresses has so interfered with the patient's previous equilibrium that he now seeks help?" The answers given by Kalis et al.[5] include: a recent disruption of object relationships, a bind with a previous source of help, an identification with another person followed by disequilibrium, a surge of unmanageable (and possibly unfamiliar) impulses, and a threat to current adjustment because of changes in the environment. Curiosity about these current events should be at least as important to the therapist as knowledge of early life events and their influence on character. Recent changes in the life situation furnish an obvious starting point; curiosity about them should not be delayed pending knowledge of childhood and adolescence.

Secondly, the therapist should work collaboratively with the patient to define mental health, improvement, or relief in the patient's terms. The therapist must respect the patient's ability to formulate his own expectations and goals. All too often a therapist considers his job not done until a patient understands the origin and meaning of his symptoms. To be sure, the patient's statement, "I don't know why you think I should come, now that I'm feeling so well," may be his resistance to engaging in an intensive psychotherapeutic effort. But it can also express the bewilderment of the successfully treated truck driver, housewife, bookie, or student.

A third attitude is the therapist's willingness to hear of termination early, or even his willingness to bring it up himself when he senses it in the air. Patients often feel shy about mentioning this, sometimes because the popular media have taught them that therapy is lengthy and dramatic, and to talk of termination after six undramatic but productive sessions indicts themselves and their therapist, whom they have come to like; or they feel it would presumptuous to suggest to a doctor when their treatment should end. Whatever the reason, a statement by the therapist to the improved patient such as, "It looks to me like you may not have to be coming for a great deal longer;

does it look this way to you?" may bring willing consent. If not, it offers an excellent entry into discussion of future goals of therapy.

Some attitudes of the therapist, however, may work against an early, mutual consideration of termination, despite the patient's substantial symptomatic improvement.

The psychotherapist, because the fruits of his work are less easy to assess than those of an internist or surgeon, may nurture and tenaciously hold to certain attitudes about himself and his work in an attempt to ensure his doing right by his patients. He may well see himself as a very accepting, persevering person; and, indeed, some measure of these qualities is essential. Thus to speak early of termination may sound to him like rejection and uninterest, and he may hesitate to broach the topic, however appropriate. Likewise if he is uncertain of helping the patient, he may ease his conscience by encouraging the patient to continue taking the two things the therapist knows he can offer: his time and his attention.

If the therapist believes that there is a direct relation between hours spent in therapy and weeks spent in personal growth and change, he may encourage the patient to remain in treatment after the patient is capable of consolidating his gains on his own. These considerations include, for young therapists in private practice, the simple need to make a living.

The standards of residency and psychoanalytic training programs may obstruct early termination. Patients whose cases are being presented week after week to consultants in continuous case seminars become valuable possessions of the resident and his group. The patient who quits is frequently spoken of as "lost," and the resident has to endure the implication of some malfeasance on his part. Psychoanalytically oriented programs implicitly value long-term therapy with extensive investigations of unconscious processes and character structure; at the same time, cases of quick relief of symptoms are seldom presented, sometimes being termed "just a transference cure that won't last," and are made to seem inferior efforts.

In a field where the criteria of superiority are frequently difficult to discern, who wants to have his efforts regarded as inferior? On the other hand, arbitrary limits of six to eight appointments to a patient are the basis of successful brief therapy programs in many clinics.

Another attitude of the therapist which may impede his letting go of the patient at a propitious time is his reluctance to let the patient use him primarily as an incorporation or as a transference object. Such use may seem too much like abetting the magical thinking of the patient's unconscious — the same unconscious that helped him to get into trouble in the first place — and so a lengthy but sometimes only mildly productive analysis of the transference can result.

Therapist Techniques

Several techniques may enhance brief therapy.

Spontaneity and Flexibility. The therapist should be willing to bring a variety of the abilities which enable him to be a reasonably successful person in his nonprofessional life into the treatment situation. For instance, the therapist should be as spontaneous and flexible as his temperament allows, though not more. Different patients respond to different approaches: a chronically masochistic, anxious patient who gets into one self-defeating situation after another may well find that a therapist who can be direct, active, and sometimes bantering can make the therapy situation rewarding. A patient with low self-esteem who has his fair share of appeal and wit may be helped by a therapist who can smile and laugh.

Catharsis. Catharsis is a time-honored way of helping troubled people. When a therapist senses that there are strong feelings just below the surface, he can encourage their direct expression. With patients of borderline ego strength, the therapist may also have to help modulate the intensity of expression so that disruptive flooding of ego functioning does not occur.

Conflict Identification. In conflict identification, the therapist assigns an official label or formulation to the patient's distress to give him some intellectual mastery of the situation. Many patients, especially those unused to severe emotional distress, are frightened and mystified about what is going on inside them and frequently are afraid that these feelings portend "craziness." They are anxious about being anxious, or depressed about being depressed. In the vast majority of cases, psychosis is remote. The case of Allen, the depressed student in Chapter 13, demonstrates this point.

Active Reinforcement and Reassurance. Active reinforcement occurs when the therapist openly acknowledges that he thinks the patient has made progress or moved in his own interests. This can come as a smile, a nod of the head, saying "well done," or in a variety of ways.

Reassurance, when needed and when it can be accepted, can often diminish psychic distress. This does not mean blanket, Pollyanna statements to the effect that "everything will be all right." Allen felt much reassured during the consultation session.

Some patients have been told by irate relatives that they need psychiatric treatment when, in fact, neither the patient nor the therapist is convinced of this at all. In such instances, the therapist can reassure the patient that such is not the case.

Preparation for Further Therapy. Some patients enter treatment with a symptom that is clearly an expression of many unresolved conflicts; they may also show a readiness for an intensive investigation of the underlying conflicts. In such cases, as shown in the next example, the early therapy period can be used to prepare and motivate the patient for further therapy.

Example 16-1. Mrs. Morris, a recently married 22-year-old college student, was referred by her internist because of psychogenic obesity. Five months previously, she had married a foreign student with known Hodgkin's disease. Emotional stress had always been reflected by her weight, and she had gained 30 pounds since her marriage. It quickly became clear that her marriage was influenced by a number of unconscious and preconscious motivations and conflicts. Her therapist saw her as being "perky, heavy-set, attractive, and intelligent."

Her husband was due to complete his studies and return to his home in a few weeks. The patient obviously had a number of major stresses confronting her as well as a number of unresolved adolescent conflicts still present. The therapist used his last few visits with the patient to help her see that obesity was merely a symptom of more profound psychic distress. She readily accepted the evidence for this and also the recommendation for long-term, dynamically oriented psychotherapy when she reached her husband's homeland.

Paradoxically, the therapist may need to reduce anxiety about situational factors at the same time he is raising anxiety about intrapsychic matters for the patient whose motivation for uncovering therapy is questionable but who otherwise appears to be a good candidate for it, as shown in the case of Ben in Chapter 13.

PLANNING FOR BRIEF PSYCHOTHERAPY

Thus far it would appear that brief therapy is largely a *post hoc* phenomenon; i.e., only after a patient has gotten benefit from several sessions and does not seem motivated for or capable of longer-term treatment does the therapist decide that he will be a "brief-therapy" patient. Certainly this is often the case, but one can be more systematic. There are certain constellations of personality characteristics and situations which can allow the therapist to plan from the first interview on as to whether treatment is likely to be brief or long. These plans are, of course, always working formulations which can be modified as therapy continues and as new facets of the patient's involvement with treatment become apparent.

There are those patients who strike the therapist

as being psychologically healthy people caught in a situational crisis, as in the cases of Allen in Chapter 13 and Mrs. Linden in Chapter 15. Working definitions of psychological health have been notoriously hard to come by, and I will at least partially beg the question by saying that, first, such people strike the therapist as being well put together psychologically, usually able to enjoy life, to utilize their talents, to cope with stress, and to take advantage of opportunity, and as having a "strong ego" in the psychoanalytic sense. In short, prior to the period of acute stress, they fulfill Freud's two criteria of health: they are able to love and to work, and, to add a third criterion which has become more salient since Freud's Victorian period, they can also play. Such patients often need very few visits to help them make an adjustment for which they already possess the abilities; the sessions act more as a catalyst than anything else.

Example 16-2. An unmarried 27-year-old man came to a new university to embark on a teaching career after having obtained his Ph.D. Two weeks after arriving on the campus, he became anxious and depressed and sought psychiatric help. In the first session, he spoke about loneliness, of missing old friends who were thousands of miles away, of fears that he would not be able to handle his new teaching assignments. Review of his past adjustment showed that his academic performance, his friendship and leisure time activities, his contentment with his family and his existence, his abilities to cope with stress had all been quite good. This was his first psychiatric contact.

The therapist explored with him the social and academic resources on the new campus and went over his tentative teaching plans with him; he encouraged him to acquaint himself with the campus more fully and work on solidifying his course outline prior to the next visit. A week later, the patient came in to report that he was feeling much better and was sleeping and eating well; that he had made some new friends; that he had gotten some good letters from friends back home; that he had gone over his course outline with the head of his department, who had been pleased with it; and that he felt his life was in good order and no further therapy was indicated. Therapy ended. Two months later, the patient called to report that one of his colleagues was depressed and that he wanted to arrange a referral (which was done); during that conversation the former patient said that things continued to go swimmingly. It had been apparent from the beginning that it would be highly unlikely that this patient would need more than a very few sessions.

A second group of patients are those who have a neurotic core structure, who may or may not have a contemporary derivative conflict, and who *do* fulfill the criteria for uncovering psychotherapy. In such cases, the period of early therapy serves both to help resolve the current conflicts and to prepare the patient to enter into a long-term uncovering psychotherapy, as shown in the case of Ben (Chapter 13) and in several examples reported below.

A third group of patients are those who obviously have significant neurotic core problems, who have lived in equilibrium with these problems until recent disquieting events caused a latter-day derivative conflict to appear which led the patient to seek treatment. Because the patients are not good candidates for long-term uncovering therapy, judged by the criteria in Chapter 13, there is little point in trying to work with the basic core neurosis, but considerable relief can result when one helps the patient to work on the contemporary derivative conflict, as in the cases of Colin in Chapter 13 and of Mrs. Graves in Chapter 14. Again, this kind of assessment can often be made in the initial interviews. After a period of brief therapy, either the patient is restored to his previous equilibrium and therapy can end, at least for the time being, or the patient may become a candidate for longer-term supportive treatment.

A fourth group of patients are those who are chronically psychotic or, at best, have borderline ego strength, such as Daniel (Chapter 13), who need immediate help with day-to-day problems and may well need long-term supportive psychotherapy of the sort described in Chapter 18.

SOME MECHANISMS IN THE RELIEF OF SYMPTOMS

A number of psychodynamic mechanisms are involved in the early relief of symptoms. Some of the more common mechanisms include primitive incorporation and identification, transference, object substitution, and diminishing the importance of the symptoms.

Primitive Incorporation

This is seen frequently in schizophrenic or borderline patients: the patient seems to take a part of the psychiatrist into his own psychic apparatus. If the psychiatrist has confidence that his "devoured" body part will regenerate, thus sanctioning the cannibalistic component of the act, he can be free to be repeatedly incorporated, as shown in Examples 16-3 and 16-4.

> *Example 16-3.* A married artist of 27 complained of peculiar sudden "panic attacks" (they later proved to be displacements of anger from his job). He also became unbearably anxious whenever he had to leave the city limits for any reason. After eight sessions his panic attacks had virtually gone, but leaving the city was still difficult. Shortly thereafter, he reported that he had gone on a day's outing and had overcome his fear at the Golden Gate Bridge approach by conjuring up the image of a "portable psychiatrist" — his therapist — whom he carried in his car trunk, to be consulted if he had to.
>
> (The therapist, originally from Chicago, refrained from sharing with the patient his own fantasy that being transported in the trunk of

a car was often a prelude to a most unpsychiatric form of ventilation.)

> *Example 16-4.* A handyman, age 45, a long-term ambulatory schizophrenic, said, with a peculiar smile, to his therapist, "I admire your brains." She had the distinct impression that he had preempted her cortex as his personal property and that this feeling was instrumental in the improvement he subsequently felt in his life and work.

Transference Mechanisms

In this category I place those unconsciously determined aspects of benevolence that the patient attributes to the therapist and the fostering institution. In many respects, such expectations may be a more sophisticated version of incorporation. Such trust may allow the patient to look into himself and learn about himself in a way he had never been able to do previously.

Through the transference, a patient may be able to "borrow" power and security to make decisions he could not previously make, so-called transference cures.

> *Example 16-5.* A married house painter of 28 sought therapy at the suggestion of a therapist in the state hospital where he had committed himself for exhibitionism. Before his hospitalization, he had wanted to sell paint instead of going out on jobs but had been too shy to ask for the change. After three sessions, he had asked for and obtained the store job, although this move had barely been touched on in the sessions. That he could do, after three sessions, what had been impossible for two years can be attributed to his positive transference.
>
> His exhibitionistic impulses diminished greatly in three more sessions: he dropped out of therapy at that point, probably having got a good measure of what he had come for.

The fact that the therapist accepts and likes a patient frequently makes it possible for the patient to use the therapist as a substitute object, to accept himself more, and thus to restore disrupted object relationships. Stories of middle-aged, depressed women who come to look on young psychiatrists as their good sons (that never were) and as doctors (who will take care of them in their old age) are legion. If the therapist can let himself be so used, he can often help the patient restore her real-life object relationships.

Diminishing or Detoxification of the Importance of the Symptoms

Intellectual insight occurs when therapist and patient can name a previously unnamed source of fear and can connect two previously unconnected sets of feelings or ideas. Such insight often helps to lower anxiety and discomfort.

Superficial insight (unfortunately used too often in the pejorative sense), with an affective component, is illustrated in the next example; in this case it obviously benefited the patient.

Example 16-6. A 32-year-old housewife and mother of two children — the younger of whom possibly was retarded — had made two halfhearted suicide attempts and was rescued both times by her husband. She considered her husband, in their five years of marriage, arrogantly authoritarian and constantly critical of her intelligence, femininity, and abilities as a mother. He blamed her for their younger child's so-called retardation, although the child was too young for evaluation. She wilted, became moody and depressed, and later made the attempts at suicide in reproach.

In the third session, the therapist asked that although her husband obviously had a low opinion of her, why did she agree with him, and had others in her life told her she would never amount to much? It turned out that her father had done so.

(When a patient presents a depreciated opinion of himself without good reason, questions like "Whoever told you that you were such a no-good?" may first make the patient aware that he has been unwittingly living out a significant other's opinion.)

At the next session she related how, the previous Saturday, her husband had started in on her again when she returned from the grocery store. Thereupon, she exultantly said, she took out each can from the shopping bag and hurled it against the wall, not too far from her husband's head. Three of the first depression-free days she had enjoyed in years followed. Of course she could not hurl groceries every time she got upset, but the escape was there if needed. In short, she no longer had to accept her husband's low opinion of her.

A session later she discussed separating from him, and felt "right about it inside"; she did not want any more therapy.

A final session was arranged for a month later. At that time, her good spirits and determination persisted, and therapy ended.

Sometimes the therapist can aid in the separation of the symptom per se and its implications of personal unworthiness and hopelessness, as in the case of Colin (Chapter 13). The jailing and the judge's lecture had reinforced for Colin society's opinion that homosexuality was a shameful thing. The therapist sought to restore Colin's view that it was a lifestyle that had worked for him and deserved to be continued.

The strength of unacceptable impulses can be weakened through verbalization: the errant wish disappears.

Example 16-7. A woman, recovering from a florid postpartum psychosis, told about forgetting several days in a row to pick up some duplicate car keys at the locksmith. The original set may have been lost in a tussle to get her to the hospital when she became psychotic. Although no important material emerged, she picked the keys up the next day. Talking about forgetting them removed the inhibition.

Finally, the strength of the impulse's unacceptability can likewise be weakened through verbalization; a previously unacceptable impulse now becomes acceptable.

Example 16-8. A talented college student of 19 had twice attempted suicide because of feelings of futility, emptiness, and isolation. It soon emerged that his personal standards, despite his impressive talent and intellect, were impossibly high and admitted of no childishness or weakness. Any dependency gratification or close personal relationships were firmly forbidden. No wonder he felt his life futile.

After two months of therapy, he began to see how his scorn of childishness concealed considerable wishes in that direction. As a result he considerably softened his standards for himself, though concurrently he noted increasing productivity in his intellectual and artistic efforts. Most importantly, he took increased satisfaction in his interpersonal relationships.

Therapy continued for over a year; he consolidated and expanded many of the gains of the first two months.

FREQUENT OUTCOMES OF PRESENTING COMPLAINTS

In the early period of therapy the patient's symptoms often change in intensity, quality, or importance. Five of the more common outcomes — transformations — of the presenting symptoms follow: (1) the symptom persists, but its importance changes; (2) the symptom disappears without particular insight or affective discharge; (3) numerous symptoms diminish after common, underlying causes are found; (4) superficial insight and affective discharge occur; and (5) the symptom disappears, to reappear later in better perspective.

Change of Importance of the Symptoms

The original symptom may doggedly persist but therapy focuses on something else. Such a shift should be openly remarked upon.

Example 16-9, Mrs. T. Mrs. T., an obese mother of three, at the encouragement of an endocrinologist sought psychiatric help regarding her weight after failure of treatment at an endocrinology clinic. After several weeks, an underlying depression became apparent, and treatment was directed at understanding and trying to relieve the depression. However, the patient's weight remained unchanged.

Symptom Reduction without Insight

Symptoms frequently diminish without evidence of insight or affective discharge, especially in patients who have established transferences to therapists or institutions. The passage of time, coupled with supportive measures, promotes the improvement.

Example 16-10. A 57-year-old widow was known to generations of residents of the psychiatric clinic. Every two years or so, she would become depressed and lose interest in her work, her reading, her friends, and her tennis. A supervisor who had treated her several years before advised the therapist to conduct a careful hearing of her story, followed by kind but firm advice for her to keep up her apartment, her typing, and her tennis. He predicted that amid considerable complaints that things still were not what they used to be, and with no insight whatsoever, she would return to her former level of functioning. His prediction was borne out in ten sessions.

Connecting Current Distress with Chronic Conflicts

Patients may come with several complaints that seem to them discrete, isolated, mystifying, and unpleasant occurrences in their emotional lives. After a few sessions, these symptoms may emerge as superficial manifestations of current unrecognized stresses (phenotypic), which in turn derive from nuclear, childhood conflicts (genotypic), as the example of Mrs. Graves (Chapter 14) illustrates. Furthermore, as recognition of the relationship of the symptoms to the current stresses and past conflicts burgeons, the symptoms and distress may recede spontaneously. Mrs. Graves' case is represented in Figure 16-1.

Superficial Insight and Affective Discharge

A single superficial insight coupled with an affective discharge — an emotional realization of the insight — may bring such improvement that the patient functions at a presymptom level and feels equal to meeting the challenges of his existence again. This is shown in Example 16-6, symbolized by the throwing of the groceries, and in the following example:

Example 16-11. An unmarried nurse was referred by her supervisor to the employee health service for psychiatric evaluation because when working the midnight shift, she would call in sick at least once a week at 11:30 P.M., necessitating the supervisor's last-minute search for a substitute. The illnesses, usually respiratory, were confirmed by physician's notes. On duty she worked well.

During her single session with the psychiatrist, it came out that the patient lived a lonely life, had few friends beyond her TV set, and felt close only to the grandparents who had raised her; they lived several hundred miles away. The psychiatrist asked her, "Who would take care of you if you really got seriously ill?" "No one," she replied sadly.

Her loneliness was discussed, as was the idea that the frequent illnesses and trips to the doctor were the ways that she took care of herself as she wished someone else would. The patient's work record improved remarkably after this interview, though six months later she again began to miss work.

For the patient who feels deprived of dependency gratification, the acknowledgment of the deprivation and the awareness of the psychiatrist's compassion can prove beneficial.

Reappearance in Better Perspective

The presenting symptoms may also disappear quickly, to reappear later in better perspective.

Example 16-12. A married woman of 22

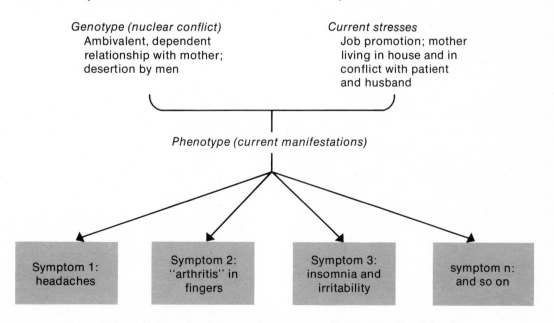

Figure 16-1. Relationship of Current Symptoms to Nuclear Conflict: Mrs. Graves.

explained on her first visit that her worries about frigidity were dubbed minor by her gynecologist because "over 80 percent of all women have some degree of frigidity." No more was heard of this for six weeks when, in discussion of her marriage, the patient told of how she got sick every time her husband laid his hands upon her. Her original complaint thus was labeled a ticket by which she entered therapy, so that she could talk about her marriage, and thereby, paradoxically, discuss what she had only been able to hint at earlier, her abhorrence of sexuality.

This is an example of a symptom being used as a symbol for itself — frigidity as a symbol of sexual conflict.

TREATMENT OF DEPRESSION

The single most frequent neurotic syndrome presented to many clinics is neurotic depression. The treatment of depression varies depending on the depth of the depression, its degree of incapacitation, its cause, and its duration. I will confine my remarks to treatment of depressions that seem clearly to be in response to life events and that may be approached by brief psychotherapy.

In mild depressions, or moderate depressions in patients with good ego strength, the major therapeutic tasks are to (1) identify the loss that precipitated the depression; (2) enhance expression of feelings, going first after feelings of loss, sorrow, and longing for the lost object, and only then after feelings of anger, resentment, or hostility; and (3) make oneself available as a temporary substitute object until the patient reestablishes his real life object relationships. In addition, the patient should be encouraged to maintain those daily responsibilities he is thinking of relinquishing because of psychomotor retardation. Antidepressant medication is not immediately called for. These principles, as well as those described previously, are demonstrated in the following example, as well as in the case of Steven G. in Chapter 17.

Example 16-13. Mrs. Osbourne, a 34-year-old mother of four, appeared with severe depression and anxiety centering around the suicide of her sister (whom she liked) three months earlier, a chronically unhappy marriage, and a fear of return of old asthma and eczema. She saw herself as a drab, luckless individual who was unable to assert herself in her marriage and who felt trapped by events and circumstances.

During her six visits, the therapist pressed her in a number of areas. He told her to try to cry about the sister's death (the patient had not been able to do so). He challenged her to try and do something for herself to test the strength of her apparent masochism. He helped her define her anxiety and depression as responses to external or internal events rather than as afflictions passively accepted from a malign fate. He challenged her poor concept of herself and got her to look more realistically at her personal, social, and physical assets which she believed she didn't possess.

During the course of her six sessions, there was a remarkable shift. She began experiencing hours and days free of depression and anxiety for the first time in years. She tried to discuss her marital situation with her husband and, when he would not communicate, made the decision at first to separate and later to divorce him.

Eight months later, at a follow-up visit, the patient reported that she had been doing well in her plans for work and further schooling. She had gotten involved with a man whom she later found out was married, and had begun to wonder how she always managed to pick "the wrong guy." Furthermore, she began to see that she was naïve about the impact she had on men. Because of these realizations, she readily accepted a referral for group therapy.

In moderate depressions, especially in patients with depressive or borderline characteristics, the negative side of the ambivalence toward the lost object may be very hard to establish with the patient, even though it seems apparent to the therapist. In such cases, displaced targets for anger may appear, expressed by sudden invectives against political parties, minority groups, ungiving relatives, psychiatrists, and others. For such patients, this may be the closest they can come to expressing the aggression that had previously been turned in against the self.

In any event, when patients have expressed strong feelings during an hour, it is only common tact and courtesy to allow them time to pull themselves together before leaving the office. In any case, the therapist should not obstinately end the session exactly at the fifty-minute mark, but should extend it to allow a recovery period.

Two more things should be observed in treating such patients. First, antidepressant medication should be considered seriously if the depression does not diminish in the first week or two of treatment. Second, the patient should be pushed to maintain his usual responsibilities even if they seem onerous at the time. The acute depression frequently will remit during the first few weeks of treatment, and the need for longer treatment can then be evaluated.

THE THERAPEUTIC CONTRACT: INITIAL AND RENEGOTIATED

After the first several sessions, often much of the presenting distress will be gone. Patient and therapist will presumably have gotten perspective on the origins of the acute stress that brought the patient into treatment and on the personality patterns and life experiences which predisposed toward the stress. The therapist will have information on the patient's strengths and weaknesses and be able to form his own judgment on the patient's need for further psychotherapy, as determined by the dynamic formulation discussed in Chapter 14, and on the patient's appropriateness for uncovering or reality-oriented psychotherapies according to the parameters described in Chapter 13.

For some patients, relief of presenting symptoms is all that the patient is really interested in or all

that might realistically be hoped for. No further treatment is indicated now, though the patient may encounter distress again in the future and wish then to return to the clinic. Patient and therapist should prepare for termination, an issue discussed in detail in Chapter 20.

Other patients may turn out to be good candidates for long-term, uncovering psychotherapy. Therapist and patient should renegotiate the therapeutic contract so that it is clear to both that symptomatic relief is no longer one of the major goals of treatment, but that increased awareness of previously unconscious processes has become the major goal, and that the development of such awareness may itself become uncomfortable and anxiety-provoking at times. The therapist should make clear that he will adopt a different stance than he might have during the initial phases. He will no longer direct the interviews as actively; he may no longer answer the questions he responded to originally; he will to a much greater degree leave to the patient the responsibility for bringing up material to be discussed; he will explain about free association; and so on. Many of the issues involved in starting long-term therapy are discussed in Chapter 19.

The patient may appear to be a good candidate for group therapy, as described by the criteria stated in Chapter 21. He should be prepared for his group experience in the manner described by I. D. Yalom.[6]

It may appear that the problem is primarily a marital couple problem, that to see only one partner to the marriage is to imagine the sound of only one hand clapping. In that case, the spouse should be brought in and seen either conjointly (both partners with the same therapist), or collaboratively (each partner with his or her own therapist). There are occasions when it is useful to see marital partners individually in the context of conjoint marital couple therapy, as described in Chapter 23.

Mrs. T. (cont'd.). In 1962, Mrs. T. started several months of intensive individual therapy in which her depression and many problems were usefully explored. It became apparent that many of her symptoms were related to a difficult marital situation. The T.'s then came for a few months of marital couple therapy, with moderate but not marked improvement in the relationship.

There were occasional visits by the wife or the couple over the next several years.

In 1969, Mr. T. came in, feeling considerable distress over a deteriorating extramarital affair. Several individual sessions with him helped put this affair in perspective with other affairs and his previously unrecognized intense needs for female approval and affirmation.

Marital couple therapy was reinstituted, with each partner testifying to his/her feelings of being neglected and abandoned by the other, and the consequent anger, resentment, and vengefulness. Five more months of marital therapy resulted in a stabilization of the relationship at a significantly more gratifying level.

Some patients who are not good candidates for dynamic (uncovering) psychotherapy nevertheless need continuing psychotherapy with a reality-oriented focus. The therapist may continue to see the patient once a week, or even less often, focusing primarily on day-to-day events and giving the patient whatever advice and suggestions he can to help the patient handle troublesome matters more effectively. Another form of supportive treatment for patients meeting certain selection criteria is described in Chapter 18.

Events of brief treatment and early therapy test the working knowledge of the practitioner, who is required to be flexible and related in developing a treatment plan which fits the needs of the patient before him. Psychotherapy is not one treatment; it is a range of treatments, all making use of the therapist's skills at interviewing, at formulation, and at managing transference with individually different patients.

REFERENCES

1. Goldstein, Arnold P., and Sanford J. Dean: *The Investigation of Psychotherapy,* Wiley-Interscience, New York, 1966.

2. Meltzoff, Julian, and Melvin Kornreich: *Research in Psychotherapy,* Atherton, New York, 1970.

3. Truax, Charles B., and Robert R. Carkhuff: *Toward Effective Counseling and Psychotherapy,* Aldine, Chicago, 1967.

4. Campbell, J., and C. P. Rosenbaum: "Placebo Effect and Symptom Relief in Psychotherapy," *Arch. Gen. Psychiat.,* **16**:364–368, 1967.

5. Kalis, B., et al.: "Precipitating Stress as a Focus in Psychotherapy," *Arch. Gen. Psychiat.,* **5**:219–226, 1961.

6. Yalom, I. D.: *The Theory and Practice of Group Psychotherapy,* Basic Books, New York, 1970.

An Example of Brief Psychotherapy

In September 1967, Steven G., a man aged 29 who was recently separated from his wife, applied for psychotherapy. He agreed to being observed by several members of the clinic staff from behind a one-way mirror. Staff members took notes at each of the six sessions: the detailed case presentation given below comes from those notes. Mr. G. was seen under the aegis of the clinic's Immediate Treatment (I.T.) program, wherein he was seen a few days after his first contact and in which the initial period of treatment was limited to six or seven visits. As part of the treatment, the patient was asked to complete a Minnesota Multiphasic Personality Inventory (MMPI) before his first I.T. visit and after his last. As luck later had it, he had taken the MMPI twice before in his life, and the staff was able to compare those with the 1967 tests as well as the one given in 1970.

BEFORE THE FIRST VISIT

First Contact

The patient first called the clinic on September 22, 1967; the social worker who took the call summarized their contact as follows:

> This bright, separated young man is applying for therapy as he is becoming more and more depressed and can't eat or sleep — (he sounded close to tears). Precipitant to current depression was his wife's leaving him. She is now filing for divorce. He appreciates belatedly that he "stifled" her freedom — that he gave no consideration to esthetic parts of living. The separation has shaken him considerably and he is now seriously considering his past lifestyle. Feels he needs professional help during this time. Separation occurred 7/1/67 after six years of marriage. There are two children, both girls, ages 2½ and 6 months. Refer to Immediate Treatment Program.

MMPI PROFILE

Mr. G. completed his pretreatment MMPI in time for it to be scored and interpreted informally before the first interview. That profile appears as Figure 17-1.

The high degree of depression and feelings of alienation, separation, and anxiety on the profile caused at least one member of the group to wonder seriously about the imminence of a schizophrenic break.

Though it may be anticipating the story a bit, Rudolf Moos, Ph.D., agreed to interpret all four of the first MMPIs "blind," that is, knowing nothing more about the patient than his sex and the ages at

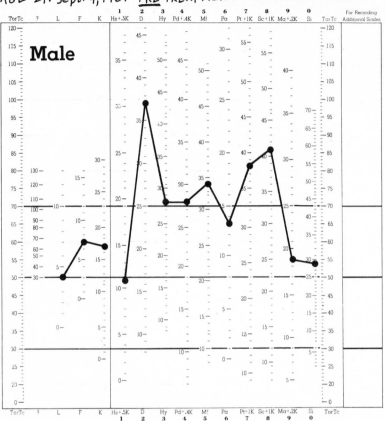

Figure 17-1   Pretreatment MMPI profile. (MMPI form copyright 1948 by The Psychological Corporation, New York.)

which he took the test. Dr. Moos did not sit in on the treatment of the patient and knew nothing about his clinical situation until after interpreting the posttreatment MMPI.

From MMPIs administered at ages 19 and 25 as part of standard batteries of tests to applicants to college and graduate school and from the pretreatment MMPI, Dr. Moos drew the conclusions shown immediately below; his comments based on the posttreatment test will be presented later. The three profiles from which he worked are shown in Figure 17-2.

PSYCHOLOGICAL REPORT – MMPI INTERPRETATION

The following is a "blind" interpretation of four MMPI profiles of S. G., taken at the following times: (1) April 1957, when the patient was 19; (2) June 1963, when the patient was 25; (3) September 1967, when the patient was 29 and just before he entered brief psychotherapy; and (4) November 1967, at the conclusion of six sessions of brief psychotherapy.

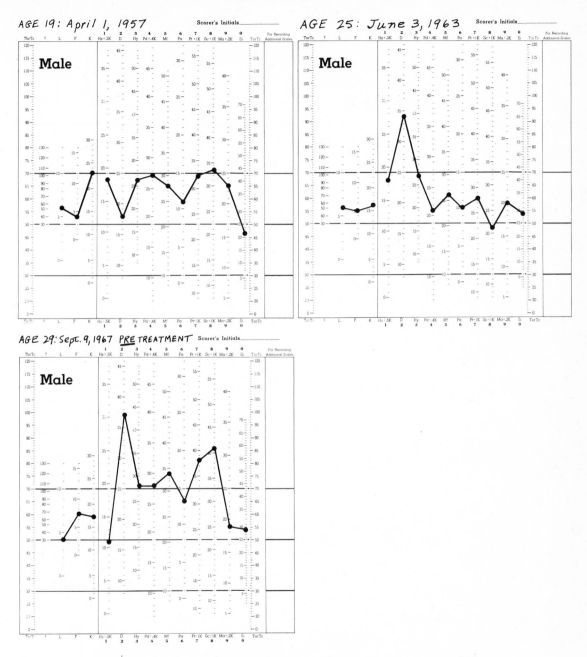

Figure 17-2   The first three MMPI profiles. (MMPI forms copyright 1948 by The Psychological Corporation, New York.)

The April 1957, age 19, profile suggests that at this time the patient was highly defended, intellectualized, and somewhat rigid (K); tended to repress, deny, be naïve and see the world through rose-colored glasses (Hy); felt somewhat passive and dependent, lonely and alienated with no very close interpersonal ties (Pd, Mf, Sc); tended to be somewhat over-sensitive and "thin-skinned" (Pa); had some concern and mild anxiety with regard to the adequacy of his functioning (Pt); but managed to remain rather highly motivated and maintain his position of having a reasonable energy level and being a "doer" (Ma).

The June 1963, age 25, profile suggests that the patient has become more open to experience, is functioning relatively adequately and does not have as strong a tendency toward denial and rigidity (lower K); that he is obviously depressed (D); that he is feeling somewhat more shy and introverted (Si); that he still manages to keep going and perhaps "smile through tears" (Ma) in spite of his subjective feelings of depression. Otherwise the basic character structure appears similar to that seen in the profile six years earlier.

The September 1967, age 29, pretreatment profile again shows obvious depression (D); an increase in feelings of alienation, separateness, and unrelatedness and lack of stable interpersonal satisfactions (Pd, Sc); and a sharp increase in anxiety (Pt). At this point the patient is clearly still able to keep functioning (K, Ma); however, he is hurting quite badly and apparently questioning some of the basic premises of his manner of living.

THE FIRST VISIT, SEPTEMBER 27, 1967

Identifying Information

The patient, Steve, was a 29-year-old space engineer who was currently separated from his wife, Joan. They had two children, both girls, aged 2½ years and 6 months. The patient referred himself to the clinic. It was planned initially that he be seen for six immediate treatment sessions at the end of which a decision would be made as to whether he should continue in therapy or not.

Chief Complaint and Present Illness

"I feel I am not adequately involved in life. And I want to find out more about myself." The patient also stated that he was having difficulty eating and sleeping, and described periods during the last three months when he had cried.

The acute aspects of the patient's illness were dated from around July 1, 1967, when he became separated after six years of marriage. He had lived alone in a one-room apartment since then, and he became increasingly depressed. He ruminated not only about his marriage but about many problems he had which considerably antedated his marriage; e.g., he had always had difficulty relating to women, he was overly involved with his father as a child and as a young man, and he had very few interests in his life outside of his work and his family.

He became increasingly despondent after the separation from his wife. His discomfort came to a peak around Labor Day; he then spent three days at a Jesuit retreat, even though he himself is not Catholic. On those three days, he described spending a day and a half alone crying by himself. The patient did not want to get divorced at the time, although his wife seemed determined to go through with the proceedings. The patient still saw his wife fairly regularly, however; their most frequent contact was when he went to her house on weekends to babysit while she went out with other men. Although he felt generally somewhat better than he did around Labor Day, "not so explosive," he still felt lonely and depressed and was sleeping only two to three hours a night. He had had some suicidal feelings around the time of Labor Day; however, he felt that this was not a problem at the time.

Past History

The patient was an only child. He made a point of stating "there were no females of my generation." As a child he had few friends of either sex. His mother was very nervous and neurotic, and he says that he was never very close to her. His relationship with his father, by contrast, was always extremely warm and intimate. It was, in fact, such a close relationship that the patient was now somewhat concerned that it may have been pathological. His father died while the patient was a freshman in college, and the patient became profoundly depressed. Although the patient majored in psychology, following his graduation he joined the service and spent two years as an engineer.

The patient was married in 1961 at age 23, and returned to graduate school to get an M.A. in electrical engineering. His wife came from a broken home. They were very dependent on one another and had very few friends; she "has a tremendous need for love." The patient developed infectious mononucleosis on their honeymoon and had not really felt good since. The patient had always been concerned in the past about with his difficulty relating to women, and seemed somewhat concerned that he had not had intercourse prior to marriage. Sex in the marriage had always been somewhat unsatisfactory, with the patient feeling that he was very selfish and that his wife was never really gratified. That there was never very much closeness in the marriage the patient attributed to many things, including the fact that he had a master's degree while his wife had less than one year of college. Because of the problems which they both felt existed, they consulted a psychiatrist fairly early in the course of their marriage. However, for a variety of reasons, this turned out to be unsatisfactory.

After the patient achieved his master's, he obtained a job with an overseas company, and apparently he has always done fairly well in his work. The marriage continued along, with a gradually worsening relationship between them. It came to something of a crisis about one year ago when they were visiting a nearby area preparing to move to the job that he presently holds. The patient stated that at that time he slapped his wife's face and felt that that was sort of a turning point in their marriage.

When the second of their two children was born in March 1967, the patient felt that if he accompanied his wife to the delivery room and stayed with her during the delivery, he would achieve the closeness that he felt was always lacking in their marriage. However, this seems to have been a rather desperate last attempt to save the marriage, and he found, much to his dismay, that they did not achieve the sort of miraculous cure that he had hoped for by witnessing the birth of his child. He went home that night very despondent and drank a fifth of bourbon, a highly unusual thing for him to do. About the same time, the patient began having an affair with another woman whom he described as having many of the same problems in her marriage that he had in his. His wife was acquainted with this woman, and he thought that it was quite possible that she knew he had had an affair with her. It may, he felt, have been a contributing factor to his wife's demands for a divorce.

Psychological Examination

The patient was an intelligent, neatly dressed, crew-cut individual who appeared somewhat outgoing and initially quite friendly. He talked in a steady stream throughout most of the hour, giving the interviewer little opportunity to interject any questions. He seemed quite animated and smiled and laughed occasionally, although it did not always seem particularly appropriate to his expressed feelings of depression. The patient had a marked tendency to intellectualize his problems, and he readily used psychological terminology. However, his insight remained somewhat superficial.

Plan

It was explained to the patient that it was thought he could obtain considerable benefit from six sessions of brief therapy. The plan as outlined to him initially was that the therapy would focus on the question of reality versus fantasy in his life, and also that an attempt would be made to help him realize and deal with those most immediate problems in his life and leave until later those areas which could be considered more long-term problems.

THE SUBSEQUENT IMMEDIATE TREATMENT VISITS

Second and Third Visits

Steve's moods had been up and down after the first visit. He called Joan (his wife) to suggest they see a reconciliation counselor; she "blew her stack" at the idea. He babysat for her over the weekend; she was abrupt with him on her return. Steve resented being excluded from Joan's life. The therapist noted that, much as Steve would like to, he didn't own Joan anymore, if ever he did.

It was obvious that the patient was going out of his way to find excuses to rejoin his wife, even though she was not interested in him beyond his usefulness as occasional babysitter. He was using each slight sign of interest from her as support for his hopes which were obviously unrealistic, since his wife had quite clearly thrown him out of the house when he had confessed his extramarital affair, and she was actively pursuing divorce.

The therapist sympathized with the patient's wish to get back together with his wife, but pointed out that the prospect was unrealistic, considering her made-up mind. Since the patient had majored in psychology, the therapist made the analogy between the patient's behavior and one of B. F. Skinner's well-trained pigeons. For the birds, behavior persisted under conditions of intermittent reinforcement — "hope springs eternal in the pigeon's breast" — but extinguished when reinforcements abruptly ceased. The therapist suggested to the patient that his occasional meetings with his wife, intermittent reinforcements, were serving to keep his hopes up for a reunion and thus perpetuate his frustration; that though it might be more painful initially, perhaps he should try to go without seeing her at all.

The therapist explored Steve's reunion fantasies but also pointed out that he was still guilt-ridden and was presenting himself as the remorseful worm. His wife, as in the manner of a woman scorned, was stepping on him. The therapist noted out loud that Steve was doing a good job of punishing himself and wondered how long he would need to keep it up.

Steve talked further about the six-month affair which, when he confessed it to his wife, led to his being thrown out of the house. He had interpreted his wife's statement months earlier to "get this woman thing out of your system" as tacit encouragement and approval of his having an affair. The woman turned out to be a coworker, not very feminine in appearance or manner, one who was having her own marital problems.

Steve found himself curious about whom Joan was seeing on weekends, what she was doing with them. He was then not particularly interested in dating other women, but instead wanted to broaden his life experiences more generally, referring positively to an encounter group he was beginning to get involved with. The therapist supported this interest.

The patient inquired if the therapist would be interested in interviewing Joan. The therapist declined, pointing out that they were no longer a marital couple, much as Steve would want to have it otherwise.

Steve was due to take a two-week business trip overseas after the second session. He was worried about how he would handle the situation when meeting old friends there. The therapist suggested, "I'll bet you're tempted to buy a half-page in the local newspaper to let everyone know how badly hurt you feel." Steve smilingly agreed.

In the third session, Steve had returned from his trip and reported a very pleasant two weeks. He had only occasionally been depressed. He told his old friends simply that he and Joan were separated but did not go into the details and was proud that he could contain himself from bursts of self-pity. He had met two attractive women there, taken each to dinner, and found those evenings enjoyable.

Fourth Session

Steve felt much better, felt he was "around the corner" as far as Joan was concerned, felt much more independent. For instance, Joan had insisted that he babysit over the previous weekend; it conflicted with his schedule, and he had refused to do so. He started dating a couple of women. He felt much freer and wanted to think about broadening his personal horizons generally. The therapist posed the question of using the remaining interviews to try to decide how these goals might best be accomplished.

More history emerged during this session. Steve's mother was never close to him and always seemed nervous and distant. Instead, he was taken care of by his father's mother, whom he remembered as a big, warm woman who held him when he was frightened. The patient's father was always very close to him, often discussing business and personal matters with him as if Steve were a colleague. His father died suddenly when Steve was a college freshman; Steve made all the funeral arrangements but never went through a formal grief reaction.

During the latter part of the session, Steve spoke about erotic fantasies he had been having when his 2½-year-old daughter, Cheri, would jump in his lap. As he talked, he began to see how he had been turning to the child for the kinds of satisfactions he had not been getting from Joan. He began to see that Joan had traits that he did not like; she was a sloppy housekeeper; she had trouble expressing tender emotions openly; and she always treated his sexual advances as if he were an animal and she a martyr. He found himself less concerned with what was going on in her life than he had been in previous weeks.

Fifth Session

The patient began the hour by explaining that he had had a "venting of emotions." "I feel aggression, hate, and anger toward Joan. I lit into her, something new." The patient noted he was saying what he really felt now, that he had not had the "personal strength" to say these things before. However, his ambivalence toward Joan was still quite evident. Regarding one incident several weeks ago, the patient recalled that when he got mad at her, she simply laughed, and at this point he had the impulse to kiss her. In response to the therapist's interpretation that the more independent the patient becomes, the more attractive he will become to Joan, the patient answered, "I'm still interested in the long run, but I'm not ready now."

The patient continued to talk about his relationship with his daughter Cheri. For the past year they had been getting into a "dependent relationship." "I was needing her love. Something didn't feel right about it to me. I had sexual arousals several times when she was on my lap." On one hand the patient feared separation from his daughter — "I can't let happen to Cheri what happened to my Dad and me." Yet on the other hand he was uncertain over their close physical relationship. In regard to the latter, he noted that as a child he himself had a warm, bosomy grandmother who had provided him with a close touching relationship. However, she died when he was six and since then he had been devoid of a touching relationship. When Cheri was born the patient noted great fears of having a son rather than a daughter. He wondered whether this was because of his former aversion to touching. Over the past year, though, the patient had slowly realized that physical touching is both natural and enjoyable.

The patient commented that he now felt in control of himself, but that basic problems were still present. In particular, he felt curious to pursue "this father thing." He didn't recall letting any emotions out when his father died and, at that time and at the time of therapy, he had no sense of sorrow. Yet he feared that listening to the last tape recording of his father (which he had never listened to in the intervening ten years) would make him start sweating and worrying.

In conjunction with talking about his father, the patient noted that relations with other men are an important thing for him to work on right now. He admitted that although he had no overt homosexual experiences, there had been times when he desired to touch either men or women. The patient defined his present concern as a dual one, wanting to start more "man-type activities" and know more men, and also wanting to get to know more women. He had sought these goals in such recent activities as an encounter group, several dates, and a recent hunting venture. In regard to these dates with other women, the patient wanted sex "only if my feelings are one-hundred percent. I'm ready for touching, but I'm a sensitive person, and I don't want to screw every girl that I meet."

At the end of the hour the patient, anticipating the next and last session, praised therapy. He wanted to find out what sort of therapy would be available if things did not work out in the upcoming months, and saw a central problem in the area of men and his relations with his father. "I'm worried most about overcoming this barrier of masculinity." The decision was made between therapist and patient to meet one more session as scheduled. Then a follow-up session in one to three months could be arranged.

Sixth Session, November 17, 1967

The patient began the hour by stating that things were "fine." He was asked how things were going with Joan. He initially stated that things were going pretty well with her and that he might as well talk about her a bit in order to get that subject "out of the way." He implied that he had several other things which he wished to speak about. The patient stated that Joan wanted to get

back together with him because she felt lonely. During the last week there had been some hugging with her. However, when he now felt "turned on," he felt as though he could show it, actually tell her that he felt turned on, and still remain in control of his emotions. He felt that he wished to live each moment as it came and that he was "trying to advise her" so that she could feel the same as he did and enjoy each moment as it came.

The therapist then commented that the patient was becoming free from having every relationship filled with "contingency clauses" and that each act no longer had to have long-term "cosmic" implications. The patient agreed. The patient went on to say that he felt more domineering and directive in his relationship with Joan and felt as though he were in control. The therapist responded, "It sounds as though you don't present yourself to her as a piece of shit floating in from the sea any longer." The patient agreed.

Steve went on and stated that he had two restraints upon any further relationships with Joan. He first wished to be treated as "an individual." He then wished to have "order in the house," something that had not been present in Joan's past behavior. He said, "If we do go back together it will be a long time from now — I am afraid to start on that path again until I have had more experiences." This was crucial.

The therapist replied with a question: "Have you ever had a purely sexual relationship with a woman without having any emotional involvement, and have you ever had a woman who loved you without you loving her in return?" The patient responded that he only had made love to two women in his entire life and that he had never had a woman love him without feeling he had to return the commitment.

The therapist told the patient that he should try to have more experiences with people who just like him for himself and for his body rather than with people whom he might plan to marry. Steve then began to think of how he might follow that prescription and stated that he was recently invited to an older woman's apartment in Saratoga but that, because of confusion about the date, he never carried through on the invitation. Furthermore, he felt that the woman was a little too old.

The patient then asked to change the subject somewhat and presented the therapist with a series of five items which he had jotted down on a sheet of paper. First, he wanted to know why he had to make everything that occurred around him so personal, why he had to explain everything in great detail to make it fit into context in his life. Second, he had recently realized that he had a fear of making concrete plans. He often waited until it was too late to make plans and then found himself with nothing to do, and he wondered why this was so. Third, he feared involvement with other people. Fourth, he had recently been forgetting to lock his car doors and laughingly stated that he got six feet away from his car almost every day, forgot locking his doors, and had to return. Fifth, he had been thinking recently about the question, "Do I believe in God?" The therapist then asked the patient, "Do you see a common theme to all these items?" The patient responded and stated that he thought it was in a failure to make a commitment, to ever make a decision.

The therapist then made an analogy and wanted the patient to comment on its relation to him: if one compared planets and stars and differentiated the two according to whether they emitted light or only reflected light, where would the patient place himself? The patient stated that he certainly had been very much a planet in the past but that now there might be some light in him and he was becoming more of a star.

The therapist then told Steve that he often waited for someone else to define a relationship. In other words, Steve would let the other person know who Steve was only after the person had let him know who he was. The therapist further elaborated by stating, "You react to people instead of presenting yourself to them." This in effect was interpreted as the underlying trouble with his relationships to both men and women, that he did not present himself but only reflected the other's expectations.

When the therapist asked the patient why he failed to commit himself, why he failed to make decisions, why he failed to define himself first, the patient was unable to respond. The therapist then suggested that the patient "stop the shilly-shallying" and take some basic steps toward defining his relationships with other people. He pointed out that each planned event with another person need not be interpreted as an extremely important event; that he could make plans, have an unpleasant evening, and learn something from that unpleasant evening. He thought that the patient would be better off making concrete plans and then seeing how they turned out rather than never making any plans at all. The therapist wondered whether the fact that this was the last session had anything to do with the patient's apparent sliding back with his relationship with Joan. Steve thought not. He stated that last Saturday night he had been taking care of the children and called Joan at the library and told her to come home and relieve him. She not only came home as requested, but she cooked him a dinner, something she had not done since their separation, fixed herself a drink, and asked him to come into the living room and sit down and talk. He considered that his increased interest in Joan was a result of her increased interest in him.

The last part of the session dealt with the issue of further treatment. Steve said he didn't really think that he needed any more at that time, that what he really needed was to see more people in a greater number of situations and acquire more life experience. The therapist agreed, underscored the strengths and constructive changes Steve had made during the six sessions. Both agreed to a follow-up session several months later.

Posttreatment MMPI Data

Steve's pre- and posttreatment MMPI profiles are shown in Figure 17-3.

Repeating Dr. Moos's interpretation of the pretreatment test and adding on his comments about the posttreatment test, we find:

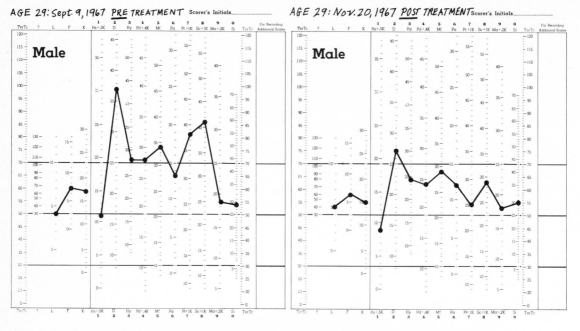

Figure 17-3 Pre- and posttreatment MMPI profiles. (MMPI forms copyright 1948 by The Psychological Corporation, New York.)

The September 1967, age 29, *pre-treatment profile* again shows obvious depression (D); an increase in feelings of alienation, separateness and unrelatedness; and lack of stable interpersonal satisfactions (Pd, Sc); and a sharp increase in anxiety (Pa). At this point the patient is clearly still able to keep functioning (K, Ma); however, he is hurting quite badly and apparently questioning some of the basic premises of his manner of living.

The November 1967 *post-treatment profile* shows some marked changes from the profile of just two months earlier. There is a large decrease in depression and anxiety (D, Pt) and a general increase in feelings of self-worth and relatedness and decrease in feelings of alienation and distance from others (Pd, Sc).

Some of the items on which the patient changes his answers from "false" to "true," pre- to post-treatment, on the Depression Scale were: "I am about as able to work as I ever

was," "My judgment is better than it ever was," "Most nights I go to sleep without thoughts or ideas bothering me," "I have never felt better in my life than I do now," "I enjoy many different kinds of play and recreation," "At times I am full of energy." Items which changed from "true" to "false" included the following: "I work under a great deal of tension," "I cannot understand what I read as well as I used to," and "I have had times where I couldn't take care of things because I couldn't get going."

Examples of items which changed from "true" to "false" on the Pt and Sc scales were "I do many things which I regret afterwards," "I have had periods of such great restlessness that I cannot sit long in a chair," "Once a week or more I become excited," "I am worried about sex matters," "Even when I am with people I feel lonely much of the time," "I often feel as if things were not real," "I cannot keep my mind on one thing." These items give examples of the specific kinds of changes which occurred during treatment.

In sum, the pre- and posttreatment profiles indicate that there were large decreases in negative affect (anxiety and depression) and increases in feelings of self-worth and interpersonal relatedness which occurred during the time this patient was in brief psychotherapy.

Thus the clinical changes which the therapist, patient, and observers noted were accurately reflected in MMPI data interpreted "blind."

FOLLOW-UP

Several Months Later

In June 1968, the therapist dictated the following note:

I have seen Steve twice since the report of our sixth immediate treatment interview of November 17, 1967, was dictated. Once was at my request in February 1968 to have a follow-up visit, and the second time we ran into each other at a local park where we had both brought our children to play in the sand piles.

On both occasions he was happy, felt life was going well, felt that he was decently well launched on seeking a new existence for himself. He has continued to participate in encounter groups and marathon groups and feels that these are productive in helping him find himself. He is leading an existence quite independent from his ex-wife and has no immediate plans for a reunion with her. He sees her periodically, especially when he goes to pick up the children to play with or babysit on weekends. He had a number of other social contacts with both men and women which he is enjoying. I would say things are "steady as she goes" with him and that there is no more need for therapy at this time. Primarily his job

now is to grow as a human being, and try to experience himself and his feelings more fully in a broad number of social and professional contacts.

Diagnosis is: Adult situational reaction. He is not on any medication. There are no plans for further psychotherapy at this time.

Three Years Later

Steve, now 32, called in June 1970 to ask for a few more sessions. He was thinking of making some major changes in his life situation and wanted an opportunity to talk them over with someone. He met with his former therapist weekly for nine sessions, and, at the therapist's request, once again took the MMPI.

Steve reported that he had been going with a woman who was due to get her master's degree; the two of them were thinking of moving into a house together. He had been growing increasingly dissatisfied with his job in particular and engineering in general, and was planning to go back to school for an advanced degree in social work. Both of these commitments made good sense, and the sessions were spent mostly in anticipating the problems that might emerge and how best to handle them. Part of his concern was that the graduate school which had accepted him was several hundred miles distant, and he was worried about the physical neglect his children, whom he had continued to visit faithfully, might suffer without his occasional supervision. Again, this concern seemed realistic since the family pediatrician had privately confided to Steve that he did not think Joan was doing an adequate job of looking after them.

Ultimately Steve worked out the plan of going to the site of his graduate school, looking for a house big enough for him, his girl friend, and, if necessary, his children; then having his girl friend come to live with him. Based on several months of such living, they would know how seriously to consider marriage and also how well they might be able to take care of Steve's children should he feel it necessary to make an effort to take custody of them.

MMPI Data. The MMPI profile from this period is shown in Figure 17-4. Dr. Moos, in ignorance of the life events Steve had described during these meetings, interpreted the 1970 MMPI profile. The last sentence of the interpretation is therefore all the more impressive. His report states:

> The patient's functioning has in a general sense remained fairly stable since the 1967 post-treatment testing. Seven of the subscales (L, F, Hs, Pa, Pt, Sc, and Si) have remained almost exactly the same during the last three years. Small, perhaps insignificant, changes, but all in the same direction as the pre- to post-treatment changes, took place in subscales K, Hy, and Sc, indicating perhaps a little more openness to experience, decrease in rigidity and in feelings of alienation.

Two subscales in which substantial changes (again consistent with pre- to post-treatment changes) have taken place in the last three years are D and Pd. These suggest decreases in the patient's feelings of depression, listlessness, and personal and social isolation. He continues to be a fairly active "doer."

There is also a fairly substantial increase in the Mf subscale from the post-treatment profile. This may simply reflect a resubstantiation of old interest patterns which had become ego alien but are now perceived as ego syntonic. Or the shift may only reflect a change in reference group (entering graduate school, for example) and/or that it is secondary to a new, more stable heterosexual relationship.

During these three-years-later visits, Steve had asked the therapist if the results of the several MMPI tests could be sent to him once he entered graduate school. Steve, after all, was to begin training in an allied field (social work), and he

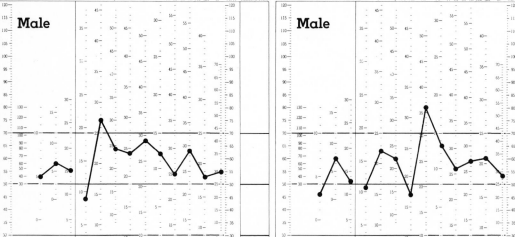

Figure 17-4 Posttreatment and three-year follow-up MMPI profiles. (MMPI forms copyright 1948 by The Psychological Corporation, New York.)

might find the results quite educational, both in what he would learn further about himself and in what he could learn about the MMPI as an assessment instrument. The therapist thought it made sense, but he wanted to check with Dr. Moos, then out of the country for several months, before making a final decision.

After discussion with Dr. Moos, both agreed to send Steve copies of his MMPI profiles and the interpretations. Furthermore, since the therapist and Dr. Moos knew that Steve's treatment might be a book chapter, they sent Steve an earlier version of this chapter, replete with profiles and interpretations, both to request his permission to use it, and, if permission were granted, to ask what changes Steve would want to have made to disguise his identity. Furthermore, the therapist was quite interested in Steve's reflections on treatment and on the accuracy of the report. Thus, several months after Steve took this last MMPI, it was scored and interpreted and sent to Steve as part of an earlier version of this chapter.

Four Years Later

By the time Steve had gotten the copy of this chapter and had a chance to think about it and respond, a year had elapsed since his previous visits, and four years had gone by since he had first come in for treatment. He sent his therapist a long and thoughtful letter; with the permission of both parties, excerpts from it are reprinted here.

October 24, 1971

Dear Dr. Johnson:

For some strange reason, receiving the write-up came as no extreme surprise, although I have never really thought about it before. It is quite an experience to read back through that period of my life, although I should add for your peace of mind that none of this is particularly stressful. . . .

In general terms, I think your write-up is remarkably accurate in both the fact and emotional overtones. I think you have captured well the essence of my problems at that time. There are obviously intonations which aren't entirely accurate, but that is the nature of human communication and I do not feel that it serves much of any purpose to pursue them. I do want to point out two areas, though, for your edification. The first relates to "Chief Complaint." In retrospect, as I recall that time, it was something like "I'm really screwed up and I don't know what is happening or where to turn and I wish to hell somebody would care just a little bit and help me." This is what I was feeling, I was really hurting and, in fact, used to lay in the middle of my fairly-bare, sterile apartment and cry and cry, hoping and praying that someone might hear me and help. (Then I would get cleaned up, smile and go to work or what have you.) So, the statement that you have is a highly intellectualized and acceptable version of my real emotions — evidence of my sensitive emotions, but strong-as-hell ego, which I will mention later.

The other point is one of clarification. To me, my guilt over playing around with another woman while my wife was pregnant was highly significant at that time and is not really emphasized until a later session, although perhaps I was fairly defended and it did not come out until those subsequent visits. My wife did not know about the other woman and that was (and still is, for that matter) a focal point for much of her behavior towards me. . . .

On the MMPI's and their interpretation, I think that at all the points in time, they are surprisingly accurate indications of the manner in which I was functioning. I might comment that I remember taking them honestly, although I remember especially the time of the pre-treatment test when I didn't give a damn what people found out and was much looser about writing down seemingly pathological answers (which, I should add, were also closely fitting my feelings at the time). It is interesting that I could behave this way on the test, but still feel I was defended in expressing the depth of my emotions one to one (see above). I might also note for the record that the April '57 test was two months after my father died and the grad-school one was at the end of the first unhappy year of engineering school and, at a time when I could not find a summer job to get me through to fall. Ah, the miseries of life!!

You might be interested in the fact that I strongly recollect and was influenced by two of your particularly directive statements. The first was convincing me to look at the immediate day, week, etc., rather than catastrophizing. The second was in regard to relying upon my wife's judgement of me as a man — and hence on to the planet analogy. Perhaps I was helped a great deal by both your support and reality-based statements such as these because of the transference which you describe. I am sure it is so, but I really doubt that it was only the factors you mention that enhanced the relationship. I am finding again and again that I am both sensitive to others and intuitive — I suspect that there was also some interaction of our basic personalities at a fairly primitive level. Now, I am getting a bit theoretical. Without rambling on for many pages, may I simply say that I have done some thinking about the matter of the match of therapist and patient. While there are clearly some base skills and techniques, I wonder if there isn't a ceiling on the work of a given pair based upon some combination of life experience (to include, but not limited to, therapy experience) and basic personality variables. I guess on a very empathetic level, I felt that, by and large, *you* could understand *me* — at least some of the time — and that is not true of most of the people I run into, professional or otherwise. The corollary to this is, of course, a vague feeling (which has never been verified) that I "know" a little about you. This probably promoted my request at one point for a more friendship-like

relationship, which you refused because it would limit my ability to deal with you in a therapeutic sense. By the way, that was another significant point for me — I am very glad you did that for both the reason given and to preclude my manipulation of the situation. It is interesting that I have had this whole situation repeated in very similar ways with two different clients, with me on the opposite side of the relationship. . . .

I would like to mention one other general, philosophical thing that comes out of my therapy experience. I think you did exactly what was fitting for the situation. As I see it, my ego became much stronger and in touch a little better with internal and external realities. Here I will get philosophical — I wonder if this is both a blessing and a detriment. That is, I have often mused on what things would be like for me if I had "allowed" myself to have a break of some sort, either at the time of my father's death or about the time I first saw you. I guess what I question is this: I wonder if I had let go of everything (or been encouraged to — I suppose I am talking a bit like Laing) then, would I have restructured my ego system in any different way — would I have been able to reprogram? That is, I now have a particularly strong ego and pretty good sense of reality and I am beginning to build both personal and vocational strength and acceptance, but I still "ain't very happy." . . .

I have wondered if good situational therapy might sometimes be an opiate which precludes confrontation with more basic personality questions. . . . In this light, I have wanted to pursue therapy but haven't known quite how. I am fairly short on funds for one reason and, for the other, I am perplexed by the choice of a person. . . . Frankly there seems to be a limit to the number of people that can do me any good.

I'd like to share a few personal things, then it's time to put this epistle to bed. I am a teaching assistant again this year ... (here Steve gives details of his work). I am finding that I am fairly respected both clinically and intellectually. ...

I have been living alone up here. The girl with whom I was involved came up, but around Christmas last year things were not going too well and I wanted less involvement and no living together – she could not take that and moved away. ... During the last year there has been another gal ... but that is cooling off. ... The next relationship that transpires will, hopefully, be with a woman who is somehow more developed, mature, what-have-you, "herself" (if I have the guts). And I'd better soon, as I'd prefer to settle down.

My children were up for a month this summer and we had an excellent time. ... The only bad part is that my ex-wife has been so financially dependent upon me for all of her needs that, with payments reduced to $200/month, she lays the "kids can't eat or have bicycles" trip on me, even though she knows I have to scrape to come up with that. She can't – I am carving my own life out now, but it is still painful to give sufficient money for your kids and know they are not getting a fair shake – besides the pain of not being with them.

So, things are really basically on the upswing – for perhaps the first time since about 1957 – but with some continuing, heavy situational press. ...

Again, it's been fun sitting here writing this long letter – I don't ever remember putting a personal and professional year on paper quite like this before. I am a little embarrassed by my rambling and sheer length – but boy, what a lot of themes to pursue with the intertwining of career, clinical thoughts, and personal happenings.

Best wishes,

Sincerely,
Steve

SUMMARY

Period of Psychotherapy

There were several factors which aided the patient's ability to make use of the brief psychotherapy. First, he was eager for help. Second, he had a positive transference to the institution, having gone to the university for both college and graduate work, and coming back once again to the same university's psychiatric clinic for help with personal problems. He was in acute emotional pain with high levels of crisis motivation. His personal situation was one which allowed him much flexibility to experiment with new styles of relating to people and experiences. He was ready to form a positive transference relationship with the therapist, a recapitulation of the close father-son relationship he had had in his youth. The therapist intervened actively with the patient, supporting and sympathizing with his sense of loss and later with his sense of anger at being rejected, yet siding consistently with reality against the patient's acting on his masochistic or self-pitying fantasies in self-destructive ways.

Three- and Four-Year Follow-up

The patient maintained the progress he had made during the psychotherapy during the follow-up period. In both clinical interviews and MMPI data, Steve demonstrated gradual improvement in his contentment with himself, his relationships, and life in general. The major area of discontent for three years was with his job; such discontent was quite consistent with his changing view of himself and of his abilities to make important life changes. The therapist agreed with Steve that leaving his job and starting anew in graduate school was a healthy move.

In his long and thoughtful letter, Steve identifies problem areas that he is still working on and raises the important philosophical issue about when crisis or situational therapy is appropriate and when more intensive, exploratory therapy would be preferable.

Not all episodes of brief psychotherapy are accompanied by such gratifying changes, just as not all long-term psychotherapy patients improve. One cannot prove in a rigorous way that Steve's improvement was caused to any significant extent by his psychotherapy, though the direct and indirect evidence points toward an important role for the psychotherapy. The MMPI data suggest greater positive changes during the three years after therapy than in the six years preceding it. Two months of growing depression prior to treatment altered significantly after the first month of treatment. It would appear from this and other cases, then, that a brief psychotherapeutic intervention can have significant and beneficial impact for the patient.

MARIO P. SASSANO, M.S.W.
CARY LEE STONE, M.S.W.

CHAPTER **18**

Supportive Psychotherapy: Thursday Afternoon Clinic

By supportive psychotherapy we mean a way of helping patients function in reality — their own and the world's — even though these two faces of reality may at times resemble each other very little. In Chapter 13, the reality-oriented approach to treatment is discussed in detail. Supportive psychotherapy is the usual name for the reality-oriented approach when it is applied to a marginally adapted outpatient. This chapter describes the practice of supportive psychotherapy in Stanford's Thursday Afternoon Clinic.

Of course, helping to *strengthen the ego* of a given patient is part of all forms of psychotherapy, uncovering as well as reality-oriented. In supportive psychotherapy this goal takes precedence over all others and leads to a way of working whose unique aspects will be the focus of this chapter.

"Supportive" derives from the Latin verb *subportare,* which translates as "to carry underneath or sustain." English equivalents are many:

> to hold up or in position; to serve as a foundation or a prop; to bear the weight or stress of; to keep from falling; to endure, bear, suffer, tolerate; to uphold by aid or countenance; to take the side or promote the cause of; to defend as valid, right, or just; to verify, substantiate; to furnish means for maintenance; to keep from fainting, sinking, yielding; to maintain in condition, action, or existence; to comfort or strengthen; to act with; to second; to back up; to bolster, stay; to countenance; to cheer, assist, encourage; to keep, nourish, nurture; to confirm, corroborate; to shield, protect, defend.[1]

These are the functions of friendship and advocacy, but unlike a friend, the therapist does not necessarily act to support the patient's habits or expressions of emotion, and unlike an advocate, the therapist does not always support the patient in getting his own way. Rather, the therapist acts to support the patient's *ego,* that part of the patient's more mature self which can act to enhance his existence, even at the cost of modifying his habits and inhibiting his desires.

Our notion of ego is close to the psychoanalytic view:[2-6] ego is a personality substructure defined

327

in terms of its functions, which may be consciously or unconsciously exercised.

Most importantly, the ego deals with reality, both internal (bodily sensations, affects, and images) and external (the demands of the environment, which of course includes the human environment: other people). Dealing adequately with reality means that the ego must *perceive* it with reasonable accuracy, must *organize* those perceptions, and then must move the self to *act* appropriately.

The patient who needs supportive psychotherapy is usually in trouble along all three dimensions of ego function: perception, organization, and action. As a result, this kind of patient hovers on the *borderline* between personality integration and disintegration,[7] is subject to wide fluctuations of mood and behavior within a short time, and, being unable to sustain a consistent ego-attitude in the midst of an intimate relationship, is usually difficult to treat with either an uncovering or a reality-oriented approach. Nevertheless, such patients can be successfully treated if the therapist considers their special needs in determing the structure, goals, and context of their therapy.

INITIAL IMPRESSIONS

To begin, candidates for supportive psychotherapy present themselves initially in ways quite different from the ways of patients for whom conventional uncovering or reality-oriented forms of psychotherapy are best. To illustrate these differences, we shall look at four intake interviews by a psychiatric resident on duty for the day. In the clinic reception room, the resident finds four young men waiting to see him. All are of medium height, weight, and coloring, all (as he later learns) are 19 years old and single, all complain chiefly of difficulty in concentrating, and all are named Jack. He takes them in the order in which they arrived, as none appears to be in an acute emergency.

Example 18-1, Jack Arthur. Jack Arthur apologizes for just dropping in without an appointment, explains that he had the day off between registration and the beginning of college classes for his junior year, states that he has been thinking all summer of applying to the clinic for psychiatric help, and adds that he really came over today more to look the place over and decide finally whether or not to make an appointment than actually to try to see a psychiatrist. He believes that part of his difficulty in concentrating on his studies arises from conflicting feelings about his declared major, prelaw. He has been trying to read ahead during the summer for some of his courses but has found his attention wandering — unusual for him because he has always been a good student. What he really loves is music, but his father, a judge, tells him that music is no way to make a living. Jack Arthur says he respects his father, even though he finds himself growing increasingly irritated at him. He doesn't want to antagonize him unnecessarily by doing anything really drastic, like giving up law for musicology, or even arguing with the old man about it. At the same time, Jack fears he may do badly in school this year if he doesn't start understanding himself better pretty soon. It's not, he adds, only the school concentration problems that worry him, anyway: he also thinks he's too shy with girls, and then he gets nervous and depressed sometimes, has unpleasant dreams, and even bites his nails. With regard to these latter difficulties, he tried to read some psychology books this last summer but they didn't hold the solution to his problems. The resident decides that Jack Arthur is probably a candidate for uncovering psychotherapy, schedules an appointment for him the following week, and tentatively plans to hold open a regular weekly hour for him for the remainder of the academic year.

Example 18-2, Jack Bigelow. Jack Bigelow states immediately that the reason he can't concentrate is that "everything's coming down" on him all at once. Until now everything was going pretty well for him. He finally graduated from high school last spring and after a while got a good job as an apprentice auto mechanic, something with a future. He was glad to be out of school, he liked making money, and he got a high enough number in the draft lottery so he thought he wouldn't have to quit his job to go in the service.* He had a fairly steady girlfriend; this was OK with him because they left each other free to date other people. He'd thought he might marry her someday, but neither of them wanted to settle down just yet.

Then last night at quitting time Jack Bigelow's boss told him he may have to let him go at the end of the week because the garage just isn't making enough money to keep on any extra help, and he's the newest man. Jack Bigelow knows that jobs are really hard to get now, what with the country in the state it's in, and he got so upset thinking about this that he couldn't even get himself to go to work today. So he was home trying to read the paper, which he usually doesn't bother to do, and he saw where they may be inducting some guys with numbers even higher than his. He doesn't want to fink out on the country, but he thinks it's a rotten war: his three older brothers have all been killed in it, and his parents couldn't take sending off still another son. While he was trying to concentrate on what to do, his girlfriend called him up at home, after she couldn't get him at work, to tell him she'd just found out she was pregnant. Jack says he's "never seen a shrink before and never thought it would come to this," but he couldn't think of anything else to do when everything happened all at once. Last year, when a friend of his had gone through something similar, the friend went to the clinic for a few weeks, got some pills to help him concentrate, and told Jack it really worked to talk things over a little bit to get himself straightened out.

After eliciting a little more information — such as how Jack has coped with crisis in the past (e.g., the deaths of his three brothers), whether or not Jack is his parents' sole surviving son, how firm the boss was about full dismissal for good versus partial or temporary reduction in working hours, how far along is the girlfriend's pregnancy — the resident concludes that Jack Bigelow will doubtless profit most from a limited number of closely spaced treatment interviews without medication for the next several weeks and accordingly schedules an appointment for a couple of days later. Treatment for Jack Bigelow will be reality-oriented. It could also be called supportive because it will be the resident's job to help Jack marshal his coping abilities — regather his ego strengths — to help him resolve the critical life problems which indeed have come down all at once upon his head. This kind of therapy, however, is usually designated by such terms as *crisis intervention* or *brief psychotherapy* rather than supportive psychotherapy.

Example 18-3, Jack Castle. Jack Castle cannot concentrate either, but he's not absolutely sure he wants to: "Maybe it's too much of a hassle, anyway." Part of the hassle is that people are coming in and going out of the commune where he's living temporarily, "and when you're just getting into somebody, then wow! he splits, and you've gotta catch some new vibes all over again." Jack Castle isn't sure, either, exactly why he came to the clinic today. He was having some acid flashbacks when he first got out of his sleeping bag this morning, and "this new chick told me to make this scene 'cause they got good downers and better shrinks than most places." Jack Castle should know: he has visited nearly every local clinic and hospital emergency room over a period of two years, plus others outside the area during his frequent wanderings around the state. As he describes it, his usual pattern is to drop in "and end up rapping with some

*This chapter was first written in 1970, when the Vietnam conflict was raging and young men were being drafted.

shrink — now, that's cool — but when they get all uptight and want to make some appointment later, well man, that's not where my head is at." Jack Castle thinks he'll stay off LSD for a while — "those flashes are heavy" — but "I just may try some of the new stuff this chick brought in today." The resident feels frustrated and discouraged because he does not see how he can do much to help this patient. Jack Castle is not subjectively in pain just now. He is not only not asking for treatment but is in fact warning that he cannot tolerate making plans and apparently moves around so much that even if he did want therapy he would not stay around long enough to follow through with any sustained treatment. The resident believes that Jack Castle would indeed require a great deal of ego support to bring any sort of order to the chaos of Jack's life, but he realizes at the same time that Jack is not yet ready. He indicates as much, to Jack's visible relief, and tells Jack that the clinic is still available to him if he should ever wish to make use of its services in the future.

Example 18-4, Jack Doane. Jack Doane has been waiting quite a while now, and the resident assumes he must be angry or anxious or both. On the contrary, Jack Doane smiles benignly at the resident as they sit down in the resident's office, looking expectantly into the resident's eyes as if waiting to be told what to do next. When the resident asks how he might be of help, Jack Doane smiles even more broadly and answers that he has no idea. When the resident rephrases his question in terms of why Jack is here, Jack answers that his mother brought him. He smiles again and tells the resident that the latter has pretty pictures on his wall. The resident tries a few more questions, but without eliciting much in the way of further clues as to why the patient has been brought to the clinic today or what is expected of him in this case as psychiatrist on duty. In trying to decide where to go from here, the

resident begins thinking that he badly needs more information before he can make an adequate case disposition, and that he's not likely to get it from Jack Doane. One of the resident's options at this point is to find out whether Jack has a prior clinic or hospital record; another is to try, with Jack's permission, to locate a responsible family member; a third is for the resident to check out his clinical impressions and tentative dispositional plans with the psychiatrically experienced clinic staff member or advanced resident on call for the day. As the resident is deciding what to do, the telephone rings on his desk.

Excusing himself to Jack, who smiles at the telephone, the resident learns from the secretary that Jack's mother has arrived in the waiting room and would like to join him and her son. When Jack smiles and nods to the resident's question — "Will it be all right with you if your mother comes to the office now?" — the resident turns back to the telephone and asks the secretary to please direct Mrs. Doane to his office. In a moment he opens the door and ushers in a small, white-haired lady whose sweet smile is a carbon copy of her son's but who is fortunately more articulate. She quickly proceeds to tell the resident that she has brought her boy to the clinic to get some pills to help him concentrate. He has spent various periods, occasionally as long as several months at a time, in the state hospital beginning when he was about 14 or 15, but Mrs. Doane has always taken him "out of that place as soon as they got him calmed down again. All he really needs is pills, anyway, and we used to could get them from the hospital, but now my husband's had a stroke and can't drive that long way to get them anymore." The state hospital had referred Mrs. Doane to the clinic for help some time ago, "But it's only now I got Jackie in, since his concentration started to go bad like, mostly since his Dad's took sick." What she means, it turns out, is that Jack mostly concentrates on his classical music collection, spending much of each day in his room listening to records. When his concentration goes bad, he starts systematically smashing his records one by one on the kitchen floor; "And that," says Mrs. Doane, smiling happily back at her beaming son, "sure does wreck up the family budget, even though we do get all his records secondhand at the thrift shop."

But Mrs. Doane is quite emphatic in her repeated statement that "Jackie's a real good boy," and needs nothing but pills; she also states that she will be "real happy" to bring him in as often as the doctor wants, especially since the clinic is so near the shopping center and she can get her errands done while her son is being seen. Other than delivering her son and calling for him, however, she certainly cannot spend time at the clinic herself, since she is much too busy taking care of her home and family of three. She also insists that her husband cannot leave the house. Mentally ruling out conjoint family therapy, at least for now, the resident writes out a prescription for enough of one of the phenothiazines to last Jack until the following Thursday, obtains Mrs. Doane's and Jack's written permission to get Jack's records from the state hospital, and asks the pair to return on Thursday at 12:30. He explains that Jack will be seen then for review of his medication, perhaps by himself or perhaps by someone else in the clinic. If someone else sees Jack, then he will make sure that the other therapist has also reviewed the records and will be as well acquainted with Jack's case, and therefore as well able to help, as himself. Mrs. Doane thanks the resident profusely for being such a nice doctor and leaves arm in arm with her son, exchanging smiles with Jack as they go out the door.

THURSDAY AFTERNOON CLINIC

What the resident had in mind for his fourth patient, Jack Doane, was, of course, the Thursday Afternoon Clinic (TAC). He did not specifically mention this clinic-within-the-clinic to the patient and his mother, nor did he explain its structure to them, because first he wanted to clear Jack Doane's formal admission with the TAC administrator. If TAC should be full, or if for any other reason Jack Doane could not become a TAC patient at present, the resident would himself carry the patient in his own treatment case load until such time as a preferable disposition could be made. If, however, as appeared likely, Jack Doane could begin next week in TAC, then the first TAC therapist to see him would explain TAC to both Jack and his mother.

Background, Goals, and Patient Population

Stanford's Thursday Afternoon Clinic, started in 1962, was modeled after Cincinnati General Hospital's Wednesday Afternoon Clinic, with TAC's aims, goals, and experiences for the past eleven years bearing a striking similarity to those at the University of Cincinnati as first described by MacLeod and Middleman.[8] TAC was originally established as an attempt to meet more adequately than before a complex of interlocking and overlapping needs felt by certain patients, by many caretaking mental health professional people, and by the community at large.[9]

The particular geographical community which TAC was set up to serve appears culturally as a university town, economically as an affluent bedroom suburb of San Francisco, and socioethnically as a homogeneous grouping of white middle-class families whose breadwinners are engaged primarily in professional and managerial occupations. To the usual visitor or householder it is a "lovely community": full of nice people who take pride in taxing themselves heavily to pay for quality education for their children, responsible city government for all, aesthetically pleasing wide streets lined with well-kept city trees and private lawns, attractive shops, and first-rate medical care for all who can afford it. In addition there is a liberal program of public assistance for the elderly, disabled, and needy, enabling them (if they choose) to function unnoticed within the dominant, affluent pattern.

TAC's patients are drawn from the members of this community who cannot fit into the dominant pattern. A common problem is the elderly psychotic widow who may appear in public talking to herself, yet sees no need to use her savings, pension, or Medicare benefits for psychiatric care. The community has long referred such patients to TAC. Another kind of problem is posed by the "failure cases" in office and clinic practices — patients who recognize that they are emotionally disturbed but who appear to be unable to use the standard forms of psychotherapy, even when financed by public funds. Such patients are often characterized as "psychiatrically disabled, but not amenable to therapy," "help-rejecting complainers — chronic, severe," "impossible patients," "strictly drug cases," "hopeless misfits," "crocks." TAC has become a welcome referral source for the professionals who must cope with this kind of patient.

In physical appearance, TAC patients look no different from any other general population group. They are male, female, tall, short, dark, light, fat, thin, old, young, neatly or sloppily dressed, from the ethnic majority, from ethnic minorities, bespectacled, glasses-free, and so on. But in age they are much more likely to be beyond 40 than under 20, and relatively few fall into the age group of 21 to 39, which is the usual range for other psychiatric outpatients. A few are married, but most are single, widowed, or divorced. Nine out of ten are partially or wholly dependent on public subsidy.

Thus, with some few exceptions, TAC patients are "no-income or low-income" people, and in their orientation to psychiatric treatment fit the Class V group described by Hollingshead and Redlich.[10] Their psychological insight is minimal; their symptoms are *ego-syntonic*; that is, they see nothing strange or bizarre about their symptoms and have little or no feeling that such symptoms are somehow "weird" or "not like me." They generally come to treatment not to understand themselves better or to change their personalities

or their habitual chaotic, crisis-ridden ways of doing things, but to get relief from their immediate symptoms. They believe that their problems are the result of physical ills and should therefore be treated by physical — i.e., chemical — means. As Mrs. Doane demonstrated, the repeated request is for "pills." All patients active in TAC are on medication; all say that they come primarily for medicine and in one way or another downgrade the "talking cure." They see little value in keeping appointments on a regular — e.g., weekly — schedule, but prefer to come in only when they "run out of pills," or when (as in emotional crises otherwise unrecognized by them) "the regular pills don't work." Diagnostically they suffer most often from one of the psychoses or severe personality disorders, frequently with attendant depression, anxiety, and psychophysiologic complaints. Most function at average intelligence levels or below. In spite of repeated crises which are similar in type, they find it hard to learn from one crisis experience how to cope with the next. Their previous experiences, if any, with uncovering psychotherapy have tended to be unsuccessful; more typically, their past psychiatric contacts have been, as in the case of Jack Doane, as repeating inpatients in state mental hospitals.

In the beginning many TAC patients were community eccentrics. For example, elderly widows were often referred by their general practitioners to the Psychiatric Clinic at Stanford, which would in turn refer them to TAC. There they received medication and a chance to mother the young residents in psychiatry (for whom they often baked and brought cookies), finding substitutes for their own long-gone sons and daughters.

Gradually TAC has acquired a more varied and challenging clientele as its population has come to reflect the changing times of an altered community. When violence escalated on the streets and on campus, middle-aged people began to seek refuge from social processes at increasingly rapid rates,[11] experiencing consequences that they could not comprehend. Younger patients, like Jack Doane, are the victims of another kind of social change —

a change in the pattern of health care delivery. Once Jack Doane would have returned at intervals to the haven of the state hospital. Now state hospitals are closing, and local mental health centers are charged with caring for these people, wherever possible on an outpatient basis. So TAC continues as it started, to attempt to meet many needs: of the patients, to be treated; of the community, to have them treated; of psychotherapists, to treat them.

Therapeutic Organization and Techniques

Daniels and Kuldau[12] have explored the concept of marginal man and his relationship to traditional society in their discussion of optimal treatment for chronic VA (Veterans Administration) psychiatric patients. They make the point that man survives not only through his ego functioning but also through his social organization. Given TAC's patient population — marginal to the larger society; alienated; often chaotic in terms of such life-patterns of organization as home, work, and other people — our first attempt is to deploy TAC itself as a steady, unchanging social organization or institution of its own. It meets without fail every single Thursday afternoon from 12:30 to 2:00. Until a recent departmental move to outpatient quarters apart from the main hospital building, TAC had its own separate waiting room, reserved during those hours for TAC patients only, with freshly brewed coffee and a separate TAC bulletin board. The coffee was tangible proof to many patients that Stanford cared about them and that they belonged. The bulletin board served a similar function, with patients occasionally tacking up original verses or other writings and with both patients and staff periodically posting clippings thought to be of general TAC interest — perhaps a state or county fact sheet on welfare rules and benefits, perhaps a newspaper notice about additional AA meetings or about the formation of a new weekly social group to help structure leisure time for the psychiatrically disabled and isolated.

Although psychiatric residents and consultants rotate through TAC on a regular basis, the senior author of this chapter has been administrator of TAC virtually since its inception, and over the years has taken his turn seeing nearly every patient for at least one treatment session, often more. The clinic office manager too has become something of an institution in her own right because she was here at the beginning of the Adult Psychiatry Clinic itself and participated from the first day of TAC in setting up a separate TAC filing and reporting system. Most important, she is the one who greets TAC patients, many of whom started at the clinic when she did. She provides them not only with continuity but also with her own blend of warmth, affection, and respect, making sure that they are seen within a reasonable space of time after their arrival and that their welfare forms are properly processed for medication and other treatment. The TAC clerk-typist fills in for the office manager when the latter is on vacation or otherwise must be away. She takes care of all the TAC files, and from the weekly treatment entries she becomes acquainted with the travails of living for the chronically ill psychiatric patient.

Both the clerk-typist and the office manager are at times heard chiding young residents for any neglect of TAC patients, however slight. Office managers, secretaries, and clerks are all too frequently omitted from professional reports on important caretaking people in the field of mental health. This omission is both unfortunate and misleading because these are the very people with whom the patient first has contact, to whom — by telephone or in person — the patient directs his first call for help. In a setting like TAC, such people provide essential continuity over time and serve as "culture carriers" for patient and therapist alike.

Example 18-5, Malcolm. After a four-year absence from TAC, Malcolm, a chronically paranoid schizophrenic man of 53, looked furtively into the clinic waiting room one day and saw — with an audible sigh of relief — the remembered face of the office manager. He approached the reception desk with courage grown out of an old familiarity. After going through the formality of re-registering for TAC, and while waiting to be seen by one of the TAC therapists, he happened to notice the TAC administrator walking through the waiting room toward him. Apparently anticipating some scolding for his long, unexplained absence, Malcolm stood up, smiled apprehensively, and blurted out to the administrator, "Where have *you* been for the past four years?"

Within this framework of institutional stability, then, TAC patients have on the whole responded well to the treatment format itself. They know that after their initial evaluation interview, which may take forty-five minutes, they will be seen for visits limited to twenty minutes, and spaced weekly, biweekly, monthly, or even less frequently, but always on Thursday afternoons and always between 12:30 and 2:00. They also know that a group of four to six doctors staff the Clinic, that the group changes every few months, and that they will rarely see a given individual therapist more than once or twice, hardly ever on two successive visits. Beginning therapists are sometimes uneasy with this format, especially at the outset of their rotation through TAC. "But how can I possibly help the patient," they will ask, "unless I really get to know him by seeing him myself every week?"

What becomes clearer to them after some experience is that most TAC patients cannot tolerate the stresses of the particular kind of personal relationship that ideally obtains between patient and individual therapist in uncovering psychotherapy. The usual TAC patient has experienced extreme difficulty both in closeness to and separation from such significant figures from his past or present life as parents, siblings, spouses, children, and former therapists; over the years the patient has learned that for him the least disorganizing way to cope with other people is to maintain a modest or

greater distance from them. The TAC treatment format is specifically designed to help this kind of patient maintain his tenuous equilibrium; it provides him with personal attention but shields him from the anxieties of intimacy and from the specter of important object loss. Often patients who become too anxious or angry in one-to-one relationships can handle institutional transference[13] which involves dependence on an institution likely to survive rather than on a person who is liable to change or leave in response to disruptive behavior.

Example 18-5, Annabelle. Annabelle, a 27-year-old single woman, has been treated for years for a gastrointestinal disorder of psychogenic etiology. She also gave evidence of very high dependency needs and a punitive superego, a combination which made for a number of changes of physicians. She finally was treated successfully by a resident in psychiatry and herself elected to come to TAC upon the departure of her individual psychotherapist. The patient recognized that what she called her tendency to "overdepend" might be something she had to "just live with," and she sensed that TAC was potentially a helpful device whereby she could in the future more comfortably regulate that tendency. She began coming to TAC as she felt the need and resisted (and continues to resent) any staff attempts at scheduling. As a consequence, TAC therapists do not tell her which week to return, or how many weeks should pass between her visits, but instead urge her to return whenever she feels like it, as long as it is on Thursday between 12:30 and 2:00 P.M. At first it was hard for her to accept even the limited hours and day of the week, but she has come to view the TAC structure as the therapists' way of abiding by her desire to maintain independence and to encourage her every effort in this direction. Her disabling psychophysiological problems were successfully dealt with during her earlier individual therapy, and she ended with her former therapist on a strongly positive note. Her transfer to TAC meant transferring the high regard in which she held that prior therapist, and she was thereby enabled to complete the psychological separation in a fairly short time. She went on, and continues — in TAC — to take meaningful issue with her present and practical problems in living.

"But what," asks the new TAC therapist, "can you helpfully do in twenty minutes" about patients' problems in living? What techniques are used, and how do they differ from those employed in the practice of dynamic psychotherapy? As described in Chapter 13, the techniques most often used are suggestion, advice, and *realistic* reassurance, with the goal of helping patients deal more rationally than before with the stresses and confusion of everyday life. It is seldom if ever helpful to TAC patients for the therapist to explore at length with them the content of their dreams or waking fantasies (which are often wish-fulfilling or bizarre); what they need is to get closer to external and current reality. For similar reasons such uncovering techniques as free association and the encouragement of childhood memories are not normally employed, nor is the analysis of defense mechanisms, nor interpretations designed to provide insight in depth, nor the identification of resistance. Knowing that the TAC patient is unable to tolerate long silences, the therapist is relatively active so as to minimize the opportunity for the patient to withdraw in fantasy or to perseverate in unproductive verbal monologues. Every effort is made to use the brief therapeutic contact efficiently. The attempt is to show genuine respect for the patient as a human being and to share the work of finding ways of coping with the many symptoms and other difficulties. As he masters these tasks, the TAC therapist learns to express warmth and empathy in such a way that the patient will feel supported and strengthened rather than threatened or overwhelmed. Sometimes the therapist will be relative-

ly permissive, listening tolerantly to the patient's ways of expressing his problems; at other times he will act more obviously as an authority figure, limiting the expression of emotion and offering sound advice, useful suggestions, and realistic reassurance. The dispensing of medication represents additional tangible evidence of the therapist's willingness and ability to help the patient, as well as providing specific symptomatic relief. The style of approach is shown by the following case.

Example 18-6, Gilbert. Gilbert, a 47-year-old bachelor, dropped in to the Psychiatry Clinic one day and asked to see someone he could talk to. Intake was being handled at that hour by the TAC administrator, who interviewed the patient for about forty-five minutes. Gilbert began by saying that he had been sure of himself for most of his life, but that for the past two years he had grown markedly less sure. In a monotonous voice he related a long, repetitive story about neighbors who took special pleasure in making his life miserable. According to him, these neighbors expended most of their waking energy throwing garbage on his lawn, cutting his shrubbery, and laughing as he walked by. No amount of his complaining to the police or the district attorney had seemed to deter these people. As if at some level he questioned his own account, Gilbert finally shook his head, lowered it, and rather sadly confessed that he was confused by his thinking: what could he do? Did the administrator think we could help him? He had come here because he had heard many good things about Stanford, and if he were to be helped anywhere, it would probably be here.

Rather than directly assault the patient's conviction that his neighbors were out to get him, the administrator replied that in his estimate much depended on how much time Gilbert gave in his life to thinking about these particular neighbors, and on how unshakable that allocation of time was. Gilbert brightened a little and admitted that he did have some question in his own mind regarding how much "time" he spent thinking about the persecutions of his neighbors. He would really, he said, like to get on to other problems in his life, like his loneliness and his chronic unemployment. He added that he wasn't sure exactly what he wanted from the clinic: maybe some counseling and something to help him "think better" – almost a prescription for supportive psychotherapy. Concurring, the administrator felt that rather than insight, this patient needed to become active as quickly as possible so as to revitalize what appeared to be a life devoted more and more to rumination. Gilbert was therefore referred directly to TAC, where he has continued in treatment for nearly three years.

At the outset he was given medication, which lessened his anxiety. His initial psychological therapy was directed toward heightening his self-esteem by helping him perform adequately in the labor market. Although this patient was a trained draftsman, he had been unable to hold down a steady job in drafting for at least two years. A chronic cause of his frustration and failure was his maladaptation to drafting and lack of information as to what other kinds of work might be available to him. After referring him to the State Department of Vocational Rehabilitation (DVR), TAC therapists participated actively in his continuing experiences with that agency. When Gilbert became suspicious at one stage of both us and DVR, we insisted on joint meetings of staff from both agencies, with the patient present. At first demurring, he told us we were taking undue precautions and that actually he trusted us. We responded that trust was an issue in his treatment, and that we had no special corner on that piece of the world; maybe in time Gilbert could trust us, but – after only a year – that might be asking too much of him. With a great deal of effort on the part of everyone, Gilbert was at length enrolled in a DVR course

in shoe repairing, where he found himself reasonably happy and began to contemplate opening his own business. The thought of becoming his own boss in the near future still appeals to him greatly.

Concurrently with employment-related therapy, we have also worked steadily along with Gilbert on enriching his meager interpersonal life. Whenever he meets with frustration and failure in the area of social functioning, he tends to return to ruminating about his neighbors, but he has been able to become a participating member in the weekly meetings of a social group composed of current and former psychiatric patients.

What Gilbert has seemed to need from TAC is an ongoing experience of consistent reality testing against his paranoid ideation. By trial and error, successive TAC therapists have learned that discussion of Gilbert's real or imagined persecution by his neighbors is nonproductive: it does not help him in the community and needlessly uses up therapy time. What does help Gilbert, however, is concentration on how he wants to use his life, and on how he can best allocate his time to regain his self-respect through limited social interaction and reemployment.

Training and Consultation for TAC Therapists

As the case of Gilbert clearly illustrates, long-term supportive psychotherapy with chronically ill patients can be demanding, exhausting, and frustrating work. For this very reason, among others, we find that one of the most important parts of TAC is the consultation hour, or "rehash." From 2:00 to 3:00 every Thursday afternoon, immediately following the hour and a half during which the patients are seen, all therapists in TAC that day meet to discuss the patients they have just interviewed. This time is used to evaluate past and current treatment approaches, to plan therapeutic strategies for each patient's next visit, and to record the results of these discussions in the continuous treatment record of each chart. Such pooling of ideas helps ensure the continuity of each patient's treatment despite changes in individual therapists from visit to visit and changes in the entire group of therapists at regular intervals of several months. In Gilbert's case, as in others, it has been crucial to use the consultation hour periodically to review the original treatment contract: assessing how closely it is being adhered to, altering therapeutic techniques whenever necessary, and revising goals or timetables in the light of new clinical data. It is not always easy for therapists and patients in uncovering psychotherapy to recall initial treatment goals even though they are together for a long period of time; the task is even more difficult in a setting with rotating therapists. By helping each other during the consultation hour, TAC therapists have been able to demonstrate consistency to their patients in keeping their agreements to work toward contracted goals. Equally, the group sessions have fostered innovations which indicate to the patients that someone is interested. Finally, they have led us to reflect a socially shared sense of each patient back to him in many separate contacts, a markedly ego-strengthening experience.

Present at the rehash each week is a senior psychiatric consultant, normally a member of the departmental *clinical faculty,* i.e., a psychotherapist with a nonpaid academic appointment who does his daily work in a setting outside of Stanford (private practice, another hospital, or another clinic). The consultant has had extensive experience working with chronically ill patients, is accustomed to and likes teaching and group supervision, and agrees to commit his time to this purpose from 2:00 to 3:00 every Thursday afternoon for a given number of months. The consultant and the group of therapists in training begin and end their rotation through TAC at the same time, thereby sharing the TAC experience, in each of its phases, more fully than would be possible were the rotations to occur in tandem.

Until a few years ago, six residents and one consultant would serve in TAC for a period of six months at a time. During the first half of each residency year, the therapist group was then composed of advanced (third-year) residents, during the second half, of residents in their first year of postinternship training. Over the years, however, residents, consultants, and administrative staff came to agree that this system needed revision to better serve the interests of both patient care and professional training. The consensus was that six months was longer than any good therapist needed to familiarize himself with the TAC patients and to learn how to work effectively with them. And six months was indeed too long for many of the therapists to sustain an interest in work with the chronically ill. Whatever enthusiasm they might have had when they began their tour of duty had usually subsided halfway through the rotation and had often metamorphosed into antipathy by the end of their tour. Advanced residents especially began to view their assignment as "a drag." For one thing, they had — by the time they reached their third year of training — already had a great deal of experience in doing supportive psychotherapy with the chronically ill, usually on inpatient services like those at the Veterans Administration or state hospitals during their second year. For another, they were often deeply involved in research on their own special interests by the time of their third year and so resented TAC as an "interruption" of their more cherished work.

Under such conditions, TAC could and sometimes did become the negative focus, or scapegoat, for all sorts of unrelated resentments and unresolved internal conflicts experienced by residents in their final year of training — hardly a happy outcome for patients or therapists, and hardly a suitable medium for teaching or learning. At the same time, it became apparent that the amount of training, maturity, and prior psychiatric experience exhibited by first-year resident classes was steadily rising year by year with concomitant increases in certain groups of medical students in their final years of predoctoral training.

So it was that though TAC patients were no easier to work with than before, and though administrative staff continued to be aware that work with such patients could produce high levels of anxiety in beginning therapists, a decision was made to reduce the length of the TAC rotation to three months, and to staff this clinic with first-year residents and with selected medical students after the latter had first undergone training in our department. This change has worked to the benefit of all concerned. During the first and second three months of the training year, TAC then is conducted exclusively by first-year residents. During the final two three-month periods, advanced medical students join the TAC staff, with the consequently reduced number of first-year residents performing an additional supervisory role vis-à-vis the medical students. This latter activity blurs the function of the consultant to some degree, but residents, consultants, and students have all been enthusiastic about the increased opportunities now afforded by the TAC rehash for didactic teaching, peer consultation, and sharing of clinical skills. At present this mix of senior wisdom and beginner enthusiasm seems the best recipe for effective supportive work with TAC patients.

Other Aspects of Doing Therapy in TAC

Within the improved climate of feeling, each participant has found it easier to meet the many demands of TAC. At different times, as we saw in the case of Gilbert, the therapist must act as physician, psychiatrist, social worker, advocate, employment counselor, community liaison, and facilitator or consultant to other agencies. No one is equally expert at performing the many functions required or fulfilling all the roles, but TAC therapists have the security of knowing that if they make a mistake one week with one patient, a colleague can recoup the following week, and vice versa. Although each therapist has his own individual style, and TAC colleagues often enjoy arguing fine points of treatment with each other from

different theoretical points of view, TAC researchers have found that specific therapeutic interventions vary less from one therapist to another with a given patient than might have been expected from perceived differences in the way each therapist thinks about his work.[14,15] Although the role of professional colleague might thus elicit differences (as in theoretical orientation and therapeutic style), the hard realities of weekly work with TAC patients make for similarities and shared problems. Mutual support and encouragement can profitably replace competition as the motivation to learn effective ways of helping patients.

In this connection, an agonizing problem for beginning psychotherapists (and a major frustration for them in work with outpatients needing chronic care) is the notion that all cases begin with the presentation of distressing symptoms, and — after a course of psychotherapy — end by mutual agreement. Ideally, the skillfully handled therapy should end with success, i.e., with a diminution in symptoms or with a rearrangement of the patient's character structure. Or, an equally well-conducted treatment can end in accepted failure, with patient and therapist both resigned to the fact that in spite of hard work on both sides there have been no changes at the hard core of the pathology and that further therapy would only exacerbate the symptoms. In TAC there is often no such closure. Patients like Malcolm return after mysterious absences of several years, apparently with no change for better or for worse and with no end in sight. The experienced therapist learns to temper his expectations of his work with a steady awareness that the patient's life goes on or ends, with therapy hopefully a meaningful variable, but in any case one variable only. As an extremely able local psychiatrist once remarked (after working long, hard, extra hours over many days and weeks with a suicidal patient), "Really, if all that stood between my patient and death was me, then that was not enough, and never is."

Following is a case example with many turning points but never a major shift and never a wholly reconstructed life.

Example 18-7, Barbara.   Barbara was 23 when she first appeared at the Psychiatry Clinic and was treated there for about two years of intensive individual psychotherapy. Diagnostically she was described by her successive therapists as possessing a passive-dependent personality with borderline mental retardation, possible Turner's syndrome, and episodes of emotionally unstable behavior which included suicide gestures, fabrication of history, and periodic somaticization of anxiety. Although this woman was further described as having a tendency to incorporate the behavior of other people, she at no time gave evidence of incorporating the model of behavior of any one of her therapists. She responded to TAC in much the same fashion that she had reacted to individual therapy. Incapable of insight, she refused the counsel and advice of nearly all her therapists, generally electing to behave in the way most likely to get her into trouble.

For instance, she would take jobs for which her state vocational counselor told her she was not qualified, and in consequence be fired after only a few days. She would insist on medications that pharmacologically and psychologically would not only be of no help to her but would in fact be detrimental to her adjustment. When she could not get these medications from Stanford, she would invariably get them someplace else. She persisted in taking courses at school that could in no way provide her with the means to earn a living and that were additionally contraindicated on the basis of her poor academic background. She added to her burden by marrying an immature man who refused to work and who increased the pressure on her to maintain employment in a tightening labor market. At any critical point in her life when she might have benefited most from sustained therapeutic contact, she would break off therapy in one clinic and pick it up in another — sometimes, but not usually, advising the new agency of her prior psychiatric experiences.

Over the years, however, Barbara keeps returning to TAC, presenting after each absence a long list of complaints documenting her excruciating existential difficulties. Although the quality of this patient's life seems unrelentingly poor, the quantity of her living is immense. Most of Barbara's therapists have at one time or another expressed frustration so intense that it borders on despair: "Why do we sweat it, when *nothing* we do seems to make any difference?" The answer that finally seems to have made the most sense to each one is: *consider the alternatives.* Would Barbara be happier dead from suicide? Would her life be more meaningful if lived permanently behind the walls of a mental institution? Even were the answer to such hard questions an appalling *yes,* who possibly could presume to make such a decision for her?

A similar problem is posed by the following case:

Example 18-8, Charles.   Charles is a 49-year-old married man referred to TAC after three discouraging years of individual psychotherapy. Described by prior therapists as suffering from the effects of an unstable personality, complicated by chronic brain syndrome, multiple physical complaints, and long-term alcoholism, Charles defies the patience and skill of all professional people who attempt to help him. His wife and adolescent daughter, both of whom have also had extensive psychiatric contacts at Stanford and elsewhere, continue to "hate psychiatry" and to join Charles in sabotaging whatever small gains he or they or the family as a whole are temporarily able to make. If Charles gives up drinking for a while, his daughter promptly gets picked up by police for acts of juvenile delinquency, his wife engages in disastrous marital infidelities, Charles has another serious accident — not necessarily in that order — and the family cycle of angry seeking for new sources of "help" begins once again.

As therapists and clinics and other agencies each become fatigued with a case, TAC remains to try once more. Therapists are encouraged on Thursday afternoons to keep firmly in mind that even patients as trying as Barbara and Charles have human rights to be cared for as well as can possibly be done in our community. TAC therapists have therefore been instrumental in helping other physicians continue to treat the physical disorders of these patients, attorneys to bear with them as advocates of their legal rights, and other helping persons and agencies to carry on with their appropriate respective functions. When other professional people start to throw up their hands after a visit with one of our patients and say, "I can't stand it any more!" TAC therapists — who know the feeling only too well — are able to provide their nonpsychiatric colleagues with helpful insights and with the kind of sharing of responsibility that enables us all to continue doing the necessary work.

TAC therapists are also encouraged to be innovative and experimental, as a final case example will show.

> *Example 18-9, Ella.* Ella, aged 38, and divorced, came to TAC after eight years of individual psychotherapy: six years with a private practitioner and two subsequent years with a psychiatric resident. At best ambivalent about her transfer to TAC, Ella had evidenced throughout her long psychiatric history an impressive and ongoing commitment to habit-forming drugs. The first problem Ella presented was a demand that her medication be increased, including her prescription for nightly sedatives. She would tolerate no opposition from the doctor she saw initially. Viewing this hostile demand as an aspect of unfinished business left over from previous therapies, the TAC therapist offered to see the patient himself as needed during this crisis of transfer, with the proviso that the two of them responsibly document the efficacy of her long list of medications. Returning many times to this

> particular therapist, despite his otherwise rotating schedule, Ella attempted to test the limits of his sincerity by refusing (on various pretexts) to see him again until 7:00 the following Saturday morning. Willing to be manipulated to prove a point, the therapist agreed, and arrived at his office well in advance of the appointed hour. Not unexpectedly, Ella telephoned him there at 6:55 to cancel their appointment. After this incident the patient was more amenable to considering reduction, substitution, or omission of drugs, and was additionally willing to see other therapists on the regular TAC basis. Having successfully met the first angry treatment challenge, the team now had the formidable task of formulating long-term therapeutic goals. Without properly working through underlying conflicts, the patient had left an inept but still supportive mate. Her fling at what she conceived to be independence was short-lived, and she now faced the lonely realities of self-support and of single-handedly raising two children, one of whom was already showing signs of serious emotional problems. Had the transfer been handled less imaginatively, it is doubtful that Ella could have continued to work on her problems as successfully as she was in fact able to do.

SUMMARY

The Thursday Afternoon Clinic attempts to provide a flexible medium for supportive psychotherapy with the chronically disabled psychiatric patient. The hope and expectation is that TAC will reinvolve alienated persons in life. Toward this goal, all the charisma and prestige of the Stanford University Medical Center is invoked. Within this setting, the therapist is encouraged fully to exploit the charisma of his own role and branch off in whatever direction his good instinct tells him he must move to facilitate the patient's return to functioning as a member of society.

REFERENCES

1. *Webster's Second New International Dictionary* (unabridged), 1934, pp. 2534–2535.

2. Freud, Sigmund: *New Introductory Lectures on Psychoanalysis,* W. J. H. Sprott (trans.), Norton, New York, 1933.

3. Freud, Anna: *The Ego and the Mechanisms of Defense,* International Universities Press, New York, 1946.

4. Hartmann, Heinz: *Essays on Ego Psychology: Selected Problems in Psychoanalytic Theory,* International Universities Press, New York, 1964.

5. Brenner, Charles: *An Elementary Textbook of Psychoanalysis,* Doubleday Anchor Books, Garden City, N.Y., 1957.

6. MacKinnon, Roger A., and Robert Michels: *The Psychiatric Interview in Clinical Practice,* Saunders, Philadelphia, 1971.

7. Pfeiffer, Eric: "Borderline States," *Diseases Nervous System,* **35**:212–219, May 1974.

8. MacLeod, John A., and Francine Middleman: "Wednesday Afternoon Clinic: A Supportive Care Program," *Arch. Gen. Psychiat.,* **6**:56–65, January 1962.

9. Rosenbaum, C. Peter: "Supportive Outpatient Treatment," *Ment. Hyg.,* **55**(2):225–227, April 1971.

10. Hollingshead, A. B., and F. C. Redlich: *Social Class and Mental Illness,* Wiley, New York, 1958, pp. 340–355.

11. Toffler, Alvin: *Future Shock,* Random House, New York, 1970.

12. Daniels, David, and John Kuldau: "Marginal Man, the Tether of Tradition, and Intentional Social Systems Therapy," *Community Ment. Health J.,* **III**(1):13–20, Spring, 1967.

13. Wilmer, Harry A.: "Transference to a Medical Center: A Cultural Dimension in Healing," *J. Calif. Med.,* **96**:173–180, March 1962.

14. Houts, Peter S., Shirley MacIntosh, and Rudolf H. Moos: "Patient-Therapist Interdependence: Cognitive and Behavioral," *J. Consult. Clin. Psychol.,* **33**(1):40–45, 1969.

15. Moos, Rudolf H., and Shirley MacIntosh: "Multivariate Study of the Patient-Therapist System: A Replication and Extension," mimeographed, 1970.

16. Bandler, Bernard: "The Concept of Ego-Supportive Psychotherapy," in Parad and Miller (eds.), *Ego-Oriented Casework,* Family Service Association of America, New York, 1963, pp. 27–44.

Some Technical Aspects in Psychotherapy

LONGER-TERM TREATMENT

Certain issues and problems recur in psychotherapy and in training psychotherapists. Certain questions about techniques and procedures arise regularly in the minds of beginning psychotherapists and are brought up in seminars, supervision, and discussion. Some of the questions, indeed, have to do as much with supervision and learning as they have to do with the care of the patient being discussed. Some questions are relatively specific to a training program's orientation; e.g., a highly psychoanalytic program will elicit more discussion of psychoanalytic technique than a program with a different orientation.

Most training programs currently are eclectic in the best sense of the term: they present a multitude of ways of trying to understand human behavior and psychotherapy. For many beginning psychotherapists, this leads at first to a period of professional identity diffusion in the first year or two of training, but synthesis and a sense of mastery usually evolve during and after the second year, much to the therapist's relief.

Most of the issues discussed in this chapter arise during that first year. Often they arise in the context of learning to do uncovering psychotherapy, though they may also come to light while learning to do reality-oriented therapy. The litera-ture on technique in psychotherapy is large and impressive; some of the books that can be of the greatest help to the beginning therapist are mentioned below. What we will discuss in the remainder of the chapter are some of those concerns which seem, year after year, to arise and perplex psychotherapists in training.

Suggested Readings

Three sources that focus on the therapist-patient relationship and which should help the therapist in forming the working alliance crucial to all psychotherapy are Roger's *On Becoming a Person,* [1] Gendlin's "A Theory of Personality Change," [2] and Kaiser's *Effective Psychotherapy.* [3]

There are a number of books which deal more with the technical than with the experiential aspects of long-term psychotherapy. A beginning psychotherapist should come to his work having read Colby's *A Primer for Psychotherapists* [4] and Sullivan's *The Psychiatric Interview.* [5] Two other rich sources of information are Fromm-Reichmann's *Principles of Intensive Psychotherapy* [6] and Alexander and French's *Psychoanalytic Therapy.* [7] Portions of Tarachow's *Introduction to Psychotherapy* [8] are also useful. For working with schizophrenic patients, who require a somewhat different set of therapeutic reflexes, see Rosenbaum's *The Meaning of Madness,* [9] Chapter 14, "Dynamically Oriented Individual Psychotherapy," with its attendant list of suggested readings, and Mendel and Green's *The Therapeutic Management of Psychological Illness: The Theory and Practice of Supportive Care.* [10]

This list is obviously far from exhaustive; it is meant only as a beginning. Seminar leaders, supervisors, and other teachers will all have other books and articles to suggest.

THERAPY AND SUPERVISION AS LIFE IN MICROCOSM

Patients coming into psychotherapy behave neurotically: they will unwittingly bring into therapy portions of their current lives and will repeat in the therapeutic situation some variant of the earlier life events and interpersonal relationships from which their neurosis developed in the first place. They may report (or we may experience with them) a continuation (repetition), or the opposite, or some combination thereof, of the original maladaptive pattern and of the patient's need to live it out at the same time he hopes to escape from it. The psychotherapeutic situation can be seen as a living Rorschach, where the patient's lifestyle, both neurotic and healthy, is reenacted in microcosm.

Such reenactment is of course found elsewhere, but rarely in such pure culture as in the therapeutic situation, which has the distinct advantage of being relatively free of many of the usual constraints on human relationships. A feature virtually unique to the psychotherapeutic situation is that the parties to it will examine the relationship as it unfolds. The therapeutic contract is time-limited (in terms of hours per week, and, sometimes, months or years of duration) and makes the study of what the patient feels, thinks, does, and says, both in the therapy hour and outside of it, the prime focus of interest.

The therapist is not an employer who hires and fires, though therapists certainly can accept or refuse to accept a patient for treatment, or

discharge him from treatment in those unhappy circumstances where the treatment situation breaks down. The therapist is not a lover, so he will neither physically seduce nor be seduced by his patient, though he may act in a mildly psychologically seductive fashion to strengthen the therapeutic alliance, *not,* however, with the aim of bedding down the patient.

The art of managing transference requires two skills: the ability to be close and the ability to be distant. The therapist must be able to choose the right distance for his patient and to shift this distance as his patient's needs require. It is a rare pair of lovers indeed who can maintain a romance and yet have one of them be the therapist artful at managing closeness and distance in the transference! For this reason we state that no therapist should become physically intimate with his patient and still pretend that what is going on is therapy. A therapist and patient may fall in love (some have even married), but when that happens they must recognize that therapy is no longer an option for them. If the patient is to continue in therapy, it must be with someone else. As these events are always confusing, it is highly advisable that the therapist seek consultation before accepting that his emotion is really love and not countertransference.

Sadly, there are some therapists who regularly bed down attractive patients and who explain their actions, if explanations are offered, on the basis that they are trying to make the patients feel physically desirable, and accept the sexual parts of their being, or some similarly transparent rationalization for concupiscence. Seduction corrupts and degrades the original request for help and is destructive of the patient's chances for growth, no matter how elaborate the rationalization.

The therapist is neither clergyman nor parent and therefore has no strong vested interest in seeing his patient conform to religion's and society's mores and expectations. Yet he may praise a patient for making progress toward therapeutic goals; he may criticize a patient who has acted in a self-destructive or self-defeating manner when such criticism can alert the patient to behavior patterns which interfere with his becoming a more successful human being.

In short, the therapist is simply another human being with some expertise in understanding feelings, thoughts, and interpersonal relationships who seeks to help the patient increase his self-awareness and decrease the neurotic limitations the patient has quite unconsciously imposed upon himself.

Thus the patient who had been controlled by domineering parents as a child may either seek out others who will control him now, seek to control and dominate others, or avoid all situations where issues of control and dominance are likely to arise. As psychotherapy begins, we may see him manifest these concerns by asking the therapist to tell him what to do or what to say (asking for control), by talking at such a great rate that he makes it impossible for the therapist to get two words in edgewise (controlling in order to avoid being controlled), or by disparaging psychotherapy in a series of intellectual criticisms which carry the underlying message, "Since psychotherapy is not scientifically well founded and is of unproven potency, it cannot possibly have any impact on (control over) me."

To the degree that these behaviors occur with a therapist who is in fact *not* trying to control him, the patient can learn from them something of what *he* brings to a relationship that may affect its later course. If the therapist reacts controllingly, then he has justified the patient's neurotic style. Thus, the therapist is immediately confronted with his own first task — to establish his "base line" against which the patient's transference distortions can be measured. Therapists do this in different ways: some attempt to achieve this by "sterilizing" the psychotherapeutic field from their own "contaminating" responses. Others aim at careful reflections of the patient's feelings at all times. Still others attempt to resonate to everything the patient brings to therapy. Whatever his personal style, the therapist will feel the intrusion of alien affects or thoughts, things not understandable from the here-and-now interaction with the patient.

What are these intrusions about? In other words, what is transference? A musical analogy may help. The patient may be transposing what he learned as a child in the key of C minor into a current life situation in G major with much background noise, and into the psychotherapeutic situation in D flat major with relatively little background noise. The therapist hears the melody, albeit in a different key. The theme is heard clearly because the therapeutic situation is constructed to contain as little background noise as possible. The time, the office, the affective state of the therapist are all relatively stable and constant. It is not so much a matter of individual style (an extraverted, friendly, talkative therapist who is consistent can offer a stable base line as well as a classically silent analyst) as it is of commitment to a constant situation from which the *patient's* interpersonal style and intrapsychic concerns can clearly emerge.

Therapy and Supervision

One curious by-product of first hearings of therapeutic melodies for the beginning therapist is that he may unwittingly transpose the theme into a new key in his supervision of a given patient. He may approach his supervisor acting uncharacteristically helpless, befuddled, and defeated, or with a superabundance of notes or tape recordings to be gotten through frantically during a supervision hour, or with more than his usual level of doubt about the efficacy of psychotherapy. It may not be until the supervisor and therapist examine the warps of their interaction that they can begin to see the kinds of things that the patient has brought to therapy, and which, by implication, he brings to his daily life and which, unwittingly, the therapist brings to the supervisor.

One very important task of supervision for beginning (and sometimes experienced) therapists, then, is that both supervisor and therapist pay attention to how each feels about and relates to the other. If the supervisory relationship has within it the same degree of mutual respect and honesty that one hopes for in the therapeutic relationship, and the same base-line constancy, such therapeutic issues can more easily be identified and worked through. This means that the therapist must feel free to report to the supervisor all of his feelings and thoughts about the patient without fear that the supervisor will condemn him for having such feelings, just as the patient must be able to talk freely to the therapist.

Example 19-1. A resident had been presenting his work with a patient to his supervisor for several weeks. One week he presented his material in a bored, listless tone, and the supervisor found himself becoming bored, too. After twenty minutes, the resident had nothing more to report about the therapy hour under discussion.

The supervisor commented on the boredom and asked if therapy with this patient had become boring. It had; therapist and patient had become enmeshed in discussing an important project the patient had been neglecting to complete. Recent therapy hours had focused almost entirely on, "How's the project coming?" ("Well, I didn't get much done on it this week.") "What do you think is holding you up on it?" ("I'm still having trouble communicating with my project director."), and so on.

The supervisor suggested that he become less interested in the project, that he and the patient look beyond the project they had become fixated upon to other aspects of the patient's life, to her social life, to her leisure-time activities, to her relationship with her family, and so forth. They did so, and life began to return to both therapy and supervision.

Therapy for the Therapist

Supervision should not be a disguised form of therapy for the therapist. But it should be conducted in an atmosphere where all the data about the task at hand — the treatment of a given patient — are open for discussion; the feelings of the therapist about the patient and of the supervisor about the therapist are often relevant. From such supervision sessions, it may become apparent that the therapist has certain neurotic conflicts of his own which interfere with his effectiveness with patients. The therapist may bring his own melodies into the therapy hour and may listen to them instead of to the patient's. One therapist had a patient who dreamed that she was trying to reach him by phone, but every time she dialed his number, an angry woman came on the line. This therapist was in fact going through a separation in which his wife was behaving with much rancor. Though he had not mentioned this to his patient, it preoccupied him and rendered him less responsive to his patient's emotions.

When such conflicts become apparent, the therapist should enter therapy himself, even though it may be tempting to "bootleg" therapy from a particularly sensitive supervisor. While the therapist works on his own problems in his own therapy, he continues his work with patients and his supervisor.

QUESTIONS AND SILENCES

Patients' Questions

Responding to a patient's questions is often difficult for a therapist. In his search for grist for the therapeutic mill, he is of course tempted to regard the question as evidence of an underlying concern. He is usually right to regard it as such, for questions reflect a particularly urgent pressure from the unconscious. Nothing, however, is so maddening to a patient as a mysterious refusal to answer, coupled with the accusatory, "Why do you ask?" On the other hand, a factual answer at the content level of the question may seal off forever the chance to use the question as an instance of the patient's concern in a particular area.

The therapist needs to ride with the question and not be afraid ultimately to answer it when such an answer could prove therapeutic. The therapist should remember that the question belong primarily to the *patient's* urgency and that it is in the patient's best interest to have that urgency fully heard, not simply gratified. Some of the commonest questions are, "What are you getting out of all this, doctor? Is this worth your while? Am I doing (saying) the right thing?" Rarely does the therapist answer, "I think so," or "I'm very pleased with your progress," even if the therapist *does* think so or if he *is* pleased. Almost always, the therapist needs to say, as tactfully as he can manage, "It sounds as if you need my reassurance just now. Can you tell me how so?" The point is to avoid a question-for-question parry with the patient and in so doing checkmate the patient's curiosity, but rather to give it even fuller experession, to let the patient hear for himself what he *really* wants to know, and then to work with him to find the answer. One technique I often find useful is to respond to a question by saying, "I may be able to respond to your question in a little while, and certainly we'll get back to it. But right now, I wonder if you can tell me what led up to your asking the question."

Some questions about the therapist's private life inevitably come up. For paranoid patients, a simple and direct answer may decrease otherwise intolerable suspiciousness and anxiety. With most patients, the therapist ideally should not feel shame about self-disclosure when it is appropriate. Still, therapists and their supervisors must be their own best judges about determining the fine line between therapeutic self-disclosure and untherapeutic, narcissistic, or guilty confessions which serve the therapist's neurotic needs at the expense of his availability to his patient.

Not every question deserves an answer. Sometimes a patient, like a child, must endure a certain amount of psychological hunger as a part of learning what belongs to him and what belongs to others. In general, the combination of a free willingness to answer an informational question that could help the patient get a securer hold on reality, and an unstinting commitment to help the patient find the full meaning and intensity of any

question he asks, will lead the therapist to his own satisfactory answer to the problem of how to deal with the patient's questions.

Silences

Patients may have difficulty in starting an hour, or they may fall silent during it. Therapists will take the lead in breaking a silence more often in reality-oriented therapy than in uncovering therapy. In reality-oriented therapy, if a patient has trouble starting a session, the therapist may ask, "How did things go at work this week?" If a silence develops during an hour, he may say, "You were talking about work a few moments ago before you fell silent. Is there something troublesome about work which is difficult to talk about?" Or he may use free association to help get things unstuck: "I wonder if you can tell me what is going through your mind at this point."

In uncovering therapy, it is left more up to the patient to start and continue an hour. Often an initial topic will be left, only to reappear in disguised form as a *leitmotif* later in the session. When a silence occurs, the therapist should first try to sense the feeling-meaning of the silence. Does the silence represent sadness, guilt, anger, anxiety, fondness, communion, sexual arousal, and so on? Almost inevitably, as Freud observed, whatever the feeling-state during the silence, the patient is also thinking about the therapist. The patient has a fantasy about the therapist, or the patient is preoccupied with what the therapist will think about something which is on the patient's mind. Silences are, therefore, manifestations of transference, and they often conceal something the patient is ashamed or afraid to communicate to the therapist.

Sometimes a silence is far more eloquent than speech. A patient may have finally spoken the unspeakable, divulged a guilty secret, or experienced a new meaning about his existence, and he needs the sanctity of silence to let things sink in. To interrupt now would be intrusive; it could constitute nervous chatter by the therapist intent on beating an insight to death with talk. Here a silent communion between patient and therapist is called for.

But what about those many uncomfortable and unproductive silences which come up? After a while, the therapist may simply ask the patient to report what is going through his mind, or he may connect the silence with the topic which preceded it. If he has a sense of the feeling behind the silence, he may try to help the patient identify it: "As we've been sitting here, I get a sense that you are feeling angry (sad, anxious, and so forth)." To get at the transference elements, the therapist may ask or suggest, "Does your silence have anything to do with therapy or with me?" Inexperienced therapists are often reluctant to ask such a question because they are afraid the patient would consider it faintly ridiculous to be thinking about the therapist when there are so many other important people and events in his life. But the therapist and therapy are often extremely important in the patient's life, especially during therapy hours, and the therapist does well to keep in mind that silences almost always involve him. Not that he has to get to the transference aspects of each silence, but he should certainly count on their existence.

When a silence comes at the end of the hour, the therapist may merely comment, "Our time is up for today." Or he may say that and add, "Perhaps next time we can try to understand what made you silent today." The patient leaves the office musing on what went on. For depressed and borderline patients, however, or for patients who are in the grip of strong and uncomfortable emotion at the end of the session, an unbroken terminal silence may presage several days or a week of anxiety and despair. The patient leaves the office perturbed and perplexed and the mood persists. In such cases, the therapist should interrupt several minutes before the end of the session, asking about the feeling and transference issues which may be involved, or he may choose to set a forward-looking tone by saying, "Our time is nearly up for today. What kinds of things might be

coming up this week with Barbara?" thus helping the patient to do some anticipatory coping with situations he expects to confront soon.

PARADOX, PRESCRIPTION, AND PREDICTION

Patients will often report behavior inside or outside of therapy as though they were (1) not aware of the motivations for it or (2) aware of the motivation but unable to control the behavior, presenting the motivation as something not under their control, but rather "unconscious" or "because those people out there think I should," or something of the sort. If the therapist thinks either that the motivation is closer to awareness than the patient realizes or that the patient can exert more control over his behavior than he gives himself credit for, the therapist may use paradox, symptom prescription, and prediction as ways of bringing about these changes.

Paradox

Watzlawick, Beavin, and Jackson[11] point out that paradox always involves two levels of communication at the same time, the content level of the communication and the metacommunication, which is a comment on how the communication is to be received. Paradox exists when the metacommunication contradicts the communication itself: paradox is a tension between the explicit level of communication and the implicit meaning of the communication.

Example 19-2. A patient complained that she was seriously irritated by an uncontrollable urge to gorge herself on food, count to three, then vomit the food in the bathroom. Her inability to control the sequence was particularly upsetting to her.

The therapist asked her if she knew a foreign language. She knew Italian. He said, "Why don't you try counting up to three in Italian?" The behavior stopped altogether after she followed his instruction.

The patient's communication had been, "I eat, I count to three, I vomit, and it is uncontrollable." The response to the therapist's symptom prescription had demonstrated that, paradoxically, at least one part of the sequence was controllable, and, by implication, perhaps the rest of it. Note that if the therapist had said explicitly, "You can control this," the patient would surely have come back with, "But I can't," and they would have been at an impasse. Paradox avoided the impasse.

A more subtle use of paradox is the implied interpretation, which often carries an element of surprise. The therapist used a kind of paradox when he said to the patient who was screaming at her husband, "You're not attacking him hard enough." Her attack had received an unexpected reaction; she had expected censure for her need to challenge her husband. By strongly supporting her right to challenge him, the therapist paradoxically frustrated her self-defeating tactic of attacking him hysterically. This is the paradoxical aspect of praise.

Prescription

Symptom prescription may depend upon paradoxical effect for its therapeutic effectivness. Often, in fact, patients also are quite apt to benefit from straight forms of behavior or symptom prescription. Thus, it is sometimes helpful to suggest to a patient that he do something to either test out an interpretation or try to develop some new form of behavior. Traditionally, there has been a reluctance to step into the patient's life and try to get him to do anything. At times, however, it is very helpful to do just this.

> *Example 19-3.* After two years of therapy in which a difficult marital situation had been somewhat improved, a 34-year-old woman lamented the frequency with which she got into "hollering" contests with her eight-year-old daughter. One source of conflict concerned the girl's bedwetting, which occurred once or twice a week. Each evening the mother nagged

the daughter, urging her to avoid liquids and to urinate just before going to bed. Sometimes the daughter obeyed; sometimes she didn't.

In therapy, evidence emerged that the patient was treating her daughter as her own quite controlling mother had treated her. Furthermore, the patient felt that her self-esteem as a mother was being injured if she did not persist. A power struggle between mother and daughter was developing, and what was getting lost sight of in the struggle was that sleeping in a wet bed was more undesirable and unpleasant for the daughter than hearing about it was for the mother.

Accordingly, I suggested to the mother that she and her husband very carefully avoid any mention of evening liquids or bedtime urination, after explaining to the daughter that they were going to try to change their ways. I suggested they hold to this line for a week, even if it meant a wet bed every night. I further suggested that the mother try to examine her own feelings and thoughts during the week.

By the end of the first week, the girl had not wet once (nor did she for the two weeks following). The mother was pleased with the outcome of the experiment, since it relieved her of the burden of having to nag the daughter. Furthermore, it brought into sharp focus her need to maintain a controlling, infantilizing relationship with her daughter, interfering with the daughter's growing needs and abilities for independent living in many areas of her life. Some very useful recollections of how her own mother had hampered the patient's growth emerged, as well as an increasing awareness that she did not have to mother in the same fashion.

Additional dividends of the experiment came as the patient found herself able to help the daughter organize her own play space, where she could sew doll clothing and leave her dolls and tools in disarray as she wished, rather than, as previously, use the mother's work table, only to arouse the patient's ire when the girl failed to clean up. The patient reported considerably more pleasure and less acrimony with her daughter in the weeks following the experiment.

Prediction

In Chapters 2 and 3 (suicide) we described how, in the case of a patient recovering from a severe depression, one can predict that depressed and suicidal feelings may very well recur. The prediction not only helps forewarn the patient, but it may also bring the benefit of paradox: the watched pot may not have to boil; the neurosis may not have to assert itself. In addition, a prediction is a statement of a stereotyped (predictable) response to a situation. By identifying the response in this way, the patient may both be freed of having to react in such a stereotyped manner and also find new and healthier ways of coping.

Example 19-4. Tom, a 27-year-old married graduate student in anthropology, was quite vulnerable to loss. If his therapist had to cancel an appointment or went on vacation, or if Tom's wife had to leave town to visit an ailing relative, Tom would sink into an angry apathy, get no work done, eat and sleep too much, and indulge himself in reading novels.

His wife was once again due to leave town to visit the relative whose illness was now terminal. The therapist asked Tom to predict how he would react to her departure. Tom predicted he would go through his usual cycle. At a session five days later, Tom reported the following:

"I took Marilyn to the train station Saturday, came back home and slept for the rest of the afternoon. I got up and ate and was tempted to start a new novel, but found myself thinking about this project at work, mulling it over and over in my mind. I slept well that night and had a good dream I'll tell you about. When I woke up Sunday, some-

thing had jelled, and I went in to work and made really good progress on the project. The pace has continued good through today. But I'm not sure I trust what's going on. I know I'm angry with Marilyn for 'deserting' me, just as I have been in the past, but I think what I am doing now is saying to her in effect that I'll show her I can live without her. It's not the best motivation in the world, maybe, but it's certainly working better than the old way."

APPOINTMENTS AS INDICATORS IN THERAPY

A regular appointment schedule is part of the base line of therapy. The therapist commits certain hours each week for work with a given patient. Some therapists make discussion of their policies about missed or cancelled appointments and whether or not the patient will be expected to pay for them a part of the original treatment contract; this is especially true for therapists in private practice. Likewise, therapists inform patients in advance when the therapist knows he will be unable to keep an appointment or will be on vacation.

Patients usually have feelings and reactions to their appointment schedule. If they come regularly and punctually, they can express their feelings during their sessions. They can say they are comfortable with the schedule, that they look forward to their therapy days. They can say they find the schedule confining or inconvenient, or that they do not like to have to adapt to someone else's schedule. They can express anger, dismay, or concern when the therapist has to cancel a session, or they can express relief at the money they save when a private therapist goes on vacation.

When patients are late for appointments or fail to keep them, they are often expressing through behavior some aspect of their feeling about therapy and their lives. Asking for extra sessions, too, may be a truncated way of trying to communicate with the therapist about therapy. Thus just as dreams, questions, silences, productivity, and posture all can convey feelings about treatment, so can the way the patient keeps, or fails to keep, his appointments be a source of information in treatment.

The Absent Patient

How to determine the meaning of a missed or cancelled appointment and how to deal with it is often difficult for beginning therapists. Experienced therapists vary widely on how to handle such matters. Some choose to make a statement of policy about missed appointments as part of the initial treatment contract for intensive psychotherapy; others wait to see if the issue comes up spontaneously during the course of treatment.

Meaning of Missed Appointments. An appointment may be missed for purely realistic reasons, for dramatic effect, for unconscious reasons (as when someone "forgets"), or for some combination of all these reasons, e.g., a patient on his way to an appointment has an auto accident, and there is reason to suspect emotion increased the hazard. The more reality enters the situation, the harder it is to establish unconscious determinants, and the beginning therapist should be cautious about interpreting accidents and the like as resistance. On the other hand, a patient who "just didn't feel like coming yesterday" is probably demonstrating nonverbally some kind of resistance to, fear of, or dissatisfaction with therapy, and he can be encouraged to substitute a verbal statement for the nonverbal one.

A fear of therapy can be expressed by missing appointments, in dreams in early therapy (a therapist asking a patient to enter a dark room is a common such dream), by expressing doubts about psychotherapy as a form of healing or helping, or in direct verbal statements. One of the most common fears is that of being found out, of overexposure. Much of the patient's neurosis he regards (often unconsciously) as dirty linen, as shameful secrets of disgusting or reprehensible fantasies or behavior. He may fear that the therapist

(who is often assumed to have psychological x-ray vision) will discover these and punish him accordingly. He may fantasy that the therapist will chastise him, discharge him forthwith from treatment or issue some other kind of harsh response.

Other patients may fear (and rightly) psychotherapy for its potential for releasing storms of pent-up emotions, storms which the patient unconsciously fears could destroy patient and therapist alike. The emotions involved are usually anger or sexuality.

> *Example 19-5.* Early in therapy, a male patient reported this dream. "I am on an ocean liner, and we are having a party as the voyage starts. As we get out to sea, the wind comes up and I spot an enormous black whale bearing down on the ship. The whale hits the ship and breaks it up and there is a mad scramble for the lifeboats. Only a few of us make it to a lifeboat, and the whale leaves us alone. I think we finally got rescued."
>
> From the patient's associations to the dream, the following meanings emerged: therapy was a voyage into the unknown, starting with a party of people who were known; the ship was his familiar neurosis; the people were the significant others in the patient's life. The storm represented the anticipated emotional upheavals of therapy; the whale was the feared therapist, who allowed only a few to survive. (The whale also represented the patient's father, who had been a domineering person, capable of wrecking the patient's self-esteem.) The fact that the patient and a few others survived the storm and were rescued represented the patient's unconscious expectation that when all was said and done in therapy, he would have profited from it i.e., have been rescued from his neurosis.

Again, it is important to respect the emotion. Patients are often overimpressed with their own destructiveness, but they are also in a better position than we to know how dangerous the process of opening things up can be. More than one flight from treatment or overt psychosis has resulted from the therapeutic tack of analyzing away rather than hearing out resistance to therapy. Rogers and his colleagues[12] have presented clear evidence that therapy can be harmful to some patients. A wise approach is to let the resistance speak right alongside the motivation for treatment. If it is in the patient to change and the conditions for treatment are right, most patients will opt for continuing therapy. Those who drop out will at least view therapy as a place where they have been allowed to choose, and they may return when life conditions permit. We must condemn the procedure of seducing or intimidating patients into changes, a procedure that reflects the attitude that the therapist knows better than the patient how much the patient can handle.

When patients start having such dreams as the one reported above, or missing appointments, or showing other signs of anxiety about therapy in midtherapy, this may signify that they are on the brink of an important discovery about themselves and are unconsciously both pleased and alarmed at what its implications might be.

Missing appointments may represent *acting out in the transference*. There was a day when the term *acting out* meant what it was supposed to mean: an unwitting repetition of an unresolved childhood conflict in which persons in the current environment are reacted to as if they were figures in the child's unconscious register of the emotional situation around him. The single woman who goes through several unhappy romances with older, married men who never seem to divorce their wives and marry her, is acting out her original role as loser in the oedipal drama. The man who does something to defeat himself every time he becomes eligible for promotion at work is acting out his own version of this theme. When the intherapy behavior of the patient comes more and more to seem to be a stereotype, apparently aimed at getting the therapist to see him in a certain way, and with a loss of opportunity to examine his own motivation, he is *acting out in the transference*. He does this instead of *remembering* or *reexperiencing*

something which, until it is put into words, will persist as behavior.

In recent years, many have come to use *acting out* loosely to signify socially deviant or disapproved of behavior, such as delinquency and sexual promiscuity. There is danger in our using a theoretical concept as a veiled way of making moral judgments. There is a need for a term which allows us to examine the neurotic use of action as a defense against self-exploration, or as an intensification and dramatization of an unproductive and neurotic way of behaving. In general, *acting out* fills that need, and we use it to refer to any neurotically determined, stereotyped behavior, even if it is the compulsive sort of work which might lead to winning a Nobel prize at the cost of a severely constricted emotional life.

It is only natural for patients to play out, live out, and act out their emotional states. The therapist is always striving to clarify, and he will want patients to understand what they are doing. But he should avoid "jumping" a patient every time the patient resorts to action to solve a conflict. If the patient cannot act out his neurosis, he may also feel inhibited when it comes to acting upon his healthy impulses.

To return to missed appointments, they may represent an acting out in the transference. They frequently occur when issues of power versus helplessness, success versus failure, reunion versus abandonment, and so on are important to the patient.

Example 19-6. Dr. Campbell was the therapist of Ben, the graduate student in physics mentioned in Chapter 13. He noted to the patient that every time he (the therapist) had to cancel or change an appointment, the patient would miss an hour, or come late, or come early and embarrassedly wait an extra hour, and so forth. The therapist had earlier commented to Ben that he thought the patient had tended to repress competitive strivings with his fellow graduate students, burying them behind a "Mr. Nice Guy" facade.

Ben didn't feel there was much evidence for his alleged competitive strivings, nor did he see more than coincidence between changes in the therapist's schedule and his being irregular about appointments. Any time the therapist suggested these connections, the patient pleasantly but contemptuously dismissed them as "Campbell's hypotheses, I and II, as yet unproven."

Once the therapist had to cancel an appointment. At the next session the patient arrived twenty minutes late, his face red as a beet, and explained, "I was working when it was time for our appointment, and I only 'remembered' it ten minutes later. As I was driving over, I found myself thinking, 'That damn Campbell. He's probably not any older than I am, and yet he can come and go and cancel appointments as he damn pleases, and I have to conform to *his* schedule, but he doesn't have to conform to *mine!*' "

The fat was in the fire, and Campbell's hypotheses were on their way to being proven.

Sometimes missing appointments signifies *disappointment with therapy*. Such disappointments may be quite realistic. It may be, for instance, that the patient has received as much benefit from therapy as he can for the time being, but does not feel permitted to say so directly. Consciously he tells himself he is resisting treatment, but his valid emotion expresses itself nonverbally by causing him to miss appointments. On the other hand, there may be a disappointment of a less realistic kind in a patient who harbors the belief that therapy will cure him magically of all of his difficulties, and he becomes angry with the therapist for withholding his magic. Such a patient needs to come to grips with the fact that therapy will require considerable effort on his part, and he can only do so once he has frankly discussed his sorrow that his wish for a nonarduous, automatic solution cannot be granted.

Dealing with Late or Missed Appointments. Late or missed appointments should be dealt with in

such a way as to maximize potential therapeutic learning for the patient. For therapists in private practice, financial matters must also be considered.

There are several things a therapist can do. First, the therapist should have some reading, writing, or dictating to do while he waits for the unannouncedly late patient. If he sits in his office with nothing to do, tapping his foot impatiently while waiting for the patient to show up, he will be getting too angry to be of much use to the patient. The patient, on arrival, will sense this, and, to the extent that he needs to provoke and defeat his therapist, will have discovered a dandy technique. I have found having a stack of psychiatric journals of the "I've got to get around to reading these someday" variety in my office is an excellent way of whiling away time for late patients: the patient can be late and I can get some reading done in the meantime. On the other hand, some patients may come later and give the therapist more time to himself as part of a neurotic need to please. Thus the therapist should watch to see that patients are not acting out to help him do what he cannot, i.e., limit his workload.

There will be occasions in which the therapist will want to phone or write the late or absent patient. Therapist practice varies widely here. The therapist will be guided by his own curiosity and concern. When patients are in precarious emotional balance, e.g., suicidal or schizophrenic, it can be therapeutic for the patient and reassuring to the therapist to phone, during or after the hour, to find out what is happening. When patients are better integrated, this solicitousness can be somewhat infantilizing. It is often valuable to wait until the next session to inquire about the reasons for having missed the previous one. Waiting also gives the therapist a chance to experience his own reaction to the missed session; such reactions may vary from relief and anger to sorrow, and may help illuminate for the therapist some nonverbal aspects of his transaction with the patient. Some therapists are able to introduce their own reactions into the discussion with the patient so that both may be clearer as to what is going on.

If a patient has missed several sessions, and attempts to phone him to get him to come in have been unavailing for one reason or another, one can write him. It is wise in such a letter to specify a date after which the therapist will no longer be expecting him, so that the therapist does not have to remain in a state of suspended animation for several weeks. A sample of such a letter follows.

Mr. Henry Thompson
521 River Drive
Oakdale, Michigan

Dear Mr. Thompson:

You have not been here for our last few scheduled sessions, and I have been unable to reach you by phone. I am wondering if you want to continue in psychotherapy with me. I will hold our usual 1:00 P.M. hour open for you for next Tuesday, February 20th, and would appreciate your calling to let me know if I should expect you. If I don't hear from you, I will have to assume that you are not interested in further psychotherapy at this time.

Yours sincerely,
Joseph W. Campbell, M.D.

When a patient is late for a session or misses one but comes for the next, the therapist should first await some mention of it by the patient. If none is forthcoming, the therapist should bring it up. Whether the reason for the absence comes from therapist's or patient's initiative, in reality-oriented therapy the therapist often will accept the explanation without much further comment, unless it looks as if the patient needs help in expressing some concern about or dissatisfaction with therapy. In uncovering psychotherapy, on the other hand, the therapist will want to understand the meaning of the tardiness or absence as much as he would want to understand a dream, free associations, or other communications from the patient.

The therapist's task will be easier if he welcomes the communication than if he regards it as a hostile threat to therapy. Techniques vary. One source of such understanding is to ask the patient what his fantasies are about how the therapist felt about the event. If the patient thought the therapist might have been concerned, relieved, bored, angry, and so on (whatever the therapist's real feelings were), some potentially valuable information has been gained. Patient and therapist can explore whether the patient has unconsciously allowed being at the right place at the right time to be a determining factor in his other relationships, whether parents and significant others in earlier years used reunions and separations as nonverbal parameters in forming relationships, and so forth. Another technique is, if the patient has given a bland explanation, simply to look at the patient and ask, "What do you suppose the *real* reason is?" Often a simple expression of concern, such as, "I wondered why I didn't see you last time," goes the farthest in opening up the whole topic. Whatever the technique, the goal should be the same: to open up the affective channels of therapy, to allow emotion its fullest say.

The relation of missed appointments to the therapeutic contract varies as to how the initial therapeutic contract was set up. If a policy about missed appointments was not defined at the time of setting up the contract, I think it is unfair to charge for one; this smacks too much of ex post facto judgment. If it was not discussed initially, one or a few missed appointments may bring the issue up for definition later. The usual contract is that the therapist agrees to set aside certain hours of his time, e.g., Tuesdays at 11:00 A.M. and Thursdays at 2:00 P.M., for the patient, and that the patient is free to use the hours as he sees fit, e.g., to come or not; if present, to talk or be silent.

Whenever the issue comes up, there are varying practices as to how missed appointments can be handled; four of the most common are reported here. Again, it should be remembered that therapists in private practice have to make a living, and financial concerns enter into their considerations in a way that they don't for therapists who are salaried and whose income is not affected by patients who fail to keep appointments.

Some therapists will not charge a patient for a missed appointment if the patient has given sufficient, i.e., twenty-four to forty-eight hours, notice. Other therapists observe this practice, adding the proviso that the therapist must also be able to fill the hour with someone else in order to escape loss of income.

A second approach is that therapist and patient will discuss each missed appointment at the following session and examine the reasons for it, no matter how much or little warning the patient has given. Discussion will center primarily around these questions: (1) is there anything the patient could have done differently to be able to come? (2) did the patient's reasons for missing the session reflect a substantial contribution of neurotic over-determination, or, by and large, did they seem to be realistic and reasonable? If the patient could have arranged things differently, or if his reasons for missing seemed neurotic, then he is charged for the session; otherwise he is not. For patients who have used illness or the press of other obligations as a way of avoiding emotionally difficult situations, such a review can be most illuminating, even if painful.

A third approach is that of defining therapy as an ironclad contract, from which no deviation will be allowed save that of terminating or taking a vacation from therapy. In this method, a major accident or illness can be considered a vacation from therapy for a week or more, but minor illnesses are not. This is a particularly stringent approach, one which I do not find attractive personally, but one therapist who employs it has told me, "It is remarkable how many patients find they can make hours in spite of colds, flu, and other inconveniences once we agreed on this contract. In fact, some of them have been amazed at how they have gone through three or four years of therapy without having caught a single cold." And he was not being sarcastic.

Finally, it can be left to the patient solely to decide whether he thinks a given absence from therapy was justifiable or not. For patients who have been excluded from important decision making earlier in their lives, or who have been inclined to get into power struggles with significant others, this approach can yield much useful material.

This list is not meant to be all-inclusive. Each therapist will ultimately work out a system that best fits his temperament and style. Nor does it follow that a therapist should find only one system and apply it universally: what might be therapeutic with one patient might be destructive with another. Consultation with an experienced therapist on a given case may make it easier for the beginning therapist to decide which policy to follow.

Extra Appointments

There are times when patients or therapists want to schedule extra appointments or increase the frequency of sessions. Increasing the frequency from once a week to two or more times a week may, in fact, reflect the shift from ego-oriented psychotherapy into uncovering psychotherapy, as part of a renegotiated treatment contract.

Patients in acute emotional crises, e.g., a broken romance, impulsive sexual behavior followed by guilt and anxiety, or a serious reverse in school work, may feel overwhelmed and want to see their therapist to unburden themselves and gain some advice and reassurance. Such requests should be honored, either by a session or by a long phone call. The delicate and taxing job of managing a potentially suicidal patient for whom hospitalization is somehow not appropriate will often require extra sessions.

Therapist and patient should be aware that such extra sessions will be for the duration of the crisis, and that, when some resolution has been achieved, the frequency of sessions will probably revert to their former level. Sometimes such a crisis will open a patient up to be willing to examine himself more intensively than he might have otherwise, and a period of long-term uncovering psychotherapy will be the result.

Sometimes the request for an extra session comes for neurotic and overdetermined reasons, and here the therapist has to exercise his judgment as to whether it is in the best interests of treatment to grant the request or not. Often such a request will come at a time when the therapist or the patient is about to go on vacation or must cancel an appointment for other reasons. In such cases, the unconscious meaning of the request may be, "Give me something extra now to replace what I am going to lose later," or it may be, "I still feel too helpless and need something extra now to tide me over while we are separated." Sometimes the request reflects unconscious rivalry with other patients, e.g., "Does my therapist care as much for me as he does for patients he is seeing more often?"

As with direct questions, dream interpretation, and so on, the only way patient and therapist can help the patient figure out what the meaning of the request for an extra session might be is to be curious. However he gets at the material, he will want to know about the circumstances under which the wish for the extra session originated, the fantasies the patient has had about the extra session. The therapist's intuition, based on his knowledge of the patient's dynamics, will sometimes guide him to make helpful conjectures. Once he understands what the patient wants and needs, the therapist can decide about the request for the extra session, and he is in an excellent position to explain how he came to his decision. Should he want to turn the patient down, he should be prepared to say just why he doesn't think it advisable or necessary now. When an unreasonable request is refused for a good reason by the therapist who has taken the trouble to understand even the angry, demanding patient, the patient will often feel psychologically received and usually continue in treatment.

Follow-up Appointments

Requests for follow-up appointments may come weeks or months after the formal termination of therapy. Therapists often make them. Therapy which has been valuable does not end with the last appointment! Many an analysand can testify that months and years after the last visit, he will find himself thinking about his behavior and dreams, especially at troublesome times, when he uses the tools he acquired during his formal therapy to do self-analysis. Sometimes he will decide that self-analysis is not enough, and will want to reenter therapy to continue work on troublesome problems. These may either be old problems returning to reveal a new facet still to be resolved, or they may be new ones which have surfaced just because some old impediments had been removed. But it is also to be remembered that new life circumstances can bring up entirely new issues. For instance, the patient whose therapy allowed him finally to marry may find, some years later, that the birth of a child provokes a new set of anxieties unanticipated during former therapy.

A single follow-up visit may have a profoundly helpful effect in a patient who was helped by therapy. The effect is rather like a "booster shot" in an already immunized person, a small dose bringing an anamnestic response. It is as if a patient who made substantial gains in therapy had acquired a certain amount of psychological immunity to certain stresses to which he previously was vulnerable. As time passes that level of immunity begins to wane, but only a single session may be required to restore his former degree of immunity to psychic infection, as shown in the case of Mrs. Graves in Chapter 14.

One too infrequently practiced reason for a follow-up visit is simply for the therapist to find out how his patient has done since formal therapy ended. If such a session is being held at the therapist's behest, the patient should not be charged for it. If the patient makes a brief, friendly "social call" after therapy has ended, it should not be billed for. This can reinforce the patient's sense that he has graduated and thus be quite therapeutic.

REFERENCES

1. Rogers, Carl: *On Becoming a Person,* Houghton Mifflin, Boston, 1961.

2. Gendlin, Eugene T.: "A Theory of Personality Change," in P. Worchel and D. Byrne (eds.), *Personality Change,* Wiley, New York, 1964, pp. 100–148.

3. Kaiser, Hellmuth: *Effective Psychotherapy,* Free Press, New York, 1965.

4. Colby, Kenneth M.: *A Primer for Psychotherapists,* Ronald, New York, 1951.

5. Sullivan, Harry S.: in Helen S. Perry and Mary L. Gawel (eds.), *The Psychiatric Interview,* Norton, New York, 1954.

6. Fromm-Reichmann, Frieda: *Principles of Intensive Psychotherapy,* University of Chicago Press, Chicago, 1950.

7. Alexander, Franz, and Thomas French: *Psychoanalytic Therapy,* Ronald, New York, 1946.

8. Tarachow, Sidney: *An Introduction to Psychotherapy,* International Universities Press, New York, 1963.

9. Rosenbaum, C. Peter: *The Meaning of Madness: Symptomatology, Sociology, Biology and Therapy of the Schizophrenias,* Science House, New York, 1970.

10. Mendel, Werner M., and G. A. Green: *The Therapeutic Management of Psychological Illness: The Theory and Practice of Supportive Care,* Basic Books, New York, 1967.

11. Watzlawick, Paul, Janet H. Beavin, and Don D. Jackson: *Pragmatics of Human Communication,* Norton, New York, 1967.

12. Rogers, Carl R., Eugene T. Gendlin, Donald J. Kiesler, and Charles B. Truax (eds.): *The Therapeutic Relationship and Its Impact,* University of Wisconsin Press, Madison, 1967.

C. PETER ROSENBAUM, M.D.

CHAPTER 20

Continuation, Transfer, and Termination as Events in Psychotherapy

In outpatient clinics where psychiatric residents and medical students see patients in psychotherapy, disposition decisions must be made when the therapist goes off service and cannot continue to see all his patients. In other instances, therapists will periodically review their case loads and see whether all the patients currently in treatment should remain in treatment. The options open to therapists are usually those of (1) continuing with the patient, (2) transferring the patient to a new therapist or new form of therapy, or (3) ending formal therapy with the patient.

When patient and therapist decide to continue, some patients of the advanced residents who are going into private practice will start having their sessions in the therapist's private office; fees may or may not be changed from the clinic fee. Patients being transferred may go to a new therapist directly or take a planned vacation from therapy. Some patients will be found to be more suitable for group therapy than individual therapy and may be transferred to group therapy while continuing individual therapy until the transition has been made. Other patients, more in need of supportive therapy, will be transferred to a program such as Thursday Afternoon Clinic. When patients are terminated, it is wise to leave a bridge to the therapist and/or clinic by suggesting that the patient call the therapist if necessary if something troublesome arises in the future, or call him at some prearranged date, or call the clinic as necessary if the therapist himself will not be available.

CRITERIA FOR DECISION MAKING

There are a number of criteria that allow therapists and patients alike to work toward one or another of these ends.

Criteria For Continuation

As a first criterion it is probably necessary but not sufficient that the therapist and patient have enjoyed working together. Not all therapists like all patients, much as they might strive toward this particular version of psychiatric perfection. If, even after discussion with supervisors, a therapist finds he does not like a given patient, he probably should not continue with him. However, dislike, especially with very hostile patients, may be a condition of relating to the patient, as Searles has pointed out. If the therapist enjoys his relating to the patient, then that may be incentive enough for him to continue. He has to ask himself, however, whether the patient is actually progressing, aside from the fact that they are en rapport. If therapy has ceased being work for therapist and patient, if it has become pleasant but primarily social, both should face this fact and discuss the possibility that treatment seems to be at an end or at least at an impasse.

A second criterion for continuation is that the patient has been making, and continues to make, psychotherapeutic progress. He is grappling with his problems and working at them and showing signs of mastery over previously neurotically limiting kinds of feelings and behavior.

A third criterion is that the patient is a particularly good teaching case. Going over sessions with a consultant or in a continuous case seminar provides a rich return to the therapist and his group. As long as continuation is at least moderately therapeutic to the patient, his value for teaching may justify continuation in a clinic where there are many competing demands for service.

There are some *apparent* criteria that therapists should watch out for; they may lead to poorly thought out decisions. The first is the thought, "This patient can't get along without me," whether patient or therapist is first to think or voice it. To be sure, there are times when patients urgently need psychotherapeutic help, especially at times of emotional crisis. But often therapy settles into a comfortable pattern of the patient unnecessarily taking a helpless, dependent role and the therapist unwittingly abetting it. At such times it behooves therapist and patient alike to examine the relationship to see if it is persisting beyond the likelihood of significant therapeutic progress being made, just as the smile on Alice's Cheshire cat persisted after the cat itself had disappeared.

Closely related is the feeling that the patient is

not ready to fly solo, not ready to meet life without therapy. It is a persistent fantasy of patients, even when they are as sophisticated as psychiatric residents, that treatment will cure them of *all* their neurotic ills and should not end until that goal has been achieved.

> *Example 20-1.* Four college students, each of them in formal psychoanalysis, formed a W.T.A.I.O. (When the Analysis Is Over) club, each supplying his own version of cure. One student said, "W.T.A.I.O., I will be able to carry a tune." He selected this goal because his father, a professional musician, had absolute pitch, and the student was convinced that his imperfect sense of relative pitch was a neurotic defense against oedipal competition. After three and a half years of otherwise productive and useful analysis, he still couldn't carry a tune; some things just don't yield to therapy.

In the same vein, therapists should examine the wish to continue with a patient because the therapist has not "done enough." How much is enough? Consultation with colleagues or supervisors can be most helpful here. Most therapists are kind and compassionate people who want the best for their patients, who want to see them overcome neurotic handicaps to successful living, and they often feel a sense of failure or inadequacy when patients do not make all the progress the therapist had hoped for. One way of compensating for such feelings is to continue therapy, even beyond the point of diminishing returns, in hopes that by dint of the passage of much therapeutic time, something good will happen. Gaining the perspective required to know how much is enough requires experience; for beginning therapists, consultation with experienced therapists is one way of developing that perspective in their work with a given patient.

Criteria for Transfer

If a therapist is going off service and cannot continue with a patient who otherwise fulfills the criteria for continuation given above, the therapist will want to arrange for the patient's transfer to an incoming therapist. Other patients will appear to be good candidates for group therapy or for supportive therapy, and suitable transfer can be arranged.

Sometimes a therapist finds that he cannot work with a particular patient. Though intellectually the therapist thinks the patient is a good candidate for psychotherapy, they somehow don't mesh. Or, if things were going well at the beginning, some later developments may result in disengagement. Perhaps the patient's depression has become so profound that he has exhausted this therapist, or frequent suicidal threats and attempts have overburdened the therapist's capacity to deal with him. If the therapist has conscientiously sought consultation from supervisors and colleagues and still finds himself repelled at the thought of further sessions with this patient, then he should seek a new therapist for the patient.

Transfers are often made for more positive reasons. A patient may have gotten about as much as he can from this therapist, but there is more to be gotten from another one. He may have worked through many complexes about men with a male therapist and now needs to work with a female therapist to elicit deep feelings about women. Perhaps the patient needed at first to work with a gentle and soft-spoken person who could be tender; now he needs more to be initiated into the use of assertiveness and aggression in an adaptive way and can learn better from a tough, outspoken therapist. Such transfers are not uncommon in Jungian analysis.

Similarly, it may develop that a different treatment modality (e.g., behavior modification, group, couple, or supportive therapy) holds more promise for the patient at this point. If he agrees, and the current therapist is not able to provide the new form of treatment, a transfer should be arranged.

Transfer from one individual therapist to another is often difficult in a clinic where therapists leave because their rotation has ended. In our clinic, only about 50 percent of all patients

recommended for transfer for such administrative reasons come in for more than one or two visits with the new therapist, even when the procedure has been carefully worked out between patient and departing therapist. Thus such administrative transfers are an unpredictable procedure, and either continuation or a carefully handled termination is preferable.

Criteria for Termination

The happiest circumstance for termination, of course, is completion of therapy. Initiation and individuation have progressed well; the patient is living much more freely and independently than when he first came for treatment. Many of the goals of treatment described in Chapter 13 have been attained.

Another criterion for termination is that the patient has made good progress, therapy seems to have reached the point of diminishing returns, and the resulting plateau is not merely a period of resistance in therapy (some periods of bland resistance are inevitable in any intensive psychotherapy). For such patients, either taking a vacation from therapy for several months (for students, the summer vacation often presents a naturally occurring hiatus) or stopping altogether is in order.

Another, very different criterion is that the patient has simply become dependent on therapy itself, has become a "therapy addict." Though all therapeutic motion has ceased, he believes that he will be saved if only he keeps coming. Certain of these patients will indeed need therapy forever and may profitably be transferred to a supportive treatment program. Others should be weaned before their magical belief in Nirvana-through-therapy-unending seriously cripples their abilities to cope on their own.

Finally, some patients' problems are simply not amenable to psychotherapy. Often this cannot be predicted at the beginning of therapy; it can only be realized in retrospect after several weeks or months of treatment. Termination with dependent

patients and those whose problems are not amenable to psychotherapy requires delicacy and tact
on the part of the therapist, as Colby[1] discusses,
so that the ending of treatment does not come to
represent defeat and hopeless incurability to the
patient. It is cometimes very helpful to say, "I
think you *could* come forever, but it would be
doing a disservice to your own ability to handle
your life."

PSYCHOLOGICAL FEATURES OF TRANSFER AND TERMINATION

The topic of transfer or termination always
arouses anxieties in patients and often in inexperienced therapists, and these frequently disguised
anxieties are often linked to separation anxieties
of earlier years, ones often involved in the original
problems for which the patient sought treatment.
Schiff[2] describes many of these issues quite
cogently in his article "Termination of Therapy."

The Patient's Feelings

One sign of such anxieties is either the occurrence of new psychological symptoms or the
recrudescence of old ones. In fact, sometimes the
entire course of therapy may unconsciously be
reenacted during its closing phase, much as the
recapitulation and coda of a symphonic finale
may restate all the previous themes.

Particularly, themes of helplessness and rage at
abandonment may become prominent. There will
always be a dependent part of anyone who has
enjoyed a significant and rewarding relationship
which will want to continue the relationship and
will become angry at its impending dissolution, no
matter how much the more reality-oriented part of
the ego may recognize that the time to end has
come. This is particularly true in psychotherapy,
where the patient, by the simple act of assuming
patienthood, has ultimately had to deal with the
helpless child in him who will protest the ending
of therapy, as he protested the ending of his own
childhood.

A common defense is to deny dependency.
Patients nearing the end of therapy, who were
previously reliable about keeping appointments,
may start missing sessions, coming late, and so on.
Often this turns out to be a nonverbal statement
of the theme, "It is not you (therapist) who are
abandoning me (patient); it is I who am leaving
you first."

One clue as to the issues which will come up
around termination is how the patient has reacted
to disruptions during therapy. Each time a therapist has to cancel a session, or goes on vacation, a
naturally occurring minitermination takes place.
The same issues around separation, the same
themes of helplessness, rage, and dependency, arise
at these times. Indeed, to the extent that these
have been acknowledged, dealt with, and worked
through during therapy, the patient will be better
prepared to face them as true termination or
transfer comes up.

The Therapist's Feelings

Therapists, too, will have mixed feelings about
the interruption or end of a profitable relationship. Though the therapist may be pleased with his
patient's progress, he may also feel guilt about
abandoning the patient before *everything* could
have been accomplished. The therapist may overes-
timate, or, more frequently for beginning therapists, underestimate his importance to the patient;
the therapist may need to confront his own
feelings of loss, as shown in the example below. In
the kind of intensive psychotherapy with schizophrenic patients that Searles[3] describes (a relationship more intense than most work with neurotics), this issue is particularly important. The
kinds of feelings Searles describes in the following
example nevertheless occur, usually in more muted
form, as termination with a neurotic patient
approaches.

Example 20-2. I think, for example, of a
woman who was, at the beginning of our work
some years ago, extremely unintegrated in her

personality functioning. She behaved, from one session to the next, and often from one moment to the next, like a galaxy of utterly different persons. She has become, over the years, partly by dint of much hard work on the part of both of us, much better integrated. . . . But we have lost much too. . . . The beer hall bouncer I used to know is no more. The captured American pilot, held prisoner by the Germans but striding proudly several paces ahead of the despised prison camp guard, is no more. The frightening lioness has gone from her den. The incarnation of paranoid hatred, spewing hostility at the whole world, has mellowed into someone unrecognizably different. The endearing little girl can no longer hide the adult woman who is now part of her. . . . It is as though a whole gallery of portraits, some of them beautiful and some of them horrible, but all of them free from diluting imperfections, have been sacrificed in the formation of a single, far more complex and many-sided portrait, the relatively well-integrated person who now exists.[3]

The Therapist's Behavior

Sometimes therapists handle their feelings about termination by abandoning the style that they had maintained during therapy and acting in unconscious collusion with the patient, even when such behavior serves no therapeutic purpose or may even dilute the therapeutic potential of dealing with termination. The ordinarily non-self-disclosing therapist may start answering personal questions he had previously left unanswered in a way which diminishes the meaning of the experience.

Example 20-3. During the three-year follow-up sessions with Steven G. (Chapter 17), Steven suggested that he and the therapist call each other by their first names and get to know each other socially. His rationale was that since he was about to start training in an allied field, social work, the therapist might become a friend and teacher. The therapist felt that this request represented Steve's wish to minimize the sense of loss at the time, and that it would be more useful to investigate the meaning of the request rather than to accede to it. Furthermore, the therapist pointed out to Steve that if he entered into a social relationship with him, his future availability as a therapist would be jeopardized and that the therapist would be neither fish nor fowl.

At the next session and in the letter he later wrote, Steve thanked the therapist for not having acceded to the request. He was then able to discuss some of his feelings about the impending separation, feelings which would have been masked if the therapist had acted differently.

Example 20-4. A residential treatment center for hyperactive and hyperaggressive children was being phased out of existence, and the morale among both staff and children was extremely low. Many children were to be returned to the same inadequate foster homes and children's asylums from which they had come, and the staff felt guilt and despair after several years of hard work with them. Many felt they hadn't done enough for the patients and ignored, out of guilt, all they *had* done.

A few weeks before the unit's closing, one of the children asked a staff member for the key to the front door, a request that he probably wouldn't have thought of previously. And the staff man gave him the key, in violation of one of the cardinal rules of the unit. In two minutes the kids had bolted through the open door, and it took several hours to retrieve the last of the escapees.

When the staff later met to consider what had happened, it quickly became clear to all that the staff's collective guilt about the ending of the project manifested itself in the decidedly untherapeutic relinquishing of the front door key.

By keeping the patient's and his own feelings and behavior in focus, the therapist can help the patient examine how he handles *this* separation, presumably prototypic of past and future separations. He can help him face and master his feelings of helplessness and anger, especially when they are out of proportion to the event. He can help the patient to examine his needs to continue to view himself as weak and helpless, even after therapy has generated considerable evidence to the contrary. It can be a time to review progress during therapy and take stock of gains made and to define further goals for the immediate and distant future. Experienced therapists show remarkable agreement on the point that termination of therapy can be a most productive period.

Other Technical Features of Termination

Timing is important both at the outset of treatment and as the time of transfer or termination approaches. It is wise when a long-term treatment contract is being established to let the patient know of the probable maximum length of time the therapist will be working with him. For psychiatric residents, this often amounts to a statement such as, "I'll be here in the clinic until next June. If therapy is still in progress then, that is probably when we will have to end." Patients who have had previous contacts with clinics may already be aware of the July–June residency year.

Some patients will remember such a statement, others will "forget" (repress) it. In either event, eight to ten weeks before the probable transfer or termination, it is wise to remind the patient about it. To focus nearly exclusively on termination issues substantially more than ten weeks away sometimes converts the last few months of therapy into a lame duck session in which not much gets accomplished. On the other hand, to give the patient less than eight weeks' opportunity to work through his feelings about termination may deprive him of a useful therapeutic experience.

The patient should usually participate in making the decision as to which of the available options would be most useful. Therapist and patient can use the last several sessions to take stock of what has happened in their work, what changes have taken place, what kinds of previously troublesome situations the patient is now handling better, what still unresolved issues will need attention in or out of therapy, and so on. Together they should strive to reach a firm decision about which path to follow.

If the decision is to discontinue therapy (rather than to transfer), some of the symptoms of separation anxiety described above may appear. The therapist may be tempted to reverse his decision and provide for additional therapy, but in most cases he is best advised to hold firm to the decision he and the patient have arrived at even while examining the patient's feelings about it. In cases where the therapist is unsure about it, consultation can be helpful. If the therapist can, while being genuine, convey to the patient his feeling that the patient has made progress and has mastered troublesome situations, patients will often find this reassurance useful during and after the latter stages of therapy.

After the Fact

Maintaining a bridge with the therapist or the clinic can often be very helpful. If the therapist will remain in the area, he can tell the patient, "If something comes up, call the clinic and they'll put you in touch with me and we'll arrange a session or two. If it looks like it is going to take longer, I'll help arrange more therapy." He should then be willing to honor his promise promptly. In most cases, a session or two with the patient is sufficient to reassure him that the therapist is still available and interested — which is often what the call was really about, whatever its manifest content — and no further sessions will be necessary, as with Mrs. Graves (Chapter 14). In those instances where the patient genuinely needs more therapy, the therapist should help arrange it and be available to the new therapist to give him information during the period of transition.

THERAPY BY MAIL, PHONE, AND TAPE

If either therapist or patient is leaving the area and the patient is willing and interested, it is possible to conduct long-distance therapy. If the patient's or the therapist's move is to be permanent, it is generally better to arrange a transfer to a new therapist who will take over the treatment. However, if the move will only be temporary, or if the patient is moving to an area where no psychotherapists are to be found, or if the patient no longer needs intensive psychotherapy but still wants to maintain contact with his therapist, the two can maintain contact through letters, phone calls, or tape recordings. I have had several patients, many of them quite articulate and psychologically minded people, who moved from the area, who continued working on their problems independently, and who would write from time to time, with my encouragement, telling how things were going, discussing problem areas, etc. In return, I have tried to respond in writing much as I might have during a therapy hour, trying to help the patient clarify and work on the issues he raised.

Example 20-5. One therapist's patient was due to leave because of a job transfer, yet he very much wanted to continue therapy. The patient's adjustment had been precarious, and therapy was one of the stabilizing influences in his life. He was moving to a remote, rural area where there were no therapists.

His therapist set up a contract with him that he would save the patient's usual treatment hour, Tuesday mornings at 10:00, to read any letters he received from the patient and to respond to them. He would continue to bill the patient for this time. The patient was quite reliable in sending a weekly letter, and the therapist was equally reliable in responding to it. Two or three times a year the patient would return to the area and have a "live" therapy session in which he and the therapist tried to consolidate the work that had gone on by mail. At the end of two years, the patient felt

sufficiently secure in his adjustment that he and the therapist were able to terminate their long-distance therapy.

Example 20-6. An intelligent and potentially very articulate young man who had often found it difficult to communicate intimately with people had enjoyed a frank and intimate friendship with someone who later became a psychotherapist. Their lives diverged, and over the next several years contacts between them were sporadic.

Eventually, the man found himself in a very difficult marital situation, impulsively left his wife in Indianapolis, and relocated in New Orleans, where he knew no one. He was extremely anxious, lonely, and depressed, yet he couldn't stand the thought of returning and facing his wife.

He called the old friend, now a therapist; they spent nearly an hour on the phone. In that and most subsequent contacts, the old friend served primarily as a therapist concerned for his friend. The therapist suggested that the friend-patient write, which the patient was glad to do. He wrote fast and furiously, sometimes sending one or two ten-page letters in a single day. He described the factors leading up to the flight, the day-by-day experiences in New Orleans, his hopes, his fears — everything. The therapist responded at least two or three times a week, albeit not at such great length.

To complicate matters, the distraught wife got in touch with the therapist to ask if he knew where her husband was, how he was doing, etc. With the patient's permission, the therapist told the wife that the husband was alive and well, but that he could not give out more information. The wife was persistent, but so was the therapist.

In time the patient realized that he would have to come out of hiding sooner or later and confront his wife, something he was able to do two months later. By this point, the frantic volume of letters, interspersed with occasional phone calls, had diminished. The patient returned to Indianapolis to talk with his wife and arrange for a divorce. He went back to New Orleans, where he had found work and was beginning to build a new life for himself. The therapist helped him enter formal psychotherapy there, though he received weekly letters from the patient as progress reports.

Ultimately the acute crisis was over; the patient had arranged the divorce, was doing well professionally and personally in New Orleans, and the correspondence virtually ended. During the four months of the acute crisis, the patient had written more than seventy-five letters during his Herzog-like hegira. A year later he remarried; the correspondence is now limited to an exchange of Christmas cards; all seems to be going well for him. Some months after his life had stabilized, he asked the therapist to return his letters, which the therapist did. Both symbolically were saying that this episode of crisis and need was over, that the patient was released from patienthood, and they were back to being friends.

ON BEING THE NEW THERAPIST

Thus far we have discussed issues confronting a therapist-patient relationship which is about to end. If the patient is to start with a new therapist, there are several issues both will have to deal with.

Borderline and Psychotic Patients

It is rare for a patient to meet with a new therapist before the last session with the old one, even if the patient is being treated in a clinic and will continue with a new therapist in the same clinic. By and large, this is satisfactory, but for patients who have severe problems with intimacy, such as borderline, paranoid, and schizophrenic patients, it is often helpful for the new therapist to sit in on the last few sessions with the old therapist, being relatively quiet at first and more active and responsive later.

This serves several purposes. The most important is that it allows the patient to become familiar with the new therapist before treatment with him begins formally. The patient can see what he looks like and hear what he sounds like. He will not be starting therapy with a stranger but rather with an acquaintance. Another purpose served is that it allows the new therapist a chance to sample the flavor of the interaction with the old therapist. He can pick up many emotional overtones and intuitions (which are often extremely important in working effectively with such patients) in a much more vivid way than mere description by the outgoing therapist would allow for. A third response is a smoother and less ambivalent handing of the baton of treatment from one therapist to the other. During the sessions, the first therapist can say to the second, "This issue of mother's trying to control everything in Daniel's life that we've just been talking about is one that has come up over and over again, and I'm sure it's something that will come up frequently in your work with Daniel, too. Daniel, do you think that's a fair statement?" Daniel can then proceed to explain things further; in a sense he is already beginning to engage in treatment with the new therapist by imparting information from his current therapy.

Neurotic Patients

Such borderline patients represent a minority in most clinics. Neurotic patients predominate; they can handle a transition much more easily. For them, if there is unsettled business left over from the previous therapy, as almost inevitably there is, the new therapist must be ready to hear about it. Some patients may not have been fully able to express their disaffection with some of the ways a former therapist did therapy or their anger at having to end their treatment with him. They may be able to berate him only retrospectively, in the presence of the new therapist. Other patients may not have been able to express their fondness and gratitude to former therapists and again can only acknowledge them belatedly.

Inexperienced therapists may be discomfited by

strong outpourings of feelings about a former therapist. It feels too much like marrying a divorcee only to hear at great length about the former husband. If anger at the former therapist predominates, the new therapist will wonder, "When will I get mine? If this patient sees someone in treatment after we terminate, will I get raked over the coals in the same way?" Conversely, if adoration of and gratitude toward the former therapist are prominent, the new therapist may wonder, "What a saint he must have been. How can I ever follow in his footsteps?"

Indeed, for patients where unresolved issues of rivalry (often stemming from childhood) are important, setting up a three-person situation — former therapist, patient, new therapist — can be an unconscious, or even conscious, way of seeing if the new therapist will engage in rivalrous behavior. Will he tacitly support attack on a former therapist, saying in effect, "Yes, it's too bad you had to spend all that time with that incompetent when you could have had *me* for a therapist"? Will he tacitly erode gratitude toward a former therapist, saying in effect, "Please don't speak so highly of that saint; the more important he is in your eyes, the less important I must be"?

If he is aware of these potential traps in the patient and in himself, the current therapist can do what he has to do: listen carefully to the patient talking about someone who is extremely important, in this case a former therapist.

Even if most of the business of separation from the former therapist seems to have been settled, even if there are few diatribes or paeans, even if the transition seems smooth, there may be more work for the new therapist to do than he is at first aware. A patient who was working effectively with the former therapist was probably in the stages of late confrontation and initiation, following our four-stage model. Contact had been established for a long time. The patient starts with the new therapist apparently still at the levels of confrontation and initiation. It seems as if they will be excused from having to go through the period of contact and early confrontation.

Such is not the case. What the patient has

brought is a kind of "passive immunity," one which tends to wane in six to ten weeks. The two can act as if they were immune to the struggles of a beginning relationship because of the good past relationship. When that fades, they *must* face beginning again; they are, after all, two people who were total strangers just two months ago.

Therapists who are not prepared for this phenomenon of a waning passive immunity may become discouraged. Why are things slowing down now when they were going so beautifully before? What happened to that insightful patient who started off so intelligently? Have I failed to live up to the standards set by the former therapist? Probably not. Probably the new therapist must prepare for a new beginning, one which comes paradoxically weeks after treatment had seemed to start. He and the patient must establish their own contact, their own way of confronting issues. Both need to realize that contact with this therapist will be different (which the patient may initially see as worse) from that with the former therapist. The new therapist's way of confronting problems will be different (which the patient may initially see as worse) than the former therapist's.

As new therapist and patient come to know each other and gradually develop respect for each other, they will move into a period of genuine confrontation and initiation, and they will probably arrive there much more quickly because of the work with the former therapist. If the new therapist can allow himself to hear about his predecessor without being rivalrous toward him, the patient can close an old chapter in his life and get more rapidly into the new one.

REFERENCES

1. Colby, Kenneth M.: *A Primer for Psychotherapists,* Ronald, New York, 1951.
2. Schiff, Sheldon K.: "Termination of Therapy," *Arch. Gen. Psychiat.,* 6:77–82, 1960.
3. Searles, Harold F.: "Oedipal Love in the Countertransference," *Int. J. Psychoanal.,* **40**: 1–11, 1959.

DIANA SILVER ARSHAM, Ph.D.
ROBERT J. UNDERWOOD, Ph.D.

CHAPTER **21**

Other Approaches to Therapy

PART I: THE THERAPIST AS A BEHAVIOR MODIFIER

The subject of the following case example was treated in a psychiatric hospital unit in consultation with a primary therapist. The case will be employed throughout this chapter as a vehicle for illustrating many aspects of behavior modification.

Example 21-1, Edith. Edith, a 53-year-old married housewife, was hospitalized with a diagnosis of depression, characterized by anorexia, insomnia, and fear of leaving her house. Since the death of her mother two years previously, Edith had become increasingly inactive and withdrawn. Her mother's home had served as the site for large weekly family gatherings, the organization and hostessing of which involved much of Edith's time and energy. Since the loss of her mother, Edith had not developed any additional social ties or activities to fill the vacuum. Typically, Edith rose at 10 A.M. and took occasional naps and watched TV throughout the day. Bart, 62, her husband, an energetic and youthful traveling salesman, would come home to find his tearful wife in bed, complaining of depression and loss of appetite. He would at first be irritated that the housework was left undone and that his dinner was not prepared, but in an effort to "help and understand" his wife, he proceeded to cook dinner for them both. At the time of Edith's hospitalization, Bart had assumed all the household responsibilities, including the ironing of his shirts and the preparation of their meals.

It is obvious that Edith's case can be treated with crisis intervention, drugs, milieu, couple therapy, and relationship therapy, all described elsewhere in this book. In this chapter we want to focus on the specific contribution that behavior modification made to Edith's treatment. We shall describe first the principles that apply to the process of behavior change in all psychotherapy; then we shall turn to specific techniques of "behavior therapy." The reader will note that "behavior modification" both supplements the uses of individual and group therapy described elsewhere in this book and adds quite specific methods of its own. Each major approach to psychotherapy may be identified by its own particular set of assumptions about the nature of the therapeutic process. Behavior therapy or behavior modification is no exception and has several assumptions on which the practitioner bases the therapy. These assumptions of the behavioral approach have to do with the focus of therapy and the nature of the therapeutic relationship.

BASIC ASSUMPTIONS OF THE BEHAVIOR MODIFIER

Behavior Is Learned

The first and most elemental of assumptions in behavior therapy focuses on the nature of behavior itself. The behavior therapist sees most behavior as learned, both that which is considered adaptive and useful to the client as well as that which is considered a problem and in need of modification. This notion allows the behavior therapist to use in the therapeutic situation the large body of knowledge about human learning which has been accumulated through the decades in experimental psychology. Furthermore, the necessity of generating parallel theories of normality and abnormality (as is often the case with the analytic theories) is eliminated by the unitary concept of behavior acquisition. In short, the behavior therapist sees all behavior acquisition as governed by the same learning principles, with social value judgments; that is, the decision that the client's or patient's behavior is adaptive (normal) or maladaptive (abnormal) is made by observers (society). Ullmann and Krasner[1,2] have written extensively on the sociopsychological approach to "changeworthy" behavior. Bandura[3] has explored the "reciprocal relationship" between the individual and his environment.

Behavior Is Shaped by Environment

Another assumption is that behavior is a function of the present environment as well as the learning history of the individual. The therapist, therefore, devotes considerable time in therapy (1) reconstructing the client's learning history, i.e., the environmental circumstances, social and physical, under which behaviors of interest were acquired; and (2) discovering the nature of the client's present environment, i.e., present circumstances, social and physical, which maintain or inhibit the behavior in question.

Once the therapist has an understanding of these past and present environmental factors, he is able to begin to formulate a behavior modification plan (treatment plan) wherein social and physical environmental factors are modified so that maladaptive behavior is unlearned (diminished) and adaptive learning is enhanced.

The reader will note that the behavior therapist does not include in the formulation of the treatment plan information which has to do with underlying or unconscious psychological factors. Most behavior therapists consider the popular belief in the existence of underlying "psychic conflicts" as causes of behavior to be academic, since, they believe, behavior may be modified without the use of such concepts.

> *Edith (cont'd.).* In discussing with Edith and Bart the events that happened immediately before and after the appearance of her depressed behaviors (crying, inappropriate daytime sleeping, etc.), the behavioral consultant and the primary therapist noted that prior to the depression, Edith's mother died and the family gatherings stopped; thus a significant source of behavioral reinforcement was lost. It was further noted that after the appearance of the symptoms, Edith and Bart seemed to have developed an interdependent way of functioning which actually reinforced Edith's depressed behavior. For example, while Edith was "too upset" over the death of her mother to cook dinner or to do other household chores, Bart inadvertently encouraged her *not* doing these activities by assuming them for her and increasing the amount of attention he paid to her depressed behavior.

Nature of Therapeutic Relationship Is Collaborative

The most significant aspect of the therapeutic relationship in behavioral therapy is the fact that therapy is a contractual arrangement between therapist and client in which the goals, methods, and outcome criteria are discussed and agreed upon at the outset of therapy.

Edith (cont'd.). The therapist reviewed with Edith and Bart the behavior changes which would be regarded as progress in therapy. Edith said that she was depressed and described a behavior pattern which consisted of crying and staying in bed all day. The therapist noted additional behavior depicting depression, i.e., Edith's appetite and sleep disturbance and social withdrawal. The goals for therapy were formulated from among these observed behaviors: crying, staying in bed, appetite and sleep disturbance, and social withdrawal. The therapist, Edith and Bart agreed in the beginning of therapy just what level of change in these behaviors would constitute progress, i.e., reduction in the frequency of crying, increase in the amount of food and number of meals eaten, increase in the length of nocturnal sleeping time, and increase in social activity. These criteria also included the substitution of new, more adaptive behaviors for old maladaptive ones, for instance, getting up for the day's activities instead of staying in bed all day. The therapist and Edith worked out a graded schedule of activities that Edith agreed to attempt. The ward staff were instructed to notice and praise (reinforce) Edith when she was seen doing the activities, e.g., making her bed or finishing her lunch.

In behavioral approaches to therapy, the relationship between client and therapist is seen as collaborative rather than dependent, as is the case in many of the more traditional, medically based therapies. The therapist's responsibility is to provide information and technique for change, not change itself. The client always maintains the responsibility for his own behavior. The therapist is teacher more than healer, the client more student than patient. The therapist's issue is not "cure" but development of skills and increments of goal attainment. The client provides the therapist with critical feedback about the effectiveness of the behavior modification techniques, so that

the therapist may alter them accordingly and introduce additional techniques. The client, after acquiring enough information about the principles of learning and behavior changes, might suggest and implement variations in his own treatment. Ultimately, the goal of behavior therapy is for the client to assume total responsibility for his own treatment and to learn techniques for modifying his behavior in the future.

Edith (cont'd.). In the collaborative relationship that the therapist developed with Edith, Edith set up her own schedule of ward activities and responsibilities and kept a diary of how she progressed through that schedule each day. She and the therapist reviewed the diary during each session and noted movement toward therapy goals.

Evaluation of Progress Is Quantitative and Continual

It is characteristic of behavior therapy that periodic and objective evaluation of behavior change and progress is an integral part of the treatment plan. This evaluation documents which behaviors increased during treatment, which old problem behaviors dropped out, and which new adaptive behaviors were developed. This process of evaluation does not, as in some therapies, take place at the conclusion of therapy, but rather is an integral part of the treatment itself, taking place at each step along the therapeutic path. The process by which evaluation provides feedback about treatment progress and therefore alters treatment progress is not unlike the process by which the ship's pilot provides feedback to the helmsman about the ship's progress and thus changes the ship's course from time to time.

Edith's and her therapist's daily review of her diary illustrates one example of the continual quantitative evaluation of progress in behavior therapy. This use of "homework," Edith's noting and recording outside of the session, is another technique often employed by the behavior therapist.

APPROACHING TREATMENT IN BEHAVIORAL TERMS: WHAT THE THERAPIST DOES

The behavioral approach to treatment offers a variety of possible plans for any given problem behavior. This flexibility allows the therapist to "tailor" his treatment to his client's particular problem behaviors and to generalize and transfer any particularly successful technique from one circumstance to another. This flexibility can occur in conjunction with other more traditional psychotherapies with significant benefit to the patient. For example, a patient with a severely debilitating phobic response might be treated by a behavior therapist for the strategic removal of that phobic response in order to make the patient available and able to continue in his psychoanalytically oriented treatment. In that situation, behavior therapy might act in much the same manner that the chemical behavior modifiers (tranquilizers) function — eliminating highly disruptive behaviors and consequently making the patient accessible to traditional therapy. In the paragraphs below the major behavioral treatment techniques are presented separately for the sake of convenience and clarity; however, they usually are used in varying combinations.

Now we shall begin to look at the behavioral approach to psychotherapy in a more concrete and specific manner. We shall outline a number of approaches and techniques frequently used by behavior therapists in working with clients. The reader should understand that these approaches are presented in a fairly abbreviated fashion, intended for illustration rather than detailed discussion (which can be found in the references).

Reinforcement

Whether a behavior is repeated will depend upon its consequences. Some consequences of the behavior will *increase* its probability of occurring again, and these consequences are called reinforcing. For a radio listener whose behavior is turning a radio knob on or off, pleasant music is a stimulus which reinforces turning on the radio. It is a *positive reinforcer*. A blaring commercial is an unpleasant stimulus that reinforces turning off the radio; because its disappearance is reinforcing, the commercial is a *negative reinforcer*. Both kinds of reinforcers increase the behavior (knob turning) that controls their appearance or disappearance, respectively. Consequences meant to *decrease* the probability that the behavior will occur again are called *punishment*. Both removing a positive reinforcer and presenting a negative reinforcer are punishing.

> *Edith (cont'd.).* The functional analysis of Edith's behavior revealed that the following contingencies had developed. Edith received most of her husband's solicitous attention (positive reinforcement) as a result of her complaints of loss of appetite, loss of sleep, and her apparent inability to do housework. The goal for treatment was to reverse this contingency so that the reinforcement would follow desired behavior rather than the undesired behavior.
>
> In the hospital treatment setting, it was arranged that Bart's visits with Edith and his praise of her were directly related to her carrying out desired behaviors. The complete treatment plan for Edith, of course, was a much more elaborate plan of systematically shifting reinforcement contingencies and manipulating environmental circumstances than merely changing Bart's scheduled visits; however, the reader should be aware that each of these arrangements followed the same reinforcement model. There was no decrease in Bart's overall attentiveness to Edith. He merely responded positively to Edith's adaptive, nondepressed behavior and paid less attention to or ignored (and thus punished) her depressed behavior.
>
> Within one week's time, smooth transfer was begun of the reinforcement contingencies from hospital ward to home environment.

Edith's part in the plan was to outline for herself, Bart, and the staff the minimal activities, such as setting the kitchen table for lunch, she felt she could complete during the first visit home. When she returned to the ward after her first visit home, she was smiling and reported to all that she had followed through with her behavioral contract. This procedure was repeated several times until discharge, with each visit including more behavioral objectives for activities within the home and outings, such as going to the grocery store for just a loaf of bread. After discharge Edith and Bart continued meeting with the primary therapist who reviewed Edith's diary of progress.

Various types of positive and negative reinforcers have been systematically employed in institutional settings, where more control of the environment is possible. The reader is referred to Ayllon and Azrin[5] for a description of a "token economy" approach to the use of positive reinforcement in the structuring of an entire ward milieu.

Anxiety Inhibition

There is no doubt that in behavior modification literature the most widely publicized technique has to do with the inhibition of anxiety responses by developing incompatible responses. Wolpe[6] developed a clinical procedure which is called "systematic desensitization" and involves the development of an incompatible response (physical relaxation) to anxiety as a means of decreasing the incidence involved in anxiety response. This procedure has been most successful in the treatment of focal symptoms, particularly of a phobic nature, where intense anxiety is associated with clearly definable physical or social environmental stimuli.

The technique involves a number of steps, the first of which is a functional analysis of the anxiety-generating stimuli. The therapist determines from the client the precise nature of the anxiety-evoking situations in decreasing order of ability to evoke the anxiety response. Once this hierarchy of anxiety-stimulus situations has been established, the therapist then proceeds to train the client in "deep relaxation" techniques. It will be this deep relaxation which will comprise the emotional response incompatible to anxiety later in the treatment procedure. Once the client is able to assume a state of deep relaxation effectively and quickly, the next phase of treatment begins. Imagined stimulus situations from the established hierarchy are paired with the deep relaxation state, beginning with presenting the *least* anxiety-provoking situation with the relaxed state, and progressing slowly over a period of sessions up the hierarchy, until finally the ultimate anxiety-provoking situation is paired with the relaxation and subsequently loses its ability to evoke anxiety.

The goal in using systematic desensitization is for the client to be able to imagine the initial stressful situation without anxiety. The following vignette illustrates this process.

Example 21-2, Lawrence. Lawrence is a 43-year-old business executive who was transferred to the San Francisco Bay area after a long-sought-after promotion. Shortly after his arrival in San Francisco he entered therapy when his intense fear of heights made his daily commute trip across the Golden Gate Bridge a nightmare of anxiety which seriously affected his functioning.

In this case the behavior therapist began the functional analysis by determining the exact nature of the phobic situation, that is, whether the phobic response to height was limited to bridges or included airplanes, high buildings, and mountains, etc. The therapist and client then constructed an anxiety hierarchy which ranged from standing on the first rung of a stepladder at the low-anxiety end and progressed through various gradations of anxiety-provoking scenes up to walking across the Golden Gate Bridge (as the maximum anxiety-provoking situation). Next, the therapist trained Lawrence in relaxation techniques so that Lawrence could quickly, at the therapist's signal, put himself in a state of complete relaxation. This instruction in relaxation actually took several sessions.

The final stage of treatment began with the therapist presenting the least anxiety-provoking stimulus to Lawrence while Lawrence was in a state of complete relaxation. The stimulus was presented again and again until Lawrence was finally able to imagine the stimulus scene without any disruption of his relaxed state. Each successive anxiety-provoking stimulus in the hierarchy was presented to him in similar fashion with each repetition, continuing until Lawrence was able to experience each in turn without a disturbance of his relaxed state.

Therapy was concluded and considered successful when Lawrence was able to travel across the Golden Gate Bridge with little or no anxiety.

Aversive Procedures

Aversive conditioning or punishment has been a historical technique employed by society with varying degrees of success to eliminate undesirable behavior of its members. Behavior therapists, also with varying degrees of success, have employed unpleasant consequences following a client's behavior as a means of decreasing the rate of occurrence of problem behavior.

The aversive approach is generally not the treatment of choice, since there are many negative ethical and aesthetic factors associated with the techniques.[7] Nevertheless, there are some situations where aversive procedures are useful, particularly when they are introduced in conjunction with developing alternative behaviors of the client by positive reinforcement. The aversive procedure stops a maladaptive behavior, at least temporarily, and the positive reinforcement promotes and maintains adaptive behavior in its place.

Because of the generally negative aura surrounding aversive techniques, they are usually employed only in the most extreme cases where the maladaptive behavior is destructive or life-threatening. Land and Melamed[8] report a case where electric shock was successfully employed to terminate chronic ruminative vomiting in a 9-month-old infant. Rachman and Teasdale[7] predict that as behavior therapy techniques continue to develop, more positive methods will replace the aversive techniques.

Social Learning Techniques

There are a group of behavior modification techniques which have in common the fact that they are the by-products of ongoing research into the dynamics of the acquisition of adaptive social behavior. An extensive review of these social learning techniques can be found in Bandura.[3] Space limitations restrict the review of social techniques in the present chapter to two of the more widely employed methods, "modeling" and "assertive training."

New behavior can be established and behavior already in the individual's repertoire can be modified when an individual is placed in contiguity with other individuals who already possess the desired behaviors. This process is particulary potent if the "model" is seen by the individual as a positive figure. Certainly in all forms of therapy the therapist in some degree serves as a model of appropriate behavior for the patient; however, there are behavior modification techniques, particularly with children, where the modeling value of the therapist is the primary source of therapeutic input and the vehicle for behavior change. The Role Model Program at Letterman General Hospital in San Francisco is an example of such an approach to behavior change in children. This program involves the pairing of children who have been identified as "mild behavior problems" with nonprofessional "therapists" who serve as models for the children. Professional supervisors work out with the models a regimen wherein the desired behaviors and attitudes will be displayed on a consistent basis in a recreational setting to the subject child. The findings from this program have tended to support the conclusion that individuals will adopt behaviors and attitudes prevalent in their social environment. The social environment can frequently consist of one person, the therapist. The following case describes a modeling procedure.

> *Example 21-3, Harold.* Harold was a 6-year-old first grader who was referred for treatment by the school counselor for inappropriate and destructive classroom behavior which occurred when he experienced anger.
>
> Behavior analysis suggested that Harold's disruptive anger responses occurred in all anger situations and seemed to be the result of absence of socially appropriate anger responses in his behavior repertoire. The therapist model, in conjunction with the supervisor, devised a series of situations which would appear to be anger-provoking for the model and which could be imbedded in the context of a play session (between model and child) such that the child would repeatedly witness the model's appropriate response to the anger situation; e.g., when the model was the loser in a game, he expressed mild verbal irritation and sought a rematch, expressing the attitude, "If at first you don't succeed, try, try again."
>
> As Harold began to demonstrate more appropriate behavior, the model differentially reinforced Harold's new, socially acceptable anger responses.

Assertive Training

Assertive training[6] is one of the more broadly useful behavior modification techniques available to the psychotherapist. Assertive training is derived from the learning principles governing stimulus generalization and transfer of learning. A basic part of assertive training involves the transfer of behaviors learned in a simulated circumstance to real life situations. Typically, patients use assertive training to learn adaptive responses to anxiety-provoking life situations. By rehearsing alternative social behavior and experiencing reinforcement from the therapist, the client is able to handle a heretofore stressful situation more effectively.

The first level of application of assertive training is merely a method of encouraging self-assertion, something that the reader may have experienced and used already. Further along on the therapeutic continuum, assertive training involves a more detailed, systematic procedure, including the breaking down of the problem situation into a series of more manageable segments with each segment being practiced and well reinforced prior to an in vivo attempt at the integrated behavior pattern.

This technique is useful for a whole range of problems that clients might present to their therapists, from the relatively nonemergent situation where a socially inadequate adolescent wishes to learn more socially effective heterosexual dating behavior to the crisis situation where a distraught teenager is brought into an emergency room after a desperate attempt at self-abortion. In the former situation the therapist might arrange situations where the young man can practice approaching women and get feedback and reinforcement from the therapist as the appropriateness or inappropriateness of his responses. In the latter case the young woman might similarly be encouraged to practice approaching her parents about her pregnancy and in turn practice and expand her repertoire of possible alternative reactions and responses to them. In either case, the therapist and client would determine a range of possible responses, arrive at a few useful alternative approaches, and finally try out these approaches through role reversal. The following case illustrates an approach to assertive training:

> *Example 21-4, Patricia.* Patricia, a 16-year-old high school junior, was seen in the emergency room for acute anxiety as a result of an attempted self-abortion. In the process of crisis intervention, the therapist learned that Patricia had a long-standing difficulty in communica-

ting with her parents and had not been home for two days. Her feelings of isolation had intensified upon learning that she was two months pregnant. Patricia and the therapist concluded that if she could tell her parents of her pregnancy, she would be much less anxious.

The first step in Patricia's assertive training involved the therapist's obtaining a detailed description of her fantasies of what she thought would happen when she told her parents of her pregnancy. This account included what her parents would say and the sequence of their statements in a dialogue as well as what emotional and physical sensations Patricia would experience at the time. During the first two sessions Patricia became very agitated and the therapist employed the relaxation techniques mentioned above in conjunction with the assertive training procedures.

Patricia next explored with the therapist the whole sequence of events which made up the problem or the anxiety-provoking situation of telling her parents. The situation included four components: (1) she makes up her mind that she will go home; (2) she encounters her closest friend, Annabell, along the way and informs her; (3) she approaches her mother to tell her that she has something to discuss with her and her father; and (4) she sits down with her parents to discuss the issue. In each event, the therapist played the role of the key individuals to whom Patricia would respond, practicing variations in her responses until she felt comfortable with the dialogue. The therapist, also serving as a model, actively arranged and paced Patricia's learning of assertive behavior, systematically reinforcing her as she approached her goal of informing her parents.

SUMMARY

No matter what the therapeutic situation — crisis, regular clinic contact, or consultation — the therapist can be a behavior modifier. The therapist

systematically employing principles of learning can actively involve the client in his treatment program and can teach the client techniques for modifying his own behavior to deal more effectively with stressful situations.

The reader should be aware that the behavioral approach to therapy, like other approaches, has some limitations. The limits of applicability are a subject of debate and research; however, for the present purposes the general rule can be stated that as the ambiguity of the presenting symptoms increases, the applicability of the behavioral approach decreases. Nevertheless, the limiting factor remains the therapist's ingenuity and skill in behavior analysis.

C. PETER ROSENBAUM, M.D.

PART 2: GROUP THERAPY

Group therapy has taken its place along with the various individual therapies as a major form of psychotherapeutic treatment. Indeed, for certain patients, it may be a more potent force for constructive change than individual psychotherapy. Just as there is wide variation in the types of individual psychotherapies and the way they are practiced, there are many forms of group therapy. The primary focus of this section will be on interactional group therapy with emphasis on here-and-now phenomena, as described by Yalom [9]; the reader interested in learning more about traditional psychoanalytically oriented group therapy may consult Foulkes and Anthony [10]; those interested in psychodrama may consult Moreno [11]; for milieu and social systems approaches, such as Synanon, see Yablonsky. [12]

Most of the approaches to therapy described in our book include (1) a statement of the theoretical underpinnings of the approach, (2) a statement of when the approach might be useful and when it might be harmful or inappropriate (indications and contraindications), and (3) a description of the techniques the therapist uses. Group therapy is so important and complex an approach that space limitations prohibit a description of all three aspects of it here. Instead, we will focus almost entirely on indications and contraindications for group therapy so that the reader will have some real understanding of which patients he might properly refer for group treatment or, if he has had requisite training, place in one of his own groups for treatment. Again, those readers who wish to learn more about the theory and practice of group therapy are referred to Yalom[9]; the material presented here is largely based on Chapters 7 and 10 in this book.

For many patients, group therapy is the treatment of choice. Sometimes it takes place with concurrent individual therapy, sometimes not. Sometimes a period of individual therapy is needed to prepare a patient for group. Interactional group therapy takes time to effect changes in group members. It usually takes a minimum of six months of meetings once or twice a week before significant change takes place. For this reason, group therapy generally is not appropriate for patients who want or need brief therapy or crisis intervention.

In the past, many patients experienced referral to group therapy as rejection, as being sent for second-best treatment. In recent years, however, so many people have either been personally involved in or have at least heard about group experiences, such as T groups and encounter groups, that often they will approach a therapist and ask for group therapy.

PATIENTS WHO MAY DO WELL

The patients who are likely to profit from group therapy are those who see their problems in interpersonal terms, and for whom the pain of interpersonal failures provides the motivation to endure the stresses of joining a therapy group. Patients who enter with complaints such as, "I feel shy with other people," "I can't seem to make friends," "I always think I am worse than other people," are all describing themselves in interpersonal terms.

Not all patients will describe their presenting symptoms in terms of chronic interpersonal distress. During initial contacts they may describe primarily intrapsychic conflicts or an acute interpersonal stress, such as a failing marriage, or a behavior pattern of long standing, such as homosexuality, seemingly unrelated to other personality factors. Sometimes evaluation for group will uncover some of the interpersonal conflicts that underlie the presenting complaint.

Patients who are being considered for group therapy should have one or more evaluation sessions. For the patient who does not formulate his problems in interpersonal terms, the therapist may offer a translation into such terms as he comes to see the interpersonal factors in the genesis of the patient's distress. How well the patient accepts and understands such translations is an important part of the evaluation and of the preparatory phase of treatment. If the patient grasps the therapist's formulation readily, he augurs well for his ability to work effectively in the group. If he has trouble grasping it, or if it seems to evade him entirely, he may do poorly in interactional group therapy, and a different form of treatment is probably in order.

The patient may enter the group still quite vague about the interpersonal dynamics of his situation, passively accepting referral to group therapy because he feels in sufficient distress to accept the suggestions of the interviewer. It may take weeks or months before he finds his goals shifting in the direction of seeking greater interpersonal fulfillment, e.g., improving in his abilities to be intimate with others, to be able to care better for others, to be able to affect and hear others in a more profound manner, to be more assertive, and so forth.

Example 21-5, Rose. Rose, a 23-year-old, single secretary, came to therapy with several complaints. She had stomach pains which were associated with stress and for which medical treatment had not provided relief. She had a very self-destructive relationship with a man who led her into masochistic sexual practices, who enjoyed beating her up before and during the sexual act; and she began to take a good deal of delight in that form of sexual expression. Now she wanted to find another man; occasionally she went out barhopping but found it to be relatively unrewarding.

Work was extremely unsatisfying. In previous work as an elementary school teacher, she also was tense and anxious. She went through long periods of depression and hopelessness. Her one brief attempt at individual psychotherapy failed.

She was strikingly self-denigrating during her first interview. She was quite colorless and, in fact, throughout much of the long course of therapy, the most striking thing about Rose, as the residents who observed the group would always say, was that she was "gray on gray." She never took a risk in the group; she rarely said anything spontaneous or unexpected. Her statements were full of clichés. She always underestimated the kinds of accomplishments she had made in life and in therapy.

Her history was one of having very few friendships, of feeling rejected and shunned by both men and women. She still had strong, childlike dependency feelings toward her parents and also toward her surrogate mother, whom she chose. Early in therapy, she said she wanted to convert to Catholicism and move to Italy; she had lived two years with a devout woman of Italian parentage and had been well taken care of.

In short, Rose could describe easily the difficulties she had in finding gratifying interpersonal and work situations. She entered group therapy dubious about the group's potential for helping her, just as she was dubious about life in general. She came initial-

ly, one sensed, almost because she saw no other possibility for help, not because she had particular optimism about what would happen in treatment. Nevertheless, she did well.

PATIENTS WHO MAY DO POORLY

There are some patients who do not in general make good group members and who should not be referred. In fact, as Yalom points out, at this stage of our knowledge it is easier to define those patients who will probably make poor group therapy members than those who will make good ones.

In making such selections, it is very important to define *what kind of* and *whose* group is involved. There is a wide variety of groups in this country which put helping people as their core task; in addition to the interactional group therapy that Yalom describes, there is a myriad of groups such as milieu groups, psychoanalytic groups, and so on and such self-help groups as Alcoholics Anonymous, Recovery Inc., and Synanon, which seek to deal with special problems and use their own system of values and techniques.

In interactional group therapy, the attitudes of the therapist organizing a group will strongly influence patient selection. Some group therapists will screen *out* certain kinds of patients and then include *everyone else* who applies for treatment.

For general interactional group therapy, it would appear that patients who, either through direct evidence or from strong inference, show the following attributes are not likely to be good group candidates: brain damage, severe paranoia, extreme narcissism, hypochondriasis, suicidal predisposition, addiction to drugs or alcohol, acute psychosis (especially if it is manic-depressive psychosis), or sociopathy. As Yalom notes:

These patients seem destined to fail because of their inability to participate in the primary task of the group; they soon construct an interpersonal role which proves to be detrimental to themselves as well as to the group. Consider the sociopathic patient, an exceptionally poor risk for outpatient, interactional group therapy. Characteristically, these patients are destructive in the group. Although early in therapy they may become important and active members, they will eventually manifest their basic inability to relate, often with considerable dramatic and destructive impact.

There are certain personality traits or configurations which are often challenged or threatened in interactional group therapy and which lead to early termination, i.e., dropping out of the group, with concomitant loss of morale for both the dropout and the group. Among those noted by Yalom are the following:

1. Inability to make an initial commitment for at least three months' work with the group: this may be due either to external factors (e.g., imminent change of location) or internal factors (e.g., wish for a "quick cure").

2. Patients who present with severe external stress or in crisis: for instance, they may be caught up in an impending marital breakup. It was noted earlier that patients who present in an acute crisis do not have the psychic energy available to become profitably involved in uncovering individual therapy; the same is true for group therapy. Some patients just simply cannot get involved initially with the group to be able to make use of its potential support and help during the inevitable frustrations and additional stresses of the first few meetings. In contrast, once a patient has become an important member of a cohesive and maturing group, the group itself can become a potent support in helping him deal effectively with future severe external stresses.

3. Group deviancy: The patient who is so extremely different from others in the group in one or more major ways that he perceives himself (and is perceived by the group) as "not one of us." Sometimes these differences are because of markedly different communicational styles; at other times they are because of age (consider the problem of the 40-year-old businessman in a group otherwise composed of college students); chronic schizophrenic patients who had "sealed over" their primary symptomatology but who were nevertheless strange and bizarre in their dress and behavior had difficulty in being accepted into a group.

In short, Yalom's work suggests that the central issue of group deviancy is that the patient is unable to communicate on the same psychological and interpersonal wavelength as the others in the group, that he cannot actively participate in the norms and the tasks which grow from the maturing group.

The problem of "group deviancy" is often a figure-ground problem: there are those patients who would be deviant in one group, but easily accepted in another. Thus referral for group therapy must include considerations of *which group;* both referring and accepting therapist should have some knowledge of the kind of group and the nature of its membership before any referral is made. As Yalom notes:

> Patients, then, become deviants because of their interpersonal behavior in the group sessions and not because of a deviant life style or past history. There is no topic, no form of past behavior, too intimate or too hot for a group to accept once therapeutic group norms have been established. I have seen individuals with life styles including prostitution, exhibitionism, voyeurism, kleptomania, and histories of various heinous criminal offenses accepted by a group.

THE EFFECTS OF GROUP THERAPY

Patients in group therapy seek improved interpersonal functioning and an increased ability to enjoy their relationship with others. They seek, also, internal changes and improvements in how they see themselves. Just as with individual therapy, and life in general, it is difficult to love others as long as one despises himself. How the group works to bring about these changes is beyond our scope; an example of changes which took place in one patient are shown below.

Rose (cont'd.). Rose was in the group, which met twice a week for an hour and a half, for two years. She was quite reliable in coming. By the end of two years, both she and the group felt the changes she had made were substantial and most beneficial and that she probably no longer needed to come. One of the two therapists in the group arranged a follow-up appointment with her as she was terminating with the group.

Five months after her last formal session, she saw the therapist for her follow-up interview. What follows is from the therapist's notes of that session:

Rose has changed rather dramatically since the time when we first saw her in evaluation. She rather systematically took charge of the interview, and I mainly asked about each of the major areas and she covered them very thoroughly.

She has an excellent job as a librarian at the Chemistry Library in Woodside, and she is applying for the one at Berkeley. She thinks she might get it; in the past she would not even apply for a job because she was so convinced she would fail. She is earning a good salary and is due for a large raise (approximately $10,000 compared to a salary of $6,500 she got before she started the group). Furthermore, she likes her job, finds it interesting, and has much more contact with people.

She feels better. She is not anxious or depressed; she is excited every day about going to work; she is not lonely; she does not find herself desperately searching for people to be with.

She stopped seeing her old boyfriend and is going with someone else. It probably won't be permanent, but it is much better than previous relationships. They fight a lot and he refers to her as a "demanding bitch," which is a real tribute to therapy. It is inconceivable that anyone would have thought of Rose as a "demanding bitch" before therapy. She fights with him. He always picks on her, criticizes her for having a dirty apartment, and she answers him back in kind; this undoubtedly makes her interesting. She is enjoying sex with her new boy friend; he is a good lover, and she is orgasmic with him. There is little need for any kind of the masochistic sexual gratification she had known previously.

She has a large circle of friends, and keeps quite busy, and is grateful for some time alone. She has moved into a larger and better apartment, and on the whole treats herself much better.

Her health is good. She has no recurrence of the pains, cramps, and heartburn which were one of the main reasons for her coming into therapy.

She has a good self-concept. Her self-esteem is high and she does not knock herself. She is a vibrant, alive, interesting woman, something that could not have been said when she first entered therapy.

We talked about things that were left undone in the group. She feels that perhaps she left the group too early, and that she could have done some more important personal things. A big unmet need was her relationship with her parents which still continues at an infantile level. She moved into a new apartment, but didn't tell her parents about it until later because she feared their criticism. She is still not completely open with other people.

Former group members have wanted to see

her socially; she didn't want to, but could not tell them so openly.

We reviewed several critical incidents in therapy. One was an interpretation made at a meeting where I pointed out that she and Sally had both arrived at a masochistic position, though from markedly different routes; that in Rose's case it was a self-destructive way of asking for love.

Her encounter with Blanche, an older woman in our group, also stands out in her mind. The realization that older people have problems, too, was important for her and helped her understand older people in a way she hadn't before. The discussion around death was very important to her, especially in the meetings taking place around the time she had her breast biopsy. She saw then that death was inevitable, and that only she could take responsibility for her life.

In addition to the gains cited above, the group was useful to her in another way. In contrast to her previous, unsuccessful encounter with psychotherapy, which had left her quite pessimistic about it, she now has much faith in it and knows that if serious problems ever recur, she would again apply for treatment and this time with confidence that it could help her.

In summary, then, patients who view their problems in interpersonal terms, and whose histories indicate that they can relate usefully, if limitedly, to others, and who are willing to make a three months or more time commitment are most likely to profit from group therapy. Patients lacking these traits, or whose intrapsychic defense structure or interpersonal style would be severely challenged or threatened by interactional group therapy are not good candidates. Some patients might be good candidates for one group, poor candidates for another, and the nature and probable composition of the group must be taken into account.

C. PETER ROSENBAUM, M.D.

PART 3: OTHER TREATMENT APPROACHES

Behavior modification and group therapy are only two of a growing number of treatment approaches. Crisis intervention, milieu treatment, uncovering and reality-oriented psychotherapies, couple therapy, the use of medication, and psychiatric consultation are all discussed in this and other books.

There remain still other treatment approaches which are beyond our scope to discuss in detail in this book. Yet they are important, and many readers will want to learn more about them. We will list a few of the most important of them here, with references indicating reliable sources of information about them. They include *child and adolescent psychiatry*[13-16] (itself a recognized subspecialty field), with which *family therapy*[17,18] is closely affiliated. As these names imply, a disturbed child or adolescent often is the most conspicuously troubled member of a specific social system — the family — which is itself under strain; the treatment of this specific ecological group may be the most effective approach.

Hypnosis[19-24] has been discovered, abandoned, and rediscovered many times over the last two centuries. The problem of effectiveness in treatment, as with other modalities, is to distinguish what belongs to hypnosis, as such, and what belongs to psychotherapy for which hypnosis may be an adjuvant. Hypnosis has been used in connection with psychoanalytic therapy and behavior therapy, so that hypnotic therapy is not any one thing. It has been used successfully in pain relief (obstetrics, burns, dentistry, terminal cancer), in control of smoking and obesity, and in a variety of psychoneurotic conditions, including traumatic neuroses of war, where it has served as an uncovering technique as well as a symptomatic one.

Psychiatric consultation to social systems[25,26]

has burgeoned over the last three decades. The general hospital is only one such social system; others include schools, prisons, industrial organizations, halfway houses, and community mental health centers (in which the psychiatrist's voice is only one of many; the others include other mental health professionals and members of the community). Often the consultation is indirect; i.e., the consultant is not asked to see a particular patient, student, prisoner, or client, but rather to look at interactions between individuals, between individuals and groups, between group and community, and so on, to see what he can contribute to making the system under consideration function more smoothly and effectively.

The concept of *community psychiatry* [25,26] develops the idea that a full panoply of mental health services be available to all the persons living in a specified geographic area, usually called a "catchment area." The panoply often includes crisis intervention centers, drop-in clinics, outpatient clinics of a more traditional variety, day-care centers, night-care centers, halfway houses, drug and alcohol rehabilitation, and short-term hospitalization (often on the psychiatric unit in a general hospital). The costs of service are underwritten by some combination of local, state, and federal funding.

Community psychiatry and psychiatric consultation to social systems obviously have much in common. Certainly these two approaches taken together represent a vast change from the situation of thirty years ago when, for lower- or middle-class patients, public outpatient clinics with long waiting lists or remote and often poorly staffed giant state mental hospitals were virtually the only resources available. Now, many people are being treated promptly, appropriately, and close to home.

REFERENCES

1. Krasner, L., and L. Ullmann: *Behavior Difference and Personality: The Social Matrix of Human Action,* Holt, New York, 1973.

2. Ullman, L., and L. Krasner: *A Psychological Approach to Abnormal Behavior,* Prentice-Hall, Englewood Cliffs, N.J., 1969.

3. Bandura, A.: *Principles of Behavior Modification,* Holt, New York, 1969.

4. Skinner, B: *Science and Human Behavior,* MacMillan, New York, 1953.

5. Ayllon, T., and N. Azrin: *The Token Economy: A Motivational System for Therapy and Rehabilitation,* Appleton-Century-Crofts, New York, 1968.

6. Wolpe, J.: *The Practice of Behavior Therapy,* Pergamon, New York, 1969.

7. Rachman, S., and J. Teasdale: *Aversion Therapy and Behavior Disorders,* Routledge, London, 1969.

8. Lang, P., and B. Melamed: "Avoidance Conditioning Therapy of an Infant with Chronic Ruminative Vomiting," *J. Abnorm. Psychol.,* 24:1-8, 1969.

9. Yalom, Irvin D.: *The Theory and Practice of Group Psychotherapy,* Basic Books, New York, 1970.

10. Foulkes, S. H., and E. J. Anthony: *Group Psychotherapy: The Psychoanalytic Approach,* 2d ed., Penguin, Baltimore, 1965.

11. Moreno, Jacob L.: "Fundamental Rules and Techniques of Psychodrama," in Jules H. Masserman and Jacob Moreno (eds.), *Progress in Psychotherapy,* Grune & Stratton, New York, 1958.

12. Yablonsky, Lewis: *Synanon: The Tunnel Back,* MacMillan, New York, 1965.

13. Shirley, Hale F.: *Pediatric Psychiatry,* Harvard, Cambridge, Mass., 1963.

14. Harrison, Saul (ed.): *Childhood Psychopathology,* International Universities Press, New York, 1972.

15. Kanner, Leo: *Child Psychiatry,* Charles C Thomas, Springfield, Ill., 1972.

16. Sinn, M. J., and A. J. Solnit: *Problems in Child Behavior and Development,* Lea and Febiger, Philadelphia, 1968.

17. Bloch, Donald A. (ed.): *Techniques of Family Psychotherapy: A Primer,* Grune & Stratton, New York, 1973.

18. Erickson, Gerald D., and Terrence P. Hogan: *Family Therapy: An Introduction to Theory and Technique,* Brooks/Cole, Monterey, Calif., 1973.

19. Cheek, D. B., and L. M. Le Cron: *Clinical Hypnotherapy,* Grune & Stratton, New York, 1968.

20. Fromm, Erika, and R. E. Shor: *Hypnosis: Research Developments and Perspectives,* Aldine-Atherton, Chicago, 1972.

21. Haley, Jay: *Advanced Techniques of Hypnosis and Therapy. Selected Papers of Milton H. Erickson, M.D.,* Grune & Stratton, New York, 1967.

22. Hilgard, E. R.: *The Experience of Hypnosis,* Harcourt Brace Jovanovich, New York, 1968.

23. Wolberg, L. R.: *Hypnoanalysis,* Grune & Stratton, New York, 1964.

24. Grinker, Roy R., Sr., and John P. Spiegel: *Men Under Stress,* McGraw-Hill, New York, 1945.

25. Caplan, Gerald: *Principles of Preventive Psychiatry,* Basic Books, New York, 1964.

26. Bellak, Leopold (ed.): *Handbook of Community Psychiatry and Community Mental Health,* Grune & Stratton, New York, 1964.

JOHN E. BEEBE III, M.D.
C. PETER ROSENBAUM, M.D.

CHAPTER **22**

The Use of Dreams in Psychotherapy

In patient's dreams, we meet their natural, unreflected, instinctive reactions. It is in just this play of nature during sleep that some of the most transforming energies are released, as everyone who has gone to sleep depressed and has awakened refreshed after a vivid, remembered dream can testify. Psychotherapy attempts to relate to this unconscious transforming power with conscious insight so that the dream solutions to conflict can be carried over into waking life if they are effective, and criticized or modified where they appear to lead the dreamer into dangerous or unprofitable conflict resolution.

In this chapter we shall illustrate how one young man's psychotherapy was helped by the inclusion of his dreams. Throughout we shall adopt two perspectives: first, that the dream offers an objective statement about the dreamer which he cannot make about himself in any other way; second, that the dream is a tentative, sometimes symbolic, attempt to deliver new information to the dreamer in a form which he can accept. These perspectives reflect many contemporary trends[1-5] in the understanding of dreams, yet leave open the question which the many followers of Freud and of Jung have so often debated,[6] as to whether the motive of dreaming is to disguise or to illuminate the dreamer's ultimate, unconscious intentions. In our view, we can only say that the dream offers the dreamer what his own mind thinks he is ready for. As he looks into his dreams, he may indeed find painful or embarrassing issues expressed in an acceptable, bearable form; or he may encounter just the reverse: familiar thoughts given a shocking, repulsive guise, forcing him to revalue them. In either case, the dream makes of the dreamer's emotions something new, rearranging emotional elements to achieve a new perspective, offering new information.

The task of dream interpretation is first (following Freud) to recognize the important emotional issues contained in the imagery of the dreams, and then (following Jung) to recognize the new statement the dream makes about these issues. The dream is thus a reservoir of information for the psychotherapist, suggesting which themes are pertinent to the therapy and what ways are best to approach these themes. The psychotherapist helps the patient receive the information delivered by his dreams so that it can become part of a conscious repertoire for coping, a working knowledge of the effective and ineffective aspects of the dreamer's own instinctive responses. The attempt at integrating the information that the dream contains — the dream analysis — is a pragmatic art, and no two therapists practice it in quite the same way. Dream analysis typifies the psychotherapeutic collaboration, the "working alliance": the two who work together must decide on experiential grounds what is true, and what is of value. Neither can tell what will be valuable until they actually attempt the interpretation.

The emphasis in this chapter will be on what is gained by letting dreams have their say in treatment. Our method will be to let the dreams themselves illustrate our belief that the respectful use of this material helps psychotherapy to become more focused, more thoroughgoing, and more effective.

CLINICAL APPROACHES TO DREAMS

Dreams often rephrase a patient's waking feelings as a tangible sequence of symbolic actions, permitting inferences about the content, the meaning, the purpose, and the value even of transient emotions. Moreover, the feelings expressed during sleep tend to change or extend the emotional attitudes which are present when the dreamer is awake. Thus the dreams serve both to clarify and to supplement the statements which a patient can make about his waking feelings.

Using the dream to shed light on the patient's emotional reactions, the psychotherapist may find evidence of: (1) repetitions of emotional conflicts carried forward from the patient's past; (2) concealed responses to the persons and institutions in the patient's current life (including his surprising reactions to himself); and (3) energy for inner or outer developments in the patient's future. These three ways of relating dreams to events in the dreamer's emotional life reflect the sometimes overlapping contributions of Freud,[7,8] Adler,[9] and Jung.[10,11] Further development and combination of these three basic viewpoints have led to the current psychoanalytic,[12] culturalist,[13] and psychosynthetic[14] ways of working with dreams.

Applications of all three ways of viewing dreams to emotional problem solving in the here and now characterize the "focal-conflict,"[15] existentialist,[16,17] and gestalt[18] approaches to dreams. Contemporary analytical psychologists[19] prefer

to determine from the dreams themselves which emotional issues in the dreamer's life the therapy ought to address and to use the dreams as a monitor of the success of the therapy in dealing with these issues; dreams are given a preeminent, guiding role in the treatment, refocusing the work as new themes appear in them.

Methods of Dealing with Dreams

There are several ways of handling dream material. Later in this chapter we shall present a detailed case example in which a modification of a Jungian approach is demonstrated. In a more traditional psychoanalytic approach, the therapist asks the patient for more and contributes less. Although they will vary in the amount of emphasis they give to different steps in interpretation, most therapists employ the following sequence:

1. Get a verbatim report of the entire dream (even therapists who do not often take notes during an hour may well do so here).

2. Ask if further elements of the dream come to mind during the report.

3. Allow the patient to associate *freely* to the dream, letting one thought lead to another, as the dream becomes a stimulus to catharsis.

4. Ask the patient to associate in a *focused* way to the dream, recovering the emotions, nuances, and memories which are connected with each dream element, with special emphasis on those that the therapist's intuition tells him may be important. (In the gestalt approach to dreams, the patient is asked to pretend he "is" the dream element and to describe himself in the first person: e.g., "I am an old house. I have dark rooms and a musty smell, but my front parlor is nice," and so on.) In this important step, the patient should be helped to recapture the experiential richness of each significant dream element. Often even a trivial-seeming element will turn out to have a fund of affective resonance for the patient, if he is allowed to dive back and recover it.

5. Seek for elements of "day residue," split-off thoughts or feelings which preoccupied the patient in the day or days before the dream, and which the dream has chosen to emphasize, satirize, or otherwise respond to.

6. Ask the patient to try to make sense out of the dream, both in terms of its manifest content (i.e., the dream as remembered) and its latent content (i.e., the symbolically expressed ideas which are revealed through the processes of association).

7. Offer the patient some of the therapist's associations to the dream (amplifications of its symbols and ideas about its meaning), to see if any of them strike a responsive chord. (Frequently, further recall will occur at this point, confirming or rejecting the suggestions as to meaning, and any of the preceding steps can be repeated, based on the new material.)

As patients become practiced in working with their dreams, they will automatically provide the associations along with the dream, and will have spent some time by themselves on the interpretation; so that the therapist can concentrate more on sharing his own ideas, based on his knowledge of the patient, and less on procuring associations from the patient. At the beginning, more time is spent asking questions, helping the patient to discover the rich flow of repressed or dissociated emotional life that so often makes its first appearance in his dreams.

In this chapter we shall show how past conflicts, present reactions, and future possibilities all made their appearance in the dreams of a young man, Eric, in once-a-week treatment for eighteen months. The dreams effectively trace Eric's development as he was helped to face the necessity of giving up an adolescent way of relating to his family in order to establish an adult identity. As the patient accomplished his emotional separation from the world of adolescence and began to enter adult life, he found himself experiencing many paradoxical emotions and no little grief. It was his dreams which helped him most to clarify what was happening to him and to trust the process in which he found himself. Through them he found the courage to develop a more mature and satisfying way of relating to his family, freeing his energies for his own life.

Though we will concentrate on Eric's therapy, it should be noted that many of the issues and techniques described apply to work with many patients. There were times when Eric needed support, acceptance, and guidance. There were times when he was confused about his problems and goals and needed help in clarifying them. There were times when he needed greater self-knowledge, needed to be more aware of how his unconscious conflicts influenced his life. There were times when he needed to test new behaviors and ways of dealing with his world, to take the risks of growing into a somewhat different person. Thus his therapy was intended to be, alternately, supportive and ego-oriented, modifying of behavior, and uncovering. His dreams became a major way of helping him in all these modes.

Example 22-1, Eric. Eric was 22 when he entered psychotherapy, a year after graduating from college. He entered feeling ashamed, depressed, and defeated: he had had fantasies of killing himself. A year earlier he had overturned plans to marry a woman of whom his divorced mother had approved and to take a job that his family had set up for him. After ending the engagement he "escaped" to the distant West Coast to pursue the literary ambitions that had been nurtured in his sheltered undergraduate years, leaving behind his mother and a 24-year-old sister who suffered from a chronic respiratory illness.

During the year he had drifted among a group of fraternity friends who had shared creative ambitions, women, and drugs during their college years. Under the spell of the leader of this group, Bert, several other members of the group had also made their way to the West Coast. The year had passed and Eric had accomplished little except to write a few rock songs that had scant prospect of being performed. He was barely supporting himself with a part-time job in a bookstore. At his first interview he told his psychotherapist, "I feel like a golden ass."

Obtaining Dream Material

An early problem for the psychotherapist is finding the right way of asking the patient what his dreams have to say about his predicament. Therapist differ on this point. Some prefer not to ask for dream material but to wait until the patient spontaneously reports dreams. Others explain in the initial interview that they are interested in the patient's dreams as well as in his waking fantasies. Often at this point the therapist will ask the patient if there is any dream which stands out or that he would like to share. Frequently, the patient will say that he does not remember his dreams. This statement can be a test of the therapist's interest. The insecure therapist, none too confident of his ability to work with dream material, may hurry along to other issues at his point in the interview. The experienced therapist will wait, giving the patient time to find a dream. Often this silence will last several minutes, as there is a considerable shift required to share dreams rather than the familiar thoughts of waking consciousness. The therapist may help the patient who is having particular trouble by saying, "Usually there is one dream that stands out, from all the years." At this point, the patient may relate a long-standing dream, often a recurrent dream from childhood.

The therapist's response to this first recounted dream is critical. He must give it attention if he wants his patient to feel he can bring other, current dreams to the psychotherapy sessions. Many therapists offer a simple interpretation at this point. Others make comments which "befriend"[20] the dream, relating to its mood, its elements, and its action with lively interest. The point is to establish that dream material can be talked about comfort-

ably and that the therapeutic effort can benefit if the leads that the dream provides are pursued.

Eric (cont'd.). The image of the golden ass intrigued the therapist, who commented on the vivid picture it gave of Eric's feelings about himself. "There's a book, *The Golden Ass,"* Eric said. "I picked it up at the library the other day."

"I know it," the therapist replied. "Psychologists have written no less than four studies of it, because it contains a tale about the psyche, called 'Amor and Psyche.' "

Pleased by the fact that his therapist seemed to share his interest in literature, Eric ventured to say more about the source of his image: "I had a dream in which I was being led across the stage by a woman. I was the golden ass and she was leading me by a rope around my neck."

"It's interesting that it was a woman," the therapist said. "At the end of *The Golden Ass,* the narrator has a vision of the goddess Isis and is initiated into her cult."

"This woman had a white toga on," the patient reported. "You know, I didn't find out about that book until after I had the dream. I was in the library looking to see if there was such a thing as a golden ass. There was another scene in the dream — a man holding a torch out with people lying dead at his feet. I did find a picture like that in the book!"

Both patient and therapist remarked at the coincidences between the dream and the book, which was in fact a current interest of the therapist. The therapist gave the patient the name of one of the commentaries in case he was interested in following it up.

In this interchange, we see the process of befriending a dream and the kind of collaboration that process engenders. Talking about fantasy material is a kind of play between patient and therapist in which chance associations, coincidence, puns, and inspirations are allowed free reign and the rigorous "scientific" attitude (that might govern the introduction of evidence in a court of law) is correspondingly relaxed. Various names have been proposed for the mode of ego-consciousness required for this sort of play — paralogical, mythopoeic, imaginal — all pointing to the need to relax logic to let the images organize their own spontaneous structures, as they do in myth or poetry. When this activity occurs between two persons, each begins to pick up on the other's imagery and to play with it. Eventually the unconscious itself will continue this activity; the patient's dreams will start to play with the ideas offered by the therapist's reactions in the therapeutic hour (as indeed the therapist's dreams may begin to register the effect of the patient's psyche on his own thinking).

Therapist influence on patient dreams is unavoidable[21]; it has been said that patients of psychoanalysts (Freudians) have Freudian dreams, i.e., dreams rich in the bodily and libidinal symbolism dealt with in that approach; patients of analytical psychologists (Jungians) have Jungian dreams, i.e., dreams rich in archetypal and mythic themes. Therapists vary widely on how much they let themselves consciously influence and interplay with their patients' dreams. The point of following dreams is not to uncover fresh content in a sterile surgical field for clean dissection, but to see how the patient's unconscious handles its contamination by another. In what the patient takes up or rejects, approaches or avoids, the therapist can see most clearly the needy, angry, open, and fearful parts of his patient's psyche. The dream is a monitor of the state of the transference.

At the beginning, the therapist enabled Eric to make a first sharing of fantasy material by following up with resonant interest the first bit of unusual, symbolic imagery that the patient offered in his initial struggle to describe himself. The ensuing discussion led to the discovery of a common interest in a particular book, a classic of fantasy literature. By bringing up the professional nature of his interest in this book, the therapist returned discussion to the realistic task, the psychotherapy, and Eric in turn related the image

to a dream, starting a dialogue in which dream statements were welcomed for what they might add to the therapeutic inquiry. Often both patient and therapist will find much to enjoy in working with fantasy material, and they should let themselves play: paradoxically, playing furthers the work of relating to dreams. (Some patients will find it difficult to play — a fertile point for further therapeutic inquiry.)

Freud, Jung, and Eric's First Dream

Freud and Jung each made unique contributions to the understanding of dreams. Freud was more interested in the way dreams are constructed: looking for evidence of unconscious solutions to conflict, he studied the ways recent life experiences ("day residues") were transformed in the process of dreaming. He attributed these changes to the action of unconscious defenses against libidinal conflicts, stirred by the events of the day. With the help of the patient's free associations, he could use the dream to uncover these conflicts and the defenses erected against them. Jung's contribution lay in exploring the usefulness of the dream transformations. Jung stressed the merits of the dream's symbolic language, as if it were the best way to exchange information about unconscious events with the conscious mind.

Freud was concerned with the translation from manifest content to latent content; Jung was concerned with the manifest content as it revealed a new idea or unexpected statement. One therapist[22] has pointed out that Freud may be said to be concentrating on the root of the tree, where moisture collects and is transmitted, while Jung attends to the crown, where the exchange of oxygen and carbon dioxide occurs; both regions are vital to the health of the tree.

Let us look first at how a psychoanalyst (Freudian) might interpret the dream. (For convenience, we will work with only the first scene.) A psychoanalyst would search for some evidence of the mental mechanisms described by Freud as the "dreamwork." Two of the more important mechanisms are *symbolization* and *condensation.* In symbolization, an idea, thought, or feeling is represented by a symbol. In condensation, two or more thoughts or feelings are represented in a single dream symbol. In waking life, condensation is an important part of wit, puns, and humor, where the expression of a forbidden impulse (usually sexual or aggressive) is merged with a more innocent one, e.g., Groucho Marx telling one of his antagonists, "I'd horsewhip you if I had a horse."

In the past Eric has felt both that he has been led by three women in his life (his mother, his sister, and his former fiancée) and that he has led them on, made asses of them. (This and other attributions of preconscious and unconscious factors in Eric were verified during the course of his treatment, thus permitting these assertions about them in this analysis of his first dream. Had there not been such corroborations, such statements about Eric's feelings would remain unsupported speculation.) Thus, in this dream, the three women are symbolized and condensed into a single woman.

Part of Eric still wishes to be passively "pulled along" by a strong woman, as became evident during the early weeks of treatment, and part of him would resent being "led by the neck" by her. Thus, being pulled along is an ambivalent *wish fulfillment* in the dream. The conscious perception of feeling "led by the neck" had crossed Eric's mind the day before the dream; it constitutes a *day residue* transformed into a dream symbol.

Another mechanism of the dream work is that of *plastic representation,* in which a more or less abstract word, idea, or feeling is represented in a symbolic object. In Eric's case the metaphor of feeling led by the neck appears in visual form. *Reaction formation,* the replacement of a thing by its opposite, is shown in the white toga: it gives an air of purity and exaltation to what Eric perceives as rather a dirty and shabby chapter in his life, one about which he feels quite guiltily depressed. In fact, it was Eric who in a sense has been (mis)leading these women; so this reversal of

role is both a reaction formation and a *displacement* (the shifting of an unacceptable idea or emotion from the appropriate object to a more neutral one); in this case the displacement protects Eric from having to feel he has been leading these women on: in the dream it is they who are leading him on.

Eric reports the dream with some wonder and amazement. In the process there will be some *secondary elaboration;* i.e., he will unwittingly rationalize and make more intelligible the plot and actors in the dream. Only through free association and other attempts at interpretation will the *latent content* — the hidden message he did not want to hear but will need sooner or later to comprehend if therapy is to proceed — emerge from the *manifest content.* Only then will Eric be fully aware of how he has misled the women in his life (for which aggression he is consciously feeling guilty), how he feels the need to be punished (led by the neck, as an ass) for having besmirched the women's image (restored to whiteness as a wish to deny what he had done).

Now let us see how an analytical psychologist (Jungian) might work with the same material. He would work with the manifest content (the golden ass and the woman in the toga) to see what they might yield in new and surprising ideas, as shown in this vignette from that session:

Eric (cont'd.). Indeed, to Eric's depressed frame of mind it came as a surprise that there could be anything golden (valuable) about the asinine way he thought he had been behaving.

New too was this image of woman. In her classic dress she seemed to connote wisdom, spirit, authority. The spiritual aspect was new: he had not seen that in the women he had known; they had tended to meet more his material needs. His mother, a good, practical provider, had always seen to his needs for food, shelter, and clothing. A series of girlfriends in college had met his needs for sex. When his well-meaning mother had begun to arrange every aspect of his future material existence with his intended bride, he had fled this maternal influence. Yet here he was being led by a woman of another sort — who seemed a positive figure, a spiritual mother, who would influence not his physical, but his psychological development.

To understand this new feminine image in her own terms, an analytical psychologist would use not the method of *association* (by which familiar figures would no doubt turn up) but the method of *amplification.* Here the dream image is compared not with similar images in the life of the dreamer but with similar images in the long life of human fantasy, drawing freely upon comparative symbolism from folklore and mythology. Here the parallels with the Latin fairy tale *The Golden Ass* become important, not just a pleasant coincidence. In that tale, the Ass is an enchanted man, and as so often occurs in such stories, his transformation back into human form is accomplished through the agency of a woman, the Greco-Roman goddess Isis. Isis arranges that the man shall return to the human form in the midst of a procession dedicated to her.

By amplifying Eric's dream, we see a possibility not explicitly stated in the dream itself: Eric could be led out of his asinine condition by the woman in the toga. Only if this possibility fits the feeling and the mood of the dream as remembered by Eric would it be acceptable as a suggestion "of where this dream is leading." But it is often a mistake to withhold such conjectures from patients on the grounds that "the patient didn't know the story when he had the dream," or "that part of the story wasn't in the dream." As moviegoers know, one doesn't always have to have seen a film before to know how it will end, and the unconscious has a remarkable propensity for remembering the endings of the many possible human stories.

To restate the dream, Eric is in an asinine state, but he is submitting to a spiritual mother who he hopes can lead him out of this condition. What could this mean? Since Eric was contemplating

psychotherapy at the time he had this dream and wrestling with the feeling that he could probably not be helped, this dream perhaps conveys the idea that there is something positive in the new dependency he would have to accept were he to enter treatment. A Jungian would say that it is not so much the fulfillment of a wish as a *compensation* for Eric's conscious attitude of despair. It offers to Eric's doubts a classical picture of a process of being helped. At the same time, the dream does not make a moral statement or a promise; it only gives an *objective picture* in symbolic form of what Eric can expect from psychotherapy — a ritual expiation, no more, no less. Whether he can stand to submit, like the ass, to the process of being led is up to him, but this is the rite to which he must submit if he is going to regain his human form (his psychological health). The idea of rite is conveyed not only by the action and cast, but by the setting, the stage.

Jung used the patient's associations to the various dream elements (focused, not free) to *establish the context* for the dream. Here Eric's statement "I feel like a golden ass" seems to provide the context. Thus the dream comes in answer to an implicit question: "What can a talented ass like me expect of psychotherapy?" The answer the dream provides is: a rite of initiation. Although the outcome of the rite is not clear, the imagery strongly suggests Eric's potential for transformation at the hands of another.

Who this other may be is always a problem in interpretation. It is easy to see the woman as the ideal psychotherapist, the spiritual mother. It is somewhat harder to recognize in her a part of Eric. Jung often pointed out that when men try to symbolize the activity of the unconscious, they fall back upon the most potent image of otherness, the opposite sex. Thus for men, the unconscious is often perceived as a woman — a powerful, unknown woman. And indeed, Eric's therapy would involve him in submitting to his unconscious, in listening to his dreams, in accepting the reality of his own emotions. And for patients who are suited for intensive psychotherapy, the unconscious is often the "ideal psychotherapist," showing the patient what he has neglected and now must include in his everyday living if he is not to live against his emotions.

As Eric's dream illustrates, there are three levels in any interpretation.[23] First is what Jung called the *objective level,* at which most Freudian dream interpretation is made: Eric's dream is seen as a statement about his relationship to the women in his life. Second is the *subjective level,* at which Jungian interpretation is often made: the dream is seen as a statement about Eric's relationship to the feminine — the unconscious emotional life — within himself. Last is the *transference level,* at which the interpersonal interpretation is made: the dream communicates Eric's intentions in seeking therapy to his potential therapist. The three levels of interpretation all combine to enrich the understanding of the dream.

Of course, the therapist does not attempt a complete interpretation at all three levels with the first dream that is presented to him! Indeed, much of the information on which the interpretations offered here are based was not available to the thereapist when the initial dream was offered, especially the intensity of Eric's feeling that he had made an ass of himself, that he had in fact sunk into a dehumanized condition. Only with much hearing of Eric's feelings did the therapist come to know the exact state of despair with which Eric had entered therapy. Gradually he came to see that the ass represented Eric's reality, not just a clever metaphor for it.

A Note of Caution

Therapists associate vividly to their patients' dreams. Listening to a dream is like hearing a short story read aloud: the listener constructs his own images and scene. As he listens the therapist strives to employ his critical faculties in the knowledge that he ultimately wants to understand the dream, making use of his skills in dream interpretation. Many therapists tend to draw from dreams what is revealing of psychopathology and to ignore what is creative or reparative. Often the therapist feels a

pressure to "be psychological," ignoring the fun of dreams.

Inexperienced therapists may be awed by how their senior colleagues seem always to get a wealth of information from even a brief dream fragment, not realizing that their senior colleagues are not nearly as likely to report a patient's dream which left them baffled and confused. Yet there are such dreams, many of them. Indeed, it is rarely if ever that a dream can be totally analyzed, that each symbol and nuance can be fully understood. There are many dreams where significant portions remain a mystery despite the best efforts of the patient and the therapist. Sometimes these mysteries are solved weeks and months later (the dream was premonitory in that sense: it was a statement from the unconscious that anticipated developments for which consciousness would be ready only later). It is because of these factors that inexperienced therapists may feel an unjustified pressure to interpret each dream totally, seeking to emulate what they perceive to be the abilities of their experienced colleagues, rather than allowing themselves to remain perplexed and intrigued by those parts of dreams they do not, in fact, understand.

The pressures to look for psychopathology, to be psychological, and to emulate experienced colleagues may lead to premature and simplistic interpretations which drearily restate the obvious, failing to discover anything new. For example, the therapist might have responded to Eric's first dream by saying, "You must feel like you're being led around by women."

Quick interpretation of any variety — Freudian, Jungian, interpersonal, existential — can only interfere with the therapeutic process, which always requires a careful discovery of the depth and extent of the patient's feelings. Jung made it his rule to say to himself before venturing an opinion on a dream, "I have no idea what this dream means."[24] Only then could he trust himself to examine the dream, open to the new possibilities a seemingly familiar symbol might offer. It is even harder for the beginner to avoid jumping to conclusions.

Indeed, a single dream has so many possible meanings that it is almost impossible to verify which meaning is correct, even if it seems plausible or acceptable to the dreamer, whose own sense of rightness must always be the final authority. One needs to hear a series of dreams to understand the movement in a given patient's psyche, and we shall continue the case of Eric later in this chapter by offering such a series. In discussing the first dream, the therapist need only make sure that he has created a climate in which the patient will want to share his subsequent dreams; then the initial work will have been more than adequately accomplished.

The Brain, Dreaming, and Remembering

Since the discovery in the 1950s of rapid eye movements and the development of technology for measuring electroencephalographic (EEG) patterns through an entire night of sleep, much valuable information has been collected to the benefit of the psychotherapist who works with dreams. In talking with patients about their dreams, it is particularly helpful to know about the kinds of dreams and their recall. A very useful source of this information is Ann Faraday's *Dream Power*.[25] Much of the basic information can be found in early articles by Dement[26,27] and the more recent elaborations in the books by Hartmann[28] and Medow and Snow.[29]

The key finding has been that there are two states of sleep: sleep in which rapid eye movements do not appear and the EEG patterns (stages II to IV) are slow and synchronized (S); and sleep in which rapid eye movements (REM) do appear and the EEG pattern (stage I) is rapid and desynchronized (D). About 75 percent of the night is spent in non-REM, S sleep, but four or five times a night (at about ninety-minute intervals), the normal subject emerges from this deep level into REM, D sleep, in which he must spend 25 percent of his total sleeping time. In contrast to the S state — which is quiet and restful — the D state is stormy, accompanied by much physiologic evidence of heightened arousal, including penile erection in men. The D state is often preceded and followed by tossing in the sleep (as if the dreamer were preparing for the curtain to go up), but during the REM period itself, motor paralysis obtains. (Patients sometimes awake still unable to move and are extremely frightened.) Only in the S state can sleep-talking or sleepwalking occur.

There are also two states transitional to sleep: the state of falling asleep (in which *hypnagogic* phenomena are recorded) and the state of awaking from sleep (in which *hypnopompic* phenomena occur). Thus, when a patient reports a "dream," he may be recalling (1) an event during S sleep (a non-REM dream) (2) an event during D sleep (an REM dream), or (3) a hypnagogic or hypnopompic phenomenon (a "dreamlet").[30] Only REM dreams fulfill the definition of "an experience that involves vivid and complex multimodal imagery, a progression of events, and sense of reality."[31] By contrast, non-REM dreams are more like background thoughts, being shorter, less vivid, less visual, less dramatic, less elaborated, less emotional, less active, more plausible, more concerned with current problems, more purely conversational, and more thoughtlike than REM dreams.[32] Dreamlets are strange, hallucinatory visions, often accompanied by unusual sensations. Often they resemble REM dreams, but they are shorter and less dramatic in structure (sometimes resembling a tableau or pageant rather than a play).

Many writers regard only the REM dreams as true dreams. It is in REM dreams that we most often find the distortions which many identify with dreaming. Freud understood these distortions as the effect of censorship upon latent dream thoughts. Jung saw them as evidence for the autonomy of the psyche's symbol-producing faculty, which he saw as possessing an archaic style of language all its own. Rossi[33] has interpreted these distortions as the way new personality structures look when first laid down by protein synthesis during the REM periods.

But it is a mistake to devalue non-REM dreams

just because they are more thoughtlike. Both kinds of dreams play a part in psychotherapy, as the following example shows.

> *Example 22-2, Alan.* Alan, a 28-year-old professional man, had the following typically REM dream in his analysis:
>
> "I was in a classroom with other students, possibly a nursery school. I was absorbed in the positive maternal atmosphere created by the teacher, humming at her desk. I felt at one with the other students, who were all working quietly at their different desks. I didn't actually see anyone in the room, nor did I need to, so contained was I within the pleasant classroom atmosphere. Suddenly an angry male figure, 'The Father,' entered the room, harshly interrupting the comfortable atmosphere with angry words directed toward the motherly teacher.
>
> " 'How could you let this happen?' the father demanded. 'Look at him!'
>
> "I was suddenly acutely conscious of myself and my surroundings. Now I could see that all the other students were wearing red tunics and I a coat of many colors."

In his analytic work, Alan often returned to this dream. It marked the stage of his therapy when he first became aware of his positive mother complex, which had separated him from his father, whose criticism he could not accept — his unresolved Oedipal conflict. Further, in the biblical figure of Joseph, who wore the first coat of many colors, the young man thought he had found a solution to this conflict, which had made it hard for him to adjust to the masculine world of work. Although Joseph was in many ways a mother's son[34] — narcissistic, gifted, eager to please, preoccupied with dreams, concerned with nourishing others, and alienated from his more ordinary brothers — he did succeed in finding a successful masculine identity within the patriarchal biblical world. He became the Pharaoh's right-hand man.

Alan reasoned that he could succeed by staying within his organization, putting his varied talents to the disposal of some higher executive, whose top assistant he could eventually become; the ultimate authority could rest in someone else. For a time, he pursued this role within his own organization with outstanding success. As he carried out assignments faithfully and imaginatively, he was given more to do and was promoted to a job very like the one Joseph had held in Pharaoh's realm.

Then — about two years after the first — came a dream of another type. It followed a day when one of Alan's clients had expressed his keen interest in cosmology — he had even described himself as a cosmologist. The patient mentioned this curious occurrence to his superiors at work, who dismissed the client as a harmless eccentric.

> *Alan (cont'd.).* In this dream, Alan found himself at a dim crossroads, along with three vague, ghostlike men with painfully grinning clown faces who were positioned like characters in a Noh drama. Suddenly, the thought came to him, "Not Joseph, but the cosmologist!"
>
> In working on this peculiar dream (which is a typical non-REM dream), Alan came to recognize that a cosmologist is not a man like Joseph, who works at another's side, but a man like Moses, a lawgiver, who discovers a new order, mapping out the world plan of his particular culture, an authentic father figure.[35] Alan then realized that it was not enough for him to play the dutiful son doing what the "fathers" in his particular organization thought was best, but that he had to map out his own career directions if he were to succeed in professional life and fulfill himself as a man.

The first dream, of the REM type, gave Alan a vivid picture of himself which he could use in reconciling his father's demands with his mother's indulgence, so achieving a first kind of positive identity for himself as a man. The second dream, of the non-REM type, gave him a new idea which he could use at an existential crossroads in his life to give up his overattachment to the earlier solution and develop still further as a man. Both the REM vision and the non-REM revision counted as nodal points in the course of Alan's psychotherapy.

Remembering Dreams. Patients are often guilty or defensive about their ability to remember dreams, as if they were resisting the process of psychotherapy. Actually, as Cohen[36] has pointed out, the recall of dreams is quite influenced by the intensity of the dream images themselves (the more vivid images are better remembered) and by the amount of interruption immediately upon awakening (even a short activity, such as answering a phone, can cause the dream to vanish). Being less vivid, a non-REM dream is particularly hard to remember unless one awakes from a non-REM period and immediately writes it down.

Under laboratory conditions, nearly everyone who is awakened from one of his four or five nightly REM periods reports a vivid dream. Within each of these REM periods, several distinct REM episodes occur: a patient may potentially report ten to twenty episodes just from the REM portion of a single night's sleep.[37] Whether discrete episodes belonging to the same REM period should be regarded as separate dreams or as "acts" of the same dream play is a moot point; usually the patient makes this judgment when he records successive episodes.

The following summary of facts about recall is drawn from Faraday[38] and Cohen,[39] based on research findings. If the subject is allowed to go right back to sleep and is awakened in five minutes, his recall is blurred; if he sleeps for ten minutes before he is awakened again, the dream is usually lost. For a REM dream to be remembered, the subject must waken in the midst of a REM period and stay awake for ten minutes, concentrating on fixing the dream in his mind. Shorter periods of pondering the dream are usually accompanied by forgetting the next morning.

For persons sleeping in their own beds rather than a laboratory, remembering is best if the awakening is sudden — as by a buzzing alarm or telephone — rather than gentle and gradual, as by a clock radio. Awakening should be followed by a ten-minute period of alert inactivity, during which a memory trace is laid down. Distraction by other activities (including turning on the light and searching for a pencil to write the dream down) may significantly impair recall.

There is evidence that dreams which touch upon issues the patient may find embarrassing to talk about with the therapist are not recalled the next morning (though they may be told to a dream experimenter during a night awakening).

The use of drugs or alcohol which suppress REM sleep also blurs the consciousness required for recall; stopping the use of even a small quantity of drugs, such as barbiturates, may enable the patient to remember his dreams.

Usually, people recall only those dreams which occur during the last REM period before awakening, dreams from a difficult night punctuated by many awakenings (as during an illness), and nightmares which awaken the dreamer into a panicked, wide-awake state. Moreover, personality differences separate those who habitually recall their dreams from those who do not. Research has indicated that nonrecallers are trying to look *away* from their dream images during sleep, while recallers are accepting the dream images passively. Nonrecallers usually have a lower tolerance for anxiety. When they do recall dreams, it is usually on nights following days which have been unusually unpleasant.

Frequently, dreams are recalled because the patient is trying to recall his dreams to tell his psychotherapist; autosuggestion given just before going to sleep often works. Scrupulous dream recallers awake during the night after dreaming, quietly scoop the dream fish into the net of a permanent memory trace, and record their impressions in a dream diary. Such conscientious patients may present an abundance of dream material to the psychotherapeutic hour, posing a problem of deciding *which* dream to discuss, as well as the appropriateness of this much emphasis on dream material.

Recording Dreams. It is important to have an accurate record of the patient's dreams. Some therapists have an uncanny recall for dream material; most find that they make substitutions when they try to recall dreams from memory. In a communication so compact, so precise, and so important as a dream, every image counts — like every word of a telegram. It makes a difference whether the patient turned to his right or to his left, whether the girl was wearing red or blue, whether the group consisted of three or of four persons. Often such details become meaningful only months or years after the dream is first mentioned.

Therefore, a good practice is to write the dream down as the patient tells it during the therapeutic hour. This practice, far from interrupting the therapeutic contact, actually reinforces the idea that the dreams will be taken seriously by the therapist and encourages the patient to bring them. The therapist can keep copies of the patient's dreams in a folder. A stenographer's notebook is ideal for recording dreams; associations can be recorded in a parallel column. With practice, the therapist can learn to get the dream reports down nearly verbatim.

Jungian therapists in general ask more frequently for dreams and spend more time on them in therapy than do therapists of other backgrounds. With practice, a Jungian can cover three or four dreams in a session, providing he first fully understands the patient and his conscious predicament. The great bulk of such therapy may be by way of dream analysis, as was true in the case of Eric. In contrast, while Freudians welcome dreams as part of therapy, they do not seek them with such intensity, and if a patient started filling his hours nearly exclusively with dream material, the Freudian analyst might suggest somewhat earlier than the Jungian that he is using dreams as a resistance against looking at waking behavior and thought. Still, a patient in Freudian analysis who failed to bring up any dream material would have this pointed out to him, and Jungians, too, recognize resistance via emphasis on dreams. Much

of the material being presented immediately below represents a Jungian outlook; the emphasis and techniques would be present in less prominent and somewhat moderated form in psychoanalytic and existential therapies.

Many patients will get into the habit of keeping a dream diary. A few will tape-record their dreams, bringing the tapes to the therapeutic hour. Some patients will type out their dreams, unasked, and bring the therapist a copy. While it is not always possible to discuss every dream in a therapeutic hour, the therapist should allow himself time at least to read whatever dreams are brought to him. Often he can allude to such dreams as issues which come up in the therapeutic sessions which seem to have been touched on by the imagery in the dreams. Thus the dreams that have been shared are included, even if not always interpreted in detail.

Only after the patient and therapist are well into a working collaboration should the therapist ask the patient for copies of his dreams, and then only after thought. Many patients do not mind such homework. Others resent it, and the therapy session may become too much like a college class or, as one patient put it, "a responsive reading." Nevertheless, when both patient and therapist keep copies of the dreams, therapy is a truly collaborative effort, with each of the partners assuming a measure of responsibility for the unconscious communication which has grown up between them.

DREAMS IN THE COURSE OF THERAPY

Initial Dreams

Initial dreams are extremely important and should be noted down, no matter what the orientation of the therapist or his practice of concentrating on later dreams in therapy. Initial dreams can predict the entire course of therapy and can identify initial problems, the kinds of emotion which therapy can release, and possible pitfalls the therapist would be wise to anticipate.

In Chapter 19, the dream of the patient on the ocean liner wrecked by a great black whale, with the patient ultimately being rescued, allowed the therapist to ask the patient if he feared getting launched into therapy might stir up severe emotional storms; the patient was able to confirm this and talk further about his fears.

> *Example 22-3.* At his second interview a college student reported this dream to his therapist:
>
> "Last night I dreamed I was coming here for my session today, and at the end of the session I asked you if you thought there was anything *really* the matter with me. You smiled and shook your head 'No,' but above your head there was a neon sign that kept flashing on and off, 'Dementia praecox, dementia praecox!' "
>
> The student knew from his psychology courses that "dementia praecox" was the old name for insanity, and his fear that he would be found mad quickly became apparent as he associated to the dream. The therapist, having observed the student's basically healthy ego functioning, he was able on the one hand to reassure him that he would not go mad and on the other to ask him about thoughts, feelings, and experiences that the patient thought were abnormal, so that they could proceed to work on them.

Initial Dreams and Treatment Choice. Initial dreams can help the therapist decide whether his initial treatment will be primarily uncovering or primarily reality-oriented. Dreams can be both problem-solving and problem-revealing. If the representations of the patient in early dreams are passive, are having things done to them, and especially if these are bad things, such as being attacked by animals, falling into an abyss, entering a foreboding dark room — if the dream somehow gives the therapist the willies — the patient's ego may not be able to tolerate uncovering work at first (though it might well later). If, on the other hand, the patient is active in his dreams and copes well with adversity, he may well be suited for an uncovering approach, especially if he meets the criteria cited in Chapter 13.

The dream is like a bridge thrown up between the conscious and the unconscious.[40] It can be used to lead the dreamer up or down in whichever direction seems right for his ego to go. In working with patients whose egos are weak, it is best to stay with the manifest sense the dream makes, confining interpretations to the dream's own immediate level of impact. With patients who have stronger egos, a rigorous exploration of the latent dream thoughts is often in order, but even here the dream should be allowed to speak at the manifest level. How these considerations apply to Eric's early treatment is shown in the following vignette:

> *Eric (cont'd.).* The night after his first appointment, Eric recorded this dream:
>
> "I am running on a road, very fast. I think I am being pursued. I have a headlamp attached to my belt and was running down the road just like a car. Pretty soon I had to use a pogo stick and bounce myself along. I crawled under a fence, and I managed to lock myself in a pen right under a freeway overpass."

Here the torch of the man in the first dream standing over the dead people (probably a hypnopompic image) has become a headlamp. Eric's energies had been bent mainly on escaping a marriage and a job that he felt was wrong for him. Running away is eventually a regression, and the childishness of this solution is aptly conveyed by the image of the pogo stick. Eric's associations did not help much with the pen, the low fenced-off place where Eric must endure a period of confinement. At this stage in the therapy, the therapist could only conjecture that this image of confinement meant that Eric could no longer stave off his depression, that he could not run any more without treatment. Indeed, the therapist worried about the "closed world of suicide" in hearing this image.

The dreams showed certain signs of ego strength, including the good headlamp (i.e., his intelligence)

and his determination to save himself. Still, the
therapist noted how Eric's depression had weakened his ego: the way he was driving himself, like a
machine; the way he blundered, self-destructively,
into the closed-off pen. Although Eric's intelligence argued for an uncovering approach, his
suicidal depression would require considerable
realistic support from the therapist. In the end, the
therapist decided to combine an uncovering with a
reality-oriented approach.

Dreams can also be helpful in supportive psychotherapy where medication is being used. Note
that in the following example, it was only after
months of treatment that one of the patient's
therapists asked for a dream, the initial dream of
therapy.

> *Example 22-4.* George, a 55-year-old, chron-
> ically depressed plumber, had been seen
> monthly for refills of his amitryptyline pre-
> scription. He complained, almost seeming to
> enjoy it, about how his wife was always
> bothering him, but, not being psychologically
> minded, could not enter into any discussion of
> how he might be contributing to the situation.
>
> One session, George reported a mildly sar-
> castic remark his wife had made. The therapist,
> new to George's case, asked him if he ever
> dreamed.
>
> George said, "Why, yes. Last night I had a
> dream about my little dog. I was holding him
> in my arms, and he was looking up at me ever
> so tenderly, when suddenly he seemed to
> droop his head like he was going to die."
>
> The therapist asked George about the dog. It
> turned out that he loved his pet above all other
> things because the dog was always sweet and
> cheerful.
>
> The therapist asked George if this dog might
> not be his own cheerful disposition, which had
> faded into despondence after his wife's sar-
> castic remark. George seemed to like this idea.
>
> At his next monthly session, George related
> another dream. "The dog was there again,
> sitting at my feet and looking up at me. As I

watched, its face turned into a vicious wharf
rat." George went on to say that he had seen
wharf rats in his younger days, working on the
harbors "around some people that were hardly
better than wharf rats they were so mean."
George had once seen a wharf rat leap and bite
a man.

Pursuing the lead of the previous month's
session, the therapist asked George if he was
ever mean, if he ever lashed out. "Well, if you
put it that way, doctor, I guess I do. Oh, I
don't like that dream. I hate to think my little
dog would turn into a wharf rat."

"Yet that's what seems to happen to a good
disposition when a person gets mean," the
therapist observed.

This was the first picture George had ever
had of his mood problem, and he marveled at
the insight it gave him. Then, for the first time,
George allowed himself to admit that he
launched nightly into verbal attacks against his
wife, not unlike the content of his monthly
sessions. His wife's occasional barbed remarks
were her weak defenses against the things he
said. "I can be pretty cruel, doctor," George
admitted.

The following month, George brought his
wife to the medication clinic with him. She
turned out to be a quiet, timid woman,
somewhat frightened of her husband. She
reported that George upset her with his critical
remarks, but that lately there had been some
improvement. For the first time, she had been
curious to see his doctor, and George had been
willing to bring her. This contact opened the
door to some much-needed couple work.

DREAMS IN THE STAGES OF CONTACT, CONFRONTATION, INITIATION, AND INDIVIDUATION

For the remainder of this chapter we shall
concentrate on Eric's dreams during his eighteen-
month course of once-a-week psychotherapy. By
so doing, we hope both to show how dreams are

used in the various stages of the transference described in Chapter 12 and also to present a detailed example of the processes of uncovering, intensive psychotherapy described in Chapters 13 and 19. Material taken directly from therapy hours will be indented; the therapist's internal speculations and more general discussion of theory and technique will be printed with normal margins.

Contact

In the stage of contact, the major task is that therapist and patient feel en rapport, feel that sufficient trust and warmth exist for them to proceed. Eric had come to therapy ambivalently, as do most patients, and he was also trying out an encounter group to see what it would be like. His attitudes about treatment are shown in the following three dreams:

> *Therapy*. Dream: My face was that of a clown's. Then I got shot full of buckshot.
> Dream: My friends from the encounter group had gathered. It seems we are all to see my individual therapist for some reason. As we sat around discussing what we were to do, I felt myself withdrawing. My chair was in a strange position, moved forward to draw a tighter circle. The nurse tried to tell me I could see the psychiatrist either Tuesday or Friday and that I had to make a choice. I thought she had said we were going to meet the doctor today, and I kept repeating it, trying unsuccessfully to remember the time of the appointment. Finally I began to scream and fainted on the floor.
> Dream: I seem to be waiting with my friend Ned outside a grocery store. I can see sailboats preparing for their launch. We're waiting for the wind. Suddenly I notice a beautiful girl, blond with very large breasts, and she is walking off with a friend of mine. Ned tells me that I could have this woman if I wanted her; so when she reappears from the grocery store, I ask her to go to bed with me. At first she

hesitates, then one of her friends shows up too. They strip and get into bed with both Ned and me. She has one orgasm before I do and tries to call it quits, but I tell her that she is wrong and can have more, so we continue.

The first two of these dreams seemed fairly clearly to reflect Eric's fear of entering therapy. At first glance, the third of these dreams had nothing to do with the therapy at all. However, Eric's associations to the grocery store ("a place where you get your supplies") and the sense of anticipation conveyed by the atmosphere of waiting for the launching of the sailboats convinced the therapist that this dream marked the beginning of a positive transference to the therapist.

Before we continue with the interpretation of the third dream, it is well to cite a helpful rule. Often one can understand a dream if one prefaces it with the statement, "It's exactly as if. . . ." Then one simply continues with the dream itself. Thus, this dream of Eric's can be stated, "It's exactly as if I am waiting with my friend Ned outside a grocery store, where I can see sailboats preparing for their launch." The interpretation then becomes largely a process of finding a reference for the "it" in the sentence. In this case, following his intuitive hunch, the therapist decided to see if the dream meant, "Starting to work with you as my therapist, it's exactly as if. . . ." From them on, it was a matter of seeing if this interpretation made sense.

> *Therapy*. The therapist conjectured that Eric might be responding to his own efforts to create a comfortable atmosphere. At the level of their egos, he and Eric could be relaxed, like two friends. Who then was the beautiful woman with big breasts that he was offering to Eric, like a good friend?

Here the therapist had to draw on his knowledge of unconscious symbolism. As we have seen, the unconscious of a man — the pattern and history of his emotional responses — is often personified by a woman. Jung called this figure the "anima,"[41] but Freud, too, had some conception of this figure, although he did not pursue the matter deeply.[42] The therapist recognized that in treatment his own unconscious was as active a participant as his conscious. This figure with big breasts could represent a positive maternal capacity in the therapist, which had also been responded to in the dreams of other patients. (Here, as we see, the therapist's self-knowledge is essential.) Thus Eric was being offered some of the therapist's unconscious — relationship and mothering. At the same time, another copulation was occurring: could that be the therapist making contact with Eric's unconscious?

Indeed, the transference relationship — with its strong overtones of incest — is often symbolized by a sexual activity involving two brother-sister couples.[43] When patient and therapist are man and woman, the "other couple" is the woman's unconscious (masculine) and the man's unconscious (feminine). The four-person sexual act represents the totality of involvement between the consciouses and the unconsciouses of both partners. Such an arrangement — often in a strangely public setting — adequately expresses the peculiarity of transference, which has been described as "the most personal relationship in the most impersonal setting."[44]

What then of the woman having had her orgasm before Eric? This made the therapist think. He was older than Eric and felt himself to have already resolved most of the issues Eric was struggling with emotionally, particularly the separation from home. It would be easy to lose patience, since he had already "come" to the insights Eric had yet to find. In treatment, it would be necessary for him to wait until Eric "came" to such insights on his own. Eric's insistence on this point seemed a good sign to the therapist that an authentic contact had been achieved in the early hours and that Eric would overcome his fear of therapy enough to make necessary demands of the therapist.

As is customary, Eric's therapist made few of these interpretations out loud. Indeed, he was none too sure of them; they were simply what

made sense at the time. To the third of these early dreams, the therapist said only, "It seems as if things are just getting started — and whoever she is, she'll have to wait for you." (This left open the question of whether the woman in the dream was a part of the therapist or a part of Eric. If the latter, she might symbolize Eric's impatience.)

Therapy. Later in this hour, Eric confessed that he had had a previous contact with a psychiatrist. The previous year, when he was still at home, Bert had convinced him to lie to get out of the draft. Eric had gone to see a psychiatrist, had pretended — quite falsely — that he was actively homosexual, and had gotten a letter excusing him from the draft. After this experience, Eric felt at once exposed (since he did harbor fears about his potential for homosexuality, which was now a matter of public record) and ashamed (since he had taken a coward's way out). Worse, all this manipulation had been unnecessary: his draft number was too high for him to be called, and he had known that before he had arranged to see the other psychiatrist. Somehow Bert had caused him to doubt his own mind. The therapist strongly suspected that Eric had done all this just to give himself reasons to say he wasn't good enough to marry his fiancée and to break the engagement.

After this confession, Eric put the question to his therapist, "Can you still help me?"

Now the therapist could see why Eric had to persuade the woman in the dream to wait for him. If she did indeed represent the "mother" he hoped to find in therapy, he had good reason to expect that she would lose interest in him, once she "knew" him. Indeed, a part of the therapist was now tempting him to be done quickly with Eric, to be satisfied with this confession as the major part of their work together. The dream, however, indicated that there was "more to come," that he should not let himself be satisfied with just this first bit of understanding.

Therapy. The therapist said, "Well, I think this gives us something to work on, rather than a reason to stop our work. It sounds as if you need to find out why you did such a self-destructive thing."

Much relieved, Eric readily agreed to this search for understanding as a goal for their work. At the next session, he said, "I like you, because you don't always say what I expect you to say." He dropped the encounter group and settled into serious intensive work. The stage of contact had been achieved.

Confrontation

In the stage of confrontation, therapist and patient begin to confront the troublesome issues which have thus far been largely out of awareness. It is here that the therapist can point out sometimes unpleasant facts to the patient, who must now pay attention to them even though he may largely have ignored similar observations made by family and friends in the past. The task for Eric was to confront the things he was doing to himself that contributed to his depression.

Therapy. Dream: I was in a race with other young men. Everyone else had on tennis sneakers; I had on fancy boots that I had bought recently. I was running around the house where I live. After I had gone one and one-quarter laps, I had to get over a barrier, which was a gutter spout. Beyond that was a void into which I hesitated to leap. Moreoever, my shoes were too slick, and so I fell back, and went back to the starting point.

In working with Eric on this dream, the therapist pointed out that in the ancient world, initiation rites, by which young men left the state of childhood and entered the state of full participation in adult life, often involved a race.

"I could use an initiation all right," Eric said.

The one and one-quarter laps was easily enough interpreted: Eric had left home one and a quarter

years before. If by leaving home Eric had intended an initiation (which in primitive tribes does indeed begin with a separation from the mother), it looked from this dream as if he had run into a major obstacle which could cause him to fail in his goal.

Somehow, as Eric and his therapist discussed the dream, the slick shoes seemed responsible: if he had had tennis sneakers like the rest, he could have continued the race.

Therapy. The therapist asked Eric about the "fancy boots," which indeed he had worn to the session. They were shiny and conspicuously expensive.

Eric admitted he had paid for them with money his mother had sent him. She often sent him money for clothes, together with letters which pointed out to him how irresponsible he was. In fact, when he had bought these shoes, he had thought to himself, "This is a regression."

The therapist said, "Well, if you want your initiation to work, you'll have to give up depending on your mother for money. Of course, that'll mean facing the unknown — I suppose the risk of ending up in the gutter."

At this point Eric brought forward his great fears of not being able to support himself. Shortly after this session, he was able to increase his earning power with a better-paying job, and he stopped accepting money from home for any of his living expenses. Not long after, he had another dream.

Dream: I was supposed to go to the beach with Bobby Kennedy this day. I had been allowed to invite some friends but didn't. A small Econoline bus — yellow — pulled up and out jumped six uniformed men, apparently guards. One of them was Kennedy disguised so that he wouldn't be shot. I got in and Ethel was sitting on one side. I went to the back of the bus. We got to a very beautiful beach and the waves settled gently on the sand. But then suddenly the tide began to move in and pushed everybody back from the beach almost to the road. A group of men I had noticed to my left were playing volleyball on high ground, so I nonchalantly joined them. I noticed they were playing quite sloppily. I asked the driver, who couldn't hit the ball uphill, if I could please serve for him. He replied that it was his serve. After a while I seated myself on a rock and was approached by a graying, middle-aged man who asked me if I would like to take a ride in his Stutz Bearcat, the Spade model, making a stop for tea or a drink. I asked him where we would stop for a drink, and he replied, "My place, of course." I replied, "No, thanks," that I wasn't like that and he would probably have trouble if we went.

This dream followed a letter from his mother in which she implored him to show some responsibility and come home to her. Here she was playing on a quite vulnerable spot in Eric, his idealism. Indeed, during the period he had been most caught in playing the savior to his mother and sister (the man who would recoup the family fortunes), Robert Kennedy had been his ideal. Ethel Kennedy was a woman of about his mother's age.

Here, in a nutshell, was Eric's identity problem. Until he had forced his way out of the part with some distinctly unheroic acts, he had sought to become a man by playing the part of his mother's hero, living out her idea of what a man should be, rather than finding his own. To the degree that he still felt guilty about leaving her, her ideas of what was right for him still had possession of him, like the bus in which he was a passenger. This was her trip.

Indeed, in her letters, his mother made all this quite explicit, in the guise of concern for his security and her own. (Hence the disguise. And, as Jung points out, a woman's opinions are often symbolized by a crowd of male figures.)

Although his mother's wishes for him had their beautiful, idealistic side (symbolized by the seduc-

tive beach), the fact remained that living out her intuitions (yellow, the color of the bus, is often a symbol of intuition) of what he might be could only be an unconscious solution to his problem. Indeed, if he allowed himself to return now to trying to be what she wanted, he would only engulf his own fragile identity in the tide and undertow of his divorced mother's needs, aptly symbolized by the sea. This regression could not be.

Yet entry into the conventional masculine world was closed to him. Neither the inept volleyball player nor the homosexual playboy could offer him much worth having in the way of masculine support. Their images led the therapist to ask Eric about his father.

As it turned out, Eric's father (the son of a rich, indulgent mother) had long before succumbed to his own mother complex. He had become alcoholic, and though he had overcome this problem while married to Eric's mother, he had remained ineffectual, becoming a petty manipulator in the business world after leaving the marriage when Eric was thirteen. Throughout Eric's college years, Eric and his sister had grown accustomed to being offered inappropriate, seductive gifts at vacation times, while regular support money was withheld or erratically given. Thus the volleyball player and the seductive older man were two sides of Eric's father (at least as he saw him, still in part through his mother's eyes).

Thus, there was no man in the family to show Eric the way to identity. To the therapist, there was something both poignant and reassuring about Eric's sitting on that rock. Often a rock symbolizes one's innermost determined sense of self, and despite the inability of either mother or father to help Eric to an identity that was his own, he did appear to have this rock.

"It felt good under me," Eric observed.

It was clear that a conventional solution -- identification with his father's values -- would not be possible for Eric. If he were to find his way, it would have to be along individual lines. The next dream was the first to suggest what these might be:

> *Therapy.* Dream: I was standing with a group of men at the top of a hollow, looking down into a cavernous hole. All seemed afraid to approach it. I was lowered into the hole and was looking around. I ran across a very soft spot of soil. I dropped to my knees and started digging. As I dug deep I struck some symmetrical-looking stones. I called the others and the excavation began. As they were excavating, a few people from the team decided to scour the walls in search of any other markings. Two openings were found; one on either side. One group enters one cave and I the other. My side is cafeteria-like; we discover glasses, silverware and some dishes, while the other team discovers beautiful pottery and stoneware and some artifacts mostly in very good condition. Meanwhile, the team leaders are marking our findings. The symmetrical stones are finally uncovered, and it seems that these stones form letters from the scripts of the Holy Grail. There are clues on how to discover it.

In working on this dream, the therapist felt that the "cavernous hole" represented the patient's depression — which in turn reflected the hole left in his life by the loss of his father in early adolescence. Yet in going into this problem (as indeed the therapy had been doing), the basis for a solution to it seemed to emerge. At this point it seemed no more than a fantasy, a wish, or a hint, but the "letters of the Holy Grail" seemed like archetypes of writing itself, going back to that time before Gutenberg, when printed letters were indeed rare and precious, guarded by priests. Could not this mean that Eric's future did indeed lie in his interest in writing? Of some interest to the therapist was that not only these precious letters were uncovered, but also a practical means of support — the cafeteria.

The therapist pointed out to Eric that the dream indication was extremely positive for his at least trying to make a go of his writing. At this point, Eric began to work regularly on a piece of writing which was to engage him for much of the next stage of his therapy.

Initiation

In the stage of initiation, the patient must try out new behaviors and new ways of experiencing things if he is to escape from a neurotic web of limitations which interfere with his abilities to master his own life. It is akin to the role of adolescence in different cultures: in leaving childhood behind, various experiments in living, some culturally encouraged and some frowned upon, some successful and some unsuccessful, must be undertaken.

During this period of Eric's therapy, much of his energy was spent working on a piece of writing for publication. This involved him in doing much research, indeed in the very period of the Grail legends. He found himself increasingly saying no to members of his college group who wanted to stay with him, to girlfriends who threatened to interrupt his work, and to his mother and sister, who had begun calling him, urging him to come home.

A series of dreams reflected these changes.

> Dream: My mother is lying on her deathbed. Her face is badly marred. Part of it is bandaged. Her lips are yellow with pus from a fever. She gives me a lamp and makes me kiss her. I give her a check for $10.

In this dream, what is dying is Eric's identification with his mother (in dreams, often one's affect toward a person is represented as that person). Or, in other words, he is getting over his mother complex. The $10 was not hard to figure out: Eric's parents had divorced exactly ten years before he had this dream; the money represented the years he had given to being her man. The recognition of the time he has given her enables him to be brutally unsentimental: he has given her enough, and he can set himself free.

Dream: My father was playing golf on a golf course with two women. I came in out of the woods and made a foursome. I walked on the green. I wasn't playing (I hadn't all day). I caught up with him. He sank his putt, looked up and said, "Oh, hi, have you decided to join us? C'mon to the next tee."

We went up to the next tee. Two women bickering — family squabble. "Look at these people," father said. "Aren't they funny? We're past our games." I said, "I want to communicate with you as a real person. We're playing this game!"

In this dream, Eric was able to confront his father directly with his particular style of seduction. Now "out of the woods" himself, i.e., less depressed, Eric was beginning to face some unpleasant family issues squarely. The father would often set his mother and sister quarreling by strategic phone calls which drove Eric's sister into hysterics. Then Eric would be called upon by one of the women, also by phone, to intervene. To his inquiry, his father would say over the telephone, "You know how hysterical women are." Eric had always felt helpless in the face of such maneuvering. Now he was beginning to refuse to "play the game"; he needed the energy for his own tasks.

At this point, the family began fighting back hard (as is inevitable when one member breaks out of a long-established pattern, even if to the ultimate benefit of all concerned). Many difficult-to-turn-down requests were made of him, all having the same basic message: be the way you used to be. The therapist was frequently called upon to support Eric in standing up to these requests. Here is how Eric's dreams monitored this period.

Dream: Being chased, sought after, shot at, killed. Somebody at point-blank range putting bullet in neck. I know who it is. When I wake up it's a man, but I can't remember who." (In other dreams it is one or two men; in yet another, a gang of men.)

Dream: Kept trying to get away from a gang of men in an old Buick. Twice they killed me. The third time I got away, ran back to my place, finding my old clothing in drawers; from the time that I lived at home.

In describing the bullet that went through his neck, Eric noted that its path was through the mouth and out his neck, "along the vocal tract," as he put it. Indeed, a long-standing symptom was his stuttering, which tended to clear up as he began successfully to resist his family's pressure to conform with aspects of their way of communicating in which he could not believe.

The old Buick was the family car. All these dreams seemed to offer the threat of regression, of a return to old ways of doing things, of being pursued by old habits of communicating which had landed him in a depressed state. In fact, they came at a time when he was doing well at giving up these old ways, which may indicate that the habit-patterns had now become anxieties rather than behaviors.

After this sequence of dreams, Eric's anxiety began to become less, as is indicated by the following two dreams:

Dream: Swimming in water, afraid. Looked down in the water, saw a snake. It turned out to be just a little black snake and didn't hurt me.

Dream: In a pit with poisonous and other kinds of snakes, including cobras, rattlers, green snakes, copperheads, and diamond backs, but this time there was no fear. I danced around, light on my feet, and walked out again.

These two dreams represent the mastery of fear which can be expected when an understanding of one's own emotions occurs. Snake dreams generally represent primordial instincts: the unknown or unconscious itself. To be unafraid of the snake is to be unafraid of one's own instincts. At about this time, Eric no longer was stuttering, no longer feared that he would kill himself, and was not terrified by his occasional homosexual impulses.

He was on good terms with the animal in himself. As if to emphasize the point, he had the following dream:

> Dream: A killer gorilla is on the loose and is killing single women. I'm visiting my parents when I hear about the murders. I guess who he will strike next — my old girlfriend. So I quickly go to see her. But when I lift her head to give her some water, it turns out to be my mother. I tell her I'll protect her, and the killer (who is a huge man) walks in. He says he will sit there until she marries him. A king comes in and hides behind a pillar to observe. He finally leaves distraught.
>
> Next there is a curious scene. All the clowns pour out and circle the stadium before the release of the lion. They welcome him and let him run around. Next the king's court procession in whiteface is released to march around. This time my old girlfriend is playing the queen. She goes into the bathroom to change headdresses when I notice behind the door a gorilla climbing over the stall coming after me.
>
> I run into a men's room and lock the door behind me, but the window is too small to escape from; so I go back and try and save my girl. As I try to convince her of the danger, the gorilla breaks in with a drawn knife and says he is going to kill me.
>
> Suddenly the curtains dividing the rooms are drawn and the procession of judgment dressed in black enter, and they take away the knife. We disrobe the gorilla, who is now small and black, and tell him we will take him to a mental hospital. He gives me his stamps and tells me to sell them for money to buy cigarettes for him. We trail past many ancient stone buildings to a beach where there is a crowd. My friends have gone with me. They discover that the killer is a homosexual and ask me what to do with him. I shrug and walk away.

In this dream we see the four-act structure that Jung noted in many dreams, as a dramatic process of conflict resolution proceeds. In the first act,

there is *exposition* of the problem — the dream begins with a return to an old way of coping, a visit home. There, an uncivilized element, a bit of untamed instinct, threatens the status quo. Naïvely, Eric attempts to function as hero and protector to his "girl," who turns out to be none other than his mother, a second sign that this is a regression, not mature coping. Later, the untamed element turns out to be homosexuality; it appears so threatening at first because Eric is afraid of it.

At a personal level, the distraught king who leaves the scene is a repetition of his father, who offered him so little identity support. At an archetypal level, this the the typical problem of the man who becomes his mother's son-lover. He is abandoned by the truly masculine world of the fathers.

In the second act, there is *development* as he makes an effort to cope with the problem by releasing various defenses — humor (the clowns), courage (the lion), and dignity (the king's court procession) — all in the service of shoring up the heroic mode.

In the third act, a *culmination* to his efforts to function as a hero is reached: the men's room window (i.e., this masculine viewpoint) is too small to allow escape, and his mother is strangely refractory to rescue.

Heroism is a dismal failure, and his anxiety is at its peak. Finally, in the fourth act, a *solution* is reached, but by means of a new element, the procession of judgment, which represents Eric's capacity for appraising his problems. By submitting the difficulty to feeling-inquiry, he discovers that his once irrational fear is really a human problem, for which there can be no sure heroic answer, only the uncertainties of treatment (the mental hospital).

Eric's shrug suggests the insignificance of this issue to the larger scheme of his life, but he does not find a definitive solution in this dream, nor did he in his therapy. He simply walks away from the problem. Yet, as Jung observed, this is the common path of much conflict resolution: the basic problems of life are not solved, they are outgrown. The major part of Eric's initiation was complete. He was now ready to become his own man.

Individuation

In this stage of treatment, therapy and the therapist diminish in their importance. The patient is more autonomous, more able to make his own decisions and to carve out a lifestyle which will be congruent with his own abilities and interests. Indeed, the patient may come to resent the constant introspection which therapy demands, as if his new identity were a millipede which never dared walk before treatment; now that therapy has given it its coordination and rhythm, the patient fears that too much inspection of how movement came about might once again result in paralysis. How Eric moves toward autonomy is shown in the following vignettes.

> Dream: I had hiked a great distance with a friend. We came to a ridge. On one side was a river and two cities. One metropolis and another suburb on the side of the river. The river had a lot of sailboats, was very beautiful-looking except for the skyline. They were building and building new high rises out into the river, huge monoliths. We met what looked to be a goat boy in the mountain. He took us to the top of another ridge where we could see that the river extended into a valley which was lush and green. I asked him why the valley wasn't used for agriculture and he just shrugged, said it was full of swamps and was no good. We climbed down, and I rested by the road. As I lay there, a lamb came and rested his head on my chest. I caressed it, and it licked me. A tourist came along and wanted to know about the sheep. I couldn't tell her much. She wanted to show me the city from an observation booth. I told her how it had once been beautiful but now they were filling it with monolithic buildings. I then showed the tour buses the right road to take to get to the

city, and I also started walking toward it. I tried rowing across the river to get to it, but a whirlpool dragged my boat under and almost me with it, but I managed to swim back to shore where I was safe.

For Eric this dream represented an overview of his life. The friend, he felt sure, was his therapist. The "goat boy" was a part of himself — the natural man, whom he had come to enjoy now that he was not so afraid of his family and of himself. The undeveloped marsh he saw as his own creativity, and the goat boy's shrug worried him here: he still had to fight against his laziness. The metropolis looked very much like the city where he had grown up, and to which the dream made it clear he would not be returning. The more he thought about this dream, the more clear it became that he would have to develop the undeveloped territory in himself if he were ever to amount to anything.

At about this time, he showed his piece of writing, now completed, to his therapist. It showed promise, but it ran out of steam. The lazy shrug which the goat boy had given to the undeveloped marsh was showing in the undeveloped work. After careful deliberation, the therapist confronted Eric with what he felt to be the weakness in his work. This was a painful time for them both, because both knew that only Eric could carry his therapy forward from this point on.

Then came the dream which seemed to bring home to Eric the reality of all he had been through. At the time that he had it, Eric had been in therapy just a year.

> Dream: I walked into a room where my cousin Pam was reading a postcard. She had just begun to read when I walked in. I flopped myself on the floor right away so as not to disturb her. I think the letter was about someone returning home. I looked around this room and saw all my relatives and my family, yet I greeted no one. Suddenly this gathering turned into a wedding reception and dinner

was served. There were many tables, but not everyone was anxious to sit down. There were scattered people seated at the red tables, here and there, but most of the people just stood and looked at the waiters who scurried between the tables.

At this point I greeted my father, threw my arms about his neck and began to weep, although I tried hard not to show any emotion. I did the same for my mother and sister, hugging them at the same time. I had to leave them, for I was in pursuit of three robbers. I took to horseback and roamed the countryside. I caught up with them in a barn. Suddenly I heard gunfire, I tied nooses around the necks of the robbers and pulled them back to the wedding as quickly as possible. By the time I got there, dead bodies were strewn everywhere. All my family had been killed, and there was a stunned cardinal father giving the last rites and planting flowers by the dead bodies. I knew then the robbers had been decoys to lure me away so that the event, which I thought I could have prevented, could take place.

For Eric, this dream was the turning point of his therapy. The three robbers, he felt, were his breaking the engagement, turning down the job, and trying to evade the draft. In his guilt over these things he left home, to redeem himself, he thought, for an eventual return. But as this dream put it so eloquently, these things were only decoys: life had really meant for him to leave home; he was one of those who have to break from the parental mold, and there was no way now to go home again: psychologically speaking, his parents were dead.

This dream was followed by another, in which he assumed more direct responsibility for the changes in consciousness which had occured.

  Dream: I dreamt I killed Robert Kennedy and was jumping over fences to get away from pursuing police. As I jumped over the fence I dropped a red pen on the ground and would

pick it up and proceed. Finally, after running through a few intersections, a girl in a car was waiting to pick me up. I decided to drive but couldn't get the window to latch. The police were everywhere, but no one seemed to bother us as we drove away with the window finally latched.

In this dream, Eric has finally terminated his role as mother's hero, and although the police pursue him (a symbol of his mother's attempts to use conventional pressures to get him to return to her), he gets away with a woman (i.e., an emotional life) having nothing to do with his mother. We notice, too, that he gets over the barrier that he could not pass in the early dream of the race. Surely the red pen is a symbol of his writing, in which his feeling of manhood is rooted (the pen being also a phallic symbol). The latching of the window represents his hard-won achievement of ego-integrity against the criticisms of his mother, as indeed he had resumed writing after the honest but wounding criticisms of the therapist.

As is usual in therapy, this dream was a bit ahead of the actual developments in his life, but it was accurate in predicting a potential for freedom from anxiety where his parents were concerned. The next dream shows the advantage of this achievement:

  Dream: Digging into the ground and finding all the money I could want.

Money in dreams is often a symbol of energy, and indeed at this point in his therapy, Eric began to have real energy for his life. He began another piece of writing, developed many new social contacts, and began to think about his next steps, which involved using these contacts to get his writing published.

At this juncture, Eric had a dream which made him think again about this way of starting a career.

  Dream: I called a number to try and reach Albert Einstein because I had recently been to a course where I heard his lectures and read everything he wrote. I called, but Margaret

Mead answered and said that everyone wanted to speak with him, but I couldn't. I awoke, acutely disappointed.

Here his old problem of not being able to reach the father and being stuck with the mother is presented in a different light — as the unavailable independent thinker versus the available authority on socialization, in a hilarious invidious comparison. The temptation for Eric at this point was to concentrate on getting the work he had already done accepted rather than develop his original ideas further, which meant more hard and lonely work, in poverty. The dream made him realize that approval alone was not enough for him, and he determined to stick out the painful process of learning to do something original and good. This decision was marked by a follow-up dream in which he did meet Albert Einstein in a bus station. As he put it in associating to this dream, the bus is a "common carrier," handling everybody. Many patients discover that their own individuality appears in the most ordinary contexts, rather than in prestigious places. Eric discovered that he had to give up his concern with importance in order to get in touch with his own personal genius.

At this point, the basic guidelines for Eric's further development had been laid down. He knew his goal — to become a good creative writer. He knew he had to work hard, and he had learned to watch out for the temptations of immediate prestige. His dreams had been so helpful that he found himself turning more and more to them for inspiration. And then he had the following dream:

Dream: I was in a light canoe, rowing through a thick underbrush along a deep creek. Hundreds of birds of all varieties — popinjays, sparrows, bobwhites, etc. — and some small animals — rabbits, squirrels, etc. — lived along the creek's banks. As I passed, some of the animals fled, others remained. As I reached the end of the creek, it seemed that it turned into a tunnel ending where a great number of birds had gathered, grounded. As I went to pass through the opening into the great river, an

owl and a lion jumped up to block my approach. As I reached up to drive the owl away, he bit my finger and I was forced to retreat.

Working on this dream, Eric's therapist was reminded of Jung's many warnings about the dangers of overavid exploration of the inner world. Jung found that many of his patients, after painful probing of their "personal" unconscious material, would come to enjoy the process of self-exploration and would start to assimilate material from the wider, deeper source of emotion he called the collective unconscious. Jung often warned that this process was not for the young, who could too easily use it it to avoid establishing themselves in life.

This dream is a good example of how the dreams themselves monitor the dangers of uncovering: had it come at the start of therapy, it might have been a warning not to move into dream material. Coming at this point, it represented a natural limit to the amount of work Eric should do on himself in therapy at this time. It was as if Eric's own instincts, represented by the animals, could sense the danger, and with great authority prevent him from going further with his introversion. He was forced to accept this healthy resistance and curb his curiosity. At this point, both Eric and his therapist realized that psychotherapy was coming to an end, and they began to think toward termination.

A particular issue was Eric's first visit home, now that he had found his identity. The therapist urged him to wait for the right time to make this return, to wait for some sign from his family that they could meet him where he now was. At first, it seemed to Eric that there never would be a right time. Marking this waiting period was the following dream.

Dream: I had to transport cadavers from an abandoned house somewhere on another planet to earth. The cadavers were anti-matter and so the settings had to be perfect in order for the bodies to be shipped without blowing up the transporter. I had two machines — the second of which was the more accurate as to what settings should work. I seemed totally apprehensive and was unable to procure the correct readings.

Here the problem of relating the events which occur in "the reality of the psyche" to the realities of everyday life is acutely presented. For Eric, the "cadavers," i.e., the deaths of his old ways of relating to the various members of his family, were absolutely real — but these changes had occurred on another plane. Now he had to return to visit his family carrying the knowledge of the changes he had undergone in therapy.

At this point, that scene in his initial dream in which a man was holding a torch over some dead bodies became clear to the therapist. It was clear to the therapist that Eric would have to carry consciousness for all the members of his family about the changes that had occurred. The rest of the family, not having been in psychotherapy, could not be expected to understand them.

The two machines, for Eric, were his therapist's intuition and his own: the therapist's, he felt, was more accurate. He took the advice and despite a scheduled vacation from work elected to wait until a real sign came from his family.

Not long after, this sign came. His sister decided to move from home and get an apartment of her own. She had become much less hysterical, and many of her respiratory symptoms had cleared up. This seemed directly related to Eric's refusal to act as a go-between in her battles with their father. His mother issued an invitation for him to join them in marking her move away from home. His father even offered to pay his way.

This visit went smoothly. Eric showed his mother a finished piece of writing that deeply impressed her: she could accept that he was serious in pursuing this goal. He returned to his therapist with plans to leave treatment in order to go to another city to pursue the technical studies he would need for the specialized writing that was his bent. Eric agreed to keep in touch with the

therapist through informal contacts, just to assure his gains.

The night after his final session, Eric had the following dream:

> Dream: I was driving an old family car. I went to see Bert, the leader of my college group, who had given me the original advice to lie to the first psychiatrist, to escape the draft. Bert got in the car with me, but I wouldn't let him drive the car. The final image was of a parking space in the new city for which I was headed.

Having worked through the termination with his therapist, Eric was ready to try out his hard-won individuation in his personal life. Having learned to stand up to his mother and father, he now could even stand up to a once all-powerful peer. As he put it in telling this dream to his therapist at an informal contact several months later, "I seemed to have separated our natures; I was strong enough to say no."

COMMENT

Much of psychotherapy proceeds in the dark. The therapist and patient struggle to understand each other as issues of therapy are brought out, tested, resisted, and worked through. In many other chapters of this book, we describe the conscious techniques by which this process may be facilitated. In this chapter, we hold up the mirror of dreams to the conscious work of therapy. Dreams catch the reflection of the meaning of the therapy to the life of the patient.

REFERENCES

1. Mackenzie, Norman: *Dreams and Dreaming,* Aldus Books, London, 1965.
2. Becker, Raymond de: *The Understanding of Dreams,* Michael Heron (trans.), Hawthorn, New York, 1968.

3. Kramer, Milton (ed.), with Roy M. Whitman, Bill J. Baldridge, and Paul Ornstein: *Dream Psychology and the New Biology of Dreaming,* Charles C Thomas, Springfield, Ill., 1969.

4. Jones, Richard M.: *The New Psychology of Dreaming,* Grune & Stratton, New York, 1970.

5. Faraday, Ann: *Dream Power,* Hodder, London, 1972.

6. Mackenzie: op. cit., chap. 7, "The Dream Debate," pp. 176–207.

7. Freud, Sigmund: *The Interpretation of Dreams,* James Strachey (trans.), Basic Books, New York, 1959.

8. Freud, Sigmund: *On Dreams,* James Strachey (trans.), Norton, New York, 1952 (paperback).

9. Shulman, Bernard: "An Adlerian View," with discussion by Kurt A. Adler, in Milton Kramer (ed.), op cit., chap. 5, pp. 117–140.

10. Jung, C. G.: "General Aspects of Dream Psychology," in *The Structure and Dynamics of the Psyche,* vol. 8, in *The Collected Works of C. G. Jung,* Pantheon, New York, 1960, pp. 237–280.

11. Jung, C. G.: "The Practical Use of Dream Analysis," in *The Practice of Psychotherapy,* vol. 16, 2d ed., in *The Collected Works of C. G. Jung,* Pantheon, New York, 1966.

12. Altman, Leon L.: *The Dream in Psychoanalysis,* International Universities Press, New York, 1969.

13. Bonime, Walter: *The Clinical Use of Dreams,* Basic Books, New York, 1962.

14. Rossi, Ernest Lawrence: *Dreams and the Growth of Personality,* Pergamon, New York, 1972.

15. French, Thomas M., and Erika Fromm: *Dream Interpretation: A New Approach,* Basic Books, New York, 1972.

16. Boss, Medard: *The Analysis of Dreams,* Ryder, London, 1957.

17. Caligor, Leopold, and Rollo May: *Dreams and Symbols: Man's Unconscious Language,* Basic Books, New York, 1968.

18. Perls, Frederick S.: *Gestalt Therapy Verbatim,* Real People Press, Lafayette, Calif., 1969.

19. Whitmont, Edward C.: *The Symbolic Quest,* G. P. Putnam's for the C. G. Jung Foundation for Analytic Psychology, New York, 1969.

20. Hillman, James: *Insearch: Psychology and Religion,* Scribner's, New York, 1967.

21. Sampson, Harold: "Discussion," to Bill Domhoff's "Home Dreams Versus Laboratory Dreams," Milton Kramer (ed.), op. cit., chap. 10, p. 221.

22. Osterman, Elizabeth: Personal communication.

23. Kirsch, Thomas B.: Personal communication.

24. Jung, C. G.: "On the Nature of Dreams," in *The Structure and Dynamics of the Psyche,* vol. 8, op. cit., p. 283.

25. Faraday: loc. cit.

26. Dement, William C.: "The Psychophysiology of Dreaming," in G. E. von Grunebaum and Roger Caillois (eds.), *The Dream and Human Societies,* University of California Press, Berkeley, 1966, chap. 4.

27. Dement, William: "Psychophysiology of Sleep and Dreams," in S. Arieti (ed.), *American Handbook of Psychiatry,* Basic Books, New York, 1966, vol. 3, pp. 290–332.

28. Hartmann, Ernest (ed.): *Sleep and Dreaming,* Little, Brown, Boston, 1970.

29. Medow, L., and L. Snow (eds.): *The Psychodynamic Implications of the Physiologic Studies on Dreams,* Charles C Thomas, Springfield, Ill., 1970.

30. Faraday: op. cit., p. 51.

31. Dement: "The Psychophysiology of Dreaming," op. cit., p. 98.

32. Faraday: op. cit., pp. 41–42.

33. Rossi: loc. cit.

34. Henderson, Joseph L., and Maud Oakes: *The Wisdom of the Serpent,* George Braziller, New York, 1963, pp. 20–22.

35. Perry, John Weir: *Lord of the Four Quarters,* Collier Books, Macmillan, New York, 1970, pp. 18–23 (paperback).

36. Cohen, David B.: "To Sleep, Perchance to Recall a Dream: Repression Is Not the Demon Who Conceals and Hoards Our Forgotten Dreams," *Psychology Today,* pp. 50–54, May 1974.

37. Dement: "The Psychophysiology of Dreaming," op. cit., p. 99.

38. Faraday: op. cit., chap. 3, "Why We Forget Our Dreams," pp. 52–67.

39. Cohen: loc. cit.

40. Alex, William: "Dreams, the Unconscious, and Analytical Therapy," published by the C. G. Jung Institute of San Francisco, 1971, p. 1.

41. Jung, C. G.: "Concerning the Archetypes, with Special Reference to the Anima Concept," in *The Archetypes and the Collective Unconscious,* vol. 9, part 1 of *The Collected Works of C. G. Jung,* Pantheon, New York, 1959.

42. Grinstein, Alexander: *On Sigmund Freud's Dreams,* Wayne State University Press, Detroit, 1968, chap. 17, pp. 392–422.

43. Jung, C. G.: "The Psychology of the Transference," in *The Practice of Psychotherapy,* vol. 16, 2d ed., in *The Collected Works of C. G. Jung,* Pantheon, New York, 1966, p. 227. 227.

44. Whitney, Elizabeth: Personal communication.

Couple Therapy

People who live together, whether married or not, often have problems in their relationship for which they seek help. When they are seen with the primary purpose of helping them in their maladaptive relationship, their treatment is termed *couple therapy*. There are several forms of couple therapy that are currently being practiced, varying in terms of the theoretical treatment orientation of the therapists (e.g., psychoanalytic, dynamic, behavioral, Rogerian, eclectic) and in the number of people included in the sessions.

Individual marital therapy is essentially individual psychotherapy with a focus on marital problems (one therapist, one patient). In *concurrent marital therapy* both spouses are treated individually by the same therapist, and in *conjoint marital therapy* both spouses are treated together by the same therapist (one therapist, two patients) or by a cotherapist team (two therapists, two patients). In *marital group therapy* (or couple group therapy) several couples are treated together by one therapist or, more commonly, by two cotherapists (two therapists, six to ten patients).

This chapter will focus on conjoint couple therapy with some discussion of cotherapist team and couple group treatment.

In conjoint couple therapy the couple is seen together and the treatment centers on their relationship rather than on individual conflict. Such treatment could not come into vogue as long as psychiatric thinking was dominated by the notion that personal neurosis was the crucial determinant of interpersonal conflict. For if the core problem is the behavior of a particular individual, the treatment of choice is individual psychotherapy. Only with the realization of the importance of situational factors in the genesis and resolution of interpersonal conflict did the interest shift from the study of the individual to the study of the interaction between individuals and the behavior of individuals under specific environmental conditions.

The work on family and marriage by sociologists, psychologists, and anthropologists became highly relevant to the couple therapist. Normative studies[1,2] delineating specific tasks and crises of marriage help put the problems a couple presents in perspective: some may be due to a breakdown in communications, others to psychopathology, and some in response to inherent stresses of marriage or to a combination of the above.

With the shift in theory came a shift in practice from individual to joint sessions or a combination of the two.[3] A parallel development occurred in the treatment of families, but the two areas are not identical and grew in response to different needs.

Family therapy developed from the interest in the families of schizophrenics aroused by Sullivan's[4] insights into the role of interpersonal processes in its etiology. If such problems were influenced by peculiarities in communication in a family (e.g., the double-bind hypothesis[5]) perhaps treating the family as a whole was the appropriate treatment for the sick person as well as a means of prevention for the rest of the family. This led to developing specific techniques of family therapy[6-11] that were first applied to families with ill members but later extended to families with a wide range of problems. Therapy was no longer concerned with individual psychopathology but was seen as an opportunity for new growth for the individual, the family, or the couple.

Couple therapy in the form of marital counseling has long been practiced by the clergy and various lay therapists, often with an explicit aim of preserving the marriage. With the growth of social psychiatry, family therapy, and behavior therapy, couple therapy began to appeal more to psychotherapists. The idea of dealing with a problem in the setting in which it occurs and with the people actually involved became widely accepted as a basis for therapy. Another impetus came from Masters and Johnson's work with sexual dysfunction. Suddenly there was a method that promised good results which could be used to help couples, irrespective of the final outcome of their marriage.

The very process of treating the couple together conveys some of the therapist's attitudes. For example, the therapist considers open communication important. He conveys this message indirectly by encouraging each member of the couple to talk freely in the presence of the other (even though he does not insist that they share all), thus implying that what they have kept hidden is probably not as shameful or disruptive to the relationship as they may have assumed. The fact that the therapist holds both spouses responsible for their interaction irrespective of the degree of individual psychopathology tends to reduce individual guilt or blame.

The treatment approach described in this chapter combines a dynamic psychotherapeutic approach with an acceptance of the importance of the effects of the social institution of marriage. The techniques described are often more active

and interactive than traditional psychoanalytic therapy, though they avoid heavy use of prescriptive suggestions utilized by some family therapists such as Haley,[6] Jackson,[12] Zuk,[13] Virginia Satir,[9] and Bach and Wyden.[14]

INDICATIONS FOR COUPLE THERAPY

Couple therapy is indicated when a couple seeks treatment for problems that are attributable to their relationship. This is fairly simple to determine when they request help with problems such as sexual incompatibility or inability to communicate. It becomes more complicated when they are vague or tentative in their complaints, covertly resentful, or when one member attempts to recruit the therapist to rescue him or her from an impossible marriage.

The important point to determine is that the unhappiness exists in the *relationship,* not only in the individual: the couple aggravate and provoke each other rather than provide mutual support or allow for personal growth. If couple therapy is to succeed, the therapist must establish that both members are involved with each other, are unhappy with their relationship, and want to change it. The fact that each may also have individual character or neurotic problems does not constitute a contraindication to couple therapy unless it is of major proportions. However, if one member of the couple is overwhelmed by severe individual pathology, he will need individual therapy before productive couple therapy can be started.

A second possible indication for couple therapy is the case of a person making progress in individual therapy but coming to a standstill around the issue of his marriage. Bringing in the spouse for a few joint sessions or a period of couple therapy may clarify the issues, diminish feelings of being left out by the spouse who is not in therapy, and help resolve interactive marital problems. A therapist can sometimes circumvent months of difficult resistance by this procedure. Such joint sessions can also be helpful when a spouse does not accept important new behaviors by the person in therapy and thus sabotages individual treatment. In general, a certain flexibility has to be maintained as to the timing and alternation of individual and couple sessions.

Couples with difficulties associated with termination of marriage, such as separation, divorce, or dispute over allocation and care of their children, may request or be referred for assistance. Joint sessions can be used to try to obtain a civilized, less vindictive settlement. Many couples are locked in angry isolation and are reluctant to deal with their spouses except through their lawyers. Some courts have come to realize the importance of direct communications in the presence of a neutral third party and have set up specific clinics to that end. Most frequently the couples seek individual help, and it is up to the treating professional to suggest joint sessions. Such meetings should be time-limited, task-oriented, and gently directed to resolution of specific issues rather than allowed to deteriorate into mutual recriminations or attempts by one spouse to pressure the other. The sessions frequently are painful. What helps the therapist is the knowledge that they can be important for the future of the children and in reducing the pain associated with lengthy court fights.

It is important for the success of couple therapy that both members be motivated for treatment. When only one member is interested and the other is a reluctant participant, it is likely that treatment will be interrupted or undermined, in more or less subtle ways, by the unwilling partner. At times this type of interaction — one eager and one reluctant participant — is indicative of the problems in the marriage and characteristic of the way a couple approaches new situations or fights with one another. What one member cherishes the other belittles. An early interpretation may allow the passive partner to express his feelings openly or expose the hidden resistance of the apparently more enthusiastic member and thereby launch treatment. However, if the interpretations fail, it is preferable not to recommend couple therapy but to work out a plan for individual therapy for one or both.

HOW COUPLE THERAPY IS INITIATED

There are several ways in which a couple enters treatment. Couples may come together to a therapist on their own initiative or be referred by a family doctor, a clergyman, a social agency, a lawyer, or a court. They may have a well-formulated marital problem for which they seek help or they may present vague dissatisfactions. Understanding how the couple came to seek treatment is important for assessment of individual and couple motivation and expectations for treatment. As in individual therapy, the presenting complaint may be merely a ticket of admission which hides covert, often unconscious, concerns. For example, couples may say that they want to save the marriage when they really do not. They may simply be proving to themselves and their partners that they have done all that they could do to rescue the situation, including couple therapy. Only when that final step predictably fails do they feel justified in leaving. Others seek a powerful ally in a familial power struggle; still others come because they want to end the marriage but are afraid to do so on their own. Many come under covert or outright pressures from peers, family, lovers, or spouses.

These issues should be explored early so that the therapist can form an opinion as to the real issues that the couple is struggling with and needs to work on.

It is important that the therapist share his impressions with the couple, check whether his conclusions seem reasonable to them, elicit their reactions, and work out mutually acceptable goals with them. Such assessment and discussion are part of the process of establishing a therapeutic contract and indeed constitute the initial phase of therapy.

Initial Interview and Evaluation of Couples

The goals of the first interview are ambitious. One tries to understand both the presenting and the underlying problems of the couple. One inquires about their strengths and habitual modes of coping with stress. One needs to determine whether they are motivated for and capable of change, and, if so, whether the timing is right and treatment is practical in their specific circumstance. Finally, one has to decide on the mode of therapy that is best suited to them. Concurrently the interview provides an opportunity for the couple to get an impression of the therapist and decide whether they can trust and work with him or her.

The first interview may proceed along the following lines:

1. Make the couple comfortable.

2. Restate to them what you know about their problems from phone calls or other prior information.

3. Encourage them to present the problem or problems as they see them. Let them decide spontaneously on who presents his view first, but later encourage the other member to give his own version. Show interest in specific incidents rather than in broad generalizations; feelings are attached to specific events.

4. Obtain a history of the problem. When did it start? How bad does it get? Has it changed over time? What have they done about it? Have they sought professional help in the past? How did it go? Why have they decided to get treatment *now*?

5. How do they usually handle problems? Do they fight? How? Can they tell us about it? (People are frequently unable to answer this question because they are unaware of their own behavior. It is important to ask it, however, because it begins the therapy process of having them pay attention to the way they feel and act in specific situations.)

6. Obtain a history of the marriage. When did they marry, and what were the circumstances? What were their reasons? What was it like at first? Later? Now? What did they expect of marriage? Have their expectations changed? In what way?

7. What was their parents' marriage like? How did their parents get along, reach decisions, resolve differences? Do they see themselves like their parents? In what ways? How did they fit into the home picture?

8. Sexual history. How do they get along sexually? Now? Originally? Has there been any change? Do they feel free with each other? Do they talk about sex? If not, do they have nonverbal ways of letting each other know how they feel?

9. Observe the couple's interactions. Does one dominate? Do they compete for attention? Do they listen to each other? Does each respond to what the other actually says or does each respond to a preconceived idea of what the other usually says? Do they ignore each other, act indifferent to each other, hurt each other, respect each other? Do they care for one another? Are they self-centered? Can they correct each other?

This approach differs from the evaluation of individuals in that the emphasis throughout is on the couple as a unit. Every question has to be responded to by each spouse, even if they cannot agree and each gives a different version. The interviewer remains neutral and does not take sides. This is important because the attitude of the therapist during the initial interview is interpreted by the couple as a harbinger of his attitude during therapy; a couple may actually test the therapist by trying to provoke him to take sides and to act as a judge determining who is right. However, their trust and confidence in his abilities as therapist diminish if he actually does. They may be aware on some level that they distort their presentation, not necessarily by lying but by their choice of material, special emphasis, or omission of situations where they feel they have acted shabbily. Thus the neutrality of the therapist is crucial. How can they confide in him if he is judgmental? How can they trust him if he is easily deceived?

When pressed to take sides the therapist can state his position that the important issue is not who he thinks is in the right but what the couple considers important and how they go about resolving their differences. They do not have to agree with each other, but they have to be able to accept the fact that they have differences and to learn to reach decisions despite diverse viewpoints.

Individual history is important for the light it sheds on what a person takes for granted, on his expectations from marriage, norms of expression or suppression of feelings in his family, or particular vulnerabilities.

Example 23-1. A couple married for two years comes for therapy because they are concerned about their terrible fights. The wife says that even though she knows that her husband loves her, she frequently feels like walking out on him. He procrastinates, is not demonstrative, and often sulks and withdraws for days on end. The husband quietly interjects that he does not withdraw for days on end. She angrily says that he does. He looks hurt and stops talking. The therapist encourages the husband to present his version verbally rather than by his behavior. The husband says that his wife is volatile, unpredictable, and irrational, and that she criticizes him all the time.

In asking about past history, the therapist learns that the husband comes from a wealthy family. His controlled, soft-spoken father was frequently absent from the home, which was run by a cold, efficient, quiet, and undemonstrative mother. Both parents rarely tolerated overt expressions of feelings.

The husband considers his upbringing and early life happy. He had prepared for the ministry, with the blessings of the family, then suffered a change of heart, left the church, and began dating. His wife was his first love.

The wife is an only child born to a lower-class German family during World War II and raised by her mother alone under difficult and unstable circumstances. The mother was very emotional and they quarreled continuously.

She met her husband-to-be in the United States, where she had come to study; they fell in love and married after a tempestuous courtship in spite of his family's opposition. Soon after the honeymoon the wife began to resent the husband because he did not stand up to his family on her behalf nor was he as dominant as she expected men to be.

The past history makes several things clear:

1. The norms of expression of feelings are diametrically opposed for each spouse as are the levels that they take for granted.

2. Each seems to have significant personal problems.

3. Each married a partner drastically different from the people he grew up with. Each probably has an important fantasy attached to the marriage.

4. They are romantically attached to each other and each seems to mean a lot to the other.

The crucial issue for both is their relationship. A lot is at stake for them, yet alone they are unable to handle it. Couple therapy is indicated.

Indeed they responded well to a year of weekly conjoint therapy. The husband learned to express his feelings more readily and verbally; the wife's provocativeness diminished as she was getting a clearer emotional response from the husband; the severity and frequency of their fights decreased to levels acceptable to the couple.

When one partner feels too inhibited or threatened to express himself in the presence of the other, the therapist should see each member individually once or several times, followed by joint interviews. The contents of the individual sessions are confidential, and it is up to the patient to bring them up in the joint interviews. Frequently, however, the opportunity to discuss "forbidden" or "hidden" matters with the therapist reduces the anxiety or shame attached to them and makes it easier to bring them up in joint sessions. Sometimes, of course, the patient emerges with a renewed determination to keep quiet, which should be respected by the therapist.

Requests for individual sessions may represent wishes for greater individual attention and an exclusive, privileged relationship with the therapist. Treatment may be sabotaged if the therapist falls in with such maneuvers and, by frequent individual sessions, allies himself with one member. Even if he is scrupulous in remaining neutral, his effectiveness is diminished if he feels hampered in his freedom to discuss issues with the couple or if he begins to have difficulty in keeping straight what can and cannot be said in a joint session. Alertness to such possibilities can lead to appropriate clarifications and interpretations to the individuals involved and is essential for continued treatment. Another possibility is that such requests represent a real need and should be honored by referral for individual treatment.

Observation of the couple's interactions is the single most important part of the evaluation, especially if the couple enters in a heated interaction. One can learn a great deal more about the problems, the characters of the participants, and the way they feel about each other from their behavior than from an interrogation. For the couple, an opportunity to engage in such an interaction in the presence of a neutral third party can be therapeutic.

Example 23-2. A third-year law student, flamboyant, handsome, and articulate, comes in with a weepy, self-effacing wife who cowers in the corner. They are clearly in the midst of an argument. When encouraged to continue, she blurts out that it was her idea to consult a psychiatrist together with her husband because she could take it no longer: her husband doesn't love her. The husband reacts angrily. In a long vitriolic outburst he says in essence that he is sick and tired of a depressed nobody; that after a long day at school he expects a loving, tender, sexual wife. The wife responds to his anger by almost visibly shriveling up and withdrawing in fear. The therapist encourages her to speak up; she sobs, and whispers that

since her husband prefers the television to her, she has no wish to sleep with him. She goes on to complain of his lack of involvement, of his absences from home, etc. The entire session is spent in this exchange, with the therapist principally encouraging the wife to express her feelings in words that can be heard. At the end of the hour they agree to return for continued evaluation.

Next week the wife looks transformed: pretty, seductive but still shy. The husband is friendly, pays attention to her and seems more relaxed. He relates that they continued to talk after the first session, and he realized that she actually had a legitimate point, that he had been neglecting her. He decided to come home early. She became more cheerful and stopped complaining. He began to enjoy her company and realized that he no longer felt angry with her. They had had some good lovemaking. At this point the therapist began a more formal evaluation. The clear difference in the couple between the first and second sessions suggested several things: that changes could occur, that therapy could help, and most important of all, that the couple had an investment in each other and in their marriage.

This couple reported a satisfactory relationship after a few conjoint sessions.

From the outset the therapist needs to be flexible and responsive to the needs of the couple. Those who have repeated failures in therapy or have severe problems with self-esteem are not likely to give a good history during the initial contact. Many may be suspicious of psychotherapy. They may need time to evaluate the therapist. In such cases, it is preferable to let the patients control the interview and concentrate on observations of the couple. The nonverbal clues plus the response to the first sessions may be useful material for evaluation and recommendations. If at the end of the evaluation the therapist decides to recommend couple therapy, how does he proceed?

CONTINUING THERAPY

There is no sharp demarcation between evaluation and treatment. Both occur concurrently and continuously. Yet, as we have indicated, it is important to set aside one or several initial sessions for evaluation at the end of which specific recommendations are made by the therapist. This gives the couple an opportunity to discuss various treatment alternatives with the therapist and to have a voice in the choice of treatment and in formulating goals of therapy.

The initial phase of therapy consists of establishing a working atmosphere where people feel comfortable and willing to share their problems, conflicts, and difficulties. The nonjudgmental attitude of the therapist helps the process of disclosure as well as serves as a model to the couple. Instead of a perpetually frustrating round of "Who is at fault?" one switches to an attitude of "What really happens?" and "What can be done about it?"

The therapist encourages the couple to talk and listen to one another; he points out their distortions and helps them establish ground rules for their interactions. He may translate nonverbal messages so that feelings and reactions become explicit and thereby more amenable to change. When a member is intimidated by the other or by his own feelings of inferiority, the therapist tries to make the couple conscious of the nature of these feelings and thereby begin the process of exploring for areas of possible change for the timid member or for both.

It is preferable to offer interpretations tentatively, subject to correction by the couple. The therapist may be wrong, especially when he interprets feelings, but more important, such an approach enhances an active participation by the couple in the therapeutic process and minimizes excessive dependence on the therapist. It helps maintain a balance of power.

The goals at this point in therapy are twofold: (1) to help each member understand the effect he has on the other and how the reaction of the spouse in turn influences his next response, and (2) to formulate the couple's problems explicitly and specifically.

Example 23-3. A handsome, well-mannered, correct, distant, and controlled married couple requests couple therapy. Joanne states in a low, measured, and unemotional tone that they have been married for four years and have had trouble for two of them. She wonders if they should separate. Bill is only interested in his work; they no longer have anything in common. Bill objects mildly. He has indeed been very busy since they have recently moved, and he is engaged in an important project, but he sees no real problem. He does not think that they need outside help. He has agreed to come only to humor Joanne. Perhaps she feels restless and should find some work to occupy herself. Joanne thinks that Bill really prefers her at home.

Their backgrounds are similar. They were childhood sweethearts and married during college. The one significant difference in their upbringing is that the role expectations in their homes varied. Bill spent a great deal of time with his father and brother and was taught to consider women to be silly, irresponsible, and basically ornamental. Joanne's home was dominated by active, responsible women, and she was reared to expect to be included fully in all major decisions in a marriage.

At the end of the first session the therapist comments that they both seem reluctant to express their true feelings; that Joanne seems depressed, while Bill acts as if he were wrongly accused. When they agree, the therapist adds that it is important for them to tell each other how they actually feel so that they can make a reasonable decision either to stay together and try to improve their relationship, or to separate, rather than to pursue their current course of drifting resentfully into a separation.

The second session is very different in tone. They are both less restrained. Joanne cries, confessing: "We had to get married" and "We gave the baby away for adoption so that Bill could finish school." Originally she had wanted another child, but Bill had objected and now she defiantly states that she no longer wants any. Bill responds angrily. He likes and wants children. Anyhow he cannot stand Joanne when she is crying. In recent months she is always depressed. He feels helpless. Everything he suggests, she rejects. There is nothing he can do that is right for her.

It seems that the wife's depression is partly a belated reaction to the loss of the baby, to her guilt about having given it away, and partly to her anger and envy of the man who can shrug it all off and immerse himself in work. The recent move to a new environment two thousand miles away from home reawakened the problem. The husband is angry and self-righteous. He has done right by his wife; he has married her; and now she is reneging on her proper role and is not taking proper care of him. Each is surprised to hear what the other is saying. They begin to get a glimpse of their anger and their needs.

The third session is taken up by the husband discussing his work. Since they alternate in presenting their needs, the therapist goes along with it and shows interest in Bill's problems at work. Joanne hears them for the first time and Bill is heartened by her intelligent, sympathetic response.

Thus therapy starts by establishing an atmosphere where Joanne and Bill can reveal their respective needs, but these are not treated as individual problems but rather as issues which affect their relationship. The focus is not on the dynamics of the husband's threatened masculinity, evoked by feeling helpless with his wife. Nor is the focus on the wife's homesickness and dependency. Instead one concentrates on the issues between them, how they react to each other's needs once they discover them, what they want from each other, what they are frustrated with or angry at each

other for. Their individual past is taken up primarily in terms of clarifying how it is distorting their ability to hear each other or to provide what the other wants.

As they understand each other better, they work out ways of coexisting, such as the husband letting the wife "cry it out" once she agrees to go out with him willingly on another preplanned day. Several sessions are devoted to exploring their conscious expectations and feelings about marriage, comparing their own solutions to those of their parents. Indirectly it helps them work out their separation from home, as well as enabling them to build up methods of problem solving. They work out an agreement to postpone (not to forego) childbearing for a couple of years during which time the wife would work, a suggestion that was actually made by the husband during the initial visit. At that time, however, it was not acceptable, probably because of its hidden implication that the wife was avoiding motherhood and being difficult and unreasonable.

As treatment progresses, more time is devoted to "working through." The techniques used may involve clarification, interpretations, role playing and specific advice for trying out new modes of response, as well as transference interpretations.

In couple therapy, there is less need than in individual therapy to promote and use transference to the therapist in order to reexperience the conflict in therapy and make it amenable to resolution. The conjoint couple approach is more pragmatic, with heavy emphasis on ways of dealing with the specific effects of the conflicts in the marriage. The assumption is that a couple can be helped to find realistic alternatives to their neurotic interaction by concentrating on interpreting individual pathology only to the extent necessary to change specific behaviors. At the same time the meaning of behaviors of the spouse that maintain the pathological interaction is explored.

The attempt is to disturb the marital equilibrium sufficiently so that a search for new behaviors will ensue. If the new interaction satisfies individual needs, the force behind the neurotic behavior will presumably diminish.

In Example 23-1, when the issue of the wife's profound distrust of men surfaced, the husband's first reaction was surprise. "Do you actually mistrust me?" he had asked. Later he inquired about her childhood, and they began to share, for the first time, a detailed and emotionally charged review of her experiences. At home during the following weeks, both became alert to the specific manifestations of the wife's mistrust as well as the husband's tendency to interpret them as personal rejections (the area where their neuroses "fit," where her pathology played into his). Instead of falling into pointless arguments, as in the past, they alerted each other to what each thought was going on, refrained from "getting even," and in the process developed new ways of interacting.

It was not necessary to analyze the wife's neurotic conflicts in the area of her feminine identity or relationship to men. It was sufficient to help her change some of the more superficial specific manifestations. This was enough to reduce the pressure on her husband, who could then refrain from inflaming her further and act in a way that alleviated her anxiety (instead of becoming sullen and withdrawn, reassure her). As her unconscious fears failed to materialize, she could trust her husband first in minor matters and later extend her area of trust so as to try other ways of being emotionally close besides fighting. In actual practice this process is rarely as straightforward as it sounds on paper. Characteristically it consists of tentative trials, some successes, setbacks, new trials, and so on. When a sadomasochistic interaction is very firmly fixed, as in Example 23-1, this process may not be sufficient, and a period of individual therapy may become necessary.

Marital partners often project unrealistic images on the other. Not infrequently profound disappointment and estrangement occur when one or both members perceive discrepancies between the actual and the ideal. This is particularly important in cases of narcissistic object choice where a member sees his partner primarily as an extension of himself rather than as a separate individual. In Example 23-3, Bill identifies with his wife and considers her actions mainly in terms of how they reflect on him. He resents her wish to go to work because he thinks it suggests that he is not much of a man. Only after a period of therapy where he works out the reality of their existence as separate individuals can he see that her working is an assertion of her own needs rather than a reflection on him.

COUNTERTRANSFERENCE AND TRANSFERENCE

Countertransference is the reaction of the therapist to his patients. It includes both a realistic assessment and an unreasonable response based on the therapist's unresolved or partially resolved conflicts.[15] Transference is a patient's inappropriate response to a therapist, derived from the patient's past experience. In this section we will emphasize those aspects of countertransference and transference that are relevant for work with couples.

Countertransference

As already noted, some marital problems can be attributed to the state of marriage.[16] Many couples present themselves with problems complicated by situations that are not very different from those faced by their therapists. Thus a therapist may be tempted to influence the couple to try the kind of solutions he has found useful in his own life and overlook a crucial difference in opinions, religion, traditions, or social pressures. Indeed a therapist has to know himself well and have experience before he develops a sense that enables him to distinguish between behavior that is maladaptive and one that is based on a conception of roles different from his own. This is particularly true in areas where the therapist holds strong convictions, e.g., sexual behavior and roles, relationships with parents, other couples, etc. The therapist may delude himself that his patient's attitudes are neurotic simply because they differ from his own.

For years some therapists believed that the place of a woman was in the home. When faced with a troubled couple where the wife was independent or dominant, they tended to attribute the marital strife to the "reversal of roles." Passing such judgments is not a legitimate function of the therapist and is indeed a manifestation of countertransference.

When a therapist first learns new therapeutic techniques, he may in his enthusiasm apply them indiscriminately and at best be totally ineffective.

Example 23-4. A third-year-resident proud of his success in a clinic for sexual dysfunctions interviews a couple who complains of poor communication and profound unhappiness with each other. He discovers early that they have had no intercourse since the birth of their fourth unplanned child and that the wife is uninterested in sex. Instead of completing the evaluation and thoroughly investigating other aspects of their lives, he recommends a course of sex therapy and gives them specific suggestions along the lines of Masters and Johnson's treatment of frigidity in women. The couple carries out his suggestions halfheartedly and change therapists after a few sessions.

The new therapist helps them work out a compromise solution that fits their religious and moral beliefs. They achieve a cordial relationship devoid of real closeness, but one that keeps up appearances, provides a home for their children and relieves them of their guilt. The wife embarks on a discreet sexually and emotionally satisfying affair and the husband spends many months away from home on business.

The real issues in this marriage were not sexual even though there is no doubt that the wife's profound disrespect and dislike for her husband resulted in a poor sexual adjustment in the marriage. Had the resident been free to allow the couple to choose the areas of work, his therapy would have gone much better, but his own needs and attitudes prevented him from being useful to the couple.

Another situation where a therapist is unable to respond to the needs of a couple occurs when he overidentifies with them or feels threatened by their lifestyle. Under the pressure of his countertransference feelings, he may, without being aware of it, cut off a particular line of discussion by interjecting a question, by concentrating on a side issue, or by giving premature suggestions. Sometimes he may feel threatened by one member of the couple. He may overidentify with the member whom he perceives to be like himself, who takes a similar role in the marriage, or who reacts in a way that he would like to but does not. A therapist may unconsciously compete with one member and thus encourage one and prevent the other from expressing himself.

Example 23-5. A wife begins treatment with a barrage of complaints. Her husband is indifferent to her. He is always preoccupied and off in his own world. He avoids any real responsibility in the home. She has to prod and pressure him all the time.

The therapist is getting more and more irritated with her. With a knowing glance he turns to the husband and says, "How can you stand this?" The couple cancel their next session.

Here the therapist's overreaction offended the wife. He could have invited the husband to express himself in a more neutral way, such as "How do you see it?" which would have encouraged an examination of their interaction. Instead the therapist flatly rejected the wife's version because of his personal reaction to her and thus sabotaged treatment.

Countertransference reactions which are not conscious are often troublesome. When the therapist is aware of and can articulate his countertransference feelings, he can try to avoid acting on them. This does not mean that a therapist can never express an opinion or temporarily take sides in an attempt to clarify issues. But he must avoid expressing his own needs through his patients.

For example, a therapist may have strong personal needs to be helpful. In working with a couple composed of a dominant and a weak person, he may feel tempted to rescue the weak one. This might be satisfying to the therapist but is not helpful to the couple and places the therapist in a powerful, paternal position with the couple. It would be preferable if he encouraged the weak one to speak up for himself or demonstrated to the couple how a member uses his weakness to advantage. Many couples pressure the therapist to decide who is in the right and try to get his approval at the expense of the other. This may be very appealing to the therapist's vanity and sense of importance, but is a trap nevertheless.

> *Example 23-6.* An overwrought wife tearfully protests that her husband is having an affair and refuses to give it up. The husband answers calmly that he cares for both women, that he gets something from each one and that he doesn't see why he must decide between them. Why should his wife mind? He loves her as much as he has always done.
>
> The therapist identifies with the wife. The husband seems so self-satisfied. But since the therapist is aware of her feelings, she keeps silent.
>
> Later it becomes clear that the couple is engaged in a struggle for dominance. The wife had kept the upper hand by withholding sex. The husband felt humiliated yet helpless because of his fear of loneliness and rejection. The affair changed the marital balance. It gave a boost to the husband's self-esteem and allowed him to regain control.
>
> Had the therapist sympathized with the wife, her role in the struggle would have become evident much more slowly or not at all.

Some therapists find couple therapy superficial, personally safer, and less difficult than individual work. Since there is always another person pres-

ent, the interpersonal distance is greater, the therapist's individual defenses are less threatened, and they get less involved.

For other therapists couple therapy offers a challenge because it requires that the therapist handle himself as a distinct and separate person. It is not possible to hide behind the guise of an "impartial screen" and one has to be constantly on the alert to distinguish between the needs of the couple and the countertransference of the therapist.

Transference

Transference manifestations can be handled directly in couple work. The therapist may recruit one member to comment on a distorted perception of the therapist by the other. Habitual patterns of response to a spouse can be pointed out when the same type of behavior is directed toward the therapist and dealt with in the here and now of the therapy situations. Unrealistic expectations from a spouse or a therapist often become very clear very quickly in couple therapy.

> *Example 23-7.* A wife reacted negatively to a female therapist during the first session and wanted to stop treatment. The husband persuaded her to return because to him her criticisms seemed far-fetched and inappropriate. Upon her return she was able to talk about her inability to trust women — they drop you in a minute for any man — and her anger at her own mother, a promiscuous, self-centered woman who did not care for her and who pushed her to seek support from the father. It became clear that the wife's reaction to the therapist was similar to her reaction to most women: she avoided female friends, turned to men for affection and was excessively dependent on her husband. The transference problem led directly to an examination of the basic struggle in the marriage, namely that the husband wanted a wife, not a dependent child, while the wife wanted her husband to mother her.

Frequently, the couple reacts to the therapist as if he were their parent, and competes for his attention using the type of behavior that elicited results during childhood. If the therapist is alert to this possibility, he can understand and, when appropriate, use it to illustrate the manner in which a particular person courts attention, asks for help or asserts himself.

Patients in individual therapy often seek direct gratifications in the sessions. This problem need not occur in couple work. A person who is of central importance in real life is a participant in the sessions, and the therapist is not the only provider of emotional gratification. The insights gained in therapy can be put to direct and immediate use. The couple can try out new solutions in the office and at home. The therapist is more clearly a catalyst, a benevolent parental figure, a teacher, but not a major provider of emotional gratifications, if he has successfully dealt with his countertransference.

TERMINATIONS

When a couple has resolved pressing problems and developed methods of dealing with conflict, it is time to consider termination of treatment. It is not necessary for them to have solved all their problems, nor is it possible to guarantee happiness. It is impossible to predict when or what kind of new challenges will arise. It is important to concentrate on developing ways of facing conflict, of dealing with one another, and of learning to communicate clearly.

Termination in couple therapy is similar to that in individual therapy in that it involves dealing with feelings of mutual fondness and dependency. Unlike individual work, it is rare to encounter profound dependency or inability to separate from the therapist, nor does one usually have to deal with feelings of anger or rejection toward the therapist. Since the goals of therapy are fairly explicit, the point of termination is usually obvious and is frequently initiated by the couple.

During the last phase of treatment the couple generally works through the anxiety of having to provide each other with mutual stimulation and support without the aid of the therapist. Ending therapy means giving up illusions about what could have been accomplished and accepting realistic limitations and compromises, which at times can be difficult. Some couples try to prolong therapy because they are fond of the therapist and have grown used to a time and place to air their problems. Knowing that they can return if they need to helps, as does a scheduled follow-up appointment. Some therapists prefer to terminate gradually — after all, therapists grow fond of their patients, too — and end with less frequent meetings. In those cases where divorce or separation are agreed on, termination of joint sessions may lead to individual therapy for one or both, preferably by a colleague. The change in therapists may be interpreted as a desertion by some patients, but for the most part the couple is so heavily involved in the termination of the marriage that the reaction to a change of therapist is secondary. A minority of cases develop a strong transference reaction in which the change of therapists becomes symbolic of the breakup of the marriage, and dealing with it takes precedence in any new therapy. It is difficult for the original therapist to see both individuals in therapy when a couple breaks up. Rancor, suspicion, rivalry for attention, and a strong pressure to take sides cloud the therapeutic relationship. It takes a very capable therapist to handle such a situation, and it is probably preferable to refer the couple to a colleague, though the therapist should make every effort to be supportive during the process of referral and be available until the new therapeutic relationship is well established.

MODES OF CONJOINT COUPLE THERAPY

A therapist can see a couple alone or in a group, by himself or with a co-therapist. Masters and Johnson[17] have been instrumental in popularizing the use of a male and female co-therapist team. Our experience bears out their assertion that for each patient the presence of a person of the same sex as the patient is often reassuring and helpful.

To the extent that people feel more comfortable in the presence of a person of the same or opposite sex, co-therapists offer natural allies.

There are certain considerations that apply to a co-therapist team, whether they work with individual couples or with a group. It is essential that the co-therapists establish a working relationship with each other and spend the time necessary to know each other well. They need to reconcile their theoretical approaches, be comfortable in each other's company, and respect and be sensitive to their individual styles of expressing themselves and working with patients.

A team that is covertly hostile, competitive, or engaged in a sexual seduction may convey messages that encourage hostile or sexual behavior by the couple or in a couple's group. A well-working team can use their relationship to model how distinct individuals, at times holding different opinions, can be fond of each other and be able to work well together. Observing such an interaction can be helpful to the couples because it touches on a central problem of marriage, namely how to preserve individuality in a dyadic relationship.

Co-therapists can take sides on issues and model a disagreement where a single therapist may be hampered by the need to maintain neutrality. The co-therapist can support an alternative position or point out that the other therapist took sides, and allow the couple to express their reactions to it. Either way provides for a more lively, real, and active consideration of important issues. For the therapists, especially when they are beginners, the co-therapist's presence minimizes countertransference reactions, reduces anxiety, and enhances the heuristic value of the sessions. Couples who benefit from therapy seem to fall into two groups: those who improve rapidly and those who take much longer to get better. For the "chronic group," couple group therapy led by a male and a female co-therapist team seems to work best. For the therapist, it is pleasanter to work with a co-therapist. He can tolerate more exasperating couples, be less concerned with taking sides, less defensive if he prefers one member of a couple, and freer in exploring alternatives.

For the couples, groups accelerate the pace of therapy. It seems as if couples begin to work out their own problems while they are observing other couples, so that when they become the focus of therapy they proceed on a deeper level. This clinical observation was unexpected and surprising at first. On reflection the situation is analogous to that in Bandura's[18] experiments of patients with snake phobias. He found that such patients improved more rapidly when they observed a therapist handling a snake than when they were given instructions to do this in his presence. In our groups the couples identified with one another and modeled their behavior on that of the other couples or on that of the therapists. Thus, as in Bandura's cases, even when couples were silent, they were actually actively engaged and working on their own problems.

In couples' groups, too, a couple can be more objective about the problems of others and therefore come up with good solutions that are welcomed by the troubled couple. When they realize that they can help solve problems that are not very different from their own, they gain in self-confidence.

A group provides a great deal of support. The presence of other couples who are struggling with similar or worse problems is reassuring. Persons of the same sex may express sympathy for and articulate role-related problems in ways that clarify the issues. The couples develop friendships and help each other during crisis periods. When these friendships pose problems, as when couples develop strong sexual feeling for one another, the group can consider, not simply theoretically, but with feeling, the types and degree of involvement couples or individuals wish to have with others and the emotional consequences of these activities. Naturally individual solutions differ and the group frequently moves on to consider a related problem, namely how much individual freedom is compatible with a close couple relationship. This is an important problem and a frequent source of resentment in a marriage.

TRENDS IN COUPLE THERAPY

The interest in marital couple therapy has increased sharply over the past few years, a period that has marked its emergence as a subfield in the area of mental health. It is a truly multidisciplinary field with active participation by psychiatrists, psychologists, social workers, sociologists, and counselors. Gurman[19] counted the number of scientific journal articles devoted to marital couple therapy during the past thirty years and noted a fourfold increase to 119 articles from 1967 to 1968.

Interest in community mental health and in public health leads to an interest in marital and family problems. Here is a segment of the population with distinct, commonly encountered problems that have a wide impact on the community and on future generations.

Well-placed, timely help is likely to have an immediate impact and a long-term preventive effect. The usual techniques of crisis intervention employing an interdisciplinary team are applicable, and outcome research can have definable goals.

Many family therapists have been shifting to work with couples in recent years as it has become increasingly evident that a central issue in many disturbed families is a disturbed marriage. This is true also of some child therapists. Because of the relatively clearly definable goals of therapy, couples lend themselves to research on effectiveness of psychotherapy. Behavior modification techniques are also easily applicable for the same reason: many of the recent journal articles deal with couple therapy from these points of view.[20]

An important impetus to marital couple therapy will probably continue to come from approaches initiated by Masters and Johnson. Clinics for the treatment of sexual dysfunction utilizing modifications of their techniques have opened throughout the United States in recent years and are very popular.

It is difficult, and at times impossible, to clearly differentiate interpersonal difficulties from sexual problems; the two areas blend and reenforce one another. Many people who request sex therapy are not good candidates for it though they might benefit from couple therapy. Others find that once they have resolved their sexual problems, they are ready to work on other aspects of their relationship. Some people divorce once they have overcome sexual dysfunction.

Thus it seems likely that the clinics for the treatment of sexual dysfunction will have to develop more precise methods of couple evaluation than are available at present and will probably branch out to provide help for couples in other areas of their lives. One hopes this increased interest will lead to more effective and readily available treatment for couples.

REFERENCES

1. Goodrich, Wells: "Towards a Taxonomy of Marriage," in J. Marmor (ed.), *Modern Psychoanalysis,* Basic Books, New York, 1968, pp. 408–423.

2. Ranch, H. L., D. W. Goodrich, and T. D. Campbell: "Adaptation to the First Years of Marriage," *Psychiatry,* 26:368–380, 1963.

3. Alger, I.: "Joint Sessions: Psychoanalytic Variations, Applications and Indications," in S. Rosenbaum and I. Alger (eds.), *The Marriage Relationship,* Basic Books, New York, 1968.

4. Sullivan, Harry Stack: *The Interpersonal Theory of Psychiatry,* Norton, New York, 1953.

5. Bateson, G., D. Jackson, J. Haley, and J. H. Weakland: "Towards a Theory of Schizophrenia," *Behavioral Sci.,* 1:251, 1956.

6. Haley, J.: *Strategies of Psychotherapy,* Grune & Stratton, New York, 1963, chaps. 6 and 7.

7. Ackerman, N. W.: *The Psychodynamics of Family Life,* Basic Books, New York, 1958.

8. Lidz, T.: *The Family and Human Adaptations,* International Universities Press, New York, 1963.

9. Satir, Virginia: *Conjoint Family Therapy, A Guide to Theory and Technique,* Science and Behavior Books, Palo Alto, Calif., 1964.

10. Ferber, A., M. Mendelsohn, and A. Napier: *The Book of Family Therapy,* Science House, New York, 1972.

11. Beels, C. C., and A. S. Ferber: "Family Therapy: A View," *Fam. Process,* 8:280–318, 1969.

12. Jackson, D.: "The Marital Quid Pro Quo," *Arch. Gen. Psychiat.,* **12**:589 et. seq., 1965.

13. Zuk, G.: "Family Therapy: Formulation of a Technique and its Theory," *Arch. Gen. Psychiat.,* **16**:71–79, 1967.

14. Bach, George, and Peter Wyden: *The Intimate Enemy,* Avon, New York, 1968.

15. Greenson, Ralph: "Loving, Hating, and Indifference toward the Patient," paper presented at the American Psychoanalytic Association Meeting in Hawaii, May 1973.

16. Rapoport, Rhona: "The Study of Marriage as a Critical Transition for Personality and Family Development," in Peter Lomas (ed.), *The Predicament of the Family,* International Universities Press, New York, 1967.

17. Masters, W. H., and V. Johnson: *Human Sexual Inadequacy,* Little, Brown, Boston, 1970.

18. Bandura, A.: "Psychotherapy Based upon Modeling Principle," in A. E. Bergin and S. L. Garfield (eds.), *Handbook of Psychotherapy and Behavior Change,* Wiley, New York, 1971, pp. 653–708.

19. Gurman, A. S.: "Marital Therapy: Emerging Trends in Research and Practice," *Fam. Process,* **12**(1):45–54, March 1973.

20. Gurman, A. S.: "The Effects and Effectiveness of Marital Therapy: A Review of Outcome Research," *Fam. Process,* **12**(2):145–170, June 1973.

The Telephone
in Outpatient
Psychotherapy*

It is unquestionable that the telephone is playing a large role in contemporary psychotherapy. Although relatively little has been published to date, articles are beginning to appear discussing the use of the telephone in a number of different therapeutic settings. It has been described as an important adjunct in the practice of outpatient psychotherapy, particularly with patients for whom the dimension of psychologic closeness-distance presents crucial problems. [1] It has obvious relevance to emergency psychotherapy, where it may even be used as the sole medium of communication, as in suicide prevention centers [2] and other telephone services which are designed for crisis intervention with drug users, adolescents, or acutely violent individuals.

These telephone-based services have even developed a body of information surrounding the special use of the telephone by particular types of patients, such as anonymous callers [3] or telephone masturbators. [4] In the emergency room the telephone provides special ways of dealing with the acutely ill patient. [5] During hospitalization, it

provides a special kind of communication with the outside world, and virtually every inpatient unit must establish special rules to prevent abuse and enhance therapeutic use of the telephone. Following hospitalization, it allows a regular, long-term follow-up on patients who live far away from the hospital. [6] During psychiatric and psychologic consultation, it has obvious uses in speeding and enhancing communication with the consultant as well as with the patient. In addition to these areas, the telephone has been used in such special situations as long-distance case supervision, [7] long-distance hypnosis, [8] and international psychiatric consultation regarding Peace Corps volunteers.

Individuals vary considerably in their affinity for the telephone, and, as a result, both therapists and patients vary in their particular uses of the phone. For example, in a recent unpublished survey of 58 psychiatrists made by Miller and Beebe in the San Francisco area, 97% used the telephone for handling emergencies in the course of treatment, 45% used it as a planned adjunct of face-to-face contact with certain patients, and 19% used it as a primary or sole mode of treatment. This variation in use was accounted for in part by the different ways the clinician rated the telephone as a medium of

*Reprinted in full by permission of the author and publisher from Warren B. Miller, "The Telephone in Outpatient Psychotherapy," *Am. J. Psychother.,* 27(1): 15–26, 1973.

communication. Thirty-eight per cent rated it as easy or very easy, 45% rated it as "so-so," and 16% rated it as difficult or very difficult.

These data reinforce the notion that, for the telephone, like so much else in psychotherapy, it is important for the therapist to know his own reaction to the medium, how comfortable he is with it, and how much he can accomplish with it. In addition to individual differences, there are generally shared perceptions of the telephone as a medium. For example, in the same survey, Miller and Beebe found that anxiety and depression, the two most common mental states associated with unplanned telephone calls, presented different problems to the therapists. The psychiatrists questioned generally agreed that depression was the most difficult mental state to evaluate over the telephone, while anxiety was the easiest.

The telephone is an important and powerful medium of communication. It has strengths and weaknesses, and the clinician should know these and his reaction to them in order to use the telephone in his practice optimally. The rest of this chapter will be devoted to a discussion of the properties of the telephone medium, the way patients use and abuse these properties, and how the therapist may use them in the service of his treatment. The emphasis will be on outpatient and emergency psychiatry.

PROPERTIES OF THE TELEPHONE MEDIUM

The telephone has five properties which will be considered in the following discussion: its spatial property, its temporal property, its single-channel property, its mechanical property, and its dyadic property. Of course, all of these contribute at once to the overall quality of the medium, but separating them out will help in identifying some of the special ways the telephone is used and reacted to.

The spatial property of the telephone refers to the way the medium completely alters the spatial relationships of two people who are communicat-

ing. Since anyone who has access to a telephone can call anyone else who has a phone, and in our society virtually everyone has access to a phone, in a sense the whole world enters the psychotherapist's office via this medium. To be sure, barriers are constructed to prevent just this sort of thing from happening. Nevertheless, anyone can call and, if persistent, generally make contact. Thus, the psychotherapist's territory is no longer limited to his office. He is available to and therefore responsible for people at a great distance from him.

It is a curious aspect of the telephone that, while it allows action from a distance, at the same time the speaker is extremely close to the listener; in a sense, his lips are only inches from the listener's ears. This leads to an unusual kind of intimacy. McLuhan[9] has pointed out that the "French phone," which is the name for the union of the mouthpiece and earphone in a single instrument, brings together the voice and the ear in an especially close way, suggesting the intimacy of love-making because of the association of auditory intimacy with the absence of visual stimulation.

The telephone also has significant temporal properties which bear on the psychotherapeutic setting. Communication with the patient is not definitely limited to any period of time, such as a therapy session. Even though the patient's office time may be formally limited to one or two hours each week, the patient has access to the therapist during all the remaining hours of the week.

A third important property of the telephone is that it is single-channeled. That is to say, communication is entirely limited to the auditory channel of communication. This means a great reduction in the ordinary counterplay of messages in which a person reinforces what he is saying verbally through his body language, or perhaps contradicts his verbal statement, thus giving a mixed message. With the loss of visual clues, visual imagery or fantasy on the part of the telephone user tends to be increased. This may account for some people's need to doodle while talking on the phone and the strong tendency toward visual fantasy about the other person which everyone has experienced while talking on the phone with someone he does not know. In addition, auditory communication has its own special properties which tend to impress themselves on telephone communication. It is almost exclusively verbal and tends to be sequential and rather more logical than would be the case in face-to-face communication.

The telephone as a machine has a number of mechanical properties. It is a concrete object and as such is rather impersonal to relate to and through. It does not require the same kind of sensitivity involved during direct personal contact. Similarly, it does not tune in to the recipient's state and so may be extremely intrusive or "insensitive" when the call is coming in.

A final important property of the telephone is that it is dyadic. Although it is possible for three or more people to communicate simultaneously, in fact, this rarely happens in psychotherapeutic practice, and the telephone seems to reinforce dyadic communication and thus two-person problem solving. As a result, when many people are involved in a psychologic or interpersonal crisis, communication and efforts at resolution which take place over the telephone tend to occur via multiple dyads rather than in triadic or small group form.

PATIENT USE AND THERAPIST REACTION

Spatial properties of the telephone result in characteristic patient uses. Dependent patients or patients who are anxious about loss of dependency gratification use the telephone to maintain closeness and reassure themselves that support is close at hand. Some patients who have especially pressing oral needs feel a pseudointimacy through their repeated use of the phone. Their telephone behavior may even become highly eroticized and result in a very troublesome type of positive transference and avoidance of therapy.

Some patients who are extremely ambivalent,

such as chronic schizophrenics, may use the telephone to achieve some degree of closeness while simultaneously maintaining their distance and their control over their feelings and the therapeutic relationship. Somewhat similarly, hostile and controlling patients may use the telephone to express some of their anger or to manipulate because they feel safer doing this at a distance. Finally, a number of lonely or chronically depressed patients who withdraw and become isolated may periodically make efforts to break out of their isolation by using the action-at-a-distance quality of the telephone.

The therapist often reacts to his patient's use of the spatial properties of the telephone with feelings of increased responsibility because he can be reached from anywhere. Sometimes this is accompanied by a feeling of decreased control, especially when the patient is distancing himself in order to maintain his own control of the therapeutic relationship. The therapist may feel frustration at the distance-keeping, the covertly hostile use of the phone from a distance, and the demanding dependency of frequent faraway calls. Especially if he feels most comfortable confining therapy to the four walls of his office, several calls from a patient will often leave him with a feeling that the therapy is going on beyond his territory and thus outside of his competence and control.

Example 24-1. A 21-year-old, married woman applied to a psychiatric clinic for help. She and her husband had been having considerable marital conflict, and she had moved close to her parents while he remained at an Air Force base 100 miles away. She was upset by the conflict and separation and had sought comfort from an old boyfriend who lived in the same apartment building as her parents. Her husband found out about this relationship and telephoned her, urging her to come home, and threatening otherwise to kill her and her boyfriend.

Because she still felt considerable love for her husband, she was torn between returning to live with him and staying with her parents. She was quite uncertain about what course to follow and pressed the therapist very hard for definite advice. After a long initial therapy session, she decided she would go home to her parents' house, at least temporarily, and return for another session the following day. That evening, the therapist received an urgent call from her. She reported that her husband had driven up to see her, and she agreed to spend the evening with him. They argued, and he attacked her physically. She fled to her parents' apartment, from which she was telephoning. The therapist talked with the patient for a while until she calmed down and then talked with the father briefly. The father had called the police, and the situation seemed to be at least temporarily in hand.

The following day the patient did not arrive for her scheduled appointment. Instead, she telephoned from across the country where she had flown that morning to stay with her sister. Again, she expressed great uncertainty as to what course to follow and pressed the therapist to give her definite advice. He urged her to return home to live with her parents and to continue in psychotherapy. She agreed to do this and made arrangements for an appointment the following week. Later that day, the therapist received a telephone call from the patient's husband. He was intoxicated and quite mournful about his wife's leaving him. However, when the therapist suggested that he and his wife might both benefit from psychotherapeutic help, he became angry and hung up the phone. Eventually, the patient did return to live with her parents and kept her next therapy appointment.

In this case, a patient who was beginning therapy was able to continue leaning heavily on her psychiatrist while living through a crisis in the marriage and coping with her distress and marital problems through much geographic mobility. The psychotherapist was brought more deeply into the marital crisis and experienced feelings of responsibility, together with decreased control, because of the extreme anxiety and precipitous actions on the part of the couple. He was frustrated by the husband's distance-keeping, but appreciated the usefulness of the telephone in working with the patient's extreme dependency.

The spatial property of the telephone may be put to use by certain manic or grandiosely delusional patients when they are attempting to extend their spheres of influence over greater and greater areas. The following case illustrates this point.

> *Example 24-2.* A university graduate student became extremely anxious while preparing for his oral examinations. He contacted many of his friends in the graduate school, talking with them for long hours about his graduate work. Soon his behavior became somewhat agitated, and he included a number of his professors in his pressured and never-ending search for a sympathetic listener. Over a period of several days this behavior took on manic proportions. He became grandiose in his thinking and spent money excessively.
>
> He began to telephone people he knew all over the country, talking to them at length about his problems and his accomplishments. He made several large purchases over the telephone. When efforts were made to get him psychiatric help, he eluded his friends and family while keeping in touch with them through telephone calls from different parts of the state. He was finally found and committed to a state hospital, but even while there, he continued to use the ward telephone to call his friends and relate at lengths his grandiose psychotic schemes.

Because the telephone can be used at any time, it tends to be used by patients who are impulsive, present-oriented, and unable to tolerate anxiety. These patients call when they are anxious or beset by their life problems rather than wait for the designated therapeutic hour. A constructive response to this type of patient is well illustrated in Example 24-1, where the therapist allowed the patient to work out very pressing problems over the telephone but always in the service of eventually establishing regular office visits.

Since the time is itself valuable, patients may also call outside of therapeutic hours in order to test the therapist's interest in them. Therapists often react to these patients with anger at their poor planning and demandingness. Whether or not he is able to turn these kinds of telephone calls to a constructive use, the therapist almost always finds he has to set firm limits on how much use of the phone he will accept.

The single-channel property of the telephone appeals to certain patients who want to maintain anonymity or protect themselves in various ways from being examined too closely by the therapist. In some cases, the caller wishes only to explore the possibility of treatment in a way which protects him from an imagined omnipotent scrutiny. In other cases, the caller, while very much in need of help, is simultaneously very suspicious. As one study revealed,[10] the use of the telephone and the withholding of his name seemed to instill in the patient a sense of power and control. Thus, by boosting his self-esteem, this tactic became a way for the patient to cope with his feelings of powerlessness and worthlessness.

Some patients wish to avoid visual contact with a psychotherapist for other reasons. They may feel shame in talking about a subject, being able to approach it only when they cannot be seen; or, they may be overwhelmed by the therapist's visual presence and be better able to talk with him when that presence has been screened out through the telephone.

Example 24-3. A 29-year-old, married woman came into psychotherapy because of an incapacitating fear of leaving her home. She was having some marital difficulties with a husband who drank a great deal and who spent large portions of his free time away from home. She was also concerned about her angry feelings toward her 5-year-old daughter. Her phobia made it particularly hard for the patient to come to therapy, and she frequently failed to keep her appointment. On these occasions she would telephone her therapist and discuss some of her current problems, as well as her symptoms, over the phone. He tolerated her telephone calls but pressed firmly for her to come to therapy. As the therapy progressed, the patient was able to make appointments more regularly.

As the relationship between her and the therapist became more intense, the therapist began to receive a different kind of telephone call. These were not in place of the therapeutic hours, but rather occurred in the intervals between them. When these calls occurred, the patient was extremely upset and usually somewhat intoxicated. The patient usually began by talking about her immediate problems with her husband, but then tended to shift her attention to material being discussed in the therapy hour. Initially, the therapist insisted that the patient bring this material to the next session. On one occasion, however, he let her talk at length and was surprised to hear her pour out a great deal of premarital and extramarital sexual material about which she felt very ashamed. She indicated that she had always been reluctant to discuss this with him face-to-face, but following this telephone call, she was able to explore this material in the therapy hours. As a result, the telephone calls markedly decreased in number.

As a result of the absence of visual clues, the therapist may have an uneasy feeling of not understanding everything that the patient is saying, or, more generally, of being out of control. This results from several different effects. First, the absence of visual cues creates for the therapist a kind of "telephone blindness" which makes it hard to grasp and evaluate the patient's state. This may account for the greater difficulty in evaluating depression as compared with anxiety over the telephone, which was reported earlier. (Perhaps depressed patients tend to convey essential information through nonverbal cues.) Second, when visual cues are missing, the therapist may develop his own visual fantasies, and these can be extremely misleading. Finally, therapists who themselves communicate in visual, nonverbal ways may feel awkward and unable to reach or influence the patient over the telephone.

The mechanical properties of the telephone actually appeal to certain kinds of patients. The impersonal property together with the dependence on verbal communication may appeal to the obsessional or to the schizoid patient; and, the concrete and machine-like property of the telephone may appeal to the concrete thinking of the chronic schizophrenic. However, therapists generally react in an opposite way. To them, because communication in the telephone medium is mediated through a machine, it lacks warmth and is interpersonally awkward.

The dyadic property of the telephone may result in its use by patients who wish to shut other people out from their communication with a psychotherapist. Thus, especially in couple and family therapy, and to some extent in group therapy, patients will call the therapist on the telephone in order to gain a private ear, often hoping to gain an ally. As a result, the therapist may fail to see or be unable to clarify the role other people are playing in the problem presented by the patient. This also applies to patients in ongoing, individual therapy who make repeated phone calls from home. Seeing such a patient with his family in the office, even if briefly, may tell the therapist a great deal which he cannot discover during a telephone call because of the dyadic constraints.

THERAPEUTIC USES OF THE TELEPHONE

Some of the frustration psychotherapists feel with the telephone is a result of their frequently passive role in the initiation of calls. This need not be the case. The therapist, too, can be active, either by initiating calls himself or by suggesting certain uses of the telephone to the patient. Let me consider some of these therapeutic uses of the telephone.

First of all, the telephone is an excellent medium for giving support and structure to an insecure and unstable patient. It is easy for a shaky patient to call the therapist and reassure himself of the latter's interest and availability, and it is not particularly time-consuming for the therapist. In this regard, the San Francisco survey reported above found that while only 26% of the clinicians made interpretations over the telephone, 78% gave reassurance and 86% allowed ventilation. This special kind of giving-of-self need not be limited to emergency or crisis situations. In fact, many patients will benefit from frequent short telephone contacts as a sole mode of treatment or as an adjunct to regular therapy sessions. Thus, a number of respondents in the Miller and Beebe survey expressed the belief that the telephone was better and safer than giving pills to very dependent, long-term patients.

It is impressive how much structure can be added to a patient's life by the simple method of instructing him to telephone at a particular time on a particular day: "It is nice to talk to you, Mrs. Jones. Call me at two o'clock again next Tuesday. I'll be interested to hear how the job interview goes." Simple instructions such as these can actually help a patient to organize his entire week. Some psychotherapists who follow a number of their long-term, borderline schizophrenic patients through a form of telephone therapy keep telephone hours, for example, from 8:00 to 8:30 several mornings each week. Their patients have the understanding that they will be in their offices and near the telephone, ready to help during that time period each day.

When an impulsive or action-oriented patient is working during therapy at putting feelings and impulses into words, it may be useful to instruct him to telephone his therapist for a talk whenever he feels especially like acting from impulse. This helps the patient learn to verbalize in stress situations and not just during the therapeutic hour. This kind of prescription for the impulsive patient falls under the general principle of "extending the world of therapy through the telephone." Another example of this principle consists of instructing the patient to telephone and talk when he is experiencing something which he is unable to recall or discuss during therapy. Thus, patients, especially those who are not psychologically minded, are encouraged to do the therapeutic work when and where their behavioral or emotional problems take place. Finally, this principle is also helpful for the following types of patients: those who feel ill at ease in the therapist's office and express themselves better when they are on their own territory; those who feel especially threatened in the physical presence of the therapist; and, those who feel they have lost control when they are expected to come to the therapist's office and talk. The instruction to call the therapist and talk from their own territory and on their own initiative may give them just the degree of confidence or sense of control they need.

A final and particularly important therapeutic potential of the telephone lies in its enabling the psychotherapist to contact several "significant others" who are involved in the patient's current problem and thus bring them more completely into the treatment process. This use of the telephone is most helpful in crisis intervention, particularly during the first few visits when the patient may arrive alone and without those people who have been most important in the development of a crisis.

Example 24-4. A 19-year-old woman was brought by the police into the emergency room in a mute, extremely withdrawn state. Through psychiatric examination, it was possible to establish that she had recently lived in a nearby college commune where she had been taking large amounts of drugs. Several days before being picked up by the police, she had apparently wandered away from the commune

in a fearful and disoriented state. The emergency psychiatrist called the commune on the telephone and discovered that the patient had no strong ties with them, having lived there for only a few weeks following her arrival from Canada. The psychiatrist then called her parents' home in Canada. Her father, a local government official, answered the telephone and was very surprised to find out about his daughter's condition. However, he stated that she had left home against his wishes and therefore he did not feel responsible for her present condition.

Since the phone call had been made late at night and had awakened the patient's parents, the psychiatrist decided to call back the next day and hospitalize the patient in the meantime. The patient was admitted to the psychiatric ward and given phenothiazines. By the following day, much of the patient's psychotic behavior had disappeared, although she remained withdrawn and occasionally displayed odd affect. The psychiatrist called the patient's parents again. The father answered again, but this time his attitude had changed considerably. He reported that he and his wife had discussed matters at length, and that he was making plans to leave Canada and come down to help his daughter. This made it possible to keep the patient in the private hospital rather than send her back to the state hospital to begin the slow bureaucratic process of transfer back to Canada. It also made it possible to include the father in the initial treatment process.

In some cases, the telephone can be used by the patient himself during an acute crisis to contact someone who plays an important role in his current problem. The following case is reported in an article by Beebe[11] and expanded upon in Chapter 10.

Example 24-5. A young Coast Guard recruit was brought to the hospital in the acute phase of a severe schizophrenic episode. He was perplexed, grandiose, and delusional. Early in his inpatient stay he asked whether his mother was dead or alive. Because of this, he was urged by his inpatient unit physician to call home. His father answered, and the patient sounded so confused on the phone that the father hung up and called back to the inpatient unit. As a result of this call, it was learned that the patient's parents were separated and that the mother could be reached at another number. The patient then called her himself and, after a short conversation, he became much more lucid.

Beginning at that time and continuing over the next few days, his psychosis cleared. During this time, he revealed that prior to his enlistment his contradictory parents had seemed to be forcing him to enlist in military service and yet indicating he might not be able to make it. As a result, he had felt both angry at them and doubtful of himself. During his first week of active duty, his anxiety about his situation and his rage at his parents had mounted steadily until he became delusional about having killed his mother. Later, during hospitalization, the patient reported that the original telephone call to his mother had been extremely reassuring and had enabled him to cope much better with his acute disorganization.

When a patient in an acute crisis is being interviewed in the psychotherapist's office and is talking a lot about a particular person, it is often helpful to use the telephone to call the "significant other" during the interview. The therapist may himself gather information from the other person or may let the patient and the other person talk together, observing and listening in on another extension. This not only helps in understanding the nature of the interaction between the patient and the other person, but also may allow the therapist to guide the interaction so that beginning resolution may take place.

OTHER ISSUES RELATED TO THE TELEPHONE

Use of the telephone in psychotherapy introduces a definite problem in the area of confidentiality. Because the telephone is so easy to use and because it facilitates the quick flow of information among a large number of people, much private and personal material gets communicated to people who have no personal ties or strong sense of responsibility to the patient. This is complicated by the fact that, unlike written communication, the telephone leaves no permanent record as to what was actually said. This may make the giver of information less careful about how much he says and how carefully he says it, and it may give the receiver of information more opportunity to enlarge upon the message on the basis of his own unconscious processes.

Another special issue related to the telephone is the question of charging a fee. Because the patient is not in the office, and because most telephone calls are so brief and seemingly trivial, it might appear unnecessary and perhaps even ludicrous to charge a fee. However, for certain patients with whom contact is maintained solely by phone, or who consume a considerable amount of time over the telephone it is appropriate and even obligatory to discuss fees and then charge according to some reasonable plan.

Example 24-6. A 23-year-old, unmarried woman came to a psychiatric clinic in acute distress. During the initial interview, the patient told a vague and rambling story of multiple interpersonal conflicts with her family and boyfriends. The psychiatrist agreed to see her for brief psychotherapy and prescribed a minor tranquilizer for several days. The patient appeared for her second interview seductively and colorfully dressed. She talked further about her interpersonal difficulties but was obviously distressed by the interview and the proximity of the therapist.

She failed to appear for her third appointment but, over the next month, called the therapist on several occasions. At first, she identified herself, apologized for missing her appointment while expressing her eagerness to get help, and resolved to come in for her next appointment. As time went on, however, her telephone calls changed in character. She began to disguise herself by using different names and different voices. Because of the reaction she elicited from her psychotherapist by her failure to keep appointments, she began to phone other psychiatrists on emergency call and talk to them. After several months she became notorious among all the psychiatrists on call at that hospital for her hysterical and deceptive behavior. She was well known by the operators and even by some doctors in non-psychiatric clinics. Although her behavior was looked upon with a mixture of anger and amusement, it was nevertheless apparent that she was attempting to cope with considerable personal distress.

Finally, a plan was worked out to give her the kind of help which would avoid the problems she felt in the close interpersonal contact of a face-to-face interview. She was assigned as a case to a particular psychotherapist who agreed to treat her in telephone therapy. She was told that all of her telephone calls would be referred to him as early in the contact as possible. She was not encouraged to come in for a face-to-face interview, but rather was encouraged to telephone her therapist whenever she needed to. She was also told that she would be charged for each telephone contact she made. With this plan in operation, the frequency of the patient's calls decreased markedly, as did her use of deception and evasion, and she was able to maintain a moderately stable relationship, via the telephone, with her assigned therapist.

A final special issue related to the telephone is the power and influence it lends the user. This is dramatically illustrated by the following story,

which appeared in the *New York Times*.[12]

On September 6, 1949, a psychotic veteran, Howard B. Unruh, in a mad rampage in the streets of Camden, New Jersey, killed thirteen people, and then returned home. Emergency crews bringing up machine guns, shotguns, and tear gas bombs, opened fire. At this point, an editor of the *Camden Evening Courier* looked up Unruh's name in the telephone directory and called him. Unruh stopped firing and answered,
"Hello."
"This Howard?"
"Yes. . . ."
"Why are you killing people?"
"I don't know. I can't answer that yet. I'll have to talk to you later. I'm too busy now."

Somehow, for a few moments, the telephone had made it possible to establish communication with a man in the midst of a frenzied, psychotic self-defense.

The previously discussed special properties of the telephone, individually or in combination, are what make it a powerful instrument. It jumps spatial barriers to interpersonal contact; it can be used at any time to reach persons ordinarily inaccessible; because it is a machine, it has its own demand quality and can be very intrusive; it allows the gathering and giving of a large amount of information quickly. Because of these qualities, the psychotherapist has an expanded capacity to listen, to change perception, to introduce new ideas, to suggest courses of action, and generally to help reestablish the equilibrium of disturbed interpersonal systems.

The potential power of the telephone is clear. The critical issue for the therapist is how to make use of it. His decisions will depend upon his awareness of how the medium can be used, its undesirable side effects, his own personal feelings about the medium, and his reactions to the kinds of patients who typically use it. This chapter provides a general introduction to these matters.

SUMMARY

The telephone is becoming an increasingly important tool in psychotherapy. The evidence indicates that individuals, both therapists and patients, react to and use the telephone in different ways. Aside from these individual differences, almost all therapists use the telephone in their practice to some extent. Because of these two factors, it is important to examine the properties of the telephone as a medium of communication and relate these properties to the way patients use the medium, the potential uses of the medium in a planned way by psychotherapists, and several special issues that arise in association with the use of the telephone in psychotherapy. This chapter has discussed these relationships and, in some cases, illustrated them with clinical material.

REFERENCES

1. Rosenblum, L.: "Telephone Therapy," presented at a meeting of the American Psychological Association, San Francisco, September 1968.
2. Litman, Robert E. et al.: "Suicide-Prevention Telephone Service," *J. Am. Med. Ass.,* **192**:21, 1965.
3. Tabachnick, N., and D. J. Klugman: "No Name — A Study of Anonymous Suicidal Telephone Calls," *Psychiatry,* **28**:79, 1965.
4. Brockopp, G. W., and D. Lester: "The Masturbator," case reports of the Erie County Suicide Prevention Center.
5. Beebe, John E.: "Allowing the Patient to Call Home: A Therapy of Acute Schizophrenia," *Psychotherapy,* **5**:18, 1968.
6. Catanzaro, R. J., and W. G. Green: "WATS Telephone Therapy: New Follow-Up Technique for Alcoholics," *Am. J. Psychiat.,* **126**:1024, 1970.
7. Wolf, A., E. K. Schwartz et al.: "Training in Psychoanalysis in Groups without Face-to-Face Contact," *Am. J. Psychother.,* **23**:448, 1969.
8. Owens, H. E.: "Hypnosis by Phone," *Am. J. Clin. Hypn.,* **13**:57, 1970.
9. McLuhan, Marshall: "The Telephone," *Understanding Media,* New American Library, New York, 1964, chap. 27.
10. Tabachnick and Klugman: loc. cit.
11. Beebe: loc. cit.
12. *New York Times,* Sept. 7, 1949.

JARED R. TINKLENBERG, M.D.

CHAPTER 25

Drugs and Psychotherapy: General Issues

The appropriate use of drugs greatly increases the range of behavioral disorders which can be effectively treated by the clinician. For certain types of psychiatric disorders, such as the functional psychosis, drugs are the foundation for all other types of therapy.[1] Since most evidence suggests that in the future psychopharmacology will play an increasingly important role in the management of behavioral disorders, it behooves the clinician to be familiar with the appropriate use of drugs. This chapter outlines general guidelines intrinsic to the effective use of psychotropic agents. The following three chapters present more detailed information regarding the use of drugs in three different clinical situations: (1) psychotic reactions, (2) anxiety disturbances, and (3) mood disorders (mania and depression).

The use of psychotropic drugs in treating patients can be divided into two phases: (1) treatment planning and initial implementation and (2) maintenance therapy. In the treatment planning phase, information is obtained from a variety of sources so that plans for therapy can be formulated. An appropriate (initial) question is "Does this patient demonstrate behavioral patterns which could be usefully modified by drugs?" Because there is an ever-burgeoning number of potent psychotropic agents which are useful in certain clinical situations and contraindicated in others, precision in answering this question is essential. In addition, an even wider array of drugs with even greater specificity will undoubtedly become available in the future. Precision is also important as a greater variety of nonpharmacological treatment becomes available to patients in many communities. There may be a choice of different therapeutic modalities, and so the problem is one of selection: "Which particular treatment modality or blend of modalities is indicated for this patient?" Furthermore, in some parts of the world there is an increasing tendency toward use of the team approach, with several different individuals being involved in the therapeutic effort. The physician is often most active in initial diagnosis and treatment; others may be more involved in continuing care. Thus, skillful initial treatment planning, including decisions about drugs, is of paramount importance.

Accurate personal and family history data are often illuminating. Has the patient had episodes of behavior in the past which are similar to the present one? The past is an excellent predictor of the future: if the patient previously responded well to certain medications, they should be repeated. Familial response patterns to psychotropic medications and their close chemical relatives should also be taken into consideration. If a close blood relative with a similar behavioral disorder responded well to a given drug, one might first try that drug in the absence of other guidelines.

PATIENT PARTICIPATION

A prime consideration in treating psychiatric patients is establishing and maintaining trustful respect between patient and therapist. This therapeutic alliance can be greatly facilitated by making the patient an active participant in each stage of the therapeutic process.

During initial treatment planning, it is usually helpful to discuss treatment goals openly with the patient, including what behavior one wishes to modify with drugs. For example, often one will discuss with an acutely disturbed psychotic patient the goal of reducing anxiety to the point of drowsiness during the day when the patient is left alone in a quiet room. I will say, "We'll want to adjust the dosage of this drug so that you'll be relaxed enough to occasionally catnap during the day and get a good sound sleep during the night." When patients are actively included in the treatment planning and understand the guides for drug taking, they are more cooperative in taking medication.

The clinician must realize that people will view drugs very differently. Some may view the drug as the irrational authority of a domineering parent; others may hope the drug will relieve their distress but fear that such relief will evict them from their present enjoyed status as a sick patient. Two different depressed individuals might resist medication in such diametric ways as, "I'm not worth the medication, and I'll be contributing to the shortage of drugs in India," to, "I haven't suffered enough in my depression and need to do more penance." A normally active, assertive male might respond to suggestions of drugs with, "Good. Now I know I'm sick."

A clinician may be able to determine some of the patient's conscious and unconscious inclinations toward medications by obtaining a detailed history from the patient, from his relatives, and, if indicated, from former therapists about how faithfully the patient took the medication, about what he did when he found that taking a given drug was ineffective, and so forth. If the patient is particularly opposed to any form of medication, then the clinician must balance the possible gains from drug effect against the increase in negativity and resistance on the part of the patient forced to take medication.

The patient should be told about the course of pharmacological treatment as it is planned, including the period of time before clinical changes can be expected, guides for adjustments in medication dosages, frequency of drug dosage changes, and expected period of time during which the drug will be administered. Patients need to know why dosages will be varied until the proper one for that patient has been found. Thus, one might say to the patient, "Different people require different doses of this medicine. We will have to regulate the dosage depending upon how you respond, and this will be determined partially by what else is happening in your life. You will have to be aware of how you are responding to the drug — changes in your thoughts, your feelings, and your behavior. So we will work together, and you will tell me about any changes so we can adjust the dosages appropriately." For sophisticated patients, an analogy with insulin may be useful; e.g., "Just as diabetic individuals require different amounts of insulin, depending upon what they eat and how much they exercise, you'll benefit from different amounts of this drug depending on the stress in your life."

Different behavioral guidelines will be required for different patients, but these must be considered in the total clinical context. For some patients, a specific phenomenon such as agitation may provide a useful index for drug titration; for others it may be worthless. For example, when panic is accompanied by auditory hallucinations, it is often part of a psychotic reaction that responds to antipsychotic drugs; however, the panic of agoraphobia is usually made worse by phenothiazines. Thus, blind adherence to a single "target symptom" is poor strategy.

The patient should be told about possible side effects, particularly those most likely to occur. Severely depressed people may not complain of the side effects of a dry mouth, or the orthostatic hypotension, impotence, urinary retention, and constipation, but in many instances will surreptitiously stop taking the medicine. The cost of medication should be discussed because for some patients this is a major reason for premature discontinuation of drugs. Most patients should be told that all psychotropic agents have certain risks just as the use of aspirin or penicillin entails certain risks. The best realistic protection from adverse side effects for the patient is the ready availability of the physician. Phone calls should be encouraged, as relatively few patients are likely to abuse this privilege. For example, it is wise to request the patient to telephone you when he experiences any marked change in his behavior, thoughts, or feelings.

Not only patients but also treatment staff should be included in initial treatment planning. These people, who often become very skilled observers, can provide invaluable clinical information which cannot be otherwise obtained. In addition, overall therapeutic effectiveness and staff cooperation is enhanced. Where appropriate, selected members of the patient's family can usefully be included in this stage of therapy. Incorporating patient, staff, and family in planning often prevents one of the major reasons for treatment failure: the patient stops taking his medication.

PSYCHOLOGICAL CONTRIBUTION TO DRUG EFFECTS

The clinician should bear in mind that even with potent psychotropic medications, psychological variables are very important determinants of the "drug effect." Each clinician should develop his own style in administering drugs so as to convey maximal confidence in the drug's therapeutic properties. Adequate knowledge of drugs and their side effects results in an increased confidence that, communicated to the patient, may enhance overall effectiveness of the total therapy program. In addition, thorough knowledge of expected side effects and how to treat them will decrease premature discontinuation of potentially effective drugs and prevent premature change of medications.

The clinician is always balancing psychological and pharmacological considerations when determining treatment plans. If a patient has a very strong preference for a certain type of medication and the clinical indications are moot, then one might reasonably comply with the patient's request while adding an admonition such as, "I think another type of drug will turn out to be best for you, but I'm willing to try your preference, as these drugs are quite similar." Patient and therapist should then agree on the behavioral indices for improvement, on what adjustments might be required, and on how long a trial period should be attempted. However, when there are very strong indications for one particular pharmacological treatment which the patient is resisting, one should be prepared to consider overriding the patient's wishes.

ALLERGIES

In initial planning, the psychiatrist should assess the likelihood that certain drugs are absolutely contraindicated because of possible allergic or idiosyncratic responses. He should inquire about the specific drug under consideration, related drugs, and unusual responses to other drugs. For example, if the patient is psychotic and I am contemplating the use of a phenothiazine, I will ask the patient (and other information sources), "Are you allergic to any medications? Have you ever taken_____?" (Name several common phenothiazines.) "Have you ever taken_____?" (Specific trade and generic name of the phenothiazine I'm considering.) If the patient describes an unusual drug reaction, full details should be obtained. Many patients will initially claim they are allergic to a psychotropic drug, although later information clearly indicates that they merely experienced a physiological side effect of that drug. For example, an "allergy" to phenothiazines often turns out to be the common side effect of muscular rigidity from excessive extrapyramidal stimulation. In such instances, phenothiazines can and should be used if clinically indicated. On the other hand, if there are suggestions of drug-induced blood dyscrasias, angioneurotic edema, urticaria, breathing difficulties, or other severe allergic reactions, all chemically related drugs are absolutely contraindicated. In addition, if the patient gives a personal or familial history of asthma, hay fever, allergic rhinitis, or allergic reactions to a wide variety of antigens, the use of any drug entails increased risk and should be approached with special caution. The clinician is well advised to remember that inappropriate use of drugs is one of the relatively few psychiatric treatments by which a patient can be quickly killed — via allergic reactions. All details of the allergy history should be legibly recorded on the patient's record, including the patient's negative response to the specific question regarding the drug to be prescribed. I clearly label and underline information about allergies at the top of my initial clinical note; this practice both underscores the importance of allergic reactions to all treatment personnel and makes this vital information always accessible in emergency situations.

OLD AND NEW DRUGS

There are already far more psychotropic drugs on the market than the clinician can or should master. The time-honored dictum is to become familiar with one or two drugs in each pharmacological class. The psychological advantages of effectively and confidently using a familiar drug probably outweigh the actual pharmacological differences among the various drugs within a given class. One must expect that new psychotropic agents will continue to be introduced to the market with great fanfare and that pharmaceutical companies will accentuate the assets of their products and minimize the liabilities. The history of clinical pharmacology is replete with examples of new drugs heralded as both safe and efficacious which turn out to be neither. There should be more evidence for a therapeutic breakthrough in psychopharmacological treatment than is found in clinical reports accompanying most drug advertisements. Especially recommended for balanced objective drug evaluations are the reports appearing in the well-edited *The Medical Letter* and the *Journal of Clinical Pharmacology and Therapeutics.* Clinicians should remember that the probability that newly introduced drugs will be more effective than old drugs is very small, whereas the risks of unforeseen serious adverse reactions are appreciable.[2] One might wisely follow Osler's aphorism, "Be not the first to embrace a new treatment nor the last to relinquish an old."

REFERENCES

1. Hollister, Leo E.: *Clinical Use of Psychotherapeutic Drugs,* Charles C Thomas, Springfield, Ill., 1973, p. 45.
2. Modell, W.: "The Hazards of New Drugs," *Science,* **139**:1180–1185, 1963.

Drugs and Psychotherapy: Antipsychotic Agents

Antipsychotic agents include three major pharmacological groups of drugs: the phenothiazines, the butyrophenones, and the thioxanthenes; as well as a small number of unrelated chemicals. These drugs are also called the major tranquilizers, ataractics, or neuroleptics. The term *antipsychotic* will be used in this chapter because it most accurately refers to the clinical uses and properties of the drugs — the amelioration of those psychotic disorders marked by problems of perception, thinking disturbances, inappropriate emotional changes, and alterations in attention, symptoms especially prominent in the schizophrenias. The term *tranquilizer* is misleading because antipsychotics do more than simply calm or pacify patients.

INDICATIONS

The many kinds of psychotic conditions encountered are described in Chapter 5, "Evaluation and Treatment of Psychotic States." The agents described in this chapter are mainly used in the treatment of functional psychoses marked primarily by thought disorders, e.g., the schizophrenias. They are only rarely used in functional mood disorders (e.g., mania and depression), where other

families of drugs are useful, as described in Chapter 28, "Treatment of Depression and Mania." Similarly the antipsychotic drugs described in this chapter are only occasionally used in toxic and organic psychoses. For the most part, then, this chapter deals with the treatment of the schizophrenias and related states, many of which are described in detail in Rosenbaum.[1]

At times, of course, the presenting clinical picture is one of a disturbed patient who is between the extremes of definitely psychotic and clearly nonpsychotic. In such borderline cases, a well-monitored trial of antipsychotic drugs is warranted; if the drug induces a clinical improvement, the diagnosis of psychosis is likely. If there is no response or the patient becomes worse, a diagnosis of psychosis becomes questionable and a shift to other types of psychotropic medication or other treatment is indicated. When psychotic reactions accompany definite organic disorders, such as with drug overdose or vascular insufficiency, the initial focus of treatment is on remediable etiological factors. Antipsychotic agents may be used in addition if still warranted.

Antipsychotic agents should *not* be used in the treatment of bad trips, e.g., paranoid and anxious reactions to lysergic acid diethylamide (LSD), marihuana, mescaline, and other psychedelic agents. The reasons for this prohibition plus the suggestions for proper management of such bad trips are given in Chapter 8.

CLINICAL EFFECTS

Most antipsychotic drugs have anxiety-reducing characteristics. In psychotic individuals these anti-anxiety effects often occur without accompanying marked sedation. These agents induce consistent improvement in such psychotic symptoms as inappropriate or blunted affect, hallucinations and other altered perceptions, emotional withdrawal, delusions and other thought disturbances, paranoid projections, and unwarranted hostility. Antipsychotic drugs reduce the intensity and intrusiveness of distressing psychotic ideation and feeling. Statements such as, "Yes, I still hear something like voices, but I can no longer hear what they're saying," are frequent clinical testimonials to the usefulness of these drugs.

The antipsychotic drugs reduce a wide range of motor activity, especially the bizarre or stereotyped movements of the psychotic individual. These motor-inhibiting properties can be particularly helpful in curbing the belligerent physical assaultiveness intrinsic to some psychotic reactions. More frequently, antipsychotic drugs provide blanketing relief from excessive motor responsiveness to external or internal stimuli. However, motor inhibitions can be experienced as unpleasant "chemical straitjacketing," particularly with young, athletic people whose typical response to anxiety is increased physical activity.

In nonpsychotic individuals, however, antipsychotic drugs usually induce marked sedation. Some experienced clinicians use these differential sedating effects as an empirical test for psychosis; an individual who can tolerate high doses of antipsychotic drugs and not fall asleep or become distressed must be psychotic. Or conversely, it is healthy to get sleepy or sick from these potent drugs. Although the sedating properties of the antipsychotics are sometimes used for treating anxious or depressed patients who clearly are not psychotic, the antianxiety drugs described in the next chapter offer a wider range of effectiveness and safety. Hollister describes the use of these potent antipsychotic agents in treating nonpsychotic patients as analagous to driving a tack with a sledge hammer. It can be done, but a deft touch is required, and any mistake is likely to be painful. The best sedatives are sedatives, not antipsychotic agents!

Most of the antipsychotic drugs can be used to potentiate analgesics and some have antiemetic properties. However, use of the antipsychotics for these purposes is outdated since there are newer, more effective antiemetic and analgesic drugs with fewer adverse side effects (unless you are treating a patient who is vomiting or in pain *and* is schizophrenic).

In the treatment of psychosis, the appropriate use of antipsychotic medications is essential and, as described by Hollister, should be considered the cornerstone of all other treatment endeavors.[2-4] A number of intensive studies have shown that treatment regimes which do not include antipsychotic medication are usually ineffective. Thus, a predominant consideration of the clinician in treating psychotic patients is to establish and maintain adequate tissue levels of an appropriate antipsychotic agent. The next two sections of this chapter describe how this objective can be achieved by effective treatment planning.

Mechanism of Effect

The exact mechanisms whereby antipsychotic drugs exert their effects have not been defined. Hence there is a plethora of models available to explain the antipsychotic actions of these drugs. A currently popular model attributes these effects to the regulation of the action of brain neurotransmitters by stabilizing the membranes of the synaptic clefts so that norepinephrine, dopamine, and other neurotransmitters do not have ready access to their receptors. Other models emphasize the effects of these agents on the three major integrating systems of the brain: the limbic system, the hypothalamus, and the reticular activating system. Alterations in the brain systems might cause the central nervous system to be generally less responsive to external and internal stimuli.

One intriguing feature of most clinically useful antipsychotic drugs is their ability to induce excessive extrapyramidal stimulation. This stimulation, which is manifested by several different motor syndromes, including one that closely mimics Parkinson's disease, is probably mediated by a decreased availability of the neurotransmitter dopamine. Possible relationships between dopaminergic mechanisms and psychosis are a fertile area for contemporary research.

Another interesting characteristic of the antipsychotic drugs is that they normalize some of the deviant behavior of the psychotic individual. However, in normal people, these drugs do not markedly alter attention, thoughts, or perceptions, although they do exert profound soporific effects. This type of drug which primarily ameliorates psychopathology is termed *reparative*. A common example would be aspirin, which reduces fever but does not lower the temperature of normal individuals. By contrast, the antianxiety drugs discussed in the next chapter are termed *compensatory* because they affect normal physiology in a direction similar to their effects on pathological processes.

CHOICE OF DRUGS

Within the phenothiazines, the antipsychotic group most extensively used, there are three subtypes, based on the type of side chain attached to the basic phenothiazine nucleus. These subtypes are the aliphatic, the piperidine, and the piperazine. Details on the structure and pharmacology of these compounds can be found in Denber and Hollister.[5,6] Some well-known drugs are listed by both generic and proprietary names in Table 26-1; the second column lists the drugs in their estimated dosage equivalent to the most extensively used phenothiazine, chlorpromazine (Thorazine®).

Table 26-1 Antipsychotic Drugs — Names and Dosage Guide

Generic and Trade Name	Estimated Equivalent Dose (mg)	Usual Oral Range (mg/day)
Phenothiazines		
Aliphatic:		
Chlorpromazine (Thorazine)	100	200–1,500
Triflupromazine (Vesprin)	25	50– 200
Piperidine:		
Thioridazine (Mellaril)	100	200– 800
Piperazine:		
Acetophenazine (Tindal)	20	60– 120
Carphenazine (Proketazine)	25	75– 600
Fluphenazine (Prolixin, Permatil)	2	2– 40
Perphenazine (Trilafon)	10	12– 96
Prochlorperazine (Compazine)	15	75– 200
Trifluoperazine (Stelazine)	5	10– 75
Butyrophenones		
Haloperidol (Haldol)	2	3– 30
Thioxanthenes		
Chlorprothixene (Taractan)	100	100– 800
Thiothixene (Navane)	2	10– 60

The last column gives the usual daily dose range for each drug.

The phenothiazines are by far the most prominent and widely used and form the major consideration of this chapter. There are special qualities of nonphenothiazine groups, however, which deserve consideration. Even though less is known about the butyrophenones and thioxanthenes, their side effects, and their range of efficacy, they do not have cross-sensitivity to the phenothiazines or to each other. They are useful when the patient is allergic or unresponsive to phenothiazines. In addition, one of the butyrophenones, haloperidol, seems particularly useful in the treatment of agitation, mania, chronic or frequent assaultiveness in psychotic patients, head banging, and the rare disorder of Gilles de la Tourette's disease, characterized by tics and involuntary vocal utterances. [7] Because the onset of excessive extrapyramidal stimulation is abrupt and almost invariable with haloperidol, most clinicians increase the dosage of this drug a maximum of only 1 to 3 mg/day. Anti-Parkinsonian agents are usually initiated at the outset and should be given for several days after haloperidol has been discontinued. The liquid preparation of haloperidol is very concentrated and should be diluted with water or juice so that less of any given dose can be inadvertently lost. The thioxanthenes exert less sedation and extrapyramidal stimulation than haloperidol and thus are especially indicated for patients in whom drowsiness or Parkinsonian symptoms are to be avoided.

Dosage

Dosage schedules vary widely, as Table 26-1 reveals, and are influenced by several factors. These factors include (1) age, weight, and physical condition of the patient; (2) severity of symptoms; (3) stage in the course of illness at which treatment is being designed; and (4) appearance of undesirable or dangerous side effects. The upper limits of the dosage ranges given in Table 26-1 for chlorpromazine and their equivalents for other drugs are higher than those in the *Physician's Desk Reference* (PDR). [8] The PDR schedules are often conservative and should not assume the definitive importance they sometimes do. The side effects of the phenothiazines are many and varied; they will be described in some detail later in this chapter. Suffice it to say here that the recognition and management of side effects of phenothiazine

administration should be fully in the clinician's mind when he starts their use.

Starting Drug Treatment. Dosages described in this section will be in terms of orally administered chlorpromazine unless otherwise specified. The usual initial dose ranges from 10 mg (as would be appropriate for a small, debilitated, elderly woman) to 150 mg for a large, young, agitated male. Vital signs should be regularly determined because of the cardiovascular effects described below. Assuming such signs remain stable, intervals between dosages depend on the time course of peak sedative and cardiovascular effects; these usually occur three to four hours after oral administration and one to two hours after intramuscular (*never* intravenous) administration. During the first twenty-four hours of treatment, one should not exceed a total dose of 750 mg of chlorpromazine; in the second and third twenty-four-hour periods, the maxima are 1,000 and 1,500 mg, respectively. Increases greater than these are of dubious value in treatment of the psychosis and carry increased risks of cardiovascular reactions and seizures. If, even while using these maximum dosages, the patient remains seriously anxious, agitated, or assaultive, the addition of a sedative agent such as a barbiturate is indicated.

Oral preparations have a greater margin of safety than intramuscular ones. Liquid preparations diluted with juice reduce contact irritation, are more predictably absorbed than pills, and hence may be preferable initially. Patients should rinse their mouths thoroughly after each dose. Intramuscular injections can be used when patients overtly or covertly refuse oral administration, but intramuscular injections must be given with great caution because of the greater risks of hypotension, cardiac arrhythmia, and subcutaneous necrosis. [9] Speed of onset is not an indication for parenteral administration, since the onset of effects after an intramuscular (IM) injection is about ten minutes, while the onset of an oral preparation is about twenty. The saving of ten or fifteen minutes is seldom worth the increased risk to the patient, particularly since conventional sedatives or physical restraints can be used to control agitation. When the IM dose is mandatory, it should be given deep in the gluteal muscles at a dosage of one-half to one-third the oral dose. Antipsychotic preparations should not be given intravenously because of the greater dangers of cardiovascular difficulties and other problems.

When beginning treatment with antipsychotic agents, supine and standing pulse and blood pressure should be closely monitored. Any irregularities in vital signs require the next dose to be held. Arrhythmias should be investigated with an electrocardiogram tracing.

Therapists usually start with about 250 mg daily in divided doses, increasing the dosage by 100 to 200 mg/day until the desired amelioration is achieved, side effects become intolerable, or the maximal dosage limits for the drug are reached and more medication becomes risky. In the acute phase of treatment, the daily dosage is given three or four times a day so that the patient can more readily adjust to side effects and to assure that the nursing staff will observe the patient frequently for untoward reactions.

Clinicians who are pharmacologically unsophisticated often prescribe antipsychotic medications in dosages that are too small. These agents should rarely, if ever, be used in the placebo dosage range. If the clinician must resort to subterfuge in treatment, the therapeutic relationship is in trouble and should be reexamined. Placebo-range doses carry little potential for sustained benefits, but the risks of allergic sensitization persist.

Extrapyramidal motor symptoms are a frequent occurrence with phenothiazine administration. They should be looked for and, if they appear, treated. Use of anti-Parkinsonian drugs prophylactically, i.e., before the appearance of symptoms, is indicated only when high doses of an antipsychotic drug with pronounced extrapyramidal stimulation will be used, or in patients with a personal or family history of extrapyramidal disorders.

Restricting the use of anti-Parkinsonian agents reduces the possibility of untoward drug-drug interactions, allergic reactions, sensitizations, and unnecessary expense.

On the other hand, if extrapyramidal signs such as Parkinsonian symptoms, dystonias, and oculogyric crises do appear, the patient cannot be expected to maintain a trusting relationship with his physician if the physician did not also treat the extrapyramidal symptoms. The piperazine group of phenothiazines and the butyrophenones are particularly likely to induce extrapyramidal effects. Anti-Parkinsonian drugs are started with low doses and gradually increased if needed. Since most of them are rapidly metabolized, divided dosages should be administered twice daily. Some commonly used anti-Parkinsonian medications and their dosages are given in Table 26-2.

The effects of most phenothiazines are quite similar. It is much better for the beginning clinician to acquaint himself thoroughly with the effects of a few of these drugs than to be only superficially familiar with the action of many. The same applies to the effects of and knowledge about anti-Parkinsonian agents. Over the course of several weeks, most patients adjust to excessive extrapyramidal stimulation of the antipsychotic drug so that the dosage of anti-Parkinsonian drugs can be tapered.[10] Both phenothiazines and the anti-Parkinsonian medications usually have significant anticholinergic properties; therefore these

Table 26-2 Anti-Parkinsonian Agents and Doses

Generic Name	Trade Name	Daily Dosage (mg) (divided into 2 to 3 doses)
Benztropine mesylate	Cogentin	1– 8
Biperiden	Akineton	2– 8
Procyclidine	Kemadrin	2–20
Trihexyphenidyl	Artane	2–10

drugs should be used with caution in conditions worsened by parasympathetic blockage, such as prostatic hypertrophy, narrow-angle glaucoma, coronary artery insufficiency, and paralytic ileus.

Continuing Drug Treatment

Nearly all schizophrenic patients respond to treatment within four weeks. General adaptation, affective state, sleep patterns, and specific symptomatology improve. Such changes should be frequently discussed with the patient, his relatives, and the treatment staff. If the patient has not responded substantially within four weeks, the diagnosis should be reconsidered and assessments made to assure that the patient is actually taking the prescribed medication.

The most common reason patients do not "respond" to medication is that they do not take it. For some patients, several days of parenteral medication to assure adequate tissue levels is useful; for others, liquid preparations or a tablet crushed and administered in jelly is helpful, especially if regurgitation is prevented by carefully observing the patient for the following half-hour. One should not change drugs before these maneuvers have been tried and adequate trial of an effective dose level has been established. Premature change of medication is inefficient and may needlessly sensitize a patient to a drug. If, however, the diagnosis has been affirmed and the patient has not responded during the four-week period despite adequate dosage levels, a change to a medication from a different chemical subtype is indicated. Dosage of the new drug can be determined from Table 26-1, for example, 5 mg of trifluoperazine for each 100 mg of chlorpromazine the patient had been taking.

Combinations of different antipsychotic preparations are usually no more effective than adequate doses of a single agent.[11] However, since the patient's acceptance of the medication regime is an essential component of adequate treatment, and since some patients tolerate specific antipsychotic side effects poorly, in certain clinical situations the use of two agents might permit reduction in the dosage of a preparation which induced particularly distressing side effects.

Long-Term Management

As previously emphasized, the single most important factor in successful long-term management of psychotic patients is usually the maintenance of effective levels of medication. Adequate medication is necessary if psychotherapy and milieu treatment are to be helpful. After the first few weeks, the dosage schedule should be consolidated to reduce unnecessary dosage throughout the day.[12] Most commonly, either the entire daily dose, or at least its major portion, is taken one hour before bedtime. Evening administration has several advantages: the soporific effects aid sleep and reduce the need for sleeping pills; the side effects of cardiovascular change, motor inhibition, extrapyramidal stimulation, and sedation take place primarily during sleep; and single large doses are more financially economical for patients and require less personnel time.

Long-acting and sustained-release forms of phenothiazines are available for both oral and intramuscular administration. The sustained-release oral forms are not recommended; they are unnecessary, the amount of absorbed medication is unpredictable, and they are costly.[13] A few intramuscular depot preparations, such as fluphenazine enanthate and fluphenazine deconate, are currently available and provide sustained release. These and similar compounds which will undoubtedly become available in the future are particularly useful in treating patients who cannot or will not come under regular medical supervision and who have shown unreliability about taking medicines for a variety of reasons, such as poor judgment, fear, avoiding expense, and so on. Such long-acting medications are injected once every one to three weeks in doses of 25 to 50 mg with doses adjusted, as always, to the patient's response.

Following hospitalization, patient, therapist, and family must constantly monitor symptoms and behavior to be sure the patient is maintained on adequate but not excessive levels of medication. It is often tempting for patients to reduce or stop medication after a while for several reasons: patients weary of the unpleasant side effects; they resent the nuisance of following a regular medication schedule; they are indignant at the implication of "once mentally ill, always mentally ill" that the medication raises; they resent the limitations the medication may exert in their daily lives, e.g., that they must be careful about driving, operating dangerous machinery, and mixing phenothiazines with alcohol, antihistamines, and other drugs.

Some patients, especially those with acute first psychotic episodes, may indeed do well without psychotropic medication once they recover fully from the psychotic experience. Others, however, especially those who have had several psychotic episodes but who have not been chronically psychotic, do poorly when phenothiazines are reduced or eliminated. Unfortunately, it is difficult to predict which patients will require long-term maintenance. The most common signs of inadequate medication are a reemergence of sleep disturbance, recrudescence of psychotic behavior, growing anxiety, and pervasive unease around others.

Relapses necessitating rehospitalization are more common after discontinuance of antipsychotic drugs.[14] Characteristically, these psychotic exacerbations do not immediately follow cessation of medication; instead, there is a lag of several weeks to several months before regression is apparent. Unfortunately, the lengthy lag period often misleads patients, their families, and sometimes unwary clinicians. The apparent freedom from need of medication and the exhilarating "I don't need drugs any more" is taken as a sign of recovery, and the later regression is inappropriately attributed to extraneous events rather than to inadequate medication.

Balanced against the increased possibility of psychotic relapses upon reduction or cessation of medication are risks inherent in continuing treatment with potent psychotropic agents. Since some of these risks, which are discussed in subsequent sections on complications, appear to be caused partially by the total cumulative amount of medication taken, the most desirable course is to slowly reduce the maintenance to the lowest level compatible with adequate function. Delicate titration and ongoing clinical surveillance are required.

TREATMENT PLANNING

General Remarks

There is far more to treatment planning than knowledgeable use of psychotropic medication. Many of the personal and psychological issues described in the preceding chapter apply to all uses of medication, whether it be antipsychotic, antianxiety, antidepressant, or antimania. As that chapter discussed, effective use of medication is predicated on a collaborative working alliance between doctor and patient.

It is usually helpful to discuss with the patient the benefit he will get from the medication. With paranoid patients concerned with control of their internal and external environments, one can say, "This medication will help you control your thoughts and feelings. It will help you keep your ideas organized. This will help you sort out your imagination from what is really happening." With hypochondriacal patients, one can emphasize how the medicine will help him relax and reduce his somatic discomfort. I usually avoid the term *drug* because of its negative connotation.

Acute patients often have slept poorly preceding treatment, and phenothiazines often have pronounced sedative effects in the early days of administration. Thus, one can say to the patient, "You look tired, and you tell me you haven't been getting enough sleep. Together, we will be adjusting the dosage of your medication so that you occasionally nap during the day and sleep soundly every night." For patients who are experiencing disturbing hallucinations, one may say, "We will adjust your medicine so that these voices are less frightening. We may not be able to make them go away completely, but we can make them less distressing." If the patient is assaultive, destructive, or overactive, one can titrate medication until the psychotic elements of these behaviors are reduced; the patient will then become amenable to other modalities of therapy. Conversely, if emotional withdrawal is a prominent aspect of the clinical picture, a guide for the level of antipsychotic drugs will be the level of accessibility of the patient to others. Delusions and other specific thought disorders are less useful indices for drug titration, as they do not sensitively reflect clinical improvement. Thought disturbances commonly persist in less compelling intensity for extended periods beyond the time when other parameters have markedly improved.

As much as possible I make initial treatment planning a joint endeavor between patient, treatment staff, and, where feasible, the family. These potent drugs often produce dramatic improvement in the psychotic patient's condition; therefore, the therapist is able to maximize his role image as a helping agent for the patient and his family. This, in turn, enhances subsequent therapeutic endeavors.

The common side effects of the medication warrant discussion with the patient. For example, with chlorpromazine the patient should be warned about orthostatic hypotension and advised against suddenly standing up after he has been sitting or lying down. The most common side effects to be anticipated with the patient are described below in the section "Contraindications and Complications."

A correctly predicted side effect engenders confidence and respect for the therapist's clinical ability, and the chance of a surreptitiously discontinued medication because of troublesome side effects is reduced. Finally, discussion of drug effects may enhance the psychological sophistication of the patient by encouraging him to discuss his perceptions and feelings openly. I often start interview sessions by asking about probable side effects. These factors interact to enhance the overall objective of maintaining trusting respect between patient and therapist that is so essential to successful therapy.

The Resistant Patient

Some patients will resist taking medication as prescribed. The clinician must formulate his treatment plan and especially decide how much coercion will be used. If antipsychotic medication is essential for the management of the patient and adequate nursing personnel are not always available to give parenteral injections to an unwilling patient, one might say, "We will not be able to keep you in our hospital unless you can cooperate with us. Part of this cooperation involves taking medication. If you cannot cooperate at this time by taking your medication, I'm afraid we'll have to transfer you elsewhere." Or if one has the manpower and the mandate to treat all resistant patients, one might say, "You'll have to take this medication. I'd prefer you take it by mouth, but if necessary, we'll have to give it by muscle." After a few parenteral injections, most patients will take the medication orally. On the other hand, if the clinical situation is borderline and the need for antipsychotic medication is moot, one might state, "This medication will probably be helpful to you, but it's not worth a disagreement right now. If you don't improve rapidly, I'll have to insist that you take medication." In every case, the clinician is obliged to carry out his stated decisions or risk loss of credibility and effectiveness.

Some patients tolerate antipsychotic drugs poorly and demonstrate an inadequate clinical response. As these patients tend to be young, less psychotic than most schizophrenics, with retention of insight, pronounced somatization, and an intense need to remain in active control of their activities, they may represent a schizophreniform group rather than true schizophrenia. The ability to tolerate these drugs without marked distress seems to be directly correlated with the severity of the psychosis. Occasionally these patients will markedly benefit from a change of medication to another chemical group.

The Resistant Therapist

Some clinicians either resist entirely the use of medication in the management of psychotic patients or use doses so low that they are pharmacologically ineffective. These therapists often emphasize contemporary trends toward the relativity of all experience and can at times persuasively argue about how drugs interfere with the creative reintegration of the patient and impede the working through of the psychotic element of his life experience. However, despite some concerted investigation, sufficient systematic evidence is still lacking to support these views. There may indeed be a small subgroup of patients for whom a psychotic episode can be a "growth" experience, but at this time it is quite difficult to select such patients prospectively. In addition, antipsychotic drugs used in appropriate doses do not interfere with learning; to the contrary, the acquisition of information may be enhanced with these drugs by increasing the attention span and reducing excessive anxiety.

In most cases, without these drugs psychotic patients are usually less accessible to other modalities of therapy. They can easily become difficult management problems and seriously interfere with the therapy of other patients.

CONTRAINDICATIONS AND COMPLICATIONS: THEIR RECOGNITION AND MANAGEMENT

Antipsychotic drugs produce a host of side effects. Some are a nuisance; some are distressing; some are dangerous. It is our purpose here to call attention to the most serious and most prevalent of these side effects and to give some information about their immediate management. Most side effects are best monitored by direct clinical observation rather than by laboratory tests, although routine laboratory measures are useful in

the first few weeks of therapy to establish the patient's base-line values. More detailed discussions of this topic are to be found in Hollister,[15] Klein and Davis,[16] Redlich and Freedman,[17] and Rosenbaum.[18]

Contraindications

The few absolute contraindications of the antipsychotic drugs are comatose states, severe acute infections, drug intoxications, the presence of bone marrow depression, or clear evidence for previous serious allergic reactions to that chemical group of antipsychotic preparations. Antipsychotic drugs should be prescribed with great care for individuals with histories of blood dyscrasias, especially agranulocytosis. Extrapyramidal, endocrine, renal, and cardiovascular disorders, including arteriosclerosis and hypertension, enhance the risks of the use of these drugs and hence require reassessment of expected clinical benefits to be derived. Similarly, in suicidal patients only a sublethal dose should be prescribed at any given time, although it is difficult to take a lethal overdose of antipsychotic medication unless the patient is debilitated or other drugs are used concurrently.

Complications

Central Nervous System. The most common CNS side effects are those of sedation, extrapyramidal phenomena (including Parkinsonism, dyskinesias, akathisias and paradoxical agitation), lowering of the seizure threshold, potentiation of CNS depressants (especially alcohol, barbiturates, and antihistamines), and production of toxic confusional states.

Sedative effects are most common with chlorpromazine, thioridazine, and butyrophenones. For agitated patients who are sleep-deprived, the sedative effect may be initially beneficial. Patients showing such effects should exert caution about driving or engaging in other activities which demand unimpaired consciousness. When sedation is not wanted, encouraging physical activity is often useful. Sedative effects usually wane significantly after a week, even though the primary antipsychotic activity persists; doctor and patient can anticipate this expectation in the early days of treatment. If excessive drowsiness persists, change to another chemical subtype should be helpful; however, amphetamines or other CNS stimulants are contraindicated.

Extrapyramidal signs are found most commonly with use of the piperazine subtype of phenothiazines and the butyrophenones. The symptoms are quite distressing to patients and are not correlated with therapeutic effectiveness. In addition to Parkinsonian signs, one also encounters dyskinesias involving coordinated, involuntary, and stereotyped rhythmic movements; dystonias marked by spasmodic bodily movements; torticollis; opisthotonus and oculogyric crises, and akathisias, or "restless feet" syndromes, marked by incessant restlessness. Most extrapyramidal overactivity can be rapidly reversed by oral anti-Parkinsonian agents (see Table 26-2). Intramuscular administration can be used in urgent cases. Extrapyramidal signs persist several days after phenothiazines have been discontinued; anti-Parkinsonian drugs should therefore be continued for a few days before gradual tapering off. Where extrapyramidal signs do not respond to anti-Parkinsonian medication, a change to another antipsychotic drug is indicated.

Another type of extrapyramidal disorder, variously termed *tardive dyskinesia, persistent dyskinesia,* or *irreversible dyskinesia,* occurs in patients under long-term treatment with antipsychotic drugs.[19] Characterized by repetitive, uncontrolled movements of the tongue, jaw, and mouth, this syndrome seems to be related to the total cumulative dosage of antipsychotic drugs, although the risk is apparently increased in female patients and in patients who are chronically ill or brain-damaged or who have a previous history of Parkinson's disease. Tardive dyskinesia may be unmasked or aggravated by sudden discontinuance of antipsychotic drugs; reinstituting the offending agent may produce improvement. Although this disorder is

considered irreversible, some improvement usually, but not always, occurs with time. Management of this disorder is often difficult, especially since anti-Parkinsonian drugs are not effective. Cautiously reducing the dosage of the antipsychotic agent but retaining overall therapeutic effectiveness is the difficult-to-achieve clinical goal.

Because antipsychotic drugs lower seizure threshold, patients with a history of seizure disorders should be followed closely. Since antipsychotic drugs potentiate CNS depressants, such depressants should be avoided or very carefully administered.

Toxic confusional states may result from antipsychotic medication, especially in the elderly; such states are marked by an organic brain syndrome with symptoms of recent memory loss, disorientation, and often by visual or haptic hallucinations of vermin or small animals on the bedclothes. Toxic states may be difficult to differentiate from the primary psychosis for which medication was started; a change of medication may be the only empirical way to make the determination.

Autonomic, Anticholinergic, and Cardiovascular Effects. The most common autonomic system effects are the anticholinergic effects of dry mouth and subsequent oral infections, nasal congestion, constipation, blurred vision, difficult urination, and, in males, impotence (especially with thioridazine). All may be treated symptomatically. Anticipation of these side effects at the time medication is started may help patients to be willing to bear with these discomforts for the greater good of improving their psychological condition. Male sexual potency often returns by changing to another phenothiazine.

Among cardiovascular phenomena, orthostatic hypotension is common during the first week or two of administering chlorpromazine and thioridazine. In young, healthy patients the hypotension is a nuisance best handled by care in rising from lying or sitting positions. In older patients, sudden drops in blood pressure can be serious, and careful monitoring of blood pressure, pulse, and electro-cardiogram are part of good medical management. Orthostatic hypotension usually diminishes or disappears after the first ten days of treatment.

Cardiac arrhythmias, especially premature ventricular contractions, occasionally occur. Ventricular arrhythmias have been noted, especially with high doses of phenothiazines, and may in fact have been responsible for cases of sudden death. Abnormalities of cardiac function call for cessation of the drug and for immediate cardiological consultation.

Metabolic and Endocrine Effects. Edema, weight gain, feminization phenomena (breast engorgement, lactation, menstrual irregularities, false pregnancy tests in women and impotency in men) in otherwise healthy patients are transient effects and can be treated with reassurance; at other times a reduction in dosage or a change to another compound is required.

Miscellaneous Complications. A wide variety of skin problems has been associated with antipsychotic agents. They frequently occur early in treatment and often subside spontaneously. Photosensitive skin eruptions may be reduced by protective clothing or sun-screening preparations; simple lotions may also alleviate skin problems.

Agranulocytosis, resulting directly from the toxic effect of antipsychotic agents on the bone marrow, is a rare but serious complication. It occurs somewhat more frequently with the use of antipsychotic drugs which require high dosages and is usually manifested during the first month or two of therapy. Clinical observation, informing the patient and relatives about early signs of fever and infection, and perhaps a daily temperature are probably the most useful monitoring techniques.[20] When agranulocytosis or other blood dyscrasias are encountered, medication should be stopped immediately and consultation sought from an internist.

Uninterrupted administration of phenothiazines over the years may lead to pigmentary deposits in the skin and cornea of certain individuals. Corneal deposits threaten vision. Patients who have taken antipsychotic medications for months or years should be checked regularly for these effects. Another visual problem, pigmentary retinopathy, may result from high doses of thioridazine. This complication, which may cause irreversible impairment, can usually be avoided by restricting the dosage of thioridazine to less than 800 mg/day.

CONCLUSIONS

After surveying the range of complications associated with antipsychotic drugs, one can be rightfully impressed by their potency and by the importance of administering them only in clinical situations which clearly warrant their use in preference to other drugs with fewer serious side effects. I restrict my use of antipsychotics to situations in which psychosis is probable or certain, or in which there is a history of predisposition to drug dependence. In other situations, antianxiety drugs with wide margins of safety and fewer serious complications are preferable. However, one should note that severe side effects occur rarely; most side effects are mild and easily controlled. If antipsychotic drugs are indicated, one should use them. They have provided by far the most potent treatment for acute and chronic schizophrenias. In problematic instances, consultation with standard texts and experienced clinicians can lead to significant and sometimes dramatic improvement for patients who as recently as 1950 were considered hopeless.

REFERENCES

1. Rosenbaum, C. Peter: *The Meaning of Madness: Symptomatology, Sociology, Biology and Therapy of the Schizophrenias,* Science House, New York, 1970, chaps. 1 and 2.

2. Hollister, Leo E.: *Clinical Use of Psychotherapeutic Drugs,* Charles C Thomas, Springfield, Ill., 1973, p. 45.

3. Grinspoon, L., J. R. Ewalt, and R. I. Shader: *Schizophrenia: Pharmacotherapy and Psychotherapy,* Williams & Wilkins, Baltimore, 1972.

4. May, P. R. A.: *Treatment of Schizophrenia: A Comparative Study of Five Treatment Methods,* Science House, New York, 1968, pp. 1–352.

5. Denber, Herman C. B.: "Tranquilizers in Psychiatry," in A. M. Freedman and H. I. Kaplan (eds.), *Comprehensive Textbook of Psychiatry,* Williams & Wilkins, Baltimore, 1967, pp. 1251–1262.

6. Hollister: op. cit., pp. 14–25.

7. Goldstein, B. J. (ed.): "Haloperidol – Clinical Experience and Treatment," *Int. J. Neuropsychiat.,* Suppl. 1, pp. 32–129, August 1967.

8. Baker, Charles E.: *Physician's Desk Reference to Pharmaceutical Specialties and Biologicals, 1972,* Litton Publications, Oradell, N.J., 1972.

9. Man, P. L., and C. H. Chen: "Severe Shock Caused by Chlorpromazine Hypersensitivity," *Brit. J. Psychiat.,* **122**:185–187, 1973.

10. Klett, C. J., and E. M. Caffey, Jr.: "Evaluation of the Long-term Need for Anti-Parkinson Drugs by Chronic Schizophrenics," *Arch. Gen. Psychiat.,* **26**:374, 1972.

11. Hollister: op. cit., pp. 38–42.

12. DiMascio, A., and R. D. Shader: "Therapeutic and Pragmatic Import of Drug Administration Schedules," in T. Rothman (ed.), *Changing Patterns of Psychiatric Care,* Crown, New York, 1970.

13. Hollister, L. E., S. H. Curry, J. E. Derr, and S. L. Kanter: "Studies of Delayed-action Medication, Part V: Plasma Levels and Urinary Excretion of Chlorpromazine in Four Different Dosage Forms Given Acutely and in Steady-state Condition," *Clin. Pharmacol. Therap.,* **11**:49, 1970.

14. Prien, R. F., J. Levine, and R. W. Switalski: "Discontinuation of Chemotherapy for Chronic Schizophrenics," *Hosp. Community Psychiat.,* **22**:20–23, 1971.

15. Hollister: op. cit., pp. 46–54.

16. Klein, D. F., and J. M. Davis: *Diagnosis and Drug Treatment of Psychiatric Disorders,* Williams & Wilkins, Baltimore, 1969.

17. Redlich, Frederick C., and Daniel X. Freedman: *The Theory and Practice of Psychiatry,* Basic Books, New York, 1966, pp. 321–326.

18. Rosenbaum: op. cit., chap. 12.

19. Hershon, H. I., P. F. Kennedy, and R. J. McQuire: "Persistence of Extrapyramidal Disorders and Psychiatric Relapse after Withdrawal of Long-term Phenothiazine Therapy," *Brit. J. Psychiat.,* **120**:41–50, 1972.

20. Litvak, R., and R. Kaelbling: "Agranulocytosis, Leukopenia and Psychotropic Drugs," *Arch. Gen. Psychiat.,* **24**:265–268, 1971.

JARED R. TINKLENBERG, M.D.

CHAPTER 27

Drugs and Psychotherapy: Antianxiety Agents

Antianxiety agents encompass several different groups of drugs, including the benzodiazepine derivatives, represented by chlordiazepoxide, diazepam, oxazepam, and flurazepam; meprobamate and congeners; certain barbiturates, the sedative-antihistaminics; and the sedative-antidepressants. These drugs are also called minor tranquilizers, anxiolytics, sedatives, and calmatives. In clinical practice other compounds such as the phenothiazines and thioxanthenes are used for their antianxiety effects, especially with patients in whom severe anxiety is accompanied by psychotic symptoms. The precise pharmacological mechanisms whereby these drugs exert their effectiveness are unknown.

Anxiety may be defined as persistent feelings of apprehension or dread, often about vague, unspecified future events. Accompanying this extremely dysphoric state may be unpleasant symptoms in almost any part of the body — headache, dizziness, abdominal discomfort, palpitations, and muscular tension. Irritability, persistent fatigue, distractibility, and insomnia are common behavioral concomitants of anxiety. Anxiety differs from fear. With fear, the causes are immediate and clearly discernible; the individual's reaction is rapid and marked. However, with anxiety, the etiology is usually vague, and the response is attenuated. It is important to realize that anxiety refers to many different conditions. Anxiety may be a symptom reflecting the vicissitudes of living, a concomitant of a physical illness, a manifestation of pervasive neurotic conflict, or a component of other psychiatric disorders including severe disturbances such as psychosis and depression.[1]

Anxiety should usually be treated when it is severe enough to cause discomfort, to interfere with the patient's daily functioning, or to otherwise disable the individual. Ideally, treatment consists not only of drugs, but also of psychotherapy and judicious alteration of the patient's environment. Most clinicians believe that the proper use of antianxiety agents does not retard psychotherapy, but instead permits the patient to more effectively utilize psychotherapeutic help. However, one should remain aware that moderate levels of anxiety have adaptive functions in alerting the individual, in mobilizing and directing energies, and in providing the persistent motivation that is required to cope successfully with difficulties. Care should be taken that these constructive forces are not unduly subdued by pharmacological agents.

CLINICAL EFFECTS

The effects of the antianxiety drugs depend on their chemical composition. The benzodiazepine derivatives, meprobamate and congeners, and barbiturates all exert to varying degrees central nervous system depression; many of their effects are similar to the familiar sedative-hypnotic, alcohol. Depending on the dosage, these sedating antianxiety agents can induce mild sedation with some impairment of cognitive functioning, pronounced sleepiness, or profound coma. Most of these drugs also have anticonvulsant and muscle-relaxant effects. Unlike the antipsychotic agents discussed in Chapter 26, most of these sedating drugs may be abused; tolerance — raised dose sensitivity level so that a given dose does not exert its usual effect — and withdrawal reactions on abrupt cessation of high doses do occur with most of these antianxiety drugs. Although differences in pharmacological effects do exist among these sedating agents, for most clinical purposes their similarities outweigh their differences.

Other drugs used for their antianxiety effects, including the sedative-antihistaminics, the sedative-antidepressants, and certain antipsychotic preparations, induce a variety of peripheral autonomic effects and hence are sometimes termed *sedative-autonomics*. Perhaps because of these uncomfortable effects, such as dryness of the mouth and visual disturbances, this group of antianxiety agents, in contrast to the sedative-hypnotic group discussed above, is seldom abused and hence may be especially useful for individuals with a history of alcoholism or other drug dependencies. The sedative-autonomics also tend to lower seizure thresholds, to increase muscular tone, and to invoke generalized motor restlessness. Patients who poorly tolerate these side effects generally prefer one of the sedative-hypnotic antianxiety agents described above.

CHOICE OF AGENTS

As with antipsychotic agents, the patient's past history of response to antianxiety drugs is a helpful guide in selecting the specific drug to be used. If the patient describes a preference or a favorable outcome with the prior use of a given antianxiety drug, that drug should be selected again. But when the patient has not previously taken an antianxiety agent, or when the results were not favorable, one is left on uncertain ground. Despite intensive efforts by skilled clinical investigators, there is little information that will help predict a priori what specific antianxiety drug would be most beneficial. The usual dictum is to learn thoroughly the use of a few agents so that they can appropriately be administered with enthusiastic confidence. Again, skillful exploitation of nonpharmacological variables is often of critical importance.

If there is no historical information to influence

Table 27-1 Dosage Guide for Antianxiety Drugs

Generic and Trade Names	Single Dose (mg)	Usual Oral Range (mg per day)
Benzodiazepines		
Chlordiazepoxide (Librium)	10–50	15–300
Diazepam (Valium)	5–20	10–75
Oxazepam (Serax)	15–60	30–150
Flurazepam (Dalmane)	15–30	30–90
Glycerols		
Meprobamate (Equanil, Miltown)	200–400	800–1,600
Tybamate (Solacen, Tybatran)	250–500	750–2,500
Barbiturates		
Amobarbital (Amytal)	65–200	200–800
Phenobarbital (Luminal, others)	16–32	32–100
Sedative-Antihistaminics		
Hydroxyzine (Atarax, Vistaril)	25–50	75–400
Diphenhydramine (Benadryl)	25–50	100–400
Sedative-Antidepressants		
Doxepin (Sinequan)	25–50	100–200

the initial choice of the antianxiety drug, several practical considerations guide many physicians to the use of one of the benzodiazepines. Perhaps most important is that even in very high doses, the benzodiazepines are virtually never lethal, except when combined with other drugs.[2] This safety factor is an important consideration in clinical practice since reducing the risks of intentional or accidental overdose is always a concern. Even if the patient is not a likely candidate for self-destruction, there is always the possibility of accidental ingestion by children or intentional overdose by others who have access to the patient's medication.

The relatively long duration of action of the benzodiazepines and the usual absence of tolerance with repetitive use generally tend to preclude extensive abuse, especially in comparison with the short-acting barbiturates.[3] The long duration of action also permits more sustained antianxiety effects with less frequent doses, often no more than once or twice a day.

Meprobamate and its homologue, tybamate, are quite rapidly deactivated and hence must be given at intervals of about six to eight hours if sustained antianxiety effects are required.[4] With meprobamate, significant tolerance can rapidly develop and necessitate higher doses; profound withdrawal reactions do occur. Tybamate, on the other hand, is not associated with withdrawal reactions, perhaps because it is cleared so rapidly from the plasma.[5]

The barbiturates, although presenting the advantage of being relatively inexpensive antianxiety agents, exert considerable sedation and hence are less useful in clinical situations where the patient must remain alert. Also, the short- and intermediate-acting barbiturates such as pentobarbital, secobarbital, and amobarbital are associated with the rapid development of tolerance, pronounced withdrawal reactions, and frequent abuse by some individuals. However, phenobarbital and other longer-acting barbiturates are seldom linked either with abuse or withdrawal reactions, probably because of their relatively slow rate of onset and sustained duration of effects.

As the terms imply, the sedative-antihistaminic and sedative-antidepressant agents may be especially useful where anxiety is mixed with other clinical syndromes. Most of these agents have peripheral anticholinergic effects; nasal stuffiness, dry mouth, and other anticholinergic symptoms limit their acceptability by some patients but on the other hand make abuse unlikely. However, some patients tolerate the side effects and gain more therapeutic benefit from these sedative-autonomic drugs than from the sedating group discussed above.

INITIAL DOSAGE SCHEDULE AND TREATMENT PLANNING

After questioning the patient about possible allergies and his use of any other psychoactive agents, including over-the-counter proprietary preparations which might synergistically interact with the antianxiety agent, an initial oral dose in the moderate range is prescribed. If possible, the first dose should be taken in the evening when mental acuity for driving or other risky tasks is not required. The patient should be warned about the dangers of sudden drowsiness and imparied psychomotor function. In addition, he should be cautioned about the concomitant use of sedating proprietary preparations, alcohol, and other drugs with central nervous system effects.

As with most drugs in clinical psychiatry, dosage schedules of antianxiety agents vary widely among different patients. For a given patient, the dosage is determined by both the anxiety reduction required and the patient's tolerance of any side effects.

As is the case with antipsychotic agents, the long duration of action of antianxiety drugs often obviates the need for prescribing them more frequently than once or twice per day. Also in parallel with antipsychotic preparations, an ideal time for administrating antianxiety drugs is an hour or two before bedtime so that the hypnotic effects can facilitate sleep while the long plasma half-life provides continued mild sedation the next day without undue drowsiness. If additional anxiety reduction is required during daytime hours, small doses can be given about two hours before anxiety relief is most urgently needed.

The patient should be informed that since anxiety is usually episodic and fluctuates with changes in one's life, the need for antianxiety medication will also change. It is sometimes helpful if the patient keeps a diary of when he needs additional anxiety reduction and especially what environmental events, feelings, and thoughts were antecedent to his increased anxiety. Such a diary serves multiple purposes: enhancing psychological awareness and sophistication, identifying areas for special attention in psychotherapy, and planning for future medication needs. The next therapy session can appropriately begin with a detailed discussion of fluctuations in anxiety and medication needs. Advantages of explicitly integrating the medication regime with other components of psychotherapy are again apparent.

Dosages of antianxiety agents will be changed more frequently than will dosages of antipsychotic agents where steady tissue levels are often required for months or years. Most clinical conditions requiring the use of antianxiety agents improve within a few days or weeks; antianxiety medications should be reduced in dosage concordantly as the patient's anxiety subsides. Treating patients for months or years with an unchanged antianxiety regimen is usually unjustified; dosage schedules which are unchanged for prolonged periods of time usually indicate a lack of therapeutic sophistication.

Injectable forms of antianxiety drugs often constitute the initial treatment of severely agitated states resulting from acute psychotic reactions, toxic delirium, drug withdrawal syndromes, and other conditions where anxiety is extreme. Doses are usually about one-half the oral dose, but titration is required for each patient. After the patient has been adequately sedated with parenteral administration, antianxiety drugs are usually given by mouth.

Combining various types of antianxiety drugs does not usually offer advantages over simply increasing the dosage of a single preparation.[6] However, as discussed in Chapters 26 and 28, there are instances where adding antianxiety agents to an antipsychotic or antidepressant regimen may be helpful.

CONTRAINDICATIONS AND COMPLICATIONS

An antianxiety drug is definitely contraindicated when there is known hypersensitivity to that specific drug or a closely related drug. In other words, a given antianxiety drug should not be used if that drug has induced urticaria, angioneurotic edema, breathing difficulties, hemolysis, or other signs of a generalized allergic reaction. Antianxiety drugs should be used with special caution when there is liver or renal impairment, blood dyscrasia, or depression of the central nervous system from any cause. By far the most common side effect of these drugs is drowsiness, which usually subsides with continued use. Other less common, usually mild side effects include tremor, ataxia, postural hypotension, lightheadedness, mental confusion, a variety of skin eruptions, and abdominal pain. Rarely, blood dyscrasias and impairment of liver function occur. Although teratogenic effects have not been established with antianxiety drugs, treating pregnant patients with these or any other potent drugs requires that potential therapeutic gains be judiciously weighed against the possible risk of fetal harm.

The fact that only a small proportion of people who abuse drugs were initiated into drug taking by physicians does not obviate the need for care in prescribing practices. Patients who have a past history of alcoholism or other forms of drug abuse require special surveillance; for such people, particularly useful are antianxiety drugs with low abuse potential, e.g., the sedative-autonomics. Although continuous monitoring of the amount and frequency of drugs prescribed is required, one should not avoid using the antianxiety drugs when they are indicated because of vague fears about possible future dependency. If antianxiety drugs are needed to relieve disabling discomfort or reduce anxiety so that therapy can proceed, they should be used.

Toxic Doses

Even in very high doses the benzodiazepines and sedative-antidepressants virtually never have a fatal outcome when they are taken alone.[7] When combined with alcohol or other drugs, the effects of the other drugs usually predominate. Large doses of meprobamate, tybamate, and the sedative-antihistiminics present a greater lethal risk, especially when combined with other drugs. Excessive doses of barbiturates present significant suicide risks; in the United States barbiturates are common agents for intentional self-destruction. For these reasons, prescription doses of barbiturates should be kept small; whenever possible, safer antianxiety drugs should be used. The emergency treatment of an overdose of an antianxiety agent entails ridding the patient of the drug, frequent observation, and supporting vital functions (see Chapter 7 for details).

CONCLUSIONS

The judicious use of antianxiety drugs can greatly facilitate the treatment of many patients who demonstrate excessive anxiety stemming from a wide range of different sources. The benzodiazepines are the most commonly used antianxiety drugs, perhaps because they have virtually no suicide potential and relatively low abuse potentials. Meprobamate and homologues, barbiturates, certain antihistaminics, and some antidepressants are also useful in selected clinical situations. As with most psychotropic agents used in psychiatry, nonpharmacological factors have important effects on treatment results; the physician should enthusiastically convey his conviction that the prescribed antianxiety drug will be helpful. The dosage schedule necessarily varies both among different patients and according to the changing clinical course. Prolonged use of high doses is seldom necessary. Although the physician should be aware of the potential for abuse with most antianxiety drugs, when clinically indicated, they should be used.

REFERENCES

1. Wittenborn, J. R.: *The Clinical Psychopharmacology of Anxiety,* Charles C Thomas, Springfield, Ill., 1966, pp. 17–29.

2. Davis, J. M., E. Bartlet, and B. A. Termini: "Overdosage of Psychotropic Drugs: A Review," *Dis. Nerv. Syst.,* **29**:157–246, 1968.

3. Hollister, Leo E., F. P. Motzenbecker, and R. O. Degan: "Withdrawal Reactions from Chlordiazepoxide (Librium)," *Psychopharmacologia,* **2**:63–68, 1961.

4. Hollister, Leo E., and G. Levy: "Kinetics of Meprobamate Elimination in Humans," *Chemotherapia,* **9**:20–24, 1964.

5. Shelton, J., and Leo E. Hollister: "Simulated Abuse of Tybamate in Man: Failure to Demonstrate Withdrawal Reactions," *J. Am. Med. Ass.,* **199**:338–340, 1967.

6. Hollister, Leo E.: *Clinical Use of Psychotherapeutic Drugs,* Charles C Thomas, Springfield, Ill., 1973, p. 134.

7. Davis et al.: loc. cit.

Treatment of Depression and Mania

The use of drugs in the treatment of affective illness has increased dramatically during the past decade. This chapter presents the major drugs used in the treatment of depression and mania, together with their indications, contraindications, side effects, and doses suggested for treatment. It should be noted at the outset that the treatment of affective illness does not lie in the use of drugs alone; rather, drugs should be used as an effective adjunct to psychotherapeutic intervention. For this reason, the physician who prescribes amitriptyline (Elavil®)* to a suicidal patient has only just begun to treat his illness. The psychiatrist is well advised to assess the patient's current life situation by eliciting a description of his current mood, his current stresses, and his methods of coping with them. Only after a thorough review of the patient's affective state has been achieved should the physician prescribe psychopharmacologic agents to an inpatient or an outpatient.

The lethality of depression is profound. More than 25,000 suicides are recorded each year in the United States. The majority of these individuals have seen a physician within two weeks of their suicide. For this reason the use of drugs in this patient population should be viewed as a two-edged sword: the drug can be used as a therapeutic tool, or it can be used as a means of committing suicide. Thus adequate safeguards must be maintained by the physician who is prescribing for this patient population. Only enough drug to last the patient until his next visit should be prescribed. No refills and no PRN prescriptions should be issued to patients with suicidal potential. Because it takes approximately two weeks for most antidepressants to effect a clinical response, it is important for the physician to follow the patient closely during this time of high risk in order to ascertain the patient's suicidal potential.

TREATMENT OF DEPRESSION

Clinical Aspects of Depression

Numerous diagnostic classifications have been proposed to delineate various subgroups of depressed patients; some of these were described in Chapter 5. One such system is especially important in psychopharmacology and relates to the presence of agitation or retardation. This breakdown is important because several of the antidepressants are more effective in the treatment of agitated patients than retarded patients. Patients with an

---

*All drugs mentioned in this chapter will have their generic names given first, followed by the proprietary name in parentheses.

agitated depression show very high levels of anxiety with increased psychomotor activity, agitation, and repetitive speech. Thus the agitated patients tend to wring their hands, pace, and not show the slowness of speech and movement observed in retarded patients.

An analysis of the patient's history of affective disease is important in distinguishing patients with manic-depressive illness from patients with psychotic depression. If a patient has had a recurrent series of affective illnesses, he is likely to respond to lithium carbonate; if not, he would be a candidate for tricyclic antidepressants.

Studies on the efficacy of drug treatments in affective illness should be reviewed with the following ideas in mind. First, affective disease is self-limited: patients who are incapacitated for more than six months probably have been misdiagnosed. Furthermore, the placebo effect is quite strong in affective disease: roughly 20 percent of depressed patients improve on placebos.[1] The use of antidepressant medication increases the rate of response to approximately 70 percent.[2]

The Tricyclic Antidepressants

The tricyclic group of antidepressants represents the most widely used class of compounds available to treat affective illness. More than ten tricyclic compounds are commercially available to the physician; five will be discussed here. Imipramine (Tofranil®) is the drug of choice in the treatment of retarded depression; amitriptyline (Elavil®) is the drug of choice for patients with agitated depression.[3] Both compounds should be started in doses of 100 to 150 mg/day for the first week of treatment. Following this, doses should be advanced to as much as 300 mg/day of imipramine (Tofranil®) and 200 mg/day of amitriptyline (Elavil®). Therapeutic effects of these compounds are usually seen between the seventh and twenty-fifth day of treatment. Patients should be maintained on these drugs for at least one month before switching to a different compound if no therapeutic effect is observed. If the patient

responds, he should be maintained on the drug for up to three months, at which time the medication may be discontinued only if the patient is being seen periodically by his treating physician.

Because amitriptyline (Elavil®) may be effective in the treatment of insomnia in some cases of depression, dose schedules utilizing this compound may be weighted such that the patient receives a maximum dose in the evening. For this reason, a typical regimen might include 25 mg with breakfast, lunch, and dinner and 50 mg prior to retiring in the evening. Consideration of the weight of the patient should influence the total dose employed.

Because of the relatively long period of time required for tricyclic drugs to achieve symptomatic change, several drug houses have introduced demethylated antidepressants, which are reputed to act somewhat more quickly than the methylated compounds. Drugs such as desipramine (Pertofrane®) and nortriptyline (Aventyl®) may act slightly faster than imipramine (Tofranil®) and amitriptyline (Elavil®), yet clinical evaluation of these compounds is not as nearly complete as for the methylated drugs. There is little evidence that the demethylated forms of the tricyclic drugs act prior to one week after initiating drug treatment.

Protriptyline (Vivactil®) is a tricyclic antidepressant which may produce clinical response in less than one week. It is an activating agent and lacks the tranquilizing and sedating properties of amitriptyline (Elavil®). This drug may activate anxiety in patients with retarded depression. Although protriptyline (Vivactil®) may act more rapidly than other tricyclic compounds, a review of the literature suggests that in six comparative studies it was not found to be more effective in the treatment of depression when compared with amitriptyline (Elavil®) or imipramine (Tofranil®).[4]

Tricyclic antidepressants should not be given to patients who are currently receiving monoamine oxidase inhibitors (described in the next section of this chapter) or who have received these inhibitors within the previous two weeks. Patients who are comatose or have a history of agranulocytosis, hepatic disease, or severe glaucoma should not be given tricyclic compounds.

The route of administration of the tricyclic drugs is usually oral. However, imipramine (Tofranil®) and amitriptyline (Elavil®) are available for parenteral use and can be given in doses of 25 mg IM three times a day for up to three days to initiate therapy in patients who are unable to take the compounds by the oral route.

The tricyclic drugs are retained by the body for a short period of time, their half-life being approximately twenty-four hours. One should wait at least two days after stopping tricyclic compounds before administering drugs such as monoamine oxidase inhibitors, which may cause serious side effects when administered in conjunction with tricyclic compounds.

A rapid urinary color test for the presence of imipramine (Tofranil®) has been developed by Forrest et al.[5] This is particularly helpful in determining whether patients are indeed taking their medication and also in determining when the drug has been eliminated from the body prior to starting monoamine oxidase inhibitors.

The incidence of side effects in association with tricyclic therapy is uniformly low. However, there have been adverse effects reported involving almost every organ system in the body. Approximately 10 percent of patients receiving tricyclic antidepressants show a fine tremor. Orthostatic hypotension is also a relatively common side effect. Tricyclic drugs have atropinelike side effects such as drug-induced glaucoma, urinary retention, and impotence. Patients may complain of dryness of the mouth (this is best treated by encouraging them to suck on hard candy). Abnormalities in the EKG include a quinidinelike effect with a prolongation of the QT interval with flattened T waves. Nausea and vomiting are extremely rare. A wide range of allergic reactions including contact dermatitis and urticaria have been reported. Agranulocytosis is extremely rare, but several cases have been noted. The best approach to handling minor side effects of tricyclic antidepressants is to decrease the dose

slightly in an attempt to maintain the patient on enough drug to help his depression while at the same time minimizing his side effects. If agranulocytosis develops, or if the side effects become severe, the drugs should be discontinued immediately.

The administration of tricyclic antidepressants to patients with a history of manic-depressive illness is *contraindicated*. Hypomanic excitement followed by acute mania may develop in these patients, and for this reason the appropriate treatment for their depression is the administration of lithium carbonate.[6] Other investigators have noted the precipitation of acute psychotic symptoms in schizophrenics treated with imipramine (Tofranil®).[7] In patients with severe physical disabilities, such as cerebral damage, hemiparesis with aphasia, and Kimmelstiel-Wilson's disease, amitriptyline (Elavil®) is reported to have fewer side effects than imipramine (Tofranil®) and should be used as the treatment of choice.

Recent evidence[8] indicates that the chronic administration of tricyclic antidepressants is effective in the prophylaxis of recurrent depressions in patients without a history of mania. Prophylactic doses in this VA–NIMH study ranged from 75 to 200 mg if imipramine (Tofranil®) daily.

Monoamine Oxidase Inhibitors

Iproniazid, a drug first used in the treatment of tuberculosis in 1951, was found to produce euphoria in many of the TB patients. It gained acceptance as an antidepressant following this observation and ushered in a group of antidepressants all of which block the enzyme monoamine oxidase.

Those patients with severe depression who do not respond to tricyclic antidepressants should be given a trial of monoamine oxidase (MAO) inhibitors. In this class of compounds there are over five drugs which are commercially available. Three drugs will be mentioned here; phenelzine (Nardil®) probably has the fewest side effects of any drug in this class; nialamide (Niamid®) has the smallest effect on the peripheral autonomic system and consequently is very useful in the treatment of elderly patients with labile blood pressures or patients likely to develop orthostatic hypotension; isocarboxazid (Marplan®) is probably the most toxic of the three drugs, yet it is the most effective compound when used with caution. Table 28-1 lists these drugs and their recommended dosages.

As with tricyclic antidepressants, MAO inhibitors should be started at a low dose, which should then be elevated over a period of one to two weeks.

In addition to being used in patients who do not respond to tricyclic drugs, MAO inhibitors are effective in the treatment of the profoundly retarded depressed patient. These compounds may provide more activation than the tricyclic drugs, and they may be more effective in those patients who show a low degree of spontaneous activity.

The MAO inhibitors are metabolized slowly, their effects lasting up to ten days. Thus the physician must wait at least two weeks after discontinuation of MAO inhibitors before starting drugs with which they might be incompatible, such as tricyclic compounds.

MAO inhibitors should not be given to patients with liver damage. The three MAO inhibitors mentioned are all hydrazines and have potential hepatotoxicity. Neither should patients with pheochromocytoma, a history of mania, or impaired renal function, or who are currently receiving tricyclic antidepressants, receive MAO inhibitors.

Patients given MAO inhibitors must be instructed to abstain from any food rich in tyramine, a compound which releases norepinephrine and epinephrine from storage vesicles. These foods produce a hypertensive crisis in those people receiving

MAO inhibitors. Foods rich in tyramine include cheese, snails, chianti wine, and chicken liver.

Side effects of MAO-inhibitor administration include irritability and insomnia. These symptoms may progress to a psychosis and possibly mania in patients with a prior history of manic-depressive illness. Some patients have complained of neuralgias in association with MAO administration. The most disturbing side effect which may be observed in patients on MAO inhibitors is a hypertensive crisis. Other side effects include orthostatic hypotension, intrahepatic obstructive jaundice with biliary stasis, maculopapular rash, and agranulocytosis.

If any of these side effects occurs with severity, the MAO inhibitors should be discontinued. Patients with hypertensive crises should be treated with 5 mg of phentolamine (Regitine®) intravenously; MAO inhibitors should be used for at least one month prior to switching to another treatment modality if no therapeutic response is noted. Usually activation and a lessening of depression is observed within the first week of treatment.

MAO inhibitors should not be administered with narcotics, adrenalin, amphetamines, or barbiturates. Both the sedative and depressant actions of barbiturates are increased with combined use of MAO inhibitors. In addition, blood-clotting time in patients on anticoagulants is further delayed and the anticholinergic effect of anti-Parkinsonian drugs is increased.

Combined Therapies

The MAO inhibitors can be combined with electroshock therapy. This is also true of the tricyclic compounds. Both drugs may also be given with major antipsychotic compounds such as chlorpromazine. The physician should be cautioned against the administration of tricyclic antidepressants in conjunction with compounds such as Cogentin® or Kemadrin®. Because both types of compounds have atropinelike toxicity, patients receiving both may develop acute urinary retention.

Table 28-1   Monoamine Oxidase Inhibitors

Monoamine Oxidase Inhibitor	Average Daily Dose (mg/day)
Phenelzine (Nardil)	45–75
Nialamide (Niamid)	75–200
Isocarboxazid (Marplan)	20–30

Electroshock Therapy

With the advent of drugs effective in the treatment of affective illness, the hope that electroshock therapy (ECT) would become unnecessary increased. Electroshock therapy has numerous shortcomings, including the necessity for frequent hospitalization, interference with memory, and lack of aesthetic appeal. Nevertheless, the present consensus seems to be that drugs have not yet replaced ECT. Greenblatt's classic study demonstrated that in the treatment of 281 depressed patients, ECT ranked as the most effective treatment after a short-term follow-up.[9] This placed it well above phenelzine (Nardil®), imipramine (Tofranil®), placebo, and isocarboxazid (Marplan®) in effectiveness. At present, the administration of ECT should be confined to patients who clearly have not responded to adequate trials of both tricyclic antidepressants and MAO inhibitors or to patients who are in grave risk of suicide and who cannot be placed in an environment to minimize the risk of suicide. The populations of patients most likely to show improvement with ECT are those with involutional melancholia and severe psychotic depression.

ECT should be administered with appropriate muscle relaxants such as succinylcholine together with a short-term hypnotic, usually a barbiturate derivative. Patients with a history of subarachnoid hemorrhage, fractured vertebrae, or the presence of an intracranial aneurysm should not be given ECT.

Stimulant Drugs

Amphetamines, because of their rapid effects in increasing activation, have been used for many years in the treatment of depression. However, they have not proven to be very effective. Their disadvantages are many; they cause anorexia, habituation, jitteriness, and a rapid development of tolerance. In addition, toxic amphetamine psychoses are frequently seen in patients using high doses of amphetamines.

The oral administration of 10 to 30 mg of dextroamphetamine sulfate in a single dose produces wakefulness, increased awareness of surroundings, quicker response to environmental stimuli, and a decreased sense of fatigue. Ban reports that this dose increases confidence, decisiveness, initiative, and concentration.[11] Moreover, administration of amphetamines is associated with euphoria, elation, and increased motor activity and speech. At present these drugs are used in the treatment of hyperkinetic children, narcolepsy, and pyknolepsy. They may be given occasionally to normal, healthy adults when it is necessary for them to be alert over an unusually long period. Until recently, a number of physicians would prescribe dextroamphetamine sulfate for the purpose of weight reduction. This practice has come under severe attack, and at present it is bordering on unconscionable medical practice to administer the drug for this purpose.

In the treatment of hyperkinetic children, the weight of the patient is extremely important in ascertaining the drug dose. Because of the appetite-suppressant action of amphetamines, these drugs should not be given before meals. Because of the rapid buildup in tolerance and habituation, amphetamines should not be administered for more than three months. All patients who are started on amphetamines should have a trial dose of 2.5 mg orally to ascertain whether sensitivity exists. If there is any evidence of agitation or depression, further administration of the drug should not be attempted.

The side effects of amphetamines are numerous. Precipitation of an acute schizophrenic episode characterized by severe paranoid manifestations with auditory and visual hallucinations has been well documented. Amphetamines, particularly the sulfates, are capable of inducing a toxic confusional state, but more often produce a transient delirium with disturbance of memory. Neurological symptoms of headache, dizziness, vertigo, and tremor have been noted. Characteristic cardiovascular effects of amphetamine use are tachycardia and hypertension.

Amphetamines are respiratory stimulants, and an overdose may produce rapid, shallow breathing. Severe toxic reactions have been seen in patients treated orally with as little as 30 mg of dextroamphetamine sulfate. Symptoms of overdose include irritability, tension, restlessness, tremor, and shock. The treatment of overdosage is systematic sedation with phenothiazines or barbiturates.

Other drugs which have been used as stimulants include methylphenidate hydrochloride (Ritalin®), pipradrol (Meratran®), and phenmetrazine (Preludin®). These compounds, although extremely effective for a short-term lift in mood, are not the drug of choice in the long-term treatment of the depressed patient. It is of note that methylphenidate hydrochloride (Ritalin®), is being used effectively in the treatment of hyperkinetic children.

TREATMENT OF MANIA

Lithium Carbonate

Lithium carbonate is probably the most potent drug in the armamentarium of the psychiatrist. When employed in therapeutic doses, lithium carbonate is effective in the treatment of nine out of ten manic patients. Unfortunately, the margin of safety between therapeutic and toxic blood levels of lithium is extremely narrow; thus, monitoring blood levels is essential, especially in the initial phases of treatment.

There is evidence that lithium carbonate is effective not only in the treatment of mania but also in the treatment of patients with recurrent depressive episodes.[8,10]

The patient started on lithium carbonate should be given four to six capsules containing 300 mg of lithium carbonate daily for the first few days until his blood-lithium level reaches 1.2 Meq/liter. When this is achieved, the number of capsules should be reduced and the patient's blood level maintained between 0.8 and 1.2 Meq/liter. The usual number of capsules for maintenance dose is three or four per day. Signs and symptoms of lithium toxicity occur when blood levels exceed 2.2 Meq/liter.

Because of the competition between sodium and lithium for transport across cell membranes, sodium intake should be maintained relatively constant. If sodium intake is increased while the patient is maintained on a constant intake of lithium, blood-lithium levels will decrease.

When the patient is started on lithium carbonate, blood samples for lithium determination should be taken every other day until the lithium level becomes stable on a maintenance dose. Following this, patients should have blood drawn at least once a month for lithium-level determinations.

Side effects of lithium carbonate treatment include nausea, diarrhea, vomiting, fine tremors, polyuria, polydipsia, ataxia, and muscular weakness. Death because of overdose is associated with convulsions and coma. Patients with a history of renal or cardiovascular disease should not be given lithium carbonate.

Once an acute episode of the mania is controlled, patients should be maintained on lithium carbonate for a minimum of one year. If this is found to prevent recurrent cycles of the illness, patients may be maintained on the drug for life. At present, there is little evidence on the effects of lithium carbonate on the human fetus. For this reason the drug is contraindicated in the treatment of pregnant women. Those women of childbearing age should be advised to follow the birth control method of their choice during the course of lithium carbonate therapy.

SUMMARY

For the depressed patient selected as a candidate for chemotherapy, the first drugs of choice are the tricyclic antidepressants. Patients with retarded depression should be treated with imipramine (Tofranil®), and those with agitated depression with amitriptyline (Elavil®). Those depressed patients who do not respond to tricyclic antidepressants should be given monoamine oxidase (MAO) inhibitors. Phenelzine (Nardil®) is the best MAO inhibitor with which to start. Those depressed patients who have had recurrent episodes of mania and depression may be started on lithium carbonate, which is the treatment of choice for the acutely manic patient. Furthermore, it is found to be effective in the prevention of recurrent manic-depressive psychosis. Stimulant drugs, such as amphetamines, should not be administered to patients with depression. The use of these compounds should be confined to the treatment of hyperkinetic children.

REFERENCES

1. Ball, J. R. B., and L. G. Kiloh: "A Controlled Trial of Imipramine in the Treatment of Depressive States," *Brit. Med. J.,* **5159**:1052–1055, 1959.

2. Ottman, J. E., and S. Friedman: "Comparison of Marplan and Tofranil in the Treatment of Depressive States," *Am. J. Psychiat.,* **117**:929–930, 1961.

3. Kielholz, P., and W. Poeldinger: *Compr. Psychiat.,* **9**:179, 1968.

4. Klein, Donald F., and John M. Davis: *Diagnosis and Drug Treatment of Psychiatric Disorders,* Williams & Wilkins, Baltimore, 1969, p. 194.

5. Forrest, I. S., et al.: "A Rapid Urine Color Test for Imipramine (Tofranil, Geigy): Supplementary Report with Color Chart," *Am. J. Psychiat.,* **116**:1021–1023, 1960.

6. Bunney, W. E., Jr., H. K. H. Brodie, D. L. Murphy, and F. K. Goodwin: "Psychopharmacological Differentiation between Two Subgroups of Depressed Patients," *Proceedings of the Seventy-eighth Annual Convention of the American Psychological Association,* 1970, p. 829.

7. Newman, R. A., and W. R. Fisher: "Imipramine as a Psychotomimetic Drug in Borderline Schizophrenics," *Am. J. Psychiat.,* **212**:77–78, 1964.

8. Prien, R. F., C. J. Klett, and E. M. Caffey, Jr.: "Lithium Carbonate and Imipramine in Prevention of Affective Episodes," *Arch. Gen. Psychiat.,* **29**:420–423, 1973.

9. Greenblatt, M., et al.: "Differential Response of Hospitalized Depressed Patients to Somatic Therapy," *Am. J. Psychiat.,* **120**:935–943, 1964.

10. Goodwin, F. K., et al.: "Lithium Carbonate Treatment in Depression and Mania," *Arch. Gen. Psychiat.,* **21**:486–496, 1969.

11. Ban, Thomas A.: *Psychopharmacology,* Williams & Wilkins, Baltimore, 1969, p. 195.

Abortion Consultation

Abortion consultation in the United States is rapidly becoming voluntary rather than mandatory. Even before the January 1973 Supreme Court ruling abolishing all restrictive abortion legislation during the first three months of pregnancy, psychiatric abortion consultation was no longer required in New York under that state's radically altered 1970 abortion law. Under 1968 laws in California and Georgia, and even in Massachusetts with its nineteenth-century abortion law, the custom of mandatory consultation had been quietly neglected or dropped entirely prior to the Court's decision. With such far-reaching changes in process, it is important at this time to review the use of abortion consultation as it becomes a part of ordinary medical practice.

Because the psychiatrist will no longer be necessary to provide the legal excuse[1] and societal sanction for what was formerly taboo behavior, the distinction between counseling and consultation, often blurred in the past, can now be made explicit. As recently as 1965 Tietze[2] estimated only 8,000 legal abortions were performed annually in the entire United States. In 1970 there were more than 180,000 reported legal abortions,[3] and in 1971 there were 480,259 registered abortions in this country.[4]

Clearly the day of the psychiatrist in the role of society's agent often allied with and sometimes against the woman seeking an abortion is past. No longer will the consultant be required to search for clues suggesting suicide or psychosis to justify a woman's abortion request. The outgoing era saw the psychiatrist acting as a quasi-judge, the abortion committee as a quasi-jury, and the obstetrician-gynecologist as a quasi-executioner. As this primitive period ends, we can plan for more rational treatment of the abortion problem and more humane care for the women involved.

There is an important distinction to be made between *abortion counseling* and *abortion consultation,* which could not be made as long as the state coerced the woman into seeking either counseling or consultation. Most women do not need formal psychiatric consultation before having an abortion, but many women welcome warm, empathic counseling.[5] Counseling properly performed in a dignified atmosphere should be voluntarily available to all women undergoing abortion.

The purposes of abortion counseling are "to aid the woman in making a decision about an unwanted pregnancy — help her implement the decision — (and) assist her in controlling her future fertility." The basic principles of good counseling are first that counseling be freely entered into, second that counseling be supportive and nonjudgmental, regardless of the circumstances of the pregnancy, and third that the counseling be an educational experience. Good counseling can be performed by

---

*From 1968 to 1970, Dr. Asher initiated the national abortion reporting system in the United States Public Health Service.

a wide variety of individuals from differing backgrounds. "A woman sympathetically counseled and supportively aided in dealing with an unwanted pregnancy hopefully will be able to integrate the experience in such a way as to prevent its recurrence."[6] Thus, the immediate goal of counseling is curative, and the long-range goal is preventive.

Abortion consultation, in contrast, will be necessary for a relatively small percentage of the estimated 2 million or more women annually who will eventually be obtaining legal abortions in the United States. [7] Consultation is most appropriate for those women and couples for whom it is highly likely that a continued pregnancy will indeed cause serious emotional turmoil, for whom being pregnant may constitute a crisis rather than a life event, and for whom that crisis requires psychiatric help in minimizing anguish and maximizing healthy coping. This chapter will be devoted to describing those circumstances in which psychiatric consultation in pregnancy and possible abortion should be sought and the manner in which the consultation should be conducted. Though abortion will be the most likely result of a consultation, abortion as an outcome should not always be the foregone conclusion, as will be shown in Example 29-4.

INDICATIONS FOR ABORTION CONSULTATION

Seven conditions are listed below as possible indications for psychiatric consultation. [8] None is absolute; each is based on clinical experience and serves to alert the clinician to possible trouble ahead. When a given patient shows signs of two or more of these conditions, the likelihood of emotional complications of continued pregnancy is greater, and the need for psychiatric consultation is increased. These conditions are:

1. History of major tranquilizer usage, psychosis, or psychiatric hospitalization

2. History or question of mental retardation

3. History of previous severe postabortal or postpartum reaction

4. History of strong religious or ethical training opposing abortion

5. History of multiple previous unplanned pregnancies

6. Clinical picture of marked guilt with depression and suicidal fantasies

7. Clinical picture of a woman being coerced

Once the basic decision to ask for abortion consultation is made, two questions must be answered: first, when should the consultation occur; and second, to whom should the woman be referred?

It is desirable but not always possible to obtain psychiatric consultation *prior* to abortion. If the patient objects, the counselor or operating physician may have to be satisfied with recommending consultation should "problems occur" postabortally. When the counselor or physician feels very strongly that the situation requires consultation prior to abortion, he should clearly state why and recommend referral rather than permit lengthy and dangerous equivocation.

Abortion consultation need not be carried out by a psychiatrist. It always has been only because of medicolegal tradition. Successful abortion consultants may come from a variety of disciplines including appropriately trained psychiatric nurses, social workers, clinical psychologists, and psychiatrists.

Common sense would suggest that women who have been *placed on major tranquilizers, been diagnosed as psychotic,* or *had psychiatric hospitalizations* have a higher risk of unfavorable psychic sequelae after abortion. Ekblad's classic follow-up study of 479 Swedish women concluded that preabortal emotional difficulties are correlated with postabortal complications.

A study of the connection between various factors in the women's mental constitution or environment and the occurrence of self-reproaches shows that the psychically abnormal find it more difficult than the psychically normal to stand the stress implied in a legal abortion. This means the greater the psychiatric indications for legal abortion are, the greater is also the risk of unfavorable psychic sequelae after the operation.[9]

Furthermore, abortion as a recognized life stress fits into the category of those events testing ego strength and coping mechanisms which could be defined as a crisis.[10] Major tranquilizers are, of course, often prescribed without a history of psychotic behavior, but their previous use should be taken into account in deciding whether consultation is appropriate.

The issue of abortion of a *mentally retarded mother* is an extraordinarily complex ethical question.[11,12] Only in the future will rational guidelines appear to help decide the questions raised by the pregnant adolescent, or adult woman who desperately wants a child but is not capable of understanding the implications of her action, let alone raising a child which might itself be retarded. At present we feel that to perform an abortion on a retarded mother without adequate psychiatric consultation would be at best foolish and at least callous.

That pregnancy even when normally completed can present a direct assault on a woman's ability to function has been recorded since the time of Hippocrates.[13] Common sense again indicates that in aiding a woman with a *history of postpartum difficulties* or, more specifically, *previous postabortal emotional complications,* particular care should be taken to elucidate the circumstances of the current pregnancy. The purpose of the consultation would not necessarily be to influence the woman's decision, but rather to identify the areas of weakness which require support in order to help prevent a recurrence of the previous difficulties.

Example 29-1. A 24-year-old divorcee sought treatment to talk about an abortion she had had two years previously. She was employed and living with her ex-husband's best man. Her only previous psychiatric contact had been some brief therapy at the time of the abortion.

She viewed herself as a "phony and at times not a real person, especially because of my bleached hair, my nose operation (I had a hook nose just like my father, it was disgusting), and getting my breasts made bigger."

Following her abortion, she developed an intense curiosity about the fetus. She worked in the hospital where the abortion was performed and was able to find the specimen jar containing her fetus. She remembers no particular reaction at that time. However, soon thereafter she began to have fantasies that the abortion never took place, that she had carried the pregnancy to term, and that her father had forced her to give up the baby. Furthermore, she believed the baby had been a girl and was now living in Europe. This psychotic fantasy was well encapsulated, since the rest of her mental status examination was normal. When she appeared for a second abortion, which will be discussed later, acute psychological trouble was the predictable outcome.

Women who have been raised in a fundamentalist or conservative *religious or ethical background strongly opposed to abortion,* if they consider abortion at all, are very likely to equate abortion with murder. They risk experiencing great shame and guilt at either the contemplation or completion of an abortion. The emotional fervor which attends the issue is well expressed by the statements of contemporary Fetal Rights or ProLife organizations. It would seem prudent to explore in greater depth with women from such backgrounds (or those whose husbands have come from such backgrounds) the possible emotional consequences of having an abortion.

Women who have had *multiple unplanned pregnancies* should be evaluated. The causes of "unplanned pregnancy" are many. Some are true accidents, such as when a pregnancy occurs with an IUD in place. Some result from misinformation or lack of information, such as the woman who thinks that ovulation always occurs at the time of menstruation, or who thinks it never does. Some pregnancies occur because of discrimination against the woman who seeks contraception, often because she is too poor, too young, or single. This happens far less often than formerly, but still far too often in some areas of the country. Some unplanned pregnancies result because couples habitually plan poorly. For them, to practice contraception successfully would represent a definite deviation from their general "hang loose" lifestyle. Other pregnancies, particularly with couples unsure about having a third child, or couples who are using contraception for spacing of births rather than family size limitation, are neither planned nor unplanned. These pregnancies fall into a third category which we might call "partly planned"; as a result, they are often caused by contraceptive "failure."* Failures from withdrawal or rhythm, (a notoriously unreliable method), not replenishing the foam, or forgetting to grease the rim of the diaphragm suggest the in-between, partly planned state masking a conflict of motives.

Pregnancy as a way of trying to resolve unconscious conflict is often seen more clearly in the adolescent woman who is not able to accept her emergent sexual drives, is therefore not able to rationally seek contraception, and as a result becomes pregnant when her drives win out, as shown in Example 29-2. The most difficult cases psychologically are the women who rationally reject pregnancy, but who, acting out of unconscious motives, become pregnant. The conflict for them is thus flushed into the open, but not resolved by their actions. Rather, it then focuses

on the inexorably expanding fetus. The decision to abort or not follows after extensive ambivalent agonizing. However, if the unconscious motivations are not dealt with then or soon after, the experience may leave no imprint and a subsequent pregnancy will quite likely ensue.

Example 29-2. A 17-year-old unmarried college-bound high school senior had three unplanned pregnancies and abortions in two years. She first had sexual intercourse at age 15 with her boyfriend, who was a college freshman at the time. Since they were not able to plan their sexual activity rationally, they were unable to plan contraception, and used denial and rationalization in thinking that pregnancies "happened only to other people."[15] It happened to her. Her parents helped her arrange an abortion, but there was no follow-up discussion with parents or physician about future sexual activity or contraceptive use. She made an appointment to visit Planned Parenthood with her boyfriend; he injured himself on the day of the appointment, and she did not keep it. She again became pregnant and had an abortion.

Following the second abortion she started on the pill, stopped shortly before her boyfriend was to leave for six months, and became pregnant a third time. Parents and boyfriend brought great pressure to bear for a third abortion. After having it, she was given an IUD and started psychotherapy to try to work out a number of unresolved issues about sexuality, fertility, and abortion.

Three issues emerged clearly in therapy. The first was that she had an intense desire to have a child. A second issue was that in her relationship with her boyfriend she often felt used and unsure of herself. A third theme was the persistent though not overwhelming sense of guilt about ending the lives of what she termed "babies."

The evidence for her craving to have a child came from conscious fantasies (especially

---

*Westhoff et al., who are demographers and not psychologists, summarize their data as follows: "Another finding consistent with GAF results is the low effectiveness of contraception practiced during the first two birth intervals — a time when nearly all couples are practicing contraception to postpone rather than to prevent pregnancies. . . . As couples approach desired family size, the effectiveness with which they practice contraception increases sharply — so much so that this improved contraception would appear to be a substantial factor in the family limitation being attained in this country."[14]

while baby-sitting) and unconscious wishes (dreaming of having babies, looking for babies, and taking care of babies). Her mother was sterile; both the patient and her younger sister had been adopted. The patient remembered, when she was age 3 and her mother brought her sister home, announcing that the new baby at her house was *her* baby. The clear inference is that by adolescence she had not yet resolved the competitive aspects of her relationship with her mother.

Her boyfriend had been her first and only sexual partner. Her fear about their relationship — unable to feel secure in that relationship or to develop another one — explained in part why she sought a child who would without ambivalence need her and thus increase her sense of self-value.

Her degree of guilt about the three abortions was not unusual for someone brought up in our culture with its differing attitudes about when life "begins," when a fetus becomes a child, and the nagging doubt that abortion might in some emotional sense be murder.

In the work with her after her third abortion, she resolved many of the psychological issues verbally and maintained contraception successfully with an IUD. Follow-up shows that she is continuing to do well in school, at home, and with friends in her growth toward adulthood. Had abortion consultation been available to her during her first pregnancy, one or perhaps two subsequent pregnancies and abortions could have been averted.

When severe *depression, guilt,* or *suicidal thinking* appear early in pregnancy, immediate psychiatric consultation can provide support prior to a possible abortion. If abortion is decided upon and performed, the previously established therapeutic alliance will make it easier for the patient to accept further psychotherapy in an attempt to understand more fully the depression and suicidal feeling. In some cases the preabortal period will be deceptively tranquil, followed by a stormy post-abortal course.

Reasons for the depressive reaction will vary widely. They may range from grief over the impending loss of a desired child to loss of self-esteem (the "good girl" image shattered) to loss of the sexual partner as a result of pregnancy. Brief therapy may be sufficient to deal with the feelings raised by the loss, or it may turn out that long-term therapy is indicated to treat more deep-seated characterologic problems, as seen in the following example of a woman with low self-esteem plagued by suicidal thinking.

Example 29-3. An attractive 30-year-old separated woman with no previous history of psychiatric hospitalization was told during marriage that she might be infertile. Following her divorce, she became pregnant by her boyfriend. She decided on abortion because she was working and because the relationship with the boyfriend was not stable. She was intellectually strongly in favor of abortion, had no difficulty getting psychiatric authorization, and went through the abortion itself uneventfully. Three months later she started a six-month psychiatric hospitalization for depression and suicidal behavior. She repeatedly castigated herself for "murdering the baby," while at the same time inveighing against the men (her boyfriend, the psychiatrist, and the obstetrician-gynecologist) who had "railroaded" her into the operation. While on the ward, she banged her head on the wall and mutilated her arms and abdomen with pins in order to find some release from her guilt and anger. She required periodic hospitalization over the next year and a half for recurrent suicidal behavior and preoccupations.

When she was a child, her father, who had very much wanted a boy, was cold and rejecting of her, encouraging only culturally defined masculine interests, such as playing Little League ball, attaining academic excellence, and aspiring to medical school. She had long been discontent with her looks and had cosmetic surgery performed on her ears and nose after high school.

This surgery, as it is for many young women, was just one symptom of her grave doubts about her feminine identity; her fear about sterility during marriage was another. The fetus therefore had many conscious and unconscious meanings for her: it was proof that she was a woman; it might turn out to be the son her father always wanted and thus lead to his acceptance of her; it could be a symbolic phallus that would finally win the father's love. The dissonance between the conscious decision for abortion and these potent unconscious wishes to have the baby were poignantly shown in her diary when she first learned she was pregnant:

"I don't believe it. Do you believe it? Me pregnant? After trying to conceive a year and a half in my marriage, and knowing I must be sterile, and now, I AM PREGNANT. Oh God, wow. I am SoooOOOOO happy. You don't know, A baby, a baby in me. No, it can't be for real. . . . I am so happy. I dance for joy and cry and feel so good. . . . Of course, I will get an abortion, but I am sooo ecstatic now. . . . Me, I am going to have a baby. . . . It is too wildly wonderful. Sit still, Carol, baby, and dig it."

The contrast between "Of course, I will get an abortion," and "Me, I am going to have a baby," predicts the intense conflict she was to suffer following the abortion. At an unconscious level the loss of the fetus recreated in her the frustration she felt at not being "man enough" to win her father's love and approval, the last straw after all the childhood efforts had failed. For her the abortion destroyed both the evidence of her womanhood and the hope of her father's acceptance.

Like childbirth, abortion may call up for reexamination all the unresolved conflicts of a woman's childhood relationships. In this example, the adult superstructure collapsed at the stress and at this writing has only partially been rebuilt.

A woman may be *coerced* into having an abortion for a wide variety of reasons. Women are also coerced into having children. Neither situation represents a very happy resolution of conflict. As in the previous example, the woman may feel coerced externally or railroaded, when in fact the coercion arose from within. In the following example the woman is caught in a cross fire between her experientially based emotional feeling toward pregnancy and her societally based ethical opposition to having more than two children. Such cases will become more frequent as pressures for population stabilization become more widespread.

Example 29-4. A 30-year-old wife of a psychologist and mother of two young children became pregnant although she was using a diaphragm and foam most of the time. Neither member of the couple wanted a third child because of their commitment to Zero Population Growth. However, she expressed sadness that times were such that "You can't do something as pleasurable as having children." They had been married for seven years in a stable, satisfying relationship. For her, childbirth and child rearing were a great source of gratification. She remembered her "healthy and vibrant" feelings during pregnancy itself and "the incredible emotional relationship" with the newborn infant.

She had had both her children by natural childbirth, and her husband had helped with the deliveries. The abortion was planned using general anesthesia at 4½ weeks' gestation. Her husband was scheduled for a vasectomy the following week.

Three days before the scheduled abortion she began to get shaky and started crying a great deal. She felt that she could not go through with it and did not. A day after the abortion was scheduled to have taken place, I saw her together with her husband. He was a soft-spoken, extremely supportive individual whose primary concern was his wife's welfare. He shared her strong ethical views on limiting family size to two children. Another date for the abortion had been set. I recommended that she not push herself excessively and that she follow her feelings. If she again found that she could not go through with it, she should realize that though there would be guilt in either situation, the guilt about the third child would probably be less than the guilt about the abortion. She, in fact, found that emotionally she could not go ahead and have the abortion. Once she had accepted this and decided to have the child, she felt relieved and happy about the decision.

In this case the coercion was largely self-induced and represented an internalization of rapidly changing societal values. Consultation clarified for her that these values did not have nearly the force of her strongly positive emotions about pregnancy and childbirth. The relief she felt at ending the ambivalence and her successful course in continuing the pregnancy support this view.

Unlike the woman in Example 29-2, whose father and boyfriend forced her to have the abortion, the psychologist's wife had the support of her husband in the decision. The divorced woman who attempted suicide (Example 29-3) was so seriously out of touch with her own ambivalence, though it was easily discernible in the diary, that she in a sense coerced herself with near-tragic consequences. She later projected this sense of coercion onto the men (boyfriend, psychiatrist, and gynecologist) who in helping her obtain the abortion thought they were being supportive.

The problem of coercion is a complex one. It may go by totally unnoticed initially, as with the divorced woman. It may occur and be surmounted, as with the high school senior. It may lead to paralysis and indecision which can then be worked out successfully with proper consultation, as in the example of the psychologist's wife.

AREAS OF CONSULTATION

Once the ground rules of the abortion consultation are defined, there are ten areas which should be systematically covered. These ten areas are listed below and then described more fully in the order they might naturally be taken up during the consultation. As in any psychiatric interview, though, if the patient seems to be getting unduly anxious or embarrassed at any point, the interviewer can move quickly on to more neutral territory and return to the more sensitive issues later, when the patient may feel more comfortable. The consultation should end with the patient and consultant anticipating the patient's reaction to either continued pregnancy or abortion, according to the decision jointly reached during the one or two consultation sessions. The patient should then be cognitively prepared to cope with the experiences to follow.

The *definition of ground rules* precedes all else. Is the consultant being asked primarily to give pro forma approval to an abortion already decided upon by the patient and others in her life, to satisfy a medicolegal requirement, or is the consultation being sought to help the patient come to a decision and then follow through with a minimum of conflict and distress? Consultant and patient should discuss this question early in the consultation so that they can proceed with similar expectations to deal with the remainder of the tasks confronting them. When help with making and implementing a decision is the basic work to be done, the ten areas to be covered are as follows:

1. Learn how the woman feels about the pregnancy and possible abortion.
2. Clarify the circumstances of this pregnancy.
3. Discuss the emotional and psychological responses to this pregnancy.
4. Learn about the patient's fantasies and fears about pregnancy and abortion.
5. Obtain a careful sexual history.

6. Discuss the effect of the pregnancy on the patient's social environment.

7. Discuss the effect of the pregnancy on important others in the patient's life.

8. Obtain a psychiatric history and, when indicated, psychological testing.

9. Meet with significant others when needed.

10. Help the patient arrive at a decision and anticipate reactions either to continued pregnancy or to abortion.

How does the patient *feel about the pregnancy and possible abortion?* Most women in our culture have mixed feelings about abortion. A totally positive or totally negative view may be an indication of trouble, or it may merely represent a necessary amount of denial given that particular woman's character structure. The consultant should attempt to explore with the woman both sides of her ambivalence, if present, and the missing side if absent. Some women will see absolutely no alternative to the abortion, and it may turn out that the consultation is really serving the needs of the woman's partner or some other important person. In that case, the woman may want to invite this person to see the consultant with her. In other situations, the woman may be truly torn between conflicting needs and pressures. Hopefully, as these contradicting forces are carefully explored and weighed with an objective but sympathetic consultant, the decision will become easier to make.

The specific *circumstances of the pregnancy* need clarification. One must know the length of gestation: first trimester abortions can be done by simple suction curettage; second trimester abortions require injection of hypertonic solutions or hysterotomy, both more complex procedures than simple curettage. The woman's emotional reaction to any previous pregnancies needs discussion. If any of them ended in spontaneous or induced abortions, investigate carefully the circumstances and feelings at that time. Finally, the use or nonuse of contraception should be openly discussed in detail.

This may be a significant index of the woman's unconscious wish to become pregnant, or it may reveal a profound lack of birth control information which the consultant can help correct. If the woman's unconscious or scarcely preconscious desire to become pregnant was dominating her behavior, it is very important to help her to an open recognition of her true feelings. In that way she will be in a much better position to deal with the current pregnancy; in addition, she will be better able to assert control over her future reproductive life.

The *responses to the pregnancy itself* are of great psychological importance. Many of them, such as dreams and fantasies, since they are more emotional than rational, indicate the deeper feelings and motivations involved. The 30-year-old divorced woman (Example 29-3), uncertain about her ability to become pregnant, did her own pregnancy test and recorded her reaction:

> "Okay now, Carol, stay calm and do this test right. One drop of reagent; one drop of my urine. Now I'm waiting. My God, it's agglutinating. No, wait. Oh my God, it is. IT IS. Where's a lamp? I've got to see this for sure. Are my eyes playing tricks? NO . . . IT'S FOR REAL, CHICKY. YOUR TEST IS POSITIVE AND YOU ARE PREGNANT. YOU ARE PREGNANT. *I AM PREGNANT. I AM PREGNANT.*

The strength of these feelings of joy and exultation was fully matched by the gloom and despair which enveloped her in a suicidal, self-mutilating depression following the abortion. This woman's immediate response could have been of some predictive value which, had it been known, would have resulted in a slower, more careful approach to the abortion.

The 17-year-old high school girl in Example 29-2 had a series of dreams following the second abortion. All involved happy scenes with babies. As therapy progressed, it became clear that besides representing a continued neurotic need for children, the dreams on another level expressed a healthy, optimistic recovery from the recent loss.

Thus, with this patient one could have felt safe in recommending her for a third abortion, which she handled quite well. In brief therapy she learned to understand the neurotic as well as the adaptive components of her dreams.

A woman's *fantasies or fears about getting pregnant, initial or early fantasies once she knows she is pregnant,* or *fantasies about a previous abortion* all may be helpful in advising about a current abortion decision. The woman who, in spite of using the pill correctly, finds it impossible to relax during intercourse may feel guilty about her sexual behavior, or she may unconsciously wish for that which she appears to fear most: pregnancy. The 24-year-old divorced woman in Example 29-1 who saw her fetus in a pathology specimen jar developed a well-encapsulated psychotic delusion that she had carried the pregnancy to term. She first discussed the delusion two years after the abortion, but rejected a recommendation for further psychotherapy. Six months following that she was admitted for a second abortion and developed a hysterical psychotic episode. The abortion was delayed, and with support she eventually was able to carry through with the procedure. However, her inability to master the previous abortion experience appropriately by giving up the delusion that the fetus was still alive was a good indicator that the subsequent abortion without intervening therapy or consultation would represent a crisis for her.

Because feelings about abortion in many ways reflect underlying attitudes about sexuality in general, a *careful sexual history* should be taken. Early and later traumatic sexual experiences, masturbation, menarche, first intercourse, and orgasm are all important sexual events which may need review. Attitudes about menarche and masturbation will suggest the degree of sexual repression under which the woman was raised. Her age and feelings at the time of first intercourse may provide important clues as to whether she will see the abortion as a form of punishment for her sexual desires and activity. Many women in our present-day society will have varying degrees of

difficulty with their own orgasms, varying from complete absence of orgasm to dissatisfaction with the timing or frequency. This too should be discussed as an aid to relieving sexual inhibitions in general which may directly or indirectly influence the reaction to the abortion experience in particular.

The *effect of the pregnancy on the woman's social environment* may be quite specific or quite vague. She could lose her job or be thrown out of school; less concretely, she may feel a silent sense of rejection or disapproval among those who know. The possible effects can be explored. What would happen at school or on the job? Would she share the information with her friends, or would she feel it essential that she be the only one to know? Might she in fact lose her job, her status as a student, or even her friends if the pregnancy were known? Is there confirmation available in reality for the feared reactions, or do her fears seem exaggerated or even projected views of her own negative feelings about the pregnancy? All these questions require thorough consideration; though an abortion may occur in secret, the social network will be affected directly by her actions. She herself may react and reverberate to these feared judgments for months to come if they are not clarified ahead of time.

The *effect of pregnancy on important other persons* in the woman's life is a critical area of discussion. The pregnancy and abortion may represent a crisis in the relationship with the woman's sexual partner, whether he be boyfriend, "old man," or husband. A casual affair or one-nighter resulting in pregnancy may precipitate a crisis in the woman's longer-term relationships. If her partner knows about the pregnancy, it may be appropriate to see them together before the abortion. Often, however, the woman does not want her sexual partner to know that she is pregnant, even if he is her husband, though this obviously bespeaks a troubled relationship; it is important to let the woman make up her own mind. In doing so the meaning of the secrecy should be clarified. She may feel the relationship is over and not want the child to serve as an excuse for prolonging the bond. Conversely, she may desperately want a commitment from her partner and be afraid that the pregnancy will expose her dependency on him and open herself to rejection by him.

The question of involving parents, especially when the woman is an adolescent, can be very delicate. The consultant again must be guided by a primary responsibility to the patient. Some adolescents fear parental punitiveness about sexuality and pregnancy. In other cases, sharing the crisis with parents may break down communication barriers not only about sexuality but also about many other matters, and the crisis may serve both to bring unexpected parental support and to ease the transition into adulthood. It is as if the parents breathe a sigh of relief that the responsibility for their daughter's sexual behavior is finally lifted from their shoulders and placed where it properly belongs — on her shoulders. Other individuals of importance may be siblings or special friends. Though it is rare to see such people conjunctively in consultation, at times it is quite appropriate and helpful.

The consultant should obtain a *psychiatric history* and, when indicated, *psychological testing.* One should inquire about previous psychiatric treatment and hospitalization, use of psychotropic medication, and awareness of emotional problems not directly connected with the pregnancy. The consultation can, in fact, be a "ticket of admission" for a course of psychotherapy which deals with far broader issues than pregnancy and abortion. One should be particularly sensitive to information about dependency needs and feminine identification. One can forgo a formal mental status examination unless there is suspicion of a particular organic or psychotic complication of functioning which deserves attention.

Sometimes psychological testing can illuminate unclear areas of possible postabortion complications. The Minnesota Multiphasic Personality Inventory (MMPI) can help identify depression, guilt, strange ideas, and energy levels, all of which

can combine to lead to self-destructive behavior. Rorschach responses predominating in images of mutilation, viscera, and so forth, can also have important predictive value. The 30-year-old divorcee (Example 29-3) who was hospitalized for depression and suicidal preoccupation following abortion was tested later; the tester said, from the MMPI data, "I fear that she could alternate between acting self-destructively on her bizarre ideas and just sitting around obsessing about them, to the exclusion of reality around her." However, the Rorschach "was the most distressing," as she presented "a very disturbing theme over and over again, namely her damaged and mutilated self." On Card II, where people usually see two bears with their noses together separated by a space, she saw "the skin of a reptile that has pins stuck around the edges. I have a feeling that it's me. It looks like it's been pulled apart and stretched." In this particular case, psychological testing prior to abortion would have been interpreted by this patient as a gross interference with her right to abortion. However, in other cases in the future such testing could be recommended not as a precondition but rather as an aid to abortion. Her postabortal course could surely have been eased had the danger signals present in her diary been detected by the judicious use of psychological testing.

It is at times most important for the consultant to *meet with significant others* in the patient's life. This certainly was true in Example 29-4, the happily married psychologist and his wife. However, by acting as both mediator and clarifier in a conflict situation, it may be easier to work effectively as the woman's ally in the final decision-making process as well as in the postabortal period. The consultant may want, with the patient's consent, to speak directly to the operating physician who made the initial referral in order to discuss concerns about the emotional implications of the procedure; it might even be appropriate to have a three-way meeting take place if there are specific questions to answer or fears which need to be allayed.

Finally, the patient should be helped *to anticipate her reactions,* pre- and postabortally. Some women do very well once the ambivalence is worked through. For others, the immediate pre-abortal period may continue to be one of great stress even after the decision is made. Tranquilizing medication, soporifics, mobilization of family members and friends, and supportive therapy all may be appropriate and necessary with individual patients. A mild to moderate feeling of depression in the postabortal period is common, even in women who have undergone spontaneous abortion. One might think there would be no guilt component to these women's reactions, but this is not always so. Induced abortion magnifies such underlying guilt and regret. Anticipation of such feelings and follow-up counseling can markedly diminish these reactions.

The longer-term sequelae which are frequently seen are the *gestation reaction* and the *anniversary reaction.* Both are periods characterized by thoughts of "the child," what sex it would have been, renewed feelings about the male partner, sleep and appetite disturbance, and depression with feelings of guilt and regret. The gestation reaction occurs nine months after conception took place, the time when the fetus would have been born. Like the anniversary reaction which may occur on the first, second, or even later anniversaries of the abortion itself, the gestation reaction is usually self-limited, indicates some degree of unresolved feelings about the experience, and can be a propitious time to gain better perspective on the abortion experience through further therapy.

CONCLUSION

Abortion consultation, like abortion counseling, is coming into its own all across the nation. Because psychiatric consultation will no longer be required as a ruse to obtain abortion, the consultant can be restored to a more comfortable role as agent of the client or patient rather than of society at large.[16]

The rapidly spreading acceptance of legal abortion as an ethical and moral right of all women in place of illegal abortion as a punishment for female sexual behavior will mean a diminution of societally induced guilt about abortion. However, the cases chosen as examples in this chapter all represent situations wherein the women's internal psychodynamics were critical in determining her decision to abort or not to abort, her course, and the outcome. In the future both consultants and abortionists will be able to pay more attention to these factors as societal attitudes become increasingly less rigid. Knowing indications for consultation and areas to cover should help make the consultant more effective as an ally of the patient.

If ever voluntary contraception becomes universally available and effective, present-day attitudes about abortion may become antiquated curiosities subject to anthropologic investigation. Until then, however, abortion will remain an important issue for all women, a sensitive issue for many, and a life crisis for a few. For women in the last category, skillful and empathic consultation in conjunction with supportive counseling is essential.

REFERENCES

1. Halleck, Seymour L.: "The Power of the Psychiatric Excuse," *The Politics of Therapy,* Science House, New York, 1971, pp. 135–156.
2. Tietze, Christopher: "Therapeutic Abortions in the United States," *Am. J. Obstet. Gynecol.,* **191**:784–787, July 1968.
3. Center for Disease Control: *Abortion Surveillance,* U.S. Government Printing Office, 1970.
4. Ibid., 1971.
5. Ford, C. V., et al.: "Therapeutic Abortion: Who Needs a Psychiatrist?" *Am. J. Obstet. Gynecol.,* **38**(2):208–213, August 1971.
6. Asher, John D.: "Abortion Counseling," *Am. J. Public Health,* **62**(5):686–688, May 1972.

7. Tyler, Carl W., and Jan Schneider: "The Logistics of Abortion Service in the Absence of Restrictive Criminal Legislation in the United States," *Am. J. Public Health,* **61**(3): 491, March 1971.

8. Asher: loc. cit.

9. Ekblad, M.: "Induced Abortion on Psychiatric Grounds. A Follow-up Study of 479 Women," *Acta Psychiat. Neurol. Scand. Suppl.,* **99**:234, 1955.

10. Bloom, B. L.: "Measurement of Crisis Phenomena," in Howard Parad (ed.), *Crisis Intervention: Selected Readings,* Family Service Association of America, New York, 1965, pp. 304–305.

11. Adams, M.: "Social Aspects of Medical Care for the Mentally Retarded," *New Engl. J. Med.,* **286**(12):635–638, May 23, 1972.

12. Curran, W. J.: "Rights for the Retarded: A Landmark Decree," *Am. J. Public Health,* **62**(2):264–265, February 1972.

13. Zilboorg, G.: "The Dynamics of Schizophrenic Reactions Related to Pregnancy and Childbirth," *Am. J. Psychiat.,* **8**(4):733, January 1929.

14. Westoff, C. F., R. G. Potter, and P. C. Sagi: *The Third Child: A Study in the Prediction of Fertility,* Princeton, Princeton, N.J., 1963, pp. 233–234.

15. Miller, Warren B.: "Psychological Antecedents to Conception in Pregnancies Terminated by Therapeutic Abortion," to be published.

16. Szasz, Thomas: *The Ethics of Psychoanalysis,* Dell, New York, 1965, p. 21.

WARREN B. MILLER, M.D.

CHAPTER 30

Psychiatry and Physical Illness: The Psychosomatic Interface

The psychiatrist as physician has knowledge of and experience with the basic processes of disease. It is quite natural therefore that a psychiatrist be expected to know how disease states affect the mind, both through their direct physiological effect on the central nervous system and through their indirect symbolic effect. He can also be expected to understand and deal with those complex relationships which exist between psychological events and the onset or worsening of a physical disease or the prolongation of recovery from it. In short, the psychiatrist is expected to be proficient and understanding in dealing with the interface between the mind and the body, between the psyche and the soma.

The psychosomatic interface has traditionally been discussed under four headings: organic brain syndromes, psychological reactions to physical illness, conversion disorders, and psychophysiological disorders. This chapter will discuss and summarize those four traditional areas within an adaptational framework. At the conclusion, there will be an integration of this material using a general systems type of approach.

ADAPTATION TO PHYSICAL ILLNESS: ORGANIC BRAIN SYNDROMES

The organic brain syndromes are the broad psychological and behavioral disturbances resulting from dysfunction of the chief organ of adaptation, the central nervous system, as a result of organic illness which either involves it directly or affects it indirectly through systemic influences. Although there is some current evidence that psychiatric syndromes such as schizophrenia, manic-depressive psychoses, certain character disorders, and drug and alcohol dependencies have significant organic determinants in the sense that they may have biochemical and neurophysiological causes, the organic brain syndromes are different in that they are associated with organic disease states which affect the central nervous system in a general and diffuse way. (See also Chapter 5.)

This diffuse disruption of the central nervous system results in a general cognitive and integrative dysfunction which produces a core psychobehavioral syndrome common to all organic brain syndromes. The features of that core have been categorized in several different convenient and somewhat arbitrary ways. In this discussion they will be grouped under seven headings which may be remembered by the simple mnemonic EMOJIAC, which may be explicated as follows. E stands for emotions. These are characteristically labile when the patient is subject to the influence of arousing stimulation and are otherwise generally flattened. M stands for memory. This is impaired, particularly short-term memory as compared with long-term memory; immediate (one or two minutes') recall may be especially impaired. O stands for orientation. This is usually but not always disturbed. Orientation to time is generally the first to be affected; orientation to place is next to be impaired as the disorder becomes more severe; and in the grossest central nervous system deficits there is a disorientation to person. J stands for judgment. This may be poor, often because of lack of comprehension and poor appreciation of consequences. Frequently there is also an impulsivity of thought and behavior which affects judgment. I stands for intellective function. This is characteristically disrupted, as manifested by poor general knowledge, by difficulty with cognitive manipulations such as arithmetic calculations, and by limitations in abstract thinking as indicated by proverb interpretation or determination of similarities. A stands for attention. Impairment of this function is indicated when the patient reveals gaps in his intake of environmental material when, for example, he is asked to repeat to an interviewer a short story or a series of digits forward. It is also indicated by his being highly distractible and unable to focus his attention, such as when he rambles during his response to a specific question. C stands for concentration. This function may be disrupted in varying amounts, from the point where the patient notices some difficulty accomplishing his usual tasks to the point where he is unable to concentrate upon requests as when asked to perform serial subtraction of 7. In addition to the material embraced by the EMOJIAC categories, perhaps the most important clue to the presence of a brain syndrome lies

in the fluctuating nature of the signs. Apart from changes in the metabolic and other organic causes of the syndrome, these fluctuations appear to result from the patient's changing ability to mobilize the central nervous system to overcome the deficit and function more effectively. As a result, marked variations in the extent of impairment from day to day and even hour to hour will be apparent.

Most standard psychiatric mental status examinations (MSE) have been designed so as to elicit information relevant to all seven of these categories. However, no special MSE is actually necessary to identify the presence of an organic brain syndrome. Rather, the clinician need only suspect its presence and observe the patient's behavior and responses during the interview.

In addition to the core brain syndrome, there are particular features associated with each case which make it specific and unique. Historically this has resulted in the development of a variety of typologies.[1] Within the last forty years a general consensus has developed on the distinction between the acute and chronic types of brain syndrome, with the former being reversible and the latter irreversible.[2-4] Recently, the trend in several psychiatric texts[5,6] has been to identify three distinct clinical pictures: *delirium, dementia,* and the *dysmnestic syndrome.* The first typically has a rapid onset, is reversible, and results from involvement of all parts of the central nervous system; a dementia may be either slow or rapid in onset, is irreversible and therefore prolonged, and has associated with the it the involvement of specific cortical centers which cause specific functional deficits; the dysmnestic syndrome (characterized by the memory loss, disorientation, and confabulation seen in Korsakoff's psychosis) also has a variable onset, tends to be irreversible, and is thought to be connected with the impairment of the specific cortical areas associated with memory.

There are two variables which seem to play an important role in the type of clinical picture seen in association with an organic brain syndrome. The first of these variables is the *time course* of the syndrome. This refers to the relative speed of onset of the underlying dysfunction and to the duration of its presence. When its onset is sudden, over a period of minutes or hours, there results a clouding of consciousness, apprehension and agitation, and perplexity. When the development of dysfunction is more gradual, over a period of weeks or months, the individual has more opportunity to adapt to the deficits. In such instances the syndrome may be apparent only under stress or when familiar and supportive structure is removed. This may be observed in the so-called sundowner syndrome, where a hospitalized patient seems to have clear mentation during the day but as soon as the sun goes down (i.e., when both physical and social stimulation decrease) develops confusion and becomes a management problem. Irrespective of the speed of onset, when the organic brain syndrome is of long standing, as happens in irreversible posttraumatic conditions and those conditions associated with aging, the individual has the time to adapt his daily routine and even his lifestyle so that the clinical picture does not reveal the typical signs of organicity but presents more prominently with denial of the deficit, various defensive and adaptive rigidities, marked orderliness, and emotional or disorganizing reactions to stress.

The second variable to play a significant role in the clinical picture associated with organic brain syndromes is the *character structure and basic adaptive style* of the involved individual. The neurotic, behavioral, and psychotic disturbances seen in association with brain syndromes — particularly the acute ones — are manifestations of basic personality features. In these disturbances, the brain syndrome seems to act either as a releaser of latent, ordinarily controlled (or repressed) aspects of personality or as a special kind of stress which calls forth especially primitive and maladaptive aspects of the individual's response repertoire.

The following two examples illustrate two kinds of behavioral disturbances seen in association with brain syndromes.

Example 30-1. Psychiatric consultation was requested for a 29-year-old woman who was recovering for three days following routine abdominal surgery. The physicians and nurses on the ward complained that she was "becoming hysterical." By this they meant that at times she became very emotional and demanding. This occurred particularly at night, when she complained bitterly of difficulty falling asleep and seemed to be frightened and upset by the most minimal disturbances. During psychiatric interviewing the patient tended to ramble, was distractible, and had a poor memory for recent events; nevertheless it was discovered that she was having frightening dreams during much of the night. It also was learned that she had always had a low tolerance for sleeping medication. A review of the chart revealed that she was being given large doses of postoperative pain medication as well as routine doses of sleeping medication. It appeared that she was overmedicated. Psychiatric impression was of a mild organic brain syndrome secondary to sedative medication with associated anxiety reaction and exacerbation of passive dependent character traits. Within twenty-four hours of decreasing her pain and sleeping medication, the patient was completely cooperative. She was fully aware of her environment and able to cope well with routine hospital and postoperative stresses. She remembered preoperative events clearly and in general seemed to be an entirely different "personality."

Example 30-2. A 45-year-old Mexican-American male with chronic renal failure was in the hospital for renal dialysis. Although his family was extremely supportive, the long course of his illness had resulted in their visiting him with decreasing frequency. He was awaiting a kidney transplant and receiving periodic dialysis. It was in this setting that on one occasion he became extremely suspicious and distrustful of the house staff and made an effort to escape from his room by jumping out the window. Psychiatric examination revealed a gross organic brain syndrome associated with delusions and hallucinations. Blood urea nitrogen was markedly elevated and other blood chemistries were abnormal as well. The patient was restrained and dialysis was begun. With clearing of the patient's renal function, his psychotic process completely receded and he became his previous friendly, somewhat timid self. Work with the patient's family mobilized their concern and support and helped prevent reoccurences of the psychotic state even though the patient continued to experience varying degrees of organic brain deficit while awaiting a transplant.

Although it is commonly recognized that a local organic disease or a systemic toxic process can disrupt the central nervous system in a gross, diffuse, and nonspecific way, it is less often appreciated that certain *psychological and symbolic factors* can, through excess or deficiency, produce a very similar clinical picture. The more common factors which can do this are extreme anxiety, sensory deprivation and/or monotony, sleep deprivation, and social and symbolic isolation.[7-9] Since it is not unusual to find most if not all these factors affecting patients who are in the hospital with serious organic disease, it is important to recognize how their effects can actually summate with the disruption of an organic brain syndrome, making the latter clinically more apparent and, in some instances, stressing the patient beyond his compensatory capacities.

Example 30-3. A 72-year-old widow was hospitalized for a generalized dermatitis. Although somewhat depressed and withdrawn, she was doing well until she developed a secondary infection with staphylococcus. As a result she was placed in isolation on precautions. This severely reduced the number of social contacts she had and the overall amount of stimulation to which she was exposed. Within twenty-four hours, the patient became markedly depressed,

agitated, disoriented, and, at night, hallucinatory. The medical staff recognized the organic brain syndrome and the associated depression but did not appreciate the precipitating nature of the move to isolation. Psychiatric consultation was requested, and the psychiatrist recommended the usual types of orienting stimuli such as the presence of a calendar and a clock by her bed and the regular volunteering of orienting information by each nurse to enter the room. He also suggested a definite effort on the part of the nursing staff and the patient's family to provide regular social and physical stimulation. Although this program was definitely helpful, the patient remained moderately withdrawn and liable to nighttime disturbance until she was moved off isolation and back to the open ward.

ADAPTATION TO PHYSICAL ILLNESS: PSYCHOLOGICAL REACTIONS TO ILLNESS

Organic illness affects the individual not only through its direct physiological influence on the functioning of the central nervous system as discussed in the previous section but also through higher-level, symbolic processes. Each illness has special meanings and poses certain problems to the sick person. He responds with a variety of short- and, in some cases, long-term modifications of his behavior. These processes of coping and adaptation have undergone important initial exploration and description during the last several decades.[10-13]

The stresses to which sick individuals are subject may be placed in three categories. First is the *loss* of functional ability and the debilitation, pain, and threat of death which result directly from the disease itself. Associated with these stresses are similar ones which result from the various threatening procedures and experiences to which the patient may be subjected during the course of his evaluation and treatment. Second is the *dependency* and passivity and the resulting regression which the patient must accept, especially during the early phase of a severe illness. A corollary stress which may occur toward the end of an illness is the resumption of previous levels of self-determination and emotional investment in the outside world with its associated need to "de-regress." In illnesses which leave a permanent residual, this recuperative psychological process may even assume the proportions of new identity formation. Third and last is the *separation* and aloneness which follow the removal of the sick individual both psychologically and spatially from his supportive social network. To understand an individual's adaptive psychological responses to illness, all three stresses must be considered. During the development and resolution of an illness and its attendant stresses, certain intrapsychic and interpersonal adaptations occur normally. These sequences are in turn shaped by social norms and custom. Thus, as the outward signs or inner symptoms of an illness first develop, the individual becomes aware of the changes and pays increasing attention to his physical condition. Depending on his own past experience with illness, his usual level of concern about bodily function, and his characteristic response to signals of danger, he will live for a period of time with the signs and symptoms more or less on the periphery of his attention. Sooner or later, however, they will take a central place in consciousness, and the individual will attempt to interpret what he is experiencing in a way which helps him cope with the signs and symptoms and understand them within a rational framework. In some cases his interpretations will lead him to explain away or discount the significance of what he perceives. In other cases they will lead him toward a concerned attention or even preoccupa-

tion. Depending on the direction of these interpretations and on the severity and course of the disease, sooner or later the individual will be led to action. At first this may simply involve discussing the possible meaning and significance of what he is experiencing with a family member or friend. At some point, however, a remedy will be looked for, and this may eventually involve his seeking professional help. Wherever in this sequence the individual begins to perceive himself as ill and, drawing upon cultural norms regarding illness behavior, starts to act as a sick person, he assumes what Parsons[14] has called the *sick role*. This sequence of psychological and behavioral events is depicted in Figure 30-1.

In our society, there are certain rights and duties associated with being sick and the assumption of the sick role. First of all, the sick individual is exempted from the execution of his usual obligations and responsibilities and from the performance of his usual social roles. Second, the individual is not held responsible for his being ill. In other words, he is exempted from personal responsibility for his ill state. Third, he is expected to give up the sick role as quickly as possible. This is closely tied to the fourth feature, the individual's responsibility to seek help and, if possible, improve his condition. This last feature usually leads the individual into a distinct "patient role," where he acquires a whole new set of rights and obligations, including the right to be taken care of and the obligation to follow the doctor's orders and give up some of the privileges of his nonsick status. It is through these sets of expectations associated with illness behavior that social custom ensures not only that the patient is protected from too much demand during his illness, but also that

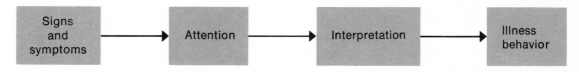

Figure 30-1 The sequence of cognitive events that lead from the development of a symptom (or sign) of physical illness to the behavior associated with "being sick."

he is hastened out of his sick and patient status as quickly as possible.

With this general discussion of the psychological and social aspects of becoming ill and recuperating from illness as a background, we may go on to discuss and illustrate some maladaptive reactions to illness. Generally these take two forms, which represent the extremes on a continuum. One extreme form is exemplified by the *denier*. This is the individual who typically takes great pride in his self-reliance, health, and ability to control his own life, including his bodily functions. Such an individual will often delay attending to signs and symptoms and then will avoid interpreting them in terms of illness as long as possible. He will be reluctant to acknowledge to his family and friends that he is ill, and even more reluctant to ask for help from a physician. If he cannot avoid becoming a patient, he will minimize his illness and avoid his appointments or treatments. If he is hospitalized, he will create problems with the staff by denying or minimizing his illness and attempting to resume his usual activities too quickly. In general, this sort of individual comes to treatment too late, often after the disease has progressed extensively, and when he does come to treatment, resists it in a variety of ways. The net result is inadequate therapy. Psychiatric consultation may be requested by a concerned but frustrated physician for help with treating and managing a reluctant patient.

The other extreme form is exemplified by the *hypochondriac*. This is the individual who is extremely dependent and anxious in the face of physical illness even of the mildest sort. He tends to be hyperalert to the signs and symptoms of illness and too quick to interpret any bodily changes as a signal of disease. Correspondingly, he is prone to discuss the slightest physical problems with family and friends and quick to present complaints to a physician. In the face of real and severe physical illness, this individual will tend to rely excessively on others for help and reassurance and be overconcerned with the problems of

treatment and self-medication. If he is hospitalized, he is inclined to regress to an anxious and dependent state, often characterized by a demanding and controlling quality. In general, this sort of individual comes to a physician too early and too often. As a result of his behavior he often creates antagonism and may be rejected by his family, friends, and physician for excessive complaints and demands; on the other hand he may be medically and surgically overtreated, exposing himself to the eventuality of iatrogenic complications. Psychiatric consultation may be requested because of the pronounced psychological and physical invalidism which tends to result from even the most minimal organic problem.

The majority of ill people fall between these two extremes, and their pattern of adaptation to disease is especially influenced by two factors: the *time course* of the disease and their own *character structure*. It appears, for example, that a disease is more readily denied when it has a rapid onset and a rapid remission. The following case was discussed at a coronary care unit (CCU) staff meeting concerned with patient management.

Example 30-4. A 63-year-old business executive was stricken with severe precordial pain while playing tennis. His friends wanted to take him immediately to the hospital, but he objected, insisting that he would soon be all right. Finally, after the pain had continued for forty-five minutes, he was brought to the emergency room, where he was diagnosed as having a myocardial infarction and admitted to the coronary care unit. On the day following his admission, he was depressed, anxious, and irritable. In spite of his physicians' and nurses' requests, he insisted on doing as much for himself as he could, short of getting out of bed. He carried on a long argument with his primary physician over whether he could have a telephone in his room. This was strictly against the rules, but he insisted he needed it to conduct some business activities and his physician finally agreed. On the second day following admission, the patient ambulated himself on numerous occasions in spite of his doctor's orders that he remain on strict bed rest. This was possible because the pain, which had been severe on the day of admission, had completely disappeared by the second day following admission. At this time he was transferred off the CCU. During the rest of his hospital stay the patient never raised any questions about the condition of his heart and seemed not even to acknowledge that he had had a heart attack. Within a few days of his transfer the patient was so eager to get home that his physician decided to discharge him to be cared for at home rather than continue the struggle with him in the hospital. At the time of his discharge the patient was already talking about returning to work. Once he had returned home, this energetic and active man with a well-documented and severe myocardial infarction found it almost impossible to even recall the fact that he had been acutely ill a short time before.

On the other hand, diseases which have a gradual onset and a chronic, relatively unremitting course may lead over a period of time to an extensive amount of relearning and psychological compensation.

Example 30-5. A 47-year-old married woman was admitted to the hospital for cardiac catheterization and a general evaluation for open heart surgery. She had had rheumatic fever as a child and had a long-standing multivalvular involvement which considerably limited her mobility and activities. Her heart condition had always caused her considerable worry. She had never had children and had spent most of her married life at home, closely attended by a solicitous husband. During the three months prior to admission she experienced increased shortness of breath and fatigue, and her personal physician suggested

that she might profit considerably by open heart surgery. Cardiac evaluation in the hospital indicated that this in fact was the case, but when the surgeons visited her to make arrangements for surgery, she became very anxious and uncertain about her decision. Psychiatric consultation was requested, and after several interviews the psychiatrist determined that the patient was not motivated to have her chronic heart disease repaired, even partially. Consciously, she feared the pain and trauma of surgery and the small but real risk of death. On a less conscious level she was much more anxious about the demands that her husband would place upon her and the lifestyle changes that he would expect of her as a result of an improved cardiac condition. After further discussions with the psychiatric consultant and her attending physician, she somewhat reluctantly decided not to undergo surgery but rather to continue with her invaliding cardiac symptoms and condition.

In addition to the time course of a disease, the character structure of an individual also figures significantly in his adaptation to it. Kahana and Bibring in particular have developed this theme.[15] Using traditional psychoanalytic character types, they discuss the relationship between individual dynamics, the meanings of illness, and the patient's maladaptive behavior in the face of physical illness. For the *oral* personality, illness brings a fear of helplessness and a great need for personal care which is manifested during illness by the demand for boundless attention, interest, and support; for the *compulsive* personality, illness threatens loss of control over himself and his environment, and his behavior becomes rigid and controlling while he shows signs of shame and guilt; to the *hysterical* personality, illness means a personal defect and the threat of being unattractive, unappreciated, and weak, and as a result it stimulates exaggerated, dramatic, and captivating behavior. The following two examples illustrate how one patient with a *masochistic* personality and another with a *paranoid* personality reacted to their respective illnesses and what kinds of problems in medical management each presented to the house staff.

Example 30-6. Psychiatric consultation was requested for a 41-year-old married woman with a congenital back deformity which for many years had left her slightly limited in movement and in mild to moderate pain. She had two teenage children of her own and for about ten years had worked hard as the secretary-receptionist and general assistant to a physician in a small community where she lived. This man was somewhat incompetent in the management of his overall private practice, and the patient had spent a great deal of time helping him with his management, worrying about him, and getting him out of financial difficulty. Her own husband worked as a truck driver and was away much of the time. The patient's disability had become much more pronounced in the six months prior to admission. This development followed the sudden death of her physician-employer, after which she became much more concerned with her own health. As the patient put it herself, "I have always packed my worries in a bag and carried them around with me." Once she no longer had the job with the physician, she "had to find something else to worry about." The patient's childhood and early adult history suggested that she was a woman who had learned to achieve balance in her psychological life by always having a problem to worry about. In addition, she had always found it important to be concerned with other people rather than herself. The psychiatric consultant saw the task of medical management as one of helping her to find another set of problems and concerns outside of herself and her physical health which could bind her attention and energies and could satisfy her need to give to others. The patient's family was involved in

the disposition, primarily by getting them to appreciate the importance for this woman of having a focus of work and attention outside of herself and the family. The patient found a volunteer job in a local hospital and was gradually able to return to her previous level of ambulation and general functioning. One thing which made this possible was the encouragement on the part of her physicians to get back to work "for the sake of your family."

Example 30-7. Psychiatric consultation was requested for a 60-year-old married man who had been hospitalized for treatment of an open fracture of the left arm resulting from an accidental fall. The patient had always been a rather suspicious, argumentative, and distant individual. This was his first hospitalization during his adult life, and he responded by becoming irritable, dissatisfied, and, eventually, suspicious of the staff and convinced of the deliberate inadequacy of their care. His hostile attitude alienated the staff to the point where they avoided him and his care did actually worsen. As a result of this type of interaction the patient was on the verge of signing out of the hospital, in spite of the fact that he needed to be on continuous I.V. medication and have his wound checked frequently. In dealing with this patient's hostility and need for control, the house staff had responded by attempting countercontrol. The psychiatric consultant, after perceiving this patient's paranoid personality trends, decided to respond in a different way. At the time of the interview the patient had packed his bags and was sitting out in the hall with the I.V. still running. The psychiatrist did not attempt to express disapproval of the patient's leaving. He told the patient quite explicitly on several occasions that whether or not he left the hopsital was entirely up to him. Then he focused the discussion on the patient's future plans. As these were discussed, it became clear that the patient had no plan and was leaving only to get away from an intolerable situation. The psychiatrist then focused discussion on the various elements in this situation, agreeing with the patient on several points. The latter's adamancy about leaving softened considerably in the face of this type of interview. The patient was waiting for his wife to pick him up, and when she arrived a joint interview highlighted her reluctance to have him leave the hospital and her willingness to help him cope with the problems with which he was dealing. As a result of these interventions the patient agreed to "give the staff another twenty-four hours" to improve their treatment of him. This provided the psychiatric consultant with time to talk directly with the nurse and physician staff and to help them develop a suitable management plan which would allow the patient to feel more in control and to maintain interpersonal distance.

PHYSICAL ILLNESS AS A FORM OF ADAPTATION: CONVERSION DISORDERS

The original notion of a conversion reaction was developed by Freud on the basis of his idea that a psychological conflict, such as the wish to act on an unacceptable impulse, was defended against by converting its expression from behavior into symbolic body language. This "conversion" from a psychological to a physical mode of expression brought about relief of anxiety by simultaneously defending against the overt expression of the unacceptable impulse and allowing its expression in a disguised way.

Example 30-8. The patient was a 34-year-old married woman who lived with her husband and 2-year-old daughter on a small farm. During the time since the birth of her daughter she had become increasingly depressed and upset by the amount of housework she had. Her husband was a passive man who demanded a great deal from her, and after her child was born the patient had found taking care of the farmhouse, her daughter, and her husband a great strain. She became increasingly resentful and was having more frequent arguments with her husband, some of which resulted in their not talking to each other for several days at a time. The patient's husband was a financially successful and powerful man outside the home, and during the marriage she had formed a very deep dependency on him, one which in many ways replaced her relationship with her father. This latter relationship had been lost to her when she was forced to leave home around age 16 because of bitter arguments with her mother. The patient was therefore both consciously and unconsciously extremely reluctant to leave her husband, in spite of the great resentment she felt about her role and the demands he placed upon her.

In the context of this conflict, the patient developed some low back pain which over a period of several days progressed to paralysis of the lower right leg. She was hospitalized on the orthopedic service for evaluation, and a psychiatric consultation was requested when no physical basis for the disability could be established. During the interviews with the psychiatrist, the patient talked about her wish to leave her husband and ultimately about her concern with her own dependency and her wish to "stand on my own two feet." She also discussed her own fear of the loneliness and helplessness she might experience if she did try to establish independence. It came out that her leg paralysis had developed on the day following a severe argument during which the patient had made up her mind to leave. In the process of discussing these dynamics, the patient formed a dependent, therapeutic relationship with the psychiatric consultant. This together with some insight permitted her to give up her conversion symptom. She was transferred at that point to a psychiatric inpatient service for more extended psychiatric treatment.

In this case the paralysis expressed the patient's conflict over dependence-independence issues. She wanted to leave her husband, but her anxiety about leaving was so great that she remained indecisive. At the point that she was about to "walk away" from her husband, her foot became paralyzed and prevented this. The primary gain which resulted from this conversion symptom was the relief from anxiety which occurred when the symptom prevented the patient from leaving her husband. Once the conversion symptom was well established, the patient was physically unable to move about, had to be attended to, and eventually was hospitalized, thus increasing her dependency. This increased care and attention which she received as a result of the conversion was the secondary gain of the symptom.

Summarizing this case, then, the conscious impulse was to gain independence and the more or less unconscious wish was to remain dependent. The conversion symptom developed at a time when the patient was about to act on her conscious wishes, creating a great deal of anxiety. The bodily statement and expression of the conversion can be paraphrased as, "I cannot stand on my own two feet." In developing this symptom, the anxiety was relieved and, in fact, the patient's dependency was increased by her illness and hospitalization.

More contemporary approaches to the understanding of conversion reactions, such as the work reported by Ziegler and Imboden,[16] offer a different formulation of the psychological and somatic sequences. These authors suggest that the patient with a conversion reaction, through either a personal experience or close observation of others, has acquired a set of behaviors which represent an illness, and that in a more or less unconscious way he is enacting that illness and adopting the sick role. Although these behaviors may function to express some symbolic and personal meaning in the language of the body, their primary psychological function is, on the one hand, to communicate to and influence others in the social field, and on the other hand, to distract the patient himself from the real issues while simultaneously offering him an acceptable cogni-

tive framework for understanding how he feels. In addition, Ziegler and Imboden emphasize that conversion reactions defend not only against anxiety but also against other dysphoric affects such as depression, shame, and anger.

Example 30-9. A 46-year-old woman was admitted to the emergency room with a right hemiparesis, complaining of a sudden onset several hours earlier. Neurological examination revealed a nonanatomical and inconsistent neurological picture. Because of these physical findings and because of the patient's remarkable indifference to her symptoms, the intern asked for a psychiatric consultation. Psychiatric interview revealed two especially important pieces of background information. First, the patient's father had suffered a stroke approximately six weeks prior to her coming to the emergency room and had lived for four weeks with an identical clinical picture, a right hemiparesis. The patient had always been extremely close to her father, living with him all her life. She had taken care of him during his final illness and had been with him when he died. Although quite upset by his illness and death, the patient had grieved minimally in the last two weeks.

Second, although the patient's symptoms had become much worse during the evening prior to the emergency room visit, she had actually experienced her symptoms for the two weeks since her father's death. They had come and gone, depending to some extent on the amount of distress that she was feeling. During this period the patient imagined that she too was dying from a stroke and this worry occupied a considerable amount of her attention. At the same time it mobilized a great deal of concern from other members of the family. Working together, the intern and the consultant psychiatrist assured the patient that she did not have a neurological disease and began to focus some of her attention on the grief she was feeling for her father. The following day a

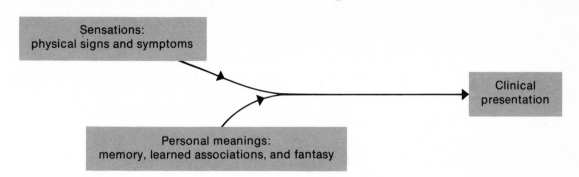

Figure 30-2   A schema illustrating how sensations and personal meanings together produce the form of clinical presentation of a physical disorder.

successful referral to outpatient psychotherapy was made.

Formulated as the enactment of an illness and the adoption of the sick role, conversion reaction can be seen as a special instance of the more general pattern in which illness is used as a *form of adaptation*. The basic elements in this adaptive process may be summarized in the following way: the pathological conditions and events of a physical illness produce signs and symptoms which arise into the consciousness of the individual, come to his attention, and are interpreted as described in the previous section. During this process they interact with memories, learned meanings, and fantasies, all of which ultimately contribute to and shape the final clinical form of the illness. This process is illustrated in Figure 30-2.

This influence of personal meanings on the physical sensations is a complex process which will be summarized in this discussion by the term *modulation*. This concept is chosen because personal meanings frequently exert their influence by either adding to or subtracting from the original physical sensations, resulting in an apparent increase or decrease of the physical signs and symptoms. Toward one end of this continuum, modulation can result in the amplification of physical symptom states. In the extreme form of this type of modulation, when the contribution of memory and fantasy is very great and the contribution of pathologically based sensations is mini-

mal or even nonexistent, we shall speak of induction. At the other end of the spectrum, modulation can result in either a dampening or a complete suppression of the physical symptom state. These various forms of modulation are illustrated in Figure 30-3.

That end of the modulation continuum which results in a decrease in the experience and clinical presentation of physical symptom states is that part of the process of reacting to illness which results in a *minimization* of the illness, an avoidance of doctors and in some cases even a total denial of the illness. This process has already been discussed in the previous section as an aspect of adaptation to physical illness. The other end of the modulation continuum includes both the *amplification* of physical symptom states and their *induction* without any underlying organic basis. It occurs both as an adaptation to physical illness and as a form of adaptation through the exaggeration or simulation of illness. The amplification of physical symptoms manifests itself as an overreaction to physical illness, hypochondriasis, and the use of physical illness to gain personal ends. Induction corresponds to what has traditionally been referred to as conversion. By using the modulation model to reinterpret the psychological basis of conversion, it becomes clear that conversion is not a separate and distinct process but rather shares features with the whole process whereby illness is either minimized or exaggerated

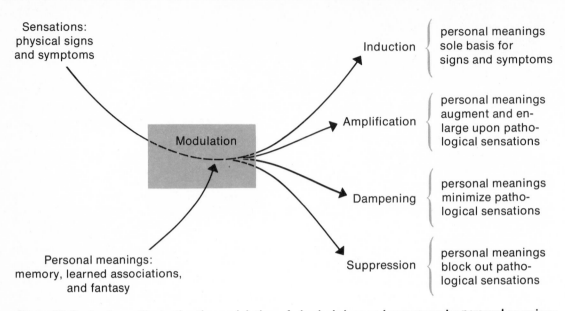

Figure 30-3   A schema illustrating the modulation of physical signs and symptoms by personal meanings.

in order to satisfy a variety of personal needs.

Conversion reactions at times seem to be qualitatively different from the other clinical phenomena explained by the modulation model. This is especially true when they are seen in their pure form, such as sudden and completely reversible paralyses, blindnesses, aphonias, and gross motor seizures. However, a careful investigation of most cases where conversion reaction is suspected will reveal some degree of organic basis for the patient's clinical presentation. In fact, some authors such as Slater[17] have argued that most cases of diagnosed conversion reaction, if followed over a long enough period of time, will develop a clear-cut organic disease process which was accounting for their original symptoms. Perhaps the best examples of Slater's point are the young women who present in neurological offices with vague and changing complaints and are initially labeled as hysterics but later develop multiple sclerosis.

Although Slater's argument may be too strongly stated, there is a marked tendency among nonpsychiatric physicians to seek consultation when a

difficult and complaining patient has physical complaints for which they can find no organic base. They tend to dichotomize between the physiological and the psychological causes of a symptom and seek either to establish a satisfactory organic base for the clinical picture or to define the patient as having a conversion reaction. Unfortunately, psychiatrists dichotomize in the same way, and so both sets of physicians tend to overlook the fact that in most cases of suspected conversion reaction there is *both* an organic and a psychological basis to the problem.

Example 30-10. A 21-year-old single woman, attending her last year at college and living at home with her parents, was admitted to the neurology service for evaluation of an unusual pain syndrome. The patient had fallen off her bicycle approximately a month before admission, subsequently developing a pain in the deep pelvic area, perineum, and upper left thigh. No organic base for persistent pain had been discovered, but the patient was progressively handicapped to the point where she required crutches to walk. While she was in the hospital, the patient was extremely withdrawn, petulant, and uncooperative. Past history revealed that the patient was the only child of a marriage that had been marked by conflict for a number of years. More recently, the patient's mother and father had argued frequently over the patient's conduct, including a marked disagreement about whether or not she was having "real pain." The father contended that the patient could "walk if she really wanted to." The history also revealed that the patient was having difficulty with her peers, especially with regard to her own heterosexual behavior. Early in her hospitalization the patient confessed to one of the nurse's aides that she had been having a series of sexual affairs which were short-lived and unsatisfying to her and about which she felt extremely guilty. Psychiatric consultation was requested when the neurological work-up was entirely negative, the working diagnosis being that of conversion reaction. Even before the psychiatrist saw the patient, however, the neurologists were surprised to find that a pregnancy test which had been suggested by a gynecological consultant was returned as positive.

At this time the focus of attention shifted from the patient's pain to the question of her pregnancy. Although she continued to require crutches to walk, her pain complaints almost totally disappeared. The focus of the psychiatric consultation revolved around making a decision regarding a therapeutic abortion, which the patient had requested while demanding that her parents not be informed. She explained that her father had attacked her physically in the past and that she was afraid of what would happen should he discover that she was pregnant. Although she remained evasive and hostile, the psychiatrist eventually worked out with the patient a plan whereby she was discharged from the hospital to live with her mother's sister. There she would not be confronted daily by her parents' arguing over the reality of her illness, and she would be able to have a therapeutic abortion without her parents' knowing. While the patient was living with her aunt, her pain symptoms diminished to the point where she was able to walk without her crutches.

A week and a half after her discharge she was granted a therapeutic abortion on mental health grounds, and the procedure was accomplished in an uneventful fashion. She continued to refuse psychiatric treatment, and since the neurologist felt that he no longer could play a role in her care, her treatment was transferred to the ob-gyn clinic. At one of her routine postabortion clinic visits, the patient complained of fevers and chills at night and excessive bleeding from the vagina. Over the next several days, she was worked up extensively for these complaints, with no positive results. The gynecologist began to suspect that her reports of excessive bleeding were highly inaccurate. During one of her visits the patient was discovered by a nurse to be running hot water over a thermometer which had been given to her. This resulted in an angry confrontation with the patient and a repeat call to the psychiatric consultant. The patient admitted that she had been trying to falsify her temperature but said this was because nobody believed that her complaints were real. At this point the psychiatric consultant agreed to help the patient get continuing medical care from the medical outpatient clinic, but also insisted that the patient's parents be brought into the case. During the next several weeks, while the patient was being followed by the internist, she continued to complain of vaginal bleeding and renewed her complaints of incapacitating pelvic and left-thigh pain. The psychiatric consultant was finally able to get the patient's mother in for an interview, and it developed that the latter knew about the patient's pregnancy and therapeutic abortion. She was extremely supportive of the patient and even agreed that there must be some organic basis for the patient's pain. The patient's father refused to come in for an interview, and her mother refused to apply pressure on him to do so, fearing that he would discover their daughter's pregnancy and feeling that he was totally unsympathetic to the patient's pain complaints. The patient herself continued to show no interest in psychiatric treatment, and eventually she and her mother decided to seek medical help for the pain syndrome elsewhere.

This complicated and frustrating case illustrates a number of the problems which can occur when a patient is referred for consultation from another medical or surgical service with a presumptive diagnosis of conversion reaction. First, this diagnosis and subsequent referral is often made after the medical work-up turns out a generally negative report. Such abrupt relabeling of his condition may leave the patient feeling rejected and confused. Second, a patient like this is frustrating and often leaves the primary physician feeling that he has been deliberately manipulated. As a result he does, in fact, reject the patient as soon as possible. Third, this case illustrates the difficulty in knowing to what degree a patient's presenting complaint has an organic basis. This woman's original trauma, when she fell from the bicycle, in all likelihood produced a temporary pain syndrome; but it seems quite possible that her pain was amplified and later perhaps even induced from memory and fantasy because of her parents' (and later her physician's) struggles with her over its seriousness, indeed even its reality. Fourth, this case illustrates how a patient will simply shift the focus of distorted complaints to a new set of symptoms when the suspected distortion is simply confronted without dealing with the basic psychological problem. Fifth, this case illustrates the great importance of key figures in the patient's psychological field in determining both the presence and the persistence of a distorted form of complaint. As has already been discussed, the amplification and induction of physical complaints serve the important psycho-

logical function of influencing the behavior of significant others in the social field. In this case, the complaint served to keep the patient bound closely to her mother and, almost certainly, in the center of her parents' struggles.

Sixth and finally, this patient's attempt to falsify her temperature illustrates and raises for discussion the problems of malingering and factitial illness. Whenever either of these is suspected, there is a natural inclination for physicians to assume that the falsification or simulation was conscious or deliberate. Although there are certainly numerous cases where deliberate and conscious efforts are made to falsify a physical sign or symptom, such behavior usually has important unconscious determinants. When considering the amplification and induction of symptoms, the psychiatrist should keep in mind the shifting and often subtle continuum between conscious and unconscious psychological processes. A patient may be totally unaware of his simulation, or he may be aware of doing it but unaware of why he does it, or he may be aware of both doing it and what motivates him but be unable to control himself. In all these instances a psychological formulation which is limited to the conscious and willful factors is incomplete. Furthermore, as was seen in this case, even when there are major conscious determinants to the falsification, the patient may feel completely justified in his behavior and may not interpret his behavior as malingering or an attempted simulation.

The time course of a conversion reaction depends on the amount of intrapsychic gratification that it provides and on the degree to which responses from the patient's social field are reinforcing. Even when a conversion reaction is primarily the amplification of an ongoing disease process, if it continues to serve a useful function, it may persist after that disease process has run its course because the patient has "learned" the syndrome and can induce it on the basis of memory and fantasy. Once this kind of adaptive mechanism has worked successfully for a period of several weeks or months, the patient invests considerable self-esteem in his "disability" and integrates it into his cognitive and emotional self-image. For this reason the chance of completely removing a conversion reaction which has been present for a year or longer is small. Quick and encompassing treatment of a newly established conversion reaction is desirable whenever possible. In addition to family and individual psychotherapy when appropriate, this should include some type of nonspecific medical treatment which allows the patient to give up the "physical illness" gracefully. Such a face-saving opportunity to give up being ill is particularly important in nonpsychologically minded patients.

It has often been stated that conversion reactions occur primarily in the setting of the hysterical personality. However, work such as that by Chodoff and Lyons[18] indicates that adaptation through the exaggeration and simulation of illness actually occurs in a variety of character and personality types. These findings fit with the modulation model, which would suggest that almost anyone is capable of the amplification of physical symptoms given certain previous experiences with illness, an appropriate stress, and a social field setting which is receptive to this kind of communication.

ILLNESS AS A FAILURE OF ADAPTATION: PSYCHOPHYSIOLOGICAL DISORDERS AND OTHER SELF-DAMAGING SYNDROMES

The concept of a psychophysiological disorder was developed in connection with a group of diseases in which there was a definite organic lesion but in which there was no clearly established primary organic cause. In these diseases, psychological factors were felt to play a major if not a total etiological role. Into this category fit some of the traditional "psychosomatic" diseases, such as peptic ulcer, ulcerative colitis, bronchial asthma, hypertension, and certain kinds of arthritis.

Dunbar[19] was one of the first to explore systematically the relationships between the psychosomatic diseases and personality. She demonstrated that each disease was associated with a particular constellation of personality traits. However, her relatively nondynamic approach was soon overshadowed by Alexander and French's psychoanalytic approach to what they called the "vegetative neuroses."[20] They theorized that the somatic manifestations of these diseases were not the symbolic expression of repressed emotions as was the case in conversion, but rather were the normal physiological accompaniment of emotions which were present in a chronic and exaggerated form. They based their concept of a psychophysiological disorder on two premises: (1) organs innervated by the autonomic nervous system become diseased as a result of an excessive and often prolonged discharge of that system, and (2) this discharge arises in certain individuals who are unable to adjust to their lives or cope with certain stresses and therefore experience excess and prolonged emotional tension.

Thus Alexander and French made a sharp conceptual distinction between psychophysiological disorders, which involved the autonomic nervous system and resulted from the chronic discharge of excess emotional tension, and conversion disorders, which involved the voluntary nervous system and resulted from symbolic bodily expression as a defense against excess emotional tension. Unfortunately, such sharp distinctions have not held up well. First, certain psychosomatic disease processes, such as psychogenic vomiting or hyperventilation, clearly involve organ systems innervated by both the autonomic and the voluntary motor system. Second, virtually any disease state, for example ulcerative colitis or asthma, although nonsymbolic in origin, takes on secondary symbolic meanings, often of sufficient proportions as to shape the individual's entire psychic life. Third, there is abundant clinical evidence that diseases involving the autonomic nervous system can be used for adaptive purposes, through both the patient's modulation of their signs and symptoms and his control over self-exposure to the conditions which are known to affect the disease process. Fourth and finally, many of the so-called psychosomatic diseases such as asthma have been shown to have significant organic etiologies.

Physicians have begun to think less in terms of specific psychological causes of the psychophysiological disorders and more in terms of a complex of causes among which a personality trait or an emotional state may be meaningfully listed. For example, Mirsky[21] studied the development of peptic ulcers in army recruits during basic training and was able to demonstrate that the development of peptic ulcers in specific individuals depends on a complex of variables, including a genetically determined tendency to produce excess pepsinogin, a personality configuration with particularly high dependency needs, and a high level of environmental stress in conjunction with little nurturant support.

Historically, the psychophysiological disorders have been assumed to result from the effect of excess emotional tension on a constitutionally determined "organ weakness." Recently, however, Miller[22] has been able to demonstrate instrumental conditioning of such autonomically controlled functions as the rate of kidney excretion, the heart rate, the blood pressure, and the peristalsis of the intestinal tract; this demonstration raises the important possibility that psychophysiological disorders may have a major learned component. The therapeutic implications of this are large because if these disorders are learned, they can be unlearned.

Two principles which are basic to the discipline of psychophysiology are helpful when considering psychophysiological disorders. The first is that of *individual response stereotypy*. This means that each individual responds to a variety of different stress situations in a more or less stereotypical way with their autonomic nervous system and ultimately with the end organs innervated by that system. For example, Malmo[23] has shown that some individuals respond to several different kinds of stress with the development of muscle tension, while other individuals respond to the same set of stresses with a form of tachycardia. Within the group of skeletal muscle responders, Malmo was

able to demonstrate that each individual responded to stress with tension and sometimes pain in very specific muscle groups.

Example 30-11. A 35-year-old married man was referred for psychiatric evaluation by a neurologist who had seen the patient for tension headaches. Past history revealed that the patient had married a Japanese woman several years prior to the referral, while he was enlisted in the Navy. For several years they had remained childless and had settled into a life which was relatively devoid of social contact, especially for the patient. He worked hard as line supervisor in a local electronics firm and devoted much of his free time to studying and taking courses in one of the adult education programs in his community. The rest of his time was devoted to working out a small business venture into which he had entered with his only friend. The patient had many compulsive personality traits and liked to lead an orderly and well-controlled life. Several years before the psychiatric referral, some interpersonal difficulty with his friend developed around their business venture, and the patient began to experience tension headaches. Approximately a year prior to referral, the patient's wife gave birth to their first child. Following the delivery, she developed jaundice and was ill for three months with the result that the patient's usual orderly life pattern was significantly disrupted. Even when his wife was well again, the new infant's arrival continued to create some confusion at home. Through all this the patient continued to experience intermittent tension headaches. Sometimes these occurred at work and he found it necessary to return home. Sometimes they occurred in the evenings at home while the patient was trying to study. At other times they occurred on weekends when he and his wife were relaxing. During the consultation the psychiatrist pointed out the relationship between the patient's personal need for order and control, the variety of problems with which he was currently contending, and the resultant high levels of tension which he experienced primarily in the form of headaches. The patient was not a good candidate for long-term psychotherapy, and the consultant confined himself to discussing with the patient ways of organizing his daily routine which would help to reduce tension and thereby the tension headaches. After several weekly meetings, therapy was concluded with the patient somewhat improved.

A second principle of psychophysiology is that of *stimulus-response specificity*. This means that there are responses specific to certain stimulus situations and that these responses occur in many different individuals placed in the same situation or recur in the same individual when he reexperiences highly similar situations. It is common with research on this principle to define situations in terms of the emotions which are aroused. This is well illustrated by Wolf and Wolff's[24] investigations of a man with a gastric fistula which allowed study by direct observation of his gastric mucosa under various stimulus conditions. These authors found a clear pattern of engorgement, hypermotility, and hypersecretion of the gastric mucosa associated with any situation which produced anger. Conversely, they found a pattern of pallor, hypomotility, and hyposecretion in situations which tended to produce fear or anxiety. The following case illustrates the principle of stimulus-response specificity at a clinical level.

Example 30-12. Psychiatric consultation was requested for a 24-year-old married woman hospitalized with an acute episode of ulcerative colitis. The patient had experienced two previous severe episodes. The first occurred at age 17 after she had ambivalently decided to leave home to be more independent and to work to support herself. Several months later, when her colitis was in remission, she met and married a young man whom she knew very superficially. In several months of dating they had seen a great deal of each other, and she had become pregnant by him. After the baby was born, they began to argue constantly. The patient was a very energetic and outgoing person, and her husband repeatedly accused her of being sexually involved with other men. By the time the baby was 1 year old, the patient and her husband had separated; they subsequently divorced. In this setting, the patient had her second episode of severe ulcerative colitis.

After successful treatment, the patient lived alone for several years, working part-time and raising her child. Then she met her current husband, a man several years her senior, dominant in his personality and very successful in his business. At the time of the psychiatric consultation, they had been married for three years. This marriage had also been filled with dramatic arguments and emotional turmoil, but throughout it the patient had been able to maintain generally good control of her colitis. However, at the time of hospitalization her husband had begun talking openly of leaving her.

During psychiatric interviews, it was clearly demonstrated that the specific conflict which presented the gravest difficulty for the patient was separation from an important source of dependency gratification. All three of her bouts of colitis had occurred while she was undergoing a major separation. During the consultation, the patient and her husband were seen together, and for the first time some of their mutual hostilities were expressed both openly and in a relatively controlled fashion. With the patient's colitis well controlled by a series of steroid enemas, she was discharged from the hospital and referred for private couple psychotherapy.

Consideration of the time course of the disease and of the role of personality structure is as useful for understanding the manifestations of psychophysiological disorders as it is in connection with other psychosomatic conditions. The time course of psychophysiological disorders depends on the length of exposure to those psychological and biological factors which contribute to the excessive autonomic discharge and the pathological end organ response. At the psychological level, because psychophysiological disorders represent, in part, a failure to cope with stress and avoid distress, the time course is highly influenced by the individual's ability either to remove himself from the stressful situation or to learn new coping measures. Thus, psychophysiological disorders seem to occur particularly in the setting of personality disorders under conditions where the individual is either prevented from removing himself from the source of stress, as in the military service or in prison, or when he is characterologically unable to remove himself from the stress, as with compulsive or dependent personalities.

As already mentioned, Dunbar associated certain personality traits with psychophysiological disorders. However, Alexander argued that it was not the manifest personality trait itself but rather the dynamic behind that trait which played the significant role in psychophysiological disorders. For example, he argued that individuals with peptic ulcers had suppressed passive longings and expectations of being loved and taken care of. Although these longings were repressed from consciousness, at an unconscious level they continued, and the expectation of love had a physiological corollary in the expectation of being fed. Along a different line, Reusch[25] has argued that there is an "infantile" personality structure in all individuals with psychosomatic and especially psychophysiological disorders. This personality is characterized by marked dependency and a rigidity of neurotic defenses. His formulation is consistent with the adaptational framework presented here since it would be in such immature and rigid individuals that coping and defense mechanisms were inadequate, leading them to experience the high levels of distress which result in excess autonomic discharge.

Psychophysiological disorders are not the only

diseases which result from failures at adaptation. There are a host of disease-producing behaviors which result from inadequate coping and/or flooding of the adaptive mental mechanisms with dysphoric affect, including accident-proneness, risk-taking, self-abuse, and masochism. These behaviors seem to have two kinds of psychological basis, one motivational and the other not. The latter occurs when inadequate coping and excessive subjective distress interfere with the operation of good judgment and decision making.

Example 30-13. A 17-year-old female was two days from her high school graduation. There was considerable excitement in the family about the oldest daughter's passing this milestone. In fact, feelings were doubly high because she was to be married on the day following her graduation. Two nights before the graduation, however, she had a severe argument with her fiancé and he stormed out of her house, saying that perhaps they ought not to get married after all. She was very upset by this development and in her search for an outlet for her tension decided to go for a drive. She borrowed her parents' car, even though they cautioned her to wait until she had calmed down a little. Half an hour later she "accidentally" drove the car across the highway divider and was involved in a head-on collision. Her spinal cord was severed at T-6 and she was left a permanent paraplegic. Psychiatric consultation was requested to help in the rehabilitation process, in particular to help the patient with a sullen depression and to help the patient's family and boyfriend with their feelings of guilt.

In other cases, definite motivational elements enter into the self-destructive behavior. This is especially true with certain personality types where self-damage becomes a way of coping with interpersonal difficulties.

Example 30-14. Psychiatric consultation was requested for a 17-year-old male admitted to the medical service with his third rattlesnake bite in as many years. Ever since early adolescence the patient had been fascinated by reptiles and by poisonous snakes in particular. He was an immature and extremely rebellious adolescent. His family strongly disapproved of his interest in snakes, and this only served to make them more fascinating to him. In late adolescence, he began to collect poisonous snakes from all over the state. This so offended his parents that they refused to let him keep the snakes at home. He built a series of cages for them in the garage and even began to manufacture rattlesnake venom for medical use by regularly milking his rattlesnakes.

His first rattlesnake bite had occurred when he was rushing to save his pet dog from a rattlesnake loose in the back yard. His second bite occurred while he casually handled one of his pet snakes. His third and most recent bite occurred while he was asleep. The patient had argued with his father about how late he could stay out at night; afterwards he decided to spend the night in his car and to bring one of his pet rattlesnakes with him. Somehow during the night the snake "accidentally" escaped from its small cage and bit the patient. During the psychiatric consultation the patient was seen individually, and afterwards his parents were willing to deal as a family with the issues raised by his rebellious behavior and his recurrent self-exposure to the dangers of snakebite. As a result they were subsequently referred for psychiatric treatment.

SYNTHESIS

The division of discussion in this chapter into four separate sections organized around traditional psychiatric diagnostic categories tends to emphasize the differences between types of problems encountered by the psychiatrist while working at the psychosomatic interface. In contrast, the use of an adaptational framework throughout the discussion tends to emphasize the similarity of problems and the lack of sharp boundaries between traditional diagnostic categories which is so frequently encountered. Psychiatrists who work in a general hospital generally learn to consider all four of the adaptational categories previously discussed in every case they encounter, even though the original consultation request may be stated explicitly in terms of only one of them. This practice evolves because patients inevitably ignore the textbooks and combine these categories in their clinical presentations. Some of the commonest combinations include the following: the adaptational problems of physically ill patients are often based on or added to subclinical and unrecognized organic brain syndromes; patients with definite organic pathology often modulate their signs and symptoms in a way that suggests conversion reaction; similarly, many patients with psychophysiological disorders modulate the expression and elaborate the secondary meanings of their illnesses so that these too take on a conversionlike quality; patients with organic brain syndromes will often exhibit either frank denial of illness or the presence of a conversion reaction; finally, failure to cope adequately with the stress of a severe physical illness may produce a psychophysiological disorder or, ultimately, lead to self-destructive behavior on the part of the patient.

To attend adequately to all the issues and sort out their complicated interplay, it is useful for the clinician to approach each patient with a set of basic questions from which the information gathering and clinical interview can proceed. These questions may be summarized as follows: (1) What are the potentially identifiable organic disease processes that are present in this patient? Here the clinician must concern himself with both the disease states already known and those which are reasonably possible but not yet established. (2) What has this patient's previous experience with illness been, both in himself and in significant others? Here the clinician must determine what manifestations of disease the patient knows directly and what he has learned about coping with illness, modulating illness, and the way illness influences potential caretakers. (3) What are the patient's styles of coping and adaptation? Here the clinician must identify typical ways the patient adapts to stress and how he modifies these adaptations when his usual methods are not available to him. (4) What are the stresses with which the patient is contending? Here the clinician must evaluate what problems the patient is facing in all areas of his life, not just those related to his health. (5) Who are the significant others in the social field? Here the clinician must discover who is currently important in the patient's life and how they are affected by the illness and the patient's reaction to it.

A way of synthesizing these questions and, in fact, all the previous discussion is shown in Table 30-1 with a simplified general systems approach.[26,27] Such an approach is warranted because of the great number of variables which affect problems at the psychosomatic interface and because of the considerable interplay of these variables.

The table organizes the clinical material in a way relevant to the different systems which operate across the psychosomatic interface. These

systems include cells, organ systems, the patient, dyadic, and other larger social systems. In the table, one axis represents the three levels of organization at which relevant systems exist, namely the biological, psychological, and sociological levels. The other axis represents three ways of organizing information gained from each of these levels. This table, and the type of multivariable approach which it represents, highlights the complexity of the material encountered by the clinician when dealing with patient problems at the psychosomatic interface. Thus it serves to emphasize the importance of a comprehensive approach to these problems and the great need for careful integration of all the types of available clinical information for understanding a particular case.

REFERENCES

1. Menninger, Karl A.: *The Vital Balance*, Viking, New York, 1962, pp. 31ff.

2. Engel, G. L., and J. Romano: "Delirium, a Syndrome of Cerebral Insufficiency," *J. Chron. Dis.*, **9**(3):227, 1959.

**Table 30-1   A General Systems Outline of the Clinical Material
Relevant to Problems at the Psychosomatic Interface**

System Level	Previous Experiences of System	Present Dispositions of System	Present Processes within System
Biological	Old trauma and disease conditioning; autonomic conditioning	Physiological capacities; response stereotypy and specificity	Disease processes (including effects on CNS); treatment processes
Psychological	Personal meanings and associations learned through experiences with and observations of illness	Character structure; coping styles	Modulation of psychological sensations and states; adaptive reactions
Social	Exposure to and learning of socially and subculturally sanctioned sick role behavior	Caretaking dispositions of nuclear family and treatment personnel	Social reinforcement and punishment processes in response to illness

3. Lipowski, Z. J.: "Delirium, Clouding of Consciousness and Confusion," *J. Nerv. Ment. Dis.*, **145**(3):227, 1967.

4. Goldstein, J.: "Functional Disturbance in Brain Damage," in S. Arieti (ed.), *American Handbook of Psychiatry*, Basic Books, New York, 1959, p. 770.

5. Mayer-Gross, W., E. Slater, and M. Roth: *Clinical Psychiatry*, Williams & Wilkins, Baltimore, 1960.

6. Redlich, F. C., and D. X. Freedman: *The Theory and Practice of Psychiatry*, Basic Books, New York, 1966.

7. Chapman, L. F., et al.: "Highest Integrative Functions in Man during Stress," *The Brain and Human Behavior*, Williams & Wilkins, Baltimore, 1958, vol. 36.

8. Weisman, A. D., and T. P. Hackett: "Psychosis after Eye Surgery," *New Engl. J. Med.*, **258**:1284, 1958.

9. West, J. W., et al.: "The Psychosis of Sleep Deprivation," *Ann. N. Y. Acad. Sci.*, **96**:66, 1962.

10. Hamburg, D. A., et al.: "Adaptive Problems and Mechanisms in Severely Burned Patients," *Psychiatry*, **16**(1):1, 1963.

11. Senescu, R. A.: "The Development of Emotional Complications in the Patient with Cancer," *J. Chron. Dis.*, **16**(7):813, 1963.

12. Chodoff, P.: "Adjustment to Disability: Some Observations on Patients with Multiple Sclerosis," *J. Chron. Dis.*, **9**:653, 1959.

13. Janis, I. L.: *Psychological Stress*, Wiley, New York, 1958.

14. Parsons, T.: "Illness and the Role of the Physician: A Sociological Perspective," *Am. J. Orthopsychiat.*, **21**:452–460, 1951.

15. Kahana, R. J., and G. L. Bibring: "Personality Types in Medical Management," in N. E. Zinberg (ed.), *Psychiatry and Medical Practice in a General Hospital*, International Universities Press, New York, 1964.

16. Ziegler, F. J., and J. B. Imboden: "Contemporary Conversion Reactions, II: A Conceptual Model," *Arch. Gen. Psychiat.*, **6**:279, 1962.

17. Slater, E.: "Diagnosis of Hysteria," *Brit. Med. J.*, **1**:1395, 1965.

18. Chodoff, P., and H. Lyons: "Hysteria, the Hysterical Personality and 'Hysterical' Conversion," *Am. J. Psychiat.*, **114**:734, 1958.

19. Dunbar, H. F.: *Emotional and Bodily Changes: A Survey of Literature on Psychosomatic Interrelationships*, Columbia, New York, 1954.

20. Alexander, F., and T. M. French: *Studies in Psychosomatic Medicine*, Ronald, New York, 1948.

21. Mirsky, I. A.: "Physiologic, Psychologic and Social Determinants in the Etiology of Duodenal Ulcer," *Am. J. Dig. Dis.*, **3**:285–314, 1958.

22. Miller, N.: "Learning of Visceral and Glandular Responses," *Science,* **163**:434, 1969.

23. Malmo, R. B.: "Physiological Concomitants of Emotion," in A. M. Freedman and H. I. Kaplan (eds.), *Comprehensive Textbook of Psychiatry*, Williams & Wilkins, Baltimore, 1967, pp. 1044–1048.

24. Wolf, S. G., and H. G. Wolff: *Human Gastric Function, an Experimental Study of a Man and His Stomach*, Oxford, New York, 1947.

25. Reusch, J.: "The Infantile Personality," *Psychosom. Med.*, **10**:134–144, 1948.

26. Miller, Warren B.: "Psychiatric Consultation, Part I: A General Systems Approach," *Psychiat. Med.*, **4**(2):135–145, 1973.

27. Miller, Warren B.: "Psychiatric Consultation, Part II: Conceptual and Pragmatic Issues of Formulation," *Psychiat. Med.*, **4**(3):251–271, 1973.

WARREN B. MILLER, M.D.

CHAPTER **31**

Psychiatric Consultation in the General Hospital

When an individual asks for consultation, he is asking for an "expert" in a specific area to give him help with a problem. Although the area of psychiatric expertise is often rather broadly defined, in the general hospital psychiatric consultation requires an ability to work in one or more of the following three ways: (1) with an individual patient at the psychosomatic interface; (2) with a patient and his caretakers, regarding the patient's emotional difficulties and the transactional problems that these create for the staff; and (3) more generally, with a variety of social systems problems which may or may not directly involve patients and their behavior.

This chapter will review some principles and concepts that should help the psychiatrist deal with the consultation process. To a large extent this process occurs in any type of consultation, as the psychiatrist will recognize from the occasions when he asks for a medical or surgical consultation for one of his patients and finds himself on the receiving end. However, because of the important relationships between a patient's psychological state, the patient-caretaker interactions, and the consultation request, psychiatric consultation is sufficiently different from other types of expert consultation that learning about it requires special attention to these general principles and concepts.

What is said about psychiatric consultation in the general hospital will often apply equally to psychiatric consultation in nonmedical settings. Thus, the principles and concepts discussed will be useful for consultation in a number of other social systems, such as those devoted to education, corrections, and welfare. However, in these other systems the process of consultation has some important differences. First, the consultee will not be a physician. This will affect the process by increasing the psychiatrist's status and authority while decreasing his familiarity with and grasp of the subject area. Second, in nonmedical settings the person about whom the consultee is asking, often generically referred to as the "client," is not a patient and does not perceive himself as such. This changes the consultation process by making the person who is identified with the problem less directly accessible to the psychiatrist-physician.

THE DOCTOR-PATIENT
RELATIONSHIP: A DYADIC SYSTEM

A doctor and a patient have a special kind of two-person relationship. Each has a special role with respect to the other which involves behavior defined by well-established social convention. The patient is expected to offer a genuine problem, to describe it as accurately and completely as he can, and to submit himself to the questions, manipulations, and general examination of the physician. He is expected to place his trust in the doctor and, if necessary, become physically and even emotionally dependent on the physician. On the other hand, the doctor is expected to provide diagnosis and treatment to the patient to the best of his ability. He is expected to pursue his examination and his therapy with the patient's improvement in mind, divorcing his own personal interests from his professional conduct. Finally, he is expected to take on the demands and needs of the patient whenever and however the illness dictates.

As Szasz[1] has written, the doctor-patient relationship varies considerably from one in which the doctor is totally active and the patient totally passive, as when the physician is doing surgery on an unconscious patient, to one of mutual participation and guidance, as when the doctor is helping the patient to manage his own diabetes. However, in all its forms the doctor-patient relationship is basically a two-person system. This suggests, as illustrated in Figure 31-1, that the relationship is a reciprocating one in which the behavior of one member is closely tied in with and affected by the behavior of the other member.

The psychiatrist, being a physician, is very familiar with the doctor role in such a relationship. For this reason, when called in consultation, he feels quite comfortable taking on the doctor role and relating to the patient in question as a physician. Unfortunately, his tendency to relate as a physician may make it difficult for him to appreciate that, as a consultant, he must attend

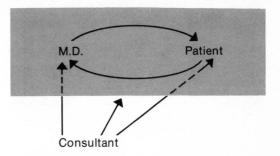

Figure 31-2 **The relationship of the consultant to the doctor, the patient, and the doctor-patient dyad.**

also to his relationship with the other physician (the consultee) and, ultimately, to how he affects the primary dyadic system, the consultee and the patient together. These three distinct relationships are illustrated in Figure 31-2.

As a psychiatrist consultant approaches a dyadic system such as the one described, there are two tendencies. The first is to work primarily with the patient, in effect displacing the other physician from the doctor-patient relationship. The second is to completely avoid the patient and work primarily, if not solely, with the consultee physician. These tendencies will be called the *consultee-displacement* and the *patient-avoidance* tendencies, respectively. The occurrence of either one depends, in part, on the nature of the problem within the dyadic system and, in part, on the psychological set of the consultant psychiatrist. For example, if the psychiatrist is busy and not currently interested in additional patient care, he may tend to avoid the patient. This can work well if the consultee's expectation is to talk about his patient to get some understanding of his patient's behavior and of his own reaction to that behavior. However, if the consultee is himself busy and wants the psychiatrist to take over (in other words, wants the psychiatrist to displace him from the doctor-patient relationship), patient-avoidance by the consultant will generate considerable resistance and resentment.

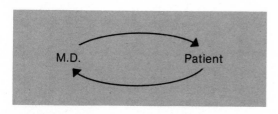

Figure 31-1 **The doctor-patient relationship as a simple system.**

In other instances the psychiatrist may have a strong patient-care orientation which leads him to move in and become the patient's physician, or at least his psychiatric physician. Again, this can work well, when the patient's difficulty is largely intrapsychic and not illness-related and when the consultee appropriately feels he cannot handle the problem. But it will create rivalry and conflict when the consultee is himself possessive of his patients and wants help from the psychiatrist which is specifically limited. It will also create difficulty where the consultee is unable to deal with his own feelings about the patient's behavior and is, in effect, trying to remove himself as much as possible from the case. In such instances the patient, often quite appropriately, objects to the psychiatrist's taking over his case, with the consequence that his initial emotional reactions to his disease and its treatment are compounded by his resentment at his own physician's apparent desertion. When this happens, the patient may well displace these feelings onto the consultant psychiatrist, with the result that he appears to be rejecting help from all sides.

In consultation there are specific problems associated with the misuse of either a patient-avoidance or a consultee-displacement tactic. With patient-avoidance these problems are inadequate understanding of the patient's problems through lack of accurate information; nonresolution of the patient's problem as a result of insufficient contact with the patient; failure to meet the consultee physician's needs and/or expectations; and threatening and/or offending the consultee physician by examining too closely his own reactions and problems with the patient. The problems associated with the consultee-displacement are persistence of the patient's unresolved interpersonal problems with his own physician, the consultee; exceeding the request of the consultee and creating resentment or competition between physicians; and persistent avoidance by the consultee physician of his own patient such that he remains unaware of his role in the development of the difficulties.

THE CONSULTATION SET

One of the chief skills in doing psychiatric consultation with a two-person system lies in maintaining all three of the relationships discussed above and illustrated in Figure 31-2 by keeping a relationship with both the doctor and the patient while simultaneously holding in mind the pattern of their two-person system and relating to it as such. Development of this skill can be achieved through adoption of the consultation set, consisting of a group of expectations and attitudes toward the objects of consultation. The group is represented below in the form of six working principles. It should be noted that these principles are applicable not only to the types of two-person systems we have discussed so far, but also apply well to the larger systems which will be discussed later in the chapter.

The six working principles are

1. The consultant is working with a system of two or more people and not with just a single individual.

2. The consultant is an outsider to the system and may need to learn special meanings, customs, and even languages that are a part of that system before he can begin to understand it.

3. Responsibility for members of the system lies primarily within the system. Although a consultant must sometimes accept major responsibility for a member of the system and may at other times have to help a poorly functioning member to move out of the system, an ever-present and major purpose of his actions is to help the system learn how to cope with its own problems.

4. While keeping his position as an outsider and observer of the system, the consultant may simultaneously become a temporary, partial member of the system to facilitate its function. (In many respects this is equivalent to becoming involved with a patient in individual psychotherapy while simultaneously maintain-

ing awareness of the interpersonal process and using that awareness to guide the therapy.)

5. The consultant's most important input to the system often is as much the gathering and synthesis of information, the contribution of concepts, knowledge, and techniques, and the provision of modeling as it is the making of decisions about the patient or the doing of therapy.

6. Educational, communicational, and facilitative skills are as crucial in consultation as the more traditional psychiatric skills of individual diagnosis and therapy.

Several case reports and some discussion of typical situations in which the above principles can be used will help illustrate their importance. The following two cases are representative of the type of experiences a psychiatric consultant encounters while doing consultation in the general hospital. The first case was seen as a result of a routine call for consultation. Request for the second case was made on a more urgent basis. In both cases the psychiatric consultant worked successfully with a doctor-patient dyad.

Example 31-1. Psychiatric consultation was requested for a 32-year-old professional who appeared rather depressed to his physician and had made several oblique references to suicide. The patient had been hospitalized for evaluation of fevers of unknown origin and symptoms of malaise and fatigue. There was a suggestion of some recurrent joint pains. The patient also had had a recurrent urethritis since contracting a gonorrheal infection six months previously. It was initially suspected that the patient had a Reiter's syndrome, but examination and testing did not definitely establish this.

After talking with the patient, the psychiatric consultant discovered that the man was seriously embarrassed by the fact that he had contracted a venereal disease. The patient appeared to be situationally depressed by the

hospitalization and the exposure of his previous illness to his physician, whom he looked upon as a peer. Upon talking further with the patient's physician, the consultant established that the physician, too, felt embarrassed by the patient's medical history and tended to avoid the patient and the discussion of medical problems when he did visit. The patient was not seriously depressed and did not wish any psychiatric treatment. However, he did respond favorably to several short interviews with the psychiatrist, particularly to the latter's comfort in discussing rather directly the implication of the patient's symptoms and the diagnostic uncertainty surrounding them. The consultant spent the main portion of his time, after the first two contacts with the patient, talking with the consultee about the patient's reaction to the social implications of his illness and his need for explicit communication in spite of his embarrassment. On one occasion, he modeled how such communication could be handled while going on rounds with the consultee physician. After one week the patient no longer showed signs of depression and was discharged from the hospital.

Example 31-2. The psychiatric consultant was called urgently to see a 51-year-old male short-order cook who, twenty-four hours following open reduction of a severe femoral fracture, was tearing at his cast and appeared to be psychotic. The psychiatric consultant spent one hour with the patient. In spite of the fact that the patient was grossly disturbed, agitated, and apparently disoriented, the interview quickly revealed that the patient had a severe delirium, based in part on a mild, chronic brain syndrome associated with chronic alcoholism. Review of the patient's chart led to the discovery that he was on several medications, including tranquilizers and pain medications in large doses. It appeared likely that these medications were significantly increasing his brain syndrome.

The consultant spent a period of time with the surgical intern discussing postoperative delirium, the association of psychotic behavior with delirium, and the management of the delirium syndrome. Some of the consultant's actions included: "giving permission" to the intern to use restraints until the patient was more manageable; suggesting reduction and simplification of the complex of medications the patient was receiving; and making this frightening patient seem more human to the intern by pointing out the relationship between the patient's present fear and his experience with an artillery bombardment during the Second World War. The consultant maintained brief supportive contact with the patient during the next several days but left the management basically in the hands of the intern. Within two days the patient was able to conduct himself appropriately on the ward and even tolerated his cast with some humor.

The following two cases illustrate situations where it was appropriate and even necessary for the consultant psychiatrist to work almost exclusively with the patient or the consultee, without fearing the complications of consultee-displacement or patient-avoidance. Example 31-3 also illustrates how certain psychiatric consultations naturally turn into opportunities for crisis intervention or short-term psychotherapy which may be pursued following the same principles discussed in earlier chapters. Example 31-4 illustrates how certain forms of psychiatric consultation border on being professional education and in-service training.

Example 31-3. A 27-year-old married woman was being treated by the medical service for acute leukemia. She had a remission following a long and difficult course of chemotherapy. However, she remained extremely anxious and childlike, irritating her physician by her demands and clinging behavior. Angry at her excessive dependency but still solicitous, he called for psychiatric consultation.

On the basis of interviews with the patient and her family, the consultant determined that she had become extremely anxious when originally told of her leukemic diagnosis and its prognosis. Subsequently, she had not had sufficient strength or encouragement to work out her feelings about dying, about the period of her life that she had remaining, or about the meaning of her life to date. Instead, she had regressed to a whining, infantile state, in effect denying her illness by her preoccupation with bodily functions.

The consultant realized that the physician was totally unable to cope with this extreme and primitive reaction to terminal illness, one which actually began before the patient had entered his care. Thus, the psychiatrist decided to initiate psychotherapy. Both the patient and her physician were relieved and grateful. The consultant-therapist saw her daily for three days, then twice weekly for two weeks, and finally, after discharge from the hospital, once weekly for several months. During this interval, she was able to work out many feelings about the prospect of an early death and to resolve a number of long-standing emotional problems in relation to her parents, her husband, and her children. She ended therapy herself while her disease was in partial remission.

During the therapy, the psychiatrist had relatively little contact with her primary physician. The latter was a mature hematolotist who was sympathetic and sensitive to the patient's predicament. He appreciated the initial management suggestions from the consultant but, after that, he concerned himself primarily with the usual hematological matters involved in treating a leukemic patient.

Example 31-4. A psychiatric consultation was requested by a physician working in the medical outpatient clinic. He was exasperated and felt helpless about a 45-year-old woman with complaints of abdominal pain whom he had followed in the clinic. He had given her a thorough gastrointestinal and gynecological work-up without positive results, and she was complaining even more than on her initial visit. The physician was bothered by some of his own feelings about her and seemed more eager to discuss these than to get the patient off his hands. The patient was interviewed for fifteen minutes during one of her regular outpatient visits. Together with the wealth of information which the consultee had already gathered, this one contact was enough for the consultant to establish a working diagnosis of psychogenic pain. The remainder of his effort went into discussing the case with the consultee during several meetings which took place over a month's time.

The consultee described how he felt impelled to do something for the patient each time she came in and how he felt increasingly helpless. The psychiatric consultant discussed the interpersonal effects of pain and pain behavior and the way in which this patient's complaining but help-rejecting style served as a form of adaptation. The consultant went on to discuss how such a patient typically makes it difficult for the caretaker to avoid doing either too much or too little. Finally, he outlined a treatment approach which involved the patient in follow-up medical care with relatively frequent, brief visits. The problems in applying this approach and the continuing reactions of the consultee to subsequent visits by the patient were discussed at later meetings. As a result of these interventions, the patient's complaints stabilized and she continued periodic visits to the clinic with persistent but tolerable pain complaints. The consultee felt quite comfortable in dealing with her complaints and setting limits on his involvement with her.

There are other two-person systems outside of the general hospital setting about which the psychiatrist gets calls for consultative help. Some of these are caretaker dyads, in which one person is officially in a caretaking position. Familiar examples of these include the social worker and his client, the nurse and his patient, the parole officer and the parolee, and the teacher and his student. Other dyads are based on common patterns of social bonding and responsibility. Examples include the parent and his child, the married person and his spouse, and two friends. In all these cases the psychiatrist may be called by one member of the dyad about problematical behavior on the part of the other member. In such instances it will often be useful for him to recall the lessons learned with the doctor-patient dyad and to adopt the consultative set while approaching them as a two-person system.

MORE COMPLEX SYSTEMS

So far we have considered consultation only in relatively simple two-person systems. In actuality, all patients are embedded in more complex systems. Because the three-person triad illustrates so well the types of problems which can occur with consultation to more complex systems, we will use the doctor-nurse-patient triad as a basis for discussion. This system is especially relevant to the psychiatric consultant in a general hospital because medical and surgical inpatients are invariably involved in such a system and usually significantly affected by it. (It should be noted that the triad we are considering is sometimes more a role triad than just a constant three-person group. In other words, since a given patient usually has several nurses — corresponding to different shifts — and sometimes a team of physicians, the triadic patterns and problems to be discussed will sometimes be less a function of individual personalities and more a function of medical roles.)

The doctor-nurse-patient triad is illustrated in Figure 31-3. From that figure it is easy to appreciate how much more complex the triad is for the consultant psychiatrist than the doctor-patient dyad. Obviously, to work quickly and be effective the psychiatrist must have some familiarity with the transactional patterns of doctor-nurse-patient

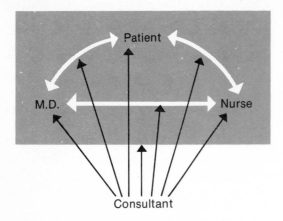

Figure 31-3 The relationship of the consultant to the various elements of the doctor-nurse-patient triad.

triads which commonly cause problems and lead to requests for patient consultation.

One of the most common types of triadic problems on an inpatient service grows out of the inability of both the doctor and the nurse to meet the needs of a particular patient for support and structure. Consultation may then be requested by either the doctor or the nurse. Sometimes the problem originates within the patient himself, as when he is seriously suicidal, frankly psychotic, markedly deviant and antisocial, or suffering from a major organic brain syndrome. These clinical syndromes can be so severe that the physician and nurse cannot be expected to draw upon their own resources and experience to deal with them adequately. Furthermore, these clinical pictures are often so overwhelming or disturbing to the doctor and the nurse that the patient is tacitly avoided until the problem forces attention by emerging full-blown in some acute, disruptive way.

For characterological or situational reasons some patients are more angry, demanding, guilt-provoking, or anxious than most. As a result they may be very distressing to a particular doctor or nurse who cannot cope with their upsetting behavior and therefore avoids them. When this occurs, the patient may turn with increased intensity to the

other professional in the triad. The latter, however, may feel inadequate to meet the increased demand and to manage the patient alone and therefore also avoids him. This leaves the patient unsupported, a good candidate for becoming a "management problem."

A similar process occurs when a patient has an unpleasant appearance, as with some facial neoplasms, or is difficult to communicate with, as in the following example:

Example 31-5. Psychiatric consultation was requested for a 63-year-old man who was recuperating slowly from oral surgery. He had had a tracheostomy and spoke, at best, with hoarse, indistinct speech. Because of the effort involved in listening to him and understanding him, his physician and the ward nurses increased their avoidance of him as his postoperative course grew long and complicated. As a result, he grew extremely irritable and depressed. Consultation was requested for his depression, with an inquiry made about the possible value of antidepressant drugs. A major portion of the consultant's work involved pointing out the avoidance process and its negative feedback effect and then helping the physician and nurses to come together to work out a coordinated plan of action. As a result, although the patient had had a four-month postoperative course prior to the consultation, he was able to go home within three weeks.

A second kind of triadic problem occurs when a patient is given conflicting messages or expectations as a result of physician-nurse differences. A common example is the patient for whom a consultation is requested because of "exaggerated complaints of pain." In such a situation it is not unusual to find that the doctor's and the nurse's expectations of pain tolerance are far apart.

Example 31-6. A 51-year-old widow was undergoing daily irrigation of bilateral nephrostomy tubes with an experimental medication in an effort to dissolve staghorn calculi. She complained bitterly of pain and was on the verge of stopping what promised to be a lifesaving procedure and leaving the hospital. The request for psychiatric consultation was made by her physician, who felt she "overreacted" to her pain.

The psychiatric consultant visited the patient on the urology ward and found her to be a chronically depressed, self-pitying woman. During this initial contact he noted that she received considerable support and sympathy from the ward nurse, who told him that the irrigation procedure had been quite painful for the few other patients who had undergone it. The consultant noted the discrepancy between the physician and nurse in their perceptions of the patient's pain. To each of them he pointed out the elements of the patient's pain response which he or she had ignored. This helped them to reach an agreed-upon middle position with respect to pain medication and expected pain tolerance. Within several days, the patient was noticeably less depressed.

A third type of triadic problem can occur as a result of the status hierarchy of doctor, nurse, and patient within the three-person system. Because authority, responsibility, and overall status are arranged linearly, with the doctor on top and the patient on the bottom, problems which occur in the execution of role performance tend to get transmitted up and down the line. Thus, if a doctor is angry in giving an order to a nurse, the nurse is likely to carry it out with some anger directed at the patient. If the doctor avoids the topic of death with the nurse, the nurse is likely to avoid the subject with the patient. This transmission of a psychological theme through members of a social system hierarchy works in the opposite direction as well. Thus, if the patient angrily complains of insufficient pain medication to the nurse, the nurse is likely to be angry and to complain of insufficient pain medication orders to the physician. Similarly, when the patient transmits to the nurse a feeling of hopelessness, the

nurse in turn is prone to communicate that feeling as her own as she interacts with that patient's physician. Because the patient is generally the most vulnerable link in this hierarchy, he is often the first one to show distressed behavior when there is a problem in it. In addition, he is the one for whom psychiatric consultation may be requested, even though the problem only appears to be his.

Example 31-7. A ward nurse requested informal consultation regarding a 34-year-old divorced woman who had been admitted to a busy general medical ward for bed rest and traction for low back pain. The patient was being given considerable pain and tranquilizer medication, although the nurse felt that she was not seriously ill and found herself dealing angrily with the patient.

Discussion between the nurse and the consultant psychiatrist revealed that the patient's physician was well known in the hospital for admitting patients with emotional problems for bed rest and supportive care, something which was directly in conflict with hospital admission policies. During the course of the consultation, the nurse-consultee realized that her anger was largely directed at the physician and decided to take up his admission practices with the nursing supervisor.

When the psychiatric consultant is evaluating an inpatient who has a number of significant relationships with staff, other patients, and family, the number of potentially important relationships becomes too great to review adequately and hold in mind. In such complex situations, it is often important for the consultant to know to what extent the problem for which he is called is determined by the patient's social field. In this connection, it is useful to keep in mind that there are certain psychological features of individuals which make them more or less social field-dependent and thus more or less vulnerable to all the conflicting pressures and tensions emanating from significant others in that social field. Those features which tend to increase social field dependency include: the presence of an organic brain syndrome, such that the patient is more stimulus-bound and has decreased integrative capacity; physical dependency, such that the patient has to rely on others for movement, feeding, physical care, and social and emotional stimulation; marked forms of characterological dependency, such that the patient habitually depends on others for support and direction; situational regression (often as a result of prolonged illness), such that the patient has become more childlike, helpless, and passive; and finally, the presence within the patient's social field of significant others, usually family members, who consistently reinforce the patient's dependency. The consultant who recognizes two or more of these qualities in a patient will often do well to concentrate a significant portion of his effort toward working with significant others in the patient's social field so that he may better understand and deal with the "patient's problem." These ideas are elaborated further in the next chapter.

LIAISON PSYCHIATRY AND COMMUNITY CONSULTATION

As the psychiatrist gains experience with consultation for single, specific problems and becomes more aware of the role that the particular social system (inpatient unit, treatment team, outpatient clinic, and so on) plays in creating or perpetuating the (patient's) problem, he tends to search for more effective ways of dealing with the recurrent problems that he has seen. He may do this by establishing a regular working relationship or psychiatric liaison with certain members of the target social system. In so doing he may choose to work with only one person, for example the clinic director, with a group of persons, for example a group of surgical interns, or with several different levels within the system, for example a group of staff nurses and a group of nurses' aides. Which ones of these he chooses will depend on his own skills and inclinations and on the exigencies of the consultee system. Whether the focus of discussion is on patient problems, interstaff relationships, or more general social system factors will similarly depend on both the psychiatrist and the system. Both Caplan[2] and Haylette[3] have described and offered classification of the methods and, to some extent, the stages of this more extensive and more formalized type of consultation. And as both of these authors indicate, such activity is a natural bridge into community and preventive psychiatry.

REFERENCES

1. Szasz, Thomas, and M. H. Hollender: "A Contribution to the Philosophy of Medicine," *Arch. Intern. Med.,* **97**:585, 1956.

2. Caplan, Gerald: *The Theory and Practice of Mental Health Consultation,* Basic Books, New York, 1970.

3. Haylette, C. H., and L. Rapoport: in L. Bellak (ed.), *Handbook of Community Psychiatry and Community Mental Health,* Grune & Stratton, New York, 1964, pp. 332–338.

Special Issues in Consultation: The Psychosocial Interface

During the past several decades it has become increasingly accepted in the fields of psychiatry and psychotherapy that the social context of behavior is of central importance, both for understanding its origins and for shaping its direction. This assumption has been discussed and supported repeatedly throughout the previous chapters of this book. In no special problem area does the major impact which the social context has on behavior have more relevance than in consultation. For this reason we shall focus closely in this final chapter on the interaction of the patient in the hospital or clinic and his social field.

Discussion in the previous chapter made it apparent how extremely complex is the social field of a hospitalized patient. For any particular patient within the hospital or clinic, not only is the number of relationships great, but the social systems and subsystems within and without the hospital of which they are a part are also numerous. The patient must relate to nurse and doctor. Each of the latter is also part of a team, and thus the patient is interacting not with these individuals alone but with small systems (teams) of individu-

als, each with its own dynamics. In addition to nurses and doctors, there are other patients and other staff. All these individuals and systems of individuals are a part of a larger social system, the hospital. Finally, interacting with the patient in this total context are other individuals in other social systems, most importantly the patient's family and its individual members. The enormous complexity of this total social field for the hospitalized patient has been discussed by the author in greater detail elsewhere.[1,2]

This chapter will discuss three aspects of the psychosocial interface of the patient for whom a psychiatric consultation is requested. First, it will examine the importance of the patient's social field in determining his psychological state. This analysis will be conducted with special reference to hysteria and conversion phenomena. Second, the social field and patient will be conceptualized in terms of a dynamic unit, the ecological group. Third and finally, this chapter will examine the way a patient's effect upon his social field is transmitted through social networks to the consultant psychiatrist. This phenomenon will be discussed with special reference to the effect this transmission may have on the process of consultation.

SOCIAL FIELD ORIENTATION AND THE MODULATION OF PSYCHOLOGICAL STATES

Chapter 30 presented a model in which it was argued that physical symptom states and the behaviors associated with them could be modulated by individuals so as to either amplify or dampen the experience and/or the expression of these states and behaviors. It was suggested that this formulation was a useful way to understand both the use of the illness for the purpose of adaptation, as in conversion and hypochondriasis, and the adaptation of individuals to the presence of illness, as in denial of illness and in under- and overreaction to illness. It should now be pointed out that the process of psychological state modulation for purposes of adaptation is a more general one which is not limited to physical symptoms and medical illness.

The number of psychological states which could be described is almost infinite. There are those states which seem to be determined by inner physiological conditions, such as being sleepy, being hungry, or being drunk; there are interest, attention, and arousal states, such as being interested in what another person has to say, being aware of another's presence, or being sexually aroused; there are affective states, such as being angry, being afraid, or grieving; there are cognitive states, such as believing a certain fact to be true or believing in a more general idea; and there are more complex identity states, such as being ill, being male, being old, being psychotic, or being a business executive. All these states and many others can and do come to be modulated by individuals for purposes of adaptation in much the same way that medical symptoms and illness states are modulated.

Modulation refers to the ability which individuals have to modify the experience and expression of states like hunger, anger, and attention, depending upon their own conscious and unconscious purposes. We generally think of psychological states as occurring under more or less specific conditions, for example, pain or hunger as a result of specific physiological changes, grief as a result of a particular loss, or anger under conditions of frustration. However, of equal importance are those background stimuli or conditions which may also become associated with those states, for example, the presence of a sympathetic person with the experience of pain, or the presence of a fearful or guilty person with the experience of anger. Though these background stimuli may not ordinarily be necessary for the occurrence of a psychological state, through their frequent association with it they may acquire sufficient stimulus value as to become a primary releasing factor. Thus, a person's experience of pain or anger may actually be cued by the presence of a sympathetic or guilty person.

Example 32-1. Psychiatric consultation was requested for a 42-year-old woman, wife of a professional in the community, who had been admitted to the medical service for treatment for her chronic lung disease. The consultation request stated that the patient was uncooperative and disobeyed ward regulations. When the consultant visited the medical ward, he found a moderately brain-damaged patient who required considerable staff attention and guidance but who was rejecting staff offers of help and angrily disrupting ward routine.

The patient had been admitted to a different service in the same hospital a year earlier; her mental status was normal at the time. During that stay she had mistakenly been given a medication to which she was known to be allergic, resulting in anaphylactic shock and cardiac arrest. Despite prompt resuscitation, she was left with moderate brain damage.

The staff that had treated her then had felt very guilty about their mistake, and the staff that was treating her now, although a totally different one, also was feeling guilty. It was as if the affect of guilt had been transmitted from one medical team to another. Their guilt led them to treat her with excessive concern and eagerness to please, and the patient reacted with the release of angry, disruptive behavior. This behavior stood in contrast to the way she had been at home, where she had neither harbored resentment over the accident nor proven difficult to live with.

The consultant concluded that the patient's ward behavior was a function of the moderate brain damage which had made her both more dependent on her caretakers and more sensitive to their nonverbal communications of excessive concern. He met several times with the doctors and nurses on the service, helped them articulate their guilt and excessive concern about the patient, and helped them to find more appropriate ways of relating to her. As their behavior came more to be shaped by the patient's needs and abilities than by their own guilt, the patient's disruptive behavior diminished markedly and she was able to cooperate much better in her own treatment.

Social Field Orientation

If a person is highly responsive to the verbal and behavioral cues of others and relies heavily on others for direction and stimulation, he is said to be high in social field orientation. Conversely, if he is independent and self-reliant, he is said to be low in social field orientation.

There are three major factors which influence a person's social field orientation at any given time: (1) his basic personality structure, (2) the more changeable aspects of the person's psychology, and (3) the current social field conditions. The normally self-reliant and independent individual may become quite sensitive to the expectations of doctors and nurses when he is taken ill; indeed, such a change is considered part of the sick role — one must act like a patient. Changes in the person's psychology, such as the psychological

changes involved in becoming ill or such alterations as the brain damage in the preceding case, can make one more social field-oriented. The arrival on the scene of a powerful and dominant figure can increase social field orientation in all its members. Thus, any assessment of social field orientation must include consideration of the individual's habitual interpersonal style, fluctuations in that style because of intercurrent psychological or physiological events, and changes in the situation (the social field).

Those persons who are habitually sensitive to others' feelings, needs, opinions, and judgments or who may be especially dependent on the presence or care of others for the fulfillment of their own needs are thus more susceptible and vulnerable to fluctuations in the social field. For these persons, the social field will have a greater impact on the modulation of their psychological states (whether it be amplification or dampening) than for those persons who are low in social field orientation.

The Development of Social Field Orientation. The concept of social field orientation is similar to Witkin's perceptual-cognitive dimension of *field dependence*[3] and to Riesman's social-psychological dimension of *outer-directedness.*[4] Since it represents a more enduring psychological characteristic of the individual, a brief discussion of its psychogenesis should provide further clarification of its meaning. As a child acquires mastery of his various modes of expression, he also learns to modulate his expressions, dependent upon the wishes and expectations of those significant others with whom he interacts. He modulates by dampening or delaying the expression of his wishes or, alternatively, by amplifying or accelerating their expression. The degree of acquisition of this ability to modulate the expression of his wishes depends both upon constitutional factors and upon the types of rewards he receives from his social field for doing so. During this developmental process, the child not only develops motor skills but acquires the ability to modulate drive, interest, affect, and cognitive states as well. Some children are even able to completely suppress or induce complex psychological states such as boredom or hurt feelings. It is noteworthy that the control which the child gains over various psychological states tends to affect both the inner psychological state and the manifest associated behavior. Thus, when a child amplifies his pain behavior in response to a painful injury because of its attention-getting property, he tends also to have a greater experience of pain. All of us have seen a minor injury, responded to by oversolicitous parents or relatives, become the occasion of piteous whimpers and sobs.

The child's reliance upon the modulation of psychological states may be increased if he possesses high levels of sensitivity to the moods, wishes, and needs of the important people in his social field. Such sensitivity allows him to identify what kinds of responses will or will not be rewarded by the social field. Thus, the developing child who is sufficiently sensitive may learn within certain limits what the other people who are important to him want him to feel, think, and do. Ultimately, for some children the psychological states of others may become more or less automatic cues to their own psychological states. In the long run, for these individuals such development may mean that their own wishes, values, and capacity for feeling may remain relatively undeveloped and undifferentiated. As a result, these children may be able to express their own wishes only by using the psychological states demanded of them by the social field as a vehicle of expression.

If a child learns to use his psychological states to achieve his own goals indirectly, he may also learn to take a more active role in this type of interaction and to produce psychological states in others through the same process. For example, the child who wants to gain a certain privilege from one of his parents may amplify or even induce a state such as boredom or upset in order to elicit his parents' concern, knowing that under these conditions he is more likely to achieve his special privilege. Thus, what starts out as a way of adapting to a certain kind of social field becomes a

way of influencing and shaping that field. In the process, the child has learned to amplify or induce psychological states in himself in order to produce related states in others.

As a result of such a learning process, certain children may acquire an unusual degree of control over some or many of their psychological states. For example, the child may be able to feel sad and cry as the situation demands, and he may be able to induce a large variety of other states to influence his parents or caretakers. It is noteworthy that as the child develops these controls, his social field simultaneously acquires greater influence over his own psychological states. This may result in the paradox that he appears to be willing a behavior which is not ordinarily under voluntary influence, while at the same time reporting that he actually feels himself to have little will with respect to this behavior. There is an important clinical analog of this paradox in the conversion patient who has no experience of will with respect to his "paralyzed" limb.

Manifestations in Adults. The manifestations in adults of social field orientation and the ability to modulate psychological states range, as might be expected, from the normal to the pathological. For example, women are far more field-oriented and tend to be more adept at modulating their psychological states. It is commonly asserted that women are more "receptive" and "intuitive," more "flexible" and less "assertive," more "indirect" and "emotional," and more "dependent." Using the concepts which have been developed above, these ideas may be translated by saying that women are more aware of and responsive to the psychological states of others, more likely to adjust their own psychological states and responses to the states of others, less likely to influence others through direct verbal expression, and more likely to need others to provide cues to their own psychological states.

Another normal manifestation of social field orientation occurs in dramatic, histrionic, and extroverted individuals. Such people have as a common trait the tendency to dramatize, to take delight in performing for others. Some become actors. The dramatic performance is enhanced when they not only "play" a part, that is, induce the behavioral state, but actually "feel" it, that is, induce the inner, affective state as well. For these people, mastery over the induction of psychological states is an important prerequisite to success in their way of relating to the social field.

At the more pathological end of the spectrum, and of special interest to the psychiatric consultant, are the hysterical personalities. Cardinal features of these personality types are the following: exhibitionism, histrionic behavior, and dramatic self-display; emotional capriciousness and inconsistency of reaction; fraudulent affects and "going through the motions of feelings"; coquetry and provocative behavior.[5] These features may be explained in the following terms: exaggerated attempts to influence the social field through the induction of psychological states; unpredictability as a result of extreme reliance on cues from the social field; inappropriately and transparently induced psychological states; and the obvious use of sexual states to influence others in the social field.

Seductiveness is almost the sine qua non of the hysterical personality. In popular thinking, it is connected with sexuality, particularly female sexuality as it is used to influence men. However, sexual seduction is merely one form of a class of behaviors, all of which may be characterized by the use of psychological states to influence other people through indirect means. Doctors may be seduced by some patients into showing interest and taking care of them. This process typically involves the amplification or induction of illness states as described in Chapter 30. Friends and relatives may be seduced by manifestations of sadness or grief into giving special attention and consideration to a bereaved individual. Persons in positions of power or authority may be seduced into giving special considerations to people who present themselves as needy, helpless, and highly appreciative. A businessman may be seduced into completing a business deal with a salesman who successfully induces in himself the states of confidence and reliability.

Seduction has a negative connotation, but most adults modulate a variety of psychological states on one occasion or another. The more prosocial aspects of this process are often referred to as *simulation,* and there are a large number of everyday terms for referring to its different forms. Thus we talk about "feigning" sleepiness, "pretending" to be hungry, "acting" drunk, "seeming" to be aware (or unaware), "simulating" sexual arousal, "affecting" anger, "professing" belief, and "playing" dumb. Modulation and induction also play a common role in the more complex types of psychological states; we speak of "simulating" illness, "acting" psychotic, "playing" a role, or more generally, of "impersonating," imitating," and "imposturing." When modulation has antisocial purposes, it is often assumed to be more conscious in its origins, and we use such words to describe it as "malingering," "fraud," "lying," "faking," "counterfeiting," "manipulating," and "swindling."

Clinical Implications

There are two main ways in which the processes that have been described are important for the consultant psychiatrist. First, the cases he is called upon to see often involve the amplification or induction of illness states. In these cases, the manifestations will vary in the extent to which they are conscious and the extent to which the personality is involved. They are thus not limited to conversion but include various hysterical syndromes and various forms of factitious and feigned illness, including Munchausen's syndrome. Example 32-2 illustrates a case in which a series of different psychological states were induced by the patient in her attempts to seduce her physicians and manipulate her social field.

Example 32-2. A 19-year-old woman on the neurosurgical service was referred for psychiatric consultation. She had been involved in an automobile accident several weeks prior to referral and had remained paralyzed in the lower two extremities since that time in spite of the fact that there was no evidence of injury of the nervous system. The neurosurgeon suspected a conversion reaction and requested psychiatric evaluation.

The patient had been brought up by her mother after her parents had separated and divorced when she was 6 years old. Her mother worked much of the time, and the patient was left largely to herself throughout much of her childhood. She completed high school without establishing any lasting relationships and went to work as a nurse's aide following graduation. It was during this period that she first came to medical attention. While working on a neurological ward, she complained to the hospital personnel physician of headaches. He noted an enlarged right pupil and immediately began an intensive neurological evaluation. At its conclusion, no specific neurological diagnosis could be made, although the patient continued to complain of headache and began to complain of other lateralizing symptoms. One day, after several months of investigation which included multiple procedures and multiple consultants, the patient was seen by a physician on the ward where she worked to be placing drops in her right eye, the one with the enlarged pupil. When she was confronted, it was discovered that the drops contained atropine. She became extremely angry at the confrontation but was unable to explain her deliberate falsification of a neurological syndrome. Finally, she was discharged from her job. It was several months following this episode that she was involved in the automobile accident.

Psychiatric examination revealed an attractive, cooperative, and pleasant woman who seemed eager to please the psychiatric consultant by providing all the information she could about her psychological status. She completely rejected the idea that she was falsifying her

paralysis or that it might be a conversion reaction. As the psychiatric consultation was extended over several interviews, it became clear that the patient was relating at a very superficial level to the psychiatrist and was defensively evading any investigation of her deeper feelings or motivations. Since no improvement in her "paralysis" occurred, it was decided to transfer the patient to the psychiatric inpatient unit where she could continue to be seen by the consulting psychiatrist.

Several weeks of insight-oriented psychotherapy produced no change in what was by then definitely diagnosed as a conversion reaction. In fact, the patient seemed to be extremely comfortable on the psychiatric unit, moving about in a wheelchair and receiving considerable attention and interest on the basis of her apparent paraplegia. After a conference about her, the staff decided to change the mode of treatment for this patient by confronting her regularly with her manipulative use of illness. As a part of the treatment process, considerable effort was made to affect the milieu of the psychiatric unit in order to change the balance of social rewards and costs for her continuing paralysis.

Within a week of instituting this new treatment program, the patient began walking, at first hesitantly, but very soon without any indication of abnormality. At about the time the patient began walking, she became more sexually seductive during individual psychotherapy. This pattern was also manifest, although to a lesser degree, in her general ward behavior. Her individual therapist refused to become drawn into her seductiveness, confronted her with it, and insisted that she begin making plans for the period following her discharge.

It was at this time that the patient first began to talk, during her individual psychotherapy, about hearing voices. Since the patient had never previously manifested any signs or symptoms of psychosis and was not currently showing any other signs of a thought disorder, and since her hallucinated voices frequently seemed to serve a communicative function to her psychotherapist, it was felt that these hallucinations were another manifestation of hysteria. During the subsequent two days, in the face of increasing staff pressure for her to deal seriously with discharge planning, the patient became increasingly agitated and antagonistic toward rules and regulations. Finally, after being placed on ward restriction, she deliberately left the ward, forcing her transfer to a locked unit at the state hospital. Follow-up information indicated that the patient became progressively antisocial during her subsequent two-month state hospitalization. She failed to manifest any further signs of psychosis and eventually signed herself out against advice.

The second way in which social field orientation and its effect upon psychological state modulation are important for the consultant psychiatrist results from the nature of the social field surrounding the patient and his position in it. Being a patient, especially one who is hospitalized, means being dependent upon others for one's care and well-being. This, in itself, makes the patient more aware of the psychoactive forces in the social field. In addition, the patient in treatment exists in an extremely complex social network which exerts profound influences upon him simply by virtue of its complexity. These two factors become additive in increasing the patient's need to scan the social field and to try to adapt himself to it. Only by understanding these processes can the consultant psychiatrist deal completely with the problems he is called to see. For this reason it will be useful to undertake a further analysis of the patient's social network and his position in it and to introduce several additional concepts which should prove useful in further understanding the dynamics across the psychosocial interface.

THE ECOLOGICAL GROUP

The people who make up a patient's social environment have traditionally been discussed by behavioral scientists in terms of several different conceptual units. To place the ecological group concept in perspective, it will be useful first to describe briefly three of the commonly conceptualized social field units relevant to most patients. They include the following: (1) Dyadic units or couples. Included in this type of unit are marital couples, parent-child pairs, supervisor-supervisee pairs, friendships, and an unlimited number of other two-person relationships which are, to some extent, emotionally based and enduring and not simply transient encounters. (2) Small groups or primary groups. Included in this type of unit are the family; the peer group (the gang, the clique, the circle of friends); the work group (the shop, the office, the management team); the recreational group (the bowling team, the bridge club, the band); and other small, rather closely relating groups of people. In each of these groups there tend to be face-to-face and relatively informal relationships between all members. In most of them, members tend to occupy either formal or informal positions and to behave according to certain roles which are associated with those positions. (3) Large organizations. This type of unit includes government bureaucracies, universities and schools, corporations, hospitals, prisons, churches, military organizations, and other large, complex, and generally task-oriented groups of people. These larger organizations tend to be formalized and have many non-face-to-face (indirect) relationships. They also tend to have well-developed and clearly differentiated roles, with each individual having a specific role and belonging to a specific role set — that group of people with whom he regularly interacts in performing his role.

In addition to these three social field units, there is another type which has never had strong conceptual development but to which there is frequent reference in clinical work, and that is that group of people customarily referred to by such terms as "social network"[6] or "significant others." Such terms generally designate those people in the social field of a patient with whom he is emotionally engaged in a "significant" relationship. Unfortunately, such terms are global and nondynamic, and so they suggest very little about how patients interact with their social fields. In an effort to deal with these problems, the concept of the ecological group will be developed in the following section as a way of thinking about the patient and all the most important people in his social field as a dynamic group or collective.

A Special Unit: The Ecological Group

Ecology is the study of the relationship between an organism and its physical and biological environment. A basic assumption of ecology has been the belief that an organism's behavior can be best understood by taking into consideration the multiple variables, on different physical and biological levels, which vary independently of each other but which together have a summated, direct influence on the organism under consideration. The term *ecological group* was originally chosen to suggest a similar relationship between an individual and the several influential people in his social environment.[7]

A general definition of the concept of the ecological group is: an individual and those people in his social field who are most important in his current life, considered together as a dynamic whole. Schematic representation of a typical ecological group is shown in Figure 32-1. The central person under consideration (the patient in a psychiatric discussion) is the *axial individual* (AI), and all others, arranged schematically in a wheel around him, are *perimeter individuals* (PI). The relative importance of two perimeter individuals to the axial individual is expressed roughly through their relative distance from him. Thus the spouse in Figure 32-1 is more important to the axial individual than the employer. The lines between individuals indicate the existence of interpersonal

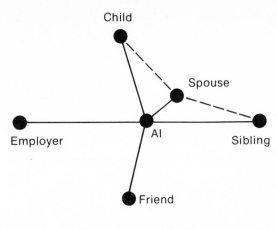

AI = axial individual

Figure 32-1   A typical six-member ecological group (see text for explanation).

forces. The solid lines indicate those relationships which directly involve the axial individual. The broken lines indicate those relationships which exist between certain perimeter individuals. As can be seen from the figure, not all members of an individual's ecological group necessarily have interpersonal ties with each other. This makes the ecological group different from other types of groups where the members all have face-to-face relationships. What makes a perimeter individual a member of anyone's ecological group are the important ties which he has with the axial individual. A specific ecological group is bound together and becomes a dynamic whole through the common focal point of the axial individual. Thus, in Figure 32-1 the spouse, employer, and friend are all dynamically related but only through the person of the axial individual.

The concept of the ecological group was developed to counteract a tendency among clinicians to think of patients as members of and in dynamic balance with just one social group, such as the family or the hospital ward, and to overlook the fact that there are usually a number of relationships, groups, and organizations within which the patient must maintain a balance. This is illustrated in Figure 32-2 where an individual and his ecological group are depicted as being drawn from three different social field units: a dyadic unit, a small group, and a large organization. This figure shows how the ecological group is functionally distinct from the three other social field units and cuts across these to include individuals from all of them.

Example 32-3 illustrates the ecological group concept. The situation is relatively simple because the ecological group cuts across only two social field units, a family and a surgical team. However, it is intended to illustrate the dynamic aspect of an ecological group and the latter's importance for adequate resolution of a patient's presenting problem.

Example 32-3. A 35-year-old married man with chronic ulcerative colitis applied for psychiatric hospitalization. Because of recurrent bouts of his colitis, which had led to several surgical procedures, he had been out of work for several years. Now, however, he stated that he could discontinue his reliance upon narcotic medication and his wife's financial support and begin to "rehabilitate" himself. The patient presented himself as a tanned, thin, but healthy-looking man. He talked about wanting to change his inactive lifestyle while at the same time raising many objections to the different plans that might lead to such a change.

The patient had had his colitis for almost

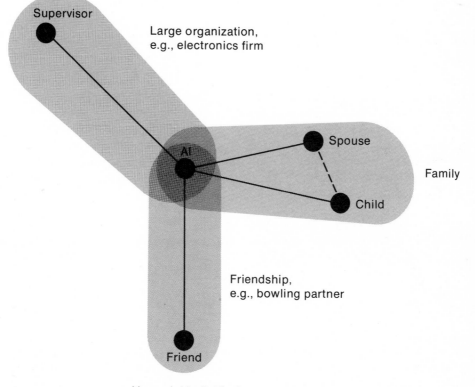

AI = axial individual

Figure 32-2   A hypothetical ecological group whose numbers are drawn from three distinct social field units in which the axial individual participates.

twenty years. At the onset of the disease there had been two psychiatric hospitalizations for several months in an effort to treat him with intensive psychotherapy. For several years after those hospitalizations, the patient had been able to work as a computer programmer. However, beginning approximately four years prior to the interview and following his third abdominal surgical procedure, during which he lost a large segment of his small intestine, he was regularly confined to the home and unable to work because of abdominal pain and difficulty with bowel control. As a result his wife went to work to support the family. It was during this period that his surgeon increasingly acceded to his demand for narcotic medication on the grounds that, in addition to relieving the patient's pain, this was a particularly effective way of slowing the rapid transit of food and liquids. At the time of the interview, the patient's use of narcotic medication had progressed to the point where he was addicted to large daily doses of Percodan®.

As the interview continued, it became clear that the patient was quite comfortable with the situation in which his wife worked to support him and he was taking Percodan® to control his symptoms and, undoubtedly, to elevate his mood. In fact, the patient revealed a strong conviction that his addiction was not undesirable and that he was a victim of society's "hangup about drugs." He believed that since Percodan® was the most effective medication in controlling his bowel function and relieving his pain, he should be allowed to continue his use of this drug without restriction.

An interview with the patient's wife revealed a bright, attractive, and assertive woman who was very supportive of her husband. Although she expressed interest in his discontinuing the use of narcotics and returning to work, she also expressed considerable annoyance at the difficulties he had encountered in obtaining the narcotic medication he needed. She also revealed considerable satisfaction in her role as family provider and caretaker of a sick husband. The overall impression she gave was of a controlling woman who indirectly exerted considerable pressure on her husband to remain in his passive and dependent role.

Discussion with the patient's social worker and surgeon revealed that both of them suspected a considerable amount of narcotic abuse on the part of the patient although their reactions to this were distinct. The surgeon indicated that the patient regularly used up his monthly narcotic prescription a week or more ahead of time and that he appeared to be taking the drug, in part, for the "high" it produced. Although he had been treating this patient with maintenance Percodan® for several years, recent changes in his level of administrative responsibility had made him more aware of and concerned about a small group of his patients who depended heavily on him for narcotic medication. Thus, on the one hand he was anxious to be free of his patient's demands for narcotics. On the other hand, however, he was clearly bound to the patient by a long-term involvement and, to a certain extent, by the patient's hostile dependency.

The social worker, in turn, indicated disapproval of the patient's overuse of narcotics for what she felt was primarily a psychiatric problem. However, she perceived significant limits in his ability to change. Because of the surgeon's growing reluctance to continue the narcotic medication, she had felt under some pressure to find a substitute program which would "rehabilitate" him and was, in turn, putting the patient under some pressure to apply for psychiatric treatment.

In tying together the various elements of this case, it appeared to the psychiatrist that the patient's application for psychiatric treatment was the result of a complex interplay between him, his surgeon, his social worker, and his wife. In reality, the patient was not motivated for psychiatric treatment but rather was responding to pressure from the social worker to "get rehabilitated." While this was superficially supported by his wife, she actually was exerting stronger influence against rehabilitation because of her preference for working independently and having the patient dependent on her. The crisis which led to psychiatric contact was precipitated in part by the patient's increasing dependency on and abuse of narcotics and in part by his physician's newly acquired apprehension about the appropriateness of dispensing maintenance narcotics. While this apprehension led the surgeon to consider more seriously other methods for dealing with the patient's demands and constant complaints of pain, it was balanced by his involvement with the patient and the satisfaction of being his primary physician.

Ultimately, psychiatric treatment was not a workable way of resolving the problems of this case. As a result of the psychiatrist's contacts with the patient, the patient's wife, his surgeon, and the social worker, the latter two worked out a plan with the patient and his wife whereby the patient remained at home where he was maintained on narcotics but with closer, more adequate controls established over his supply.

In this case the ecological group, illustrated in Figure 32-3, is composed of the patient, his wife, his physician, and his social worker. The case is comparatively simple in that the patient is participating in only two distinct social systems, the family and the surgical team. The problems in this case centered around issues often associated with maladaptation to chronic illness: characterological passivity and drug dependency. Their resolution was worked out with little disagreement among members of the patient's ecological group because of their mutually shared belief that he should remain in a passive-dependent position.

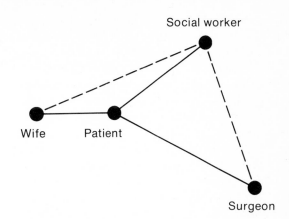

Figure 32-3   The ecological group of the patient in Example 32-3.

Eco-Strain

In cases more complex than the one used in Example 32-3, especially when the patient participates in a number of different social systems, a resolution may be much more difficult to achieve because of conflicts between the systems in the types of behavior which are expected and reinforced. Figure 32-4 illustrates the case where an individual participates in three distinct systems. As an element in System I, the axial individual has certain interpersonal forces working upon him and

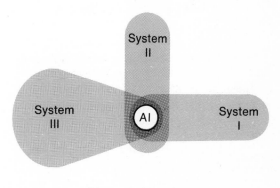

AI = axial individual

Figure 32-4   A general systems approach to describing the social field of any given individual.

emanating from him. These forces may or may not harmonize with similar sets of forces in Systems II and III. When they do not harmonize and there is an intersystem conflict of forces, there is a resultant strain within the individual. A commonly recognized example of this is called *role strain*. This exists when someone assumes two or more roles which can become incompatible, such as being a mother and a doctor, or being a coworker and a supervisor. The competition between the different behaviors which are expected in the different roles produces a tension within the individual. In the ecological group model, strain is present when the interpersonal forces between the axial individual and any two or more persons in his ecological group are in conflict. This kind of strain will be referred to as *eco-strain*. When this is persistent and relatively unchanging, it produces a low-grade tension in the individual. However, rapid or major shifts in the ecological group of an individual may produce a large eco-strain which, in turn, results in a high level of intrapsychic tension.

There are many life situations which are likely to involve an individual in conflicting interpersonal forces as a result of his participating in two independent social field units or systems. Some common examples are adolescents caught between the family system and a peer group system, newly married individuals caught between their families of origin and their newly acquired family of procreation, professionals and other salaried individuals caught between their social system at work and their families, individuals in therapy caught between their families and friends and their treatment social system. All these individuals are enmeshed in the conflicting expectations of separately functioning systems. These conflicts result in eco-strain, and often psychiatric efforts to help such individuals deal with their crises fail until this factor is taken into account.

Example 32-4. A 17-year-old male high school senior was referred by his family physician for psychiatric treatment because of bouts of anxiety in which he developed severe shortness of breath associated with hyperventilation and agonizing fears that he would die. The patient was a bright student who was very successful academically, somewhat at the cost of interpersonal relations. He was an only child who had always been in the center of his mother's attention. The anxiety attacks began during the spring of the patient's senior year and were precipitated by two major factors: an especially bad bout of hay fever symptoms which resulted from high levels of spring pollens and which significantly interfered with his breathing comfort; and the stress of deciding about whether to go to a college which would necessitate moving away from home.

The parents were seen in the course of evaluation. They were both excessively preoccupied with their son's health and said that as a result they were rather apprehensive about his leaving the home. The father was emotionally much more removed from the home, and one of the central problems seemed to be the mother's reinforcement of her son's anxiety about his breathing and overall health. From the very beginning of the psychiatric contact, discussions centered around the patient's uncertainty about leaving home and his mother's reluctance to accept his leaving.

Although the first few meetings seemed to relieve some of the family's apprehension and worry, the patient continued to have acute episodes of anxiety. When these were discussed further, it came out that the patient and his parents were still calling the family physician when the anxiety attacks occurred on evenings and weekends and that the latter was encouraging them to come into his office for immediate help and medication. Thus, although the patient and the family were discussing with the psychiatrist the issues underlying the bouts of anxiety, the anxiety itself was being reinforced by the extremely solicitous attitude of the family's physician. Subsequently, the psychiatrist contacted the family physician and encouraged him to be less receptive to the patient's and the family's calls for crisis help. The dynamic basis for the request was explained, and a coordinated effort between the physician and the treating psychiatrist was planned in which calls for help with the anxiety attacks would be referred to the psychiatrist. This plan helped to contain the escalating bouts of anxiety; the underlying problems were dealt with directly, and the anxiety attacks diminished.

The Ecological Group and Crisis Development

The ecological group assumes different importance for individuals according to their social field orientation, and it plays different roles in crisis initiation. Crises may be described as developing in two general ways: as a result of something happening directly to an individual, such as school graduation or a severe accident; or as a result of something happening to one of the members of his ecological group, such as a parent moving out of his home or the sudden loss of a close friend. Thus, we may speak of crises which are axial-initiated and those which are perimeter-initiated. The former begin in the axial individual and spread out to involve his ecological group. Intervention is usually best directed primarily toward the axial individual and only secondarily to some of the most affected individuals in his ecological group. Perimeter-initiated crises, on the other hand, begin in some perimeter individual and devolve upon the axial individual. They may take the extreme form of what Langsley and Kaplan[8] have called a "caretaker crisis," in which one of the perimeter individuals on whom the axial individual is particularly dependent makes a major change in his relationship to the axial individual or removes himself from the social field. Intervention in these cases is often best directed at both the key perimeter individual and the axial individual simultaneously.

Example 32-5. A 35-year-old unemployed man was brought in an acute psychotic state into the emergency room by his sister and brother-in-law. History revealed that he had been chronically psychotic for fifteen years, living at home with his mother, and with his sister and brother-in-law living in the adjoining house. Since his first psychotic break at the age of 20, the patient had received sporadic psychiatric care, which had recently consisted of monthly visits for renewal of phenothiazine medication. The patient's mother took care of him at home and tolerated his unusual behavior rather well. However, in the several weeks prior to his emergency room visit, the patient's mother had developed pneumonia, which had left her bedridden and unable to care for him. As a result, the patient was left much of the time to his own devices or, alternatively, in the care of his slightly hostile sister and brother-in-law. Under these conditions, the patient's chronic psychosis exacerbated to an acute state. It appeared to the emergency room physician that the precipitating stress in this situation was the acute illness of the patient's long-standing caretaker. Because of his sister's substantial resistance to assuming caretaking responsibilities for him, a short-term psychiatric hospitalization was arranged until his mother had recuperated.

In this example of a perimeter-initiated crisis, the key perimeter individual was already receiving appropriate medical attention. Intervention with her was needed primarily so that she could appreciate her important role vis-à-vis her son and perhaps avoid similar difficulties when she next was ill or indisposed. However, in many instances, the key perimeter individual's behavior change is based on psychological factors rather than on medical illness as in this illustration. When this is the case, for example, when there had been a disruptive argument or when depression and withdrawal threaten loss of an important relationship, it is essential that the key perimeter individual be actively brought into the crisis intervention.

Clinical Implications of the Model

The concept of the ecological group is designed to be clinically useful. Although other social field concepts such as the family, the doctor-patient relationship, or the married couple refer to units which are easily identified, such units generally do not present themselves as such in a clinical setting, asking for help. It is the individual who comes for help, and it is therefore the ecological group concept, with the presenting individual at its core, which may be most helpful in working with that individual.

There are several important implications of the model which suggest principles of clinical action. The first principle calls for the clinician to attend, during acute psychological disturbance, not only to the patient (the axial individual) but also to other members of his ecological group. In doing this, he will have to evaluate the role that they have played in development of the problem and, perhaps separately, the role that they may play in its resolution. He will also want to evaluate all the perimeter individuals' conflicting expectations and demands on the patient which result in eco-strain and psychological distress. A second principle of action calls for the clinician to keep in mind that the patient may not be the one who initiated the crisis, who is presenting the main obstacles to a resolution, or who is most easily worked with and influenced in the solution. The person who feels the crisis most or who is most likely to complain to a source of help may simply be the most vulnerable individual involved. Thus, looking to the patient's ecological group may provide the clinician with a person with whom it is particularly important to work actively. A third and final principle states that solutions often lie within the ecological group rather than within the patient alone or within the patient acting with the support of the clinician. This means that solutions may be achieved most easily when the clinician acts as the facilitator for the ecological system equilibration rather than as someone who primarily tries to help control the patient's behavior or stimulate some inner change.

The following example illustrates the concepts and principles which have been developed in the previous paragraphs on the basis of the ecological group model. It is a more extensive discussion of a case discussed in Chapter 30. There emphasis was placed upon the psychiatric consultant's crisis intervention and brief psychotherapy. In the material presented below, more emphasis will be placed upon the psychiatric consultant's work with the patient and her ecological group.

All the examples used to illustrate the ecological group model, including the one that follows, have been patients with medical illness. Although the ecological group concept is especially helpful in connection with psychiatric consultation in the general hospital, it is equally applicable to psychiatric patients who appear in the emergency room or in the outpatient clinic. Applications of the ecological group model to cases from emergency and clinic settings are found in the first part of this book and an earlier article.[7]

> *Example 32-6.* A 27-year-old married woman with two young children developed fever, sore gums, and swellings in her neck and was diagnosed as having acute myeloblastic leukemia. Her general practitioner made the diagnosis and referred her to a hematologist without telling her his diagnosis. Accompanied by her husband, she went to the hematologist, who told her, after his evaluation, that she had acute leukemia of the most serious type. The patient responded to this with an outburst of weeping, frenzied pacing, and extreme anxiety. Later that day, after she had regained her composure, she was referred for hospitalization for further evaluation and possible treatment with a new chemotherapeutic agent.
>
> During a hospitalization of several weeks, the patient became progressively childlike and dependent. Her physicians were very sympathetic, particularly because chemotherapy was

causing painful side effects. They tried to encourage her and urged her family to give as much support as possible. Her parents responded with considerable support; the patient's husband, however, found it difficult to visit her. He want away on several long business trips during her hospitalization, communicating very little with her and leaving the children in the hands of a baby-sitter. The patient sensed his withdrawal and, as a result, became exceedingly anxious and fearful. She began to depend a great deal on her extremely solicitous parents, but their concern and attention seemed only to increase her demands and helplessness. Eventually, her mother and father took turns staying overnight in her room and attending to every physical need.

At this point, the primary physician, a hematologist, requested a psychiatric consultation. Although the patient appeared helpless and childlike, she had actually experienced a remarkable remission from her leukemia as a result of several weeks of drug treatment. As far as he was concerned she soon would be medically able to go home, even though she was far from being psychologically ready. The psychiatric consultant first interviewed the patient and then made contact with all the family members. He concluded that brief psychotherapy with the patient was indicated, as well as some collaborative work with the patient's husband, parents, and physician. Past history revealed that this woman had always been extremely dependent upon her parents, particularly her father, and had never lived by herself or held a job independently. She flunked out of college after one year and precipitously married a man whom she had met during her freshman year. The marriage decision seemed to be a way for the patient to resolve her ambivalence about going back home to live and her uncertainty about the future.

The patient and her husband had been married for seven years when her illness occurred. The marriage had not been satisfactory, particularly in the last three or four years when there were frequent arguments. During this period, the patient maintained some happiness by devoting herself to her two young children. Her husband worked considerably in excess of forty hours per week and often took week-long business trips. This left the patient alone some of the time and led her to develop some relationships in the community where she lived and to maintain ties with her parents in a nearby community.

The psychiatric consultant initially saw the patient in daily psychotherapy. He established a close relationship with the patient and helped her to think and talk openly about the problems she was facing. What the patient appeared to appreciate most of all was a stable relationship which was supportive but not too involved. Under these conditions, she was able to discuss how frightened she was by the withdrawal and detachment of her husband on the one hand and by the infantilizing solicitousness of her parents on the other. She was afraid her husband would desert her while she was dying, and although she wanted her parents' attention and reassurance, she was upset when they gave it because then she was only reminded of her situation, and it made her feel more helpless and hopeless. She was simultaneously aware of her physician's unexpressed resentment for her clinging dependency, but she felt unable to control herself and, in turn, resented his resentment.

As well as giving himself as a source of stable and somewhat detached support while she learned to deal with the issues of a terminal illness, the psychiatric consultant also worked with the patient's ecological group. He met with her parents and encouraged them to relax somewhat in their constant attention and vigilance. They received this message with considerable relief and almost immediately stopped staying overnight with her in the hospital room. The consultant also met with her physician and discussed some of the psychological problems the patient was confronting during this crisis and how they related to lifelong adjustment difficulties. This relieved considerably the hematologist's resentment at her frustrating, childlike state and made him feel better about the "quality of life" which had resulted from his considerable effort to establish a clinical remission. Finally, the psychiatric consultant met with the patient's husband and gained an undertanding of the basis for his anxiety and avoidance behavior. Even before her illness, he had felt trapped by his wife's dependence on him. Her response to the diagnosis of leukemia had only increased his anxiety and wish to flee. As a result of his meetings with the consultant, the husband was able to be more supportive with his wife.

As the psychiatrist continued his therapy with the patient, she gained sufficient confidence and independence so that, in spite of considerable weakness, within a week she was able to go home from the hospital. Once home, she continued in psychotherapy and was able to talk through enough of her concerns about her illness and death, her parents, and her husband and children, that she decided to terminate the treatment on a regular basis after about four weeks. During this period, she was able to gain a type of psychological independence from her parents which she had never before enjoyed. Also, for the first time, she began to acknowledge and think about the very profound difficulties that existed in her marriage.

Two months after discontinuing regular therapy, the patient and her husband recontacted the therapist to discuss marital problems. As a result of several further sessions of couple therapy, they decided to separate. Six months later, they were divorced. After the divorce, the patient took an apartment with her two

children and, for the first time in her life, lived on her own. She maintained an active social life, dating one man regularly. One year after her divorce, she had an acute exacerbation. She accepted this with strength and composure. During her terminal hospitalization, she was visited by her parents and her boyfriend and realistically made arrangements for the care of her children after her death.

In this case, the patient's ecological group consisted of her husband, her two children, her mother and father, and her hematologist. These people were members of three distinct social systems: her family of procreation, her family of origin, and the inpatient medical ward. These relationships are illustrated in Figure 32-5.

All the perimeter individuals were responding somewhat differently to an axially initiated crisis

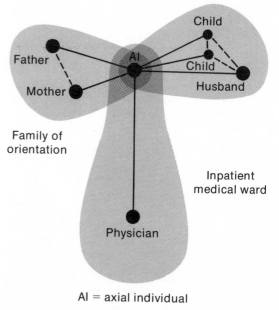

AI = axial individual

Figure 32-5 The ecological group of the patient in Example 32-6 with the members' social systems also indicated.

which had resulted from the development of acute leukemia. Because of the patient's long-standing interpersonal dependency or social field orientation, she was especially sensitive to the reaction of her ecological group to her fears and need for help. Her physician urged her to get well and explained her condition but gave little in the way of emotional support. Her parents attended to her every need and in many other ways acted as though she could not take care of herself. Her husband acted as though she had no reason to be so upset and continued his work routine uninterrupted while generally avoiding the patient until she could take care of herself. These conflicting messages and expectations created a significant eco-strain and thereby added to the patient's distress in response to her confrontation with a fatal illness.

The psychiatric consultant intervened in two ways. He conducted brief psychotherapy with the patient. Simultaneously, he met with the perimeter individuals in the patient's ecological group. In doing this he was able both to help them modify their reactions to the patient and to help the patient understand their behavior and integrate their collective messages with her own needs and plans. As a result of this intervention, the patient was able to regain her confidence and establish mastery over a painful reality. In the process a new equilibrium was achieved in the patient's ecological group, and ultimately there was a significant change in its membership.

TRANSMISSION OF AFFECT THROUGH THE SOCIAL SYSTEM

The previous sections have discussed and illustrated how the social field of a patient influences his psychological status, especially when he is psychologically disposed to be responsive to that field. In particular, Example 32-1 illustrated how the presence of a particular affect and attitude in the patient's social field resulted in the development of a reciprocal affect and set of behaviors in the patient herself. This section will consider a

third aspect of the psychosocial interface, one which represents an opposite phenomenon, namely the impact of the patient's affect and attitude on the social system and its subsequent transmission through that system. Since this chapter is concerned with the dynamics of consultation, this section will focus on the way this transmission affects the psychiatric consultant.

Whenever a hospitalized patient is experiencing a particular affect, those around him experience it as well. If he is depressed, his family, his caretakers, and the other patients all become aware of this depression and, depending upon their degree of involvement, participate in it. This participation is based upon their empathy with him. For some caretakers who are able to distance themselves completely from patients, the sharing of affect may last only as long as they are in direct face-to-face contact. But for others who are more fully involved, the transmitted affect pervades more of their lives. This is only natural, because caretaking brings involvement, and involvement means a certain merging of psychological perspective, a certain amount of mutual identification, and a certain sharing of mood and feeling.

A patient's caretakers not only share in his affect, they also communicate it to others with whom they deal regarding that patient. This may mean only a short and low-intensity communication, as when the morning nurse, in passing information about a particular patient on to the evening nurse, says, "Incidentally, Mr. Brown is really down in the dumps today." Frequently, however, the patient's affect will influence the caretakers' communications about him much more pervasively. Since disturbed affect is a common reason for psychiatric consultation request, this latter type of caretaker communication is especially likely to be influenced by the patient's mood and attitude.

Example 32-7. A resident psychiatrist on call for the psychiatric consultation service was interrupted during a therapy hour by the clinic telephone receptionist who sounded extremely anxious. She apologized and explained that she had just received a call from a medical intern for an urgent consultation. The consultation psychiatrist called the intern immediately. The latter anxiously related the story of a 42-year-old woman, on the ward for evaluation of a chronic cardiac condition, who was extremely upset about her heart, her diagnostic work-up, and her course in the hospital. When the patient herself was seen one-half hour later, she was only moderately anxious. She reported that she had been very upset a short time earlier about a scheduled procedure but that the talk with the intern had reassured her, especially since he suggested a psychiatric consultation. By the end of the psychiatric consultant's interview, it became clear that the patient's main source of anxiety was actually her marital relationship and that she would benefit therapeutically from further discussion of her marital problems. Her anxiety, which appeared to have been considerably aggravated by a morning telephone conversation with her husband, had largely subsided, and she agreed to several psychiatric interviews during the remainder of her hospitalization.

In this case the affect of anxiety was transmitted from patient to intern to receptionist to psychiatric consultant. By the time it reached the latter, its rather specific origins had been obscured and it was magnified to the point of "urgency." This type of experience is not uncommon for psychiatric consultants. It seems that the affect associated with a message is often more enduring in its movement through a social system than the content of the message. In this particular case, the affect associated with the message became magnified when its specific context was lost, whereas at the same time, the message bearers still had responsibility for seeing that it reached its destination.

In many cases, it is not just affect but also a type of interpersonal exchange which is transmitted through the system to the consultant psychiatrist.

In a sense, the process of transmission contains a capsule statement of the type of problematic interaction taking place between the patient and his caretakers.

Example 32-8. The consultant psychiatrist received a terse and demanding consultation request from a medical intern. The telephone message requested immediate psychiatric evaluation of a 47-year-old male schoolteacher who was in the hospital for adjustment of his insulin doses and control of his diabetes. During the next hour, the psychiatric consultant tried several times to reach the intern by telephone and page, but when unsuccessful went to the medical service to see the patient directly. There he encountered the intern at the nurses' station. Before anything else was said, the latter expressed his anger at the psychiatrist for not responding promptly. When the psychiatrist explained that he had been busy when the request came in but had tried to call the intern, the latter replied that it was not his fault that the psychiatrist had failed to reach him and that he wanted the psychiatrist to "find out what was wrong with this damn patient."

Further discussion revealed that this patient had been extremely controlling of his treatments and very demanding of his caretakers, blaming them whenever a problem developed, especially when they had not responded immediately to his call. As a result, all the staff, nurses as well as doctors, were very angry with him. When the psychiatric consultant saw the patient, the latter was sitting grim-faced in bed with his arms folded. Through a long and anger-filled interview, the patient related the many experiences during his hospitalization which had produced his mounting anger.

Information from the patient's past history and his current lifestyle suggested that he was a strongly counterdependent individual who deeply resented being in the hospital. He appeared to be dealing with his anxiety about his health and his characterologically based rejection of the dependent position by attempting to control his treatments and his caretakers. Inexperienced with this type of patient and psychologically unsophisticated, the medical intern had responded to this situation with countercontrol, thus initiating a rapidly escalating patient-staff conflict, with each side blaming the other.

Through patient listening and support, the consultant psychiatrist was able to soothe some of the patient's tumultuous feelings. He then had a long discussion with the medical intern and a conference with the staff nurses. In this way, he enabled them to appreciate the importance for this patient of at least partial control of the treatment process. These adjustments made it possible for the patient to remain in the hospital in a relatively anger-free state for the two days until his planned discharge.

In this case, it was more than anger which was transmitted through the social system to the consultant psychiatrist. What was transmitted was the core of the problematic doctor-patient interaction. Just as the patient was angry, demanding, controlling, and blaming of the intern, so, too, the intern was demanding and controlling in his consultation request and angry and blaming in his response to the psychiatrist's inquiries. Such reflection of the patient-doctor interaction in the consultee-consultant interaction is a recurrent experience for consultant psychiatrists and may assume several other forms. Thus, a passive-aggressive or a helpless-dependent request for help from the consultee often means that these qualities characterize the ongoing patient-staff interactions and play some role in the problem for which consultation is requested. The tendency, of course, is for the consultant psychiatrist to respond to the distorted consultation request in a negative way. This tendency can be avoided, however, if the psychiatrist appreciates the extent to which the patient's affect and interpersonal style create

reciprocal effects in the social field, thus influencing the entire consultation process.

COMMENT

The goal in this chapter has been to consider in some depth the psychosocial interface between the patient in the general hospital or clinic and the social system in which he is embedded. This interface has been described and conceptualized in ways which should help the psychiatric consultant better understand the patients he is called to see and better appreciate the dynamics of the consultative process. However, the usefulness of such concepts as the modulation of psychological states, social field orientation, the ecological group, and the transmission of affect through a social system need not be limited to psychiatric consultation. They are useful in the emergency room in the psychiatric clinic as well, and thus this concluding chapter introduces concepts which bring the reader full circle back to the problems and concerns considered in the very beginning of this book.

REFERENCES

1. Miller, Warren B.: "Psychiatric Consultation, Part I: A General Systems Approach," *Psychiat. Med.,* **4**(2):135, 1973.

2. Miller, Warren B.: "Psychiatric Consultation, Part II: Conceptual and Pragmatic Issues of Formulation," *Psychiat. Med.,* **4**(3):251, 1973.

3. Witkin, H. A.: "Psychological Differentiation and Forms of Pathology," *J. Abnorm. Psychol.,* **70**(5):317, 1965.

4. Riesman, D.: "From Morality to Morale," in M. McGiffert (ed.), *The Character of Americans,* Dorsey, Homewood, Ill., 1964, pp. 250–264.

5. Chodoff, P., and H. Lyons: "Hysteria, the Hysterical Personality, and 'Hysterical' Conversion," *Am. J. Psychiat.,* **114**:734, 1958.

6. Bott, E.: *Family and Social Network,* Tavistock Publications, London, 1957.

7. Miller, Warren B.: "A Psychiatric Emergency Service and Some Treatment Concepts," *Am. J. Psychiat.*, **124**(7):924, 1968.

8. Langsley, D., and D. Kaplan: *The Treatment of Families in Crisis,* Grune & Stratton, New York, 1968.

Outline Form for Collecting and Recording Examinational Data in the Psychiatric Interview*

I. *THE PSYCHIATRIC HISTORY*

A. *Identifying Data.* Age, sex, race, or ethnic group, occupation, family income and socioeconomic class, marital status, composition of current household, religion, and number of interviews on which this report is based. The chief complaint or presenting problem (quotation of patient).

   Ex. What is troubling you at this time?

B. *The Development of the Present Illness:*

   Ex. When did it start and what was happening at that time?

C. *Past History:*

   1. *Infancy and early childhood;*
      Ex. What is the first thing you can remember?

   2. *School History;*
      Ex. How did you get along in school?

   3. *Vocational adjustment;*
      Ex. Where have you worked prior to this job? Before that?

   4. *Development of special interests, hobbies, habits, and social life;*
      Ex. What do you like to do for fun?

   5. *Sexual history;*
      Ex. How do you and your wife get along? Then lead into this.

   6. *Military experiences and adjustment.*

D. *Medical and Surgical History*

E. *Family History:*

   1. *Social, economic, and religious data;*
      Ex. What did your father do for a living?

   2. *Characterization of parents,* their relations to each other and to their children;
      Ex. What kind of person is your father? Your mother?

   3. *Characterization of siblings and relatives* who played a significant role in the patient's life;
      Ex. How did you get along with your (younger sister)?

   4. *The patient's position in the family constellation;*
      Ex. How was your opinion about various matters received in your family?

*By Karl A. Menninger, *A Manual for Psychiatric Case Study,* 2d ed., Grune & Stratton, New York, 1962. By permission of the author and publisher. (Abridged.)

5. *Marital history;*
   Ex. How long have you been married?

II. *PSYCHOLOGICAL EXAMINATION*

A. *Gross Identification:*
   1. *Circumstances* — reliability;

   2. *Observational data on patient.*

B. *Part Processes:*
   1. *Perception:*
      Normal — alertness, accuracy;
      Deficiencies — sensory, attention, orientation;
      Excesses and distortions — sensory, attention;
      False percepts, illusions, hallucinations, concept of body image, depersonalization.

   2. *Intellection* (cognitive):
      Level and range;
      Normal — intelligence (estimated IQ), memory, abstraction, information (knowledge);
      Deficiencies — excesses;
      Distortions — judgment (common sense).

   3. *Thought processes:*
      Normal — tempo, rhythm, organization;
      Deficiencies — retardation, blocking, incoherence, irrelevance;
      Excesses — press, intellectualization, garrulousness, circumstantiality, flight of ideas;
      Distortions — perseveration, condensation, neologisms, word salad, echolalia, stereotypy, and autism.

   2. *Thought content:*
      Normal — fantasies, dreams, preoccupations;
      Deficiencies — impoverishment;
      Excesses — obsessions, delusions, fixed ideas.
      Ex. Do you have any recurrent troublesome thoughts?

5. *Emotions* (affective):
   Normal — mood, intensity, depth, modulation;
   Deficiencies — blandness, bluntness, apathy, coldness;
   Excesses — elation, rage, depression, panic, worry, fear, suspiciousness;
   Inappropriateness — disharmony between affect and stimulation, incongruity, dissimulation.

6. *Action* (expressive behavior):
   Normal — energy level, vigor, persistence;
   Deficiencies — inertia, stupor, rigidity, inhibition;
   Excesses — restlessness, hyperkinesis, agitation, assaultiveness, destructiveness, impulsiveness;
   Inappropriateness — compulsions, tics, rituals, mannerisms, habits, stereotypy, posturing, catalepsy.

C. *Hunches, Intuitions, Fantasies, and Highly Subjective Reactions to the Patient* (usually best gotten in first interviews).

III. *INTEGRATIVE FUNCTIONING (RELATIONSHIPS)*

A. *Relations to Self:*
   1. *Self-concept* — models, body image;
      Ex. How would you describe yourself as a person?

   2. *Ego-ideal* — goals, identification of figures, ethics;
      Ex. Who would you most rather be at this time?

   3. *Super-ego* — strength, model;
      Ex. Whom in your family do you resemble most?

B. *Relations to Others:*
   1. *Quantitative* — range, diversity, intensity, and so forth;
      Ex. Do you have many friends? How many close ones?

2. *Qualitative* — type of object, modality (parasitic, domineering, and so on);
   Ex. Tell me about some of your friends.

3. *Love-hate pattern* — dominance, ambivalent manifestations;
   Ex. How do you get along with (a significant person)?

C. *Relations to Things:*
   1. *Attitude to possessions:*
      Ex. What are some of your proud possessions?

   2. *Work pattern* — interest, skill, satisfaction;

   3. *Play pattern* — interest, skill, satisfaction;
      Ex. What do you do in your spare time?

   4. *Philosophic,* social, religious interests.

D. *Relations to Therapy:*
   1. *To the clinic:*
      Ex. How do you feel about coming to a psychiatric clinic?

   2. *To the interviewer:*

   Expectations and Preconceptions {
      Conscious;
      Ex. What do you think a psychiatrist does?
      Unconscious — transferences (identify transference figure and modality)
   }

   3. *Motivation:*
      Ex. What would you like to have done for you?

IV. *REACTIONS TO DISINTEGRATIVE THREAT*

A. *Identification of Threat:*
   1. *External* — nature and severity of environmental stress.

2. *Internal* — impulses mobilized and their object;
   Ex. Hostile impulses, erotic impulses, loss of security or dependency.

B. *Reactions:*
   1. *Normal reactions* — humor, tears, fantasy, etc.

   2. *Pathological reactions:*
      (a) *First-order devices* (alarm and mobilization):
         Excessive — repression, suppression, alertness, irritability, emotionality, intellection, activity, withdrawal, autonomic lability.
      (b) *Second-order devices* (partial detachment and attempted compensation):
         Dissociation — fainting, amnesia, depersonalization (simulations);
         Substitutions (and displacements) of objects — phobic, obsessive, projections of modality — compulsions, rituals, perversions;
         Altered attitudes to the self — self-abasement and restriction, asceticism, mutilation, intoxication, narcotization;
         Somatization — in fantasy, sensation, function;
         Exploitation (secondary gain).
      (c) *Third-order devices* (transitory ego rupture with prompt restoration; episodic):
         Panic attacks;
         Catastrophic demoralization;
         Transitory dereistic excitement;
         Assaultive violence — homicidal, suicidal, sexual;
         Convulsions.
      (d) *Fourth-order devices* (persistent ego rupture or exhaustion):
         Excitement;

Hyperthymia;

Autism;

Apathy;

Delusional preoccupation;

Confusion.

   (e) *Fifth-order devices* (complete ego failure):

Continuous uncontrolled violence;

Other forms of death.

V. *PHYSICAL AND NEUROLOGICAL EXAMINATION*

VI. *DYNAMIC FORMULATION*

A. *Personality Type* (characteristic adjustment pattern).

B. *Prevailing Environment* (persistent stresses).

C. *The Critical External Stresses.*

D. *Principal Internal Stresses.* The conscious and unconscious threats to integrated functioning (e.g., resurgence of ego, alien impulses, anniversary material, recapitulations in life of a child of own conflicts).

E. *Emergency Measures.* Reactions and symptoms in response to threat.

F. *Net Result.* Assessment of physical, emotional, and social disability.

VII. *DIAGNOSIS*

A. *Present State:*
1. *Formal diagnosis* — APA (DSM - II);

2. *Informal diagnosis* — if formal diagnosis not very descriptive.

B. *Premorbid Personality*

VIII. *DISPOSITION*

A. *Psychotherapy:*
1. *Goals of treatment* — limited or extensive character reorganization;

2. *Techniques of treatment* — support, exhortation, uncovering, insight, build compulsive defenses, etc.;

3. *Probable frequency and length of treatment.*

B. *Hospitalization.*

C. *Drugs.* Which one, why, how much, how long?

IX. *FOLLOW-UP RECORDING*

A brief progress summary should be prepared every three months and upon termination. It should contain the following (plus any comments you think relevant):

Check List for Summaries

1. Visits per week; time in treatment; total visits.
2. A brief, informal characterization of your therapy with patient.
3. Changes in personality, treatment, or life situation; issues or crises in treatment since last summary.
4. Initial diagnosis, formal (APA) and informal (your own description).
5. Current diagnosis, formal and informal.
6. Have drugs been used: if so, which drug, how much, for how long, and response.
7. Were psychological tests done?
8. If treatment ended, by whose decision and why?
9. Supervisor's name if case was supervised.

Mental Status Examination

An adequate psychiatric examination consists of the psychiatric history (PH) and the mental status examination (MSE). These provide the raw data upon which diagnostic and psychodynamic formulations are based. Whereas the PH deals primarily with the *content* of individual experience, the MSE focuses on the *form* of observable behavioral responses.

The purpose of the MSE is to provide an accurate description of the patient's current functioning. This record can be used as a base line for later comparisons, as a standard for evaluating changes in past performance (inferred from history), and for comparisons between individuals, aiding psychodiagnosis.

Because of its here-and-now emphasis, the MSE is more objective than the PH, but in both procedures the psychiatrist is the measuring instrument. What he perceives, tests, and records is a function of the attitudinal set he brings to the examination. Proper timing, explanation, and emphasis on the positive value of certain tests are necessary to enlist cooperation. A perfunctory, rigid, or disinterested MSE is just as limited as a cursory history.

Usually, the *impressionistic* aspect of the MSE is collected during history taking and the *psychometric* testing is performed later, but there are no fixed rules. For example, making sure that the patient hears your name at the start of the interview may be used later for a test of recent memory. Or if a patient interprets the proverb "The hand that rocks the cradle rules the world" by saying, "My mother was that way; she always ruled me," this personalization is pertinent to both

the MSE and the PH. Thus, with the exception of explicit cognitive testing, the MSE and PH are largely conducted concurrently but are recorded separately. The following outline, which is one way of organizing the written report, may serve as a guide to the kinds of information gathered in the MSE.

I. *IMPRESSIONS OF THE GENERAL FORM OF BEHAVIOR*

In writing up the impressions of the MSE, it is necessary to state not only the kind of behavior but also its quantitative aspects (degree, intensity, range, frequency, etc.). Much of abnormal behavior can be viewed as a wide swing (positive or negative) away from a set point of rough equilibrium, taken as a level of normality within a given culture or, more particularly, for a given individual's usual mode of reactivity. Some kind of quantitative statement is thus useful for inter- and intraindividual comparisons. Careful recording of such data helps to determine changes during therapy.

A. *Appearance:* Dress (untidy, meticulous, etc.) and physical characteristics (body build, physical defects, etc.).

B. *Kinetics:* Posture, gait, gestures, mannerisms, tics, general motor activity, degree of social distance and congruent movement, tempo of reactions to specific situations, stupor, stereotypy, catalepsy, etc.

C. *Affective Expression:* This is inferred from the patient's behavior or is explicitly articulated by the patient during certain phases of the interview. Whereas the PH deals with what the patient has been feeling in the recent or remote past, the MSE focuses on what he is feeling *now*.

1. *Predominant mood or moods* — calm, anxious, depressed, indifferent, etc.
2. *Facial expression* — mobility, furrows, nonblinking stare, omega sign, peaked upper eyelids, incongruity between upper and lower halves of face, etc.
3. *Reaction to interviewer* — friendly, hostile, ingratiating, etc.
4. *Interviewer's reaction to patient* — sympathetic, fearful, interested, etc.
5. *Degree of reporting inferred affect* — for example, does a tremulous, hypervigilant patient deny that he is anxious, etc.?
6. *Changes in affect during interview* — crying, fear, joy, etc.
   (a) At what times and to what topics?
   (b) How dealt with — walking out of room, compulsive acitvity, pleas for help, etc.
   (c) Degree of control — were panic or crying spells controllable, etc.
   (d) Range of affective expression – e.g., changes in intensity versus monotony, change from beginning to end of interview, etc.
   (e) Inappropriateness of affect:
      (i) Incongruity to context – e.g., laughing when talking about close friend's death, *la belle indifférence,* etc.
      (ii) Incongruity to kinetics of behavior – e.g., laughing while crying; wide-eyed blank stare coupled with halting, disjointed smiles and grimaces.
   (f) Changes in autonomic function – sweating, tremors, cool hands, heart rate (observe carotid artery), tremors, sighing, dryness of mouth, pupil size, etc.
   (g) Effect of affect on other functions, i.e., on speech, logic, movement, etc.

D. *Speech*
1. *Quality of speech* — tone, inflection, loudness, pronunciation (slurring, lisp, etc.), tempo (slow, rapid, halting), blocking, stuttering, perseveration, etc.
2. *Quantity of speech* — free verbalization, monosyllabic answers, pressure of speech, etc.
3. *Organization of speech* — coherent, logical, relevant, circumstantial, disorganized, flight of ideas, word salad, rhyming, punning, overabstraction, amorphous vagueness, use of third person for first person singular, concreteness, shifts from concrete to abstract, goal-directedness, derailments, loss of place.
4. *Use of words* — difficulty in word finding, use of gestures to entirely supplant words, appropriateness to context (pedantic, overelaborate, imprecise, etc.), parapraxes, neologisms, condensations, etc.

E. *Symptomatology:* The MSE record describes those symptoms that are evident *during* the interview; the PH records the evolution of symptoms which took place in the past. Since the PH is best collected in an open-ended fashion, specific inquiry about various symptoms, past and present, can often be done toward the end of the interview as a prelude to cognitive testing. This approach suggests to the patient that the questions and tests are not being specifically directed to him but are a regular part of the examination of all patients. Historical information about suicidal tendencies, hallucinations, hypnagogic phenomena, frightening dreams, fugue states, *déjà vu* experiences, etc., can often be comfortably introduced in this fashion.

1. *Symptomatology involving thoughts:*
   (a) Compulsions — repetitive acts the patient feels driven to do: hand washing, counting, etc.
   (b) Obsessions — repetitive thoughts, often aggressive or sexual in nature, that enter the patient's mind unbidden and which he seems unable to control.

(c) Ruminations — repetitive or continuous speculation, often circular and about abstract matters, interfering with all other thought processes.

(d) Doubting and indecision — time-consuming uncertainties and vacillations concerning such trivial matters as which dress to wear, whether to go downtown, etc.

(e) Phobic thoughts — irrational fears, e.g., of heights, crowds, closed or open spaces, etc.

(f) Free-floating anxiety — sense of dread or impending doom, unlinked with reportable specific stimuli.

(g) Feelings of unreality — solid objects in the environment seem unusually distant or vivid, remote or evanescent, as though in a dream or a fog.

(h) Depersonalization — loss of sense of identity, feelings of emptiness or transparency, distortions of the body image, etc.

(i) Feelings of persecution — people are thought to be maliciously obstructing the patient's plans, plotting against him, poisoning him, etc. These patients may view the interview and MSE as a special kind of test that is part of a master scheme against them. Undue reactions to cognitive testing may be the first sign of these tendencies.

(j) Feelings of grandeur — ideas of omnipotence, the center of all concerns, etc.

(k) Feelings of influence — control by uncanny forces such as brain waves, atomic rays, etc.

(l) Ideas of reference — feelings that events in the outside world are in some way related to the patient. He may feel that newspapers, radio, television programs, etc., are commenting about him personally or that car horns sound for him and streetlights deliver recondite messages.

(m) Thought-broadcasting — feelings that his thoughts or feelings can be transmitted to others, that others can read his mind, etc.

(n) Self-destructive tendencies — urges to harm oneself or commit suicide. Careful attention must be paid to this information. Are the feelings overwhelming the patient at present? What plans has he made to carry out these acts? What does death mean to him? How has he controlled these impulses in the past? Now?

(o) Somatic preoccupations — overconcern with bodily functions (hypochondriasis) or bizarre distortions of supposed anatomy (somatic delusions, e.g., bowels are knotted up, semen is infiltrating the brain, etc.).

Comment: Symptoms (a) through (e) are commonly seen with neurotic distress but also occur in psychosis in conjunction with items (g) through (o), which are more indicative of defective reality testing. Of course, if any of these items turns up positive during the MSE, a careful history documenting the time, place, content, frequency, diurnal variation, relation to sleep and waking, etc., must be explored and then recorded in the PH.

2. *Perceptual symptoms* (sense deceptions):

(a) Illusions — the misinterpretation of sensory stimuli, such as mistaking a shadow for a man, or the misidentification of a person, such as calling a nurse "Mother." Illusions are particularly frequent in delirium, especially at night.

(b) Hallucinations — subjective perceptions occuring in the absence of external stimuli:

(i) Auditory — Patient may disrupt interview by cocking his head to one side, listening intently, or whispering and yelling back at the voices. In schizophrenia, the voices usually talk *to* the patient: "You're a dirty Communist . . . you shouldn't talk to him"; in delirium tremens, the voices more often talk *about* the patient: "Now he's smoking a cigarette. . . . He looks like one of those TV ads." Some obsessional patients may "hear" their own thoughts, but unlike schizophrenics, they recognize the thoughts as self-induced rather than coming from the outside. Auditory hallucinations point to schizophrenia unless proven to stem from either an acute or chronic brain syndrome.

(ii)   Visual — patient may recoil from apparitions or may laugh at antics of little men, etc. Though sometimes occurring in conjunction with auditory hallucinations in schizophrenia, visual hallucinations are most often seen in acute organic brain syndromes, such as in delirium tremens, after psychotomimetic drugs, and in temporal lobe epilepsy.

(iii) Gustatory, olfactory, and tactile hallucinations are also more common in organic syndromes.

II.   *EXAMINATION OF THE COGNITIVE FUNCTIONS*

This part of the MSE consists of more formal test questions borrowed from standardized psychometric tests. Equivocal findings should be followed up by a clinical psychologist.

Not every patient requires even the amount of cognitive testing outlined here. In general the tests are useful for distinguishing organic brain disease from the functional psychoses, in estimating intelligence, and in obtaining a base line for later comparisons. Changes over time are important for distinguishing delirium from dementia and for gauging the effect of anxiety on thought processes.

Impressions of many of these mental functions can be obtained from the free verbalizations during the anamnesis, but the specific tests are aimed at obtaining an objective record for inter- and intra-individual comparisons.

The test questions used should take into consideration the patient's age, cultural background, educational level, physical health, and history of drug taking. Easy questions should be asked first, followed by more difficult ones, until the patient is unable to respond correctly. At this point it is often reassuring to return to a question that the patient is able to handle correctly. This is particularly indicated where loss of self-esteem and depression have stemmed from the patient's vague awareness of beginning mental decline.

As a rule, a patient should *not* be given the correct answers to questions he has failed, nor should he be explicitly helped with calculations, etc., because these aids would influence later performance if repeat testing is necessary.

The following outline* is offered as a guide for testing the cognitive functions:

A.   *Orientation:* Date, place, and person. Being more than three days off as to date is highly suspicious of disorientation, but because most patients have been recently exposed to calendar information (appointment times, etc.), it is advisable to make sure that the patient knows the complete date (day, month, and year) as well as where he is (floor, wing, and name of hospital) and who the significant people are in his surroundings (nurses, doctors, etc.). Another good question is: "How long have you been here?"

B.   *Attention and Concentration:* An impression of distractability can be obtained by casually dropping a pencil or glancing at one's watch to see if such minor stimuli disrupt the patient's ongoing behavior. Distractability is frequent in manic and delirious patients. Difficulty with concentration is suggested by the patient's reporting he can no longer read the news-

---

*This format is a condensed and modified version of the mental status examination prepared by the Department of Psychiatry, University of Rochester, in 1964.

paper, which is a frequent finding in seriously depressed or organic patients.

1. *Digit span* — this test consists of asking a patient to repeat a series of digits read to him by the examiner. Patients should first be tested on retention of digits forward. When the upper range of this is determined, retention for digits in reverse order should then be tested separately. For both parts, digits should be given at the rate of one per second and should not be grouped. The pitch of the examiner's voice should be allowed to drop with the last digit of each series. If the patient fails on the first trial at any digit series, a second trial of that length series should then be given. Stop after two failures at any given series length. The following are suggested as digit series to be used:

Digits Forward	Digits Backward
3,8,6	2,5
6,1,2	6,3
3,4,1,7	5,7,4
6,1,5,8	2,5,9
3,4,2,3,9	7,2,9,6
5,2,1,8,6	8,4,1,3
3,8,9,1,7,4	4,1,6,2,7
7,9,6,4,8,3	9,7,8,5,2
5,1,7,4,2,3,8	1,6,5,2,9,8
9,8,5,2,1,6,3	3,6,7,1,9,4
1,6,4,5,9,7,6,3	8,5,9,2,3,4,2
2,9,7,6,3,1,5,4	4,5,7,9,2,8,1
5,3,8,7,1,2,4,6,9	6,9,1,6,3,2,5,8
4,2,6,9,1,7,8,3,5	3,1,7,9,5,4,8,2

Add together other combinations for longer sequences, if patient is capable.

The average expected level is from five to eight digits correct forward and from four to six correct backward. Less than five forward or less than three backward should be considered below average performance. A slight decrease in score after age 65 is considered normal. At any age, a discrepancy between digit span forward and backward of more than three points is unusual.

2. *Serial 7s or serial 3s:* This is a test of concentration in which the patient is asked to subtract 7s (or 3s) from 100 in serial fashion audibly and as fast as he can. Serial subtraction is one of the most valuable tests in detecting slight changes in attention produced by delirium. Long before arithmetical error may be manifested, the patient may betray his decreasing ability to perform the task by *heightened effort, perseveration, increase in total time of the tests, frequent hesitation or questioning, requesting a new start or becoming irritable, depreciating the test and examiner.*

Average time for serial 7 subtractions is up to ninety seconds. Four or more errors is considered marginal, and seven or more errors is considered quite poor performance. For repeated examinations, examiner should use 102, 101, 99, or 98 as starting points to minimize learning effects. If the patient is unable to do this, start with serial 3s, or let the patient use pencil and paper. Counting backward is of a lesser degree of difficulty, and finally, counting forward may be used. One may also ask the patient to recite the alphabet forward as fast as he can as a similar test with a lower degree of difficulty. It is important to get some kind of base line for later comparisons.

C. *Memory:* Both recent and past memory may be tested and estimated during the regular history taking. For recent memory, ask patient to recall your name, his route to the hospital, a recent meal, etc. In helping to determine whether the patient is confabulating, some of the above should be checked more than once with the patient and, if possible, with outside sources. In this regard, the question "Have you seen me before?" may be helpful. The patient who confabulates will often answer in the affirmative, fabricating details of a previous meeting with the examiner that did not take place. Reciting a simple story, such as the "Cowboy Story," and having the patient tell it back is a good test of recent memory and confabulation.

D. *Information:* The patient's fund of information and vocabulary are the two best indicators of his general level of intelligence and are particularly useful because of their relative insensitivity to the effects of any but the relatively most severe forms of psychopathology. That is, they are particularly helpful in determining the "premorbid" level of intellectual functioning, when there is impairment in other functions as the result of a disease process. Some suggested items are:

1. How many days are there in a week?
2. What must you do to water to make it boil?
3. How many things are there in a dozen?
4. Name the four seasons of the year.
5. What do we celebrate on the 4th of July?
6. How many pounds are there in a ton?
7. What does the stomach do?
8. What is the capital of Greece?
9. Where does the sun set?
10. Who invented the airplane?
11. Why does oil float on water?
12. What do we get turpentine from?
13. When is Labor Day?
14. How far is it from New York to Chicago?
15. What is a hieroglyphic?
16. What is a barometer?
17. Who wrote *Paradise Lost*?
18. What is a prime number?
19. What is habeas corpus?
20. Who discovered the South Pole?

Individuals of average intellectual ability should be able to answer correctly eight to thirteen of these items. Fewer than eight correct answers is suggestive of below average intelligence; correct answers to more than thirteen of these items suggests above average intellectual ability.

E. *Vocabulary:* The patient's vocabulary is probably the best indicator of his general intellectual level. This is an attribute that can be observed and evaluated throughout the interview with the patient, but it can be more specifically tested through presentation of a number of words from the following list (in order of difficulty):

1.	apple	13.	microscope
2.	donkey	14.	stanza
3.	diamond	15.	guillotine
4.	nuisance	16.	plural
5.	join	17.	seclude
6.	fur	18.	spangle
7.	shilling	19.	recede
8.	bacon	20.	affliction
9.	tint	21.	chattel
10.	armory	22.	dilatory
11.	fable	23.	flout
12.	nitroglycerine	24.	amanuensis

Patients must be able to give a reasonable definition or in any other way indicate their understanding of the *meaning* of the word. This can be done also by using the word correctly and appropriately in a sentence that indicates understanding of the meaning. Persons of average intellectual ability should be able to answer correctly eight to sixteen of these items. Fewer than eight correct answers indicates below average intelligence; more than sixteen correct suggests above average intellectual ability.

F. *Abstraction:* We are interested in the patient capacity to reason abstractly. This is a particularly important aspect of the patient's intellectual function because of its vulnerability to the effects of organic disturbances and its impairment in certain psychotic states, particularly schizophrenia. We are concerned with the patient's capacity to generalize, to think in terms of classes of objects and of events, and to understand the meaning and implication of symbols. The capacity for abstraction can be tested in a number of ways, two of which are the use of proverbs and "similarities." The use of proverbs for this purpose is subject to some criticism because of the varying familiarity of patients with various proverbs and because of the possibility of patients' responding correctly on the basis of stereotyped or habitual responses rather than the capacity to perform the reasoning function at the time the proverb is presented. That is, in testing capacity for abstraction, we are interested in the patient's ability to perform this function at the time of the examination rather than a demonstration of having possessed this capacity in the past. The test can be presented in the following way: "You know what a proverb is, don't you? A proverb is a saying. What do people generally mean when they say...." Some proverbs that may be used are:

1. Don't count your chickens before they're hatched.
2. There is no use crying over spilled milk.
3. The wheel that does the squeaking is the wheel that gets the grease.
4. A stitch in time saves nine.
5. As the twig is bent, the tree's inclined.
6. You can catch more flies with honey than with vinegar.
7. It's an ill wind that blows nobody good.
8. The restless sleeper blames the couch.
9. The tongue is the enemy of the neck.
10. The mouse that has but one hole is soon caught.

Persons of average intellectual ability should be able to give adequate responses to at least four or five of these items.

The testing of the capacity to give similarities is another method of assessing the patient's ability to reason abstractly. Here we are concerned with the patient's capacity to see objects and concepts in terms of "abstract or general classes." The test may be administered in the following way: "I am going to name some things that are the same or alike in certain ways. I want you to tell me in what way they are the same or alike. For example, in what ways are a plum and a peach alike?" Other similarities are:

1. beer and wine
2. cat and mouse
3. piano and violin
4. paper and coal
5. pound and yard
6. scissors and copper pan
7. mountain and lake
8. first and last
9. salt and water
10. liberty and justice
11. 49 and 121

Persons of average intellectual ability should be able to answer correctly five to eight of these items. Fewer than five adequate responses suggests below average intellectual functioning; more than eight adequate responses suggests above average intellectual functioning.

Note that the patient's response to similarities may be more or less abstract. For example, recognizing that both a plum and a peach "can be eaten" or "are round" or "have skins" are all correct in the sense that these are all accurate similarities. However, they are somewhat less abstract responses than recognizing that a plum and a peach are both fruits; i.e., they are members of a class of objects called fruits.

G. *Judgment and Comprehension:* As part of the examination of the patient's intellectual function, we are concerned with the extent to which the patient has been able to acquire an understanding of common modes of behavior in society and an understanding of common social mores and conventions. The extent to which a patient can perform well in this area may be an index of the extent to which he is a socially conforming individual who responds in terms of good judgment. The patient may be asked the following questions:

1. What is the thing to do if you lose a book belonging to a library?
2. Why is it better to build a house with bricks than with wood?
3. What should you do if you see a train approaching a broken track?
4. Why is it generally better to give money to an organized charity than to a street beggar?
5. What is the thing to do if a very good friend asks you for something that you do not have?
6. Why are criminals locked up or put in prison?
7. Why should most government positions be filled through Civil Service examinations?
8. Why does the United States require that a person wait at least two years from the

time he makes application until the time he receives his final citizenship papers?

9. Why is cotton used in making cloth?
10. Why should a promise be kept?

Persons of average intellectual ability should be able to correctly answer four to seven of these items. Correct response to less than four items suggests below average intellectual functioning; correct answers to eight or more items suggests above average intellectual functioning.

H. *Perception and Coordination:* The examination should contain at least a brief examination of the patient's perceptual and visual motor functioning. To this end the patient can be asked to:

1. Write his name (observe the speed and coordination the patient displays; observe the size of the letters, their accuracy, the presence or absence of tremor, etc.) on a sheet of blank paper.
2. Copy a simple circle drawn by the examiner on a sheet of blank paper.
3. Copy a simple cross drawn by the examiner on a sheet of blank paper.
4. Similarly copy a square, a diamond, and a row of dots.

Inability to perform these simple functions accurately and gracefully indicates visual-motor incoordination suggestive of brain damage or mental deficiency.

Conclusion: This MSE outline is too elaborate for some patients and incomplete for others. Each examiner will have his own preference for certain kinds of impressionistic data and test material. Experience will guide which kind of tests are administered, but for the beginner, it is best to err on the side of overtesting rather than undertesting. A psychiatric record that does not include some kind of ordered statement of the patient's mental status is incomplete.

Many of the polemics in psychiatry, as over the efficacy of psychotherapy, stem from a lack of objective means to measure changes in behavior as well as the tendency to deal in hypothetical constructs rather than explicit observations. A careful MSE is therefore a step in the right direction.

After recording the pertinent data, the examiner must *summarize* his findings in paragraph form. In drawing inferences, the psychiatrist must integrate *all* the data and not rely on a single finding, such as a neologism or olfactory hallucination, for his composite clinical appraisal.

The following proverbs serve as caveats for the usefulness and conduct of the MSE: "One swallow doesn't make a summer"; "One always paints the wolf bigger than it is"; "You can't tell the depth of the well by the length of the pump handle"; "The palest ink is better than the most retentive memory."

ADDENDUM – GUIDES FOR THE EVALUATION OF ANSWERS TO COGNITIVE EXAMINATION QUESTIONS

D. *INFORMATION*

1. 7
2. Heat it
3. 12
4. Spring, summer, fall, winter
5. Independence Day; Declaration of Independence signed
6. 2,000 lb
7. Digests food
8. Athens
9. West
10. Wright Brothers
11. It's lighter
12. Trees or sap of a tree
13. First Monday in September
14. 800 to 1,000 miles
15. Ancient picture writing; sacred Egyptian letters or script
16. Instrument for measuring atmospheric pressure
17. Milton
18. A number divisible by no other whole number except itself or 1
19. A legal writ requiring a person in custody to be brought before the court; a demand upon the court that, unless the reason for

a person's detention be forthcoming, he must be freed

20. Admundsen

E. *VOCABULARY*

Since the last third of the vocabulary list contains words that are most likely to raise questions in the examiner's mind, there are listed below dictionary definitions for the last eight words. Less elegant, precise, or detailed definitions are, of course, fully acceptable.

17. Seclude — Remove and keep apart, as from society.
18. Spangle — A small sparkling object; small metallic decoration for a dress; to adorn with spangles.
19. Recede — To move, to tend, or to incline backward; to withdraw, to cede back.
20. Affliction — Distress of body or mind or that which causes it; grief; calamity.
21. Chattel — Article of personal property; a moveable.
22. Dilatory — Tending to cause tardiness, slowness, or delay.
23. Flout — To scoff at; to jeer; to mock, insult, or treat with contempt; to sneer.
24. Amanuensis — One who copies manuscripts or takes dictation; a secretary.

F. *ABSTRACTION*

I. Proverbs

An adequate interpretation of a proverb consists of a statement of the general principle or idea conveyed by the proverb, i.e., an interpretation of the concept involving a translation from the specific referents to a broader level of applicability in terms of life, people, and philosophy. A correct translation of the principle in terms of a specific example is also acceptable. Frequently, proverbs are interpreted in terms of another proverb. If the subject responds by giving another proverb which is relevant and which, on questioning, he is able to interpret appropriately, that is also considered acceptable.

The general, more abstract meanings of the proverbs are given below and are to be used only as general guides to the appropriateness of the subject's response:

1. Chickens — Don't depend on the results of a venture until the outcome of the venture is known.
2. Milk — Little is to be gained by excessive rumination over an adverse circumstance.
3. Wheel — Desired ends are more likely to be obtained if one can get other people's attention.
4. Stitch — Preventive actions are in the long run more efficient than repair.
5. Twig — Early experiences often play a major role in determining subsequent events.
6. Flies — Positive inducements are the most effective.
7. Ill wind — Even the most adverse circumstance may have some beneficial influence.
8. Sleeper — People often tend to excuse their own shortcomings or faults in terms of external circumstances.
9. Tongue — Harm to oneself can result from one's own thoughtless actions, verbal or nonverbal.
10. Mouse — It is best not to rely too exclusively on a single resource.

II. Similarities

Responses to similarities items can vary over a considerable range of degree of abstraction. The responses listed below represent the most abstract and general level of response:

1. Alcoholic beverages
2. Animals
3. Stringed or musical instruments
4. Hydrocarbons; kinds of fuel
5. Units of measurement
6. Metal objects
7. Topological or geographical features of the earth
8. Extremes of position
9. Necessities of life
10. Social ideas or ideals
11. Perfect squares

G. *JUDGMENT AND COMPREHENSION*

Responses to comprehension items can vary over a wide range of quality from the very specific to the most general and comprehensive. Below are listed principles and/or ideas underlying the most comprehensive and acceptable answers:

1. Book — replace it or make restitution
2. Brick — more durable; more permanent; better insulated; safer; sturdier
3. Train — try to stop by signaling
4. Charity — to assure that money goes to the needy
5. Friend — try to procure it

6. Criminals — to deter people from crime; to protect society; to provide an example to others; to punish and avenge; to rehabilitate; to segregate criminals from the rest of society
7. Civil Service — to get better-qualified and better-trained people; to set standards; to prevent nepotism.
8. United States citizen — to investigate individual's past; to provide a probationary period; to keep out undesirables
9. Cotton — durable; cheap; easy to weave; easy to dye; cooler than wool
10. Promise — to maintain a basis of faith and mutual trust

Index